P9-AQG-357

REVIEW

OF

RESEARCH

CONTRIBUTORS

NANCY APFEL
K. ALISON CLARKE-STEWART
GARY D. FENSTERMACHER
RICHARD M. JAEGER
MICHAEL MACDONALD-ROSS
ROBERT NICHOLS
CHRISTINA BRATT PAULSTON
K. WARNER SCHAIE
LOUIS M. SMITH
SHERRY L. WILLIS

Theodore Lownik Library
Illinois Benedictine College
Lisle, Illinois 60532

IN EDUCATION

6

1978

LEE S. SHULMAN
EDITOR
MICHIGAN STATE UNIVERSITY

F. E. PEACOCK PUBLISHERS, INC., ITASCA, ILLINOIS

A PUBLICATION OF THE

AMERICAN EDUCATIONAL RESEARCH ASSOCIATION

370.78
R454
v. 6

Editorial Board

John B. Carroll

T. Anne Cleary

Laurence Iannaccone

William G. Spady

Kenneth Strike

Decker F. Walker

Copyright © 1979
American Educational Research Association
All rights reserved
Library of Congress
Catalog Card No. 72-89719
Printed in the United States of America
ISBN 0-87581-239-2

Contents

I. HUMAN DEVELOPMENT

1. Policy Implications of the IQ Controversy   3
   Author: *Robert C. Nichols*
   Editorial Consultants: *Arthur Jensen and Sandra Scarr*

2. Evaluating Parental Effects on Child Development   47
   Authors: *K. Alison Clarke-Stewart with Nancy Apfel*
   Editorial Consultant: *Leon Yarrow*

3. Life Span Development: Implications for Education   120
   Authors: *K. Warner Schaie and Sherry L. Willis*
   Editorial Consultants: *Rolf Monge, Susan Stodolsky and David Rogosa*

II. RESEARCH ON TEACHING AND INSTRUCTION

4. A Philosophical Consideration of Recent Research on Teacher Effectiveness   157
   Author: *Gary D. Fenstermacher*
   Editorial Consultants: *Denis G. Phillips and Bruce J. Biddle*

5. Bilingual/Bicultural Education   186
   Author: *Christina Bratt Paulston*
   Editorial Consultants: *Merrill Swain, Bernard Spolsky and Roger Shuy*

6. Language in Texts: The Design of Curricular Materials   229
   Author: *Michael Macdonald-Ross*
   Editorial Consultants: *Lawrence Frase, George Klare and John Rickards*

III. POLICY

7. About Educational Indicators: Statistics on the Conditions and Trends
   in Education   276
   Author: *Richard M. Jaeger*
   Editorial Consultants: *James Impara and Kenneth Land*

IV. METHODOLOGY

8. An Evolving Logic of Participant Observation, Educational Ethnography
    and Other Case Studies   316
    Author: *Louis M. Smith*
    Editorial Consultants: *Frederick Erickson and Paul Diesing*

I

HUMAN DEVELOPMENT

1

Policy Implications of the IQ Controversy

ROBERT C. NICHOLS
State University of New York at Buffalo

> A human being is . . . the sum of an original acted on by antenatal
> influences and the later environment. The first problem of educational science
> concerns the *relative shares* of these agencies in determining human thought and
> conduct.
>
> *Edward L. Thorndike* (1903, p. 40)

Since Jensen's (1969) famous (some might say infamous) article in the
Harvard Educational Review, there has been a lively debate over the origin and
nature of individual differences in behavior and the implications of these differences for educational policy. After almost a decade, it seems that most points of
view have been thoroughly aired, and much of the heat of argument has been
dissipated. It may now be time to review the points that have been made, to
attempt to sort out what is known from what is not known, and to assess the
educational implications.

The argument has focused primarily on individual differences in intelligence,
although several writers have maintained that other traits are equally, if not more,
important. This review will be concerned with intelligence first and will then
briefly extend the discussion to other traits. Jensen's definition of intelligence as
the large general factor underlying most mental abilities has been generally
accepted, although there has been disagreement over the appropriateness of its
operational measurement by verbal tests of IQ and academic aptitude. Historically, however, the concept of intelligence came not from factor analytic studies
but from Terman's Stanford revision of the Binet scales, which measure mainly
verbal comprehension and reasoning factors. The Stanford-Binet has been the
operational standard against which other measures of intelligence have been
validated, a role which the Wechsler tests may now be in part assuming.

ARTHUR JENSEN, University of California—Berkeley, and SANDRA SCARR, Yale University, were the
editorial consultants for this chapter.

Individual differences in intelligence are large, and people whose contacts are limited to a selected group of associates are often surprised by the wide range of abilities revealed by standardized tests. The national norms for the *Cognitive Abilities Test* (Thorndike & Hagen, 1971), for example, reveal that the lower 10% of 12th-grade students often have difficulty with such words as *forefathers, hutch,* and *curb*, while the upper 10% can usually define such words as *zealot, sinecure,* and *patronage*. The correlation between intelligence test scores and academic performance at any point in the educational system, from elementary school through college, is typically between .50 and .65. Thus it is not surprising that educators have been deeply concerned about the nature of these important differences and that emotional involvement with the issues has run high.

The argument has centered around whether individual differences in intelligence are primarily the result of genetic differences or environmental differences. Although extreme statements have been abundant on both sides, most participants in the debate seem willing to concede that both the genes and the environment are responsible for individual differences in some degree. The dispute has been over which is responsible for the lion's share. Few advocates have been satisfied with a 50–50 compromise; most seem to prefer something like 80–20. Whether the 80 is attributed to the genes or to the environment is highly predictive of a writer's position on most other issues in the debate. It is not a great distortion to characterize the debate as being between the *hereditarians* on the one side and the *environmentalists* on the other; indeed many of the participants have identified themselves with one or the other of these terms. The hereditarian position has been advocated by such writers as Jensen, Herrnstein, and Eysenck, and the environmentalist position by such writers as Kamin and Lewontin. Some of the major papers from the debate have been collected by Block and Dworkin (1976).

It is heuristically useful to characterize the extreme positions, but a majority of researchers interested in the issue probably fall in a middle or uncommitted range. It is this large, relatively open-minded jury that will ultimately pass judgment on the evidence presented by the partisan advocates. The middle ground is not represented proportionately in the literature, since partisan fervor motivates publication and, when an issue is as polarized as this one, it is difficult to write on it without seeming to take one side or the other.

Although environmentalists have tended to be on the defensive throughout the hundred-year or so history of the nature-nurture controversy, their extremely defensive stance in the most recent engagement seems to grow out of the presumed policy implications of a possible victory by the hereditarians. Environmentalists have suggested that the issue should not even be discussed, out of fear that policy makers will be prematurely influenced by the hereditarian arguments. The hereditarians have generally ignored this truce proposal, however, and the environmentalists have seen no alternative but to man the barricades.

In the policy debate it is the hereditarians who are on the defensive. The environmentalists tend to be strong advocates for liberal social programs, such as large-scale educational intervention for socially and economically disadvantaged groups. The hereditarians have generally tended to avoid explicit policy proposals, claiming only that the hereditarian position is not necessarily inconsistent with liberal social goals. The eugenic proposals that have been associated with the hereditarian theory in the past have not been strongly advocated by most current hereditarians, but they have nevertheless been critically attacked by the environmentalists.

The policy debate has often been confounded with the debate over matters of fact, and policy implications have frequently been tacitly assumed to follow from the various factual outcomes, without careful analysis. For purposes of review it seems best to consider the two intertwined debates separately, first considering the evidence for the heritability of human behavior and then some of the policy implications.

EVIDENCE FOR THE HERITABILITY OF INTELLIGENCE

It has not been feasible to interfere with human lives or human reproduction in the ways that would be required to produce conclusive experimental evidence of the degree of genetic determination of individual differences. Instead investigators have had to rely on indirect evidence and on the analysis of natural experiments that are always unsatisfactory in one way or another. The environmentalists have usually been successful in demonstrating that any study that might be cited is not conclusive, and frequently also that the data are inadequate, the analyses flawed, and the interpretation biased. The hereditarian response has been to point out that such lack of absolute conclusiveness is characteristic of almost all naturalistic studies of human behavior, and in such circumstances the answer is to be found in the convergence of evidence from a variety of sources. It is argued that the genetic theory accommodates all of the evidence parsimoniously, while the environmental theory becomes increasingly elaborate, ad hoc, and improbable (Urbach, 1974).

Space permits only a brief review of each of the several lines of evidence that have been advanced. No attempt will be made to take a strong position on the methodological controversies in each area, since rapid progress is being made in resolving questions concerning the observational facts. In most cases new data can be collected if the existing data are inadequate, and the controversy has speeded the pace and improved the quality of research.

The Meaning of Heritability

Heritability is the proportion of the population variance of a trait that is attributable to genetic differences. It is not an enduring characteristic of a person or of a trait but is descriptive of a given population at a given point in time. The heritability indicates the relative importance of genetic and environmental influences in bringing about the observed individual differences in the trait in the given population. As such, the heritability provides a means of estimating the amount of change in the trait that might result from changing the relevant environmental or genetic factors within the range existing in the population. It does not provide information about the probable effects of changes outside the range of natural variation in the population studied.

Under ideal circumstances good estimates of the heritability of human traits may be derived from studies of the similarity of various categories of relatives. For example, the correlation between separated identical twins who have had no environmental experiences in common is a direct measure of heritability. Since fraternal twins share about half of the genes on which people differ and identical twins share all, the greater similarity of identical twins represents the effect of half the genetic influence. Thus, twice the difference between identical and fraternal twin correlations is a measure of heritability. The intraclass correlation is the proportion of common variance, and it is not squared in these calculations (Jensen, 1971). Since parents and children have about half their genes in common, a measure of heritability may be obtained by doubling the correlation between natural parent and adopted child. There are a number of other special circumstances from which heritability can be estimated.

Unfortunately, the data that are available never conform neatly to all of the assumptions of the above calculations. Separated identical twins are not assigned randomly to environments; identical twins may be treated more alike than are fraternal twins; adopted children may be selectively placed; measurement is often unreliable. In addition there are a number of genetic complications, such as assortative mating, dominance, epistasis, and gene-environment interaction (Falconer, 1960). Thus, in practice it is necessary to make a number of corrections and adjustments to the simple heritability calculations in the examples above, and these adjustments sometimes involve rough estimates of unknown effects. Moreover, the standard errors of heritability estimates tend to be large, since they are usually based on differences among correlations (or among variances), which are subject to large sampling fluctuation. Therefore we should not have great confidence in the exact heritability coefficients calculated in any given study. Instead we might hope to narrow the range of probable heritabilities by considering evidence from a number of different studies, using different kinds of data with different assumptions.

Twins Raised Together

Twins form a natural experiment in which identical and fraternal twins differ in genetic similarity, yet, when raised together, do not seem to differ greatly in environmental similarity. Quantitative estimates may be made of the factors known to affect twin similarity, which permits calculation of the heritability from the observed similarity of the two kinds of twins on a given trait (Jensen, 1967; Jinks & Fulker, 1970).

Almost all studies have found identical twins to be more similar than fraternal twins on tests of intelligence as well as of most other traits. The median intraclass correlations from 17 of the larger twin studies of intelligence, involving altogether some 6,000 sets of twins, were .85 and .59 for identical and fraternal twins, respectively (Loehlin & Nichols, 1976, p. 39). All 17 studies found substantial differences between the similarity of the two kinds of twins. Depending on assumptions concerning measurement error, assortative mating, errors of twin diagnosis, and so on, heritabilities calculated from these median correlations can range from about .50 to about .80.

The major criticism of these heritability calculations concerns the assumption of equal similarity of environmental influences for the two kinds of twins. Identical twins spend more time together than do fraternal twins, and because they look alike they elicit more similar treatment from parents and others. Some studies suggest that this greater environmental similarity for identical twins is not responsible for their greater behavioral similarity (Smith, 1965; Scarr, 1968), but they have not satisfied the environmentalist critics (Goldberger, 1976, 1977b). Kamin (1974) has leveled telling criticism at the adequacy of the data and methods of analysis of many of the older twin studies of intelligence. Nevertheless, the results of these experiments continue to be confirmed by more recent studies with larger samples and better designs (Nichols, 1976, in press). Kamin's criticisms have themselves been the subject of telling criticism (Fulker, 1975).

Identical Twins Raised Apart

Separated identical twins come close to a true experiment in which genetically identical individuals are placed in different environments. Any similarity of such twins would seem to be due solely to genetic and prenatal environmental influences. However, separated identical twins are rare and difficult to find, and so far they have not satisfied the ideal conditions of a true experiment.

Jensen (1970a) reanalyzed the data for the 122 sets of separated identical twins available from the four major studies of twins raised apart; he found a correlation for intelligence of .82. However, this impressive correlation has not fared well under the intensive scrutiny of the environmentalists.

The separated identical twin evidence suffered a severe blow from the recent questioning of the veridicality of the Burt data (Jensen, 1978b, McAskie, 1978; Wade, 1967a), which contributed 53 of the 122 sets. The combined correlation for the 69 sets from the remaining three studies is .73; however, Kamin (1974) has cast doubt on the trustworthiness of this figure by pointing out the relatively large effect of age differences (since twins are the same age, any age difference in test scores will produce spurious correlation between twins), the similarity of twin environments, and other flaws. The effect of these criticisms has been meliorated somewhat by Fulker (1975), who pointed out several serious flaws in Kamin's procedures.

Siblings Reared Apart

Although the evidence is less dramatic than that for separated identical twins, full siblings separated from birth can provide evidence that is just as convincing. The environmentalists would predict a correlation near zero for such siblings, provided they were not placed in correlated environments, and the hereditarians would predict a correlation around .50. Since separated siblings are relatively common compared with twins, it should not be prohibitively difficult to obtain adequate samples and to control for correlated environments and age effects on the test scores. Thus it is surprising that only three such studies have been reported (Elderton, 1922–1923; Hildreth, 1925, 1940), and none recently. The correlations ranged from .23 to .47, but the studies can be criticized on methodological grounds, such as late separation of the sibling pairs.

Adopted Children

Adoption provides one of the best ways available of separating the environmental and the biological influences of parents on children. Studies of adopted children have recently been reviewed by Munsinger (1975) and by DeFries and Plomin (1978). Munsinger computed the average of the major correlations for IQ from the five adoption studies which he considered to have the fewest methodological defects. These average correlations were: biological parent and adopted child, .48, adoptive parent and adopted child, .19, and, from control families, parent and own child, .58.

Taken at face value these results suggest a strong genetic influence causing the adopted child to be more like the biological parent than the adoptive parent, and a weaker environmental influence causing still greater similarity of parents to their own children and some similarity of adoptive parents to their adopted children. However, these studies are not without methodological problems. As was discussed by Munsinger, and more pointedly by Kamin (1974), there were problems of selective placement, restriction of range, and lack of exact comparability of adoptive and control families. DeFries and Plomin (1978) outlined requirements for an adequate adoption study and found all previous studies to be lacking in one or more important features. Thus there is reason for controversy concerning the proper interpretation of the adoption findings.

The Munsinger review has been criticized by Kamin (1978) for errors of reporting and interpretation of data. Munsinger's (1978) reply, however, seems convincing in its claim that the average correlations quoted above are a reasonable representation of adoption findings in the literature. In addition Scarr-Salapatek (1975) and Scarr and Weinberg (in press) have questioned Munsinger's interpretation of the above-average ability usually found for adopted children. Munsinger attributed this finding to selection of superior children for placement, while Scarr and Weinberg see it as resulting from the superior home environment of adoptive families. Although both of these factors are undoubtedly involved to some degree in the consistently observed superior average performance of adopted children, a study recently completed in France by Schiff, Duyme, Dumaret, Stewart, Tomkiewicz, and Feingold (1978) suggests that the family influence is substantial. The biological mothers of 32 school-age adopted children were traced, and 20 of them were found to have additional children of school age who had not been adopted away and who were siblings or half siblings of the adopted children. The adopted children averaged about one standard deviation above their unadopted siblings on the WISC and the ECNI (a French group test), and there were corresponding differences in school failure rates. Although selection could be a factor in this study, the use of sibling controls seems to reduce its possible effects considerably.

A large adoption study is currently being conducted by Horn, Loehlin, and Willerman at the University of Texas which is reportedly free from some of the defects of earlier studies. Preliminary results for about 450 adopted children, as reported by DeFries and Plomin (1978), show smaller parent-child correlations than those discussed above, but a similar pattern. In addition there was an intraclass correlation of .28 among the 282 pairs of unrelated children raised together. This correlation is higher than would be expected from the small degree of selective placement and is presumably in part the result of the common environmental influence of the adoptive homes.

Another excellent adoption study, conducted at the University of Minnesota, has become available since the Munsinger review. This study included a sample of 101 transracial adoptions (Scarr & Weinberg, 1976, 1977b) and another sample of 104 families with 194 children who were adopted in infancy and were teenagers (16–22) at the time of the study (Scarr & Weinberg, 1977a). There was also a control group of 120 biological families comparable to the latter sample of adoptive families. The observed correlations followed the usual pattern. For example, in the teenage sample the correlation of biological mother's education with child's IQ was .21 for 150 adopted children and .24 for 237 natural children, while the correlations of foster mother's education with adopted child's IQ was .10. The major results were presented in a series of regression equations in which strikingly different effects were observed for biological and adoptive children when IQ scores of the rearing parents were added to an equation including other family demographic characteristics. The parental IQ scores substantially increased the correlation and became the major predictors for the biological children, but they had little effect for the adopted children. A similar effect for the adopted children was observed when the natural mother's education was added.

Many of the transracial adoptive families also had natural children, and an intraclass correlation of .30 was observed for 134 pairs of such unrelated children reared together. Thus the Minnesota and Texas studies are in agreement in finding substantial similarity in ability among unrelated children reared together. These findings are quite similar to the weighted average value of .32 calculated by Jencks (1972) from five older U.S. adoption studies concerning a total of 259 pairs of unrelated children reared together. As Jencks (1972) and Loehlin, Lindzey, and Spuhler (1975) have noted, this correlation suggests a greater environmental effect of the home than one would expect from the other kinship correlations.

Scarr and Weinberg also interpreted the above-average performance of the adopted children, especially the transracial adoptions, as likely to be due to the above-average environments provided by adoptive families.

Animal Studies

Although behavioral genetic studies of animals are becoming increasingly sophisticated and focused, only two general lines of evidence for genetic control of animal behavior will be of concern here.

Comparison of the behavior of inbred strains provides a simple indication of whether or not genetic differences can affect a given behavioral trait. Dog fanciers need not be told that large strain differences in behavior are typically found. Because of the ease of comparisons, a large amount of information is available about strain differences. Sprott and Staats (1975), for example, have compiled a bibliography of 1,222 behavioral studies of genetically defined mouse strains. Strain differences are observed for almost every conceivable behavioral measurement.

Selective breeding experiments provide the most unambiguous evidence of the heritability of a behavioral trait. Since Tryon's (1940) classic selection study of maze learning in rats, selection studies have shown substantial heritabilities for a variety of behavioral traits, ranging from open-field activity in mice (DeFries, Hegmann, & Halcomb, 1974) to geotaxis and phototaxis in *Drosophila* (Polivanov, 1975).

Animal studies have no direct relevance for human behavior, of course, but the ubiquity of genetic variance in animal behavior makes it seem likely that human behavior also is influenced to some degree by genetic differences.

Stability of IQ

Intelligence scores are by no means constant. Bayley (1949, 1968) has documented cases in which changes in test scores over a period of years were accompanied by other behavioral changes indicating a real change in intelligence. Compared with other behavioral traits, however, IQ scores become remarkably stable after about age six. Brodway and Thompson (1962) reported test-retest correlations of intelligence scores of .85 over a 15-year period from adolescence to adulthood, of .65 over a 10-year period from preschool to adolescence, and of .59 over the 25-year period from preschool to adulthood. In the Fels longitudinal study of 89 children, Kagan and Moss (1962) found a correlation of .54 for intelligence over a seven-year period beginning at ages 3 to 6, and a correlation of .78 over a five-year period beginning at ages 6 to 10.

These findings seem to suggest that causes of individual differences in intelligence have their major impact early in life, and that later environmental influences do little to disturb the early-established rank order of individuals. It has been argued that later environments tend to be correlated with early environments to about the extent that later IQ is correlated with early IQ. As discussed below, however, deliberate compensatory changes in the later environment do not seem to result in substantial IQ changes.

Most environmentalists seem to have concluded from this evidence that the salient environmental effects on intelligence occur early in life. The preschool period is thus considered most advantageous for intervention efforts (Bloom, 1964; Hunt, 1964).

Infant intelligence measures have little or no correlation with later IQ scores (McCall, Hogarty, & Hurlburt, 1972). This finding is ambiguous, however, in its implications for the heredity-environment issue. It could be either that the environment has not yet had its lasting effect or that genetic structures have not matured enough to permit measurement of genetic potential at early ages.

Analysis of Kinship Correlations

The correlations of intelligence scores among people with various degrees of genetic relationship, raised together and raised apart, which have been discussed above form an impressive picture of increasing similarity with increasing genetic relationship when viewed all together. Erlenmeyer-Kimling and Jarvik (1963) presented the results of 52 studies in a chart showing this relationship graphically which has been widely reprinted. The median or pooled correlations from this chart, augmented by additional studies, have been analyzed by Jencks (1972), Morton (1974), Jinks and Eaves (1974), Eaves (1975), Rao, Morton, and Yee (1974, 1976), and others using the method of biometrical genetic analysis. This method involves construction of a model based on theoretical or known genetic and environmental relationships and the calculation of the best fitting parameters for the model from the observed median correlations. These parameter estimates are said to be superior to those based on a single set of relationships, such as twins or adopted children, because they are derived from a broader observational base and because additional parameters, such as dominance and genotype-environment correlation, may be estimated. The broad heritabilities for intelligence derived from these calculations ranged from .45 for Jencks to .83 for Jinks and Eaves. This is a wide range of values for analyses of essentially the same set of data. Loehlin (1977) repeated the various analyses and found that the discrepant results were due not to differences in the analytic methods or in the data but to differences in the assumptions made by the different groups of investigators concerning such matters as dominance, assortative mating, and equivalence of environments. The unusually low value obtained by Jencks appears to be due to a particularly inappropriate set of assumptions (Loehlin, Lindzey, & Spuhler, 1975, Appendix I). When Loehlin (1977) repeated Jencks's analysis using the assumptions of Jinks and associates, he obtained a value of .68, which is more in line with the other results.

The biometrical genetic method shows promise of being able to yield heritability analyses that will in the future provide a fairly precise and generally acceptable answer to nature-nurture questions. Claims that this is now the case may be premature, however. Kamin (1974) has pointed out that the observational data are often not as firmly established as they may seem to be from the number of studies involved. They are sometimes based on arbitrary selections from several correlations reported, they sometimes involve questionable corrections for such distorting factors as restriction of range, there have been errors in calculation and in reporting, and the samples frequently leave something to be desired. Kamin also pointed out that the results of the analyses are particularly sensitive to relatively small fluctuations in certain of the correlations. Goldberger (1977a) reviewed the recent biometrical genetic analyses of IQ and pointed out inconsistencies in the models, in addition to raising questions about the data. Until the various issues in dispute are resolved it may be that more modest attempts to estimate heritability from limited sets of relationships, such as twins and adopted children, will be more convincing than the grand analyses based on all available kinship correlations.

EVIDENCE FOR ENVIRONMENTAL EFFECTS ON INTELLIGENCE

The environmentalists have not emphasized positive evidence for environmental effects, although if substantial lasting effects of environmental manipulations were demonstrated it would provide strong support for their position. There have been many studies of environmental influences, some of which will be discussed in this section.

The Effects of Schooling

The process of schooling is so intimately related to the development of the verbal comprehension and reasoning abilities that are measured by most intelligence tests that it seems almost self-evident that formal education is necessary for the development of intelligence as we know it. Indeed this does seem to be the case, although evidence for the long-term effects of schooling is scant (Härnqvist, 1977).

During World War II many elementary schools in Holland were closed, and the IQ scores of children entering secondary school after the war appears to have dropped about 7 IQ points as a result (DeGroot, 1951). One-tenth of all Swedish 13-year-olds were tested in 1961, and five years later about 5,000 males from this sample took intelligence tests on enrollment for military service. After control for the age-13 test scores and socioeconomic status, those who had completed the gymnasium scored between 7 and 8 IQ points above those who had dropped out after only seven to nine years of schooling (Härnqvist, 1968). After reviewing these and other studies, Jencks (1972) concluded that each extra year of schooling boosts an individual's adult IQ score about one point above what it would otherwise be.

Differential School Effects

The intimate association between schooling and intelligence also makes it seem reasonable to expect that differences in the quality of schools would be responsible in some degree for individual differences in intelligence and especially in scholastic achievement. The Equality of Educational Opportunity survey (Coleman, Campbell, Hobson, McPartland, Mood, Weinfeld, & York, 1966) probably deserves credit for first casting widespread doubt on this expectation. Its conclusion, based on a massive survey of some 600,000 students in 4,000 schools, was that "variations in school quality are not highly related to variations in achievement of pupils. . . . The school appears unable to exert independent influences to make achievement less dependent on the child's background" (p. 297). A number of reanalyses of the Coleman data (e.g., Mosteller & Moynihan, 1972) have failed to change the basic conclusion.

Similar negative results were found at the college level. For example, Astin (1968) found that differences in achievement on the Graduate Record Examination area tests were highly related to differences in ability and other student characteristics measured at the time of college entrance, and that the residuals were unrelated to measures of college quality.

Averch, Carroll, Donaldson, Kiesling, and Pincus (1972) at the Rand Corporation reviewed the existing research on differential school effects for the U.S. Commission on School Finance. This thorough critical review concluded that "research has not identified a variant of the existing system that is consistently related to students' educational outcomes" (p. 154). The authors explained, "We must emphasize that we are not suggesting that nothing makes a difference, or that nothing 'works.' Rather, we are saying that research has found nothing that *consistently* and *unambiguously* makes a difference in students' outcomes" (p. 145). The report pointed out that what had been investigated were the effects of existing variations within the current system. These findings, of course, say nothing about the potential effects of radical departures from current educational practice.

Effects of Compensatory Education

Even if differences in schooling are not a large source of variance in intelligence and academic achievement for students in general, they may be a potent influence for certain subgroups of students. This seems most likely to be the case for students whose achievement may have been lowered by socioeconomically disadvantaged home backgrounds. Based on this reasoning a number of compensatory education programs for disadvantaged students were started in the 1960s as part of the War on Poverty. The U.S. Commission on Civil Rights (1967) reviewed the results of these programs and concluded "that none of the programs appear to have raised significantly the achievement of participating pupils as a group, within the period evaluated by the Commission" (p. 138). This review led Jensen (1969) to begin his paper with the provocative sentence: "Compensatory education has been tried and it apparently has failed" (p. 2).

Subsequent evaluations of compensatory programs have not been much more encouraging, although the scope and quality of the evaluations have in some cases greatly improved. The Westinghouse Learning Corporation's (1969) evaluation of the effects of Head Start found that children enrolled in both summer and year-round projects of this national preschool compensatory program did, in fact, have a head start when they entered first grade, compared with students not in the program. However, by the end of the first grade all of the advantages produced by the program had been lost. Although the report has been criticized (Cicirelli, Evans, & Schiller, 1970; Smith & Bissell, 1970), it seems clear that any lasting effects were small. These findings could be due to the fact that the preschool program increased test-taking ability and social skills rather than having any real effect on cognitive ability. The findings could also be due to the fact that real cognitive gains were lost in the comparatively dull atmosphere of public schools enrolling large numbers of disadvantaged children.

To decide between these two interpretations, and possibly others, Project Follow Through was begun in 1969. Since the final results of the evaluation of this large compensatory program have only recently been released (Stebbins, St. Pierre, Proper, Anderson, & Cerra, 1977; Kennedy, 1978), it will be described in some detail. This compensatory program for grades 1 through 3, plus kindergarten in many cases, of schools enrolling predominantly disadvantaged children was designed as an educational experiment. To provide for "planned variation" contracts were awarded for the development of 17 diverse, theoretically relevant, and internally consistent compensatory education curricula, called models. One of these models was installed in each of 100 local school districts, and the developers of the model provided consultants to supervise its implementation. In each district experimental schools, which received the program, and comparison schools, which did not receive it, were identified. Evaluation data, including cognitive (Metropolitan Achievement Test) and noncognitive outcomes, were collected by an independent agency, the Stanford Research Institute. This is one of the largest educational research projects ever conducted. Over 352,000 children participated during the four-year evaluation period (although the major analyses were based on considerably smaller samples of children for whom complete data were available), and the data collection alone is reported to have cost approximately $30 million (Marciano & David, 1977).

The results were clearly negative. After several adjustments to make the outcome measures comparable a majority of the differences between experimental and control schools were found not significant. When significant differences were found the control school was superior more frequently than was the experimental school. Most models had at least one site in which the experimental school was superior, but all models had at least one site in which the control school was superior. Thus no model was found to be generally superior to the others. Models emphasizing basic skills were reported to be superior to models emphasizing conceptual or affective processes on the basic skills and affective outcomes, but House, Glass, McLean, and Walker (1978) have raised serious questions about this result.

Another large compensatory evaluation, which has also just been completed (Coulson, Hanes, Ozenne, Bradford, Doherty, Duck & Hamenway, 1977) is the Emergency School Aid Act (ESAA) National Evaluation. Beginning in 1973 the ESAA provided funds for compensatory programs in desegregating and minority-impacted schools. Seventy-four matched pairs of eligible schools were identified and assigned at random to treatment and control conditions. The *basic elementary sample*, grades 3, 4, and 5 in desegregating schools, included 34 pairs of schools; the *pilot elementary sample,* grades 3, 4, and 5 in minority-impacted schools, included 20 pairs of schools; and the *basic secondary sample,* grades 10, 11, and 12 in desegregating schools, included 20 pairs of schools. There was some attrition of schools over the three years of the program. The average per-pupil expenditures in the third program year for treatment and control schools, respectively, were $1,549 and $1,169 for basic elementary, $1,336 and $1,206 for pilot elementary, and $1,116 and $1,025 for basic secondary schools. Within each school 45 children from each grade were chosen for study at random from those eligible for ESAA programs; an additional 15 students were chosen at grades 3 and 10 to allow for attrition in the longitudinal study of effects over the three-year life of the program. These students were given tests of reading and mathematics achievement at the beginning and end of each school year.

The gain scores of students in treatment and control schools were compared at each grade at the end of each school year. The only significant differences were in the third year, when the treatment students had larger gains in reading at grade 5 and larger gains in mathematics at grade 4 than did the control students. Although two differences significant at the .05 level might be expected by chance among the 54 comparisons that were made, this may be a faint indication of increasing program effectiveness, since the differences occurred in the third year among the schools with the largest expenditure differences. For the longitudinal analysis, 904 students from the elementary sample, 302 students from the pilot elementary sample, and 177 students from the basic secondary sample were available who had taken all six sets of tests (beginning and end of each of three years). There were no significant differences in the trends of treatment and control students on either cognitive or noncognitive measures for any of the three samples.

Although the large national compensatory programs have not been shown to be generally effective, notable successes have been reported by much smaller programs, such as Gray and Klaus (1965). However, in view of the great variation in program effectiveness among local sites found in Project Follow Through, it would seem prudent to require that a program be demonstrated to be transportable to other locations before it is declared an unqualified success.

Massive Intervention

Compensatory education programs have frequently been criticized as offering too little too late. A few small programs have attempted to overcome this objection by early and massive intervention in every aspect of the child's life.

One such program that has been widely cited as showing potent effects of massive early intervention is being conducted in Milwaukee (Garber & Heber, 1977), although, as Page (1972) has pointed out, the reporting of this study leaves much to be desired. Forty infants of black slum mothers with IQs below 75 were randomly assigned to experimental and control groups. The experimental families received a massive intervention for six years, beginning in the first weeks of the infant's life. The six-year program, consisting of educational and vocational rehabilitation of the mother, provision of adequate nutrition and medical care, and intensive enrichment of the child's environment, is estimated to cost about $30,000 per child (Trotter, 1976). At 6 years of age the mean IQ of the experimental group was about 112, compared with about 82 for the control group. At age 9, after three years of public school, the means were about 106 and 79 (mean IQs are approximate, as read from the graph presented by Garber and Heber, 1977). The major strength of this study, the massive intervention, is also one of its weaknesses. It is not known what parts of the program are responsible for the gains.

McKay, Sinisterra, McKay, Gomez, and Lloreda (1978) reported that an intensive four-year program involving day-long schooling plus nutritional supplements and health care produced dramatic ability gains in undernourished preschool children in Colombia. The 50 children receiving the full four-year program were superior by almost one standard deviation to the 90 children who were exposed to only the final year, and groups receiving two and three years of the program fell in between. Most of the group differences remained on a follow-up Stanford-Binet test one year later. Like the Milwaukee study, this impressive demonstration program does not provide information about what aspects of the total intervention are producing the effects. Larger programs that will likely follow from these dramatic demonstrations should incorporate designs to show the relative effectiveness of different aspects of the treatment.

Skeels and Dye (1939) reported similarly large IQ gains from large changes in the environment of apparently retarded children.

All three of these studies involved children in extremely deprived environments. It may be that severely deprived and undernourished children are below the threshold of environmental support necessary for the normal development of intelligence, and a special process may be involved in reversing the effects of the deficiency. Jensen (1969) proposed such, a threshold effect to account for the obvious influence of extreme deprivation when he was arguing for minimal environmental influences on intelligence for the general population. If this is the case, it would not be expected that these findings would be generalizable to children in the normal range. It may be that the disadvantaged children in these programs respond to environmental enrichment in the same way as any other children would, however, and similarly great increments in enrichment might have 'similarly great effects for the majority of children. Bereiter (1970) and others have pointed out that substantial effects of extreme environmental manipulation are not necessarily inconsistent with high heritability, since the slope of the regression line is the square root of the variance accounted for. Thus, if environment accounts for 20% of the variance in IQ, the standard deviation of environmental effects is $\sqrt{.20} = .45$, and changing the salient environmental factors by, say, three standard deviations will result in a $3 \times .45 = 1.35$ standard deviation change in IQ. It would be worthwhile to find out whether or not massive intervention would also prove effective with children in the normal range.

Children Raised in Isolation

Case studies of children raised in extremely deprived environments may provide information similar to that derived from the massive intervention programs described above. There have been several reports (e.g., Gesell, 1940) of feral children who were presumed to have been reared by wolves or other animals. Typically these children were unable to adapt to human culture. These studies have been heavily criticized, especially because the early history of the children was unknown. Bettelheim (1959) suggested that the feral children might have been recently abandoned psychotic, autistic, or severely retarded children.

There have been a few studies in which the early histories of the children were known, and in these cases the outcome was quite different. These studies were reviewed by Clarke and Clarke (1976), who also included reprints of some of the papers. For example Isabelle, the illegitimate child of a deaf-mute mother, was kept in almost complete isolation with her mother during her early childhood (Davis, 1940, 1947; Mason, 1942). When discovered at age 6½ she was unable to talk and had a mental age of 19 months. With compassionate training she made rapid progress and eventually developed normal intelligence. Similar rapid development after severe retardation due to early deprivation was observed in another case involving twin boys (Koluchová, 1972, 1976).

In 1970 a 13-year-old girl, Genie, who had been raised in almost total isolation and subjected to considerable abuse was discovered (Curtiss, 1977). She suffered from extreme malnutrition and was unable to speak or understand language of any kind. She functioned at about the 2-year-old level on preschool performance scales. Genie was intensively studied over the next five years, especially from the point of linguistic analysis. She progressed rapidly in language comprehension and could communicate in English, but tests revealed gaps in her abilities. For example, she was above average in gestalt perception and part-whole judgments but scored low on tests involving sequential order. Her overall performance on the Raven Progressive Matrices was poor, but she was able to solve certain difficult items. Careful analysis of her linguistic performance suggested that her language was controlled by the right hemisphere of her brain, which is normally a nonlanguage area. Curtiss interpreted these findings as supporting the hypothesis of a "critical period" for normal language acquisition.

These cases show that extreme environmental deprivation can have marked effects, which hardly needs to be demonstrated, but they also suggest that the early stunting of intellectual development is not irreversible. The more detailed analysis in the case of Genie suggests that extreme early deprivation may have permanent effects on certain patterns of abilities. These findings seem to support both the environmentalists' claim that compensatory education can overcome the effects of environmental disadvantage, and the hereditarians' expectation that even extreme environmental manipulations do not have a great impact on intelligence.

It is to be hoped that such cases do not occur in the future, but, if they do, it seems important that they be carefully studied and thoroughly reported.

Birth Order

There is fairly good evidence from several large studies (Belmont & Marolla, 1973; Breland, 1974; Velandia, Grandon, & Page, in press) that earlier-born children in a family tend to score higher on tests of intelligence and academic achievement than do later-born children. The birth-order effects are not large, but they are important because they seem to be clearly environmental in origin. There is not a plausible genetic explanation, as there is with almost every other observed relationship of intelligence with another variable, although some unknown genetic effect that is correlated with mother's age, as is Down's syndrome, could conceivably be involved.

Breland (1974) found that the birth-order effect is larger for siblings close together in age than for those further apart. There is also a greater effect on verbal than mathematical tests for siblings near the same age. These findings suggest that the effect is due to social influences rather than to natal or prenatal biological factors. Zajonc (1976) has used the birth-order findings along with the generally observed negative correlation of intelligence and family size (which could be either genetic or environmental in origin) as the basis for a *confluence model* of intellectual development. According to this model, a child reflects the average absolute intelligence or mental age of those around him, and the absolute intelligence is, of course, diluted by the addition of children to the family. The confluence theory is consistent with a considerable body of aggregate data, such as the relationship between birth rates and reading comprehension scores in various countries. Zajonc suggested that the recent SAT score decline may be the result of the baby boom in the 1950s which resulted in larger and more closely spaced families, although this suggestion was not accepted as a likely explanation by the Advisory Panel on the Scholastic Aptitude Test Score Decline (1977). Page (1977, 1978) showed that many of these aggregate relationships could be explained on the basis of the confounding of family size with race and socioeconomic status. He also maintained that even though birth order and family size may appear to be important influences in aggregate data, they account for too little of the variance of individual scores to be considered an important determinant of individual differences in IQ.

Small effects can sometimes be of great theoretical importance, like the faint clouding of a photographic plate that first indicated the presence of radioactivity. If the critical elements in the birth-order effect could be isolated, their influence might be magnified manyfold.

Nutrition

Excellent reviews of studies of the effect of malnutrition on intelligence are provided by Loehlin et al. (1975) and by Brozek (1978). Studies in developing countries (such as Birch, Pineiro, Alcalde, Toca, & Cravioto, 1971) strongly suggest that prolonged severe malnutrition during the first two to four years of life, leading to hospitalization for kwashiorkor, results in lasting intellectual impairment of 10 IQ points or more. The difficulty of obtaining comparable well-nourished controls makes the exact extent of the impairment uncertain. Yet a relatively short period of severe malnutrition in otherwise adequately nourished people seems not to have lasting effects. This is dramatically demonstrated by a study of the results of a severe six-month famine that occurred in the western part of Holland as a result of a German transportation embargo near the end of World War II (Stein, Susser, Saenger, & Marolla, 1972). Rations were drastically reduced, and birth weights of infants declined somewhat. Some 19 years later almost all Dutch males were being given an intelligence test (Progressive Matrices) upon registration for military service, and it became possible to compare the scores of those born before, during, and immediately after the famine in affected cities with those born at the same time in control cities not affected by the famine. No significant differences were found between the approximately 20,000 men affected by the famine early in life and the controls.

Severe malnutrition does not occur frequently enough in the United States to contribute significantly to individual differences in intelligence. In Third World countries, however, it is estimated that between 220 and 250 million children under 6 years of age suffer from some degree of malnutrition (Berg, 1973). Thus nutrition may be an important factor in producing ability deficits worldwide which add to the difficulties of developing countries.

Since the massive intervention programs discussed above involved nutritional supplements and health care along with the educational program, it may be that the relief from malnutrition was a major factor in producing the impressive achievement gains of these programs.

Family Characteristics

Parental IQ and socioeconomic status (SES) are probably the most frequently proposed environmental influences on intelligence, undoubtedly because of the substantial relationship between family SES and a child's ability. But this correlation is not strong evidence for a causal relationship, since it could be partly or entirely genetic. Some support for the environmental hypothesis may be found in the generally lower, but positive, correlation observed for adopted children, although the hereditarians have usually attributed this correlation largely to selective placement.

Parental IQ and SES, as such, do not have a direct environmental impact on the child. The influence must be mediated by specific parental behaviors or other characteristics of the home that the child experiences directly. If these more immediate influences are adequately measured they would be expected to be more strongly related to the child's ability than are the usual SES measures if the relationship is environmental and less strongly related if it is genetic.

Marjoribanks (1972) assessed eight aspects of the home environment thought to influence intelligence by means of structured interviews with the parents of 90 middle-class and 95 lower-class 11-year-old boys. These environmental scales had a corrected multiple correlation of .72 with the boys' total Primary Mental Abilities test score, while the corresponding corrected multiple correlation for six SES indicators was .51. Previous studies cited by Marjoribanks also found similar results using similar environmental scales. Although the environmental scales were not reported in detail, some of the items, such as parental expectations for the education of the child and number of thought-provoking activities engaged in by the child, seem to be more reactions of the family to manifest ability of the child than causal influences. This artifact might explain the exceptionally large correlations between SES and ability typically reported in these studies.

White and Carew Watts (1973) conducted an intensive systematic in-home observational study of 31 children during the second and third years of life. The children were selected on the basis of the competence of an older sibling, on the assumption that this would identify homes differing in environmental factors which could influence ability. There were 22 children (called As) with an exceptionally competent older sibling and 9 children (called Cs) with older siblings of below-average competence. There was very little overlap between As and Cs in SES, so this was essentially a study of the ways mothers of different social classes interact with their children. Many significant differences were found, in spite of the small sample. "The mothers of A children interact more with them, engage in more intellectually stimulating activities with them, teach them more often, encourage them more often, initiate activities for them more often, and are more successful in controlling their children'' (p. 199). In a further analysis of the data for 23 of these children, Carew (1975) found that intellectual interaction between mother and child was the type of experience that correlated highest (.76) with the Stanford-Binet administered at age 3, the end of the observation period. The corresponding correlation for SES was .72. When the several intellectual interaction measures were added to SES in a regression equation, the multiple correlation increased slightly less than would be expected by chance.

These findings showing large environmental differences associated with SES and related to IQ are provocative but not conclusive, because they could be mediated along either genetic or environmental paths. Although authors of the studies have generally proffered environmental explanations for their findings, the meager available evidence suggests that genetic explanations should not be ruled out. For example, the Scarr and Weinberg (1977a) adoption study discussed earlier provided correlations of family SES with IQ scores for biological and adopted teen-age children. The multiple correlation of four family SES indicators with child's IQ was .33 for 237 biological children and .14 for 150 adopted children. The correlation for adopted children can be attributed in part to selective placement. These findings suggest that family-child correlations in studies of biologically related families should be interpreted with extreme caution. There seems to be no good reason, however, why in the future such studies should not routinely be conducted with adopted children. A substantial relationship between family characteristics and adopted child's IQ seemed to be apparent in another adoption study by Scarr and Weinberg (1976), but this finding is suspect because of methodological problems (McNemar, 1977; Nichols, 1977).

Study of the relationship between child behavior and environment, controlling for possible genetic paths, seems to be a neglected area of research. This is surprising in view of the potential importance of positive findings. I cannot escape the feeling that I must have overlooked a large body of research, but the studies cited seem representative of what is available. Research in this area should be exceptionally promising to those who propose environmental explanations for the SES–intelligence correlation.

GROUP DIFFERENCES IN INTELLIGENCE

When identifiable subgroups of the population are compared in reasonably representative samples, significant differences in ability are usually found. These group differences are important scientifically, since they permit a sort of epidemiological analysis that may provide clues to the origin of individual differences. They are also important for educational policy, since some groups have strong political constituencies that call for action relative to the group as such rather than to group members as individuals.

Racial and Ethnic Differences

The Coleman report (Coleman et al., 1966) provides the best basis for comparisons of the various racial and ethnic groups. In its large national sample, schools enrolling minority students were overrepresented. Students were tested at five grade levels, and results showed the following overall rank order of the groups studied: whites (52), Oriental-Americans (51), Mexican-Americans (44), Puerto Ricans (43), Indian-Americans (43), and blacks (39). Numbers in parentheses are mean standard scores (mean = 50; SD = 10) for the 12th-grade verbal test. Mexican-Americans, Oriental-Americans, and Indian-Americans scored somewhat higher on the nonverbal test, with the Oriental-Americans the highest of all groups tested. Studies comparing religious groups have typically found that Jews scored somewhat higher and Catholics somewhat lower than Protestants.

The difference that has received the most attention is that between blacks and whites, because these are the largest groups and the difference is the largest of all the observed group differences. The Coleman report noted that blacks on the average scored about one standard deviation below whites on both verbal and nonverbal tests in rural and metropolitan areas of all regions of the country at all grade levels. The difference is, thus, a large and pervasive one, and it has remained approximately constant since it was first carefully studied during World War I (McGurk, 1978). Group differences are most obvious to the casual observer at the extremes, where even relatively small differences between means will have a large effect on the proportional representation of the groups. The relative representation can be estimated from areas under the normal curve, assuming that the trait is normally distributed and the group variances are equal. Intelligence test scores are distributed approximately normally, and group variances do not differ greatly. There is some indication that the variance may be somewhat smaller for blacks than for whites (Kennedy, Van De Riet, & White, 1963), which would increase the differential representation at the higher end. With one standard deviation difference between the means, approximately 16 percent of blacks would be expected to score above the white mean. Thus any program selecting for IQs above 100 would have $16/50 = .32$ the number of blacks expected from random assignment. The corresponding proportion at one standard deviation above the mean (about the average for college freshmen) would be .14, and at two standard deviations, .06. There would be a corresponding overrepresentation of blacks in groups selected for low scores.

The critical question about the racial difference concerns the degree to which it is due to genetic differences. None of the available evidence unambiguously separates genetic and environmental differences between the races. Thus the approach to this question has been to examine a number of different lines of circumstantial evidence in an attempt to narrow the range of possibilities. For example, controlling for SES and other possible environmental differences does not greatly affect the racial difference in ability (Jensen, 1973), yet the degree of admixture of black and Caucasian genes as determined by blood groups, is essentially unrelated to ability measures (Scarr, Pakstis, Katz, & Barker, 1977).

Jensen (1973) reviewed the available evidence in detail and concluded that "all the major facts would seem to be comprehended quite well by the hypothesis that something between one-half and three-fourths of the average IQ difference between American Negroes and whites is attributable to genetic factors, and the remainder to environmental factors and their interaction with genetic differences" (p. 363).

After reviewing essentially the same evidence, Loehlin et al. (1975) concluded that the mean IQ differences among U.S. racial and ethnic groups:

probably reflect in part inadequacies and biases in the tests themselves, in part differences in environmental conditions among the groups, and in part genetic differences among the groups. . . . A rather wide range of positions concerning the relative weight to be given these three factors can reasonably be taken on the basis of current evidence. (p. 238)

The question that is of greatest relevance to educational policy concerns the degree to which the schools may contribute to the group differences. The Equality of Educational Opportunity survey (Coleman et al., 1966) tested children in grades 1, 3, 6, 9, and 12 specifically to obtain data relative to this issue. If a cumulative deficit, or increasing gap, for minority groups were to be observed with increasing grade level, it would suggest that the schools or other factors operating during the school years may be involved. The only cumulative deficit that was found was for blacks in the South and Southwest, where the difference widened by about half a standard deviation over the 12 years. These cross-sectional findings are only suggestive, since they may be affected by differential migration, dropout, and other factors.

A more sensitive test of cumulative deficit is provided by comparing scores of older and younger school-age siblings. An age decrement in which the older siblings score lower than the younger siblings do would provide evidence for a cumulative deficit. Jensen (1974a) found a slight but statistically significant age decrement for verbal IQ, but not for nonverbal IQ, for black siblings, and no age decrement for white siblings in a California school district. Using the same methodology in a rural Georgia school district, Jensen (1977) found a substantial age decrement for both verbal and nonverbal IQ for 826 black siblings, and no age decrement for 653 white siblings. He interpreted these results as most likely due to the markedly greater environmental disadvantages of the Georgia blacks relative to the California blacks.

In addition to the IQ differences between racial and ethnic groups there appear also to be distinctive group profiles when a number of different abilities are measured. Loehlin et al. (1975) provide a good review of this evidence. Typical are the study of Lesser, Fifer, and Clark (1965) and a replication by Stodolsky and Lesser (1967), who tested middle- and lower-class first-grade children from several racial and ethnic groups with tests of verbal, reasoning, number, and spatial abilities. The distinctive profile shapes for the various groups were characteristic of both upper- and lower-class children of the group. In other words, the profile shape was characteristic of the racial or ethnic group rather than of SES. Jews and blacks tended to be high in verbal ability relative to the other tests, while Puerto Ricans and Chinese tended to be low in this. These general group patterns have generally been confirmed in other studies.

Jensen (1969) proposed that the major profile difference between blacks and whites consists of relatively small differences in Level I abilities (rote learning and memory) and relatively large differences in Level II abilities (complex cognitive processing). This finding has been replicated in several studies (e.g., Jensen & Figueroa, 1975). Jensen (1978c) reported finding that the magnitude of black-white differences on a variety of tests is directly proportional to the loading of the tests on the general factor in factor analytic studies.

Socioeconomic Differences

In a detailed review of the literature on social class differences, Tyler (1965) remarked that "The relationship of measured intelligence to socioeconomic level is one of the best documented findings in mental-test history" (p. 336). An analysis of AGCT scores of over 80,000 white enlisted men in the U.S. Army (Stewart, 1947) found large test-score differences by civilian occupation. Professionals average somewhat more than one standard deviation above the mean; office workers and businessmen averaged from one-half to one standard deviation above the mean; the skilled trades had averages around the mean; semi-skilled workers were somewhat below the mean; and unskilled workers averaged from one-half to one standard deviation below the mean. A similar pattern of differences is found for children from homes of various socioeconomic levels, although the differences are smaller, as expected from regression to the mean.

Coleman et al. (1966) found that eight home-background factors (SES indicators) accounted for 23% of the variance in 12th-grade verbal achievement for whites and 15% of the variance for blacks. Most correlations between father's occupational status and child's ability in the literature are somewhat lower than those reported above in the section on family characteristics. Jencks (1972) reported the average correlation from a number of large studies to be .30, which is very close to the value he calculated for ninth graders in the Project Talent sample.

There have been two main lines of evidence from which it has been argued that SES differences in ability are in part genetic. First is the fact of social mobility based on ability and achievement, plus the evidence that there is a substantial heritability of intelligence. If the brightest tend to move up the SES scale and the dullest to move down, they will carry their genes with them, which will maintain genetic differences among social classes (Eckland, 1967). Herrnstein (1973) has pointed out that if IQ is highly heritable, then the greater the equality of opportunity and the greater the chances for individual social mobility, the more social class will become a matter of inherited status. Waller (1971) has shown that IQ is related to intergenerational social mobility even within families. He found that sons whose IQs were higher than their fathers' IQs (when both were tested at the same age in school) attained by middle age a higher average SES level than their fathers had attained at the same age, while sons with lower IQs than their fathers' attained a lower average SES. The correlation between the father-son differences in IQ and in SES was .29.

The second line of evidence suggesting that SES differences are mainly genetic is the general failure to reduce them appreciably by compensatory education, welfare benefits, day care, and similar environmental programs. It can be argued, however, that these programs have not greatly reduced differences on the major environmental influences associated with SES.

Firkowska, Ostrowska, Sokolowska, Stein, Susser, and Wald (1978) studied the relationship between parental education and occupational status and the Raven Progressive Matrices score for almost the entire population of 11-year-old children in Warsaw, Poland. The correlations were about the same as those typically reported in capitalist countries. For example, correlations of the Raven score with fathers' and mothers' education and occupational status ranged from .27 to .29. These correlations are of special interest because the authors reported that in Warsaw the communist society has eliminated all economic and housing distinctions associated with education and occupational status. Thus, the varying degrees of wealth and poverty that are associated with SES in the United States seem not to be a major factor in producing the ability differences between socioeconomic groups.

Sex Differences

The literature on sex differences has been thoroughly reviewed by Maccoby and Jacklin (1974), although some of the conclusions of this review have been persuasively challenged by Block (1976). There appear to be no substantial sex differences in general intelligence. The major sex differences that seem to be found consistently are that males are more dominant, active, and aggressive, and starting in adolescence they are more capable in mathematical skills and in visual-spatial ability than are females. Females score higher on tests of verbal ability, are more susceptible to anxiety, and seek more help and reassurance than do males.

The sex differences in verbal, quantitative, and spatial abilities are reported in various studies to be between a quarter and a half standard deviation. However, most studies may be grossly underestimating the extent of the sex difference by using tests that are substantially correlated with general ability. When specific abilities have been measured independently of general intelligence, the sex differences are much larger. For example, factor scores were derived from the

Project Talent test battery in such a way that measures of English language facility, memory, and mathematical and spatial ability, among others, were independent of general intelligence (Lohnes, 1966). On these measures females exceeded males by two standard deviations on the English factor and over one standard deviation on the memory factor. Males exceeded females by almost two standard deviations on the mathematics factor and over one standard deviation on the spatial factor (Backman, 1972; Lohnes, 1966). These are extremely large differences that deserve further investigation.

Cultural Bias of Intelligence Tests

An explanation that is frequently offered for group differences in ability is that some groups have had greater exposure to the content of the tests than have others. For example, Block and Dworkin (1974) said that "Standard IQ tests are without any doubt highly culture-loaded. In our view, they are all also clearly culture biased in that they require knowledge of, for example, literary, musical, and geographical facts which are differentially available to people with different sociocultural backgrounds" (p. 461). It is easy to find items in most verbal intelligence tests that seem to meet this criterion of culture bias, and citation of such items has been the major line of evidence presented by those who attribute group differences in whole or in part to biased measurement. This appeal to face validity gains credence from the fact that groups who obtain lower average scores also seem to be less well exposed to the majority culture. Critics of this position can point to certain exceptions, such as Eskimos, who do not score low (MacArthur, 1968), and American Indians, who score higher than blacks on the average, in spite of seemingly greater cultural isolation (Coleman et al., 1966).

The high culture loading of many IQ tests would lead one to expect some degree of cultural bias in the test scores, but assessment of the actual degree of bias for various subpopulations in this country must depend on evidence showing that the scores actually behave in a biased way for these populations. Therefore, the hereditarians, for whom reasonably unbiased measurement is essential for the study of group differences, have responded to the test-bias criticism by presenting evidence which suggests that the test scores do not behave in a biased way, at least not enough to cast serious doubt on the validity of observed group differences (Jensen, 1973). For example, Jensen (1947b) reported that the black-white difference is typically found to be smaller on verbal than on nonverbal, and seemingly less culture-loaded, tests of ability.

College admissions tests appear to predict college grades equally well for blacks and whites, and they do not underpredict for blacks in integrated colleges as would be expected if the tests were more biased than the college-grade criterion (Cleary, Humphreys, Kendrick, & Wesman, 1975). On the other hand, Mercer (1972) has shown that lower-class blacks and Chicanos with IQs below 70 are more capable of self-care than are middle-class whites with similarly low IQ scores.

Jensen (1974b) studied item response patterns on the culture-loaded Peabody Picture Vocabulary Tests and the culture-reduced Raven's Progressive Matrices Test in large representative samples of white, black, and Mexican-American elementary school children in California. There were large mean differences among groups (in the order of white, black, and Mexican-American on the Peabody, and white, Mexican-American, and black on the Raven), but the rank order of item difficulties for the tests and the pattern of wrong answers did not differ significantly in the three groups, as would be expected if some items were more culture biased than others. Equally difficult Raven and Peabody items for whites were also equally difficult for blacks, but the Peabody items were more difficult for the Mexican-Americans, suggesting some culture bias of the verbal Peabody measure for the largely bilingual Mexican-Americans.

THE HERITABILITY OF INTELLIGENCE

In light of the above evidence, what can one conclude about the heritability of IQ in the European and American Caucasian populations that have been most intensively studied? After the most thorough review and quantitative evaluation of the evidence up to that time, Jensen (1969) concluded that the heritability of IQ was about .80, and subsequent developments have not caused him to revise this estimate. On the basis of a similarly thorough review and analysis, Jencks (1972) arrived at a heritability of .45. Following a critical and one-sided review of much of the same evidence, Kamin (1974) concluded that the available data do not compel us to reject the hypothesis that the heritability of intelligence is zero. Loehlin et al. (1975), in an exceptionally fair and cautious review focusing primarily on race differences, allowed that the evidence is clearly inconsistent with heritabilities of 0.0 and 1.0. In another review Lewontin (1975) concluded that the heritability of IQ is utterly trivial and hardly worth the effort necessary to carry out decent studies.

How is one to reconcile such discrepant conclusions from analyses of essentially the same collection of studies? The answer seems to be that the data do allow a rather wide range of interpretations, depending on the method of analysis used and the assumptions and corrections employed. For example, Jencks divided the IQ variance into .45 due to heredity, .35 due to environment, and .20 due to covariance of genes and environment, on the basis of a path analysis which involved a specific model and specific assumptions about the data. Loehlin et al. (1975, Appendix I) showed that by changing certain paths in the model to equally (if not more) plausible positions, Jencks's data yield variance estimates of .60 due to heredity, .25 due to environment, and .15 due to covariance of heredity and environment. By a somewhat different selection of assumptions and studies (especially omitting the Burt data; see below) it seems likely that Jensen's calculations could be made to converge on a heritability of .60 as well. Thus, among those honestly attempting to arrive at the best possible estimate of heritability on the basis of available evidence, a range of values from about .45 to .80 has been reported. At the upper or the lower limit of this range, it becomes relatively easy to cite reasonably good evidence to pull the estimate back in the other direction. Thus the interested bystander, not wishing to make his own calculations and having no reason to prefer one extreme over the other, might reasonably adopt a compromise value of .60 as a working hypothesis, with a confidence interval of about .20 around this value. As we shall see, the exact value of the heritability coefficient has little importance for policy.

Kamin's analysis had a different objective from the others. He made no attempt to arrive at a reasonable estimate of heritability. Instead he tried to show that the data on which high heritability estimates have been based are faulty, and this attempt was tellingly successful. He was responsible for first calling into question the extensive and influential data collection and analyses of Cyril Burt (Wade, 1976a). Although it is still a matter of dispute whether or not Burt deliberately manufactured or altered data to fit his theory (Jensen, 1978; McAskie, 1978), it is generally agreed that Burt's data should not be used as strong evidence for any theory. Rimland and Munsinger (1977) have shown that Burt's results are not out of line with those of other investigators, however. Kamin was also able to cast some degree of doubt on the suitability of many of the classic studies for the heritability calculations usually made from them.

Kamin's trenchant criticisms have been a valuable contribution to the evaluation of previous studies and should help to improve the quality and openness of research in this area in the future, although in pointing out the errors of others he made a number of serious errors himself (Fulker, 1975; Scarr-Salapatek, 1976). However, the impression that a casual reader of Kamin might obtain—that there are no data in this area worth looking at—is clearly wrong. Kamin's proposed environmental interpretations of the remaining data that he could not dismiss on methodological grounds are individually reasonable, though often improbable. Identical twins could be treated more alike than are fraternal twins in a way and to a degree necessary to make them considerably more alike in intelligence. Separated identical twins raised in the same town or in similar circumstances could have environments similar enough to make them similar in intelligence, but hardly more similar than fraternal twins reared together, as they are reported to be. Selective placement could have operated in such a way to account for many of the findings of adoption studies; the older age of adoptive parents could account for some of the differences between adoptive and control families, and so on. Taken together, however, these post hoc explanations seem improbable. The whole is less than the sum of the parts. Where is the independent evidence to show that the proposed environmental influences have even a small effect on intelligence? Kamin may be correct in saying that no single study compels us to believe that IQ is in any degree heritable, but this hardly applies to the collection of studies as a whole.

Some comments concerning the interpretation of the heritability coefficient may be appropriate here. Heritability is a statistic descriptive of a population and is not inherent in the trait itself. It is dependent on the variability of the salient environmental and genetic factors in the population, and thus it may tell us more about the nature of the population than about the trait. If either environmental or genetic variability changes, the heritability will change accordingly. However, this does not mean that heritability is capricious or completely sample specific, as some have suggested. Roughly similar values seem to be found in most European and American studies, but some caution is probably in order in generalizing to, say, blacks, who have not been adequately studied. It seems likely that the heritability of intelligence has increased substantially over the past several hundred years, due to increased homogeneity of environmental and educational opportunities and the increased genetic diversity resulting from greater mobility of populations and consequent gene mixing. This trend is probably continuing at present.

Heritability provides an indication of the maximum effects that might be obtained by environmental manipulation within the range of environments included in the studies in which heritability was determined. In most studies environmental variation has been limited to that found in typical middle-class Western culture. Thus severe environmental deprivation, for example, could have a large effect on the development of intellectual ability, in spite of a high heritability coefficient. Similarly, if the salient environmental influences producing, say, birth-order effects were known and were intensified and concentrated, there is nothing about a high heritability coefficient to suggest that they could not have a very large effect.

Since environmental influences that are known to have substantial effects on health or on ability are fairly quickly distributed to most members of the society in developed countries, it seems likely that the major effects from environmental manipulations will be observed in changes in the average level of the population over time, while genetic effects and unknown environmental influences will be largely responsible for individual differences at a given time. This thought was first expressed by Thorndike (1905) and has been widely quoted since.

THE HERITABILITY OF OTHER BEHAVIORAL TRAITS

Genetic influences on a variety of traits of personality and interest have been investigated by comparing identical and fraternal twins reared together, and these studies have been reviewed by Vandenberg (1967) and by Nichols (1976). As a general rule identical twins are more alike than are fraternal twins on practically every trait that has been studied. Some investigators have tried to distinguish more and less heritable traits on the basis of twin studies, but findings are not consistent in this regard. A difference of about .20 between identical and fraternal twin correlations is found for a wide range of personality and interest measures. On the basis of a large twin study including a diversity of personality and interest measures, Loehlin and Nichols (1976) concluded that the data did not provide evidence sufficient to establish that the difference in similarity between the two kinds of twins was dependably different for different personality traits.

Most adoption studies have been concerned either with cognitive abilities or with psychopathology. DeFries and Plomin (1978) have reviewed adoption studies showing genetic influences in schizophrenia, criminal behavior, alcoholism, and hyperactivity in children.

Grotevant, Scarr-Salapatek, and Weinberg (1976) studied family resemblance in interests of 65 adoptive families and 89 biological control families as part of the Minnesota adoption study discussed above. Parent-child and sibling comparisons revealed that biologically related family members modestly resembled each other on the various interest scales as well as on the profile of interests, while unrelated family members in the adoptive families showed no resemblance at all in interests.

Although the evidence for genetic factors in individual differences in nonintellective traits is not as extensive as that for intelligence, the existing data consistently suggest some degree of genetic influence on most traits of personality and interest. It is likely that differences in such traits as dependability, academic interest, activity level, and cooperativeness, which are important elements in educational achievement, are, like intelligence, determined in part by genetic differences.

Sociobiology

The controversy over the new field of sociobiology has not been a part of the IQ controversy. Concern about the possible policy implications of a biological basis for human behavior is the root of both disputes, however. The basic ideas of sociobiology tend not to disturb hereditarians, while they chafe environmentalists. Sociobiology is the analysis of animal behavior in terms of its evolutionary significance or its adaptive value for Darwinian fitness. The widespread observation of animals helping other animals has led to the concept of *inclusive fitness*, in which an animal might perpetuate its genes not only by reproducing itself, but also by helping relatives, who share some or all of its genes, to reproduce. The central theorem of sociobiology is that animals tend to behave so as to maximize their inclusive fitness. Wilson (1975) and, in a somewhat simpler book, Barash (1977) have provided analyses of an overwhelming variety of animal behavior which suggests that this central theorem is almost certainly true.

Both Wilson and Barash included a final chapter in which sociobiological analysis is extended to human behavior, and this has been the source of dispute (Sociobiology Study Group, 1976; Wade, 1976b). While the IQ controversy concerns the degree to which individual differences are genetically determined, the sociobiology controversy concerns the degree to which typical patterns of behavior are dependent on the genes. For example, are such common human social patterns as masculine aggressiveness and feminine coyness, concern about lines of kinship, and the incest taboo brought about because during the long evolution of Homo sapiens, individuals who behaved in this way were more likely than others were to have their genes represented in later generations? Or are these social patterns the result of cultural evolution and learning? The sociobiologists present reasonable scenarios of how a variety of common human social patterns could have contributed to genetic survival on the African savannas where mankind evolved. These post hoc explanations, however, are not considered to be sufficient proof by the critics.

A critical assumption of sociobiological analysis is that individual differences in such traits as altruism, cheating, concern for relatives, deception, and reciprocity are to some degree heritable, so natural selection for these traits can produce genetic changes in subsequent generations. If this condition is met it seems reasonable to suppose that the average level of these traits would be determined by the evolutionary process. The heritability analyses of nonintellec tive traits discussed above are relevant to this assumption. In a persuasive critique of the sociobiology of human behavior, however, Washburn (1978) argued that the development of language has made human society categorically different from that of other animals. He suggests that cultural learning, made possible by language, has largely supplanted biological determination as the basis for human behavior.

Magoon (1978) has proposed that the point of view represented by sociobiology has implications for educational policy, in that the most effective educational practices are likely to be those that take advantage of the basic patterns of learning which have been built into the human brain by evolution.

IMPLICATIONS FOR EDUCATIONAL POLICY

Throughout most of the polemical papers of the IQ controversy is the sometimes implicit, sometimes explicit assumption that important policy issues hinge on the outcome of the debate. Yet the exact policy alternatives that depend on the heritability of IQ are rarely discussed in detail. In fact, when an explicit policy implication is suggested by one side it is usually denied by the other. For example, Lewontin (1970) said Jensen's "programmatic conclusion is that there is no use in trying to remove the [race] difference in IQ by education, since it arises chiefly from genetic causes and the best thing that can be done for black children is to capitalize on those skills for which they are biologically adapted" (p. 79), to which Jensen (1970b) replied, "I do not advocate abandoning efforts to improve the education of the disadvantaged. I urge increased emphasis on these efforts, in the spirit of experimentation, expanding the diversity of approaches and improving the rigor of evaluation in order to boost our chances of discovering the methods that will work best" (p. 97).

It seems likely that no policy issues are so clearly related to the heritability of IQ that both sides would agree that they are, in fact, policy implications of the IQ controversy. Instead there seems to be a dimension of political philosophy or world view that is related to preference for the biological over the environmental explanation of human behavior, and that is also related to preferences for a variety of educational and social policy alternatives. The controversy thus seems to be fueled not by the need to obtain the right answer in order to reveal the proper policy alternative, but by the desire to support one or another world view which leads to a given set of policy preferences. Hereditarians seem to be comfortable with individual differences as a basis for important social distinctions, while environmentalists seem somehow embarrassed by them, particularly when they are the basis for discriminations that appear to be inhumane or unfair.

Lewontin (1970) characterized the competing world views as one "in which true merit, be it genetically or environmentally determined, will be the criterion of men's earthly reward" on the one hand, and one "in which every man can aspire to the fullest measure of psychic and material fulfillment that social activity can produce" on the other (p. 92). This characterization does not quite capture the distinctive quality of the latter position, probably because Lewontin seems to have been trying to make it appear to be the more attractive alternative. Aspiration to the fullest measure of fulfillment is actually a characteristic of the meritocracy in which differential capabilities determine the degree to which the aspiration is achieved. The latter alternative might be more accurately characterized as "one in which every person receives an equitable share of the psychic and material fulfillment that social activity produces, regardless of his or her contribution to the production." For short, the dimension might be dubbed a preference for competitive vs. egalitarian social models. Hereditarians tend to lean toward the competitive end and environmentalists toward the egalitarian end of the continuum. Hereditarians frequently claim that their research is not prompted by political motives of any kind, but by the belief that open scientific research will eventually lead to desirable social ends,[1] but environmentalists (e.g., Kamin, 1974) see political motives and bias underlying almost all studies of the nature-nurture issue.

Most of the supposed policy implications of the IQ controversy seem to derive from this argument concerning who gets what from whom and how, and, since education is the major vehicle by which both ability and family status are translated into socioeconomic achievement (Duncan, 1968), many of the policy issues concern education.

If the heritability of intelligence were conclusively shown to be 0.0 or 1.0, a large majority might be convinced that one or another policy alternative would be the best course. However, the firmest conclusion that can be drawn from all of the research on the nature-nurture issue to date is that the heritability of intelligence is neither 0.0 nor 1.0. Thus there is room for both sides to find support from the empirical findings. Raising or lowering the heritability estimate by .1 or .2

may sway those near the margin, but there will always be room for argument from the extremes. Perhaps this is why the nature-nurture debate has erupted periodically for over 100 years and seems no nearer to resolution now than in the past.

Compensatory Education

One of the major policy differences between the environmentalists and hereditarians is their differential enthusiasm for compensatory education programs for racial minorities and socioeconomically disadvantaged groups. If the lower achievement of these groups is attributed to socially imposed disadvantages, the society should feel obligated to make extraordinary efforts to remedy the deficiency. If the lower achievement is attributable to inherent differences in ability, the moral obligation to compensate is not felt, although we might want to make exceptional efforts to increase the achievement of lower ability groups for other reasons. Gage (1972) stated the issue baldly:

This hypothesis [genetic basis for racial differences in intelligence] provokes intellectual and political fights because of its implications, if accepted, for legislation aimed at improving the education of Negroes and other low income students. It can be construed as implying that such legislation is futile. If that belief is accepted by political leaders, our governments will not give educators, and their research and development arms, the money they need for work toward reducing the educational and employment disadvantages suffered by Negroes and other minorities. (p. 308)

The evidence concerning the genetic basis for group differences does seem to have a bearing on the moral obligation of the society to attempt to reduce differences, although it is likely that one's sense of moral obligation affects one's interpretation of the heritability evidence more than the other way around. The heritability evidence, however, is an unnecessarily indirect and unreliable basis for estimating the probable effectiveness of a given educational program when the program can be tried directly in experiments. It would seem to be unwise for political leaders to judge the value of proposed programs on the basis of deductions from the heritability evidence. The use of heritability arguments for or against a given educational proposal as a substitute for obtaining more direct experimental evidence is more a political act than an application of science.

In the 1960s the environmentalist position was widely accepted, and hereditarians were quiescent. Ambitious compensatory programs were undertaken with unrealistically high expectations, in part because of the general belief in the environmental origin of group differences. The failure to achieve these expectations has led to a general disillusionment with education, which seems to be an undesirable outcome. The error was not that the environmental theory was wrong but that it was used inappropriately to promote untried programs on a wide scale. There seems to be danger now that the genetic theory will be used with equal inappropriateness to suppress the experimental trial of programs that might be beneficial.

Moral and political considerations aside, the answer to the question of which children, if any, should receive exceptional educational resources depends on which will benefit most, although judgment of the relative value of different benefits inevitably involves moral and political issues. Environmentalists have tended to assume that poor performance, being the result of environmental deficiencies, will respond most favorably to additional resources, while hereditarians, impressed by the high correlation of IQ and achievement, have assumed that the higher the ability, the greater the capacity to use additional educational inputs. Bereiter (1970), commenting on the data reviewed by Jensen (1969), suggested that both positions may be correct. The data appear to indicate that environmental enrichment tends to increase individual differences in achievement, with those initially higher gaining more from new resources than those initially lower. On the other hand, some environmental influences appear to operate as threshold variables, which are significant sources of variation only when below some minimal value, and disadvantaged children may be below the threshold on some environmental variables. From these observations Bereiter deduced that manipulation of nonexperiential variables, such as nutrition and health care, may produce exceptional benefits for disadvantaged children. Further, educational enrichment may produce exceptional benefits for disadvantaged children and for gifted children. As noted above, however, such deductions from heritability studies are an inadequate basis for policy, and Bereiter's proposals were wisely in the form of guides for research, not recommendations for policy.

Equality

The phrase *equality of educational opportunity* has been a slogan behind which hereditarians and environmentalists could unite for some time. Gradually, however, it has come to have distinctly different meanings for the two groups, and the unity has dissolved. In a review of the history of the concept of equality of educational opportunity, Coleman (1968) noted that until relatively recently the phrase has meant equality of access to appropriate educational resources, regardless of race, religion, sex, socioeconomic status, or other artificial impediments. Only ability and motivation would determine the level of educational achievement. "Let each become all that he is capable of being," is the way it is phrased in the motto of the State University of New York. This concept had appeal to both the competitive and egalitarian ends of the continuum, since it held that success depended on merit and unfair discrimination was swept away.

Coleman (1963) attributed the beginning of deviation from this concept of equality to the Equality of Educational Opportunity survey (Coleman et al., 1966), which revealed unexpectedly large group differences in achievement that were largely independent of the distribution of educational resources. A new criterion, equality of outcome, was adopted by environmentalists as the appropriate measure of equality of opportunity. Schools "are successful only insofar as they reduce the dependence of a child's opportunities upon his social origins. . . . Thus, equality of educational opportunity implies, not merely 'equal' schools, but equally effective schools, whose influences will overcome the differences in starting point of children from social groups" (Coleman et al., 1966, p. 72). It was Jensen's (1969) questioning of the appropriateness of this criterion on the grounds that the group differences may be in part genetic that led to the current outbreak of the IQ controversy. However appropriate or inappropriate it may seem, the achievement of equality of outcome has proved to be an elusive goal during the past decade. Gordon (1976) lamented that

Despite cumulative appropriations of what must be nearly $30 billion and an enormous amount of sometimes misdirected effort and equivocal research, we still don't know how to make school achievement and developmental opportunity independent of social position. Our best general predictor of success in school is successful birth into a middle- or upper-class Caucasian family.[2] (p. 101)

Disappointed that compensatory programs failed to remedy what seemed prima facie to be the result of unfair discrimination, many environmentalists adopted the concept of *representative equality*, in which "groups discriminated against on the basis of ascriptive characteristics of race, ethnicity, or sex have a chance equal to that of the overadvantaged groups to attain higher positions" (Miller, 1976, p. 19). This concept has led to programs referred to as affirmative action, compensatory opportunity, or positive discrimination, in which members of disadvantaged groups are given an advantage in competition for desirable educational programs or occupational positions. It is representational equality, much more than compensatory education, that has caused a parting of the ways of hereditarians and environmentalists on the equality issue. The hereditarians object to the abandonment of merit as the criterion of success and to the unfairness of reverse discrimination. The undoing of the results of past discrimination, which is a strong compensating value for environmentalists, is not an attraction to hereditarians, who do not consider mean differences in group performance to be a valid indicator of discrimination. The hereditarians prefer to concentrate on the individual, on the grounds that if all individuals are treated fairly, then groups, which are composed of individuals, will also be treated fairly, even though mean differences among the groups remain. For example, Jensen (1976) said that,

The notion of representative equality in education . . . is based on the false premise that the observed group differences in input and output are merely signs of discrimination, racism, or social injustice. I advocate focusing on individuals in education, and evaluating educational programs in terms of their effectiveness in maximizing individual potential rather than in terms of equalizing group differences. (p. 131)

Hereditarians from Galton (1869/1962) through Terman (Seagoe, 1975) to the present have typically been more interested in the high end of the intelligence distribution than in the low, since the intellectually gifted are seen as representing the best genetic material with which educators can work and the best hope for exceptional achievement in life. Environmentalists, on the other hand, tend to be more interested in those who score low, since they are seen as unfortunate victims of a harsh environment, while the gifted show by their performance that they have already received more than their fair share of advantages. There is, thus, a difference in viewpoint concerning who should be educated.

Hereditarians tend to prefer a strong positive correlation between intelligence and educational attainment, which would enhance individual differences and provide meaningful credentials by which the most able can be selected for the most important jobs. The environmentalists tend to prefer a smaller positive correlation than exists, which would reduce individual differences and allow for representational equality. Growing out of the strong environmentalist influence in the 1960s, most federal programs recently have emphasized considerations of equality over quality. In 1977, 76% of federal educational appropriations were intended to equalize educational opportunity in some way (Stormsdorfer, 1977).

These efforts appear to have been effective. Peng (1977) compared college entry rates for various groups in the National Longitudinal Study for 1972 with comparable rates from Project Talent in 1961. Overall the rate of entry into postsecondary education of high school graduates declined slightly (from 59 to 54%), and there was a considerable shift from four-year to two-year institutions. However, substantial progress was made in changing attendance patterns in the direction sought by national policy makers. Sex differences and socioeconomic differences in college attendance were substantially reduced over the 11-year period. Although race was not available in the Project Talent data, the race differences in 1972 were attributable to differences in SES and ability. When these two variables were controlled, blacks were somewhat more likely to enter college than were whites, which is undoubtedly a great improvement over 1961. On the other hand, the Project Talent data showed that in 1961 some 70 percent of the men and 63 percent of the women in the top ability quartile entered a four-year college. In 1972 only 54 percent of both sexes in the highest quarter in ability entered a four-year college. When two-year colleges were included, there was still a substantial decline in college entry of the most able high school graduates. It is likely that environmentalists would be pleased with these results, while hereditarians would be dismayed at the decline in the education of the most able.

Improving IQ and Achievement

How much can we boost IQ and scholastic achievement? This question, the title of Jensen's 1969 article, is perhaps the most important one for educational policy. Concerns about increasing or decreasing individual differences seem relatively unimportant when compared with improving the overall level of academic achievement, and there is no disagreement concerning the most desirable direction for change.

In the 1960s environmentalists were optimistic that provision of appropriate experiences could raise the IQ by as much as 20 or 30 points (Bloom, 1964; Hunt, 1961), and the available evidence suggested that average scores were in fact increasing substantially over time (Tuddenham, 1948). They reacted with disbelief (Bloom, 1969; Hunt, 1969) when Jensen (1969) suggested, largely on the basis of heritability analyses, that it seemed unlikely that educational intervention would have an appreciable effect. Over the past decade, however, the studies of school effects reviewed above, along with evidence that average ability has begun to decline (Advisory Panel, 1977), have tended to quell the optimism.

The violent swing in expectations of what education can accomplish which has occurred over the past decade appears to have been accompanied by a shift in the modal scientific opinion from extreme environmentalism to a tentative middle ground. Although this position includes substantial environmental variance, we now hear only modest predictions of what might be achieved. For example, Bereiter (1976) estimated that the average IQ might be raised by about two points by widespread application of what is known concerning "such conventional and benign means as improved prenatal and postnatal care, better nutrition, and generally greater stimulation throughout the years of growth." He pointed out that this would not be a negligible result, since it would increase by a third the number of people with IQs above 130, "who perform most of our professional and highly technical work," and it would have a similar beneficial effect at the low end.

Bereiter indicated that the reason more cannot be expected is that most of the environmental influences on intelligence are unknown, and he urged increased research, particularly in the area of heredity-environment interaction. He commented that "One of the ironies of the environmentalists' opposition to research on the genetics of human intelligence is that they thereby block efforts that might lead to discovery of environmental ways to treat intellectual deficits." Such chiding of the environmentalists for their apparent lack of interest in research to isolate the large environmental effects that they claim exist has long been a favorite tactic of the hereditarians. For example, Terman (1922) issued the following facetious challenge to the environmentalists:

It is high time that we were investigating the IQ effects of different kinds of baby talk, different versions of Mother Goose, and different makes of pacifers and safety pins. If there is any possibility of identifying, weighing, and bringing under control these IQ stimulants and depressors, we can well afford to throw up every other kind of scientific research until the job is accomplished. That problem once solved, the rest of the mysteries of the universe would fall easy prey before our made-to-order IQs of 180 or 200. (p. 119)

The environmentalists, of course, have not been uninterested in research, but in their drive to promote equality they have generally accepted as self-evident the hypothesis that the favorable environmental influences are those that are associated with socioeconomic status. Since manipulations deduced from this hypothesis have tended not to have the expected effects, it seems likely that the scope of environmentalist research will increase. The potential payoff from the discovery of new environmental influences on intelligence is great and should justify a policy of increased research.

It seems that genetic variability contributes substantially to individual differences in intelligence, yet, like the environment, the mechanism by which it contributes is unknown. Thus the hereditarians are no better off than the environmentalists, whom they chide, in terms of knowing how their favorite influence works. When the genetic mechanism is known, as in phenylketonuria, for example, it is often possible to have a large influence on the result. Loehlin et al. (1975) have pointed out the fallacy in the popular supposition that genetic variance is fixed and that only environmental variance provides hope of improvement. They suggest that, when both biological and environmental mechanisms are finally understood, it is probable that the biological will be the easier to change. The potential payoff from knowledge of the biological basis for intelligence is great and should justify a policy of increased research.

It is worth noting that, although the relative contributions of genetic and environmental factors to individual differences in intelligence may have implications for the political desirability or moral necessity of various policy objectives, as discussed above, the tactical achievement of many of these objectives depends on knowledge of the mechanism by which the genetic or environmental influences work. When the mechanism is unknown the implication for tactical policy is the same, whether the unknown mechanism is genetic or environmental. The implication is that no effective tactical policy is possible.

Eugenics

Since the correlation of intelligence scores of parent and child is about .50, the average ability of a group of children can be determined by selecting the parents. It should be noted that this result follows simply from statistical regression, and it holds true regardless of whether the parent-child correlation is due to genetic or to environmental factors or to some combination of the two. Thus, both hereditarians and environmentalists who are interested in improving the intelligence of children have a mechanism by which it can be done. The idea of actually trying to manipulate who becomes the parents of the next generation, however, has always been as appealing to hereditarians as it has been an anathema to environmentalists. It is not immediately apparent why this should be so. It might be that hereditarians envision a more permanent gain by having the improvement encoded in the genes, but one would think that the prospect of having the next generation of children raised in more favorable environments would be equally appealing to environmentalists. It might be that environmentalists are more squeamish than hereditarians are about interfering with the rights of parents, but it is usually the hereditarians who object to the attempt to promote equality by restricting the ability of successful parents to advance the fortunes of their own children. Yet, for some unknown reason, it is usually the hereditarians who make eugenics proposals and the environmentalists who object to them.

There has been a great variety of eugenics proposals, and the major papers from Galton to the present have been collected by Bajema (1976). The more ambitious and coercive proposals of the past have not surfaced since the fallacious and brutal racial policies of the Nazis made the danger of misuse of any such program all too painfully obvious. Recent eugenics proposals have been modest in scope and entirely voluntary. The leading positive eugenics proposal (seeking to increase fecundity of the most suitable parents) is the method of germinal choice (Muller, 1965) in which sperm from the most desirable males would be stored and made available to women who voluntarily choose to conceive a child with it. The leading negative eugenics proposal (seeking to restrict reproduction by the least suitable parents) is the voluntary sterilization bonus (Shockley, 1972), in which a bonus amounting to $1,000 for each IQ point below 100 would be offered for voluntary sterilization to nonpayers of income tax. It is interesting to note that the originators of both of these proposals are winners of the Nobel prize, and both have used their prestige to urge public acceptance of the eugenic idea, with equally unimpressive results.

CONCLUSION

The IQ controversy appears to be the result of the presumed implications of the heritability of intelligence for the distribution of educational resources. Since the heritability has been demonstrated to be neither 0.0 nor 1.0, the policy implications do not follow directly from the empirical results but depend instead on various political values. Additional research arising out of the controversy suggests that the initial assumption that the distribution of educational resources will have important effects on broader social problems is not correct.

For educational policy in general, the implications of genetic and environmental determinants of individual differences in intelligence are the same and are minimal so long as the mechanism by which intelligence is affected remains unknown.

NOTES

1. A paper by Jensen (1968a), based on a lecture given at the Universities of Adelaide, La Trobe, Melbourne, and Sydney in Australia during September and October 1977, expresses this idea. It is interesting to note that this lecture, which explicitly disclaims political motivation and concentrates exclusively on scientific issues, was canceled by

the authorities in three other Australian universities because of threatened demonstrations against Jensen's appearance on their campuses.
2. This is an overstatement. The best general predictor of success in school is an individual IQ test.

REFERENCES

Advisory Panel on the Scholastic Aptitude Test Score Decline. *On further examination.* New York: College Entrance Examination Board, 1977.

Astin, A. W. Undergraduate achievement and institutional "excellence." *Science*, 1968, *161*, 661-668.

Averch, H. A., Carroll, S. J., Donaldson, T. S., Kiesling, H. J., & Pincus, J. *How effective is schooling? A critical review and synthesis of research findings.* Santa Monica, Calif.: Rand, 1972.

Backman, M. E. Patterns of mental abilities: Ethnic, socioeconomic, and sex differences. *American Educational Research Journal*, 1972, *9*, 1-12.

Bajema, C. J. *Eugenics: Then and now.* Stroudsburg, Pa.: Dowden, Hutchinson & Ross, 1976.

Barash, D. P. *Sociobiology and behavior.* Amsterdam: Elsevier North-Holland, 1977.

Bayley, N. Consistency and variability in the growth of intelligence from birth to eighteen years. *Journal of Genetic Psychology*, 1949, *75*, 165-196.

Bayley, N. Behavioral correlates of mental growth: Birth to 36 years. *American Psychologist*, 1968, *23*, 1-17.

Belmont, L., & Marolla, F. A. Birth order, family size, and intelligence. *Science*, 1973, *182*, 1095-1101.

Bereiter, C. Genetics and educability: Educational implications of the Jensen debate. In J. Helmuth (Ed.), *Disadvantaged child.* (Vol. 3). New York: Brunner/Mazel, 1970.

Bereiter, C. IQ differences and social policy. In N. F. Ashline, T. R. Pezzullo, and C. I. Norris (Eds.), *Education, inequality, and national policy.* Lexington, Mass.: Lexington Books, 1976.

Berg, A. *The nutrition factor: Its role in national development.* Washington, D.C.: Brookings Institution, 1973.

Bettelheim, B. Feral children and autistic children. *American Journal of Sociology*, 1959, *64*, 455-467.

Birch, H. G., Pineiro, C., Alcalde, E., Toca, T., & Cravioto, J. Kwashiorkor in early childhood and intelligence at school age. *Pediatric Research*, 1971, *5*, 579-584.

Block, J. H. Issues, problems, and pitfalls in assessing sex differences: A critical review of *The psychology of sex differences. Merrill-Palmer Quarterly*, 1976, *22*, 283-308.

Block, N. J., & Dworkin, G. I.Q., heritability, and inequality. *Philosophy and Public Affairs*, 1974, *3*, 331-409 (part 1) and *4*, 40-99 (part 2).

Block, N. J., & Dworkin, G. (Eds.). *The IQ controversy: Critical readings.* New York: Pantheon Books, 1976.

Bloom, B. S. *Stability and change in human characteristics.* New York: John Wiley, 1964.

Bloom, B. S. Letter to the editor. *Harvard Educational Review*, 1969, *39*, 419-421.

Breland, H. M. Birth order, family configuration, and verbal achievement. *Child Development*, 1974, *45*, 1011-1019.

Brodway, K. P., & Thompson, C. W. Intelligence at adulthood: A twenty-five-year followup. *Journal of Educational Psychology*, 1962, *53*, 1-14.

Brozek, J. Nutrition, malnutrition and behavior. *Annual Review of Psychology*, 1978, *29*, 157-178.

Carew, J. V. *Social class, everyday experience and the growth of intelligence in young children*. Paper presented at the third biennial conference of the International Society for the Study of Behavioral Development, Guildford, England, July, 1975.

Cicirelli, V. G., Evans, J. W., & Schiller, J. S. The impact of Head Start: A reply to the report analysis. *Harvard Educational Review*, 1970, *40*, 105-129.

Clarke, A. M., & Clarke, A. D. B. *Early experience: Myth and evidence*. New York: Free Press, 1976.

Cleary, T. A., Humphreys, L. G., Kendrick, S. A., & Wesman, A. Educational uses of tests with disadvantaged students. *American Psychologist*, 1975, *30*, 15-41.

Coleman, J. S. The concept of equality of educational opportunity. *Harvard Educational Review*, 1968, *38*, 7-22.

Coleman, J. S., Campbell, E. Q., Hobson, C. J., McPartland, J., Mood, A. M., Weinfeld, F. D., & York, R. L. *Equality of educational opportunity*. Washington, D.C.: U.S. Government Printing Office, 1966.

Coulson, J. E., Hanes, S. D., Ozenne, D. G., Bradford, C., Doherty, W. J., Duck, G. A., and Hamenway, J. A. *The third year of Emergency School Aid Act (ESAA) implementation*. Rep. of Contract Nos. OEC-0-73-0831 and OEC-0-73-6336 (TM-5236/014/00). Santa Monica, Calif.: System Development Corporation, March 1977.

Curtiss, S. *Genie: A psycholinguistic study of a modern-day "wild child."* New York: Academic Press, 1977.

Davis, K. Extreme social isolation of a child. *American Journal of Sociology*. 1940, *45*, 554-556.

Davis, K. Final note on a case of extreme isolation. *American Journal of Sociology*, 1947, *57*, 432-457.

DeFries, J. C., Hegmann, J. P., & Halcomb, R. A. Response to 20 generations of selection for open-field activity in mice. *Behavioral Biology*, 1974, *11*, 481-495.

DeFries, J. C., & Plomin, R. Behavioral genetics. *Annual Review of Psychology*, 1978, *29*, 473-516.

DeGroot, A. D. War and the intelligence of youth. *Journal of Abnormal and Social Psychology*, 1951, *46*, 596-597.

Duncan, O. D. Ability and achievement. *Eugenics Quarterly*, 1968, *15*, 1-11.

Eaves, L. J. Testing models for variation in intelligence. *Heredity*, 1975, *34*, 132-136.

Eckland, B. K. Genetics and sociology: A reconsideration. *American Sociological Review*, 1967, *32*, 173-194.

Elderton, E. M. A summary of the present position with regard to the inheritance of intelligence. *Biometrika*, 1922-1923, *14*, 378-408.

Erlenmeyer-Kimling, L., & Jarvik, L. F. Genetics and intelligence: A review. *Science*, 1963, *142*, 1477-1479.

Falconer, D. S. *Introduction to quantitative genetics*. New York: Ronald Press, 1960.

Firkowska, A., Ostrowska, A., Sokolowska, M., Stein, Z., Susser, M., and Wald, I. Cognitive development and social policy. *Science*, 1978, 200, 1357-1362.

Fulker, D. W. Review of *The science and politics of IQ* by L. J. Kamin. *American Journal of Psychology*, 1975, *88*, 505-537.

Gage, N. L. I.Q. heritability, race differences and educational research. *Phi Delta Kappan*, 1972, *53*, 308-312.

Galton, F. *Hereditary genius*. New York: World Publishing Co., 1962. (Originally published, 1869.)

Garber, H., and Heber, F. R. The Milwaukee Project: Indications of the effectiveness of early intervention in preventing mental retardation. In P. Mittler (Ed.), *Research to practice in mental retardation: Care and intervention*, Vol. I. Baltimore: University Park Press, 1977.

Gesell, A. *Wolf child and human child*. New York: Harper, 1940.

Goldberger, A. S. On Jensen's method for twins. *Educational Psychologist*, 1976, *12*, 79-82.

Goldberger, A. S. *Models and methods in the IQ debate: Part I* (SSRI Workshop Series). Madison: Social Systems Research Institute, University of Wisconsin-Madison, 1977. (a)

Goldberger, A. S. Twin methods: A skeptical view. In P. Taubman (Ed.), *Kinometrics*. Amsterdam: North-Holland, 1977. (b)

Gordon, E. Education of the disadvantaged: A problem of human diversity. In N. F. Ashline, T. T. Pezzullo, and C. I. Norris (Eds.), *Education, inequality, and national policy*. Lexington, Mass.: Lexington Books, 1976.

Gray, S. W., & Klaus, R. A. An experimental preschool program for culturally deprivated children. *Child Development*, 1965, *36*, 887-898.

Grotevant, H. D., Scarr-Salapatek, S., & Weinberg, R. A. *Resemblances of personality and interest styles in adoptive and biological families*. Paper presented at the sixth annual meeting of the Behavior Genetics Association, Boulder, Colorado, June 1976.

Härnqvist, K. Changes in intelligence from 13 to 18. *Scandinavian Journal of Psychology*, 1968, *9*, 50-82.

Härnqvist, K. Enduring effects of schooling—A neglected area in educational research. *Educational Researcher*, 1977, *6* (10), 5-10.

Herrnstein, R. J. *I.Q. in the meritocracy*. Boston: Little, Brown, 1973.

Hildreth, G. H. *The resemblance of siblings in intelligence and achievement*. New York: Teachers College Press, Columbia University, 1925.

Hildreth, G. H. Adopted children in a private school. In G. M. Whipple (Ed.), *The 39th yearbook of the National Society for the Study of Education. Intelligence: Its nature and nurture. Part II. Original studies and experiments*. Bloomington, Ill.: Public School Publishing Co., 1940.

House, E. R., Glass, G. V., McLean, L. D. & Walker, D. F. No simple answer: Critique of the Follow Through Evaluation. *Harvard Educational Review*, 1978, *48*, 128-160.

Hunt, J. McV. Intelligence and experience. New York: Ronald Press, 1961.

Hunt, J. McV. The psychological basis for using pre-school enrichment as an antidote for cultural deprivation. *Merrill-Palmer Quarterly*, 1964, *10*, 209-248.

Hunt, J. McV. Has compensatory education failed? Has it been attempted? *Harvard Educational Review*, 1969, *39*, 278-300.

Jencks, C. *Inequality: A reassessment of the effect of family and schooling in America*. New York: Basic Books, 1972.

Jensen, A. R. Estimation of the limits of heritability of traits by comparison of monozygotic and dizygotic twins. *Proceedings of the National Academy of Sciences*, 1967, *58*, 149-156.

Jensen, A. R. How much can we boost IQ and scholastic achievement? *Harvard Educational Review*, 1969, *39*, 1-123.

Jensen, A. R. IQs of identical twins reared apart. *Behavior Genetics*, 1970, *1*, 133-146. (a)

Jensen, A. R. Race and the genetics of intelligence: A reply to Lewontin. *Bulletin of the Atomic Scientists*, 1970, *26*, 9-22. (b)

Jensen, A. R. Note on why genetic correlations are not squared. *Psychological Bulletin*, 1971, *75*, 223-224.

Jensen, A. R. *Educability and group differences*. New York: Harper & Row, 1973.

Jensen, A. R. Cumulative deficit: A testable hypothesis? *Developmental Psychology*, 1974, *10*, 996-1019. (a)

Jensen, A. R. How biased are culture-loaded tests? *Genetic Psychology Monographs*, 1974, *90*, 185-244. (b)

Jensen, A. R. Equality and diversity in education. In N. F. Ashline, T. R. Pezzullo, & C. I. Norris (Eds.), *Education, inequality and national policy*. Lexington, Mass.: Lexington Books, 1976.

Jensen, A. R. Cumulative deficit in I.Q. of blacks in the rural South. *Developmental Psychology*, 1977, *13*, 184-191.

Jensen, A. R. The current status of the IQ controversy. *Australian Psychologist*, 1978, *13*, 7-27. (a)

Jensen, A. R. Sir Cyril Burt in perspective. *American Psychologist*, 1978, *33*, 499-503. (b)

Jensen, A. R. Personal communication, January 6, 1978. (c)

Jensen, A. R., & Figueroa, R. A. Forward and backward digit span interaction with race and I.Q.: Predictions from Jensen's theory. *Journal of Educational Psychology*, 1975, *67*, 882-893.

Jinks, J. L., & Eaves, L. J. I.Q. and inequality. *Nature*, 1974, *248*, 287-289.

Jinks, J. L., & Fulker, D. W. Comparison of the biometrical genetical, MAVA, and classical approaches to the analysis of human behavior. *Psychological Bulletin*, 1970, *73*, 311-349.

Kagan, J., & Moss, H. A. *Birth to maturity: A study in psychological development*. New York: John Wiley, 1962.

Kamin, L. J. *The science and politics of I.Q.* New York: Halstead Press, 1974.

Kamin, L. J. Comment on Munsinger's review of adoption studies. *Psychological Bulletin*, 1978, *85*, 194-201.

Kennedy, M. M. Findings from the Follow Through Planned Variation Study. *Educational Researcher*, 1978, *7*(6), 3-11.

Kennedy, W. A., Van De Riet, V., & White, J. C., Jr. A normative sample of intelligence and achievement of Negro elementary school children in the southeastern United States. *Monographs of the Society for Research in Child Development*, 1963, *28*, No. 6.

Koluchová, J. Severe deprivation in twins: A case study. *Journal of Child Psychology and Psychiatry*, 1972, *13*, 107-114.

Koluchová, J. A report on the further development of twins after severe and prolonged deprivation. In A. M. Clarke & A. D. B. Clarke (Eds.), *Early experience: Myth and evidence*. New York: Free Press, 1976.

Lesser, G. S., Fifer, G., & Clark, D. H. Mental abilities of children from different social-class and cultural groups. *Monographs of the Society for Research in Child Development*, 1965, *30*, No. 4.

Lewontin, R. C. Race and intelligence. *Bulletin of the Atomic Scientists*, 1970, *26*, 2-8.

Lewontin, R. C. Genetic aspects of intelligence. *Annual Review of Genetics*, 1975, *9*, 387-405.

Loehlin, J. C. *Identical twins reared apart and other routes to the same destination*. Unpublished manuscript, University of Texas at Austin, 1978. (Based on a paper presented at the Third International Twin Congress, Washington, D.C., September 1977.)

Loehlin, J. C., Lindzey, G., & Spuhler, J. N. *Race differences in intelligence*. San Francisco: W. H. Freeman, 1975.

Loehlin, J. C., & Nichols, R. C. *Heredity, environment and personality: A study of 850 sets of twins*. Austin: University of Texas Press, 1976.

Lohnes, P. R. *Measuring adolescent personality: Project Talent five-year follow-up studies*. (Interim Report I, Proj. No. 3051, Contract No. OE-6-10-065.) Pittsburgh: University of Pittsburgh, 1966.

MacArthur, R. S. Some differential abilities of northern Canadian native youth. *International Journal of Psychology*, 1968, *3*, 43-51.

Maccoby, E. E., and Jacklin, C. N. *The psychology of sex differences*. Stanford, Calif.: Stanford University Press, 1974.

Magoon, A. J. Sociobiology and schooling. *Educational Researcher*, 1978, *7* (4), 4-10.

Marciano, R., & David, J. *Lessons learned in operationalizing the Follow Through planned variation in the field and implications for future research*. Paper presented at the annual meeting of the American Educational Research Association, New York, April 1977.

Marjoribanks, K. Environment, social class and mental abilities. *Journal of Educational Psychology*, 1972, *63*, 103-109.

Mason, M. K. Learning to speak after six and a half years of silence. *Journal of Speech Disorders*, 1942, *7*, 295-304.

McAskie, M. Carelessness or fraud in Sir Cyril Burt's kinship data? A critique of Jensen's analysis. *American Psychologist*, 1978, *33*, 496-498.

McCall, R. B., Hogarty, P. S., & Hurlburt, N. Transitions in infant sensorimotor development and the prediction of childhood I.Q. *American Psychologist*, 1972, *27*, 328-348.

McGurk, F. C. J. Race differences—20 years later. *IAAEE Monographs*, No. 5. New York: The International Association for the Advancement of Ethnology and Eugenics, 1978.

McKay, H., Sinisterra, L., McKay, A., Gomez, H., & Lloreda, P. Improving cognitive ability in chronically deprived children. *Science*, 1978, *200*, 270-278.

McNemar, Q. Statistics can mislead. *American Psychologist*, 1977, *32*, 680-681.

Mercer, J. I.Q.: The lethal label. *Psychology Today*, September 1972, pp. 44-47, 95-97.

Miller, S. M. Types of equality: Sorting, rewarding, performing. In N. F. Ashline, T. R. Pezzulo, & C. I. Norris (Eds.), *Education, inequality, and national policy*. Lexington, Mass.: Lexington Books, 1976.

Morton, N. E. Analysis of family resemblance; I: Introduction. *American Journal of Human Genetics*, 1974, *26*, 318-330.

Mosteller, F., & Moynihan, D. P. *On equality of educational opportunity*. New York: Random House, 1972.

Muller, H. J. Means and aims in human genetic betterment. In T. M. Sonneborn (Ed.), *The control of human heredity and evolution*. New York: Macmillan, 1965.

Munsinger, H. The adopted child's I.Q.: A critical review. *Psychological Bulletin*, 1975, *82*, 623-659.

Munsinger, H. Reply to Kamin. *Psychological Bulletin*, 1978, *85*, 202-206.

Nichols, R. C. *Heredity and environment: Major findings from twin studies of ability, personality and interests*. Paper presented at the meeting of the American Psychological Association, Washington, D.C., September 1976. (ERIC Document Reproduction Service No. ED 131 922.)

Nichols, R. C. Black children adopted by white families. *American Psychologist*, 1977, *32*, 678-680.

Nichols, R. C. Twin studies of ability, personality and interests. *Homo*, in press.

Page, E. B. Miracle in Milwaukee: Raising the I.Q. *Educational Researcher*, 1972, *1* (10), 8-16.

Page, E. B. *Is IQ really contagious?* Address presented at the annual meeting of the American Psychological Association, August 1977.

Page, E. B. *Separating illusion from reality: Family effects in large U.S. samples*. Paper presented at the meeting of the American Educational Research Association, Toronto, March 1978.

Peng, S. S. Trends in the entry to higher education: 1961-1972. *Educational Researcher*, 1977, *6* (1), 15-20.

Polivanov, S. Response of *Drosophila persimilis* to phototactic and geotactic selection. *Behavior Genetics*, 1975, *5*, 255-267.

Rao, D. C., Morton, N. E., and Yee, S. Analysis of family resemblance; II: A linear model for family correlation. *American Journal of Human Genetics*, 1974, *26*, 331-359.

Rao, D. C., Morton, N. E., and Yee, S. Resolution of cultural and biological inheritance by path analysis. *American Journal of Human Genetics*, 1976, *28*, 228-242.

Rimland, B., & Munsinger, H. Burt's I.Q. data. *Science*, 1977, *195*, 248.

Scarr, S. Environmental bias in twin studies. *Eugenics Quarterly*, 1968, *15*, 34-40.

Scarr, S., Pakstis, A. J., Katz, S. H., & Barker, W. B. Absence of a relationship between degree of white ancestry and intellectual skills within a black population. *Human Genetics*, 1977, *39*, 69-86.

Scarr, S., & Weinberg, R. A. I.Q. test performance of black children adopted by white families. *American Psychologist*, 1976, *31*, 726-739.

Scarr, S., & Weinberg, R. A. *The influence of "family background" on intellectual attainment: The unique contribution of adoptive studies to estimating environmental effects.* Paper presented at the Mathematical Social Science Board conference on Family Environment and Subsequent Child Development, Stanford University, March 24, 1977. (a)

Scarr, S., & Weinberg, R. A. Intellectual similarities within families of both adopted and biological children. *Intelligence*, 1977, *1*, 170-191. (b)

Scarr, S., & Weinberg, R. A. Nature and nurture strike (out) again. *Intelligence*, in press.

Scarr-Salapatek, S. Comments on H. Munsinger, The adopted child's IQ: A critical review. *Psychological Bulletin*, 1975, *82*, 623-659.

Scarr-Salapatek, S. Science and politics: An explosive mix (review of *Science and politics of I.Q.* by L. J. Kamin). *Contemporary Psychology*, 1976, *21*, 98-99.

Schiff, M., Duyme, M., Dumaret, A., Stewart, J., Tomkiewicz, S., and Feingold, J. Intellectual status of working-class children adopted early into upper-middle class families. *Science*, 1978, *200*, 1503-1504.

Seagoe, M. V. *Terman and the gifted.* Los Altos, Calif.: William Kaufmann, 1975.

Shockley, W. Dysgenics, geneticity, raceology: A challenge to the intellectual responsibility of educators. *Phi Delta Kappan*, 1972, *53*, 297-312.

Skeels, H. M., & Dye, H. B. A study of the effects of differential stimulation on mentally retarded children. *Proceedings of the American Association of Mental Deficiency*, 1939, *44*, 114-136.

Smith, M. S., & Bissell, J. S. Report analysis, The impact of Head Start. *Harvard Educational Review*, 1970, *40*, 51-104.

Smith, R. T. A comparison of socioenvironmental factors in monogygotic and dizygotic twins, testing an assumption. In S. G. Vandenberg (Ed.), *Methods and goals in human behavior genetics*. New York: Academic Press, 1965.

Sociobiology Study Group of Science for the People. Dialogue (the critique): Sociobiology—Another biological determinism. *BioScience*, 1976, *26*, 182-190.

Sprott, R. L., & Staats, J. Behavioral studies using genetically defined mice—A bibliography. *Behavior Genetics*, 1975, *5*, 27-82.

Stebbins, L. B., St. Pierre, R. G., Proper, E. C., Anderson, R. B., and Cerra, T. R. *Education as experimentation: A planned variation model. Vol. IV-A: An evaluation of Follow Through.* Cambridge, Mass.: Abt Associates, Inc., 1977. (Also issued by the U.S. Office of Education as *National evaluation: Patterns of effects,* Volume II-A of the Follow Through Planned Variation Experiment Series.)

Stein, Z., Susser, M., Saenger, G., & Marolla, F. Nutrition and mental performance. *Science*, 1972, *178*, 708-713.

Stewart, N. AGCT scores of Army personnel grouped by occupation. *Occupations*, 1947, *26*, 5-41.

Stodolsky, S. S., & Lesser, G. Learning patterns in the disadvantaged. *Harvard Educational Review*, 1967, *37*, 546-593.

Stormsdorfer, E. W. An outline of research issues and priorities. In *The National Longitudinal Study: A planning conference for new cohorts of high school sophomores and seniors to start in 1980*. Washington, D.C.: National Center for Education Statistics, 1977.

Terman, L. M. The great conspiracy, or the impulse imperious of intelligence testers, psychoanalyzed and exposed by Mr. Lippmann. *The New Republic*, 1922, *33*, 116-120.

Thorndike, E. L. *Educational psychology*. New York: Lemcke and Buechner, 1903.

Thorndike, E. L. Measurement of twins. *The Journal of Philosophy, Psychology, and Scientific Method*, .1905, *2*, 547-553.

Thorndike, R. L., & Hagen, E. *Cognitive Abilities Test*. Boston: Houghton Mifflin, 1971.

Trotter, R. Environment and behavior: Intensive intervention program prevents retardation. *APA Monitor*, 1976, *7* (September-October), 4.

Tryon, R. C. Genetic differences in maze-learning ability in rats. In G. M. Whipple (Ed.), *The 39th yearbook of the National Society for the Study of Education. Intelligence: Its nature and nurture. Part I. Comparative and critical exposition*. Bloomington, Ill.: Public School Publishing Co., 1940.

Tuddenham, R. D. Soldier intelligence in World Wars I and II. *American Psychologist*, 1948, *3*, 54-56.

Tyler, L. E. *The psychology of human differences*. New York: Appleton-Century-Crofts, 1965.

Urbach, P. Progress and degeneration in the I.Q. debate. *British Journal of the Philosophy of Science*, 1974, *25*, 99-135; 235-259.

U.S. Commission on Civil Rights. *Racial isolation in the public schools* (Vol. 1). Washington, D.C.: U.S. Government Printing Office, 1967.

Vandenberg, S. G. Hereditary factors in normal personality traits (as measured by inventories). In J. Wortis (Ed.), *Recent advances in biological psychiatry*. New York: Plenum Press, 1967.

Velandia, W., Grandon, G., & Page, E. B. Family size, birth order, and intelligence in a large South American sample. *American Educational Research Journal*, in press.

Wade, N. I.Q. and heredity: Suspicion of fraud beclouds classic experiment. *Science*, 1976, *194*, 916-919. (a)

Wade, N. Sociobiology: Troubled birth for new discipline. *Science*, 1976, *191*, 1151-1155. (b)

Waller, J. H. Achievement and social mobility: Relationships among I.Q. scores, education, and occupation in two generations. *Social Biology*, 1971, *18*, 252-259.

Washburn, S. L. Human behavior and the behavior of other animals. *American Psychologist*, 1978, *33*, 405-418.

Westinghouse Learning Corporation/Ohio University. *The impact of Head Start*. Springfield, Va.: Clearinghouse for Federal Scientific and Technical Information, U.S. Department of Commerce, 1969.

White, B. L., & Carew Watts, J. *Experience and environment: Major influences on the development of the young child*. Englewood Cliffs, N.J.: Prentice-Hall, 1973.

Wilson, E. O. *Sociobiology: The new synthesis*. Cambridge, Mass.: Harvard University Press, 1975.

Zajonc, R. B. Family configuration and intelligence. *Science*, 1976, *192*, 227-292.

2

Evaluating Parental Effects on Child Development

K. ALISON CLARKE–STEWART
The University of Chicago
with
NANCY APFEL
Yale University

KEEPING UP WITH THE TIMES: THE NEW TREND IN EDUCATION

If anyone were to inquire of any student of social progress, "What is the newest
development in the educational world?" the answer would almost surely be,
"Schools for infants and a constructive program of education for parents."

28th NSSE *Yearbook*, 1929, p. 7

Organized parental education efforts have developed rapidly in this country
(NSSE *Yearbook*, p. 20);
Organized child study groups have grown in number prodigiously within the
past few years; and books on the care and rearing of children find a ready
market.

Editorial, *The New York Times*, November 1, 1925

Rapid change in social conditions, in housing customs, recreations, social
mores . . . makes a demand upon parents for a philosophy and methods based
on today, (NSSE *Yearbook*, p. 67) [while]
The community, examining the child at the close of his preschool and most
fundamental years, and finding him wanting, consistently lays the responsibility
for this lack at the door of the home, [and], further, demands that the home
remedy the situation.

Forest (1927), p. 231

Scientists, of course, cannot take the place of mothers, but they can teach them
many useful things and enable them to do intelligently not a little that they now
do in accord with instinct or the advice of women no wiser than themselves.

Editorial, *The New York Times*, October 29, 1925

These statements—though written half a century ago—cogently convey current thinking in the United States about the education of parents. Spearheaded

---

LEON YARROW, National Institute of Child Health and Human Development, was editorial
consultant for this chapter.

by federal agencies like the Office of Child Development and the Office of Education, and following the ideas of a former Commissioner of Education that "parent education is the key to more effective education" (Bell, 1976) and "the child has the right to have a trained parent" (Bell, 1975), child-rearing courses, books, pamphlets, television programs, and home visits have reached millions of parents over the past 10 years. Among recent trends in education, the focus on training parents is significant, and efforts to inform parents and prospective parents are still increasing in variety, scope, and magnitude.

Parent education, greeted with unbounded optimism in this decade as the panacea for society's problems, is not a new idea, but one which has risen to prominence again with fresh hopes and a short memory (Brim, 1965; Lüscher, 1977; Schlossman, 1976). It may be supported by new data, take new forms, and be motivated by a new sense of anguish: "What *is* new is the intensity of the malaise, the sense of having no guidelines or supports for raising children, the feeling of not being in control as parents, and the widespread sense of personal guilt for what seems to be going awry" (Keniston & Carnegie Council, 1977, p. 4). But the arguments and assumptions on which current parent training efforts are based have not changed since 1929, as these statements from the 28th NSSE Yearbook (National Society for the Study of Education), indicate:

1. Parents are the most important influence on children's development, and the early years are the most important period (cf. Brim, 1965; Hess, Bloch, Costello, Knowles, & Largay, 1971; White, 1975).
2. Schools [or, more recently, preschools] are not doing an adequate job and are not as influential as the home (cf. Bronfenbrenner, 1974; Coleman, 1966; Jencks, 1972; White, 1975).
3. Changing social conditions, such as poverty, stress, single parenthood, divorce, maternal employment, and increasingly numerous associations outside the family have led to increased parental uncertainty and anxiety (cf. Keniston et al., National Academy of Sciences, 1976; Yankelovich, Skelly, & White, Inc., 1976–1977).
4. Surveys show that some parents [such as those of lower socioeconomic status] have not been successful in meeting their responsibilities to young children (Goodson & Hess, 1976).
5. New scientific knowledge about child rearing is available which, if disseminated, will effect behavioral change (cf. Brim, 1965; Hess et al., 1971).

What is this "new scientific knowledge" about child development and child rearing on which current parent training and education efforts are based? Is it an adequate and defensible basis for parent programs and translatable into effective program curricula? And what are the effects of current parent education programs on children's development? This chapter addresses these questions.

Since research to answer these questions is voluminous and space for the chapter is limited, not every relevant study has been described or criticized in detail. Instead, the chapter describes and evaluates the major research approaches that have been used in the study of child rearing and its effect on development, illustrates each with representative investigations, and where possible indicates the current consensus of results. Finally, based on the convergence of results from all approaches, it suggests what implications the research has for educational programs and policy.

ANIMAL STUDIES

A frequent starting point for discussion about rearing effects (Bowlby, 1951; A. M. Clarke & A. D. B. Clarke, 1976a; Hunt, 1961; Palmer, 1969) has been research on animals. The reason, clearly, is that such research provides unique information about experience and development not available from studies of human subjects, because in experimental animal studies extreme and well-controlled manipulation of the environment is possible, and animal field studies offer a wide range of naturally occurring variation. Animal research is particularly valuable for investigating environmental effects on the young, where ethics guiding human experimentation are most constraining. The following sampling of studies illustrates the usefulness of animal research for answering questions about early experience and development and anticipates the issues that concern investigators studying rearing effects in the human species.

Studies of Early Experience

Deprivation and Stimulation. Initiated by Hebb's (1949) theorizing on the importance of early experience for intellectual growth, a multitude of studies examining the effects of early sensory restriction or stimulation on later performance have been conducted (reviewed by Bronfenbrenner, 1968; Hinde, 1970; Hunt, 1961; Palmer, 1969; Rutter, 1974; Thompson & Grusec, 1970). Investigators using rats (Nyman, 1967), dogs (Thompson & Heron, 1954), cats Riesen, 1965), and chimpanzees (Rogers & Davenport, 1971) all demonstrated that a sensorily restricted rearing impairs intellectual development. Conversely, studies providing specific kinds of sensory stimulation showed that enriched experience—in particular, a range of seeing and doing—leads to intellectual enhancement in a variety of species (Forgays & Forgays, 1952; Held & Hein, 1963; Hymovitch, 1952; Meier & McGee, 1959). There seems little doubt that, in animals, a link exists between sensory experience and intellectual development.

The effects of social privation or deprivation on social-emotional development are less clear-cut. The best known example of research on this relationship is undoubtedly that of Harry and Margaret Harlow. Their monkeys raised without mothers were timid and unfriendly as youths and socially and sexually deviant as adults (Harlow & Griffin, 1965; Suomi, 1977). But while rearing in extreme social isolation is undeniably detrimental, at issue is the effect of briefer periods of mother-infant separation. That the distress caused by such separation is immediate and severe is clear (Cairns, 1966b; Cairns & Werboff, 1967; Elliot & Scott, 1961); what is not so well established are the long-term effects of such separation. Most investigators, unable to bear the dramatic and painful effects of their manipulation, have terminated the separation and their observations within a few minutes—concluding that brief separation has dire and possibly permanent consequences (Hinde & Spencer-Booth, 1971). In the few investigations that have continued past the first few minutes of distress, however, the young animals have been observed to calm and behave normally within a matter of hours—*if* the separation period involves events that elicit and maintain activity (Cairns, 1977). The problem with most studies has been that they paid attention to what the infant was deprived of (mother) but not what it was exposed to (isolation or interaction), and the latter makes a significant difference in the outcome of separation experiences.

Critical Periods. Lorenz's (1935) discovery of imprinting in birds, which must occur within a "critical period" soon after birth and is subsequently irreversible, has dominated thinking about the effects of early experience on animal learning, and the concept has been widely applied to human development as well. Research done after Lorenz's and with other species clearly suggested that the concept of a "critical" period was too restrictive, and animal researchers substituted for it the notion of "sensitive periods" during which specific stimuli have more pronounced and durable effects (Bell & Denenberg, 1963; Davenport, Menzel, & Rogers, 1966; Scott & Fuller, 1965; Wiesel & Hubel, 1963). The application of their conclusions to human learning, especially as a basis for early childhood education, has continued, however, with little modification of the original notion of critical periods. Unfortunately, the animal studies apparently documenting the critical importance of early experience did not use systematic crossover of rearing conditions at different ages (Cairns, 1977). Investigators who have used such designs subsequently have discovered that most mammals are capable of considerably more social adaptation than they had been given credit for in earlier accounts of deprivation (Cairns, 1977). Even imprinting, in some species, can be overcome by experience in adolescence (Hinde, 1970; Klinghammer, 1967), and the dire effects of rearing monkeys in isolation can be alleviated by the presence of a baby monkey, a "therapy" monkey, or an adult sheepdog—animals that interact in a reciprocal, playful, and nonintense manner (Cairns, 1977; Gomber, 1975, Novak & Harlow, 1975). Effects of isolation, moreover, are the same in adult dogs as in puppies (Cairns, 1977). The consensus of research on critical periods in animal development, according to a recent reviewer (Rutter, 1974), is that although early learning influences later learning, its effects are essentially reversible, and in some cases the effects of later experience will predominate. There can be, claims Rutter, no general rule; whether or not deprivation of stimulation in infancy has a permanent effect depends in large measure on environmental conditions in later life.

Early Social Development

Attachment.   Animal research has also been used to explore issues surrounding the development of an infant's social bond or "attachment" to its caregiver. Not only have studies of mother-infant separation demonstrated the existence of the bond, but further investigations have explored the particular qualities of caregiver behavior that engender the bond and cause different kinds of reaction to separation from the attachment object. By manipulating the conditions under which infant animals are reared, researchers have examined and discounted the belief that attachment to mother develops merely because the mother feeds the infant. Although infants did prefer a lactating surrogate mother to a nonlactating surrogate (Harlow, 1958), they formed attachments to a terrycloth surrogate that did not feed them (Harlow & Zimmermann, 1959) and to animals that they could see but not touch (Cairns, 1966a, 1966b). Apparently feeding, physical contact, or affectionate interaction are not necessary conditions for the formation of an attachment bond. In the normal course of development, however, they co-occur. More important, although the surrogates induced attachment and provided immediate comfort in frightening situations, in the long term, in comparison with a live mother, they were only marginally better than no attachment figure at all. To develop normally, infants require reciprocal interaction with another animal, not just the passive reception of attachment behavior by a surrogate (Hinde & Spencer-Booth, 1967; Wolfheim, Jensen, & Bobbitt, 1970).

Further information about attachment development is provided by studies of individual variation in young animals' reactions to separation from the attachment object. Infants showing the greatest disturbance immediately and for some months after separation were reared by individuals (Hinde & Spencer-Booth, 1970) or species (Kaufman & Rosenblum, 1969a, 1969b; Rosenblum, 1971) that were rejecting, aggressive, punitive, and restrictive. When reared by mothers who were more permissive and playful, infants were less dependent, more likely to explore, and less traumatized by a separation.

Influence of Infant on Caregiver.   Animal research also demonstrates how, from the moment of birth, the presence or absence of the infant (a condition which for obvious reasons can be more readily manipulated in animal subjects) has a marked effect on the caregiving behavior of the adult (Harper, 1971; Maccoby & Jacklin, 1974; Rosenblatt, 1969; Thoman, 1974). This finding has led to recognition of a parallel phenomenon in human subjects and to the use of dyadic procedures of assessment of environmental "effects" and social interaction in both animals and humans.

Fathers as Caregivers

Research on animals also offers information about parental behavior in its observations of caregiving by fathers. Animal studies demonstrate that in certain species, in the wild or in the laboratory, fathers assume a very active parental role and form mutual social attachments with their infants (Maccoby & Jacklin, 1974;

Redican, 1976). In field investigations of different species of nonhuman primates, for example, males have been observed to assist in births, to premasticate food for infants, and to carry, groom, defend, "teach," "discipline," sleep with, and play with their young. It has also been observed that the extent of male parental care is related positively to a more relaxed and permissive mother-infant relationship. Moreover, in the laboratory, with sufficient exposure to newborns or in the absence of a restrictive mother, adult males (who may or may not be fathers) have been observed to show parental behavior, even in species that do not typically show such behavior in the wild. These studies have provided support for looking seriously at the paternal role in humans, for, as Redican (1976, p. 359) says, "If such an aggressive and inflexible creature as the rhesus monkey is capable of positive interactions with infants, there is reason to expect at least comparable potential in less sexually dimorphic, relatively monogamous, more flexible creatures such as *Homo sapiens.*"

The investigations cited above illustrate how animal studies can offer some general guidelines or suggestions about parental effects on development. Direct application of their results, however, is foolhardy. Although such studies offer a degree of control not possible in human research, in going beyond "natural" phenomena (by investigating surrogate mothering components, for example), they may not be generalizable to real-life situations—even for animals. More than that, there is danger in generalizing from lower species to humans, since even within the subhuman species studied, variability in effects and adaptability was evident. Results of animal studies are most useful to *support* generalizations from human research, not to replace them.

NATURALISTIC STUDIES

Natural Experiments

Children in Institutions. Children growing up in orphanages and residential institutions compose a natural experiment that can offer important information about the effects of child care. Countless studies have documented the impaired language and intellect and disturbed behavior that characterize such children and limit their adult functioning (Bakwin, 1942; Dennis, 1973; Goldfarb, 1945, 1955; Pringle & Bossio, 1960; Provence & Lipton, 1962; Spitz, 1946; see reviews by Ainsworth, 1962; Bowlby, 1951; Ferguson, 1966; Rutter, 1974; Yarrow, 1961). At first, investigators observing the pale, wan, and retarded children in institutions attributed their state to deprivation of "a mother's love." It soon became clear, however, that these children were deprived of much more. Their physical surroundings were perceptually barren; they had few playthings; opportunity for motor activity was limited; and they lacked stimulating and responsive contact with any adult, not just mother. Moreover, there were questions about the children's diet, health, and heredity compared with the home-reared children by which they were judged. Early investigations did not or could not separate these confounding conditions, and so they were not helpful in identifying which components of the environment were responsible for the deficiencies observed. They did, however, forcefully demonstrate that environment makes a difference to children's development, and they were responsible for firing researchers' interest in the contributions of normal care to development.

Subsequent study of children in institutions has identified certain features that modify the effects of institutionalization. Two important factors are the length of stay and the age of the child. Development progresses normally for the first three months of infancy if physical needs are met; from 3 to 6 months, smiling, vocalizing, and motor development begin to be delayed; and by 1 or 2 years, significant retardation (by as much as 50 IQ points) is usually evident and continues for as long as the child remains in the institution. This finding has been used as an argument for the "criticalness" of early experience and as a justification for early intervention. Unfortunately for researchers, however, circumstances have not permitted the systematic study of effects of institutionalization on children admitted and released at different ages; almost always, children have been admitted to such institutions in infancy. Consequently, available data on children in institutions do not document, one way or the other, the existence of an early critical period. The obvious susceptibility of infants and young children to an institutional environment should not be confused with irreversibility of effects.

Another factor that modifies the effect of institutionalization is the quality of care the institution provides. All institutions are not equally bad. In institutions that offer books and movies, trips and outings, and an adequate number of capable caretakers who are interested in promoting the children's development, children's intellectual development is significantly less retarded than in the depriving institutions (Dennis, 1960, 1973; DuPan & Roth, 1955; Rheingold, 1956; Skeels & Dye, 1939; Tizard & Rees, 1974; Tizard & Tizard, 1970; Wolins, 1969). Still, if no close relationships develop between the children and their caretakers, emotional and social relations are likely to be impaired (Tizard & Tizard, 1971). Providing stimulation and exercise is apparently adequate for normal cognitive and motor development, but social, emotional, and to some extent, language development appear to be associated with regular interaction with an adult who forms a close relationship with the child (Bowlby, 1951; Brodbeck & Irwin, 1946; DuPan & Roth, 1955; Pringle & Bossio, 1960; Provence & Lipton, 1962; Wolins, 1969; Wolkind, 1971).

"Lost and Found" Children.　A second, and fortunately infrequent, natural experiment is provided by the discovery of children who through ignorance, prejudice, or cruelty have been forced to grow up in severe deprivation and essential isolation, until their rescue at some later age. Cases (reviewed by A. D. B. Clarke & A. M. Clarke, 1976a) such as that of Isabelle, who lived in forced isolation with her deaf-mute mother (Davis, 1940, 1947), or the twin boys

banished to the cellar by the "wicked stepmother" their father married after their own mother died (Koluchová, 1972, 1976) demonstrate the extremely detrimental effects of such deprivation. Follow-up of the cases suggests, however, that with deliberate training and/or adoption into supportive and stimulating families, even these severely retarded children make gradual progress toward normalcy and achieve functional competence by adolescence (A. D. B. Clarke & A. M. Clarke, 1976a; Curtiss, 1977). These extreme cases, though not sufficient by themselves, do offer some further evidence of the substantial reversibility of effects of early experience.

Adopted Children.   More systematic evidence for reversibility is provided by studies of children from depriving early environments who were adopted into normal "advantaged" families. Recent studies of adoption clearly contradict Bowlby's (1951) original claim that mothering delayed until 12 or 24 months is useless. The question now is not whether the effects of early deprivation are reversible, but how completely reversible they are for each developmental function (Ainsworth, 1962; Rutter, 1974). Children who are adopted in infancy, although already somewhat retarded, apparently recover completely by the time they are 4 years old (Dennis, 1973). Even the offspring of retarded parents develop normally if adopted early by a family (Skodak & Skeels, 1949) or cared for by a substitute mother (Skeels, 1966; A. M. Clarke & A. D. B. Clarke, 1976b). Children adopted after 2 years of age, however, although they recover substantially, *may* not recover *completely*. Dennis's (1973) study of children from an orphanage in Lebanon who were adopted by American or Lebanese parents found that these children, by adolescence, showed a decrement in mental age equal to the numbers of years past 2 at which they had been adopted. Tizard and Rees (1974), too, observed that children adopted past 4½ years had lower IQs than those adopted at younger ages (but unfortunately their finding was confounded by the fact that the parents adopting the younger children were better educated). A. D. B. Clarke and A. M. Clarke (1976b), arguing against irreversibility, suggest that Dennis's results may have been biased by selectivity for adoption according to age, or that catch-up might still occur in adulthood. These issues have not been resolved. In general, however, the Dennis study was relatively free of selectivity factors. At this point, the most reasonable conclusion from studies of adoption seems to be that substantial but perhaps not total reversibility of intellectual deficits follows adoption at any age. Tizard and Rees (1974) suggest an alternative to the critical-period hypothesis to explain their own and Dennis's data, which is that the remaining deficit of the older-adopted children may be the result of their having less opportunity to interact with their new parents after adoption because they spend more time in school. Perhaps additional stimulating interaction, along with adoption, could raise the intellectual level of older-adopted children. This is an important avenue of research that needs to be explored further before the issue of reversibility of the effects of early events can be settled.

Other investigators have been interested in adopted children's social adjustment as well as their intellectual performance. Their studies show that despite early adversity, most children placed in more favorable surroundings, even after infancy, developed into emotionally healthy, well-adjusted, and socially competent young people (Kadushin, 1970; Lewis, 1954; Rathburn, McLaughlin, Bennett, & Garland, 1965; Tizard & Rees, 1974). Social outcomes, like intelligence, may be somewhat less favorable the older the child is when adopted (Kadushin, 1970; Rutter, 1974). Clearly, however, a "good home" can overcome remarkably severe early disadvantages, and may even do so more effectively than restoration to the biological mother (Tizard & Rees, 1974).

Adoption studies inevitably track children going from a restricted environment to one that is more advantageous. The opposite situation—going from good to bad—has not generally been available for study but would have interesting implications for the issues of reversibility and intervention. One recent intervention did, however, essentially "adopt" infants from their high-risk mothers, giving them all the advantages of individualized care and intellectual stimulation every day (five days a week) until they started school, and then they were returned to their disadvantaged mothers (Heber & Garber, 1971). The remarkable advances in intellectual performance made by these children during their preschool "adoption" declined as soon as the program ceased. Although the decline was not to as low a level as the performance of children from similar homes who did not have the enrichment experience (the control group), at the last assessment it was still dropping, and reading achievement in the two groups was indistinguishable (A. M. Clarke & A. D. B. Clarke, 1976b). Substantial reversibility—in either direction—seems to be the rule, at least at levels that are conventionally and easily assessed.

Natural Variation[1]

Cultural Variation. Formerly the territory of anthropologists, multicultural or cross-cultural research is now an accepted, fast-growing field within child development. While presumably no longer motivated merely by a *National Geographic* curiosity, the study of child rearing and development in other cultures is still too often simply "the study of individual differences in a nice place without a guiding theory, hypothesis, or rationale" (Leiderman, Tulkin, & Rosenfeld, 1977). Nevertheless the approach can be a useful one, and no doubt it will be increasingly valuable for adding to our knowledge of parental effects on child development as it grows in popularity and methodological sophistication.

One potential contribution of this approach lies in its demonstration of cross-cultural "universals" of development. In the Mayan Indians of Mexico, for example, the emphasis in infant care is on subduing the infant's motor activity and demands, in clear contrast to American parenting practice. Yet these infants walk and talk "on time," and their performance on American IQ tests is within the normal range (Brazelton, 1977). Similarly, the course of developing a focused relationship with the mother is identical for infants in Uganda and the United States, despite substantial differences in the amount of mother-infant contact in the two countries (Ainsworth, 1977). Comparability has also been observed across a variety of cultures in the order of frequency of specific kinds of maternal caregiving behavior (Lewis & Ban, 1977) and in relations between parental behavior and children's school achievement (Kifer, 1977). Clearly, it is premature at this time to suggest that these particular phenomena and relations are "universals." Many more studies of many more cultures are needed before that conclusion can be drawn—and then, most likely, the phenomena will turn out to be universal only within certain limits.

A second useful contribution of collecting data from other cultures is to extend the range of variation beyond that observed within a single culture, so that relations between theoretically linked parent and child behaviors that fail to reach statistical significance within one culture can be tested across the wider range of practices represented by several cultures. In the area of stimulating infants' motor development, for example, American mothers are relatively homogeneous, and no significant relations have been observed. By contrast, in Africa, where mothers offer a great deal more physical contact and training to their infants, infants are chronologically early in sitting, standing, walking, and sensorimotor skills (Konner, 1977; Goldberg, 1977; Super, 1976), while at the other extreme, in Guatemala, where babies spend much of their time unattended and unstimulated, these skills are attained much later (Kagan & Klein, 1973). The problem with drawing simple conclusions from these particular observations is that, as with institutions, in different cultures many elements of the environment are confounded: social stimulation, vestibular stimulation, physical contact, deliberate encouragement, the opportunity to feed at will. To sort out these various potential influences on the child's development demands careful and systematic observation in many cultures with varying degrees of each element.

Cross-cultural research can also speak to the issue of reversibility of environmental effects. Although African and Guatemalan infants are very different at 1 year of age, for example, later, when both are mobile, and the African is given less attention while the Guatemalan seeks out more stimulation, the differences diminish and probably eventually disappear (Kagan & Klein, 1973).

Finally, a glimpse of child rearing in another culture can produce—often with shocking suddenness—a new awareness of the unconscious biases, assumptions, and values we hold as researchers and Americans. This awareness of our cultural biases can broaden our definition of "normal" parent behavior and heighten our appreciation of subcultural differences within the United States.

Although multicultural research can be helpful for exploring and understanding parental effects on child development, the usefulness of currently available investigations is limited by several methodological weaknesses. Researchers studying another culture have typically spent but a short time—sabbatical leave or summer vacation—in the foreign country, often without even knowing its language. Subject selection has been haphazard and biased by nonscientific factors. Recruitment of subjects, a problem in our own country, is an even more serious problem when agreeing to participate in a study means accepting an inscrutable stranger and an alien task. In addition, even when the testing or observation has been done by native researchers, interpretation of the results has nearly always been made by the foreign investigator. A strong tendency has existed, too, for cross-cultural investigators to study only what is important in American culture—cognition, achievement, maternal behavior, rates of development—not what is of importance for the other culture. And finally, investigators have succumbed to the tendency to generalize conclusions from studies of parents and children in Istanbul or Israel to recommendations for programs in Ithaca or Iowa, without full evaluation of the multitude of confounding factors that make the two child-rearing situations different.

Social Class. Research comparing the performance of children and mothers from different socioeconomic levels was responsible in large part for the plethora of compensatory early childhood education efforts in the 1960s and continues to motivate the parent training programs of the 1970s. Interventions were based on the premise that lower-class or low-income families are deficient in important ways for children's development, and proposed solutions went so far as to suggest that the children of the poor be sold to bidders who could offer them a "normal" middle-class upbringing (Banfield, 1970). In fact, socioeconomic status offers only a crude shorthand index of presumed differences in home environment. Modal behavior, of parents and children, is the same at different socioeconomic levels (Erlanger, 1974), and heterogeneity within social classes is generally greater than that between (Deutsch, 1973). Nevertheless, comparison of data from tests and observations of parents and children from different socioeconomic groups reveals some consistent and statistically significant differences in *mean* levels of performance.

In infancy, the differences in maternal and infant behavior are few and small, and when they occur, favor the infant in the less affluent family. Although, when interviewed, middle-class mothers may express more interest in affectionate and social interaction with their infants (Moss & Jones, 1977), there is no difference in how much they are observed to talk to the infant, show affection, or respond to distress. In fact, less affluent mothers are observed to hold and touch their infants more and look and smile at them more often. Their infants are more active, cry less, and are able to tune out redundant stimulation sooner. The only difference in observed behavior favoring middle-class infants at this age is in the quality of verbal interaction; middle-class mothers talk to the infant when they are close and not involved in another activity, and they are more likely to respond to the infant's vocalization with speech (Caldwell, 1967; Deutsch, 1973; Golden & Birns, 1968; Hindley, 1970; Kagan, 1968; Lewis & Freedle, 1972; Lewis & Wilson, 1971; Moss, Robson, & Pedersen, 1969; Seltzer, 1971; Wachs, Uzgiris, & Hunt, 1971).

Past infancy, more differences appear, and these usually favor children from more affluent and educated families. Mothers in these families are more affectionate, accepting, and egalitarian with their children. Restrictions are fewer, and discipline is more likely to involve requests and explanations rather than coaxing, commanding, threatening, or punishing. Middle-class mothers and children interact more frequently, especially verbally and with materials, and their conversations are more likely to occur face to face, to include questions and object references, and to be more varied, complex, abstract, and didactic. Their responses to the child are prompter, more consistent, and more rewarding. Their children, meanwhile, score higher in assessments of IQ, problem solving, use of complex objects, development of cognitive schemas, and school achievement, though they are not different in social behavior (Baumrind, 1971; Bayley & Schaefer, 1960; Beckwith, 1972; Bee, Van Egeren, Streissguth, Nyman, & Leckie, 1969; Cazden, 1966; Hindley, 1970; Kagan, 1968; Minton, Kagan, & Levine, 1971; Moss et al., 1969; Nelson, 1973; Olim, 1970; Tulkin & Kagan, 1972; Zegiob & Forehand, 1975).

Unfortunately, serious methodological problems in this research, too, limit interpretation of these results and applications of these findings to issues of policy or education. First, in more studies than one would hope, socioeconomic status has been confounded with race, ethnicity, religion, or family structure. Second, even within the SES index itself, variables of income, education, and occupation are confounded, and consequently it is not clear which of these aspects may be responsible for the observed differences. Exploration of education and occupation as separate factors (Erlanger, 1974) suggests they do have differential effects. Kohn (1977) proposes that the most important variable to account for SES differences is the father's occupation. Occupational demands of the father's job, he suggests, lead parents to value and encourage in their children either self-direction or conformity to authority, thus determining the quality of parent-child interaction and outcomes for the child. So far, however, this chain of events has not been demonstrated longitudinally and causally. If it were, it would certainly suggest that educational intervention, at the level of mother's caretaking behavior, at any rate, would likely be futile or maladaptive.

A third problem with the research on social class differences is that methods have been biased against lower-class participants (Sroufe, 1970). Mothers and children are often assessed with middle-class tests and observed in university settings. Fewer differences between social classes have been observed at home than at the university (Schlieper, 1975).

And finally, a methodological problem in research on social class is that these studies typically have entailed only simple group comparisons, ignoring variation *within* classes that could inform us about the *process* of environmental effects on child development. SES, a "status" variable, is less predictive of child outcomes than are a variety of "process" measures of the home environment (Beckwith, 1971a; Bradley, Caldwell, & Elardo, 1977; Dave, 1963; Honzik, 1967; Kifer,

1977; Tulkin, 1970). By itself, SES accounts for but a small percentage of the variance in children's development—much too small an amount to use as the basis for recommending policy (see Erlanger, 1974).

Working Mothers and Absent Fathers. Another kind of group comparison that has been popular in the study of parental effects on child development compares children in families lacking either a father or a full-time mother. It is not surprising that these studies have uncovered no general or consistent differences in children's behavior related simply to maternal employment or father's absence, since, like studies of social class, these group comparisons have not controlled for important factors associated with parental status. Father's absence is confounded with social, economic, and psychological circumstances— including the reasons for the absence, how the mother handles it, and whether a substitute male father figure is available to the child—and effects are specific to the age and sex of the child. (See reviews of father absence by Biller, 1974, 1976; Herzog & Sudia, 1973; Lynn, 1974.) Factors confounded with maternal employment include family status, stability, and SES; mother's age, education, and attitude toward work; the nature of the employment and the acceptability of women's working within the mother's reference group, and the father's presence and the alternative child-care arrangement (Etaugh, 1974; L. W. Hoffman, 1961, 1974; Nye & Hoffman, 1963; Stolz, 1960; Wallston, 1973). The study of working mothers is growing in popularity as the number of working mothers climbs (see statistics in National Academy of Science, 1976), but most investigators still follow what L. W. Hoffman (1974) called a "sniper approach," correlating maternal employment status with whatever child variable is at hand, without guiding hypotheses or theory. The only variables that have been systematically controlled are age and sex of the child: When mother works full time, this may be detrimental for younger children (under 3) and for boys, in the areas of emotional and social behavior, while for older (school-age) girls, in areas of achievement and aspiration, it may be beneficial.[2]

Still needed is systematic study of how maternal work status is translated into the life of the child. Clearly the situation is more complex than merely that mother is away all day; we need to explore the intervening processes of family interaction and attitudes. The one intervening variable related to employment status that has been examined in any detail is the mother's feeling of satisfaction with her role (L. W. Hoffman, 1974; Wallston, 1973; Yarrow, Scott, De Leeuw, & Heinig, 1962), but in this research, too, there are problems. The mother's satisfaction has been shown to be related to her interaction with the child: both working and nonworking mothers who are dissatisfied with their status are less involved with their children and less adequate mothers; their children are less sociable and confident (Harrell & Ridley, 1975; L. W. Hoffman, 1961, 1974). Unfortunately, however, since mothers are not randomly assigned to work or nonwork conditions, it is not clear from these investigations whether the same mothers would be dissatisfied no matter what they were doing. Therefore, the differences in their behavior reflect a general factor of dissatisfaction rather than dissatisfaction with work status per se.[3] Clearly, more thoughtful and systematically controlled work on the issues of maternal employment is necessary.

"Normal" Variation

Parental Knowledge and Attitudes.   The study of parental attitudes and their associations with child behavior was a popular area of research in the 1940s and 1950s. In more recent years, however, as a consequence of methodological criticisms of interview data (Yarrow, 1963), deliberate disregard of "black box" phenomena by behaviorists, and the discovery of new technologies for measuring behavior (Stern, 1974), this approach has been largely abandoned by child development researchers. This is unfortunate, for although interviews are highly questionable as a source of information about actual parental or child behavior or about earlier parental practices or feelings, they do afford valuable information about concurrent parental attitudes, perceptions, stereotypes, and knowledge. Information about what parents think and feel, what they know and value, and what they need to know in order to solve the tasks of child rearing is important information which offers a context for understanding their behavior (Lüscher, 1977; Parke, 1977a). Whether at a cultural or individual level, knowledge of parents' values and knowledge can help explain why parents behave the way they do and suggest which behaviors may be susceptible to change with educational intervention. Unfortunately, in this area as in the others discussed above, investigators have typically taken the easiest approach, simply correlating parent attitudes or knowledge with child performance and ignoring the intervening variables of parent-child interaction.

KNOWLEDGE.   Despite this lack of empirical evidence, the links between parental knowledge and behavior and even between parental knowledge and child outcomes have repeatedly been assumed (Bronfenbrenner, 1958; Hunt, 1961; Robinson, 1972). Bronfenbrenner, for example, argued the link from his reading of social-class and child-rearing data over the preceding 25 years: popular child-rearing literature was permissive, middle-class mothers read more, middle-class mothers were more permissive; therefore, reading (knowledge) leads to permissiveness (behavior). Unfortunately, the link is not so clear as this argument implies. A variety of investigations have not found strong evidence that there is a simple link between child-rearing advice and parents' behavior. Erlanger (1974) notes there was not a sudden jump in permissiveness following publication of that bible of permissiveness, Spock's *Baby and Child Care* (1946), and Crandall (1977) was unable to find a causal connection between child-rearing advice in magazine articles and parental behavior over the four-decade period of the Fels longitudinal study. Brim (1965), reviewing effects of parent education programs, concluded that the issue was unresolved. More recently, Lüscher (1977), in a similar review, reported that although shifts in parental knowledge, attitudes, and behavior do correspond to the content of parent education courses and articles, the relation is not strong and could be invalid because of methodological problems in the research. Since a recent survey of parents reading popular child-care books (Clarke-Stewart, 1978b) suggests that parents do not expect to change their behavior as a result of their reading—before or after reading the books—the failure to find a link between reading and child-rearing behavior may not be surprising.

A further source of information about the link between knowledge and behavior is research correlating parents' measured knowledge of child development with their behavior. One study to take this approach did find that mothers' knowledge about child development was related to their attitude and behavior toward children and to the child's development (Clarke-Stewart, 1973). Mothers who were more knowledgeable about principles of child development were more affectionate, talkative, playful, and responsive, imposed fewer restrictions and stimulated the child at an appropriate level for his development stage; their children were intellectually advanced and more social and affectionate. Mothers' knowledge of child development, however, was also highly correlated with maternal IQ—a factor that could account for both greater knowledge of child development and more stimulating and appropriate treatment of the child. Clearly, more research to separate effects of specific and general knowledge or ability is needed before recommendations for parent training programs can be made.

ATTITUDES. More research attention has been given to linking parental attitudes with parental behavior. Two major attitudinal dimensions are the focus of these investigations: emotional attitude (love/hostility) toward the child, which has been related to affective parental behavior (Clarke-Stewart, 1973; Levy, 1958; Moss & Robson, 1968; Stern et al., 1969; Tulkin & Cohler, 1973), and control or discipline of the child, which has been related to the degree and quality of controlling parental behavior (Baumrind, 1971; Beckwith, 1971b; Brody, 1969; Chamberlin, 1974) and to parental responsiveness, play, and appropriate stimulation, as well (Clarke-Stewart, VanderStoep, & Killian, in press; Tulkin & Cohler, 1973).

Investigations have also linked these parental attitudes to child behaviors. Rejection or hostility has been held to be responsible for children's poor development, especially of social behavior (Bronfenbrenner, 1961; Davids, 1968; Escalona, 1953; Heinstein, 1963; Lewis, 1954; Milner, 1951; Sears, Maccoby, & Levin, 1957; Spitz, 1951), while a positive, affectionate attitude has been linked with more positive development (Baldwin, Kalhorn & Breese, 1945; Clarke-Stewart, 1973; M. L. Hoffman, 1963; Lakin, 1957; Moss & Robson, 1968; Stern et al., 1969). Relations between parental attitudes toward control and children's behavior are less consistent, apparently complicated by differing methods of assessment and by the emotional context in which control occurs. Becker's (1964) review of discipline shows how control and emotional attitude interact: permissive discipline in an affectionate context, for example, is associated with outgoing, friendly child behavior, while in a hostile context it may lead to noncompliance or aggression. Baumrind (1967, 1971, 1977; Baumrind & Black, 1967), in the most complete recent studies of disciplinary attitudes and behavior, found no difference in children's behavior related to parental permissiveness alone. The pattern of child behavior related to warm permissiveness by Becker (i.e., sociable and cooperative) she found to be related to a third pattern of discipline, which she labeled "authoritative": it was moderate and firm, but not authoritarian. Although there is some discrepancy between Becker's and Baumrind's correlates of permissive or authoritative disciplinary attitudes (which may be the result of secular change from the 1940s and 1950s to the 1960s and 1970s), evidence regarding *authoritarian* discipline is consistent in showing that an attitude favoring strict discipline, especially if hostile or rejecting, is related to children's lower IQ, creativity, and social competence (Baumrind, 1971; Becker, 1964; Clarke-Stewart et al., in press; Hurley, 1959; Nichols, 1964).

Parental attitude by itself, however, is not as predictive of child development as parental behavior (Clarke-Stewart, 1973). Further investigation of the full chain of parent attitude–parent behavior–child response can help resolve discrepancies between studies and increase understanding of child development. In addition, we need to look at child effects on parental attitudes, not just the reverse; relations among parental attitudes, parental behavior, and child behavior are reciprocal, and should be studied from that perspective.

Maternal Behavior.   The most direct information about parental effects on child development lies in systematic observation of maternal and child behavior. Such investigation has become common in the past 5 to 10 years, and the data now available are numerous (see reviews by Clarke-Stewart, 1977a; Rutter, 1974; Schaefer, 1972). A summary of findings of that observational research, organized according to central dimensions of maternal care, follows.

CARETAKING PRACTICES.   Primarily as a result of theoretical interest in hunger/oral and elimination/anal drives, a number of early studies assessed relations between children's behavior and the mother's method and style of feeding and toilet training (reviewed by Caldwell, 1964). Although relations sometimes appeared in these investigations, they were not consistent or replicable, and most likely they were caused by other maternal variables with which feeding and toileting practices were correlated. More recent studies have indeed demonstrated that neither the amount nor the type of routine caretaking activity is related to development (Ainsworth & Bell, 1969; Bernal & Richards, 1969; Clarke-Stewart, 1973; Engel, Nechlin, & Arkin, 1975; Heinstein, 1963; Schaffer & Emerson, 1964).

AVAILABILITY.   Another early hypothesis, still implicit in current discussions about day care and maternal employment, was that the amount of time the mother was available or with the child is a critical influence on development. Recent research on this hypothesis, however, suggests that although children's intellectual and social behavior is related to the amount of time the mother spends *interacting* with the child (Beckwith, Cohen, Kopp, Parmelee, & Marcy, 1976; Clarke-Stewart, 1973; Rubenstein, 1967; Saxe & Stollak, 1971; Schaffer & Emerson, 1964), it is not related to mere maternal availability (Engel et al., 1975; Schaffer & Emerson, 1964) or the amount of time mother and child spend in the same room (Clarke-Stewart, 1973).

AFFECTION.   Warmth, affection, and tender loving care have popularly been assumed to determine the condition of children, and some support for this view has been provided by empirical research. Overt expression of maternal affection—smiling, caressing, holding tenderly—has been observed to be related to children's positive social-emotional development (Ainsworth, Bell, & Stayton, 1972; Clarke-Stewart, 1973; Rutter, 1974; Saxe & Stollak, 1971; Schaefer & Bayley, 1963; Yarrow, Rubenstein, & Pedersen, 1975). Love is not enough to influence children's intellectual or moral development and academic achievement, however. Although these cognitive aspects are sometimes related to maternal affection (Clarke-Stewart, 1973; Radin, 1971), they are not related consistently (Aronfreed, 1969; Carew, Chan, & Halfar, 1975; Crandall, Dewey, Katkovsky, & Preston, 1964; Crandall, Preston, & Rabson, 1960; Engel, Nechlin, & Arkin, 1975; Kohlberg, 1969; McCall, Appelbaum, & Hogarty, 1973; Yarrow et al., 1975). It is likely that when relations between maternal affection and the child's IQ occur it is because the mother's affection is associated with other aspects of her interaction, such as stimulation, responsiveness, or control, which have been shown to be more highly correlated with children's intellectual performance (Clarke-Stewart, 1973; Wenar, 1976).

STIMULATION.   As early as six months of age, infants' perceptual-cognitive competence is clearly related to the amount they are stimulated by the mother's rocking, jiggling, talking, playing, and stimulating with objects (Appleton, Clifton, & Goldberg, 1975; Beckwith, 1971a; Beckwith et al., 1976; Rubenstein, 1967; Yarrow et al., 1975), and this relation between child competence and maternal behavior continues as the child gets older (Bradley & Caldwell, 1976a, 1976b; Carew et al., 1975; Clarke-Stewart et al. in press; Elardo, Bradley, & Cardwell, 1975; Engel et al., 1975; Hanson, 1975; Wenar, 1976). The more the mother provides appropriate play materials and intellectual experiences; shares, expands, and elaborates the child's activities; and entertains and talks to the child, and the more stimulating the quality of her interaction is, the better the child's performance in standardized or naturalistic assessments. The relation between the child's intelligence and maternal stimulation is stronger than that between IQ and the mother's physical, emotional, or caretaking behavior (Caldwell, 1964; Carew et al., 1975; Clarke-Stewart, 1973; Elardo, Bradley, & Caldwell, 1977), sheer number of toys available (Clarke-Stewart, 1973), or until the child is over 3 years old, the child's self-initiated intellectual activities (Carew et al., 1975).

When the child begins to talk, the quality of maternal speech also becomes associated with language acquisition and cognitive development. Mothers modify their speech level in response to the child's early language skill, using shorter, simpler, more redundant sentences (Phillips, 1973; Snow, 1972), and it has been thought that this may facilitate language learning. Children's early language development (vocabulary, comprehension, syntax) has also been observed to be related to the amount, variety, and syntactic complexity of the mother's face-to-face speech to the child (Clarke-Stewart et al., in press; Nelson, 1973). When children are first learning language, they are most proficient if mothers accept their verbal attempts, talk to them about objects, respond to their attention verbally, and use sentences slightly more complex than the child's (Clarke-Stewart et al., in press; Nelson, 1973).

Later, when children are at a higher cognitive level, intellectual performance is associated with maternal speech that is more abstract (Olim, 1970); and maternal "acceleration"—by actively encouraging independence, reading to the child and encouraging him to read, teaching language, providing an intellectual model, and emphasizing school achievement—is related to IQ, IQ gain, and academic achievement (Freeburg & Payne, 1967; Hanson, 1975; Kifer, 1977; McCall et al., 1973).

RESPONSIVENESS.   It has been suggested that stimulation alone does not facilitate children's intellectual development as much as the degree to which the stimulation is responsive to or contingent upon the child's behavior. At the level of simple reinforcement of particular types of behavior, there is almost certainly a link between maternal responsiveness and child behavior (e.g., for babbling) (Beckwith, 1971b; Cazden, 1966; Jones & Moss, 1971), help seeking and achievement effort (Crandall et al., 1960), exploration and curiosity (Endsley, Garner, Odom, & Martin, 1975), cooperation (Bryan, 1975), sociability to mother (Clarke-Stewart, 1973), and compliance with requests (Lytton, 1977)). Mothers who are observed to respond positively to these kinds of behavior have children who are more likely to exhibit them in their spontaneous interactions. In addition, however, there are less obvious associations between maternal responsiveness and child performance. Frequency and duration of infant crying, for example, are negatively associated with mothers' prompt and consistent responsiveness to distress (Bell & Ainsworth, 1972; Clarke-Stewart, 1973; Dunn, 1975). Moreover, responsiveness to distress is related to infants' use of other forms of communication, to advanced cognition, to learning ability in a new situation, and to a more secure relationship with mother (Ainsworth, 1973; Beckwith et al., 1976; Bell & Ainsworth, 1972; Lewis & Goldberg, 1969; Schaffer & Emerson, 1964; Yarrow et al., 1975). Later, in the second half of the first year, the statistical relation between infants' competence and maternal responsiveness to distress declines. At this age, greater infant competence is related to the mother's responsiveness to social expressions (Beckwith et al., 1976; Clarke-Stewart, 1973; Elardo et al., 1977).

It seems that something more general than mere reinforcement of specific behaviors is responsible for the relation observed between maternal responsiveness and competence in infants and young children. A hypothesis suggested to account for the relation is that the infant learns a generalized expectancy that he can control the environment, which encourages him to explore new situations (Lewis & Goldberg, 1969). In support of this suggestion were Clarke-Stewart's (1973) observations that for children 8 to 18 months old, maternal responsiveness was more strongly related to the child's IQ score (general competence) than to the frequency of social behavior responded to. Further, when mothers were divided according to their responsiveness and stimulation, those with high responsiveness and low stimulation scores had children with higher IQs than those with high stimulation and low responsiveness scores. By 30 months of age, however (Clarke-Stewart et al., in press), no such relation was observed, suggesting, perhaps, that immediate maternal responsiveness has its beneficial effect only in the first two years of life.

CONTROL.   Another kind of maternal behavior that has concerned inves-
tigators of mother-child interaction is the amount and type of maternal discipline or control. Reviews of this literature (Aronfreed, 1969; Becker, 1964) show that most frequently evidence for this behavior has been drawn from interviews. Actual observation of disciplinary behavior is more difficult and has been done less often. When they have been observed, however, mothers' restriction of infants' physical movement and exploration has been negatively associated with overall development (Beckwith, 1971a; Beckwith et al., 1976; Clarke-Stewart, 1973). When children become mobile, physical restriction apparently becomes less influential (Clarke-Stewart et al., in press; Hanson, 1975; McCall et al., 1973) and the degree of maternal directiveness is more predictive of development. While directiveness may be an effective strategy for enhancing the perfor-
mance of very young children (Bayley & Schaefer, 1964; Clarke-Stewart, 1973), later, directing and controlling the child's activities is associated with less adequate intellectual and social development (Aldous, 1975; Bayley & Schaefer, 1964; Carew et al., 1975; Clarke-Stewart, 1973; Clarke-Stewart et al., in press; McCall et al., 1973; Nelson, 1973; White & Watts, 1973). Punitiveness or severity of penalties is another aspect of control that has been related to child development. In the Fels longitudinal data, McCall et al. (1973) found that both very severe and very lenient punishment were associated with decreasing IQ scores, from 3 to 17 years of age. IQ increased when discipline was moderate to severe, clear, and accompanied by frequent approval. This pattern of discipline is very much like the ''authoritative'' pattern Baumrind (1967) describes, in which the parent attempts to direct the child in rational and reciprocal ways, with few restrictions but firm control. Children of parents using this approach to discipline, she observed, were more friendly, socially responsible, and self-
reliant compared to children of either authoritarian or permissive parents (Baum-
rind & Black, 1967).[4]

The Child's Contribution.   Although lip service has always been paid by more thoughtful writers to the idea of parent-child reciprocity, almost all research until the early 1970s operated under the explicit or implicit assumption that the direction of influence in parent-child relations was from parent to child. It was known for some time that infants differed in activity patterns, persistence, approach, and receptivity to stimuli (Thomas, Chess, Birch, Hertzig, & Korn, 1963), and there was even scattered evidence that infants' behavior affected their mothers' behavior, as well as the reverse (e.g., Levy, 1958). But it was not until R. Q. Bell's (1968) now widely cited article summarizing evidence which demonstrated that infants' behavior affects their parents' behavior that the contribution of children to family interaction, and thus to their own environment and development, was given serious investigation. Since that time, the bidirectionality of parent-child interaction has been documented in a variety of ways.

First, there is fine-grained microanalysis of mother-infant interaction, demonstrating second-to-second reciprocity and mutual behavior cycles (Brazelton, Koslowski, & Main, 1974; Jaffe, Stern, & Peery, 1973; Stern, 1974), and examination of the effects on infant behavior when this continuous feedback between mother and infant does not exist (Thoman, 1974). Second, there is documentation of parent-child reciprocity in studies of the effects of early contact between mother and infant. When a mother is given her infant immediately after delivery she apparently becomes "attached" to the child, as a result of her own state and the infant's at that particular moment (Gaulin-Kremer, Shaw, & Thoman, 1977; Klaus & Kennell, 1976), and this attachment is later reflected in her behavior toward the child (Kennell, Jerauld, Wolfe, Chesler, Kreger, McAlpine, Steffa, & Klaus, 1974; Ringler, Kennell, Jarvella, Navojosky, & Klaus, 1975). Third, there are studies that examine the impact of individual differences among newborns on concurrent and later behavior of mothers. In one study, mothers were observed to vocalize more to babies that weighed more (Brown, Bakeman, Snyder, Frederickson, Morgan & Hepler, 1975), for example. In another, infants who were more alert and responsive at birth had mothers who interacted with them more responsively (Osofsky, 1976). Finally, the child's contribution to mother-infant interaction has been shown in changes in both maternal and infant behavior over the first year of life. The more frequent smiling and vocalizing of infant to mother at one age has been found to be correlated with the mother's greater responsiveness and sociability some months later (Clarke-Stewart, 1973). Infant social behaviors thus seem to "hook" the mother. Indeed, mothers report that it is only when eye-to-eye contact with infants begins that they think of them as human. After that developmental milestone, mothers become significantly more involved in interaction with children (Robson & Moss, 1970). Less is known about bidirectionality of influence at older ages, when parent-child patterns are relatively well established, but we might expect that documentation of reciprocity then, too, would be possible.

The Father's Role. As the child's contribution to parental behavior was ignored by researchers until recently, so was the father's role, beyond studies of his absence. Perhaps because fathers are now taking a more active role in infant care and even participating in the baby's delivery, within the past few years there has been a surge of interest in studying fathers (see Lamb, 1976b; Parke, in press). These studies have demonstrated how active and involved in interacting with their infants fathers are, implicitly suggesting that fathers are, or can be, as good at parenting as mothers. Studies have shown that fathers are "engrossed" in their newborn infants (Greenberg & Morris, 1974), and just as nurturant, affectionate, responsive, and active with infants and young children as mothers (Clarke-Stewart, 1978a; Parke & O'Leary, 1976)—at least when interaction is expected and an observer is taking notes. Unfortunately, the distinction between competence and performance limits generalization from these results; although these studies show that fathers can be as active as mothers, they do not establish how much fathers actually do take care of their children. Home observations and parental reports suggest that the opportunities for fathers to display their nurturant talents are not frequent (Kotelchuck, 1976; Lewis & Weinraub, 1974; Pedersen & Robson, 1969; Rebelsky & Hanks, 1971; Walker & Woods, 1972). Nevertheless, young children do develop close relationships with their fathers as well as their mothers (Clarke-Stewart, 1978a; Kotelchuck, 1976; Lewis & Weinraub, 1974; Schaffer & Emerson, 1964) and may prefer to play with their fathers (Clarke-Stewart, 1978a, Lamb, 1976, 1976b).

An alternative approach to demonstrating how much fathers are like mothers has been to investigate how different they are. The most consistently revealed difference is in play style: fathers are more active, physical, abrupt, and vigorous when they play with infants or young children (Clarke-Stewart, 1978; Lamb 1976a, 1976b; Lynn & Cross, 1974; Parke & O'Leary, 1976; Pedersen & Robson, 1969; Yogman, 1977). When they are with their young children, fathers engage in social play about as much as mothers do, but they do so for fun, not to stimulate the child's intellectual development (Clarke-Stewart, 1978a).

Another approach for evaluating paternal contributions to child development has been to correlate paternal variables with assessments of child development (Baumrind, 1971; Becker, Peterson, Luria, Shoemaker, & Hellmer, 1962; Bishop & Chace, 1971; Honzik, 1967). The problem in several such investigations, however, has been that in focusing on the *father*-child relation, researchers have ignored the concurrent contribution of the mother (Epstein & Radin, 1975; Radin, 1973). This exclusive concentration on father is as shortsighted as the focus only on mother. To fully understand children's development, we need to examine relations with both mother and father simultaneously, treating mother, father, and child as a triad. This approach has been taken by Pedersen and his associates (Pedersen, 1975; Pedersen, Yarrow, & Strain, 1975), but published data from their research are few as yet. The unique contribution of the triadic approach is to distinguish between *direct* parental effects and *indirect* effects mediated by the other parent. One study (Clarke-Stewart, 1978a) of direct and indirect effects suggested that in the first few years of life (from 15 to 30 months), the mother's effect on the child's intellectual development was most likely to be direct, whereas the father's was more likely to be indirect: his behavior both reflected the child's ability at an earlier age and influenced the mother's behavior at a later time. This relation might not hold for school-age children, whose intellectual performance is associated with the father's occupational success and satisfaction (Honzik, 1967); however, it seems likely that even this variable would affect the mother's behavior and be translated by her to the child.

Studying mother-father triads includes investigating the effect of the mother-father relationship on the child. Although some difference between parents' behavior offers stimulating variety and is positively related to development (Clarke-Stewart, 1977b), marital conflict and hostility or marked disagreement, inconsistency, or imbalance between two parents can have a detrimental effect. Children are more competent when the behavior of *both* parents—to each other and the child—is characterized by love and respect (Becker et al., 1962; Bronson, 1966; Honzik, 1967; Kohn & Clausen, 1956; Murray & Seagull, 1969; Parke in press; Pedersen, 1975; Rutter, 1971; Smolak, Beller, & Vance, 1977; Trapp & Kausler, 1958; Wyer, 1965).

Research Issues in Observing Parent and Child Behavior. The observational studies discussed above, although they have distinct advantages over less direct methods of collecting data, are marred by serious methodological problems which limit the educational implications that can be drawn. Although space does not permit a thorough discussion of all of these problems, the most important are mentioned below.

PROCEDURAL. First is the issue of questionable representativeness. More often than not the observations occurred in a laboratory "playroom" where, according to the few studies that have contrasted this setting with the home (Belsky, 1977; Castell, 1970), unfamiliarity, anxiety, or social pressure distorts parents' and children's "natural" behavior and curtails predictability (Lytton, 1974). In the home setting, of course, the presence of an observer can also be a disturbing influence on parent-child interaction, especially if the observer is of a different race or class (Sattler, 1970). Precautions have not always been taken to minimize the observer's effect.

Another procedural issue concerns the method of recording the observation—from microanalysis of videotapes to global ratings of extended naturalistic observations. Although research has advanced beyond simple checklist counts, what is needed now is more systematic combination of methods by combining broader with microanalytic measures or by operationalizing complex concepts like effectiveness or responsiveness into quantifiable units. The practical import of findings from microanalysis of mother-infant interaction, which is, at this moment, obscure, could be illuminated by such combinatorial efforts.

DESIGN AND ANALYSIS. Correlational analysis, which has most commonly been applied to observational data, although generally more informative than a simple test of group differences, still has obvious limitations that are often ignored in drawing conclusions from observations of parent and child behavior. Most important, used simply, correlation indicates nothing about curvilinear relations or about causal directions, although the latter are almost inevitably assumed in discussion of parent-child relations. To really find out about parental effects requires analysis of changes over time. This can be done on the second-to-second scale of the conditional probability analysis of parent and child behavior (e.g., Bakeman & Brown, 1977; Parke, 1977a). If this scale is extended over a somewhat longer time period from minute to minute, a stochastic model is appropriate (e.g., Kaye, 1977). If it is extended over a period of weeks, months, or years, a variety of analyses may be applied: sequential lag analysis (e.g., Sackett, in press), time-series analysis (Gottman, McFall, & Barnett, 1969), path analysis (e.g., Walberg & Marjoribanks, 1976), cross-lagged panel correlation (Campbell & Stanley, 1963; Crano, 1977; Rozelle & Campbell, 1969), or causal model analysis (Rogosa, in press).

Though none of these statistical techniques can *prove* causality, they can help the investigator choose between causal hypotheses by ruling out as less plausible those that do not conform to the data. To apply such statistical methods to the study of parental and child effects—which has only been done for a handful of studies—is difficult. Such analyses demand repeated observations and multiple indicators over time, and their validity is strongly dependent on the reliability of measurement (not the strong suit of observation research), inclusion of all relevant variables, and selection of the "right" causal lag. Ultimately the results of even such sophisticated analyses must be interpreted in light of intelligent, reasonable, and systematic theories (see Rogosa, in press; Walberg & Marjoribanks, 1976). Although three studies that have used some form of causal analysis (Clarke-Stewart, 1973; Kessen, Fein, Clarke-Stewart, & Starr, 1975; Rogosa, Webb, & Radin, 1978) do support the suggestion that maternal stimulation and responsiveness foster children's early intellectual development and test competence, such a conclusion must be considered highly tentative at this time, while serious efforts using advanced causal models proceed.

When data extending over a period of years are available, the further issue of predictability of outcome from infancy or early childhood to later childhood and adulthood is raised. This issue, seldom demonstrated but often assumed, is a knotty one and is of special interest to those who would invest in early childhood education and parent training programs with hopes of reaping later societal (adult) benefits. McCall (in press) distinguishes between two kinds of prediction; continuity (of developmental function) and stability (of individual differences), which have heretofore been confused. The example he uses to illustrate the confusion is the finding that the correlation between children's IQ and the IQ of their biological parents is greater than that between children's IQ and that of their adoptive parents (Honzik, 1957; Skodak & Skeels, 1949). This finding has been interpreted as demonstrating that IQ is genetically determined. In fact, however, another piece of data—evidence that the average performance of the adopted children was closer to the IQ of their adoptive parents than to that of their biological parents—indicates that rearing environment also has a significant impact. The first (correlational) finding reflects the stability of individual differences; the second (mean difference) reflects continuity of development; the former may be more genetically determined, the latter, more environmentally determined. McCall's own analysis (McCall et al., 1973) of the Fels longitudinal data demonstrates that despite high ($r = .70$) cross-age stability of individual IQ scores from 4½ to 17 years of age, mean IQ scores also demonstrated distinct patterns of increases and decreases that were predictable from environmental measures (parents' encouragement and stimulation of the child's independence and intellectual activities). Both genetic and environmental effects appeared in these data, but they were revealed by different kinds of analyses.

Most longitudinal studies of parent-child relations and child development have analyzed only individual stability and have found limited predictability from infant performance to later child or adult outcomes on social and intellectual measures (see Beckwith, in press; McCall, in press). Based on the lack of predictability of IQ from infant performance and the high stability of IQ measures thereafter (Bloom, 1964), it has been argued that the critical time for parental stimulation or intervention is in the early years, and later parental behavior does not matter (White, 1975). The argument gains additional support from the finding that although predictability of later performance from infant tests is weak, predictability from early experience (maternal behavior, family environment) is high (Beckwith, in press; McCall, in press). Unfortunately, this argument contains several critical flaws. First, there is the problem that the argument applies data about stability of individual differences to a recommendation regarding environmental effects on developmental continuity. Second, there is the fact that the nature of the IQ tests used in inferring predictability changes after infancy, and only then begins measuring the kinds of ability (like symbolic thought) assessed in later tests—abilities that are less species typical and provide a greater range of individual differences, which increases correlations. Finally, the argument is hampered by the fact that the home environments of the children for whom predictability of IQ was observed were themselves stable and unchanging (Hanson, 1975; Shipman, 1977). The finding of stability in IQ scores after three years does not mean that later family behaviors were not important, but only that their influence was not different from that measured earlier. Evidence of stability cannot be interpreted, as some have done, as suggesting either that the early period is critical (e.g., White, 1975) or that environment has no effect (e.g., Jensen, 1969). In stable environments like these, environmental factors operate continuously. There is no evidence to support the suggestion that the effects of specific attempts by parents to stimulate their children in the early years will endure if the child is later placed in a nonadvantageous environment.

Separation of the tangle of genetic and environmental contributions to child development by parents is an old, important, and not fully resolved issue—but unequivocal resolution is probably not necessary for our purposes here. There is already sufficient evidence to demonstrate that parental behavior is associated with children's behavior and development beyond the genetic component. This evidence comes from studies of children of normal fathers raised by retarded mothers versus those of retarded fathers raised by normal mothers (Scarr-Salapatek, 1975), comparison of amounts of variance accounted for by mother's behavior versus mother's IQ (Clarke-Stewart, 1973; Clarke-Stewart et al., in press), correlations between child's IQ and maternal behavior with maternal IQ or education covaried out (Honzik, 1967; McCall et al., 1973), and analyses of IQ change patterns in siblings (McCall et al., 1973). It should not be necessary to demonstrate that parental behavior is entirely responsible for children's behavior or even how substantial the environmental contribution is in order to look for educational implications in the research on parent-child relations.

There is, however, one further problem that makes the task difficult. Most investigators have sought only to document correlations between specific pairs of variables—parental control and child aggression, maternal talk and child IQ—in their search for the "essential" elements of the parental environment. When multivariate statistics such as factor analysis, multiple regression, or covariance have been applied to the study of parent-child links, however, much greater complexity is demonstrated than is revealed by any number of "single shot" studies. Multivariate analysis of a wide range of parental variables shows that all components of so-called "good" mothering—verbal stimulation, positive responsiveness, lack of coercion, affectionate involvement—are intercorrelated (Clarke-Stewart, 1973; Clarke-Stewart et al., in press; Hanson, 1975; McCall et al., 1973), but, in one study at least, after analysis of covariance, the only predictive—possibly "essential"—component of this cluster of "good" maternal behavior was the mother's deliberate stimulation of the child's independent and intellectual activities (McCall et al., 1973). If investigations include only a few variables, the danger of obtaining spurious correlations is obviously great.

Interaction Studies.   Thus far we have discussed separately studies of demographic or cultural variation in child rearing and studies of individual differences within the range of "normal" variation. This was not strictly for ease of presentation; it was necessary because most investigators have not evaluated both levels simultaneously. Most studies of "normal" family variation, in fact, have been restricted to variation among white middle-class families living close to universities. Clearly, as Brim (1975) and Bronfenbrenner (1977) have recently stressed, there are advantages to evaluation of environmental influences at all levels—from micro to macro—and to the integration of these various levels. For our purposes here, the cultural-demographic (macro) level can contribute an important context to the investigation of child-rearing styles at the micro level. It can also make it enormously difficult to answer the question: What are the "best" child-rearing practices? Perhaps the question can never be answered with a single, simple list, but only with a qualified: It depends . . . on the child, the family, the situation. There is a growing awareness of the need for ecological and contextual research, and theoretical models incorporating SES, family size, and child-rearing environment (Walberg & Marjoribanks, 1976), or micro, meso, and macro levels (Bronfenbrenner, 1977), are available. Nevertheless, the number of studies following the approach thus far has been very small. Eventually it may be possible to arrive at a number of "best child-rearing" lists—for girls and for boys; for black, white, and Spanish-speaking families; and so on—if that is still desired. As yet, however, such lists are a dim possibility. In this section we have few studies to report that have attempted even to integrate child-rearing and child development relations with a single demographic variable.

INTERACTION WITH SEX.   The one demographic variable that has been considered with any frequency is the child's sex. The reason, usually, has been to answer the question of whether boys or girls are more susceptible to environmental influences. Some studies have shown stronger correlations between child's IQ and a variety of maternal behaviors for girls (Bradley et al., 1977; Elardo et al., 1977; Kagan, 1971; Moss & Jones, 1977; Radin, 1974; Sears, Whiting, Nowlis, & Sears, 1953; Yarrow et al., 1975), while others have found the correlation stronger for boys (Bayley & Schaefer, 1964; Bing, 1963; Clarke-Stewart, 1973; Moss & Kagan, 1958; Schaefer & Bayley, 1963), and yet a third group of studies has reported no difference (Baumrind, 1971; Clarke-Stewart et al., in press; Shipman, 1977). The question is clearly unanswerable as stated.

One critical factor to account for the disagreement among studies may be the child's age. The California longitudinal studies (Bayley & Schaefer, 1964; Honzik, 1967) indicate that for boys early maternal warmth was associated with low IQ in infancy and high IQ at school age or in adulthood, while for girls early maternal warmth was related to high IQ in infancy and low (or unrelated) IQ later. But the discrepancies in the findings of the three groups of studies cannot be resolved simply by considering the ages of the respective subjects. One study examined sex differences in mother-child correlations in two comparable samples (Clarke-Stewart et al., in press). In this investigation, although sex differences did appear quite frequently in each sample, only 2 out of 105 significant correlations were replicated by *both* groups of each sex (and they were not relations involving child's IQ). This finding suggests that previously reported "sex" differences in parent-child correlations may have been due to comparing correlations for *any* two groups, not necessarily for groups differing in gender.

Another reason for separating parent-child relations for boys and girls has been to investigate the interaction between the sex of the parent and the sex of the child. These studies have found that different patterns of maternal and paternal discipline are associated with different patterns of behavior for girls and boys. For girls, independence and originality are associated with firm, even abrasive, control, while for boys, independence is associated with nonconforming and nondirective parental behavior and warm encouragement of autonomy (Aldous, 1975; Baumrind, 1971, 1977; Rosenberg, 1977). Baumrind suggests that the explanation for this difference may be that girls need to be pushed to be independent because it is not part of the traditional girls' sex role. This explanation may or may not be true, and the difference may or may not continue as sex-role stereotypes change, but the importance of the study here is its demonstration that the question of whether boys or girls are *more* affected by parental behavior is clearly simplistic. The question should be: What behaviors of mother and father have what effects on what children at what ages? Considerably more research is needed in order to investigate such complex questions as this one, questions that are raised by the attempt to look for contextual differences in parent-child relations.

INTERACTION WITH RACE. The investigation of parent-child relations within the context of race is of particular importance, since parent training programs for black mothers have most often been based on parent-child relations observed in white families. Research comparing correlations in black and white families reveals that the association between children's intellectual development and maternal stimulation observed in white families is, in fact, not as strong in black families (Bradley et al., 1977; Clarke-Stewart, 1973; Elardo et al., 1977; Shipman, 1977). Apparently this is not a function of lower mean frequency of these behaviors, since higher correlations were found between mothers' and children's emotional behaviors, which were also less frequent in black families (Clarke-Stewart, 1973).[5] Some of the difference may be attributable to a bias in assessment instruments which could attenuate correlations of black subjects; however, since assessments of black children's performance were relatively more related to other, nonmaternal environmental factors, such as teachers, school, and provision of play materials (Clarke-Stewart, 1973; Elardo et al., 1977; Shipman, 1977), the possibility exists that different processes are important in homes of different racial and cultural groups.

INTERACTION WITH SES. A somewhat parallel difference has been observed in middle-class versus lower-class families, with the observation that maternal attitudes are more related to maternal behavior in middle-class than in lower-class families (Moss & Jones, 1977; Tulkin & Cohler, 1973). This, too, could be a by-product of bias in assessment favoring more educated mothers, who would be more likely to establish rapport with the middle-class interviewer and to have greater verbal ability and knowledge of socially desirable answers. But, like the race differences, it could be a function of differing processes in the two kinds of families. Lower-class mothers and children were more affected than middle-class mothers and children by the father's attitude—again, a nonmaternal variable (Moss & Jones, 1977).

One other approach to studying contextual effects of SES has been to investigate the interaction of SES with infants' ability. In low-income, high-risk environments, it has been found, low infant ability predicts later low competence; in the middle-class home, however, stimulation can overcome an early low ability (McCall et al., 1973; Sameroff, 1974; Willerman & Broman, 1970) and enhance an early predisposition to vocalize (Kagan, 1971). Sameroff and Chandler's (1975) transactional model, incorporating SES, family environment, and initial child ability, all interacting over time, is illustrative of the interactive approach to parent-child research that is needed if we are to understand the complexities of the entire range of natural child rearing and its effects on development.

EXPERIMENTAL STUDIES

No matter how sophisticated are the statistical machinations performed on data from naturalistic observations, there is only one real way to demonstrate parental effects, one test of causal relations, and that is the experiment. Only the observation of outcomes that follow directly and inevitably from manipulation of parental behavior will *prove* that child development is the outcome of the parental environment. Direct manipulation of parents' behavior, however, is difficult at best, and perhaps impossible on a nontrivial, long-term, and "real life" level. Consequently, here, too, the issue of parent-child effects has been approached somewhat tangentially.

Institutional Interventions

One indirect route has been the modification of child-rearing conditions in residential institutions. Improvement of bad institutional care—whether it is by an additional hour of attention every day, mobiles and tape recordings, painted bulls-eyes on the infants' cribs, provision of a substitute "mother," or just someone to play with—does lead to improved development (Bakwin & Bakwin, 1960; Brossard & Décarie, 1971; Casler, 1965; Dennis & Sayegh, 1965; Hunt, Mohandessi, Ghodssi, & Akiyama, 1976; Kirk, 1958; Lyle, 1960; McKinney & Keele, 1963; Rheingold, 1956; Rheingold & Bayley, 1959; Saltz, 1973; Skeels, Updegraff, Wellman, & Williams, 1938; White, 1966). All kinds of intervention enhance the development of children in these extremely deprived environments, but the question of whether instituting similar "improvements" in the normal family environment would be beneficial is, of course, not answerable by these studies. It has been noted that supplementing "good" institutional care does not further enhance development (Clarke & Clarke, 1976a; Rheingold, 1956).

Laboratory Experiments

The most focused attempts to explore environmental effects on child development have occurred in laboratory settings where highly specific environmental events can be completely controlled and manipulated. Most experiments involve an adult experimenter (as the "parent" substitute) and measure the effects of his or her behavior on individual children's immediate behavior. These experiments are described first.

Modification of Child's Behavior

STIMULATION.   One set of experiments has demonstrated that even quite brief but repeated episodes of extra stimulation can significantly accelerate infants' development (Powell, 1974; Zelazo, Zelazo, & Kolb, 1972) or increase frequency of vocalization (Dodd, 1972). A combination of social and vocal stimulation seems to be particularly effective (Dodd, 1972; Thoman, Korner, & Beason-Williams, 1977). In the Thoman experiment newborns repeatedly heard a recording of mother talking and at the same time were either picked up or left in their cribs. Subsequently, the infants who had been picked up were more alert, less fussy, and easier to soothe whenever they heard the tape. This illustrates the benefit of combined social-physical-vocal stimulation. With older children, highly specific experimental modification of adults' speech in conversation with children has been related to the children's subsequent language: adult use of more complex language was reflected by children's use of more complex language (Nelson, 1975; Turnure, Buium, & Thurlow, 1976).

RESPONSIVENESS: A host of studies has documented the effect of systematic reinforcement of children's behavior (reviewed by Bryan, 1975; Harris, Wolf, & Baer, 1967; Risley & Baer, 1973; Stevenson, 1965). The frequency of infant vocalization, smiling, and head turning has been systematically increased by contingent reinforcement mediated by a person who looks at the infant [6] (Bloom & Erickson, 1971; Rheingold, 1961; Rheingold, Gewirtz, & Ross, 1959; Wahler, 1969; Watson & Ramey, 1972; Weisberg, 1963), and the duration of infant crying has been reduced by ignoring the cry and reinforcing positive social behavior (Etzel & Gewirtz, 1967). With older children (Risley & Baer, 1973), operant conditioning has been used to teach motor skills, to produce speech, and to modify social behavior, using reinforcers like a snack, play, tokens, candy, a smile, or praise. Experiments have explored in detail parameters of conditioning such as the schedule and timing of reinforcement and the effects of prior conditions and different reinforcers [7] (Brackbill, 1958; Stevenson, 1965). But for our purposes the interesting question is not whether children can be taught particular behaviors or behavior patterns by contingent reinforcement—it is clearly possible to increase the frequency of specific behaviors—but what are the likely long-term or general effects of reinforcement on child development.

Relevant to this question is the work of Watson and Ramey on transfer effects of contingent responsiveness. These investigators have observed that infants who were contingently reinforced for one activity subsequently learned to control another stimulus in a second conditioning situation more readily than infants who had not been given prior opportunity to control a stimulus (Finkelstein & Ramey, 1977; Watson, 1971, 1977). Moreover, contingently experienced infants were better able to distinguish between conditioning and extinction trials. These investigators also report that infants who could control stimulation came to smile and coo more to the controlled stimulus and to attend more to the controlling level. Tentative evidence is thus offered that contingent responsiveness can have long-term consequences in new situations—either because the infant develops a generalized expectancy about control in new situations or because he learns to attend to his own response performance.

PUNISHMENT.   The issue of control, explored by naturalistic and attitudinal studies, has also been investigated in the laboratory by the systematic presentation of an aversive stimulus contingent on the child's behavior. (These studies are reviewed by Aronfreed, 1969; Feshbach & Feshbach, 1972; Gewirtz, 1969; Parke, 1972, 1977b.) The typical punishment study involves giving verbal disapproval, ringing a loud buzzer, or taking away candy when the child chooses, touches, hits, or reaches toward some particular toy. These investigations have demonstrated that punishment is most effective in extinguishing the child's undesired behavior when it is consistent, intense, early in the response sequence, administered by a nurturant adult, and accompanied by a rational explanation. The last condition, is in fact, the most influential; reasoning can outweigh the effect of the other four conditions, and its effect is longer lasting. While these results suggest that punishment can be effective, the investigations also show that its effects may be limited to the particular situation and may lead to anxiety, aggression, or avoidance of the punisher.

MODELING.   Laboratory experiments have explored the effects of an adult model who exhibits highly specific behaviors to see what the child will imitate (see reviews by Aronfreed, 1969; Bandura, 1967, 1969, 1977; Bryan, 1975; Feshbach & Feshbach, 1972; Kohlberg, 1969). Whether or not the child imitates the model's behavior has been shown to depend on a variety of factors, among them, particularly, the kind of behavior and the characteristics of the model. Acts that are aggressive or bizarre are nearly always imitated; imitation of positive or neutral behavior is more dependent on the model's characteristics. It is most likely to occur when the model is powerful, prestigious, and competent, enjoys what she or he does, and gets rewarded for the behavior. The effect of the model's "nurturance" is somewhat complicated. When the model is warm and accepting, this apparently facilitates reproduction of socially neutral behavior (Mussen & Parker, 1965; Yarrow, Scott, & Waxler, 1973) and one kind of prosocial behavior (rescue of another child in distress), but it retards or does not affect another prosocial act (donation to a charity) (see Bryan, 1975). This apparent discrepancy may be because the model's warmth encourages the child to do what he wants (keep the candy and rescue the child). Experiments have also shown that children adopt less stringent standards for rewarding themselves when the model is warm (Bandura, Grusec, & Menlove, 1967). The liberating effect of warmth is likely to be attenuated, however, as the child becomes familiar with the adult's standards and enforcements and comes to value the adult's approval more—as he would with mother at home.

In the laboratory, care is taken to separate the model's warmth and helping behavior, but in real life, the mother does both. In the laboratory, care is also taken to separate modeling and reinforcement; but again, at home, the parent does both. When the combination of both modeling and reinforcement has been investigated it appears that this is especially effective in promoting imitation of the specific behaviors modeled and reinforced and of other similar ones (Bandura, 1969; Risley & Baer, 1973). Kohlberg (1969) suggests that reinforcement, like direct instruction, serves to define for the child what is successful or right, and this is why it increases imitation.

A study that provides a valuable link between naturalistic observation and these experimental studies of modeling and reinforcement was done by Waxler and Radke-Yarrow (1975), using real mothers as the models and reinforcers. In both free play and semistructured situations, the number of times children imitated their mother's behavior was correlated with the frequency of the mother's reinforcement. Apparently this was not a direct maternal effect, however; although imitation increased after reinforcement for some children, a few children never imitated, a few more imitated but were never reinforced, and for the rest, imitation and reinforcement were reciprocal. Apparently there is more than one way to facilitate imitation. Imitation was also related to the amount and kind of modeling the mother did; it was greatest when there was a *moderate* amount of modeling and when the modeling was elaborate, involved, and enthusiastic.

By demonstrating individual differences in imitation-reinforcement patterns between mother and child, this study raised the issue of children's history prior to the experiment, an issue which has typically been ignored by experimenters. This is one of several limitations of laboratory experimentation. The realm of the experiment is highly simplified and artificial. It assesses behavior on a short-term basis, without consideration of what the child knew when the experiment began or what he retains after it is over. Although such experiments hint about what might be the processes of learning at home, they do not demonstrate that parents actually behave in the ways followed by stimulating experimenters, nurturant models, or operant conditioners in the laboratory. Nor do they demonstrate that putting together all the elements from these experiments represents a picture of real parent-child interaction. Therefore although experiments are helpful in establishing what behavior changes adults *can* produce, their limitations should not be ignored in extrapolating to interaction between parents and children at home.

Modification of Parental Behavior. Although most laboratory experiments have manipulated children's behavior, a few have attempted to modify parental behavior or to find out what factors affect parents' behavior. They represent an approach that is a logical and necessary step between observational studies of parent-child relations and massive parent education interventions, but they have been infrequent. Simulated child-behavior experiments offer clear documentation of the potential effect the infant or child may have on parents' behavior. They have demonstrated that mothers go to their infants when they believe they are crying, although they cannot hear them (Moss, 1974), smile and vocalize to their infants more when the infant's social behavior appears to be contingent on their behavior (Gewirtz & Boyd, 1977b), and use less punishment with children they believe are "repentant" (Sawin, Parke, Harrison, & Kreling, 1975).

Demonstration that parents' behavior can be modified by specific minor interventions is illustrated by Price's (1977) experiment, in which viewing and discussing a videotape of the mother interacting with her infant increased the reciprocity of her interaction measured one month later. Similarly, Parke, Hymel, Power, and Tinsley (1978) found that fathers' involvement in feeding and diapering their 3-month-old boys was increased by prior exposure to a training videotape of father-infant interaction.

Parent Training Programs

The best test of causal links between parent and child behavior is afforded by the parent training programs currently in vogue. This latest incarnation of parent education—intervention with poor mothers of young children—began in the late 1960s in the wake of Sputnik, the War on Poverty, and programs for a Great Society. The twist distinguishing such parent training from its immediate predecessors—the social worker, visiting nurse, and parent discussion group—was its avowed foundation in empirical child development research.

First, proponents of parent training cited the research finding that differences in children's intellectual performance, even before they entered school, were related to the family's socioeconomic status. Clearly, it was argued, true to the then-current environmentalist *Zeitgeist*, if SES differences exist before children enter school, the reason must be in the home environment. This finding was combined with a second line of research: correlational studies of natural parent-child variation demonstrating relations between children's intelligence and the kind of care they received. The argument was then extended to place the probable reason for SES deficits in the parents' behavior. Third, would-be parent trainers cited literature on "critical periods" in early childhood as a justification for reaching children before school, and then, after Head Start "failed," before preschool. Bronfenbrenner's (1974) synthesis of evaluations of preschool programs and early parent training efforts was used as further support for parent training, on the basis of his arguments that (1) the more involved parents were in early childhood programs, the greater and longer lasting were their children's intellectual gains; (2) the younger children were when the programs were started, the greater were their gains; and (3) the longer the program continued, the longer were gains maintained. Finally, the argument for parent training was given added strength by the finding that program effects "diffused" to younger siblings, thus suggesting that programs involving parents would be more cost effective. All these pieces of evidence were used to build a powerful case for parent training programs.

Parents were billed as the "first and possibly best teachers," and parent training was hailed as the new panacea for society, offering children guaranteed protection against later deficiencies through a continuing home environment of suitable stimulation. Curricula were quickly devised, based on conventional wisdom or child development research, and parent education assumed the magnitude of a "movement." A recent computer search by the Interagency Panel on Early Childhood Research and Development (for fiscal years 1975 and 1976) revealed over 200 different programs for educating or training parents of young children.

Variation among Programs. It is impossible to describe fully the intricate variety currently available in training programs for parents. It must suffice to describe a few exemplary programs and to indicate the major dimensions on which variation occurs.

One of the earliest programs to take early childhood education to the home, the Infant Education Research Project (Schaefer & Aaronson, 1977; Schaefer, Furfey, & Harte, 1968), was not strictly a parent training program but rather a home tutoring program for young children. Young women visited 15-month-old, black male infants from low-income families in Washington, D.C. daily, for one-hour tutoring sessions that continued until the children were 3 years old. The sessions stressed language development and utilized traditional middle-class activities like reading books, labeling pictures, doing puzzles, playing games, listening to music, and taking trips.

A second program, in contrast to the Schaefer program's focus on the child, emphasized the mother. This was Ira Gordon's Florida Parent Education Infant and Toddler Program (Gordon, 1969; Gordon & Guinagh, 1977; Gordon, Guinagh, & Jester, 1977). In this program, paraprofessionals visited poor mothers and their 3-month-old infants in their homes every week over a period of one, two, or three years, teaching them to play games based on IQ tests, Piagetian scales, folklore, and laboratory experiments, and stressing the principles of matching activities to the child's developmental ability.

The Parent/Child Toy Library Program (Nimnicht, Arango, & Adcock, 1977) also focused on the parent, while the child was not present. Middle-income parents of 3- to 8-year-olds attended eight weekly sessions at a center and, through demonstration, discussion, and role playing, learned teaching techniques with toys expected to enhance children's intellectual growth.

An alternative approach to parent training was to focus on the mother-child *dyad*, an approach best exemplified by Phyllis Levenstein's Mother-Child Home Program (Levenstein, 1970, 1977a, 1977b; Madden, Levenstein, & Levenstein, 1976). Low-income mothers were visited at home by "toy demonstrators," who were social workers, middle-class volunteers, or mothers who had "graduated" from the program. The visits occurred twice weekly for seven months each year, over a one- or two-year period, starting when the child was 2 or 3 years old. The MCHP curriculum encouraged and facilitated verbal interaction between mother and child as they played with toys and books provided by the program in a developmentally sequenced order.

The most intensive and comprehensive approach to parent training can be seen in the Parent Child Development Centers (PCDCs) in Birmingham (Lasater, Malone, Weisberg, & Ferguson, 1975), Houston (Leler, Johnson, Kahn, Hines, & Torres, 1975), and New Orleans (Andrews, Blumenthal, Bache, & Wiener, 1975). These three programs differed in the ages and characteristics of participants, but all offered both intensive training in child rearing and comprehensive services for the entire family (including health care, social welfare, transportation, clothing, food, and general education). Parent training curricula were conveyed by diverse methods of instruction, including modeling, practice reinforced by other mothers, interviews with "model mothers," written materials, informal social discussion, group discussions, classes, workshops, home visits, and analysis of videotapes of the mother's interactions with her child. The broad goals of these projects focused on increasing mothers' ability to cope with stressful environments and to facilitate children's development, and fostering children's cognitive, socioemotional, and physical development.

This sampling of programs illustrates some of the variety that exists in parent training and parent education programs. Programs may focus on the mother, the child, or both. Their goals, though most often limited to raising children's IQ, range from highly specific tasks for parent or child to broad cognitive, social, and physical goals for the child and affective, verbal, and attitudinal goals for the parents. Children range in age from young infants to 5-year-olds, and their parents come from a variety of special groups including Indians, Mexican-Americans, teenagers, drug users, and child abusers. Most participating families are poor or have handicapped children. Program visits may continue over periods of weeks or years, occur daily or bimonthly, and last from half an hour to a full day. They may be individual teacher-parent sessions, group discussions or classes, television programs, or written materials, presented at home or at a school, mobile health unit, or pediatric clinic. The staff may be college students or graduates, paraprofessionals or professionals, mothers from the same neighborhood or across town. The instructional approach can be didactic, as in Kogan and Gordon's (1975) "bug in the ear" instructions; direct, as in Sonquist et al.'s (1975) explicit modeling, Morris, London, and Glick's (1976) role play, Gordon's (1969) exercises, Shearer's (undated) reinforcement, or Levenstein's (1970) toy-mediated verbal interactions; or indirect, as in Kessen et al.'s (1975) incidental modeling and nondirective discussion.

Evaluation. It is of particular interest here not only to describe parent training programs but to examine their outcomes, investigating whether they successfully modify parents' behavior and accelerate or improve children's development, and ascertaining what aspects or kinds of programs do so most effectively. Unfortunately, problems inherent in all kinds of program evaluation, and in the evaluation of these programs in particular, make that task exceedingly difficult. Reviews of even the most highly controlled kinds of parent training programs (behavior modification) conclude that while there is evidence such programs can be effective, evaluation of the programs suffers from methodological inadequacies (Berkowitz & Graziano, 1972; White, Day, Freeman, Hantman, & Messenger, 1973). Methodological problems are even greater when the jump from laboratory to life is longer, as it is in most parent training programs. Not only is experimental control inevitably lost, but evaluation of these programs is plagued by the conflict between the dual program purposes of research and service. In fact, fewer than one quarter of the programs turned up by the Interagency Panel search contained an evaluation component, and when evaluation was included, it was typically the simplest kind possible: a pretest and posttest of children's IQ or mental age, with no control or comparison group. The absence of randomly assigned controls is, quite likely, the result not only of convenience or economy but also of the program sponsors' conviction that assigning eligible families to a no-treatment condition is inhumane or unpolitical.

Some investigators have solved the problem of assigning families to control groups by merely postponing treatment for some families, called the "wait-controls" (Kogan & Gordon, 1975; Love, Nauta, Coelen, Hewett, & Ruopp, 1976; Martin, 1977). Other investigators have utilized a solution that controls for differences in parental motivation or family background by considering the older siblings of program children a control (Karnes, Teska, Hodgins, & Badger, 1970; Madden et al., 1976). This solution has not often been available, however, as it necessitates testing older sibs at the same age as target children, before the intervention begins. The quasi-experimental solution of assessing comparison groups matched on sex, race, and SES, often living in another area, has also been tried. Unfortunately, these "test-only" comparison subjects are often not recruited using the same invitation as experimental subjects, and they are frequently not pretested. When control subjects are pretested, initial noncomparability with treated subjects on other than matched variables (like family structure or child's IQ) is often revealed (Levenstein, 1977b; Slaughter, 1977). Quasi-experimental solutions may often be necessary and their results generally are acceptable (Campbell & Stanley, 1963), but it should be noted that one group of investigators employing both quasi-experimental and experimental designs found that their parent training program appeared significantly more successful in the study with the quasi-environmental design (Madden et al., 1976).

Even when the investigator creates a true random control group, there may be problems. One problem is that when control subjects live near the experimental subjects, the curriculum may be "diffused" from program mothers to control mothers or from program children to control children (Bronfenbrenner, 1974; Gray & Klaus, 1970). Another problem is that the performance of control subjects who are repeatedly tested over the duration of the program in tandem with the experimental subjects may increase substantially, a phenomenon known as the "climbing control group" (Andrews et al., 1975; Kogan & Gordon, 1975; Lambie, Bond, & Weikart, 1974). On the basis of this phenomenon, it has been suggested that mere repeated testing constitutes a (minimal) intervention, either because the child gets more practice with the items during the tests or because the mother provides more test-relevant activities at home. A systematic investigation of the phenomenon by Stedman and his associates (Haskins, Ramey, Stedman, Blacher-Dixon, & Pierce, 1977; Stedman, 1977) tested children every three months from 4 to 28 months of age; no increase in scores due to the repeated testing was found, whether or not the mother observed the testing. Unlike participants in most parent training programs, however, the mothers in this study were largely middle class; thus they may have changed less as a result of what they observed, since they were likely already providing test-related activities at home. The difference between Stedman's results and the "climbing control group" phenomenon might also be accounted for by the fact that subjects in a real test-only control group may change their behavior because they believe they are in an educational program not just a study of children's development (Kogan & Gordon, 1975; Lambie et al., 1974). Stedman's findings, however, do suggest that repeated testing per se is not responsible for either the rising scores of control subjects or the superior performance of an experimental group that is repeatedly tested while the control group is not.

Another problem in evaluating parent training programs lies in subject attrition. Not only does attrition reduce sample size and significance, but these conditions have been observed to interact with program treatment (Slaughter, 1977; Stedman, 1977), program outcome (Lombard, 1973), parental characteristics such as age (Morris et al., 1976), and the initial ability of the child (Lazar, Hubbell, Murray, Rosche, & Royce, 1977a). The issue of differential attrition is far from settled, however. Other studies or reviews have found no differences in attrition related to treatment (Andrews et al., 1975; Lazar et al., 1977a; Love et al., 1976), outcome (Lazar et al., 1977a), parents' characteristics such as socioeconomic or educational level (Andrews et al., 1975; Morris et al., 1976), or child's ability (Morris et al., 1976; Slaughter, 1977; Stedman, 1977). Interaction of attrition with program variables may be more complex than has been investigated in these studies; Gray and Klaus (1970; Klaus & Gray, 1968) found that *control* group dropouts were of relatively low SES, while *program* group dropouts had higher social status.

Assessment instruments used in evaluating parent training programs constitute another methodological hazard. Because most such programs were originally geared toward improving children's school performance, and because standardized IQ and achievement tests were readily available, it is not surprising that these became the major assessment tools used for program evaluation. Unfortunately, as is now recognized, such tests impose limitations because of their cultural specificity and stability-reflective design. Reliance solely on IQ tests, moreover, ignores possible socioemotional and motivational outcomes of programs and does not necessarily predict to school achievement (Miller & Dyer, 1975). Finally, evaluation of parent training programs demonstrates that no single measure is an adequate assessment, even of intelligence gains (Gray & Klaus, 1970; Klaus & Gray, 1968; Levenstein, 1977a, 1977b; Parkman-Ray,

1973; Slaughter, 1977). The need for more complex and multivariate strategies for assessing child outcomes of parent programs seems clear.

Similarly, multivariate assessment of dimensions of parental change is needed. Maternal behavior change has usually been assumed, and then ignored, in program evaluations. Investigators have generally not asked mothers about their goals or looked at their interactions with their children before or after imposing the program. Perhaps the reason is the lack of standardized instruments for assessing maternal behavior. Any evaluations of maternal variables that have been attempted have been based on questionnaires, maternal reports, or observations made in training sessions or structured tasks rather than natural situations. Program evaluation is further limited by biased, in-house assessments, by the exceptional (experimental and exemplary) nature of the model programs evaluated, and by the lack of postprogram follow-up. Even when follow-up evaluations are done (as for the 14 programs compiled by Lazar et al., 1977a), program effects are confounded by children's later educational experiences, and assessments are restricted to measuring child outcomes.

But the most serious limitation of program evaluations, for our purposes here, is that even when adequate evaluations have been done, most researchers have been concerned only with demonstrating the overall effectiveness of their programs. They have not investigated the *processes* of change, examining effects according to program dimensions such as length, intensity, curriculum, and mode of instruction. In the evaluation of any single program, all these program components are confounded. With great difficulty, reviewers have attempted to compare outcomes associated with specific dimensions across programs by a number of approaches: (1) ignoring confounding components and relating a common outcome (inevitably, child's IQ) to the position of programs (high, medium, or low) on each dimension, and then "taking a vote" (Bronfenbrenner, 1974; Goodson & Hess, 1976); (2) computing and testing the significance of the mean differences in outcome for each position (Bronfenbrenner, 1974; Goodson & Hess, 1976); (3) examining the range of outcomes for each position (Bronfenbrenner, 1974; Goodson & Hess, 1976); or (4) compiling raw data from different programs and correlating program dimensions with a common child outcome (Lazar et al., 1977a). The results of such attempts are essentially negative. Of the 15 dimensions analyzed by the Lazar Consortium on Developmental Continuity, only one was significantly related to program effectiveness.[8] Goodson and Hess were cautious in interpreting their dimensional analyses and concluded that differential effects were the result of unidentified factors, while Beller (in press) gave up the task of dimensional analysis entirely, claiming it was impossible at the present time. As a basis for evaluating dimensional effects, manipulation and comparison of dimensions *within* programs, while controlling other potentially confounding variables, are needed, as is more extensive assessment of outcomes other than children's IQ.

These needs were addressed in a study done in New Haven by Kessen, Fein,

Clarke-Stewart, and Starr (1975). Their home-based program held constant the age and background of subjects (12 months old, from the working and lower-middle classes), the length and intensity of the program (six months each of weekly, biweekly, and then monthly visits), the training and qualifications of the staff (college graduates, who were each assigned equal numbers of families in each treatment condition), and the instructional approach (nondidactic "light intrusion"). Evaluation, before the program began and at six-month intervals thereafter, was complex and comprehensive, assessing maternal attitudes and behavior and children's social, cognitive, and language development through tests, natural observations, and semistructured probes.

Beyond these constant variables, the study explored systematic variation in curriculum and program focus. Subjects were randomly assigned to one of six treatment conditions. The first three treatment conditions were alike in their focus on the mother-child dyad but different in curricular goals and content. In the "Language Curriculum," the home visitor encouraged the mother to talk to the child, describing ongoing activities, playing language games, and labeling toys, objects, and pictures. When the child began to speak, the mother was encouraged to respond to and elaborate on his vocalization and to engage him in dialogues. The goal of this curriculum was to promote the growth of vocabulary and comprehension and to help the child appreciate the "multifold" uses of speech.

For the "Play Curriculum," home visitors tried to help the mother arrange an environment wherein the child could discover and explore interesting and diverse objects suited to his developmental level. In this environment, interested, appreciative grownups would elaborate on the child's object interactions in nondirective ways and expand the activities he initiated.

The "Social Curriculum" was designed to provide the mother and child with frequent opportunities for playful, reciprocal interaction and to encourage continuation of such social episodes when the home visitor was not there. The home visitor first suggested activities for the mother and child to share and later joined in the activities, but always the focus was on the mother-child pair. The theme of this curriculum was the "enrichment of interpersonal connections"—through mutual looking, playing, talking, responding, and expressing affection.

While the Language, Play, and Social curricula all focused on the mother-child dyad, two comparison conditions focused on either mother (mother-only-comparison) or child (baby-only comparison). In the mother-only condition, the home visitor was friendly to the child but did not actively play with him; she directed her attention to conversation and activities with the mother. In the baby-only condition, the home visitor was friendly to the mother but her activities consisted of conversation and play with the child; the mother was not encouraged to watch or participate. The curriculum for both these treatments was a combination of the Language, Play, and Social curricula activities. The sixth and final treatment condition in the study was a test-only control.

General Outcomes. Despite the limitations of evaluation methods applied to the study of parent training programs, some general statements can be made about the short- and long-term effects of such programs on mothers and children. The *consistency* of results showing positive outcomes from such a wide variety of programs—no matter how inadequately evaluated—is impressive. It is clear that parent training programs can have immediate effects on children's intellectual performance and development. Most, though not all, programs demonstrate significant if moderate IQ gains for program children compared to control or comparison children, gains which seem to peak at about 3 years of age (Andrews et al., 1975; Boger, 1969; Gordon et al., 1977; Gutelius, 1977; Lally & Honig, 1977; Lambie et al., 1974; Lasater et al., 1975; Leler et al., 1975; Levenstein, 1977a; Schaefer & Aaronson, 1977; and reviews by Beller, in press; Goodson & Hess, 1976; Horowitz & Paden, 1973; White et al., 1973). In addition, gains in children's language ability, when measured separately from IQ, have been observed (Andrews et al., 1975; Boger, 1969; Lally & Honig, 1977b; Lasater et al., 1975). Fewer studies have assessed noncognitive variables, but those that have suggest that such variables as children's sociability, security, and cooperation may be increased by participation in a parent training program (Lally & Honig, 1977b; Lasater et al., 1975; Levenstein, 1977b).

For intellectual variables, there is also consistency of results among studies that have followed up children after the program has ended. Global measures of program effectiveness (placement in special education classes or grade retention) reveal consistent effects for most parent training programs through elementary school (Lazar et al., 1977a, 1977b). IQ gains also are maintained for a period of several years following the program but gradually decrease with time. They are usually maintained over the first one to two years (Goodson & Hess, 1976; Lasater et al., 1975; Morris et al., 1976; White et al., 1973), though not always (Gordon et al., 1977a [9]; Lambie et al., 1974). By three years after the program has ended, gains from some programs have faded to nonsignificance (Gutelius, 1977; Schaefer & Aaronson, 1972), while others are still significant (Gordon et al., 1977 [10]; Gray & Klaus, 1970; Levenstein, 1977a). Later, the difference between program and control children declines still more, although perhaps not to the level of controls (Goodson & Hess, 1976). The problem in interpreting follow-up results is that the time postprogram at which the follow-up assessment is made is confounded with children's age and with educational experience since the program. In Lally and Honig's (1977a, 1977b) program, in fact, differences between experimental and control children were no longer apparent at 6 years of age—and yet these children were still *in* the program.

Effects of parent training programs on mothers are less well known than child outcomes, but positive changes by the end of the program have been noted in maternal behavior and attitudes: mothers are more talkative, didactic, responsive, and active with children; they use more complex speech, including questions, with them; their attitude toward child rearing is less authoritarian; and they are more confident about being parents (Andrews et al., 1975; Benson, Berger,

& Mease, 1975; Boger et al., 1969; Gutelius, 1977; Leler et al., 1975; Levenstein, 1977b; Love et al., 1976; Sonquist, 1975; Wandersman & Wandersman, 1976). Nevertheless, these positive outcomes are not inevitable, especially for attitudes. No differences have been observed, in other studies, in mothers' personal sense of control, values, child-rearing philosophy, attitude, IQ, or behavior toward the child (Epstein & Evans, 1977; Lally & Honig, 1977b; Leler et al., 1975; Levenstein, 1977b; Slaughter, 1977; Sonquist, 1975; Stern et al., 1970).

Outcomes Related to Program Dimensions

CURRICULUM GOALS AND CONTENT.   Recent reviews comparing outcomes across different parent training programs have concluded that the content, emphasis, goals, and philosophical orientation of the curriculum are not related to program effectiveness as regards children's IQ or later placement in special education classes (Goodson & Hess, 1976; Lazar et al., 1977a; Vopava & Royce, 1978). The problem is, however, that few of the curricula reviewed were anything but cognitive. In the Goodson and Hess report, for example, 20 programs were cognitive and only 5 were verbal and 3 sensorimotor; clearly, this distribution did not provide a balanced comparison, even if other aspects of the programs had been comparable. It is perhaps deceptively easy to conclude that curriculum content and program effectiveness are not related. There is substantial evidence, at least, that the absence of *any* curriculum—unstructured social visits or visits from a nurse—does not lead to gains in development (Badger, 1977; Gordon, 1969; Lambie et al, 1974; Levenstein, 1977b).

The only study to probe directly the issue of differential effectiveness of curricula, Kessen et al.'s New Haven program (1975), found no differences in children's IQ test competence related to curriculum condition, further supporting Goodson and Hess's conclusion. For increases in children's functional competence (language production and symbolic or relational play) and mothers' articulate nondirectiveness, the order of curriculum groups was Language first, Play second, and Social third. This finding further supports the observation that *lack* of a curriculum is ineffective: the outcome of the Social Curriculum, which was most like the unstructured, noncurricular, social visits in the other studies, was significantly lower than that of Language and Play curricula, and not different from the performance of test-only control subjects. Language and Play curricula subjects were not significantly different from each other. Perhaps this was because of the cognitive emphasis in both these curricula, a quality which has been observed previously to increase program effectiveness with respect to maternal behavior (Barbrack, 1970). Possible explanations for the apparent superiority of a cognitive-language curriculum might include how closely the curriculum focused on skills that were tested, how much it involved the mother (Goodson & Hess, 1976), how compatible it was with the parents' goals (Sonquist, 1975), or how comfortable and involving it was for the home visitor (in the

New Haven study the Social Curriculum was always hardest for home visitors, while the toys in Language and Play curricula activities served as ice-breaking mediators). Another possible explanation is how well the curriculum enhanced the parents' (cognitive) understanding (Heinicke, 1977). Clearly the issue of curricular effectiveness needs further investigation; investigation which should include a range of outcomes for mothers and children and sensitive indicators of program content.

PROGRAM PARTICIPANTS. A major question for parent training and early childhood education concerns the relative effectiveness of programs focusing on parent versus child. Unfortunately, only a small number of studies have compared the relative effects of mother-focused and child-focused programs. Of these, one (Lombard, 1973) found that mother-focused was superior to child-focused, another (Kessen et al., 1975) found that child-focused (baby-only comparison) was superior to mother-focused (mother-only comparison), and a third (Stern et al., 1972) found no differences between child-focused and mother-focused programs in terms of children's intellectual performance.

Similarly, studies have seldom compared mother-focused with mother-child–focused programs, although, since there is evidence that home-based parent training programs produce more child gains than group classes or discussion on parenting (Brim, 1965; Chilman, 1973; Goodson & Hess, 1976; McCarthy, 1972), it may be inferred that mother-child focused programs are more effective. Radin's (1972) study demonstrated that when the mother watched the teacher instruct her child it led to greater child gains than when she merely attended parent meetings. Stedman's (1977) observation that subject attrition was less when mothers were allowed to watch their children being tested also suggests that the child may be an important part of effective intervention. For producing changes in *maternal* behavior, however, mother-focused programs may be more effective (Beller, in press; Kessen et al.'s (1975) mother-only versus Language, Play, and Social curricula conditions).

Most comparisons have been of mother-child–focused versus child-focused programs, assessed by comparing amounts of parental involvement in the child's early childhood education program or by comparing home visit and center programs. These comparisons indicate that mother-child programs have a greater effect on the mother's attitude and teaching (Adkins & Crowell, 1969; Adkins & O'Malley, 1971; Downey, 1969; Love et al., 1976; Radin, 1972). But these differences may simply reflect the fact that the mother has learned to give the "desirable" answer or exhibit the desirable behavior. No difference was found in the New Haven study (Kessen et al., 1975) between maternal behavior to the child in child-focused (baby-only) and mother-child–focused (Language-Play-Social) conditions.

There is more evidence for the greater effectiveness of mother-child–focused programs in enhancing *children's* development. More mother-child involvement produced higher or longer lasting gains in children's IQ (Adkins & Crowell,

1969; Adkins & O'Malley, 1971; Alford & Hines, 1972; Beller, in press; Bronfenbrenner, 1974; Downey, 1969; Goodson & Hess, 1976; Lazar et al., 1977a; Radin, 1972). But this evidence is not convincing either. Bronfenbrenner based his conclusion on a small sample of programs with confounded ages and frequency of visits; Lazar's comparison was between 13 high–medium parent involvement programs and only one low involvement program; and Goodson and Hess based their claim of superiority on gains of 6 versus 8–10 IQ points. Equally strong evidence exists for the claim that there is no difference between mother-child–focused and child-focused programs in fostering children's intellectual development (Gilmer, Miller, & Gray, 1970; Kessen et al., 1975; Miller & Dyer, 1975). And what is more, some studies have found that child-focused programs are more effective than mother-child programs for producing gains in children's test competence (Kessen et al., 1975), test orientation (Love et al., 1976), and school skills (Bronfenbrenner, 1974). In Klaus and Gray's (1968) combined home-visit and center program, in fact, gains in children's intelligence occurred when the children were attending preschool (child-focused) and dropped when they had only home (mother-child) visits.[11]

In addition to the question of whether the focus of the program is related to its effectiveness is the question of whether program effects are related to individual differences among children or families. It has been observed that parent programs are more effective when mothers are not employed (Karnes et al., 1970) or very poor (Bronfenbrenner, 1974; Chilman, 1973; Herzog, Newcomb, & Cisin, 1972; Klaus & Gray, 1968; White et al., 1973). Other family characteristics, too, such as the size of the household (Slaughter, 1977; Kessen et al., 1975) or the amount of contact with extended-family members (Kessen et al., 1975), may interact with treatment conditions in complicated ways. This is a complex issue that needs further exploration. Children's age, sex, and ability may also interact with program effectiveness. Differential effects have been noted for boys and girls (Gordon & Guinagh, 1977; Kessen et al., 1975; Lally & Honig, 1977b), but, unfortunately, data currently available are not sufficient to formulate any sex-related generalizations. The same is true for the interaction of children's initial intelligence or ability with program effectiveness (Goodson & Hess, 1976; Lazar et al., 1977a). Age may also be related to program effects. The problem in relating the child's age to program outcomes, however, is that age typically has been confounded with program length. Studies varying age of subjects at the beginning of the program (by about a year, in the range from 2 months to 3 years) show no significant age-related differences in immediate effects (Andrews et al., 1975; Lambie et al., 1974; Levenstein, 1977a, 1977b; Morris et al., 1976), although there is some evidence that beginning at a younger age is better in the long run (Gordon & Guinagh, 1977; Karnes, Hodgins, & Teska, 1969; Karnes, Studley, Wright, & Hodgins, 1968; Vopava & Royce, 1978). Nevertheless, the consensus is that there is no "magic age" for starting parent training programs (Beller, in press; Lazar et al., 1977a).

LENGTH AND INTENSITY OF PROGRAM. Positive results have been observed for early childhood programs varying from a few months (Palmer & Siegel, 1977) to a few years (Gordon et al., 1977). Although some studies have found no difference between programs lasting one or two years (Andrews et al., 1975; Lombard, 1973; Love et al., 1976) or two or three years (Klaus & Gray, 1968), when differences are found (Gilmer et al., 1970; Gordon & Guinagh, 1977; Gordon et al., 1977; Levenstein, 1977) they favor the longer programs and are usually reflected in longer lasting rather than larger gains, or in maternal or sibling changes rather than child changes. Caution must be applied, however, since several of these studies confound program length with child's age. Moreover, even if program duration ranging from one to three years is related to program effectiveness, beyond that length longer programs may not be advantageous (Lally & Honig, 1977b). Maintaining the program once it begins is also important; in Gordon's study, two contiguous years in the program were better than two nonconsecutive years.

A more intense program schedule and longer visits may also be more effective (Andrews et al., 1975; Gilmer et al., 1970; Kessen et al., 1975; Love et al., 1976), but the studies examining this variation have confounded program intensity with location, activities, focus, or age. Moreover, causal direction from visit length to program effect cannot be assumed. It may be that visits are shorter when the home visitor or mother is discouraged by the child's progress or when the home visitor is unable to establish rapport with the mother. According to Lazar's analysis, there is no systematic effect of intensity of visits.

INSTRUCTION TECHNIQUES. Finally, program effectiveness may be related to instructional aspects of the program. There seems to be no difference in program outcome depending on staff qualifications (Gordon, 1969; Lazar et al., 1977a; Levenstein, 1977b; Love et al., 1976; Vopava & Royce, 1978; White et al., 1973), as long as there is a curriculum to follow (Lambie et al., 1974). The structure or specificity of the instruction may be related to immediate (Lazar et al., 1977a) or later (Goodson & Hess, 1976) outcomes for the child or the mother (Boger, 1969), but this evidence is weak. The instructional format may also be related: Although parental group discussion or lectures are not very popular or effective in changing parents' or children's behavior or attitudes (Brim, 1965; Chilman, 1973; Goodson & Hess, 1976; Gordon & Guinagh, 1977; McCarthy, 1972; Radin, 1972; White et al., 1973), discussion that involves both group pressure and the mother's own child can be as effective as or more effective than individual home visits (Andrews et al., 1975; Badger, 1977; Slaughter, 1977). Merely providing mother and child with toys is not an effective intervention strategy—unless the toys are selected for their stimulating and age-appropriate properties (Badger, 1977; Levenstein, 1977b; Slaughter, 1977).

Assumptions and Evidence. Although some of the more naive assumptions on which early parent programs were founded (e.g., that a brief program could serve as a permanent "inoculation" against later deficiencies) have subsequently been disproved or discarded, the parent program movement today continues to be based on untested assumptions. In addition to instituting more adequate and fine-grained evaluations to ascertain the effectiveness of programs and program components, if we are to understand the process of parental influence on child development we must expose and explore the assumptions of parent intervention programs. Following are some of these assumptions:

1. *That what the program designer intends is what really happens.* Home visitors, though given prior indoctrination and training in program techniques, have seldom been monitored *in situ* as they interpret and implement the program—and they should be.

2. *That the message the parent training intends is what gets through to the mother.* The message that gets across may be distorted by the mother's uncertainty, anxiety, or ignorance into a more simple-minded form—for example, the mother may hear "Play with your child!" but miss more subtle suggestions about *how* to play (Kessen et al., 1975). We need to know how the program is received.

3. *That all mothers are equally ready for parent training.* Differences in maternal attitudes prior to the program have been observed to be related to their involvement in the program (Schaefer & Aaronson, 1977); their behavior (Martin, 1977), and the child's progress (Schaefer & Aaronson, 1977). Consideration of individual differences in parents' needs is necessary.

4. *That the mother's goals for herself and her child are the same as the program designer's—or would be if the mother knew better.* Compatibility between parents' and program's goals has been found to affect outcomes (Sonquist, 1975), but parents' goals have seldom been evaluated in parent training studies.

5. *That the mother changes or will change in the desired direction.* [12] While there is some evidence that desired changes in maternal behavior occur (Lasater et al., 1975), there is also evidence that mothers may change in the opposite direction from that intended—becoming more directive (Kessen et al., 1975), more extreme (Chilman, 1973), or less involved with their children (Badger, Hodgins & Burns, 1977). It may be, as Nimnicht et. al. (1977) and Schlossman (1978) have suggested, that the effect of parent training is to make the mother more anxious or unsure, which could make her adapt the program to strengthen rather than diminish her own natural proclivities. Moreover, the most essential and desirable aspects of mothers' natural behavior with their children—like sociability, responsiveness, and effectiveness—may not even be susceptible to change (Kessen et al., 1975). Naturalistic assessment of the mother's behavior with her child before, during, and after the program is important.

6. *That changing the mother's behavior causes the child's improved perfor-*

mance. Studies have found that maternal attitudes or behavior and children's IQ and behavior are correlated in intervention families (Andrews et al., 1975; Epstein & Evans, 1977; Gordon & Guinagh, 1977; Lambie et al., 1974; Levenstein, 1977b; Schaefer & Aaronson, 1977), as they are in "unimproved" families, and that a reduced correlation between maternal education and child IQ occurs in experimental families (Levenstein, 1977b). But what is needed to test this critical assumption is analysis of the relation between *changes* in maternal and child behavior over time.

Only four studies offer evidence of this kind. Kogan and Gordon (1975) observed that mothers' behavior changed during training sessions and children's changed in the posttraining period, but they found no correlation between maternal change and child change. Andrews et al. (1975) found that mothers' behavior changed prior to the time treatment effects were observed for child's IQ, but the time lags by which maternal change preceded changes in children's motor and cognitive performance were slight and could be at least partially attributed to asynchrony in scheduling assessments. They did not analyze for correlations between maternal change and child change. Kessen et al. (1975), examining both changes in group means and correlational patterns, found no evidence that changes in maternal behavior either preceded or caused increments in children's performance, and indeed, found that child changes preceded maternal changes on several factors. Forrester, Boismier, and Gray (1977) found that the correlation between children's IQ at the beginning of the program and maternal stimulation at the end was stronger than that between maternal stimulation at the beginning and child IQ at the end. Since the opposite direction of influence was observed by Clarke-Stewart (1973) for comparable variables and the same age children in families *not* participating in a parent training program, this correlational pattern may reflect a treatment effect, but what is needed is further breakdown by time periods *within* the duration of the program.

In sum, the results of these four investigations of mother-child changes, combined with the following findings:

1. That the behavior of children from child-focused programs influences the mother's behavior (Falender & Heber, 1975).
2. That mother-child interaction and children's behavior are more susceptible to program-induced change than is maternal behavior (Kogan & Gordon, 1975; Lally & Honig, 1977b) or attitudes (Lally & Honig, 1977b; Leler et al., 1975, Sonquist, 1975).
3. That, as described earlier, child-focused programs are at least as effective as mother- or mother-child–focused ones in producing child gains.

make it only too clear that we have no basis for the assumption that parent training programs "work" strictly or simply through the mother's influence on the child.

7. *That the benefits of parent training will continue after the program ends because the mother learns principles she can adapt as the child gets older or can apply in her interactions with later children.* Although mothers *report* that they generalize behavior modification techniques to other family members (Hamm & Lyman, 1973; Shearer, undated), and although younger siblings generally perform better than expected on tests of intelligence (Gilmer et al., 1970; Gray & Klaus, 1970; Klaus & Gray, 1968; Levenstein, 1977b; Miller, 1968), the degree to which mothers generalize their program-produced behaviors apparently declines over time and place. It is greatest when sibs are close in age to the target child (Gray & Klaus, 1970) and in situations in which the program was taught [13] (Gilmer et al., 1970; Levenstein, 1977b; Miller & Sloane, 1976). Evidence that mothers can adapt the principles learned in parent training programs as children get older has not been collected.

CONCLUSION

Strategies for Research

The limitations of particular research paradigms have been pointed out in the preceding pages. In concluding the chapter, some comments about the research enterprise as a basis for educational policy and practice are needed. This review has drawn upon two bodies of literature to discuss parental effects on child development: reports of educational programs for parents, which typically have not been designed as research investigations, and accounts of observational or experimental research on parents, which generally has not been intended as a basis for education. In order to derive sound recommendations for education, the results of both kinds of investigation are useful. At present, however, each approach is limited in ways that will be alleviated only by cross-fertilization between the two (Williams, 1977).

Today almost all investigations of child development are constrained by narrow strategies for research, strategies that can best be characterized as *single celled.* In the matrix of researchable areas relating to childhood—such as child development, child rearing, and children's services—the vast majority of investigations focus on problems within a single area; seldom is the domain of a research project the intersection of two areas, such as child development and family services, and almost never is it the intersection of more than two, such as socioeconomic status, parental behavior, family services, and child development (Hertz, Mangus, Mann, & Wagner, 1977). Thus research is located in single cells of a matrix. Then, too, efforts to align ongoing research with prior studies in terms of samples, variables, measures, or results are sparse, and coordination or collaboration between investigators is rare (Bell & Hertz, 1976; Hertz et al., 1977). Thus researchers occupy single cells—monastic cells. And since it is almost inevitably true that an investigator is trained in a single research paradigm (e.g., lab or field), which he subsequently applies to a variety of problems rather than exploring the same problem with a variety of methods, this research is characterized by yet a third kind of cell—researchers unable or unwilling to break away from communist cells (or prison cells?).

The outcome of this last constraint is well illustrated by the inconsistency between results of laboratory and field investigations of the effects of responding to infants' crying and vocalizing. In laboratory experimentation it has been found that ignoring a cry leads to decreased crying (Etzel & Gewirtz, 1967), while at home, over a longer period of time, ignoring a cry is associated with more frequent crying (Bell & Ainsworth, 1972). Similarly, in experiments, verbal reinforcement of infants' vocalization has been observed to increase vocalizing (Weisberg, 1963), while in the normal course of children's communication development increasing frequency of vocalization is accompanied by a decline in the frequency of maternal talk (Greenbaum & Landau, 1977). Such inconsistencies can lead to acrimonious argument (Ainsworth & Bell, 1977; Gewirtz & Boyd, 1977a, 1977c) or sterile cross-paradigmatic controversy (Kuhn, 1962). Undoubtedly there are problems and differences [14] in methodology and interpretation on *both* sides of such arguments, but the apparent discrepancies between results of lab and field studies have been exacerbated by the fact that different investigators are on the two sides, often apparently more interested in proving the other side wrong than in explicating the processes of child development.

To replace the single-celled approach to research with something more useful for resolving such differences and to provide the firmest possible basis for educational policy, a new research strategy is called for. This strategy would be:

1. Programmatic: Systematically and sequentially applying multiple assessment methods—interview, observation, experiment, and intervention—to any given problem (M. R. Yarrow, 1973).
2. Integrative or collaborative: Coordinating concepts, variables, instruments, and results with those of other investigators in the same and related areas (Bell & Hertz, 1976).
3. Interactive and contextual: Giving attention to interactions and interrelations across ecological and individual levels—historical time, sociocultural context, parental attitudes and behavior—and identifying chains or patterns of variables leading to child development (Hertz et al., 1977).
4. Complex and multivariate: Assessing and analyzing the gamut of parental and child abilities and behavior.
5. Clearly concerned with social rather than merely statistical significance: Evaluating person as well as pacing variables, at levels of assessment that probe more deeply than simple tests, and accepting as the criterion for significance more substantial indices than inconsequentially small group differences in IQ.

Implications for Education

Methodological limitations notwithstanding, the research reviewed here, representing as it does the best empirical evidence about parental effects on child development available at the present time, can be examined for its possible applications to education. This final section summarizes the generalizations that appeared consistently across the different research paradigms reviewed and points out some of their educational implications.

Generalizations about Parental Effects on Child Development

1. Permanent deprivation or enrichment of sensory and social experience clearly affects intellectual and social development. Environment does make a difference.
2. Children are particularly susceptible to environmental input in the early years. Early environment is important.
3. The effects of early environment are largely reversible by later experience. Early environment is not everything. The effects of early deprivation can be overcome by later stimulation, and the benefits of early enrichment can be lost by placement in a restricted environment—at least to the extent of being within the normal range of development. Continuing experience rather than just a particular period of experience is critical for development.
4. In the early environment, the kind of parental behavior that facilitates children's intellectual development is stimulating talk and play, encouragement of exploration and independence, and maintenance of moderate control. The kind of parental behavior that fosters new learning is contingently responsive to the infant's or young child's behavior. To support the child's socioemotional development, interaction with the parent should be regular, repeated, and reciprocal, positive, playful, and moderately permissive. Increasing the frequency of particular child behaviors can be accomplished by modeling and reward; decreasing their frequency follows from consistent and justified punishment—particularly if the adult is perceived by the child as powerful, competent, and nurturant. Parents who display these kinds of behavior facilitate children's development.
5. Parental behavior is characterized by complex patterns of related clusters of different kinds of behavior—e.g., control, affection, and stimulation. It is unlikely that a single parental behavior alone determines the child's development.
6. Parental behavior interacts with the child's individual characteristics, and the child's behavior affects the parent's, as well as the reverse. Parent and child together create a reciprocal, interactive, dyadic unit.
7. Although children's performance may be related to demographic groupings like SES, race, and maternal employment or marital status, these variables alone do not predict children's behavior as well as parents' actual

behavior does. A range of environments in different sociocultural contexts supports normal development.

Taken together, these findings can be used as a basis for instituting educational programs for children (point 1), which offer the kinds of behavior by teachers or paraprofessionals that have been shown in laboratory and naturalistic study to positively affect child development (points 4, 5), programs that start with young children (point 2) and continue through childhood (point 3), programs that are tailored to the characteristics of individual children (point 6) from a variety of sociocultural backgrounds, in families where parental care does not provide stimulating and affectionate experiences (point 7).

Another logical and perhaps even more obvious extension of the same set of findings might be the recommendation that educational programs for parents be instituted.[15] These programs would build on the supposition that parents, even more than teachers, are able to respond to the individual characteristics of their own children (point 6) and to provide early (point 2) and continuing (point 3) environments of stimulation and affection; they would train parents to exhibit the behaviors described as facilitative of child development (points 4, 5). Before accepting this recommendation as a reasonable educational policy, however, it is important to consider the findings from the research literature pertaining to the changing of parents' behavior.

Generalizations about Program Effects on Parent Development

1. Parents' child-rearing behaviors and attitudes are embedded in a sociocultural context which is affected by socioeconomic circumstances and is related to cultural traditions. There is no evidence that they are determined by expert opinion or educational literature on child care and development.
2. Parents' specific knowledge about child rearing is related to their children's development. However, since specific child-rearing knowledge is associated with more general knowledge, and since child development is more closely related to parents' behavior than to their knowledge (general or specific), there is no evidence that child-rearing knowledge influences child development directly.
3. Although educational programs have been successful in changing some kinds of parental behavior, like caretaking, amount of talking, or teaching, they have been less successful in modifying others, such as responsiveness, effectiveness, playfulness, and affection. It is the latter parental qualities, expressed in natural interaction with the child, that are most closely related to child development.[16]
4. Since parental child rearing is characterized by complex patterns or clusters of behaviors, all components of which are not equally modifiable, it is not clear that the results of changing only one component of the parents' natural style will be effective or unambiguously beneficial for child development.

5. Parent programs interact with family circumstances and individual characteristics of their clients; all parents are not equally affected by educational
intervention.
6. Positive outcomes for parents and children have been observed to result
from participation in parent programs. However, since gains are greatest
when *both* parent and child are active in the program, and since changes in
the child's behavior can lead to changes in the parent's, it is not clear that
program-produced modification of parental behavior is solely responsible
for the positive outcomes for the child.

Taken together, these generalizations about program effects on parent development reveal some of the difficulties inherent in modifying parental behavior
by educational means. They also point up the unfounded assumptions in the
presumed chain of influence on which parent education has been based:

Program		Increased		Changes in		Gains in
curriculum	⟶	parental	⟶	parental	⟶	child
		knowledge		behavior		development

Although the research reviewed does provide consistent support for expected
relations between parent behavior and child development in natural families, it
does not prove that changes in parent or child development can be induced
simply through programs that increase parents' knowledge about child rearing or
child development or that modify only a minimum number of behaviors. In brief,
at the present time, there exists no strong empirical support for the hope that
parent training will prove a societal panacea, creating brighter and better citizens in this generation or the next. Any mandate for parent education programs
must await unambiguous evaluations that demonstrate significant positive effects.[17]

NOTES

1. This review does not include investigations of differences in child rearing leading to
abnormal psychological development (e.g., schizophrenia, autism). These are reviewed by Jacob (1975).
2. One consistent difference between children of working and nonworking mothers that
has been observed is that daughters of working mothers are less traditional in their
career aspirations and sex-role perceptions; they see women as more competent and
men as warmer, and they anticipate working themselves (L. W. Hoffman, 1974).
Studies documenting this difference, however, have not explored whether this is
because the mother offers these girls a competent, nontraditional role model, because she deliberately encourages the child's independence, because the father is
more active and encourages the daughter's independence—or all of the above.
3. Since popular opinion has been, and still is, that mothers should be at home
(Yankelovich, Skelly, & White, 1977), there would be more pressure on working
mothers than on nonworking mothers to say that they were dissatisfied. This could
account for the small difference between the two dissatisfied groups (the dissatisfied

*non*working mothers being least adequate), and could support the suggestion of a general dissatisfaction hypothesis.

4. Unfortunately, Baumrind's later research (1971) looking at boys and girls separately suggests that even this generalization is oversimplified.

5. In our society it is difficult to separate class and race, and these two variables are often confounded. One study (Zegiob & Forehand, 1975) that did separate the two revealed an interesting finding that middle-class black mothers behaved like white middle-class mothers in *verbal* behavior and like black lower-class mothers in *affective* behavior. Perhaps children in these families benefit from the best of both worlds, since these are the most predictive maternal behaviors for development of white and black children.

6. Recently, questions have been raised about whether the experimental increase of these behaviors is the result of contingent reinforcement alone (Sameroff & Cavanagh, in press). Studies contrasting the effects of contingent and noncontingent stimulation on infants' behavior (e.g., Bloom & Esposito, 1975) suggest that the increased frequency of social behaviors is due at least in part to the unconditioned elicitation of smiling and vocalizing provided by (not necessarily contingent) social stimulation. The issue of elicitation versus reinforcement has not been fully resolved as yet, but for our purposes here it is sufficient to note that infants' social behavior can be increased experimentally by an adult, especially the mother (Zelazo, 1971), who smiles and talks to the infant—regardless of whether the mechanism involved is reinforcement or elicitation.

7. One currently controversial issue about reinforcement is the effect of "external" reinforcement on "intrinsic" motivation. Although there is some evidence (Lepper & Greene, 1975) that use of external incentives such as tokens, trophies, or M-&-Ms weakens children's desire to perform a liked activity, results of experiments exploring this issue are not entirely consistent (see Bandura, 1977). Since parents seldom set up "token economies" at home or award "good player" certificates when their children spend an afternoon engaged in a favorite activity, the issue is not apparently germane to our concerns in this chapter, except to qualify the notion of material reinforcement as a desirable or foolproof method of manipulating children's behavior.

8. A more recent and complete analysis of data from the Consortium on Developmental Continuity (Vopava & Royce, 1978) was more successful in uncovering program variations related to program effectiveness. Of 25 variables tested, 5 were related to children's later placement in special education classes—adult/child ratio, goals for parents, parent involvement, home visits, and child's age—but only the first two of these variables were predictive of program effectiveness with the other correlated variables covaried out.

9. Gordon's one-year program.

10. Gordon's two- or three-year programs.

11. The broadest focus in parent education is to include the father in the program. Two studies that explored paternal participation (Martin, 1977; Santilli, 1972) found that programs had the same effect on children whether or not the father was included, but there may be more maternal participation or parental growth if the father is included or at least not opposed (Chilman, 1973).

12. Another assumption about change in maternal behavior is that the amount of participation in the program causes the beneficial outcomes observed. Badger, Hodgins, and Burns (1977), for example, considered it a positive outcome of their program that mothers who attended over half the sessions were better able to "act on their plans" after the program ended. What they failed to recognize was that acting on one's plans would include going to parent education meetings, and the direction of causation, therefore, would most likely not be from participation to outcome but from personal predisposition to participation.

13. Although the older target children may also contribute to this effect on their younger siblings, it appears unlikely that this is the only or major influence, since younger sibs of children in child-focused early childhood programs were not superior to controls (Gilmer et al., 1970). Of course, the possibility exists that younger siblings in a home visiting program, like their older brothers and sisters, benefited from the *direct* influence of the parent trainer or her toys. In fact, supporting this notion, Gilmer et al. found that sibs benefited more from a home-visiting mother-child program than from a center-based mother-child program (in which, presumably, siblings had less contact with the parent trainer).

14. For example, differences in time span, operationalization, and measurement of variables, emotional context, the adult who administers the stimulation or reinforcement, the methods of statistical analysis, and so on.

15. Programs might also be instituted for prospective parents, such as Education for Parenthood. This program in the high schools was not discussed in this review since there has been no evaluation yet of the effects of participation in the program on adolescents' later behavior as parents.

16. These kinds of parental behavior have, in fact, been found to be more predictive of child development than is participation in a parent training program (Bensen, 1976; Kessen et al., 1975; Lambie et al., 1974).

17. For discussion of why the decision to institute parent education must ultimately rest on values, not data, see Schlossman 1978.

REFERENCES

Adkins, D. C., & Crowell, D. C. *Development of a preschool language-oriented curriculum with a structured parent education program* (Unpublished Final Rep.). Honolulu: University of Hawaii, Head Start Evaluation and Research Center, 1969.

Adkins, D. C., & O'Malley, J. *Continuation of programmatic research on curricular modules for early childhood education and parent participation* (Unpublished Final Rep.). Honolulu: University of Hawaii, Center for Research in Early Childhood Education, 1971.

Ainsworth, M. D. S. The effects of maternal deprivation: A review of findings and controversy in the context of research strategy. In *Deprivation of maternal care: A reassessment of its effects*. Public Health Papers, No. 14, 1962, pp. 97-165.

Ainsworth, M. D. S. The development of infant-mother attachment. In B. M. Caldwell & H. N. Ricciuti (Eds.), *Review of child development research* (Vol. 3). Chicago: University of Chicago Press, 1973.

Ainsworth, M. D. S. Infant development and mother-infant interaction among Ganda and

American families. In P. H. Leiderman, S. R. Tulkin, & A. Rosenfeld (Eds.), *Culture and infancy: Variations in the human experience*. New York: Academic Press, 1977.

Ainsworth, M. D. S., & Bell, S. M. Some contemporary patterns of mother-infant interaction in the feeding situation. In J. A. Ambrose (Ed.), *Stimulation in early infancy*. London: Academic Press, 1969.

Ainsworth, M. D. S., & Bell, S. M. Infant crying and maternal responsiveness: A rejoinder to Gewirtz and Boyd. *Child Development*, 1977, *48*, 1208-1216.

Ainsworth, M. D. S., Bell, S. M., & Stayton, D. J. Individual differences in the development of some attachment behaviors. *Merrill-Palmer Quarterly*, 1972, *18*, 123-144.

Aldous, J. The search for alternatives: Parental behaviors and children's original problem solutions. *Journal of Marriage and the Family*, 1975, *37*, 711-722.

Alford, R. W., & Hines, B. *Demonstration of home-oriented early childhood education program* (Final Rep.). Kanawha County, W.V.: Appalachia Educational Laboratory, September 1972. (ERIC Document Reproduction Service No. ED 069 391)

Andrews, S. R., Blumenthal, J. B., Bache, W. L., & Wiener, G. *New Orleans Parent-Child Development Center* (Fourth Year Rep. OCD 90-C-381). New Orleans: University of New Orleans, March 1975.

Appleton, T., Clifton, R., & Goldberg, S. The development of behavioral competence in infancy. In F. D. Horowitz (Ed.), *Review of child development research* (Vol. 4). Chicago: University of Chicago Press, 1975.

Aronfreed, J. The concept of internalization. In D. A. Goslin (Ed.), *Handbook of socialization theory and research*. Chicago: Rand McNally, 1969.

Badger, E. The infant stimulation/mother training project. In B. M. Caldwell & D. J. Stedman (Eds.), *Infant education*. New York: Walker, 1977.

Badger, E., Hodgins, A., & Burns, D. *Altering the behavior of adolescent mothers: A follow-up evaluation of the Infant Stimulation/Mother Training Program*. Paper presented at the Nassau County Coalition for Family Planning Conference, Westbury, N.Y., November 1977.

Bakeman, R., & Brown, J. V. Behavioral dialogues: An approach to the assessment of mother-infant interaction. *Child Development*, 1977, *48*, 195-203.

Bakwin, H. Loneliness in infants. *American Journal of Diseases in Children*, 1942, *63*, 30-40.

Bakwin, H. Emotional deprivation in infants. *Journal of Pediatrics*, 1949, *35*, 512-521.

Bakwin, H., & Bakwin, R. M. *Clinical management of behavior disorders in children* (2nd ed.). Philadelphia: W. B. Saunders, 1960.

Baldwin, A. L., Kalhorn, J., & Breese, F. H. Patterns of parent behavior. *Psychological Monographs*, 1945, *58* (3, Whole No. 268).

Bandura, A. The role of modeling processes in personality development. In W. W. Hartup & N. L. Smothergill (Eds.), *The young child: Reviews of research*. Washington, D.C.: National Association for the Education of Young Children, 1967.

Bandura, A. Social-learning theory of identificatory process. In D. A. Goslin (Ed.), *Handbook of socialization theory and research*. Chicago: Rand McNally, 1969.

Bandura, A. *Social learning theory*. Englewood Cliffs, N.J.: Prentice-Hall, 1977.

Bandura, A., Grusec, J. E., & Menlove, F. L. Some social determinants of self-monitoring reinforcement systems. *Journal of Personality and Social Psychology*, 1967, *5*, 449-455.

Banfield, E. C. *The unheavenly city: The nature and future of our urban crisis*. Boston: Little, Brown, 1970.

Barbrack, C. R. *The effect of three home visiting strategies upon measures of children's academic aptitude and maternal teaching behaviors* (DARCEE Papers and Reports, *4,* No. 1). Nashville, Tenn.: George Peabody College for Teachers, 1970.

Baumrind, D. Child care practices anteceding three patterns of preschool behavior. *Genetic Psychology Monographs,* 1967, *75,* 43-88.

Baumrind, D. Current patterns of parental authority. *Developmental Psychology Monograph,* 1971, *4* (1, Part 2).

Baumrind, D. *Socialization determinants of personal agency.* Paper presented at the biennial meeting of the Society for Research in Child Development, New Orleans, March 1977.

Baumrind, D., & Black, A. E. Socialization practices associated with dimensions of competence in preschool boys and girls. *Child Development,* 1967, *38,* 291-327.

Bayley, N., & Schaefer, E. S. Relationships between socioeconomic variables and the behavior of mothers toward young children. *Journal of Genetic Psychology,* 1960, *96,* 61-77.

Bayley, N., & Schaefer, E. S. Correlations of maternal and child behaviors with the development of mental abilities: Data from the Berkeley Growth Study. *Monographs of the Society for Research in Child Development,* 1964, *29* (6, Whole No. 97).

Becker, W. C. Consequences of different kinds of parental discipline. In M. L. Hoffman & L. W. Hoffman (Eds.), *Review of child development research* (Vol. 1). New York: Russell Sage, 1964.

Becker, W. C., Peterson, D. R., Luria, Z., Shoemaker, D. J., & Hellmer, L. A. Relations of factors derived from parent-interview ratings to behavior problems of five-year-olds. *Child Development,* 1962, *33,* 509-535.

Beckwith, L. Relationships between attributes of mothers and their infants' IQ scores. *Child Development,* 1971, *42,* 1083-1097. (a)

Beckwith, L. Relationships between infants' vocalization and their mothers' behavior. *Merrill-Palmer Quarterly,* 1971, *17,* 211-226. (b)

Beckwith, L. Relationships between infants' social behavior and their mothers' behavior. *Child Development,* 1972, *43,* 397-411.

Beckwith, L. Prediction of emotional and social behavior. In J. Osofsky (Ed.), *Handbook of infant development.* New York: John Wiley, in press.

Beckwith, L. Cohen, S. E., Kopp, C. B., Parmelee, A. H., & Marcy, T. G. Caregiver-infant interaction and early cognitive development in preterm infants. *Child Development,* 1976, *47,* 579-587.

Bee, H. L., Van Egeren, L. F., Streissguth, A. P., Nyman, B. A., & Leckie, M. S. Social class differences in maternal teaching strategies and speech patterns. *Developmental Psychology,* 1969, *1,* 726-734.

Bell, R. Q., A reinterpretation of the direction of effects in studies of socialization. *Psychological Review,* 1968, *75,* 81-95.

Bell, R. Q., & Hertz, T. W. Towards more comparability and generalizability of developmental research. *Child Development,* 1976, *47,* 6-13.

Bell, R. W., & Denenberg, V. H. The interrelationships of shock and critical periods in infancy as they affect adult learning and activity. *Animal Behavior,* 1963, *11,* 21-27.

Bell, S. M., & Ainsworth, M. D. S. Infant crying and maternal responsiveness. *Child Development,* 1972, *43,* 1171-1190.

Bell, T. H. The child's right to have a trained parent. *Elementary School Guidance and Counseling,* 1975, *9,* 271-276.

Bell, T. H. *Formulating governmental policies on the basis of educational research.* Address given at the University of Chicago, Chicago, April 5, 1976.

Beller, E. K. Early intervention programs. In J. Osofsky (Ed.), *Handbook of infant development.* New York: John Wiley, in press.

Belsky, J. *Mother-infant interaction at home and in the lab: The effect of setting*. Paper presented at the biennial meeting of the Society for Research in Child Development, New Orleans, March 1977.

Bensen, J. F. *Parent training in preprimary behavioral competence* (Interim Project Rep. R01-MH-22560). Coral Gables Fla.: University of Miami, December 1976.

Benson, L., Berger, M., & Mease, W. Family communication systems. *Small Group Behavior*, 1975, *6*, 91-104.

Berkowitz, B., & Graziano, A. Training parents as behavior therapists: A review. *Behavior Research Therapy*, 1972, *10*, 297-317.

Bernal, J., & Richards, M. P. M. *The effects of bottle and breast feeding on infant development*. Paper presented at the annual conference of the Society for Psychosomatic Research, London, November 1969.

Biller, H. B. *Paternal deprivation: Family, school, sexuality, and society*. Lexington, Mass.: D.C. Heath, 1974.

Biller, H. B. The father and personality development: Paternal deprivation and sex role development. In M. E. Lamb (Ed.), *The role of the father in child development*, pp. 89–156. New York: John Wiley, 1976.

Bing, E. Effect of childrearing practices on development of differential cognitive abilities. *Child Development*, 1963, *34*, 631-648.

Bishop, D. W., & Chace, C. A. Parental conceptual systems, home play environment, and potential creativity in children. *Journal of Experimental Child Psychology*, 1971, *12*, 318-338.

Bloom, B. S. *Stability and change in human characteristics*. New York: John Wiley, 1964.

Bloom, K., & Erickson, M. T. *The role of eye contact in the social reinforcement of infant vocalizations*. Paper presented at the biennial meeting of the Society for Research in Child Development, Minneapolis, April 1971.

Bloom, K., & Esposito, A. Social conditioning and its proper control procedures. *Journal of Experimental Child Psychology*, 1975, *19*, 209-222.

Boger, R. P. *Parents as primary change agents in an experimental Head Start program of language intervention* (Experimental Program Rep.), November 1969. (ERIC Document Reproduction Service No. ED 013 371)

Bowlby, J. *Maternal care and mental health* (World Health Organization Monograph No. 2). Geneva: World Health Organization, 1951.

Brackbill, Y. Extinction of the smiling response in infants as a function of reinforcement schedule. *Child Development*, 1958, *29*, 115-124.

Bradley, R. H., & Caldwell, B. M. Early home environment and changes in mental test performance in children from six to thirty-six months. *Developmental Psychology*, 1976, *12*, 93-97. (a)

Bradley, R. H., & Caldwell, B. M. The relations of infants' home environments to mental test performance at fifty-four months: A follow-up study. *Child Development*, 1976, *47*, 1172-1174. (b)

Bradley, R. H., Caldwell, B. M., & Elardo, R. *Home environment, social status, and mental test performance*. Paper presented at the biennial meeting of the Society for Research in Child Development, New Orleans, March 1977.

Brazelton, T. B. Implications of infant development among the Mayan Indians of Mexico. In P. H. Leiderman, S. R. Tulkin, & A. Rosenfeld (Eds.), *Culture and infancy: Variations in the human experience*. New York: Academic Press, 1977.

Brazelton, T. B., Koslowski, B., & Main, M. The origins of reciprocity: The early mother-infant interaction. In M. Lewis & L. A. Rosenblum (Eds.), *The effect of the infant on its caregiver*. New York: John Wiley, 1974.

Brim, O. G. *Education for child rearing* (2nd ed.). New York: Free Press, 1965.

Brim, O. G. Macro-structural influences on child development and the need for childhood social indicators. *American Journal of Orthopsychiatry*, 1975, *45*, 516-524.

Brodbeck, A., & Irwin, O. C. The speech behavior of infants without families. *Child Development*, 1946, *17*, 145-156.

Brody, G. F. Maternal child-rearing attitudes and child behavior. *Developmental Psychology*, 1969, *1*, 66.

Bronfenbrenner, U. Socialization and social class through time and space. In E. E. Maccoby, T. M. Newcomb, & E. L. Hartley (Eds.), *Readings in social psychology*. New York: Henry Holt, 1958.

Bronfenbrenner, U. The changing American child—a speculative analysis. *Journal of Social Issues*, 1961, *17*, 6-18.

Bronfenbrenner, U. Early deprivation in mammals: A cross species analysis. In G. Newton & S. Levine (Eds.), *Early experience and behavior*. Springfield, Ill.: Charles C Thomas, 1968.

Bronfenbrenner, U. *Is early intervention effective? A report on longitudinal evaluations of preschool programs* (Vol. 2). Washington, D.C.: Department of Health, Education, and Welfare, 1974.

Bronfenbrenner, U. Toward an experimental ecology of human development. *American Psychologist*, 1977, *32*, 513-531.

Bronson, W. C. Early antecedents of emotional expressiveness and reactivity control. *Child Development*, 1966, *37*, 793-810.

Brossard, M., & Décarie, T. G. The effect of three kinds of perceptual-social stimulation on the development of institutionalized infants. *Early Child Development and Care*, 1971, *1*, 211-230.

Brown, J. V., Bakeman, R., Snyder, P. A., Fredrickson, W. T., Morgan, S. T., & Hepler, R. Interactions of black-inner city mothers with their newborn infants. *Child Development*, 1975, *46*, 677-686.

Bryan, J. H. Children's cooperation and helping behaviors. In E. M. Hetherington (Ed.), *Review of child development research* (Vol. 5). Chicago: University of Chicago Press, 1975.

Cairns, R. B. Attachment behavior of mammals. *Psychological Review*, 1966, *72*, 409-429. (a)

Cairns, R. B. Development, maintenance, and extinction of social attachment of behavior in sheep. *Journal of Comparative and Physiological Psychology*, 1966, *62*, 298-306. (b)

Cairns, R. B. Beyond social attachment: The dynamics of interactional development. In T. Alloway, P. Pliner, & L. Krames (Eds.), *Attachment behavior: Advances in the study of communication and affect* (Vol. 3). New York: Plenum Press, 1977.

Cairns, R. B., & Werboff, J. Behavior development in the dog: An interspecific analysis. *Science*, 1967, *158*, 1070-1072.

Caldwell, B. M. The effects of infant care. In M. L. Hoffman & L. W. Hoffman (Eds.), *Review of child development research* (Vol. 1). New York: Russell Sage, 1964.

Caldwell, B. M. Social class level and stimulation: Potential of the home. *Exceptional Infant*, 1967, *1*, 455-466.

Campbell, D. T., & Stanley, J. C. Experimental and quasi-experimental designs for research on teaching. In N. L. Gage (Ed.), *Handbook of research on teaching*. Chicago: Rand McNally, 1963.

Carew, J. V., Chan, I., & Halfar, C. *Observed intellectual competence and tested intelligence: Their roots in the young child's transactions with his environment.* Unpublished manuscript, Harvard University, 1975.

Casler, L. The effects of an extra tactile stimulation of a group of institutionalized infants. *Genetic Psychology Monographs*, 1965, *71*, 137-175.

Castell, R. Effect of familiar and unfamiliar environments on proximity behavior of young children. *Journal of Experimental Child Psychology*, 1970, *9*, 342-347.

Cazden, C. Subcultural differences in child language: An interdisciplinary review. *Merrill-Palmer Quarterly*, 1966, *12*, 185-219.

Chamberlin, R. W. Authoritarian and accommodative child-rearing styles: Their relationships with the behavior patterns of two-year-old children and other variables. *Journal of Pediatrics*, 1974, *84*, 287-293.

Chilman, C. S. Programs for disadvantaged parents: Some major trends and related research. In B. M. Caldwell & H. N. Ricciuti (Eds.), *Review of child development research* (Vol. 3). Chicago: University of Chicago Press, 1973.

Clarke, A. D. B., & Clarke, A. M. Formerly isolated children. In A. M. Clarke & A. D. B. Clarke (Eds.), *Early experience: Myth and evidence*. New York: Free Press, 1976. (a)

Clarke, A. D. B., & Clarke, A. M. Studies in natural settings. In A. M. Clarke & A. D. B. Clarke (Eds.), *Early experience: Myth and evidence*. New York: Free Press, 1976. (b)

Clarke, A. M., & Clarke, A. D. B. The formative years? In A. M. Clarke & A. D. B. Clarke (Eds.), *Early experience: Myth and evidence*. New York: Free Press, 1976. (a)

Clarke, A. M., & Clarke, A. D. B. Some contrived experiments. In A. M. Clarke & A. D. B. Clarke (Eds.), *Early experience: Myth and evidence*. New York: Free Press, 1976. (b)

Clarke-Stewart, K. A. Interactions between mothers and their young children: Characteristics and consequences. *Monographs of the Society for Research in Child Development*, 1973, *38*, (6-7, Serial No. 153).

Clarke-Stewart, K. A. *Child care in the family: A review of research and some propositions for policy*. New York: Academic Press, 1977. (a)

Clarke-Stewart, K. A. *The father's contribution to family interaction and the child's early development*. Unpublished manuscript, University of Chicago, 1977. (b)

Clarke-Stewart, K. A. And daddy makes three: The father's impact on mother and young child. *Child Development*, 1978, *49*, 466-478. (a)

Clarke-Stewart, K. A. Popular primers for parents. *American Psychologist*, 1978, *33*, 359-369. (b)

Clarke-Stewart, K. A., VanderStoep, L., & Killian, G. A. Analysis and replication of mother-child relations at two years of age. *Child Development*, in press.

Coleman, J. S., Campbell, E. Q., Hobson, C. J., McPartland, J., Mood, A. M., Weinfeld, F. D., & York, R. L. *Equality of educational opportunity*. Washington, D.C.: U.S. Government Printing Office, 1966.

Crandall, V. C. *Changes in advice and their relations to changes in behavior*. Paper presented at the annual convention of the American Psychological Association, San Francisco, August 1977.

Crandall, V. J., Dewey, R., Katkovsky, W., & Preston, A. Parents' attitudes and behaviors and grade-school children's academic achievements. *Journal of Genetic Psychology*, 1964, *104*, 53-66.

Crandall, V. J., Preston, A., & Rabson, A. Maternal reactions and the development of independence and achievement behavior in young children. *Child Development*, 1960, *31*, 243-251.

Crano, W. D. What do infant mental tests test? A cross-lagged panel analysis of selected data from the Berkeley growth study. *Child Development*, 1977, *48*, 144-151.

Curtiss, S. *Genie: A psycholinguistic study of a modern-day "wild child."* New York: Academic Press, 1977.

Dave, R. H. *The identification and measurement of environmental process variables that are related to educational achievement.* Unpublished doctoral dissertation, University of Chicago, 1963.

Davenport, R. K., Menzel, E. W., & Rogers, C. M. Effects of severe isolation on "normal" juvenile chimpanzees: Health, weight gain, and stereotyped behaviors. *Archives of General Psychiatry*, 1966, *14*, 134-138.

Davids, A. A research design for studying maternal emotionality before childbirth and after social interaction with the child. *Merrill-Palmer Quarterly*, 1968, *14*, 345-354.

Davis, K. Extreme social isolation of a child. *American Journal of Sociology*, 1940, *45*, 554-565.

Davis, K. Final note on a case of extreme isolation. *American Journal of Sociology*, 1947, *52*, 432-437.

Dennis, W. Causes of retardation among institutional children: Iran. *Journal of Genetic Psychology*, 1960, *96*, 47-59.

Dennis, W. *Children of the crèche.* New York: Appleton-Century-Crofts, 1973.

Dennis, W., & Sayegh, Y. The effect of supplementary experiences upon the behavioral development of infants in institutions. *Child Development*, 1965, *36*, 81-90.

Deutsch, C. P. Social class and child development. In B. M. Caldwell & H. N. Ricciuti (Eds.), *Review of child development research* (Vol. 3). Chicago: University of Chicago Press, 1973.

Dodd, B. J. Effects of social and vocal stimulation on infant babbling. *Developmental Psychology*, 1972, *7*, 80-83.

Downey, J. *Project Early Push: Preschool program in compensatory education.* Buffalo, N.Y.: American Institute for Research in Behavioral Sciences, 1969.

Dunn, J. F. Consistency and change in styles of mothering. In *Parent-infant interaction* (Ciba Foundation Symposium 33; new series). Amsterdam: Associated Scientific Publishers, 1975.

DuPan, R. M., & Roth, S. The psychologic development of a group of children brought up in a hospital-type residential nursery. *Journal of Pediatrics*, 1955, *47*, 124-129.

Elardo, R., Bradley, R., & Caldwell, B. M. The relation of infants' home environments to mental test performance from six to thirty-six months: A longitudinal analysis. *Child Development*, 1975, *46*, 71-76.

Elardo, R., Bradley, R., & Caldwell, B. M. A longitudinal study of the relation of infants' home environments to language development at age three. *Child Development*, 1977, *48*, 595-603.

Elliot, O., & Scott, J. P. The development of emotional distress reactions to separation in puppies. *Journal of Genetic Psychology*, 1961, *99*, 3-22.

Endsley, R. C., Garner, A. P., Odom, A. H., & Martin, M. J. *Interrelationships among selected maternal behavior and preschool children's verbal and nonverbal curiosity behavior.* Paper presented at the biennial meeting of the Society for Research in Child Development, Denver, Spring 1975.

Engel, M., Nechlin, H., & Arkin, A. M. Aspects of mothering: Correlate of the cognitive development of black male infants in the second year of life. In A. Davids (Ed.), *Child personality and psychopathology: Current topics* (Vol. 2). New York: John Wiley, 1975.

Epstein, A. S., & Evans, J. L. *Parenting: Processes and programs.* Unpublished manuscript, High/Scope, Ypsilanti, Michigan, November 1977.

Epstein, A. S., & Radin, N. Motivational components related to father behavior and cognitive functioning in preschoolers. *Child Development*, 1975, *46*, 831-839.

Erlanger, H. S. Social class and corporal punishment in childrearing: A reassessment. *American Sociological Review*, 1974, *39*, 68-85.

Escalona, S. Emotional development in the first year of life. In M. J. E. Senn (Ed.), *Problems of infancy and childhood.* New York: Josiah Macy Foundation, 1953.

Etaugh, C. Effects of maternal employment on children: A review of recent research. *Merrill-Palmer Quarterly*, 1974, *20*, 71-98.

Etzel, B. C., & Gewirtz, J. L. Experiment of modification of caretaker-maintained high rate operant crying in a 6- and a 20-week old infant: Extinction of crying with reinforcement of eye contact and smiling. *Journal of Experimental Child Psychology*, 1967, *5*, 303-317.

Falender, C. A., & Heber, R. Mother-child interaction and participation in a longitudinal intervention program. *Developmental Psychology*, 1975, *11*, 830-836.

Ferguson, T. *Children in care—and after*. London: Oxford University Press, 1966.

Feshbach, N., & Feshbach, S. Children's aggression. In W. W. Hartup (Ed.), *The young child: Reviews of research* (Vol. 2). Washington, D.C.: National Association for the Education of Young Children, 1972.

Finkelstein, N. W., & Ramey, C. T. Learning to control the environment in infancy. *Child Development*, 1977, *48*, 806-819.

Forest, I. *Preschool education*. New York: Macmillan, 1927.

Forgays, D. G., & Forgays, J. W. The nature of the effect of free-environmental experience in the rat. *Journal of Comparative and Physiological Psychology*, 1952, *45*, 322-328.

Forrester, B. J., Boismier, N. O., & Gray, S. W. *A home-based intervention program with mothers and infants*. Unpublished manuscript, George Peabody College for Teachers, Nashville, 1977.

Freeberg, N. E., & Payne, D. T. Parental influence on cognitive development in early childhood: A review. *Child Development*, 1967, *38*, 65-87.

Gaulin-Kremer, E., Shaw, J. L., & Thoman, E. B. *Effects of delay of first mother-infant encounter*. Paper presented at the biennial meeting of the Society for Research in Child Development, New Orleans, March 1977.

Gewirtz, J. L. Mechanisms of social learning: Some roles of stimulation and behavior in early human development. In D. A. Goslin (Ed.), *Handbook of socialization theory and research*. Chicago: Rand McNally, 1969.

Gewirtz, J. L., & Boyd, E. F. Does maternal responding imply reduced infant crying? A critique of the 1972 Bell and Ainsworth report. *Child Development*, 1977, *48*, 1200-1207. (a)

Gewirtz, J. L., & Boyd, E. F. Experiments on mother-infant interaction underlying mutual attachment acquisition: The infant conditions the mother. In T. Alloway, P. Pliner, & L. Krames (Eds.), *Attachment behavior: Advances in the study of communication and effect* (Vol. 3). New York: Plenum Press, 1977. (b)

Gewirtz, J. L., & Boyd, E. F. In reply to the rejoinder to our critique of the 1972 Bell and Ainsworth report. *Child Development*, 1977, *48*, 1217-1218. (c)

Gilmer, B., Miller, J. O., & Gray, S. W. *Intervention with mothers and young children: A study of intrafamily effects* (DARCEE Papers and Reports, *4*, No. 1). Nashville, Tennessee: George Peabody College for Teachers, 1970.

Goldberg, S. Infant development and mother-infant interaction in urban Zambia. In P. H. Leiderman, S. R. Tulkin, & A. Rosenfeld (Eds.), *Culture and infancy: Variations in the human experience*. New York: Academic Press, 1977.

Golden, M., & Birns, B. Social class and cognitive development in infancy. *Merrill-Palmer Quarterly*, 1968, *14*, 139-149.

Goldfarb, W. Effects of psychological deprivation in infancy and subsequent stimulation. *American Journal of Psychiatry*, 1945, *102*, 18-33.

Goldfarb, W. Emotional and intellectual consequences of psychologic deprivation in infancy: A revaluation. In P. H. Hoch & J. Zubin (Eds.), *Psychopathology of childhood*. New York: Grune & Stratton, 1955.

Gomber, J. M. *Caging adult male isolation-reared rhesus monkeys* (Macaca mulatta) *with infant conspecifics.* Unpublished doctoral dissertation, University of California, Davis, 1975.

Goodson, D. B., & Hess, R. D. *The effects of parent training programs on child performance and parent behavior.* Unpublished manuscript, Stanford University, 1976.

Gordon, I. J. *Early child stimulation through parent education* (Final Rep.). Gainesville, Fla.: Institute for the Development of Human Resources, University of Florida, June 1969. (ERIC Document Reproduction Service No. ED 038 166)

Gordon, I. J., & Guinagh, B. A home learning center approach to early stimulation. (Final Rep., No. 5-RO1-MH-16037-04). Gainesville, Fla.: Institute for Development of Human Resources, University of Florida, December 1977.

Gordon, I. J., Guinagh, B., & Jester, R. E. The Florida Parent Education Infant and Toddler Programs. In M. C. Day & R. K. Parker (Eds.), *The preschool in action* (2nd ed.). Boston: Allyn & Bacon, 1977.

Gottman, J. M., McFall, R. M., & Barnett, J. T. Design and analysis of research using time-series. *Psychological Bulletin,* 1969, *72*, 299-306.

Gray, S. W., & Klaus, R. A. The early training project: A seventh-year report. *Child Development,* 1970, *41*, 908-924.

Greenbaum, C. W., & Landau, R. Mothers' speech and the early development of vocal behavior: Findings from a cross-cultural observation study in Israel. In P. H. Leiderman, S. R. Tulkin, & A. Rosenfeld (Eds.), *Culture and infancy: Variations in the human experience.* New York: Academic Press, 1977.

Greenberg, M., & Morris, N. Engrossment: The newborn's impact upon the father. *American Journal of Orthopsychiatry,* 1974, *44*, 520-531.

Gutelius, M. F. *Mobile unit for child health supervision* (Interim Rep., No. RO1-MH-9215). Ely, Vt.: March 1977.

Hamm, P. M., Jr., & Lyman, D. A. *Training parents in child management skills with the school as the agent of instruction.* Washington, D.C.: National Center for Educational Research and Development, February 1973.

Hanson, R. A. Consistency and stability of home environmental measures related to IQ. *Child Development,* 1975, *46*, 470-480.

Harlow, H. F. The nature of love. *American Psychologist,* 1958, *13*, 373-385.

Harlow, H. F., & Griffin, G. Induced mental and social deficits in rhesus monkeys. In S. F. Osler & R. E. Cooke (Eds.), *The biosocial basis of mental retardation.* Baltimore: Johns Hopkins Press, 1965.

Harlow, H. F., & Zimmermann, R. R. Affectional responses in the infant monkey. *Science,* 1959, *130*, 431-432.

Harper, L. V. The young as a source of stimuli controlling caretaker behavior. *Developmental Psychology,* 1971, *4*, 73-88.

Harrell, J. E., & Ridley, C. A. Substitute child care, maternal employment and the quality of mother-child interaction. *Journal of Marriage and the Family,* 1975, *37*, 556-564.

Harris, F. R., Wolf, M. M., & Baer, D. M. Effects of adult social reinforcement on child behavior. In W. W. Hartup & N. L. Smothergill (Eds.), *The young child: Reviews of research.* Washington, D.C.: National Association for the Education of Young Children, 1967.

Haskins, R., Ramey, C. T., Stedman, D. J., Blacher-Dixon, J., & Pierce, J. E. Effects of repeated assessment on standardized test performance by infants. Unpublished manuscript, Frank Porter Graham Child Development Center, Chapel Hill, N.C., 1977.

Hebb, D. O. *The organization of behavior.* New York: John Wiley, 1949.

Heber, R., & Garber, H. An experiment in prevention of cultural-familial mental retardation. In D. A. Primrose (Ed.), *Proceedings of the Second Congress of the International Association for the Scientific Study of Mental Deficiency.* Warsaw: Polish Medical Publishers, 1971.

Heinicke, C. M. *Changes in the preschool child as a function of change in the parent-child relationship.* Paper presented at the biennial meeting of the Society for Research in Child Development, New Orleans, March 1977.

Heinstein, M. I. Behavioral correlates of breast-bottle regimes under varying parent-infant relationships. *Monographs of the Society for Research in Child Development*, 1963, *28* (4, Serial No. 88).

Held, R., & Hein, A. Movement-produced stimulation in the development of visually guided behavior. *Journal of Comparative and Physiological Psychology*, 1963, *56*, 872-876.

Hertz, T. W., Mangus, S., Mann, A. J., & Wagner, C. S. *Toward interagency coordination: FY'76 federal research and development on early childhood* (6th Annual Rep.). Washington, D.C.: Social Research Group, George Washington University, 1977.

Herzog, E., Newcomb, C. H., & Cisin, I. H. Double deprivation: The less they have the less they learn. In S. Ryan (Ed.), *A report on longitudinal evaluations of preschool programs.* Washington, D.C.: Office of Child Development, 1972.

Herzog, E., & Sudia, C. E. Children in fatherless families. In B. M. Caldwell & H. N. Ricciuti (Eds.), *Review of child development research* (Vol. 3). Chicago: University of Chicago Press, 1973.

Hess, R. D., Bloch, M., Costello, J., Knowles, R. T., & Largay, D. Parent involvement in early education. In E. H. Grotberg (Ed.), *Day care: Resources for decisions.* Washington, D.C.: U.S. Government Printing Office, 1971.

Hinde, R. A. *Animal behavior: A synthesis of ethology and comparative psychology* (2nd ed.). New York: McGraw-Hill, 1970.

Hinde, R. A., & Spencer-Booth, Y. The effect of social companions on mother-infant relations in rhesus monkeys. In D. Morris (Ed.), *Primate ethology.* London: Weidenfeld & Nicholson, 1967.

Hinde, R. A., & Spencer-Booth, Y. Individual differences in the responses of rhesus monkeys to a period of separation from their mothers. *Journal of Child Psychology and Psychiatry*, 1970, *11*, 159-176.

Hinde, R. A., & Spencer-Booth, Y. Effects of brief separation from mother on rhesus monkeys. *Science*, 1971, *173*, 111-118.

Hindley, C. Ability and social class. In D. Edge (Ed.), *The formative years: How children become members of their society.* New York: Schocken Books, 1970.

Hoffman, L. W. Effect of maternal employment on the child. *Child Development*, 1961, *32*, 187-197.

Hoffman, L. W. Effects of maternal employment on the child—a review of the research. *Developmental Psychology*, 1974, *10*, 204-228.

Hoffman, M. L. Parent discipline and the child's consideration for others. *Child Development*, 1963, *34*, 573-588.

Honzik, M. P. Developmental studies of parent-child resemblance in intelligence. *Child Development*, 1957, *28*, 215-228.

Honzik, M. P. Environmental correlates of mental growth: Prediction from the family setting at 21 months. *Child Development*, 1967, *38*, 337-3⁄ ⁵.

Horowitz, F. D., & Paden, L. Y. The effectiveness of environmental intervention programs. In B. M. Caldwell & H. N. Ricciuti (Eds.), *Review of child development research* (Vol. 3). Chicago: University of Chicago Press, 1973.

Hunt, J. M. *Intelligence and experience.* New York: Ronald Press, 1961.

Hunt, J. M., Mohandessi, K., Ghodssi, M., & Akiyama, M. The psychological development of orphanage-reared infants: Interventions with outcomes (Tehran). *Genetic Psychology Monographs*, 1976, *94*, 126-177.

Hurley, J. R. Maternal attitudes and children's intelligence. *Journal of Clinical Psychology*, 1959, *13*, 291-292.

Hymovitch, B. The effects of experimental variations on problem solving in the rat. *Journal of Comparative and Physiological Psychology*, 1952, *45*, 313-321.

Jacob, T. Family interaction in disturbed and normal families: A methodological and substantive review. *Psychological Bulletin*, 1975, *82*, 33-65.

Jaffe, J., Stern, D. N., & Peery, J. C. "Conversational" coupling of gaze behavior in prelinguistic human development. *Journal of Psycholinguistic Research*, 1973, *2*, 321-329.

Jencks, C. *Inequality*. New York: Basic Books, 1972.

Jensen, A. R. How much can we boost IQ and scholastic achievement? *Harvard Educational Review*, 1969, *39*, 1-123.

Jones, S. J., & Moss, H. A. Age, state, and maternal behavior associated with infant vocalizations. *Child Development*, 1971, *42*, 1039-1051.

Kadushin, A. *Adopting older children*. New York: Columbia University Press, 1970.

Kagan, J. On cultural deprivation. In D. C. Glass (Ed.), *Environmental influences*. New York: Rockefeller University Press, 1968.

Kagan, J. *Change and continuity in infancy*. New York: John Wiley, 1971.

Kagan, J., & Klein, R. E. Cross-cultural perspectives on early development. *American Psychologist*, 1973, *28*, 947-961.

Karnes, M. B., Hodgins, A. S., & Teska, J. The effects of short term instruction at home by mothers of children not enrolled in a preschool. In *Research and development program on preschool disadvantaged children* (Final Rep.). Washington, D.C.: U.S. Office of Education, 1969.

Karnes, M. B., Studley, W. M., Wright, W. R., & Hodgins, A. S. An approach for working with mothers of disadvantaged preschool children. *Merrill-Palmer Quarterly, 1968, 14,* 174-184.

Karnes, M. B., Teska, J. A., Hodgins, A. S., & Badger, E. D. Educational intervention at home by mothers of disadvantaged infants. *Child Development*, 1970, *41*, 925-935.

Karnes, M. B., & Zehrbach, R. R. Educational intervention at home. In M. C. Day & R. K. Parker (Eds.), *The preschool in action* (2nd ed.). Boston: Allyn & Bacon, 1977.

Kaufman, I. C., & Rosenblum, L. A. Effects of separation from mother on the emotional behavior of infant monkeys. *Annals of the New York Academy of Science*, 1969, *159*, 681-695. (a)

Kaufman, I. C., & Rosenblum, L. A. The warning of the mother-infant bond in two species of macaque. In B. M. Foss (Ed.), *Determinants of infant behavior* (Vol. 4). London: Methuen, 1969. (b)

Kaye, K. Toward the origin of dialogue. In H. R. Schaffer (Ed.), *Studies in mother-infant interaction*. New York: Academic Press, 1977.

Keniston, K., & the Carnegie Council on Children. *All our children: The American family under pressure*. New York: Harcourt Brace Jovanovich, 1977.

Kennell, J. H., Jerauld, R., Wolfe, H., Chesler, D., Kreger, N. C., McAlpine, W., Steffa, M., & Klaus, M. H. Maternal behavior one year after early and extended post-partum contact. *Developmental Medicine and Child Neurology*, 1974, *16*, 172-179.

Kessen, W., Fein, G., Clarke-Stewart, A., & Starr, S. *Variations in home-based infant education: Language, play, and social development* (Final Rep., No. OCD-CB-98). New Haven, Conn.: Yale University, August 1975.

Kifer, E. *A cross-cultural study of the impact of home environment variables on academic achievement and affective traits.* Paper presented at the annual convention of the American Education Research Association, New York, April 1977.

Kirk, S. A. *Early education of the mentally retarded.* Urbana: University of Illinois Press, 1958.

Klaus, M. H., & Kennell, J. H. *Maternal-infant bonding: The impact of early separation or loss on family development.* St. Louis: C. V. Mosby, 1976.

Klaus, R. A., & Gray, S. W. The early training project for disadvantaged children: A report after five years. *Monographs of the Society for Research in Child Development,* 1968, *33* (4, Serial No. 120).

Klinghammer, E. Factors influencing choice of mate in altricial birds. In H. W. Stevenson, E. H. Hess, & H. L. Rheingold (Eds.), *Early behavior: Comparative and developmental approaches.* New York: John Wiley, 1967.

Kogan, K. L., & Gordon, B. N. A mother-instruction program: Documenting change in mother-child interactions. *Child Psychiatry and Human Development,* 1975, *5* (3), 190-200.

Kohlberg, L. Stage and sequence: The cognitive-developmental approach to socialization. In D. A. Goslin (Ed.), *Handbook of socialization theory and research.* Chicago: Rand McNally, 1969.

Kohn, M. *Class and conformity: Reassessment, 1977.* Paper prepared for the Conference on Research Perspectives in the Ecology of Human Development, Cornell University, Ithaca, N.Y., August 1977.

Kohn, M. L., & Clausen, J. A. Parental authority behavior and schizophrenia. *American Journal of Orthopsychiatry,* 1956, *26,* 297-313.

Koluchová, J. Severe deprivation in twins: A case study. *Journal of Child Psychology and Psychiatry,* 1972, *13,* 107-114.

Koluchová, J. A report on the further development of twins after severe and prolonged deprivation. In A. M. Clarke & A. D. B. Clarke (Eds.), *Early experience: Myth and evidence.* New York: Free Press, 1976.

Konner, M. Infancy among the Kalahari Desert San. In P. H. Leiderman, S. R. Tulkin, & A. Rosenfeld (Eds.), *Culture and infancy: Variations in the human experience.* New York: Academic Press, 1977.

Kotelchuck, M. The infant's relationship to the father: Experimental evidence. In M.E. Lamb (Ed.), *The role of the father in child development.* New York: John Wiley, 1976.

Kuhn, T. S. *The structure of scientific revolutions.* Chicago: University of Chicago Press, 1962.

Lakin, M. Personality factors in mothers of excessively crying (colicky) infants. *Monographs of the Society for Research in Child Development,* 1957, *22* (1, Serial No. 64).

Lally, J. R., & Honig, A. S. The Family Development Research program. In M. C. Day & R. K. Parker (Eds.), *The preschool in action* (2nd ed.). Boston: Allyn & Bacon, 1977. (a)

Lally, J. R., & Honig, A. S. *The Family Development Research Program* (Final Rep., No. OCD-CB-100). Syracuse, N.Y., University of Syracuse, April 1977. (b)

Lamb, M. E. Interactions between two-year-olds and their mothers and fathers. *Psychological Reports,* 1976, *38,* 447-450. (a)

Lamb, M. E. The role of the father: An overview. In M. E. Lamb (Ed.), *The role of the father in child development.* New York: John Wiley, 1976. (b)

Lambie, D. Z., Bond, J. T., & Weikart, D. P. *Home teaching of mothers and infants.* Ypsilanti, Mich.: High/Scope, 1974.

Lasater, T. M., Malone, P., Weisberg, P., Ferguson, C. *Birmingham Parent-Child*

Development Center. (Progress Rep., Office of Child Development.) Birmingham, Ala.: University of Alabama, March 1975.

Lazar, I., Hubbell, R., Murray, H., Rosche, M., & Royce, J. *The persistence of preschool effects: A long-term follow-up of fourteen infant and preschool experiments* (Final Rep., Grant No. 18-76-07843). Office of Human Development Services. Ithaca, N.Y.: Community Services Laboratory, Cornell University, September 1977. (a)

Lazar, I., Hubbell, R., Murray, H., Rosche, M., & Royce, J. *Preliminary findings of the Developmental Continuity Longitudinal Study.* Paper presented at the OCD conference, "Parents, children and continuity," El Paso, Texas, May 1977. (b)

Leiderman, P. H., Tulkin, S. R., & Rosenfeld, A. (Eds.), *Culture and infancy: Variations in the human experience.* New York: Academic Press, 1977.

Leler, H., Johnson, D. L., Kahn, A. J., Hines, R. P., & Torres, M. *Houston Parent-Child Development Center.* (Progress Rep., Grant No. CG60925, Office of Child Development). Houston, Tex.: University of Houston, May 1975.

Lepper, M. R., & Greene, D. Turning play into work: Effects of adult surveillance and extrinsic rewards on children's intrinsic motivation. *Journal of Personality and Social Psychology*, 1975, *31*, 479-486.

Levenstein, P. Cognitive growth in preschoolers through verbal interaction with mothers. *American Journal of Orthopsychiatry*, 1970, *40*, 426-432.

Levenstein, P. The Mother-Child Home Program. In M. C. Day & R. K. Parker (Eds.), *The preschool in action* (2nd ed.). Boston: Allyn & Bacon, 1977. (a)

Levenstein, P. *Verbal Interaction Project—Mother-Child Home Project.* (Progress Rep., Grant No. RO1-MH-18471-08.) (National Institute of Mental Health) Freeport, N.Y.: Family Service Association of Nassau County and State University of New York, June 1977. (b)

Levy, D. M. *Behavioral analysis: Analysis of clinical observations of behavior as applied to mother-newborn relationships.* Springfield, Ill.: Charles C Thomas, 1958.

Lewis, H. N. *Deprived children: The Mersham experiment, a social and clinical study.* London: Oxford University Press, 1954.

Lewis, M., & Ban, P. Variance and invariance in the mother-infant interaction: A cross-cultural study. In P. H. Leiderman, S. R. Tulkin, & A. Rosenfeld (Eds.), *Culture and infancy: Variations in the human experience.* New York: Academic Press, 1977.

Lewis, M., & Freedle, R. *Mother-infant dyad: The cradle of meaning.* Paper presented at "Language and Thought" symposium, University of Toronto, March 1972.

Lewis, M., & Goldberg, S. Perceptual-cognitive development in infancy: A generalized expectancy model as a function of the mother-infant interaction. *Merrill-Palmer Quarterly*, 1969, *15*, 81-100.

Lewis, M., & Weinraub, M. Sex of parent × sex of child: Socioemotional development. In R. C. Friedman, R. M. Richart, & R. L. VandeWiele (Eds.), *Sex differences in behavior.* New York: John Wiley, 1974.

Lewis, M., & Wilson, C. D. *Infant development in lower class American families.* Paper presented at the biennial meeting of the Society for Research in Child Development, Minneapolis, 1971.

Lombard, A. D. *Home instruction program for preschool youngsters* (HIPPY). Jerusalem: The National Council of Jewish Women and Center for Research in Education of the Disadvantaged, Hebrew University of Jerusalem, September 1973.

Lorenz, K. Z. [Companionship in bird life.] *Journal of Ornithology*, Berlin, 1935, *83*. (Reprinted in C. H. Schiller [Ed.], *Instinctive behavior.* London: Methuen, 1957).

Love, J. M., Nauta, M. J., Coelen, C. G., Hewett, K., & Ruopp, R. R. *National Home*

Start evaluation (Final Rep., HEW-105-72-1100). Cambridge, Mass: Abt Associates, March 1976.

Lüscher, K. *Knowledge on socialization.* Paper prepared for the Conference on Research Perspectives in the Ecology of Human Development, Cornell University, Ithaca, N.Y., August 1977.

Lyle, J. G. The effect of an institutional environment upon the verbal development of imbecile children: III. The Brooklands residential family unit. *Journal of Mental Deficiency Research*, 1960, *4*, 14-23.

Lynn, D. B. *The father: His role in child development.* Monterey, Calif.: Brooks/Cole, 1974.

Lynn, D. B., & Cross, A. D. Parent preference of preschool children. *Journal of Marriage and the Family*, 1974, *36*, 555-559.

Lytton, H. Comparative yield of three data sources in the study of parent-child interaction. *Merrill-Palmer Quarterly*, 1974, *20*, 53-64.

Lytton, H. Correlates of compliance and the rudiments of conscience in two-year-old boys. *Canadian Journal of Behavioral Sciences*, 1977, *9*, 242-251.

Maccoby, E. E., & Jacklin, C. N. *The psychology of sex differences.* Stanford, Calif.: Stanford University Press, 1974.

Madden, J., Levenstein, P., & Levenstein, S. Longitudinal IQ outcomes of the mother-child home program. *Child Development*, 1976, *47*, 1015-1025.

Martin, B. *Modification of family interaction* (Final Rep., Grant No. RO1-MH-22750). Chapel Hill, N.C.: University of North Carolina, Psychology Dept., January 1977.

McCall, R. B. The development of intellectual functioning in infancy and the prediction of later IQ. In J. Osofsky (Ed.), *Handbook of infant development.* New York: John Wiley, in press.

McCall, R. B., Appelbaum, M. I., & Hogarty, P. S. Developmental changes in mental performance. *Monographs of the Society for Research in Child Development*, 1973, *38* (3, Serial No. 150).

McCarthy, J. L. G. Changing parent attitudes and improving language and intellectual abilities of culturally disadvantaged four-year-old children through parent involvement. In J. B. Lazar & J. E. Chapman, *The present status and future research needs of programs to develop parenting skills.* Washington, D.C.: Social Research Group, George Washington University, 1972. (ERIC Document Reproduction Service No. ED 027-942)

McKinney, J. P., & Keele, T. Effects of increased mothering on the behavior of severely retarded boys. *American Journal of Mental Deficiency*, 1963, *67*, 556-562.

Meier, G. W., & McGee, R. K. A re-evaluation of the effect of early perceptual experience on discrimination performance during adulthood. *Journal of Comparative and Physiological Psychology*, 1959, *52*, 390-395.

Miller, J. O. *Diffusion of intervention effects in disadvantaged families.* Urbana: University of Illinois, 1968. (ERIC Document Reproduction Service No. ED 026 127)

Miller, L. B., & Dyer, J. L. Four preschool programs: Their dimensions and effects. *Monographs of the Society for Research in Child Development*, 1975, *40* (5-6, Serial No. 162).

Miller, S. J., & Sloane, H. N. The generalization effects of parent training across stimulus settings. *Journal of Applied Behavior Analysis*, 1976, *9*, 355-370.

Milner, E. A study of the relationship between reading readiness in grade one school children and patterns of parent-child interaction. *Child Development*, 1951, *22*, 95-112.

Minton, C., Kagan, J., & Levine, J. A. Maternal control and obedience in the two-year-old. *Child Development*, 1971, *42*, 1873-1894.

Morris, A. G., London, R., & Glick, J. Educational intervention for preschool children in a pediatric clinic. *Pediatrics*, 1976, *57*, 765-768.

Moss, H. A. Communication in mother-infant interaction. In L. Krames, P. Pliner, & T. Alloway (Eds.), *Advances in the study of communication and affect* (Vol. 1, *Nonverbal communication*). New York: Plenum Press, 1974.

Moss, H. A., & Jones, S. J. Relations between maternal attitudes and maternal behavior as a function of social class. In P. H. Leiderman, S. R. Tulkin, & A. Rosenfeld (Eds.), *Culture and infancy: Variations in the human experience*. New York: Academic Press, 1977.

Moss, H. A., & Kagan, J. Maternal influences on early IQ scores. *Psychological Reports*, 1958, *4*, 655-661.

Moss, H. A., & Robson, K. S. Maternal influences in early social visual behavior. *Child Development*, 1968, *39*, 401-408.

Moss, H. A., Robson, K. S., & Pedersen, F. Determinants of maternal stimulation of infants and consequences of treatment for later reactions to strangers. *Developmental Psychology*, 1969, *1*, 239-246.

Murray, E. J., & Seagull, A. Motivational patterns in the families of adjusted and maladjusted boys. *Journal of Consulting and Clinical Psychology*, 1969, *33*, 337-341.

Mussen, P. H., & Parker, A. L. Mother nurturance and girls' incidental imitative learning. *Journal of Personality and Social Psychology*, 1965, *2*, 94-97.

National Academy of Sciences. *Toward a national policy for children and families*. Washington, D.C.: Author, 1976.

National Society for the Study of Education. *Twenty-eighth yearbook: Preschool and parental education*. Bloomington, Ill.: Public School Publishing Co., 1929.

Nelson, K. Structure and strategy in learning to talk. *Monographs of the Society for Research in Child Development*, 1973, *38* (1-2, Serial No. 149).

Nelson, K. E. *Facilitating syntax acquisition*. Paper presented at the meeting of the Eastern Psychological Association, New York, April 1975.

Nichols, R. C. Parental attitudes of mothers of intelligent students and creativity of their children. *Child Development*, 1964, *35*, 1041-1049.

Nimnicht, G., Arango, M., & Adcock, D. The Parent/Child Toy Library Program. In M. C. Day & R. K. Parker (Eds.), *The preschool in action* (2nd ed.), Boston: Allyn & Bacon, 1977.

Novak, M. A., & Harlow, H. F. Social recovery of monkeys isolated for the first year of life: I. Rehabilitation and therapy. *Developmental Psychology*, 1975, *11*, 453-465

Nye, F. I., & Hoffman, L. W. *The employed mother in America*. Chicago: Rand McNally, 1963.

Nyman, A. J. Problem solving in rats as a function of experience at different ages. *Journal of Genetic Psychology*, 1967, *110*, 31-39.

Olim, E. G. Maternal language styles and children's cognitive behavior. *Journal of Special Education*, 1970, *4*, 53-68.

Osofsky, J. D. Neonatal characteristics and mother-infant interaction in two observational situations. *Child Development*, 1976, *47*, 1138-1147.

Palmer, F. H. Inferences to the socialization of the child from animal studies: A view from the bridge. In D. A. Goslin (Ed.), *Handbook of socialization theory and research*. Chicago: Rand McNally, 1969.

Parke, R. D. Some effects of punishment on children's behavior. In W. W. Hartup (Ed.), *The young child: Reviews of research* (Vol. 2). Washington, D.C.: National Association for the Education of Young Children, 1972.

Parke, R. D. Parent-infant interaction: Progress, paradigms, and problems. In G. P.

Sackett (Ed.), *Observing behavior* (Vol. 1, *Theory and applications in mental retardation*). Baltimore: University Park Press, 1977. (a)

Parke, R. D. Punishment in children: Effects, side effects, and alternative strategies. In H. Hom & P. Robinson (Eds.), *Psychological processes in early education*. New York: Academic Press, 1977. (b)

Parke, R. D. Perspectives on father-infant interaction. In J. D. Osofsky (Ed.), *Handbook of infant development*. New York: Wiley, in press.

Parke, R. D., Hymel, S., Power, T., & Tinsley, B. Fathers and risk: A hospital-based model of intervention. In D. B. Sawin & R. C. Hawkins (Eds.), *Psychosocial risks during pregnancy and early infancy*. Book in preparation, 1978.

Parke, R. D., & O'Leary, S. Family interaction in the newborn period: Some findings, some observations, and some unresolved issues. In K. F. Riegel & J. A. Meacham (Eds.), *The developing individual in a changing world* (Vol. 2, *Social and environmental issues*). The Hague: Mouton, 1976.

Parkman-Ray, M. *Analysis and modification of maternal teaching strategies in rural poor families*. Ithaca, N.Y.: Cornell University, 1973. (ERIC Document Reproduction Service No. ED 129 398)

Pedersen, F. A. *Mother, father, and infant as an interactive system*. Paper presented at the annual convention of the American Psychological Association, Chicago, September 1975.

Pedersen, F. A., & Robson, K. S. Father participation in infancy. *American Journal of Orthopsychiatry*, 1969, *39*, 466-472.

Pedersen, F.A., Yarrow, L. J., & Strain, B. A. *Conceptualization of father influences and its implications for an observational methodology*. Paper presented at the annual meeting of the Interactional Society for the Study of Behavioral Development, Guildford, England, July 1975.

Phillips, J. R. Syntax and vocabulary of mothers' speech to young children: Age and sex comparisons. *Child Development*, 1973, *44*, 182-185.

Powell, L. F. The effect of extra stimulation and maternal involvement on the development of low-birth-weight infants and on maternal behavior. *Child Development*, 1974, *45*, 106-113.

Price, G. M. *Factors influencing reciprocity in early mother-infant interaction*. Paper presented at the biennial meeting of the Society for Research in Child Development, New Orleans, March 1977.

Pringle, M. L. K., & Bossio, V. Early, prolonged separation and emotional maladjustment. *Journal of Child Psychology and Psychiatry*, 1960, *1*, 37-48.

Provence, S., & Lipton, R. C. *Infants in institutions: A comparison of their development with family-reared infants during the first year of life*. New York: International Universities Press, 1962.

Radin, N. Maternal warmth, achievement motivation, and cognitive functioning in lower-class preschool children. *Child Development*, 1971, *42*, 1560-1565.

Radin, N. Three degrees of maternal involvement in a preschool program: Impact on mothers and children. *Child Development*, 1972, *43*, 1355-1364.

Radin, N. Observed paternal behaviors as antecedents of intellectual functioning in young boys. *Developmental Psychology*, 1973, *8*, 369-376.

Radin N. Observed maternal behavior with four-year-old boys and girls in lower class families. *Child Development*, 1974, *45*, 1126-1131

Rathburn, C., McLaughlin, H., Bennett, O., & Garland, J. A. Later adjustment of children following radical separation from family and culture. *American Journal of Orthopsychiatry*, 1965, *35*, 604-609.

Rebelsky, F., & Hanks, C. Fathers' verbal interaction with infants in the first three months of life. *Child Development*, 1971, *42*, 63-68.

Redican, W. K. Adult male-infant interactions in nonhuman primates. In M. E. Lamb (Ed.), *The role of the father in child development*. New York: John Wiley, 1976.

Rheingold, H. L. The modification of social responsiveness in institutional babies. *Monographs of the Society for Research in Child Development*, 1956, *21* (2, Whole No. 63).

Rheingold, H. L. The effect of environmental stimulation upon social and exploratory behavior in the human infant. In B. M. Foss (Ed.), *Determinants of infant behavior*. New York: John Wiley, 1961.

Rheingold, H. L., & Bayley, N. The later effects of an experimental modification of mothering. *Child Development*, 1959, *30*, 363-372.

Rheingold, H. L., Gewirtz, J. L., & Ross, H. W. Social conditioning of vocalizations in the infant. *Journal of Comparative and Physiological Psychology*, 1959, *52*, 68-73.

Riesen, A. Effects of early deprivation of photic stimulation. In S. F. Osler & R. E. Cooke (Eds.), *The biosocial basis of mental retardation*. Baltimore: Johns Hopkins Press, 1965.

Ringler, N. M., Kennell, J. H., Jarvella, R., Navojosky, B. J., & Klaus, M. H. Mother-to-child speech at two years: Effects of early postnatal contact. *Journal of Pediatrics*, 1975, *86*, 141-144.

Risley, T. R., & Baer, D. M. Operant behavior modification: The deliberate development of behavior. In B. M. Caldwell & H. N. Ricciuti (Eds.), *Review of child development research* (Vol. 3). Chicago: University of Chicago Press, 1973.

Robinson, M. *Parent/Child Development Centers: An experiment in infant-parent interventions and systematic testing of social innovations* (R & D Planning Memorandum). Washington, D.C.: Office of Research Plans and Evaluation, Office of Economic Opportunity, 1972.

Robson, K. S., & Moss, H. A. Patterns and determinants of maternal attachment. *Journal of Pediatrics*, 1970, *77*, 976.

Rogers, C. M., & Davenport, R. K. Intellectual performance of differentially reared chimpanzees: III. Oddity. *American Journal of Mental Deficiency*, 1971, *75*, 526-530.

Rogosa, D. R. Causal models in longitudinal research: Rationale, formulation, and interpretation. In J. R. Nesselroade & P. B. Baltes (Eds.), *Longitudinal research in human development: Design and analysis*. New York: Academic Press, in press.

Rogosa, D. R., Webb, N., & Radin, N. *An application of causal models to data on cognitive development in lower-class children*. Unpublished manuscript, University of Chicago, 1978.

Rosenberg, M. *The dancer from the dance: An investigation of the contributions of microanalysis to an understanding of parental socialization effects*. Paper presented at the Conference on Research Perspectives in the Ecology of Human Development, Cornell University, Ithaca, N.Y., August 1977.

Rosenblatt, J. S. The development of maternal responsiveness in the rat. *American Journal of Orthopsychiatry*, 1969, *39*, 36-56.

Rosenblum, L. A. Infant attachment in monkeys. In H. R. Schaffer (Ed.), *The origins of human social relations*. New York: Academic Press, 1971.

Rozelle, R. M., & Campbell, D. T. More plausible rival hypotheses in the cross-lagged panel correlation technique. *Psychological Bulletin*, 1969, *71*, 74-80.

Rubenstein, J. Maternal attentiveness and subsequent exploratory behavior in the infant. *Child Development*, 1967, *38*, 1089-1100.

Rutter, M. Parent-child separation: Psychological effects on the children. *Journal of Child Psychology and Psychiatry*, 1971, *12*, 233-260.

Rutter, M. *The qualities of mothering: Maternal deprivation reassessed*. New York: Jason Aronson, 1974.

Sackett, G. P. The lag sequential analysis of contingency and cyclicity in behavioral interaction research. In J. D. Osofsky (Ed.), *Handbook of infant development*. New York: John Wiley, in press.

Saltz, R. Effects of part-time "mothering" on IQ and SQ of young institutionalized children. *Child Development*, 1973, *44*, 166-170.

Sameroff, A. J. *Early influences on development: Fact or fancy?* Paper presented at the Merrill-Palmer Conference on Infancy, Detroit, March 1974.

Sameroff, A. J., & Cavanagh, P. J. Learning in infancy: A developmental perspective. In J. D. Osofsky (Ed.), *Handbook of infant development*. New York: John Wiley, in press.

Sameroff, A. J., & Chandler, M. J. Reproductive risk and the continuum of caretaking casualty. In F. D. Horowitz (Ed.), *Review of child development research* (Vol. 4). Chicago: University of Chicago Press, 1975.

Santilli, M. *Effects of parent communication training on child behavior*. Buffalo, N.Y.: State University of New York, 1972. (ERIC Document Reproduction Service No. ED 061 693)

Sattler, J. M. Racial "experimenter effects" in experimentation, testing, interviewing, and psychotherapy. *Psychological Bulletin*, 1970, *73*, 37-160.

Sawin, D. B., Parke, R. D., Harrison, A. N., & Kreling, B. *The child's role in sparing the rod*. Paper presented at the annual convention of the American Psychological Association, Chicago, September 1975.

Saxe, R. M., & Stollak, G. E. Curiosity and the parent-child relationship. *Child Development*, 1971, *42*, 373-384.

Scarr-Salapatek, S. Genetics and the development of intelligence. In F. D. Horowitz (Ed.), *Review of child development research* (Vol. 4). Chicago: University of Chicago Press, 1975.

Schaefer, E. S. Parents as educators: Evidence from cross-sectional, longitudinal, and intervention research. In W. W. Hartup (Ed.), *The young child: Reviews of research* (Vol. 2). Washington, D.C.: National Association for the Education of Young Children, 1972.

Schaefer, E. S., & Aaronson, M. Infant education project: Implementation and implications of the home-tutoring program. In M. C. Day & R. K. Parker (Eds.), *The preschool in action* (2nd ed.). Boston: Allyn & Bacon, 1977.

Schaefer, E. S., & Bayley, N. Maternal behavior, child behavior, and their intercorrelations from infancy through adolescence. *Monographs of the Society for Research in Child Development*, 1963, *28* (3, Serial No. 87).

Schaefer, E. S., Furfey, P. H., & Harte, T. J. Infant education research project, Washington, D.C. *Preschool program in compensatory education: I*. Washington, D.C.: U.S. Government Printing Office, 1968.

Schaffer, H. R., & Emerson, P. E. The development of social attachments in infancy. *Monographs of the Society for Research in Child Development*, 1964, *29* (3, Serial No. 94).

Schlieper, A. Mother-child interaction observed at home. *American Journal of Orthopsychiatry*, *45*, 1975, 468-472.

Schlossman, S. L. Before Home Start: Notes toward a history of parent education in America, 1897–1929. *Harvard Educational Review*, 1976, *46*, 436-467.

Schlossman, S. L. The parent education game: The politics of child psychology in the 1970's. *Teachers College Record* 1978, *79*, 788-809.

Scott, J. P., & Fuller, J. L. *Genetics of the social behavior of the dog*. Chicago: University of Chicago Press, 1965.

Sears, R. R., Maccoby, E. E., & Levin, H. *Patterns of child rearing*. Evanston, Ill.: Row, Peterson, 1957.

Sears, R. R., Whiting, J. W. M., Nowlis, V., & Sears, P. S. Some child-rearing antecedents of aggression and dependency in young children. *Genetic Psychology Monographs*, 1953, *47*, 135-234.

Seltzer, R. J. *The disadvantaged child and cognitive development in the early years.* Paper presented at the biennial meeting of the Society for Research in Child Development, Minneapolis, 1971.

Shearer, M. S. A home-based parent training model. In J. Grim (Ed.), *Training parents to teach: Four models* (Vol. 3, *First chance for children*). Chapel Hill: University of North Carolina, undated. (ERIC Document Reproduction Service No. ED 102 778, EC 071 447)

Shipman, V. C. *Stability and change in family status, situational, and process variables and their relationships to children's cognitive performance.* Paper presented at the biennial meeting of the Society for Research in Child Development, New Orleans, March 1977.

Skeels, H. M. Adult status of children with contrasting early life experiences. *Monographs of the Society for Research in Child Development*, 1966, *31* (3, Serial No. 105).

Skeels, H. M., & Dye, H. B. A study of the effects of differential stimulation on mentally retarded children. *Proceedings and Addresses of the American Association of Mental Deficiencies*, 1939, *44*, 114.

Skeels, H. M., Updegraff, B., Wellman, B., & Williams, H. M. A study of environmental stimulation: An orphanage preschool project. *Iowa Studies of Child Welfare*, 1938, *15* (No. 4).

Skodak, M., & Skeels, H. M. A final follow-up study of one hundred adopted children, *Journal of Genetic Psychology*, 1949, *75*, 85-125.

Slaughter, D. T. *Parent education for low income black families.* Paper presented at the General Mills American Family Forum, Washington, D.C., October 1977.

Smolak, L. M., Beller, E. K., & Vance, S. *Relationships between parental disciplinary techniques and negativism in pre-schoolers.* Paper presented at the annual convention of the American Psychological Association, San Francisco, August 1977.

Snow, C. E. Mothers' speech to children learning language. *Child Development*, 1972, *43*, 549-565.

Sonquist, H. *A model for low-income and Chicano parent education.* Santa Barbara, Calif.: Santa Barbara Family Care Center, 1975. (ERIC Document Reproduction Service No. ED 113 063)

Spitz, R. A. Hospitalism. *Psychoanalytic Study of the Child*, 1946, *2*, 113-117.

Spitz, R. A. The psychogenic diseases in infancy. *Psychoanalytic Study of the Child*, 1951, *6*, 255-275.

Spock, B. *The common sense book of baby and child care.* New York: Duell Sloane & Pierce, 1946.

Sroufe, L. A. A methodological and philosophical critique of intervention-oriented research. *Developmental Psychology*, 1970, *2*, 140-145.

Stedman, D. J. *Effects of evaluation on infant cognitive development.* (Final Rep., No. RO1 MH 24005.) Chapel Hill, N.C.: Frank Porter Graham Child Development Center, August 1977.

Stern, C. *Increasing the effectiveness of parents-as-teachers.* December 1970. (ERIC Document Reproduction Service No. ED 048 939)

Stern, C. Developing the role of parent-as-teacher with Head Start populations. In J. B. Lazar & J. E. Chapman, *The present status and future research needs of programs to develop parenting skills.* Washington, D.C.: Social Research Group, George Washington University, 1972.

Stern, D. Mother and infant at play: The dyadic interaction involving facial, vocal, and gaze behaviors. In M. Lewis & L. A. Rosenblum (Eds.), *The effect of the infant on its caregiver.* New York: Wiley-Interscience, 1974.

Stern, G. G., Caldwell, B. M., Herscher, L., Lipton, E. L., & Richmond, J. B. A factor analytic study of the mother-infant dyad. *Child Development*, 1969, *40*, 163-181.

Stevenson, H. W. Social reinforcement of children's behavior. In L. P. Lipsitt & C. C. Spiker (Eds.), *Advantages in child development and behavior* (Vol. 2). New York: Academic Press, 1965.

Stolz, L. M. Effects of maternal employment on children. *Child Development*, 1960, *31*, 749-782.

Suomi, S. J. Development of attachment and other behaviors in rhesus monkeys. In T. Alloway, P. Pliner, & L. Krames (Eds.), *Advances in the study of communication and affect* (Vol. 3, *Attachment behavior*). New York: Plenum Press, 1977.

Super, C. M. Environmental effects on motor development: The case of African infant precocity. *Developmental Medicine and Child Neurology*, 1976, *18*, 561-567.

Thoman, E. B. Some consequences of early infant-mother-infant interaction. *Early Child Development and Care*, 1974, *3*, 249-261.

Thoman, E. B., Korner, A. F., & Beason-Williams, L. Modification of responsiveness to maternal vocalization in the neonate. *Child Development*, 1977, *48*, 563-569.

Thomas, A., Chess, S., Birch, H. G., Hertzig, M. E., & Korn, S. *Behavioral individuality in early childhood.* New York: New York University Press, 1963.

Thompson, W. R., & Grusec, J. Studies of early experience. In P. H. Mussen (Ed.), *Carmichael's manual of child psychology.* New York: John Wiley, 1970.

Thompson, W. R., & Heron, W. The effects of restricting early experience on the problem-solving capacity of dogs. *Canadian Journal of Psychology*, 1954, *8*, 17-31.

Tizard, B., & Rees, J. A comparison of the effects of adoption, restoration to the natural mother, and continued institutionalization on the cognitive development of four-year-old children. *Child Development*, 1974, *45*, 92-99.

Tizard, B., & Tizard, J. The cognitive development of young children in residential care. *Journal of Child Psychology and Psychiatry*, 1970, *11*, 177-186.

Tizard, J., & Tizard, B. The social development of two-year-old children in residential nurseries. In H. R. Schaffer (Ed.), *The origins of human social relations.* New York: Academic Press, 1971.

Trapp, E. P., & Kausler, D. H. Dominance attitudes in parents and adult avoidance behavior in young children. *Child Development*, 1958, *29*, 507-513.

Tulkin, S. R. *Mother-infant interaction in the first year of life: An inquiry into the influences of social class.* Unpublished doctoral dissertation, Harvard University, 1970.

Tulkin, S. R., & Cohler, B. J. Child-rearing attitudes and mother-child interaction in the first year of life. *Merrill-Palmer Quarterly*, 1973, *19*, 95-106.

Tulkin, S. R., & Kagan, J. Mother-child interaction in the first year of life. *Child Development*, 1972, *43*, 31-41.

Turnure, J. E., Buium, N., & Thurlow, M. The effectiveness of interrogatives for promoting verbal elaboration productivity in young children. *Child Development*, 1976, *47*, 851-855.

Vopova, J., & Royce, J. *Comparison of the long-term effects of infant and preschool programs on academic performance.* Paper presented at the annual meeting of the American Educational Research Association, Toronto, March 1978.

Wachs, T. D., Uzgiris, I. C., & Hunt, J. McV. Cognitive development in infants of different age levels and from different environmental backgrounds: An exploratory investigation. *Merrill-Palmer Quarterly*, 1971, *17*, 283-317.

Wahler, R. G. Infant social development: Some experimental analyses of an infant-mother interaction during the first year of life. *Journal of Experimental Child Psychology,* 1969, *7,* 101-113.

Walberg, H. J., & Marjoribanks, K. Family environment and cognitive development: Twelve analytic models. *Review of Education Research,* 1976, *46,* 527-551.

Walker, K. E., & Woods, M. E. *Time use for care of family members* (Working Paper No. 1, Use-of-Time Research Project, Human Ecology). Ithaca, N.Y.: Cornell University, September 1972.

Wallston, B. The effects of maternal employment on children. *Journal of Child Psychology and Psychiatry,* 1973, *14,* 81-95.

Wandersman, L. P., & Wandersman, A. *Facilitating growth for all the family in adjustment to a newborn.* Paper presented at the National Conference on Family Relations, New York, October 1976.

Watson, J. S. Cognitive-perceptual development in infancy: Setting for the seventies. *Merrill-Palmer Quarterly,* 1971, *17,* 139-152.

Watson, J. S. *Transfer effects of infant experience with commercial mobiles.* Paper presented at the biennial meeting of the Society for Research in Child Development, New Orleans, March 1977.

Watson, J. S., & Ramey, C. T. Reactions to response contingent stimulation early in infancy. *Merrill-Palmer Quarterly,* 1972, *18,* 219-227.

Waxler, C. Z., & Radke-Yarrow, M. An observational study of maternal models. *Developmental Psychology,* 1975, *11,* 485-494.

Weisberg, P. Social and nonsocial conditioning of infant vocalizations. *Child Development,* 1963, *34,* 377-388.

Wenar, C. Executive competence in toddlers: A prospective, observational study. *Genetic Psychology Monographs,* 1976, *93,* 189-285.

White, B. L. An experimental approach to the effects of experience on early human behavior. In *Minnesota Symposium on Child Psychology.* Minneapolis, Minn.: University of Minnesota Press, 1966.

White, B. L. *The first three years of life.* Englewood Cliffs, N.J.: Prentice-Hall, 1975.

White, B. L., & Watts, J. C. *Experience and environment.* Englewood Cliffs, N.J.: Prentice-Hall, 1973.

White, S. H., Day, M. C., Freeman, P. K., Hantman, S. A., & Messenger, K. P. *Federal program for young children: Review and recommendations.* Washington, D.C.: U.S. Government Printing Office, 1973.

Wiesel, T. N., & Hubel, D. H. Single cell responses in striate cortex of kittens deprived of vision in one eye. *Journal of Neurophysiology,* 1963, *26,* 1003-1007.

Willerman, L., & Broman, S. H. Infant development, preschool IQ, and social class. *Child Development,* 1970, *41,* 69-77.

Williams, T. McB. Infant development and supplemental care: A comparative review of basic and applied research. *Human Development,* 1977, *20,* 1-30.

Wolfheim, J. H., Jensen, G. D., & Bobbitt, R. A. Effects of group environment on the mother-infant relationship in pig-tailed monkeys (*Macaca nemestrina*). *Primates,* 1970, *11,* 119-124.

Wolins, M. Young children in institutions: Some additional evidence. *Developmental Psychology,* 1969, *2,* 99-109.

Wolkind, S. *Children in care: A psychiatric study.* Unpublished M.D. thesis, University of London, 1971.

Wyer, R. S. Jr. Effect of child-rearing attitudes and behavior on children's responses to hypothetical social situations. *Journal of Personality and Social Psychology,* 1965, *2,* 480-486.

Yankelovich, Skelly, & White, Inc. *Raising children in a changing society* (General Mills American Family Rep. 1976–77). Minneapolis: General Mills, 1977.

Yarrow, L. J. Maternal deprivation: Toward an empirical and conceptual re-evaluation. *Psychological Bulletin*, 1961, *58*, 459-490.

Yarrow, L. J., Rubenstein, J. L., & Pedersen, F. A. *Infant and environment: Early cognitive and motivational development.* Washington, D.C.: Hemisphere, 1975.

Yarrow, M. R. Problems of methods in parent-child research. *Child Development*, 1963, *34*, 215-226.

Yarrow, M. R. Research on child-rearing as a basis for practice. *Child Welfare*, 1973, *52*, 209-219.

Yarrow, M. R., Scott, P., De Leeuw, L., & Heinig, C. Child-rearing in families of working and nonworking mothers. *Sociometry*, 1962, *25*, 122-140.

Yarrow, M. R., Scott, P. M., & Waxler, C. Z. Learning concern for others. *Developmental Psychology*, 1973, *8*, 240-260.

Yogman, M. *The goals and structure of face to face interaction between infants and fathers.* Paper presented at the biennial meeting of the Society for Research in Child Development, New Orleans, March 1977.

Zegiob, L. E., & Forehand, R. Maternal interactive behavior as a function of race, socioeconomic status, and sex of the child. *Child Development*, 1975, *46*, 564-568.

Zelazo, P. R. Smiling to social stimuli: Eliciting and conditioning effects. *Developmental Psychology*, 1971, *4*, 32-42.

Zelazo, P. R., Zelazo, N. A., & Kolb, S. "Walking" in the newborn. *Science*, 1972, *176*, 314-315.

3

Life-Span Development: Implications for Education

K. WARNER SCHAIE
University of Southern California
and
SHERRY L. WILLIS
The Pennsylvania State University

INTRODUCTION

The purpose of this chapter is to relate our knowledge about life-span developmental psychology to the emerging interest in education as lifelong learning. We begin by examining several sociocultural factors which have fostered the increasing emphasis on a lifelong approach to education. Next we consider several models of life-span development and their meaning for lifelong education. The role of education at various developmental stages is discussed, and characteristics which differentiate the young adult from the older learner and which must be taken into account in designing educational programs at different periods in the life span are discussed. Finally, implications for education arising from developmental changes in adult learners are considered.

The authors assume that the primary aim of education should be optimization of individual development across the life span, although the specific objectives of education may vary both with individual development and sociocultural milieu (Baltes & Danish, 1979; Birren & Woodruff, 1973; Kohlberg & Mayer, 1972). It is a major thesis of this chapter that the individual continues to learn and change across the life span, and thus educational intervention is a viable mechanism for facilitating optimal development at all periods in life. Since approximately two-thirds to three-quarters of the life span is centered in adulthood, a major reallocation of educational resources seems implied. Therefore, much of this chapter will deal with developmental changes in adulthood and their educational implications.

ROLF MONGE, Syracuse University, SUSAN STODOLSKY, University of Chicago, and DAVID ROGOSA, University of Chicago, were editorial consultants for this chapter.

LIFELONG LEARNING: AN IMPERATIVE

Historically, educational intervention in the United States has focused on the early stages of the life cycle (Long, 1974). Such a perspective has been associated with a series of assumptions regarding intellectual development across the life span and the primary goals of education. Childhood and adolescence are considered to be the critical age periods for acquisition of all the necessary abilities and skills, while adulthood is viewed as a time of diminishing learning capacity. Thus education is viewed primarily as a process of preparation for adulthood. Formal schooling serves as a system for transmitting information to equip the child with the knowledge and skills that will be needed throughout adult life (Cropley, 1976). This perspective on education assumes a static concept of knowledge—that the knowledge and skills available during childhood are the same as those needed during adulthood.

A variety of social, scientific, and economic conditions has recently brought into serious question the effectiveness of such youth-oriented educational systems. Educational concepts under such diverse labels as *adult education, career education, education permanente* and *lifelong learning* are gaining considerable attention (Birren & Woodruff, 1973; Dave, 1976; Dave & Lengrand, 1974; Houle, 1974). The major commonality among such diverse educational concepts is that terminal education is considered to be philosophically and practically unacceptable (Long, 1974; Peterson, 1975).

Changing Age and Education Structure

Demographic changes in the United States may be contributing to a redefinition of the role of education across the life span. In this century the adult population has been increasing faster than the population as a whole. In 1900, adults aged 35 years and older accounted for 28% of the total population; in 1970, 41% of the population was from this age group (Knox, 1977). As cohorts from the post–World War II baby boom move into this age range, the proportion of the population accounted for should continue to increase.

The most rapidly increasing segment of the adult population has involved older adults. The proportion of adults 65 years and over increased from 3 to 9% from 1900 to 1970. Such a shift in the age distribution can be attributed to attenuated population growth in the mid–1900s and to an extension in the life expectancy of approximately 30 years since 1900 (Knox, 1977). A reduction of the quotas of immigrant youth has also contributed to this age shift. These changes in the age structure suggest a necessary expansion of the role of education to accommodate the educational and learning needs of the largest segment of the population—middle-aged and older adults (Carnegie Commission on Higher Education, 1973; Hiemstra, 1976).

A qualitative and quantitative shift in the educational level of the adult population has further emphasized the need for a life-span view of education.

The younger cohorts of adults in this country are better educated. While the median number of years of formal education for adults generally was 8.6 in 1940, the median in 1970 was 12.1 years for adults generally and 12.6 years for young adults (Knox, 1977). The adult population 65 years and over still has the most depressed educational level. According to 1970 census figures, only 29.3% of individuals now over 65 years were educated through high school or beyond. By 1985, the census bureau projects that 61% of those over 65 will have at least a high school education (Knox, 1977). This rapid increment in educational level of the older adult population is partially due to GI educational funding provided for World War II veterans, who would be approaching later adulthood by 1985. In addition to increases in the number of years of schooling, the length of the school year has doubled in the past century (Moses, 1971).

Johnstone and Rivera (1965) found that the higher an individual's educational level, the more likely he or she would be to seek further educational experience. Likewise, there is some evidence that the quality of an individual's prior educational experience is positively associated with the amount of subsequent learning sought in adulthood (Brown, 1960). Successive cohorts would be expected to show a continuing interest in educational activity throughout adulthood as their average educational levels increase. Educational opportunities will therefore be in greater demand as younger cohorts move into the later adult years. At the same time, of course, adults with low levels of education and thus most in need of further training will be even more educationally disadvantaged in relation to their peers.

Technological Change and Career Patterns

The accelerated rate of technological change (Toffler, 1970) occurring in almost every area of life has served as a critical catalyst for the changing concept of education. It is estimated that the body of information in the exact sciences (e.g., physics, math) is doubling every 8 to 10 years (Wroczynski, 1974). Such technological advancements are affecting the number and types of careers in which an individual is involved. Most workers in the United States today are engaged in specialized jobs that did not exist a generation or two ago. Professional and technical job roles have increased from 4% in 1900 to 15% in 1970; service occupations have increased from 3 to 12% of the job market. In contrast, farm and laborer roles have shown comparable declines. Age differences in job roles are also evident, with the older adult more likely to be involved in obsolete or shrinking job roles. For example 45% of all men now involved in the newly developed technical or professional roles are under the age of 35 (Knox, 1977).

Technological advancement is also related to the growing phenomenon of occupational obsolescence. Educators and employers acknowledge that it is not possible to prepare a student permanently for a job role in a rapidly changing society (Dubin, 1977; Long, 1974). The threat of occupational obsolescence appears particularly acute in the most rapidly expanding job roles, those involving professional or technical competence. The half-life concept of professional competence indicates the time after completion of formal education until professionals become roughly half as competent as they were upon graduation (Dubin, 1972). A recent report (Rosenow, 1971) estimated the half-life of medical knowledge to be five years. In line with this, the newly established American Board of Family Practice requires recertification every six years (Dubin, 1972). A prominent factor in the hastening of professional obsolescence is the rate of increment of new data and knowledge. In order to keep abreast of new publications, according to George and Dubin (1972), 20% of the professional psychologist's working time would need to be devoted to updating.

Closely associated with the phenomenon of occupational obsolescence is the growth in multiple career patterns across the life span. Second careers are becoming increasingly common. Training for second careers typically occurs in adulthood, after completion of the individual's formal education. According to one estimate (Kelleher, 1973), 40% of all Americans changing occupations in a given year were over 35 years of age. Technological specialization increases the number of different occupations and reduces the life expectancy of any given occupation. Thus the most spectacular increase in job turnovers has recently been among higher educated professional, technical, and managerial personnel (Troll, 1975).

Changing Role of Women

The social, educational, and economic statuses of women in society are undergoing rapid change. The participation of women in the labor force doubled, from 20% to 42%, between 1900 and 1969 (Sheppard, 1971). The trend toward earlier marriage and child rearing and a reduction in family size during the first half of this century appears related to the current increase in the number of women over 35 years entering the work force (Troll, 1975). By the 1960s more women in their forties were working than were younger women. This revolution in women's work patterns has been associated with an increasing number of middle-aged women returning to school for further training and job updating.

However, the increasing number of working women is not directly reflected in shifts in the types of job roles occupied by women. In 1966 women accounted for only 3% of all lawyers and 6% of all physicians in the U.S. (Troll, 1975). In fact, the percentage of women in high-status, highly skilled jobs was lower in 1968 than previously. The current depression in high-prestige job roles for women appears related to the increase in the number of middle-aged women entering or returning to the labor force. Such women suffer not only from an initial lower level of job-related education compared to male workers but also from occupational obsolescence.

In summary, the need for continuing education across the life span is becoming increasingly compelling. Technological advance has contributed not only to attenuation in the birth rate and extension of the life expectancy itself, but also to the increasing rapidity with which nearly every sector of the individual's life is changing. Lifelong learning is now a necessity for optimal individual development.

LIFE-SPAN MODELS

The educational researcher interested in life-span conceptualizations will need to step away from a concept of development which is synonymous with the notion of growth as differentiation. The latter concept assumes that as each new developmental plateau is reached, further development occurs through the emergence of more complex structures. For example, in the area of intellectual development it has been proposed that children do indeed start out with a unitary single-factor component, but as growth occurs it consecutively branches into a number of separate abilities organized in a hierarchical manner. In adulthood this kind of differentiation is likely to cease, and transformations will be of a more qualitative nature in response to environmental presses. In old age there may in fact once again be a return to greater simplicity of structure, if only to counteract information overload (Reinert, 1970).

Stepping away from a growth model does not mean shifting to a symmetric differentiation-dedifferentiation model à la Werner (1957), to which data might be fitted for statistical elegance by means of a simple Gompertz curve. Indeed, one of the first caveats required before the problem of explicating life-span models can be addressed (Baltes & Schaie, 1973) is to accept the notion that there is increasing variability over the life span due to maturation. Although on each specific area of development one may find modal patterns with limited variation in the acquisition of behavior during childhood, there is great variety in the expression of individual differences during adulthood. Our discussion will focus on four topics: First, we will differentiate between development and aging; second, we will distinguish ontogenetic progressions (age change) from the description of the sociocultural attributes distinguishing various birth cohorts (age differences); third, we will distinguish between three life-span models which assume stability, irreversible decrement, and/or compensable decrement during the adult phase; and fourth, we will consider the wide degree of behavioral plasticity that is most noteworthy in adulthood.

How Do Development and Aging Differ?

Some theoreticians prefer to combine the terms *aging* and *development* and address behavioral change as a developmental process which, at all life stages, can take a variety of forms in terms of directionality, range, and intensity (Baltes & Willis, 1977). Nevertheless, it may be heuristic, particularly for educators and educational researchers, to consider some subtle ways in which the emphasis of life-span developmental researchers shifts as interest moves from emerging behavior, to behavioral maintenance, and eventually to deficit phenomena.

One of the remarkable aspects of early development is the relatively isomorphic relationship between changes in the physiological structures which seem to be essential in supporting a given behavior and the observed behavioral function (Flavell, 1970). Not only can we specify that noteworthy behavior change will occur in almost all surviving organisms between birth and maturity, but we can also note that the bandwidth of adaptive behavior is quite narrow, and the absolute number of time units separating the attainment of a given behavior by the least and most advanced children is quite brief. Most organized activities by children are primarily related to the acquisition of cognitive skills and have competitive rather than socializing attributes. Little attention is given to the implications of the child's cognitive activities for the welfare of others.

As young adulthood is reached, the isomorphic relation between structure and function breaks down (Schaie & Marquette, 1975). The attainment of the Piagetian stage of formal operations is *not* tied to the development of a specific physiological structural property of the organism (Piaget, 1972), nor can performance level in the elderly be clearly tied to specific physiological decrement (Birren & Renner, 1977). But perhaps more importantly, the developmental tasks (Havighurst, 1972) of the individual change, and the goal objectives of individual behavior are no longer primarily directed toward skill acquisition but toward the application of acquired skills to responsible social roles and societal tasks (Kohlberg, 1973; Schaie, 1977/78).

The life-span—oriented researcher will therefore be attuned to the predominance of emergent behaviors in childhood, the transformation of behaviors in terms of both small- and large-unit societal goals in young adulthood and early middle age, and the maintenance of behavior within a successively less stable physiological structure in terms of relatively egocentric goals during old age. It is most likely that as members of a species, the basic behavioral constructs found to be important in children, such as self-care, social interaction, problem solving, and language functions, will continue to be worth noting throughout life. But it is not at all certain that the same observable behaviors (phenotypes) will be reliable indicators of the latent behavioral constructs (genotypes). In other words, while the building blocks of behavior remain identical throughout life, their pattern of organization is likely to alter due to changes in the effectiveness of the physiological maintenance mechanisms and in environmental supports and societal expectations (see also Schaie, 1978).

Ontogenetic Changes vs. Intergenerational Differences vs. Effects of Sociocultural Change

Anyone seriously interested in life-span models will soon find that such models are closely related to assumptions about aging as well as selection of appropriate data bases. This chapter cannot present in detail the issues related to the interpretability of data obtained from cross-sectional, longitudinal, or the newer sequential data collection strategies (Baltes, Reese, & Nesselroade, 1977;

Botwinick, 1973; Friedrich & Van Horn, 1976; Goulet, 1975; Schaie, 1965, 1970, 1973b, 1977; Wohlwill, 1973). Nevertheless, it would be remiss if we did not call attention to the assumptions implicit in the more commonly used research designs and then indicate how they relate to life-span models.

We would first like to note that the traditional cross-sectional method compares, at one point in time, individuals from two or more age groups who by definition must belong to different birth cohorts. Longitudinal studies, on the other hand, compare the same individuals over two or more points in time. The former method therefore confounds ontogenetic change with generational differences, while the latter confounds ontogenetic change with the effects of sociocultural change occurring between times of measurement (or what the sociologists call *period effects*). For most behavioral variables these confounds are bound to be large, and it is unlikely that findings of cross-sectional age differences will agree with those obtained from longitudinal age changes (see Schaie, 1967, for a conceptual discussion and Schaie, in press), for extensive research evidence). Further, it has been argued that many age differences reported in the research literature might be more parsimoniously interpreted to be generational differences, and there are serious questions whether results of single-cohort longitudinal studies of human behavior can be interpreted in a meaningful fashion (see Schaie & Gribbin, 1975a).

Several alternative strategies have been suggested which have come to be known as *sequential methods*. The researcher interested in age changes wishes to find functions which describe ontogenetic changes across the life course and must therefore demonstrate that such functions do not simply describe the impact of specific historic events on a single birth cohort. In this instance the same age range should be monitored for two or more successive cohorts, using a design we have called the *cohort-sequential* method. In this manner it is possible to segregate the effect on intraindividual ontogenetic variance from intraindividual generational difference variance. Further complications arise in educational research when variation between and within grade levels may be important. Grade level can take on an alternate role in defining membership of a cohort (see Goulet, 1975).

Researchers studying age differences frequently want to obtain information on the question of whether there are generational differences which account for behavior difference between the young and old at a particular point in time. In this case, however, we need to know whether such differences remain stable or are an artifact of particular age-cohort combinations occurring at a single measurement point. This is best accomplished by use of the *time-sequential* design, which involves two or more replications of the age range covered by a specific cross-sectional study.

Finally, we should note that many developmentally oriented investigators are not really interested in aging per se. What they want to know is whether there are stable generational differences or sociocultural changes which may determine behavior change over time. This argues for the *cross-sequential* method in which two or more cohorts are sampled at two or more measurement points in order to differentiate between the effects of differential early-life experience or other generation-specific variance and period effects introduced by sociocultural change.

One further caution is in order. The choice of research strategies implies certain prior assumptions about thè nature of the data. Thus utilization of the longitudinal and cohort-sequential methods implies postulating trivial period effects, the cross-sectional and time-sequential methods postulate trivial cohort effects, and the cross-sequential method postulates trivial age-related effects.

Alternate Models of Adult Development

As we have noted above, it seems reasonable to argue that during childhood behavioral development can generally be viewed as undirectional, with the direction representing the emergence of more differentiated from less differentiated behavior, as well as the attainment of higher levels of performance or behavioral intensity. No such assumptions seem reasonable for most behavioral variables past adolescence. In our previous writing, moreover, we have called attention to at least three different models, all of which fit at least some available data sets for some portion of the adult life span (Schaie, 1973b).

The first of these models states that once maturity is reached, henceforth adult behavior will remain stable. The *adult stability* model may be suitable for a limited number of behaviors which are biologically mediated but whose biological base remains stable from maturity to death. More important to educators, it is a model which must be seriously considered for the so-called crystallized abilities (Cattell, 1963), if one assumes that in this case the organism has mastered all information made available by the environment. Another important instance involves many personality traits and attitudes (e.g., ego strength, dominance, conservatism) which, barring profound life crises, should be expected to remain stable over the life span (Schaie & Parham, 1976).

Postulating the stability model for a particular variable, of course, implies that the investigator's interest must shift away from a study of age. What is of interest now are shifts in the asymptotic levels attained at maturity for successive generations and the effects of transient cyclical events due to time-specific input. Obviously, situational variables may mimic what seem to be developmental phenomena. Changes in educational curricula which are introduced in one school system before they were acceptable to the professional community at large might have such effects.

If the stability assumption is indeed valid, then data from cross-sectional studies comparing different age groups are direct estimates of cohort differences; those from longitudinal studies yield evidence of cyclical variation; and the cross-sequential method is the experimental strategy of choice, since it permits differentiation of cohort and period effects. Examples of this approach have been provided in studies of the Primary Mental Abilities for samples measured repeatedly by Schaie and Labouvie-Vief (1974) and for independent random samples by Schaie, Labouvie and Buech (1973). In these studies it was found that for the middle adult range, from the thirties to the sixties, there was little change within individuals that could be attributed to aging on ability variables which did not require highly speeded tasks for measurement. Cross-sequential analyses, however, detected substantial generational differences, as well as secular trends involving individuals at all ages. We suspect that these results in major part reflect both changes in educational level for successive population cohorts and changes over proximal time periods in our efficiency to program and transmit sociocultural information to adults.

A second model, the one which seems implicitly to underlie most traditional discussion of life-span processes, implies *irreversible decrement* past the growth peak. This model is superficially most attractive because if data were to fit the model, it would then be possible to fit age functions and compute functional ages in a manner similar to the mental age concept used with children (see Schaie & Schaie, 1977b, for a detailed discussion of the functional age concept). It is an insidious model, however, because it focuses the researcher's attention primarily on those few behaviors where performance is dominated by peripheral sensory functions and psychomotor speed, which do indeed seem to show systematic age-related decrement. Moreover, these variables may be the very ones which are most likely subject to compensation by means of prosthetic environments. In other words, the model is likely to fit only for a limited number of variables and is most appropriate for the analysis of data in populations of advanced age (say the late sixties and older), where by reason of increasing physiological pathology, irreversible decrement must be expected.

But since this model specifies that ontogenetic changes will occur regardless of environmental input, it is imperative to segregate variance which is maturationally determined from that which may be generation-specific if we wish to learn and generalize about both levels and slopes of decrement functions. That is, we need to know over what age range we can predict systematic age decrement as against age differences attributable to generational shifts in level of performance. Note that the irreversible decrement model implies the absence of period effects, since no compensatory environmental impacts are deemed to be effective.

An example of the application of the cohort-sequential method appropriate to test these questions is provided in a study of the Primary Mental Abilities in which seven-year age changes were contrasted with seven-year cohort differences (Schaie & Parham, 1977). Results suggest that until the sixties there are no age changes on power tests, but substantial cohort differences prevail. From the sixties on both age and cohort differences are found, with age changes accounting for progressively larger amounts of individual-difference variance as the eighties are reached. For highly speeded tests, however, cohort differences are relatively unimportant, while decremental age changes are detected as early as the forties.

Many life-span researchers consider a third model, which we call *decrement with compensation*, more likely to fit behavioral data and, interestingly enough, much easier to test. We might argue that for many behavioral variables beyond a minimal base level, environmental input in childhood may affect growth in observed performance only minimally, since the organism as yet has not reached its asymptote. During the adult phase, however, biologically determined decrement might be compensated in part by environmental input of a quasi-prosthetic nature. The decrement-with-compensation model may be quite appropriate for variables involving fluid intelligence, temperament, and other personality traits; in other words, variables where generational differences seem relatively unimportant, but where changes in educational technology and sociocultural processes may well obscure maturational events. Let us note, further, that data fitting the decrement-with-compensation model will probably either show a moderately accelerating decrement gradient or be compatible with the terminal-drop concept, that is, severe behavioral decrement shortly prior to death (Siegler, 1975), when compensatory input no longer suffices to stabilize the behavior under scrutiny. Obviously, the latter circumstance is difficult to differentiate from an adult stability model. That is why it is probably wise to collect data whereby both the stability and decrement-with-compensation models can be examined.

Tests of the decrement-with-compensation model require the application of the time-sequential method, which is designed to differentiate age and period effects. An example of this approach is provided by a study of ontogenetic and sociocultural change in expressed attitudes of social responsibility (Schaie & Parham, 1974). In this study it was argued that one might expect both age and cohort differences in the expression of social responsibility. Empirical findings, however, supported strong cyclical trends implicating sociocultural effects, but with differential impact depending upon the age of the respondents.

Plasticity of Adult Behavior

Having pleaded the need for different sets of assumptions in research covering the life stages past early maturity, we now need to go a step further to suggest that not only are there likely to be different developmental functions for different behavioral variables, but also we may expect substantial individual differences in maintenance patterns and modifiability (Baltes & Schaie, 1976; Baltes & Willis, 1977; Labouvie-Vief, 1976). We take the general position that behavioral deficit from a young adult level of functioning must generally be attributed to a combination of genetic propensities, unfavorable environment, and physiological functions through adulthood. We would then expect much greater variability in behavioral competence than is observed during childhood. The extent of such variability may, however, not always be obvious across the total population of adults because of the countervailing trend of increased probability of physiological pathology which inhibits expression of many behaviors as well as the increasingly constricted environment and role reduction in later life (Gordon, 1971). But the *range* of observed behavior increases markedly, and we find that many elderly individuals perform well above the average of young adults (Schaie & Parham, 1977; Schaie & Strother, 1968). Indeed, the fact that we can document an increasing number of individual instances of lack of individual decline on important psychological functions suggests that the average decrement observed beyond the sixties may well be pathology related or modifiable by social intervention.

Of further importance in this context are recent findings that behavior modification paradigms with the elderly are quite successful. Thus, apparent low-level function on intellectual variables, whether due to obsolescence or decrement, has been successfully modified by several researchers (Hoyer, Labouvie, & Baltes, 1973; Labouvie-Vief & Gonda, 1976; Plemons, Willis & Baltes, 1978). Even quite simpleminded changes in instructional or reinforcement conditions may result in increased performance (Birkhill & Schaie, 1975). Considering further issues such as individual differences in life-style and environmental interaction, it has been found that there is very little decrement in function at most ages over periods as long as 14 years in individuals who have a complex environment and who are involved in many interpersonal contacts, while substantial decrement is noted in those living isolated lives (Schaie & Gribbin, 1975b).

It follows, then, that we must be much more analytic in considering the circumstances under which an individual's behavior remains stable or undergoes change over the life span. Nevertheless, those interested in educational planning, in addition to knowing that the range of individual variability is substantial and that many older individuals can well profit from technologies appropriate for young adults, must still take due note that for many of today's adults there are age changes which must be taken into account.

Life-span Developmental Models and Education

The relevance of a life-span approach for education is based on several assumptions. First, it is assumed that education, as an applied science, involves application and utilization of knowledge from several disciplines and that life-span developmental psychology is generating a relevant knowledge base. The linkage between life-span development and education is particularly relevant if the primary goal of education is the facilitation and optimization of individual plasticity—that is, if individual development is modifiable through both macro sociocultural change and micro-level ontogenetic life events. Education too is based on the assumption that behavior is modifiable and thus subject to educational intervention strategies.

Developmental Discontinuity.   A life-span perspective suggests that qualitative and quantitative developmental changes occur across the life course, resulting in developmental discontinuity. Such developmental discontinuity implies the need for qualitatively different educational goals and instructional strategies at different life stages. For example, an educational focus on skill acquisition in childhood shifts to an emphasis on social application of such skills in young adulthood. The acquisition-to-application shift is suggestive of different levels of Bloom's hierarchy (1956). Likewise, the three adult development models of stability, decrement with compensation, and irreversible decrement suggest different educational approaches. While a stability model suggests emphasis on maintenance of acquired skills and knowledge, a decrement-with-compensation model focuses on the design of compensatory strategies involving quite different educational foci and strategies. Such model differences are similar to the "teaching to the weakness vs. teaching to the strength" concept.

Moreover, such developmental discontinuity implies differential developmental antecedents across the life course and a shifting relationship between maturational neurophysiological structures and cognitive functions. Maturational influences may predominate in childhood such that emergence of a behavior occurs within a relatively narrow chronological age period. Thus, age-graded educational intervention may be merited in view of uniformity in development sequences deriving from this isomorphy between physical structure and cognitive function. However, experiential factors appear to become more salient in adult cognitive functioning and the structure-function relationship breaks down. The educational implication is that educational endeavors in adulthood should be organized by criteria other than chronological age. Developmental tasks and social roles based on experiential factors and social expectancies may be more useful indices for defining educational programs in adulthood.

Dialectical Relation between Social Change and Individual Development. A life-span approach maintains that individual development occurs in the context of social change and that such macro-environmental influences can result in differential developmental patterns for cohorts experiencing different slices of history (Riegel, 1976). The implication for education is that there must also be a dialectical relationship between the educational system and social change. That is, education must be responsive to the changing social milieu and thus to the changing nature of the student population. Students of the same grade level but from different cohorts may well differ in terms of academic performance and attitudinally related variables. Note the recent decline in performance on college entrance exams. All aspects of the educational endeavor, including curricula, instructional technology, and assessment, must be continually reexamined for possible cultural obsolescence.

ROLE OF EDUCATION AT DIFFERENT LIFE STAGES

Early and Middle Childhood

Childhood has traditionally been considered the period for development of social and intellectual skills related to effective functioning within a particular society. It is a period of emerging behavior, and preschool and primary early education has focused on knowledge and skill acquisition. Recently greater attention has been given to cognitive abilities and processes rather than specific factual information (Evans, 1977; Lay, 1971). Such factual information quickly becomes obsolete in a rapidly developing society. Accelerated change suggests the need for basic cognitive abilities which facilitate the individual's adaptiveness and flexibility in changing environments. Thus in focusing on cognitive processes, early childhood education assumes a preventive function in facilitating the a priori development of strategies for coping with change.

The research literature suggests that the child's development of certain attitudes as well as cognitive abilities has a significant impact on later development. It is suggested that certain attitudes developing in early childhood, such as achievement motivation and sex role types (Kagan & Moss, 1962), may be significant to a lifelong learning approach. For example, perceptions of age-specific and life roles begin to develop in childhood, and thus learning should be perceived as a lifelong endeavor rather than an age-specific role (Houle, 1974). Likewise, need for achievement has been shown in educational settings to develop in childhood (Atkinson, 1964; Kagan & Moss, 1962) and to be subject to modification (Atkinson, 1964). The changing age structure of the society and the impact of environmental change on career patterns suggest the need to examine attitudinal development with regard to work roles and the perception of aging. Research (Ahammer & Baltes, 1972; Hickey, Hickey, & Kalish, 1968; Seefeldt, Jantz, Galper, & Serock, 1977) suggests that the individual's perception of age-graded stereotypes develops early in the life span. Seefeldt et al. (1977) reported stereotypic views among children of physical and behavioral aspects of aging. Age segregation in the formal educational process provides little opportunity for children to interact with older adults and thus to challenge stereotypes of aging. Perception of work roles has also been found to have early developmental patterns (Kirchner, 1973).

Interestingly, one of the first steps toward a lifelong learning approach may have been the extension of early education into the preschool years and even infancy. Some perspectives gained from the compensatory education movement in the 1960s may be useful as lifelong learning expands into other age periods which have not been within the traditional educational domain. Such perspectives appear to support some of the concerns of a life-span approach. First, early intervenors became increasingly aware of the qualitative differences in cognitive functioning in infants and young and middle-aged children. Such qualitative changes imply the need for different educational goals, instructional strategies, and even assessment batteries at different developmental periods. Early childhood education has not been a simple extension downward of the elementary grades (Cropley, 1976). Furthermore, the need for a conceptual or theoretical framework for explicating the relationship between these developmental periods became evident. Piagetian theory appears to be one of the few theories which deals with qualitative change across early developmental periods (see Flavell, 1963, for a discussion of Piaget's theory). Finally, since the target of early intervention was the culturally disadvantaged child, educators became increasingly aware of the impact of sociocultural variables on development. For example, the influence of sociocultural variables on language development became a focus of much research. Thus expansion of the learning process across a wider age span illustrates the relevance of some of the life-span models previously discussed.

Adolescence and Young Adulthood

The period of adolescence marks a qualitative developmental shift from emergence to transformation of abilities and skills. The nature of such a transformation may be considered from several perspectives. In Piagetian theory, adolescence is the period during which there is a transformation from concrete to formal operational thought. However, formal reasoning tends to occur primarily in modern technological societies and varies with individuals according to the substantive area in which it develops (Piaget, 1972). It may be that with further rapid technological advances future career options will increasingly require formal reasoning. Both Piagetian theory and recent training research (Hornblum & Overton, 1976; Tomlinson-Keasey, 1972) suggest that formal reasoning is susceptible to educational intervention.

Transformation is also evident as the general intellectual and social abilities developed in childhood are channeled into acquisition of adult role competencies, particularly those involving career preparation. Such transformation of general intellectual and social abilities developed within a school setting into adult role competencies involves more than a simple transfer of a particular skill into a different context. As Schaie (1978) has recently noted, real-life tasks involve a cluster of skills rather than isolated abilities. Moreover, while the same generic intellectual abilities (genotypes) may be involved in success in both academic and job settings, the behavioral expression of these abilities (phenotypes) in different settings can vary greatly. Thus the complex of abilities involved in career-related tasks would be best developed through a problem-centered, multidisciplinary approach within the job setting itself (Cropley, 1976; Wroczynski, 1974). In contrast to the prior educational pattern of compartmentalizing learning into a series of academic courses and isolating career preparation from the workplace, the present approach would require the student to integrate knowledge of several disciplines (marketing, English, public speaking, psychology) in solving a real-life problem (selling a product).

The need to integrate work and study in young adulthood has been strongly recommended in the United States by Coleman (1972) and in several European countries (Bengtson, 1974). Coleman maintains that the isolation of the adolescent from adult-oriented contexts has seriously delayed development of adult role competencies. If work and study were integrated, school-based activities per se would be reduced, while education within the workplace would be expanded. The passive, teacher-oriented learning of the classroom would be replaced by self-initiated, active, experiential learning—an educational model more consistent with future learning across the adult life span. Partially in line with these suggestions, the Oregon Board of Education has prescribed a new set of high school graduation requirements focusing on six life competency roles: learner, individual, producer, citizen, consumer, and family member (Long, 1974; Shaffer, 1974). Likewise, the extensive literature on career development education (Holland, 1973) advocates a lifelong education.

The integration of work and study in adolescence is in line with the lifelong learning approach to combining work and continuing education across the adult life span (Houle, 1974). Rapid technological advancement and multiple career patterns make it unfeasible to crowd lifelong vocational training into a few years in adulthood (Carnegie Commission, 1971). Multiple entry points into both the educational system and the job market must be made available during adolescence and continue across adulthood. Such an approach could result in a reduction in the time required for initial job preparation, in contrast to the increasing length of college or vocational education during the past few decades. It is likely that certain job-related skills are best learned after a period of on-the-job experience. A future task for the educator is to determine the optimal timing for training for certain occupational skills.

Middle Adulthood

One of the most important challenges for a lifelong learning approach involves the formulation of educational opportunities for the middle-aged adult. Currently, adults in early middle age (35–40 years) are the most active consumers of formal continuing-education courses. This age group is also heavily involved in organizations and civic participation. Schaie (1973a) has suggested that educational intervention in middle adulthood may have the greatest impact for society, due to these adults' positions in the power structure of society.

Projections for future later-middle-age cohorts, the age group which Neugarten (1975) calls the "young-old" (55–75 years), suggest an increasing demand for educational opportunities from this age group also. Neugarten predicts that by the year 2000 the young-old population will include approximately 15% of the entire population. With a 2% per year reduction in the mortality rate and the anticipated reduction in modal age of first retirement to 55 years, it is predicted that the postretirement life span of men in this age cohort would double, from the present 13 years to 25–28 years. The significant increase in leisure time as well as the anticipated improvement in health and educational level suggest this age cohort as a prime consumer of education. Compared to earlier age periods, little is known about the middle-aged learner (Knox, 1977; Troll, 1975). It appears that cognitive psychology and educational research have focused primarily on the acquisition phase of learning, and thus on the younger learner. Due to an increasing experiential history, the task for the middle-aged learner increasingly becomes the maintenance and transformation of information rather than acquisition de novo. Rapid environmental change increases the situations requiring unlearning of material or the relating of new information to much prior learning. Within a lifelong learning approach, formal educational institutions must become increasingly sensitive to qualitative developmental changes in the adult learner (Huberman, 1974). Furthermore, multiple entry points into the educational system must be created to accommodate the expanding adult population of students which will approach continuing education with a variety of learning backgrounds.

The middle years are particularly salient in women's changing role in relation to work and education. Whereas fewer men continue to work as they get older (from 44 on), more women work between 45 and 54 than at younger—or older—ages (Troll, 1975). Such data illustrate the contrasting life patterns of the sexes, since in middle age the woman is initially freed of the child care role which has made extensive time demands in early adulthood. Such initial entry or reentry into the work world during middle age often requires career preparation or retraining. Education must become increasingly sensitive to the educational and personal needs of women undergoing role changes. Alternative educational programs and credentialing would allow consideration of the competencies acquired by such women through volunteer work or in relation to their child care role.

DIFFERENCES BETWEEN YOUNG AND OLD LEARNERS

A major concern for the systematic analysis of life-span changes in learning processes and thus relevant instructional technology is the fact that there are systematic changes in a number of basic processes between the life stage at which formal education has traditionally centered and the stages at which adult education or second career training are most likely to occur. The chronological ages at which relevant behavior changes occur differ by area of function and depend to some extent on the individual's life course. Nevertheless, even though many adult experiential phenomena occur with great chronological latitude (see Neugarten & Datan, 1973), there are at least several well-defined changes from young adulthood into late middle age which occur for most aging individuals. This section will summarize some of the clearer findings from the research literature for the areas of sensory and perceptual function, learning and memory, intellectual abilities related to educational competence, and differential motivation. A more extensive version of this section may be found in Schaie and Quayhagen (1978).

Sensory and Perceptual Differences Between Young and Old Learners

Visual Acuity. Age-related changes in the structure of the eye include lessening of transmission ability and accommodation power of the eye beginning at ages 35 to 45. Progressive thickening in the cortex region of the crystalline lens renders it less transparent, resulting in interference with the optical functions of transmitting and refracting light, as well as decreasing accommodative power. The yellowing of the lens not only reduces the amount of light to the retina but also results in loss of sensitivity to the shorter wavelengths of the visible spectrum (Weale, 1965). The older adult therefore has greater difficulty discriminating between blue, blue-green, and violet colors. Changes in the accommodative power of the eye further affect distance vision, sensitivity to glare, binocular depth perception, and color sensitivity. Circulatory and metabolic changes in the retina around age 55 to 65 years also result in reduction of the size of the visual field, along with decreased sensitivity to flicker and to low quantities of light.

Fozard, Wolf, Bell, and Podolsky (1977) conclude that it is the brightness gradient of the image on the retina that is critical in determining visual acuity. Corrective lenses can improve visual acuity by increasing retinal illumination, but acuity can also be sharpened by increasing the contrast between the object and its surrounding field or by increasing overall illumination.

There is evidence from a number of studies that age-related changes occur in visual perception. Older people tend to adhere to initial perceptions in a given stimulus situation and show evidence of resistance, or possibly inability, to reorganize their perception. Whether this phenomenon is due to a personality trait of cognitive rigidity or to a decline in visual acuity which limits discriminability of objects is not yet clear (Corso, 1971).

The combined impact of physical and perceptual deficits in the overall visual functioning of the older adult has been studied by Pastalan, Mautz, and Merrill (1973). In order to duplicate relevant environmental experiences of the aged person with ''normal'' sensory losses, these investigators attempted to simulate the effects of yellowing of the lens, increased lense opacity, and light scatter in combination. It was found that these age-related decrements have a limiting effect upon the older adult's use of buildings, facilities, and environmental space. Also, structural changes in the eye would suggest that visual aids should have distinctly outlined configurations and adequate illumination level.

Auditory Acuity. The most common auditory deficiency with advancing age is presbycusis, a sensorineural bilateral loss of auditory acuity for the high frequency tones, due to physiological degeneration in the auditory system (Corso, 1977). Such changes produce functional decrements in the auditory thresholds for pure tones, speech and pitch discriminations, and information for processing of dichotic stimuli. Such deficits may interfere with older adults' ability to communicate and therefore limit their range of interaction.

Corso (1971) reports sex differences in auditory sensitivity, with the hearing level of men higher than that of women at or above 2000 Hz, but below that of women for frequencies of 1000 Hz and below. This finding may be due to exposure to differing amounts of environmental noise. Some degree of hearing loss is found from about 32 years of age for men and 37 years for women (Lebo

& Reddell, 1972). Impairment in pitch discrimination has been noted as early as the fourth decade (Konig, 1957). However, Corso (1971) has suggested that age-related performance decrements may reflect different criteria of judgments (such as cautiousness) rather than functional losses in the auditory sensory modality.

Because presbycusis affects high-tone auditory sensitivity, there is a loss in discrimination of consonants with high frequency components in their acoustic patterns, such as *s, t, q, f,* and *g*. As a result, older adults have greater difficulty in discriminating phonetically similar words, with subsequent difficulty in following normal conversation. Increased noise levels can enhance these difficulties (Corso, 1971, 1977).

Older adults need additional information-processing time in the perception of speech (Calearo & Lazzaroni, 1957). Complete intelligibility could be obtained for subjects over 70 years of age, for discrimination of words presented at the normal rate of 140 words per minute if the intensity was sufficiently increased. But as the rate of presentation was increased, intelligibility decreased to 45 percent, regardless of intensity.

Schaie, Baltes, and Strother (1964) investigated auditory sensitivity in relation to intellectual functioning in persons over 70 years of age. All individuals showed acuity loss at higher frequency ranges with age. But men were found to have significantly greater acuity loss than women for the higher frequencies and showed greater impairment in intellectual functioning. Substantial associations have also been found between hearing loss and intellectual functioning as measured by subtests of the WAIS and the Raven Progressive Matrices (Granick, Kleban, & Weiss, 1976).

Educational programs can alert the adult learner to an understanding of the impact that sensory deficits can have on social, psychological, and cognitive behavior. Furthermore, educators need to regulate their presentation rate of auditory inputs and to adjust intensity and frequency to a level appropriate to the age of their students, in order to achieve optimal communication.

Perceptual Speed. Birren (1965) attributed age-related slowness in behavior to a slower mediation process in the central nervous system. Whether central or peripheral processes are most strongly implicated in the reduction of perceptual speed has recently been investigated by means of studies of perceptual masking. *Perceptual masking* is the failure to recognize a stimulus or signal if the first stimulus is followed too quickly by a second stimulus. The masking techniques employed in recent visual perception studies (Turvey, 1973) allow the experimenter to localize decrements and to distinguish between peripheral and central masking. No qualitative differences in central perceptual processes have been found between young and older adults (Walsh, 1976). However, in a study using experimental techniques specific to peripheral masking, Walsh, Till, and Williams (1978) found a slower operating rate for the peripheral perceptual system of the older adult over 60 years of age, as compared with the young.

In information-processing studies with techniques other than masking, a longer scanning time was needed for the older subjects to extract information when a target object was embedded in a complex display (Rabbitt, 1965). With a changing display task, Talland (1966) found that rate of presentation and task duration were important variables. But response bias such as practice effects, boredom, or fatigue can affect results.

Research results point to a slower processing mechanism for incoming stimuli with advancing age. This suggests a need for a self-paced or slower presentation rate of stimuli, consideration of varying complexity effects, and greater redundancy in stimulus material.

Age Differences in Learning and Memory Which Affect Educational Technology for the Older Learner

It is currently accepted that many of the observed deficits in learning abilities which are assumed to be age-related should be interpreted as performance differences rather than as decreased ability to learn. Decrements with increasing age have also been noted in memory, and current research is attempting to ascertain whether the observed age differences should be attributed to information acquisition, retrieval, or storage mechanisms, or to other factors.

Acquisition. Since age differences in short-term memory are minimal, age-related acquisition difficulties must be looked for at the deeper level of processing required for retention in secondary or long-term memory (Craik, 1977). Variables implicated include pacing, redundancy of cues, and meaningfulness of content.

Deficits have been noted for older persons on *paced tasks* (Arenberg & Robertson, 1977; Kinsbourne, 1973). When the learning period is slow, older individuals benefit from increased response time. However, when older learners are rushed, increased response time will not help. Although some age differences in performance have been found, even with self-pacing tasks the benefits of self-pacing for the older learner should not be ignored.

Craik (1968) concluded that the elderly make less efficient use of linguistic *redundancy* when a lower performance level was found for older subjects in two experiments designed to test the effect of redundancy in English text. In other studies it has been found that retrieval cues become less effective as more items are nested in a category, in which case noncued or random recall results in better performance for older subjects (Hultsch, 1975; Tulving & Pearlstone, 1966). Craik (1977) suggests that older adults may fail to remember events due to an overabundance or redundancy of functional items associated with the retrieval cues.

Age differences also have been found in relation to *meaningfulness of content*. However, the evidence is somewhat confused, with generalizations limited to specific situations (Botwinick, 1973; Craik, 1977). In a concept identification study, Arenberg (1968) found that older subjects had difficulty with abstract dimensions but their performance increased with the more concrete dimensions. The results of a similar study in which older adults were found to benefit disproportionately from the use of meaningful tasks as compared to nonsense tasks (Hulicka, 1967) suggests that older adults may refuse to learn meaningless tasks, even though learning occurs for meaningful materials which reflect real-life situations.

Information Retrieval. Although there is insufficient evidence to indicate faster loss of stored material with increased age (Craik, 1977), several retrieval processes have been found to place the older learner at a disadvantage. Those studied most intensively include the roles of response competition, effects of cross-modal presentation, and, in particular, performance on classification problems.

Age-related decrements have been noted when attention must be divided between two incoming stimuli, incoming stimuli and memory, or memory and response. Older persons tend to concentrate on one task and let the other deteriorate markedly (Craik, 1977). The negative effects of divided attention are also found in dichotic listening studies in which different stimuli are introduced to each ear simultaneously (Moray, 1970). Greater age differences have been found if a memory task is presented visually rather than auditorily. When older subjects were asked to reorganize material, even greater performance decrements were apparent (Craik, 1977).

Cross-modality effects have been studied by means of presentations to dual sensory modalities and to dual encoding systems within the sensory modality. Using auditory cues along with a visual presentation was found to improve memory in both younger and older adults (Arenberg, 1968). But hearing the cues seemed to be the critical variable, with better recall for the auditory-augmented conditions (Penney, 1975). However, visual stimuli augmented by active auditory vocalization tend to impair rather than improve recall in the elderly for early items in a list; such items were better recalled under a visual-only condition (Arenberg, 1976). This finding indicates that active auditory augmentation would not be feasible where long term memory is important.

Parham and Schaie (1976) investigated dual coding effects on recall of auditory and visual presentation using combinations of conflicting verbal-symbolic and pictorial stimuli. Better performance occurred when pictures accompanied the verbal stimuli, whether the verbal was presented by auditory or visual means. But cognitive overload in processing seemed to occur when the same encoding system (verbal symbolic) was tapped by different modalities, as was the case when verbal stimuli (passive auditory) were accompanied by visually presented words. These findings suggest that stimuli which enhance dual encoding, such as pictorial stimuli accompanied by verbal (auditory or visual) stimuli, may also enhance recall.

Age-related decrements have been found in organizational ability, and when instructions in efficient organization are given to older adults, performance has been found to improve (Hultsch, 1974). However, when older persons are asked to reorganize material, the added complication of divided attention produces even poorer performance. When they are taught a learning strategy, overall improvement is noted on successive tasks, but the learning effect varies as a function of age and stage of the task. Older subjects require more time to overcome negative transfer effects and to show improved performance.

The generalizability of training effects has been studied by Labouvie-Vief and Gonda (1976), who trained individuals to perform complex reasoning problems by strengthening their covert self-monitoring strategies. Training conditions involved cognitive self-guidance, anxiety reduction, or unspecified training. Cognitive strategy training produced significant increments in intellectual performance across tasks and over time. Subject-generated strategies may be more effective with older subjects than strategies imposed by the experimenter, since the unspecified training group showed the strongest training effects.

The educator planning to develop programs for older learners must thus be aware of at least several qualitative and quantitative differences which require attention, both in curriculum planning and in the development of teaching materials. We shall defer a discussion of general implications for educational programming to the final section of this chapter, but note that the most important variables seem to be the need for redundancy of cues, the appropriate selection of instructional pacing, and close attention to age- and cohort-relevant meaningfulness of content. Retrieval of information seems further enhanced by careful use of several media, as long as the same encoding system is addressed by several modalities, rather than creating conflict by requiring the simultaneous use of different systems.

Intellectual Abilities Related to Educational Aptitude

Should We Measure Intelligence or Competence?   Intelligence can be defined in this context as a spectrum of genotypic factors (latent variables or constructs) which may be derived from phenotypic (directly observable) expressions of adaptive behavior as measured across situations. And competence is defined as the phenotypic expression of a combination of genotypic intelligence factors, which, given minimal motivational incentives, will permit adaptive behavior within a specific situation or class of situations (Schaie, 1978).

In practical terms, the construct of intelligence relates to the basic cognitive skills required for many adaptive behaviors. An intelligent person has *acquired* such skills, while a competent person is able to *express* a particular combination of intellectual abilities in a specific life situation (see Connolly & Bruner, 1974).

Intelligence is basic to an understanding of cognitive behavior, and competence is the manner in which intelligence relates to the problem of daily living. Multifactor batteries measuring intelligence defined by factor analytic methods, as well as Piagetian tests, have not done well in predicting competence, either within a specific situation or across situations (Kamin, 1974). Traditional intelligence measures assume the presence of competence motivation in the young, which allows assessment without regard to the meaningfulness of the task. But older adults may require ecologically relevant and valid measures to elicit maximum performance. Current measures used for the assessment of cognitive functioning are inadequate, since their validity as measures of competence pertains to situations which are quite different from those faced by middle-aged and older adults (Schaie, 1978).

Why bother, then, with the assessment of intelligence at all? Indeed, if we knew all specific outcomes of interest, we might do better to construct tests of behavioral competence for all likely situations. Work in vocational and job assessment has shown this approach to be prohibitive, particularly when differential prediction or placement is required. But if tasks are developed which indeed refer to basic intellectual genotypes, we can then map out the relation of profiles on such tasks to a wide array of criterion situations of interest.

Valid assessment of education aptitude in adulthood requires: (1) the development of a taxonomy of adult situations which are transindividual and transcultural in scope, (2) the development of intelligence tests based on phenotypic tasks that are relevant to real-life situations, extending across ages and cohorts, (3) investigation of the effects of personality and situationally induced motivational variables on cognitive tasks, and (4) achievement of generalizability through ecologically valid measures.

Criterion Group Problems: Age or Cohort-Appropriate Norms? Thomae (1976) stresses the need to consider interindividual variability as well as cohort specific differences in performance and behavior of older adults. Not only may cohort differences be influenced by such variables as health, education, occupation, varying environmental stimulations, and test-specific personality variables, but these variables also result in interindividual variability in performance of age-specific groups (Mathey, 1976; Thomae, 1976). Rudinger (1976) further notes that sex differences may show both cohort and interindividual variability. The meaningfulness of tasks may differentially affect younger and older adult learners, thus making performance comparisons between them difficult and of questionable validity. Other variables of import which may differentially influence the older learner are cautiousness, risk taking, speed of response, and sensory acuity. When comparing cognitive performances, a question yet to be resolved is the degree to which there may be factor stability or change in the organization of abilities in older adults as compared with the young (Schaie & Gribbin, 1975a).

But the major issue in using available assessment tools remains whether we want to compare an individual with his own performance over age (and time), or we want to know where a person stands with respect to his own cohort or as compared with young adults who have had quite different socialization and early educational experiences (see Schaie & Schaie, 1977a). Further, age-corrected norms based on cross-sectional data have at best transient value, especially where corrections have been obtained from nonrepresentative samples, as is typically the case (Green, 1969; Matarazzo, 1972). Regular follow-up studies of normative samples are therefore needed to provide current norms for test users.

Situation-Relevant Assessment Tools.   Both incentive and performance level can be maximized by using situation-relevant assessment tools. In order to achieve contextual relevancy, test batteries should be tailored to the interests and goals of groups of individuals. Such a procedure involves consideration of personal, situational, and task variations, since differing situations require differing performance measures of success, and the nature of the tasks should be determined by the interests of the subjects to be tested. For example, Krauss and Schaie (1976), in their attempt to explore ecologically valid measures for the assessment of spatial rotation skills, employed a technique which used playing cards of various shapes and sizes. It was argued that the utilization of stimulus material with which subjects would be familiar and comfortable ought to enhance the likelihood that one could validly assess the construct of interest rather than measure ability to handle unfamiliar tasks. Besides selecting situations of relevance to the older learner, tasks must also maximize performance motivation in the test situations.

Scheidt and Schaie (in press) developed a taxonomy of situational attributes as a means of determining how older adults of varying backgrounds differentially adapt to classes of situations. This taxonomy, derived from analysis of the literature and from situations generated by direct contact with older adults, makes it possible to estimate previously undetermined behavior in any situation by the comparison of sociophysical and psychological behavior similarities across situations. The development of situation-relevant assessment tools should permit identification of the relationships between competent performance and varying situational contexts, while respecting individual differences.

Differences in Intellectual Performance across Age.   In general, cross-sectional studies tend to identify peak ages of performance and age at which significant decrement occurs at much earlier points than are found in longitudinal or sequential studies. As indicated earlier in this chapter, these findings reflect the positive trend in cohort differences found over the past half century. Some of these problems have been addressed by the use of sequential methodologies (Baltes, 1968; Schaie, 1965, 1973) which have attempted to separate ontogenetic change from generational differences. While the sequential methods allow analyses which provide a more detailed description of the data than the traditional cross-sectional and longitudinal designs, they are nonetheless subject to confounds of sampling representation, as are the traditional developmental methods (Horn & Donaldson, 1976). Furthermore, developmental studies are subject to generalizability difficulties because of generational differences, sociocultural trends, ontogenetic changes, and differential attrition and mortality across successive cohorts (Schaie, 1977, 1978).

In spite of these methodological problems it seems fair to conclude that for those abilities where speed of response is not of intrinsic importance, ontogenetic age changes in healthy populations are observed reliably only in the early sixties and do not become of great practical import for educational application until even later in life (Schaie, 1974; Schaie & Parham, 1977). Thus cohort differences appear of substantial importance in accounting for age differences through late middle age, while some decrement in function becomes implicated beyond the sixties. Contrary to the argument of some (Horn & Donaldson, 1976), this pattern does not seem to differ markedly for measures identified as either fluid or crystallized (see Botwinick, 1977).

Figure 1 illustrates the limited magnitude of age decrement for an estimate of Educational Aptitude (a linear combination of the Primary Mental Abilities tests for vocabulary recognition and inductive reasoning). This figure (from the senior author's sequential studies) indicates proportion of performance as a function of the level of a 25-year-old reference group, based on the longitudinal study of successive random samples from the same cohorts (shaded bars) and from repeated measurements of the same groups (solid bars). These data were obtained from studies of panel members and comparison of independent samples assessed seven years apart. Cumulative age changes were then computed by adding the appropriate seven-year segments (Schaie & Parham, 1977; Schaie, in press). We concluded that the independent-samples study (shaded bars) reflects changes with age in the general population, but that the data for the panel (solid bars) are probably more characteristic of population groups which would seek continued educational exposure. At the extreme right of Figure 1 we provide the lower bound of the middle 50% range (-1 probable error) for the 25-year-old group. It is of particular interest to note that even at age 81, within-generation performance level is above the lower bounds of the middle or 50% range for individuals at age 25. Thus it would seem that reasonably healthy community-dwelling adults, if they were ever educable by reason of intellectual abilities, would retain such educability throughout life, even though both content and technology of education will differ over age and time.

Motivational Variables Affecting Adult Learning

Cautiousness and Risk Taking. Early studies of cognitive ability and cautiousness concluded that in later life cautiousness occurs as a function of decline in cognitive ability. However, Botwinick (1973) suggested that the reverse may be true; that is, that decline in ability may be attributed to an age-related increase in cautiousness. Wallach and Kogan (1961) and Botwinick (1966, 1969) have investigated cautiousness in relation to risk taking using "life situations" with problems and consequences specific to the generations studied. Sex and educational level did not differ in terms of cautiousness. Older adults were more cautious and often exercised the option of not selecting a risky course of action, regardless of success. But when the option to avoid a decision in a risk-taking situation was removed, no age differences in cautiousness were noted.

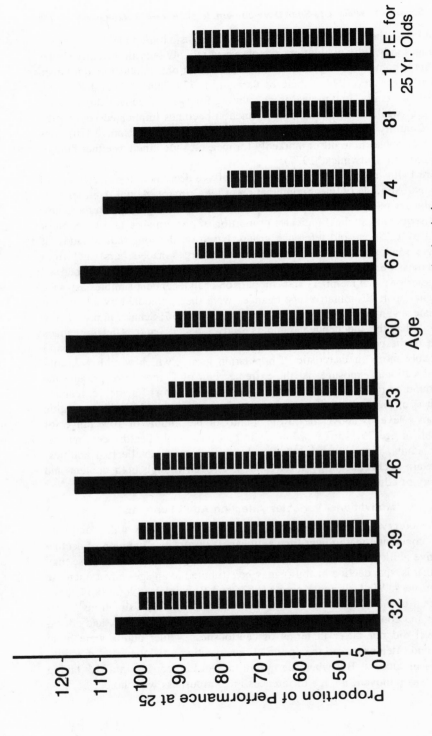

Figure 1. Performance at different ages on an index of educational aptitude as a proportion of performance at age 25.

Note: Solid bars from panel data; shaded bars from independent random samples.

Birkhill and Schaie (1975) investigated high and low risk levels in situations where the omission of responses was differentially reinforced. Older subjects in a low-risk situation performed better only when they had the option to omit responses, and they were more hesitant to become involved where risk was high. Performance was improved when subjects in high-risk conditions were discouraged to omit responses. Okun and DiVesta (1976) studied cautiousness in relation to need for achievement. The older adults they studied were more cautious, chose the difficult levels to maximize success (which would minimize obtaining potentially threatening feedback information on ability), and were less likely to raise their aspiration levels after attaining success. It is apparent that motivational factors such as cautiousness may influence the performance of older adults on measures of cognitive ability, thus causing an overestimation of age-related decrements.

Changes in Value System. Payne, Summers, and Stewart (1973) found substantial differences across three generations in judgments about behaviors having social and personal implications, with the oldest generation the most severe in its judgments. A theoretical model of adult cognitive development has recently been proposed (Schaie & Marquette, 1975; Schaie, 1977/78) which includes stages of life that incorporate the effects of environmental press and under which value changes may be subsumed. The four adult stages of development are: acquisitive, achieving, responsible, and reintegrative. These stages also fit the data presented by Lowenthal, Thurnher and Chiriboga (1975).

During the *acquisitive* stage (high school age), intellectual skills are acquired for participation in the human experience within a protective environment. In terms of value perceptions, Lowenthal et al. found high instrumental material values among both boys and girls of high school age, with the boys giving predominance to personal achievement in occupational attainment and social success, while the girls focused on personal achievement in self-actualization.

In the *achieving* stage, the young adult strives toward goal orientation and role independence, integrating this independence with assumption of responsibilities. In the newlywed members of this stage, Lowenthal et al. found a decline in instrumental-material values, with men having high personal growth values which may be attributed to a nurturant orientation.

The *responsible* stage of development consists of a pattern of long-term goal integration and increased problem-solving skills. For some individuals at this time an additional stage is reached, that of executive abilities with responsibility for societal systems and the development of cognitive strategies capable of integrating complex hierarchical relationships. Middle-aged adults were found by Lowenthal to have an abatement of personal growth values for men, and both sexes gave priority to interpersonal-expressive values. Women also showed a rising concern for ease and contentment, as well as higher social service values.

In the *reintegrative* stage, there is a relinquishment of occupational and familial responsibilities as well as a simplification of cognitive structures by selective attention to meaningful demands. This stage incorporates the preretire-

Theodore Lownik Library
Illinois Benedictine College
Lisle, Illinois 60532

ment stage of Lowenthal in which there was found to be a decline in interpersonal-expressive values for both men and women and in instrumental material values for men. There was also a subsequent increase in ease-contentment and hedonistic values in older men.

In his most recent conceptualization of moral development, Kohlberg (1973) proposes adult stages of principled moral thought which first appear in young adulthood. These stages are subdivided into a social contract, utilitarian orientation stage, and a higher stage of universal, ethical principled orientation. Cognitive-moral reflection based on personally experienced questioning of commitment is necessary to move into the principled thought stage in adulthood.

Havighurst (1976) offers some meaningful comments on how value and life stages are or are not currently served by instrumental education. If adult learning is to be maximized at various stages, planning and implementation of educational goals means incorporating an awareness of the individual's stage of values and competencies. For students in the stages of increasing responsibility, learning would be more goal directed and specific to the nature of the individual's responsibilities. But as values change from instrumental to expressive, enrichment courses may need to replace more goal-oriented professional training.

Social Conformity.   An individual is said to conform socially when he comes to agree with a new opinion or judgment which he had not held previously. Klein (1972a, 1972b) investigated age differences in such conforming behavior on visual perceptual and auditory detection tasks and found that older persons were more susceptible to social influences. When the tasks increased in complexity, conformity occurred more frequently for all subjects, but there was a larger increase in conforming behavior for the older age group.

Age functions as a normative criterion for role definitions and age-related expectations and sanctions, as well as for age-appropriate behavior (Nardi, 1973). Maintaining that age-related expectancies can act as a constraint on social behavior, Neugarten, Moore, and Lowe (1965) investigated the interaction between perceived societal age norms and perceived personal norms. They found that the older group (age 65+) had a higher degree of congruence between personal and societal norms which may represent the internalization of age norms through the adult socialization process.

If older adults are more influenced by social pressures, they are also more likely to be targets in advertising schemes and frauds. Educating these individuals toward greater self-assurance in recognizing and coping with complex and ambiguous judgments might well improve competence in coping with the requirements of daily living.

EDUCATIONAL IMPLICATIONS OF CHANGES IN THE LEARNER ACROSS THE LIFE SPAN

Life-span models and differences between young and old learners have several implications for a life-span approach to education. While educational specialists have given some attention to these issues at earlier points in the life span, comparison of learning functions across a greater portion of the life span brings them into sharper focus. In this section we will examine implications related to educational goals, instructional methodology, and the context for lifelong learning.

Expanding the Concept and Goals of Education

A life-span approach suggests that ontogenetic-individual development must be studied in the context of sociocultural change. Interactions between the individual and the environment are involved in defining both normative patterns of development and individual variability. Traditionally, education has tended to define goals in terms of either normative or differential views of individual development. Emphasis on normative patterns of development has led education to focus on developmental tasks in defining educational goals. In contrast, emphasis on individual differences has resulted in a concern for differentiation and individualization of educational objectives. Such an orientation is reflected in the current concern for cultural pluralism.

A life-span perspective would consider both normative and differential developmental patterns in the context of social change, and thus it would suggest three sources of educational goals. These are normative developmental patterns, individual variability, and sociocultural change influences (Baltes & Danish, in press). Educational goals focusing on normative developmental patterns have been particularly critical in early stages of the life span. A traditional area of education has focused on socialization of the child for adult roles and thus has emphasized normative developmental tasks and universal academic skills. In a life-span approach to education, individualization of educational goal setting becomes increasingly important with the wider range of individual differences in development during the adult life period. Educational goals during adulthood may vary both qualitatively and in the timing of achievement.

Moreover, recognition of social change in educational goal setting emphasizes the dynamic nature of the educational process. Educational goals and methodology must be sensitive and adaptive to social change. However, this suggests not only that education must be responsive to social change but also that education can be involved in directing the nature of this change. It is evident that education can remediate for obsolescence due to social change and can also provide individuals with generic skills for coping, adapting, and optimizing their development in relation to future change.

Instructional Methodology

The Increasing Importance of Noncognitive Factors in Learning. The concept that intelligent behavior may be a function of cognitive abilities plus performance-related, noncognitive factors has been discussed in the child development literature in relation to the performance-competence distinction (Flavell & Wohlwill, 1969). The influence of the child's limited linguistic capacity in assessing intellectual development through verbal means, and the necessity of screening for sensory deficits before evaluating intellectual competence in the exceptional child, are illustrations of such noncognitive factors.

A careful examination of the learning differences discussed in the preceding section suggests that noncognitive factors (e.g., sensory deficits, motivation, response speed) play an even more important role in learning performance in adulthood. A current research thrust in adult psychology is to ferret out the learning changes in later adulthood that are due to cognitive and to noncognitive factors (Woodruff & Walsh, 1975).

Instructional Pacing. Some cross-age learning differences have been related to the increasing time required for the aging adult to acquire and retrieve new information from memory (Craik, 1977). Providing a longer acquisition and response period has been shown to improve the adult's learning performance. Furthermore, the amount of material and the number of task demands presented at a given point in instruction have been shown to influence learning in later adulthood (Craik, 1968, 1977). Such findings suggest the utility of a self-pacing approach, with the number of task demands and the amount of information presented being carefully regulated. Initial research by Siemen (1974) suggests that a programmed instructional approach can be effective with the older adult. In addition, the mastery learning approach developed by Bloom (1968), as well as the competency-based method in general (Torshen, 1977), provides accommodation for variations in learning pace.

Motivation to Learn. Prior to adulthood, motivation to learn seems to have a strong extrinsic component, since education of the young is compulsory. Continued learning in adulthood, however, is primarily self-initiated. The intrinsic nature of motivation in the adult learner poses an enormous challenge to education. Dubin (1977) sees motivation as the key factor in updating the obsolete worker. House (1961) suggests three motivational orientations in the adult learner: goals, social activities, and learning. While the goal-oriented learner usually is pursuing vocational or professional goals, the activity-oriented learner seeks social contact and interaction. In relation to the academic system the goal-oriented learner may well enter a certification or credentialing academic program, while for the activity-oriented learner a nondegree program would probably be more appropriate.

Increasing Individual Differences in Learning. Individual variability in almost every type of intellectual capacity increases across the life span. The greater range of individual differences in adulthood should be of primary concern to the educator. Extreme individual differences in an intervention population (e.g., exceptional child, disadvantaged child) have usually required an individualized instructional approach. Such an individualized orientation would seem imperative in adult instruction. Variability in noncognitive factors related to learning and in motivation, as well as in cognitive ability, must be considered in designing instructional approaches for the adult learner.

The increasing importance of individual variability in adulthood should provide a fertile area for educational trait-treatment interaction/research (Berliner & Cahen, 1973). The type of studies investigating the relationship between learner aptitudes and instructional approaches initiated by DiVesta, Sanders, Schultz, and Weener (1971), Kropp, Nelson, and King (1967), and Cronbach and Snow (1977) are particularly relevant in mapping out appropriate instructional strategies for the adult learner.

The Changing Nature of the Instructor-Learner Relationship. As indicated previously, the role of the teacher across the life span appears to change from director of learning to that of a facilitator or resource person (Houle, 1974; Huberman, 1974). Whereas society and the educator direct the education of the young, the content and method of learning in adulthood are largely determined by the learner. Developmental changes in the learner across the life span suggest the need for qualitatively different types of teacher training for educators working with different age groups. The techniques of the high school or even college instructor may be inappropriate in teaching middle-aged or older persons. Teacher training institutions must be involved in translating the information concerning adult learning into a delineation of skills required of the adult educator.

Much has been said about changing characteristics as the learner ages, but we should not forget that career teachers age as well. Thus principles applying to the adult learner may equally apply to the teacher's own continued updating and learning endeavors.

Extending the Educational Context

As the role of education broadens conceptually and lengthens temporally, the context for education must also expand. With lifelong learning only a small portion of the individual's education would actually be acquired within a classroom. Except for the years of formal schooling, most of the individual's education is experiential and active, rather than receptive, and occurs in the context of daily living. Thus the home, workplace, and public facilities are all contexts for education. Education can extend geographically across the individual's total life space as well as temporally across the life span.

In summary, a lifelong approach to learning broadens the concept of education beyond the traditional youth-oriented preparation for adulthood. Education serves preventive, facilitative, and remedial, as well as preparatory, functions. The focus of educational intervention extends beyond the acquisition of academic and vocational skills to enabling the individual to master developmental tasks associated with each period in the life-span. Early education assumes preventive as well as preparatory functions as the intervenor's understanding of the relationship between developmental periods across the life span increases. Rapid technological changes suggest that learning in adulthood serves both facilitative-adaptive and remedial roles. Thus, a lifelong view of education suggests a reallocation of educational opportunity across the life span to accommodate to the changing learning needs and capacity of the individual. The individual continues to change across the life span due to ontogenetic and sociocultural factors. A life-span approach to education focuses on such individual and societal change. Lifelong learning seeks to optimize the nature and direction of these development changes.

REFERENCES

Ahammer, I. H., & Baltes, P. B. Objective versus perceived age differences in personality: How do adolescents, adults, and older people view themselves and each other? *Journal of Gerontology*, 1972, *27*, 46-51.

Arenberg, D. Input modality in short-term retention of old and young adults. *Journal of Gerontology*, 1968, *23*, 462-465.

Arenberg, D. The effects of input condition on free recall in young and old adults. *Journal of Gerontology*, 1976, *31*, 551-555.

Arenberg, D., & Robertson, E. A. Learning. In J. E. Birren & K. W. Schaie (Eds.), *Handbook of the psychology of aging*, pp. 421-449. New York: Van Nostrand Reinhold, 1977.

Atkinson, J. W. *An introduction to motivation*. New York: American Book, 1964.

Baltes, P. B. Longitudinal and cross-sectional sequences in the study of age and generation effects. *Human Development*, 1968, *11*, 145-171.

Baltes, P. B., & Danish, S. J. Intervention in life-span development and aging: Issues and concepts. In R. R. Turner & H. W. Reese (Eds.), *Life-span developmental psychology: Intervention*. New York: Academic Press, in press.

Baltes, P. B., Reese, H. W., & Nesselroade, J. R. *Life span developmental psychology: An introduction to research methods*. Monterey, Calif.: Brooks/Cole, 1977.

Baltes, P. B., & Schaie, K. W. On life-span developmental research paradigms: Retrospects and prospects. In P. B. Baltes & K. W. Schaie (Eds.), *Life-span developmental psychology: Personality and socialization*, pp. 366-395. New York: Academic Press, 1973.

Baltes, P. B., & Schaie, K. W. On the plasticity of intelligence in adulthood and old age. *American Psychologist*, 1976, *31*, 720-725.

Baltes, P. B., & Willis, S. L. Toward psychological theories of aging and development. In J. E. Birren & K. W. Schaie (Eds.), *Handbook of the psychology of aging*, pp. 128-154. New York: Van Nostrand Reinhold, 1977.

Bengtson, J. Trends and problems in the development of recurrent education in Sweden. *International Review of Education*, 1974, *20*, 508-513.

Berliner, D., & Cahen, L. Trait-treatment interaction and learning. In F. N. Kerlinger (Ed.), *Review of Research in Education, 1*, pp. 58-94. Itasca, Ill.: F. E. Peacock Publishers, Inc., 1973.

Birkhill, W. R., & Schaie, K. W. The effect of differential reinforcement of cautiousness in intellectual performance among the elderly. *Journal of Gerontology*, 1975, *30*, 578-583.

Birren, J. E. Age changes in speed of behavior: Its central nature and physiological correlates. In A. T. Welford & J. E. Birren (Eds.), *Behavior, aging and the nervous system*, pp. 191-216. Springfield, Ill.: Charles C Thomas, 1965.

Birren, J. E., & Renner, V. J. Research on the psychology of aging: Principles and experimentation. In J. E. Birren & K. W. Schaie (Eds.), *Handbook of the psychology of aging*, pp. 3-38. New York: Van Nostrand Reinhold, 1977.

Birren, J. E., & Woodruff, D. Human development over the life span through education. In P. B. Baltes & K. W. Schaie (Eds.), *Life span developmental psychology: Personality and socialization*, pp. 305-337. New York: Academic Press, 1973.

Bloom, B. S. (Ed.). *Taxonomy of educational objectives, Handbook I: Cognitive domain.* New York: Mackay, 1956.

Bloom, B. S. *Learning for mastery: Evaluating comment.* Los Angeles: Center for the Study of Evaluation of Instructional Programs, University of California, May 1968.

Botwinick, J. Cautiousness in advanced age. *Journal of Gerontology*, 1966, *21*, 347-353.

Botwinick, J. Disinclination to venture response versus cautiousness in responding: Age differences. *Journal of Genetic Psychology*, 1969, *115*, 55-62.

Botwinick, J. *Aging and behavior: A comprehensive integration of research findings.* New York: Springer, 1973.

Botwinick, J. Intellectual abilities. In J. E. Birren & K. W. Schaie (Eds.), *Handbook of the psychology of aging*, pp. 580-605. New York: Van Nostrand Reinhold, 1977.

Brown, M. A. *The relationship of the quality of collegiate education to the continuing education of college alumni.* Unpublished doctoral dissertation, University of Chicago, 1960.

Burns, R. W. (Ed.). *Sociological backgrounds of adult education.* Syracuse, N.Y.: CSLEA, 1970.

Calearo, C., & Lazzaroni, A. Speech intelligibility in relationship to the speed of the message. *Laryngoscope*, 1957, *67*, 410-419.

Carnegie Commission on Higher Education. *Less time, more options: Education beyond the high school.* New York: McGraw-Hill, 1971.

Carnegie Commission on Higher Education. *Toward a learning society: Alternative channels to life, work, and service.* New York: McGraw-Hill, 1973.

Cattell, R. B. Theory of fluid and crystallized intelligence: A critical experiment. *Journal of Educational Psychology*, 1963, *54*, 1-22.

Coleman, J. S. How do the young become adults? *Review of Educational Research*, 1972, *42*, 431-439.

Connolly, K. J., & Bruner, J. S. *The growth of competence.* New York: Academic Press, 1974.

Corso, J. F. Sensory processes and age effects in normal adults. *Journal of Gerontology*, 1971, *26*, 90-105.

Corso, J. F. Auditory perception and communication. In J. E. Birren & K. W. Schaie (Eds.), *Handbook of the psychology of aging*, pp. 535–553. New York: Van Nostrand Reinhold, 1977.

Craik, F. I. M. Short-term memory and the aging process. In G. A. Talland (Ed.), *Human aging and behavior*, pp. 131-168. New York: Academic Press, 1968.

Craik, F. I. M. Age differences in human memory. In J. E. Birren & K. W. Schaie (Eds.), *Handbook of the psychology of aging*, pp. 384-420. New York: Van Nostrand Reinhold, 1977.

Cronbach, L. J., & Snow, R. E. *Aptitudes and instructional methods.* New York: Irvington Publishers, 1977.

Cropley, A. J. Some psychological reflections on lifelong education. In R. H. Dave (Ed.), *Foundations of lifelong education*, pp. 186-234. Oxford: Pergamon Press, 1976.

Dave, R. H. *Lifelong education and school curriculum.* Hamburg: UNESCO Institute for Education, 1973.

Dave, R. H. (Ed.). *Foundations of lifelong education.* Oxford: Pergamon Press, 1976.

Dave, R., & Lengrand, P. Lifelong education and learning. *International Review of Education*, 1974, *20*, 425-537.

DiVesta, F., Sanders, N., Schultz, C., & Weener, P. Instructional strategies: Multivariable studies of psychological processes related to instruction. (Semiannual Rep., Advanced Research Projects Agency No. 1269, ONR Contract No. N00014-67-A-0385-0006). University Park: Department of Educational Psychology, Pennsylvania State University, 1971.

Dubin, S. Obsolescence or lifelong education: A choice for the professional. *American Psychologist,* 1972, *17,* 486-498.

Dubin, S. *A learning model for updating older technical and professional persons.* Paper presented at the meeting of the American Psychological Association, San Francisco, August 1977.

Evans, E. *Contemporary influences in early childhood education* (2nd ed.). New York: Holt, Rinehart, & Winston, 1977.

Flavell, J. H. *The developmental psychology of Jean Piaget.* New York: Van Nostrand Reinhold, 1963.

Flavell, J. H. Cognitive changes in adulthood: In L. R. Goulet and P. B. Baltes (Eds.), *Life-span developmental psychology: Research and theory,* pp. 248-253. New York: Academic Press, 1970.

Flavell, J., & Wohlwill, J. Formal and functional aspects of cognitive development. In D. Elkind & J. Flavell (Eds.), *Studies in cognitive development: Essays in honor of Jean Piaget,* pp. 67-120. New York: Oxford Press, 1969.

Fozard, J. L., Wolf, E., Bell, B., & Podolsky, S. Visual perception and communication. In J. E. Birren & K. W. Schaie (Eds.), *Handbook of the psychology of aging,* pp. 497-534. New York: Van Nostrand Reinhold, 1977.

Friedrich, D. K., & Van Horn, K. R. *Developmental methodology: A revised primer.* Minneapolis, Minn.: Burgess, 1976.

George, J. S., & Dubin, S. S. *Continuing education needs of natural resource managers and scientists.* University Park: Department of Planning Studies, Continuing Education, Pennsylvania State University, 1972.

Gordon, C. Role and value development across the life cycle. In J.W. Jackson (Ed.), *Role: Sociological studies IV.* London: Cambridge University Press, 1971.

Goulet, L. R. Longitudinal and time-lag designs in educational research: An alternate sampling model. *Review of Educational Research,* 1975, *45,* 505-523.

Granick, S., Kleban, M. H., & Weiss, A. D. Relationships between hearing loss and cognition in normally hearing aged persons. *Journal of Gerontology,* 1976, *31,* 434-440.

Green, R. F. Age-intelligence relationship between ages sixteen and sixty-four: A rising trend. *Developmental Psychology,* 1969, *1,* 618-627.

Havighurst, R. J. *Developmental tasks and education* (3rd ed.). New York: David McKay, 1972.

Havighurst, R. J. Education through the adult life span. *Educational Gerontology,* 1976, *1,* 41-51.

Hickey, T., Hickey, L., & Kalish, R. Children's perceptions of the elderly. *Journal of Genetic Psychology,* 1968, *112,* 227-235.

Hiemstra, R. Older adult learning. *Educational Gerontology,* 1976, *1,* 277-236.

Holland, J. L. *Making vocational choices: A theory of careers.* Englewood Cliffs, N.J.: Prentice-Hall, 1973.

Horn, J. L., & Donaldson, G. On the myth of intellectual decline in adulthood. *American Psychologist,* 1976, *31,* 701-719.

Hornblum, J. N., & Overton, W. F. Area and volume conservation among the elderly: Assessment and training. *Developmental Psychology,* 1976, *12,* 68-74.

Houle, C. O. *The inquiring mind.* Milwaukee: University of Wisconsin Press, 1961.

Houle, C. O. The changing goals of education in the perspective of lifelong learning. *International Review of Education,* 1974, *20,* 430-445.

Hoyer, W. J., Labouvie, G. V., & Baltes, P. B. Modification of response speed deficits and intellectual performance in the elderly. *Human Development,* 1973, *16,* 233-242.

Huberman, M. Looking at adult education from the perspective of the adult life cycle. *International Review of Education,* 1974, *20,* 117-137.

Hulicka, I. M. Age differences in retention as a function of interference. *Journal of Gerontology*, 1967, *22*, 180-184.

Hultsch, D. F. Learning to learn in adulthood. *Journal of Gerontology*, 1974, *29*, 302-308.

Hultsch, D. F. Adult age differences in retrieval: Trace-dependent and cue-dependent forgetting. *Developmental Psychology*, 1975, *11*, 197-201.

Johnstone, J., & Rivera, R. *Volunteers for learning*. Chicago: Aldine, 1965.

Kagan, J., & Moss, H. A. *Birth to maturity: A study in psychological development*. New York: John Wiley, 1962.

Kamin, L. J. *The science and politics of IQ*. Potomac, Md.: Lawrence Erlbaum, 1974.

Kelleher, C. Second careers—a growing trend. *Industrial Gerontology*, 1973, *17*, 1-8.

Kinsbourne, M. Age effects on letter span related to rate and sequential dependency. *Journal of Gerontology*, 1973, *28*, 317-319.

Kirchner, E. P. *An assessment inventory for the day care child* (Vol. 2). University Park: Center for Human Services Development, Institute for the Study of Human Development, Pennsylvania State University, 1973.

Klein, R. L. Age differences in social conformity on a task of auditory signal detection. *Proceedings of the 80th Annual Convention of the American Psychological Association*, 1972, *7*, 661-662. (a)

Klein, R. L. Age, sex, and task difficulty as predictors of social conformity. *Journal of Gerontology*, 1972, *27*, 229-236. (b)

Knox, A. B. *Adult development and learning*. San Francisco: Jossey-Bass, 1977.

Kohlberg, L. Continuities in childhood and adult moral development revisited. In P. B. Baltes & K. W. Schaie (Eds.), *Life-span developmental psychology: Personality and socialization*, pp. 179-204. New York: Academic Press, 1973.

Kohlberg, L., & Mayer, R. Development as the aim of education. *Harvard Educational Review*, 1972, *42*, 449-497.

Konig, E. Pitch discrimination and age. *Acta Otolaryngologica*, 1957, *48*, 475-489.

Krauss, I. K., & Schaie, K. W. *Errors in spatial rotation in the elderly*. Paper presented at the meeting of the American Psychological Association, Washington, D.C., 1976.

Kropp, R. P., Nelson, W. H., & King, F. J. Identification and definition of subject matter content variables related to human aptitudes. (Contract No. OE-5-10-297). Tallahassee: Florida State University, 1967.

Labouvie-Vief, G. Toward optimizing cognitive competence. *Educational Gerontology*, 1976, *1*, 75-92.

Labouvie-Vief, G., & Gonda, J. N. Cognitive strategy training and intellectual performances in the elderly. *Journal of Gerontology*, 1976, *31*, 327-332.

Lay, M. Preschool and elementary school. In A. N. Charters (Ed.), *Toward the educative society* (Publications in Continuing Education). Syracuse. N.Y.: Syracuse University, 1971.

Lebo, C. P., & Reddell, R. C. The presbycusis component in occupational hearing loss. *Laryngoscope*, 1972, *82*, 1399-1409.

Long, H. Lifelong learning: Pressures for acceptance. *Journal of Research and Development in Education*, 1974, *7*, 2-12.

Lowenthal, M. F., Thurnher, M., & Chiriboga, D. *Four stages of life*. San Francisco: Jossey-Bass, 1975.

Matarazzo, J. D. *Wechsler's measurement and appraisal of adult intelligence* (5th ed.). Baltimore, Md.: Williams & Wilkins, 1972.

Mathey, F. J. Psychomotor performance and reaction speed in old age. In H. Thomae (Ed.), *Patterns of aging*, pp. 36-50. Basel, Switzerland: S. Karger, 1976.

Moray, N. *Attention: Selective processes in vision and hearing*. New York: Academic Press, 1970.

Moses, S. *The learning force: A more comprehensive framework for educational policy*

(Publications in Continuing Education, Occasional Paper No. 25). Syracuse, N.Y.: Syracuse University, 1971.

Nardi, A. H. Person-perception research and the perception of life-span development. In P. B. Baltes & K. W. Schaie (Eds.), *Life-span developmental psychology: Personality and socialization*, pp. 285-301. New York: Academic Press, 1973.

Neugarten, B. L. The future and the young-old. *Gerontologist*, 1975, *15*, 4-9.

Neugarten, B. L., & Datan, N. Sociological perspectives on the life cycle. In P. B. Baltes & K. W. Schaie (Eds.), *Life-span developmental psychology: Personality and socialization,* pp. 53-69. New York: Academic Press, 1973.

Neugarten, B. L., Moore, J. W., & Lowe, J. C. Age norms, age constraints, and adult socialization. *American Journal of Sociology*, 1965, *70*, 710-717.

Okun, M. A., & DiVesta, F. J. Cautiousness in adulthood as a function of age and instructions. *Journal of Gerontology*, 1976, *31*, 571-576.

Parelius, A. Lifelong education and age stratification. *American Behavioral Scientist*, 1975, *19*, 206-223.

Parham, I. A., & Schaie, K. W. *Dual coding in memory: Effects of age, sex and intelligence.* Paper presented at the 29th annual meeting of the Gerontological Society, New York, 1976.

Pastalan, L. A., Mautz, R. K., & Merrill, J. The stimulation of age-related sensory losses: A new approach to the study of environmental barriers. In W. F. E. Preiser (Ed.), *Environmental design research,* Vol. 1, pp. 383-391. Stroudsburg, Pa.: Dowden, Hutchinson & Ross, 1973.

Payne, S., Summers, D. A., & Stewart, T. R. Value differences across three generations. *Sociometry*, 1973, *36*, 20-30.

Penney, C. G. Modality effects in short-term verbal memory. *Psychological Bulletin*, 1975, *82*, 68-84.

Peterson, D. Lifespan education and gerontology. *Gerontologist*, 1975, *15*, 436-441.

Piaget, J. Intellectual evolution from adolescence to adulthood. *Human Development*, 1972, *15*, 1-12.

Plemons, J. K., Willis, S. L., & Baltes, P. B. Modifiability of fluid intelligence in aging: A short-term longitudinal training approach. *Journal of Gerontology*, 1978, *33*, 224-231.

Rabbitt, P. An age-decrement in the ability to ignore irrelevant information. *Journal of Gerontology*, 1965, *20*, 233-238.

Reinert, G. Comparative factor analytic studies of intelligence throughout the human life-span. In L. R. Goulet & P. B. Baltes (Eds.), *Life-span developmental psychology: Research and theory,* pp. 468-484. New York: Academic Press, 1970.

Riegel, K. F. *Psychology of development and history.* New York: Plenum, 1976.

Rosenow, E. C., Jr. *Medical knowledge of self-assessment programs.* Paper presented at the 173rd annual meeting of the Medical and Chirurgical Faculty of the State of Maryland, Baltimore, April 14, 1971.

Rudinger, G. Correlates of changes in cognitive functioning. In H. Thomae (Ed.), *Patterns of aging,* pp. 20-35. Basel, Switzerland: S. Karger, 1976.

Schaie, K. W. A general model for the study of developmental problems. *Psychological Bulletin*, 1965, *64*, 92-107.

Schaie, K. W. Age changes and age differences. *Gerontologist*, 1967, *7*, 128-132.

Schaie, K. W. A reinterpretation of age-related changes in cognitive structure and functioning. In L. R. Goulet & P. B. Baltes (Eds.), *Life-span developmental psychology: Research and theory,* pp. 485-507. New York: Academic Press, 1970.

Schaie, K. W. Intervention toward an ageless society? *Gerontologist*, 1973, *13*, 31-38. (a)

Schaie, K. W. Methodological problems in descriptive developmental research on adulthood and aging. In J. R. Nesselroade & H. W. Reese (Eds.), *Life-span developmental psychology: Methodological issues,* pp. 253-280. New York: Academic Press, 1973 (b).

Schaie, K. W. Translation in gerontology—From lab to life: Intellectual functioning. *American Psychologist,* 1974, *29,* 802-807.

Schaie, K. W. Quasi-experimental designs in the psychology of aging. In J. E. Birren & K. W. Schaie (Eds.), *Handbook of the psychology of aging,* pp. 39-58. New York: Van Nostrand Reinhold, 1977.

Schaie, K. W. Toward a stage theory of adult cognitive development. *Journal of Aging and Human Development,* 1977/78, *8,* 129-138.

Schaie, K. W. External validity in the assessment of intellectual development in adulthood. *Journal of Gerontology,* 1978, *33,* 695-701.

Schaie, K. W. The primary mental abilities in adulthood: An exploration of psychometric intelligence. In P. B. Baltes & O. G. Brim, Jr. (Eds.), *Life-span development and behavior* (Vol. 2). New York: Academic Press, in press.

Schaie, K. W., Baltes, P. B., & Strother, C. R. A study of auditory sensitivity in advanced age. *Journal of Gerontology,* 1964, *19,* 453-457.

Schaie, K. W., & Gribbin, K. Adult development and aging. *Annual Review of Psychology,* 1975, *26,* 65-96 (a).

Schaie, K. W., & Gribbin, K. *The impact of environmental complexity upon adult cognitive development.* Paper presented at the biennial meeting of the International Society for the Study of Behavioral Development, Guildford, England, 1975 (b).

Schaie, K. W., Labouvie, G. V., & Buech, B. U. Generational and cohort-specific differences in adult cognitive functioning: A fourteen-year study of independent samples. *Developmental Psychology,* 1973, *9,* 151-166.

Schaie, K. W., & Labouvie-Vief, G. Generational versus ontogenetic components of change in adult cognitive behavior: A fourteen-year cross-sequential study. *Developmental Psychology,* 1974, *10,* 305-320.

Schaie, K. W., & Marquette, B. W. *Stages in transition: A biosocial analysis of adult behavior.* Paper presented at the International Society for the Study of Behavioral Development, Satellite Symposium, Kiryat Anavim, Israel, 1975.

Schaie, K. W., & Parham, I. A. Social responsibility in adulthood: Ontogenetic and sociocultural change. *Journal of Personality and Social Psychology,* 1974, *30,* 483-492.

Schaie, K. W., & Parham, I. A. Stability of adult personality traits: Fact or fable? *Journal of Personality and Social Psychology,* 1976, *34,* 146-158.

Schaie, K. W., & Parham, I. A. Cohort-sequential analyses of adult intellectual development. *Developmental Psychology,* 1977, *13,* 649-653.

Schaie, K. W., & Quayhagen, M. [Life-span educational psychology: Adulthood and old age.] In J. Brandstaetter, G. Reinert, & K. A. Schneewind (Eds.), *Probleme und Perektivlen der Paedagogischen Psychologie.* Stuttgart: Klett, 1978.

Schaie, K. W., & Schaie, J. P. Clinical assessment and aging. In J. E. Birren & K. W. Schaie (Eds.), *Handbook of the psychology of aging,* pp. 692-723. New York: Van Nostrand Reinhold, 1977. (a)

Schaie, K. W., & Schaie, J. P. *Concepts and criteria for functional age.* Paper presented at the conference titled "Aging: A challenge for science and social policy," Institut de la Vie, Vichy, France, 1977. (b)

Schaie, K. W., & Strother, C. R. The cross-sequential study of age changes in cognitive behavior. *Psychological Bulletin,* 1968, *70,* 671-680.

Scheidt, R. J., & Schaie, K. W. A taxonomy of situations for the elderly: Generating situational criterias. *Journal of Gerontology,* in press.

Seefeldt, C., Jantz, R., Galper, A., & Serock, K. Children's attitudes toward the elderly: Educational implications. *Educational Gerontology*, 1977, *2*, 301-310.

Shaffer, J. Reinforcement in lifelong socialization and learning. *International Review of Education*, 1974, *20*, 497-501.

Sheppard, H. L. *New perspectives on older workers*. Washington, D.C.: W. E. Upjohn Institute for Employment Research, 1971.

Siegler, I. C. The terminal drop hypothesis: Fact or artifact? *Experimental Aging Research*, 1975, *1*, 169-185.

Siemen, J. R. *Learning from programmed material as a function of age*. Paper presented at the 27th annual meeting of the Gerontological Society, Portland, Ore., 1974.

Talland, G. A. Visual signal detection as a function of age, input rate and signal frequency. *Journal of Psychology*, 1966, *63*, 105-115.

Thomae, H. Background and aims of the Bonn longitudinal study of aging. In H. Thomae (Ed.), *Patterns of aging,* pp. 1-11. Basel, Switzerland: S. Karger, 1976.

Toffler, A. *Future shock*. New York: Random House, 1970.

Tomlinson-Keasey, C. Formal operations in females from eleven to fifty-four years of age. *Developmental Psychology*, 1972, *6*, 364.

Torshen, K. P. *The mastery approach to competency-based education*. New York: Academic Press, 1977.

Troll, L. E. *Early and middle adulthood*. Monterey, Calif.: Brooks/Cole, 1975.

Tulving, E., & Pearlstone, A. Availability versus accessibility of information in memory for words. *Journal of Verbal Learning and Verbal Behavior*, 1966, *5*, 381-391.

Turvey, M. T. On peripheral and central processes in vision: Inferences from an information-processing analysis of masking with patterned stimuli. *Psychological Review*, 1973, *80*, 1-52.

Wallach, M. A., & Kogan, N. Aspects of judgment and decision making: Interrelationships and changes with age. *Behavioral Science*, 1961, *6*, 23-36.

Walsh, D. A. Age differences in central perceptual processing: A dichoptic backward masking investigation. *Journal of Gerontology*, 1976, *31*, 178-185.

Walsh, D. A., Till, R. E., & Williams, M. V. Age and differences in peripheral perceptual processing: A monoptic backward masking investigation. *Journal of Experimental Psychology: Human Perception and Performance*, 1978, *4*, 232-243.

Weale, R. A. On the eye. In A. T. Welford & J. E. Birren (Eds.), *Behavior aging and the nervous system,* pp. 307-325. Springfield, Ill.: Charles C Thomas, 1965.

Werner, H. The concept of development from a comparative and organismic point of view. In D. B. Harris (Ed.), *The concept of development,* pp. 125-148. Minneapolis: University of Minnesota Press, 1957.

Wohlwill, J. F. *The study of behavioral development*. New York: Academic Press, 1973.

Woodruff, D., & Walsh, D. A. Research in adult learning: The individual. *Gerontologist*, 1975, *15*, 424-430.

Wroczynski, R. Learning styles and lifelong education. *International Review of Education*, 1974, *20*, 464-473.

II

RESEARCH ON
TEACHING AND INSTRUCTION

4

A Philosophical Consideration of Recent Research on Teacher Effectiveness

GARY D. FENSTERMACHER
Virginia Polytechnic Institute and State University

Like most of us, educational researchers may find that criticism of their work comes in three varieties. Criticism of the first kind is useless because it is uninformed or unintelligible. Criticism of the second kind is useful because it is pertinent to the research effort and directed to reparable defects. Criticism of the third kind, though apparently significant, cannot be heeded because the remedy is unknown or because its implications are that the shop must be closed and a new calling found. Except for some contributions in philosophy of science, educational researchers of my acquaintance place most philosophical criticism of their work in the first and third categories. Wolman (1971), for example, thought the deficiencies of philosophical criticism were serious enough to warrant an attempt by psychologists to build their own philosophy of science, rather than having to depend on the often misguided and destructive critiques of philosophers. Lazersfeld (1962) concluded that many philosopher-critics have no idea of the workaday world of the empirical researcher, and as one consequence the social scientist may "have to muddle along without benefit of the explicating clergy" (p. 470).

The educational researcher's preference, understandably, is for criticism of the second kind. This kind of criticism can be met and resolved without radical transformation or destruction of the ongoing research enterprise. Criticisms of research design characteristics or data analysis techniques are more likely to be attended to than criticisms that expose deeply rooted assumptions or unantici-

BRUCE J. BIDDLE, University of Missouri, Columbia, and DENIS C. PHILLIPS, Stanford University, were the editorial consultants for this chapter.

Note: To the editorial consultants, and to David Berliner, Leigh Burstein, Fred Ellett, David Ericson, Nikki Filby, Marjorie Powell, Thomas Romberg, Barak Rosenshine, Betty Shumener, Richard Shavelson, and Kenneth Strike, my thanks and appreciation for their perceptive criticisms of the second kind on an earlier version of this chapter.

pated ethical implications. The researcher's preference for criticism of the second kind is strengthened by the sometimes irksome and ungracious manner in which philosophers couch criticism of the third kind. Louch (1966) prefaced an extended philosophical critique of social science methodology with the comment that "triviality, redundancy, and tautology are the epithets which I think can be properly applied to the behavioural scientist" (p. 9). Wilson (1972) concluded his philosophical reconstruction of educational research with the observation that *"most people (even researchers) will do anything rather than think*, and this is particularly obvious in educational research" (p. 129).

Despite the popularity among educational researchers of criticism of the second kind, this review of recent research on teacher effectiveness employs criticism of the third kind. My interest is in the conceptual and ethical features of this research. The perspective from which I shall raise philosophical considerations is that of philosophy of mind and social philosophy, not philosophy of science. This review suggests not ways of tinkering with what we already do, but ways of rethinking what is now done. I hope to show that criticism of the third kind can be heeded because there are remedies for conceptual and ethical problems, and these remedies lie within the province and power of the educational researcher. The arguments set forth do not require the abandonment of social and behavioral science research as we now know it, nor will the educational researcher who agrees with them be required to close up shop and find other work. I agree with Fodor (1965); if a philosopher's view of human behavior requires "that most of psychology will have to be abandoned without hope of replacement, that shows that something is wrong with the view, not that something is wrong with psychology" (p. 166). And I concur with Peters (1974) that a philosopher who questions the underpinnings of a researcher's work is obligated "to make clear what the implications of his analysis are for how psychologists should spend their time" (p. 53). Unfortunately, though I agree with Peters, my success in complying with his dictum will be limited. I lack the necessary sophistication in research design and methodology to offer complete specifications for the conception of teacher effectiveness research argued for in this chapter. However, I think the blueprint presented here is clear enough to at least test the conception through collaboration between educational researchers and philosophers of education.

The main line of argument in this review may be paraphrased as follows. Many educational researchers, when they seek assistance from philosophy, look to philosophy of science for guidance on such matters as the nature of evidence, the logic of explanation and proof, the conceptual features of causation and probability, and criteria for hypothesis formation and theory construction. Assistance of this type is often sought in order to improve what is already underway (assistance of the second kind?), rather than to transform the character of the enterprise itself. Though the value of philosophy of science to educational research may be great, it provides little assistance on how to think about the phenomenon of education. That is, philosophy of science may be a boon to the improvement of educational research, but it is not likely to add much at all to our understanding of what it means to do research in or on education.

Because of this limitation inherent in the nature of philosophy of science, philosophy of mind and social philosophy may prove productive areas of inquiry. It is in these two subfields that we may seek conceptions of education that are *productive of research that is valuable to education.* Here I am equivocating on the term *education,* and doing so intentionally. On the one hand, the term serves as a synonym for schooling; on the other hand, it refers to a conception of the process of becoming an educated person, in the grand and noble sense. Though there is nothing wrong with studying schooling in order to add to our knowledge of what it is and what goes on there, the results of this kind of research can be misused (sometimes disastrously) if they are simply turned back on the schools, with the expectation of improving what goes on there. This point is perhaps the most important one to be made in this chapter. Any respectably elaborated research design and methodology may be employed to study schooling, if the sole point of doing so is to test some hypotheses about schooling and maybe add a brick or two to the edifice of knowledge. But if the research is undertaken for the point and purpose of changing what goes on in schools, then the researcher incurs obligations of theoretical development that have heretofore received scant attention, except from a small segment of the educational research community.

It will be argued in this chapter that to change schooling in ways that are productive of well-educated persons, the researcher should possess a conception of schooling that accounts for the fact that the school situation is made up of persons who act intentionally within a complex social system. In addition to taking account of intentional behavior within a social system, the researcher should possess a theory of education, a theory of what it means to be an educated person and of the process of becoming one. Lacking a conception of intentional behavior within a social system, the educational researcher is not able to determine what fosters change in any direction. Lacking a theory of education, the educational researcher will not be able to detect and determine what is to count as a change in the preferred direction. Neither the philosophy of science (specifically that portion of it that is preoccupied with commentary on the natural sciences) nor criticism of the second kind is of much value in helping educational researchers meet the requirements of an adequate conception of the school situation, or a rationally justified and morally defensible theory of education. But an intentionalist account of human behavior based upon considerations from philosophy of mind, and a rule-role conception of social situations based upon considerations from social philosophy, combined with a well-grounded theory of education, may be employed as the basis for useful and constructive criticism of the third kind.

TEACHING TEACHERS TO BE EFFECTIVE

The argument begins where most teacher effectiveness research ends: with an examination of the implications for practice. At issue is the proposition that knowing what accounts for effective teaching constitutes knowledge of how to produce more effective teachers. Though not universally held, this proposition is implicit in many studies of teacher effectiveness. On occasion, the proposition appears quite explicitly:

We should not want to denigrate other realms of educational research, but it seems to us vital that funds be sharply increased for studies of teaching if we are to solve such problems as the selection and education of teachers for effective performance of their jobs, [and] the examination of the effects of innovations in educational practice, . . . (Gage, 1974, p. 5)

The Beginning Teacher Evaluation Study (BTES) illustrates the point. The BTES is a five-year, multimillion-dollar study sponsored by the California Commission for Teacher Preparation and Licensing, with funds from the National Institute of Education. The commission sought funding for the study in the belief that if its regulations for licensing teachers and its criteria for approving teacher preparation programs were based on findings from research on teacher effectiveness, then enforcement of these regulations and criteria would increase the number of more effective teachers. Though the investigators to whom the research was subcontracted cautioned the commission on overzealous application of correlational findings, no one denied the proposition that if we learn what makes teachers effective, then we know quite a bit about how to make teachers effective.

Before becoming enmeshed in the distinction between learning what makes teachers effective and teaching teachers to be effective, it may prove helpful to examine some of the current research on teacher effectiveness. Because much of this research has been extensively reviewed elsewhere (Berliner & Rosenshine, 1977; Cruickshank, 1976; Dunkin & Biddle, 1974; Gage, 1972; Joyce, 1975; Marliave, 1976; Medley, 1977; Rosenshine, 1970a, 1970b, 1971, 1976a, 1976b, 1977; Rosenshine & Berliner, 1978; Rosenshine & Furst, 1971, 1973), I will not belabor what is readily available in other publications. Our immediate point of departure is a category of teacher effectiveness study called process-product research. These studies have the same general design characteristics. Students in several classrooms are tested before and after instruction. Teachers are observed, and their behavior is recorded during the interval between the tests. Data from the tests are then analyzed in relation to the descriptions of teacher performance during the interval, as the researcher attempts to account for varying degrees of student gain from pretest to posttest by identifying significant relations between student gain (product) and teacher performance (process).

For example, Stallings (1975, 1976, 1977) observed 288 primary school classrooms in six Project Follow Through models. To describe teacher behaviors, she used the Classroom Observation Instrument developed by the Stanford Research Institute. To assess student outcomes, she used the Metropolitan Achievement Tests, Raven's Coloured Progressive Matrices (a nonverbal problem-solving test), and the Intellectual Responsibility Scale. Between each of these tests and the classroom processes coded on the observation instrument, 340 correlations were possible; just over 100 were found to be significant at the .05 level for each of the three outcome measures. Among her findings were that "time spent in reading and math activities and a high rate of drill, practice, and praise contribute to higher reading and math scores" (1977, p. 113). A key conclusion of her studies was that "what occurs in the classroom does contribute to achievement in basic skills, good attendance, and desired child behaviors" (1977, p. 113).

Brophy and Evertson (1974, 1977) used an observation instrument based upon the Brophy-Good Dyadic Interaction System to record selected behaviors of approximately 40 experienced second- and third-grade teachers. Information was gathered on 371 variables, which were in turn related to student results on five subtests of the Metropolitan Achievement Tests. They found that effective teaching behaviors were different in high–socioeconomic status (SES) schools from those in low–SES schools, that maintaining the active engagement of students in appropriate learning tasks was positively related to achievement gains, and that teacher behaviors frequently recommended in teaching methods texts tended to show a low or zero correlation with learning gains.

In their several studies of teacher effectiveness, Soar and Soar (1976) and Soar (1977) used different observation instruments, among them the Teacher Practices Observation Record, the South Carolina Observation Record, and Flanders Interaction Analysis. They examined data from these instruments in relation to student outcomes measured by subtests of the Iowa Tests of Basic Skills. Integrating the findings from four such studies, Soar (1977) hypothesized an "inverted U" phenomenon: "measures of teacher behavior which represent direction and control of pupil learning tasks show greatest pupil gain at intermediate levels; with the extremes of either high or low control being associated with smaller amounts of gain" (p. 98). The evidence also suggested a "differentiated U" phenomenon wherein learning of low-level cognitive objectives proceeds best "under relatively tightly structured, closely focused learning conditions," while more complex cognitive learning is enhanced "in settings in which pupils have more freedom to explore and interact with subject matter" (p. 99). The inverted and differentiated U phenomena suggest to Soar that a more careful distinction should be drawn between teacher control of student behavior and teacher control of student thought processes. Contending that it is commonly supposed that in order to free students' thought processes for complex cognitive tasks, teachers must also relinquish control of their behavior, Soar states that the data indicate that close teacher control of student behavior does not necessarily interfere with complex cognitive or creative growth. In humorous but hopefully helpful paraphrase: the body need not wander in order for the mind to wonder.

Perhaps the most extensive (in duration and dollars) process-product study of teacher effectiveness is the Beginning Teacher Evaluation Study (BTES). Although planned in four phases, only Phases II and III are research studies. Phase II was completed in 1975 by the Educational Testing Service, under the direction of McDonald and Elias (1975–1976). Phase III, under the direction of Berliner and Fisher, is scheduled for completion by the Far West Laboratory in June 1978. The purpose of Phase II was to generate hypotheses for later confirmation in Phase III and to develop measurement systems for the dependent and independent variables. Because the Commission for Teacher Preparation and Licensing (the study's sponsor) stipulated in advance its interest in the determinants of effective instruction in reading and mathematics, certain characteristics of the sample were predetermined. The Phase II sample consisted of 95 teachers and 2,500 second- and fifth-grade students in 43 schools. Outcome measures were obtained through an array of specially designed tests and subtests of the California Achievement Tests in reading and mathematics. Student achievement levels were assessed in the fall and again in the spring of the school year. Two different observation instruments were used, the APPLE system, or the Anecdotal Process for Promoting Learning Experience (Lambert & Hartsough, 1976), and the RAMOS system, or Reading and Mathematics Observation System (Calfee & Calfee, 1976). An indirect measure known as Work Diaries (Elias & Wheeler, 1976) was also used; participating teachers used the Work Diaries to describe their curricular and instructional activities. During the period between the fall and spring testing, each teacher was observed from three to eight times, and a total of nearly 400 observation days was accumulated. In the technical summary of the final report for Phase II, McDonald and Elias (1976) report that their results show that teacher performances do make a substantial contribution to what children learn. Though the best predictor of students' spring achievement scores is their fall scores, the second best predictor is what the teachers do in the classroom.

Phase III of the BTES was originally planned as a large-scale field study to test hypotheses generated in Phase II. However, problems in coordinating the two phases, and the nature of results emerging from the work of Stallings, Brophy and Evertson, and Soar, and of Harnischfeger and Wiley (1975, 1976; Wiley & Harnischfeger, 1974), led to the redesign of Phase III. This phase is now focused on the tripartite relationship between teacher behavior, student behavior, and student outcomes. A major concern of the Phase III research is with the amount of time *allocated* to academically appropriate learning tasks in relation to the amount of time students spend actively *engaged* in these tasks. The heuristic premise guiding Phase III research is that *"academic achievement is a function of student aptitude and the amount of academic learning time spent by the student''* (Far West Laboratory, undated, p. 14). The notion of academic learning time (ALT) was synthesized from the findings of previous research which, taken together, suggest that the variance in student achievement not accounted for by background characteristics and aptitude is explained by the relative amount of time students spend actively engaged in learning tasks appropriate to the instructional objectives (Marliave, Cahen, & Berliner, 1977). During the data gathering stage, classroom behavior patterns of students and teachers were observed with an instrument designed to tap the instructional and learning activities considered critical for a test of the ALT hypothesis (Marliave, Fisher, Filby, & Dishaw, 1977). Pupil outcomes were assessed in the usual pretest-posttest fashion, using specially developed achievement tests (Filby & Dishaw, 1977). In addition to the main study, a small-scale intervention study is included in Phase III (Berliner, Filby, Marliave, Weir, & Fisher, 1976; Berliner, Filby, Marliave, & Weir, in press). The purpose of the intervention study is to determine whether the researchers can increase the ALT of selected target students in 11 of the 48 classrooms in the Phase III sample. The intervention study is especially relevant to the thesis of this chapter, and more will be said about it shortly.

Enough of the recent process-product studies have been cited to show that it is the clear contention of this body of research that teacher performances can have direct, positive, and significant effects on student achievement. This finding is the result of posing this general question: What relationships obtain, if any, between teacher performances P_1, P_2, P_3, . . . P_n and success at learning tasks K_1, K_2, K_3, . . . K_n by students assigned to complete these tasks? This question is extremely inclusive; one needs to venture on a kind of fishing expedition to find answers to it. Indeed, given the high number of correlations reported in several of the studies just mentioned, it is obvious that some researchers either had little idea of what to look for at the outset or were reluctant to prejudge the potential relationships between process and product by arbitrarily restricting their data gathering categories, or both. Whatever the reason, many possible relationships were analyzed, and some were found to be significantly correlated. Having isolated specific, positive correlations, the process-product researcher is in a position to raise this question:

Q1   Do teacher performances P_1 and P_2 result in success at task K_1 by students assigned this task?

If P_1 is interpreted as organizing the class for independent seatwork, P_2 is interpreted as monitoring each student's progress on the assigned task, and K_1 is a subtraction without regrouping task, then the process-product research described above indicates that the answer to Q1 is affirmative. Stated more accurately, the students in a given classroom are more likely to master a subtraction without regrouping task (K_1) if the teacher organizes the class for independent seatwork (P_1) and closely monitors each student during that seatwork (P_2). These particular teaching performances are among those that make up a model of teaching called *direct instruction*, a model formulated on the basis of results from many recent studies of teacher effectiveness (see Rosenshine, 1976a; Berliner & Rosenshine, 1978). From an affirmative answer to Q1 it may seem permissible to infer that a teacher who employs P_1 and P_2 will be more effective in obtaining student success at K_1 than a teacher who does not employ these practices. However, sound methodological principles bar this inference until a second question is answered:

Q2 Why do P_1 and P_2 result in student success at K_1?

If one tries to answer Q2 by stating that P_1 and P_2 result in success at K_1 because these two Ps have been shown to be significantly correlated with this K, many eyebrows will be raised. Presumably we all know that a significant correlation between $P_1 - P_2$ and K_1 will not alone support the conclusion that a teacher's use of P_1 and P_2 is the cause of the students' success at K_1. But there is a noticeable tendency to view significant correlations as placeholders for causal relationships:

> As is well known, a causal inference cannot be made directly from a significant correlation between two variables. The complementary principle is, however, frequently ignored, namely, that when a significant correlation is found a causal relation exists somewhere—perhaps between the two variables or between the two variables and a third, or any of a number of possibilities. Although these logical possibilities can be thought of, the design of a study allows us to eliminate some of them as implausible, and to infer that others are more plausible. (McDonald & Elias, 1976, p. 50)

Though it requires more than a bit of stretching to attribute causation where only correlation has been established (it's like contending that where there are rocks there are arrowheads), we may not object too strenuously to the particular attribution occurring here because there also happens to be a certain intuitive appeal to the claim that the more successful a teacher is in keeping a student on task, the more likely that student is to master the task. However, even if we accept the correlation as a placeholder for causation, the relationship is not explained merely by describing what kind of relationship it is. That is, regardless of whether the relation is correlational or causal, we still don't know why it obtains under the given circumstances. A theory of some sort is needed to explain the efficacy of P_1 and P_2 for student success at K_1. Despite the absence of explanatory theory and the tenuousness of the placeholder relationship, there exists the not uncommon tendency to move right along to answering a third question:

Q3 What should teachers do in order to be effective in getting students to succeed at K_1 and tasks like it?

The answer, of course, is that teachers should do P_1, P_2, and practices like them.

This sequence of reasoning from Q1 through Q2 to Q3 is a kind of triple play. By answering one question, Q1, all questions are answered simultaneously. By coupling a few assumptions and presuppositions with a knowing wink at the absence of explanatory theory, all three questions get knocked off the playing field in the haste to move from modest correlational findings to imperatives for teacher training. The triple play is not an intentionally adopted strategy of teacher effectiveness researchers, but some come perilously close to encouraging it:

If the correlational findings are valid in situations other than the initial context of data collection, and *if* the cause and effect relationship is, in fact, in the direction of teaching behaviors causing pupil achievement, then a trained group of teachers whose instructional methods approximate the ''optimal'' methods should have higher mean classroom achievement than they would if their teaching strategies did not conform to the recommended methods. (Crawford & Gage, 1977, p. 118)

This quotation exemplifies the Q1 to Q3 shift, but not the triple play. Crawford and Gage (quoted above) are obviously concerned that the relationship questioned by Q2 indeed be causal rather than correlation serving as a placeholder for causation. Were they successful in demonstrating the causal efficacy of P-type (direct instruction) practices for success at K-type (basic skills) tasks, their case for Q3 (teachers who follow the optimal methods should obtain higher mean classroom achievement) would presumably be much stronger. Conventional research wisdom has it that experiments should be run in order to determine whether P-type practices are causally efficacious for success at K-type tasks. Suppose that these experiments were performed, and they demonstrated a causal relation between a prescribed range of Ps and success at a given range of Ks. Would we not now feel better about the shift from Q1 to Q3? Would we not now feel more confident in recommending that teachers employ P-type practices? And might we not be just a bit less reluctant to caution or criticize policy makers who mandate P-type practices? We know that triple plays take place, but we try to avoid them whenever we can. But if causality were demonstrated, we would feel better about it all.

Now, suppose further that the more successful a process-product researcher is in demonstrating causality between certain Ps and success at Ks, the less educative will the process of preparing teachers become. That is, the more we learn about what teacher performances are productive of basic skills acquisition by students, the more we will treat these performances as basic skills to be acquired by teachers. The greater the extent to which P-type practices become conceived as the basic skills of teaching, the more likely we are to treat them as the givens for effective teaching and insist upon their mastery as part of any program of teacher preparation. Of course, this reasoning is mere supposition— for the moment. I shall argue this case shortly but first want to state more clearly the way in which the Q1 to Q3 shift gets into our thinking in the first place. John Stuart Mill (1874) is illuminating on the matter:

The art proposes to itself an end to be attained, defines the end, and hands it over to the science. The science receives it, considers it as a phenomenon or effect to be studied, and having investigated its causes and conditions, sends it back to art with a theorem of the combination of circumstances by which it could be produced. Art then examines these combinations of circumstances, and according as any of them are or are not in human power, pronounces the end attainable or not. The only one of the premises, therefore, which Art supplies, is the original major premise, which asserts that the attainment of a given end is desirable. Science then lends to Art the proposition . . . that the performance of certain actions will attain the end. From these premises Art concludes that the performance of these actions is desirable, and finding it also practicable, converts the theorem into a rule or precept. (pp. 653–654)

In Mill's scheme researchers play the part of Science as they seek answers to Q1 and Q2. The answers to these questions become the "theorem of the combination of circumstances" by which the end may be attained. Those who answer Q3 play the part of Art. The role shift from Science to Art can become quite muddied. What is the status of teacher effectiveness researchers who, upon answering Q1 and Q2, walk into their teaching methods classes and tell prospective or in-service teachers to employ P-type practices? Or those who recommend these practices in their textbooks? Or those who justify research projects to funding agencies by describing the many things that have been learned for the improvement of practice? In these cases, the researchers appear to be the ones who convert the theorems into rules or precepts. On the other hand, legislatures, school principals, and teacher licensing agencies may also play the role of Art, converting the theorems handed to them by Science into rules or precepts. At first glance it may seem that even though the role differentiations can become blurred, the end result is not problematic. If the theorems are valid, then their conversion to rules and precepts is justified. It is this point that should be placed in dispute but frequently is not.

An important reason, I think, why the point is not the object of debate is that the educational researcher is not fully aware of the ambiguous status that he or she maintains relative to the roles of Science and Art. Part of the explanation for this lack of awareness may reside in the common insistence of contracts and grants agencies that researchers not only *justify* their answers to Q1 and Q2–type questions by making evident the connection between these answers and answers to Q3, but also that they *initiate* and *control* their inquiries into Q1– and Q2–type questions so that answers to Q3–type questions follow more or less naturally from answers to the prior questions; the RFP (Request For Proposal) procedure for funding educational research may easily serve the functions of initiating and controlling inquiry. The second and perhaps more revealing reason why there is not more discussion on the proper terminus of educational research involves the nature of social science inquiry itself. It is almost as if, by definition, one cannot do social science without becoming enmeshed in an ambiguity of Art and Science roles. Ryan (1970) meets the point head-on in stating that "the social sciences are preeminently 'policy sciences'; . . . they have been developed by and for men who have wanted to use the knowledge they could gain to bring about changes of one or another kind'' (p. 197). Social scientists, and educational researchers as a species of social scientist, want to improve the state of affairs as well as learn more about it. The desire that one's work have ameliorative effects can be a powerful inducement to avoid questioning the process of converting theorems into rules and precepts, for in a way, few among us fail to experience pleasure in the awareness that our work is the basis for policy development. Every educational researcher who has riddled the musings of a practitioner with the retort that ''we have no empirical evidence to substantiate that claim'' is implicitly contending that someday, somewhere, a Q1 to Q3 shift will be available to handle the situation under discussion.

Given that through the necessity to obtain funds for research or through a conscious commitment to amelioration, the educational researcher can become a willing participant in the Q1 to Q3 shift, what implications follow for the preparation of effective teachers? A central implication is that one becomes an effective teacher by following the rules and precepts developed by the conversion of theorems. Learning to be effective is thus a matter of learning the rules and obeying them. The more answers process-product researchers find to Q1–type questions, and the more successful they are at answering Q2–type questions, the more answers there will be for Q3–type questions—and the more rules and precepts there will be to be learned and followed. Complete success for product-process research on teacher effectiveness leads to a completely rule-governed program for preparing effective teachers. That there is something less than felicitous about such an outcome involves far more than the simple *reductio ad absurdum* just employed. A look at some recent work in philosophy of education will enable us to fold back yet another layer of the nature of research on teacher effectiveness.

Green (1971) has contended that the purpose of teaching is to lead students from what it is subjectively reasonable for them to believe to what it is objectively reasonable for them to believe. That is, a student comes to school with a certain set of beliefs that, given his or her experiences, seem plausible (subjectively reasonable) to him or her. But if the weight of established evidence available to humankind is brought to bear on these subjectively reasonable beliefs, it can be shown that some, many, or perhaps all of these beliefs are not reasonable in an objective sense. Education, for Green, is largely a matter of transforming a person's subjectively reasonable beliefs to objectively reasonable beliefs. The transformation from subjective reasonableness to objective reasonableness is undertaken by developing the student's capacity to reason and by presenting evidence for or against subjectively reasonable beliefs. ''The determination of 'what is reasonable for *me* to believe,' in the light of what men have discovered to be defensible beliefs, is the project any man embarks upon when he sets out to think'' (Green, 1971, p. 106). Though this particular way of stating what is meant by education is unique to Green, his general thesis is comparable to that argued by many other contemporary philosophers of education (Arnstine, 1967; Dearden, Hirst, & Peters, 1972; Ennis, 1969; Greene, 1973; McClellan, 1976; Peters, 1966; Scheffler, 1960, 1965, 1973; Soltis, 1978).

If Green's view is applied not to the teaching of students, but to the teaching of teachers, a view of teacher preparation emerges that is very different from that implied by the Q1 to Q3 shift and its concomitant conversion of theorems to rules and precepts. Rather than converting theorems to rules, theorems are used as grist for the mill in testing the beliefs of teachers which appear to them at the outset to be reasonable beliefs. On this revised view, there are no triple plays, simply because one cannot shift blithely from Q1 and Q2 to Q3. Answering Q2 clearly marks the terminus of Science's role in process-product research, and Q3 becomes a question not for the researcher *qua* Science or the policy maker *qua* Art, but for the teachers themselves. Writing a hundred years ago, Mill could not anticipate the incredibly complex organizations and institutional structures that might lead to role ambiguity for Science and Art, so it may have seemed to him unnecessary to specify carefully who is Art. For Mill it could be the case that the person who must obey the rule is the one entitled to decide whether a given theorem shall be converted to a rule. Though Mill's intentions on this matter are not clear, Green's and those of other philosophers of education are: one participates in the education of a fellow human being not by mandating compliance with preestablished rules, but rather by encouraging reflection on the bearing of facts upon the learner's beliefs. In this view, the results of process-product research are used as evidence for the evaluation of the subjectively reasonable beliefs of teachers, as a part of the process of transforming the teachers' beliefs from subjectively to objectively reasonable.

A review of some of the major points made thus far should bring the application of Green's thesis into sharper focus. Two schema for getting from research to practice have been identified. The first is a conversion schema, involving three questions:

Q1   Do teacher performances P_1 and P_2 result in success at task K_1 by students assigned this task?

Q2   Why do P_1 and P_2 result in student success at K_1?

Q3   What should teachers do in order to be effective in getting students to succeed at K_1 and tasks like it?

It has been argued that the standard procedure in process-product research has been to answer Q1, assume an answer to Q2, and supply the Q1 answer in the form of a rule as an answer for Q3 (the triple play), or alternatively to answer Q1 and Q2 independently, and then supply the Q1 answer in the form of a rule as an answer for Q3. In both cases, the terminus of the activity is a rule or precept to be followed by teachers. The difference between the first and second cases is that the second case is the stronger one; if it can be determined that teacher performances (Ps) are causally linked to student success at tasks (Ks), then the justification for and confidence in converting the Q1 answer to a rule is increased.

Thus to the extent that process-product researchers perceive one of their main tasks to be establishment of causal links between Ps and Ks, the upshot of success will be more rules and more confidence in them. Complete success at this effort yields a completely rule-governed program for preparing teachers thought to be optimally effective at teaching whatever tasks the research has explored. The difficulty with this result has little to do with whether the links between Ps and Ks are correlational or causal; rather, it is the fact that it is miseducative. The conversion schema fails because of the way the knowledge it yields is used.

The second schema for getting from research to practice is the transformation schema. In this schema, the answers to Q1 and Q2 are not converted to a rule by those who formulated the answers, by those who paid for the answers, or by those who are elected or appointed for the purpose of making rules. Rather the answers to Q1 and Q2 are presented as evidence to those who, in the conversion schema, would be expected to follow the rules. The purpose of presenting the results of research as evidence is to encourage the transformation of teachers' beliefs from being subjectively to objectively reasonable. Rule conversion *may* be an outcome of the transformation process, but only if the conversion is undertaken by those who are expected to follow the rules. At this point in the argument, it is contended that the transformation schema is superior to the conversion schema because the former avoids the rulebound approach to the preparation of teachers implied by the latter. The transformation schema does not require a definitive answer to Q2 before an answer to Q1 may be presented as evidence (the question of causation need not be settled or an explanatory theory constructed before a researcher informs a teacher of what has been learned from a correlational inquiry). Finally, the transformation schema is superior because it is consistent with (indeed, it is derived from) at least one generally accepted philosophical view of the nature of education, whereas the conversion schema cannot claim such parentage.

If the transformation schema were to be adopted as a guide to how teachers may benefit from research on teaching, then the character of this research would have to be altered. Rather than presupposing that the causes for predetermined outcomes are "out there" somewhere in an ordered universe of schooling waiting for discovery by imaginative researchers (as we so often think of research in the natural sciences), the researchers' attentions would turn to the subjectively reasonable beliefs that teachers already hold. An examination of these beliefs and the study of evidence bearing upon them would become the initiating focus for teacher effectiveness research. What the researcher committed to the transformation schema ultimately seeks is knowledge that enables teachers to enhance both their own educations and the education they provide for their students. This knowledge is gained not by pursuing answers to Q1 and Q2, but by discarding these questions in favor of inquiries designed to reveal the subjectively reasonable beliefs of teachers.

This section began by questioning the proposition that knowing what accounts for effective teaching constitutes knowledge of how to produce more effective teachers. What may at first sight appear to be a relatively simple and straightforward proposition cannot be considered either simple or straightforward after further inquiry. To assume the truth of this proposition is to become ensnared in many difficulties. The proposition works only when we view the results of research on teacher effectiveness as immediately convertible to rules, by persons or agencies other than teachers, for teachers to follow. Were it not for the relative ease with which triple plays have been made in the past, and the enthusiasm for such triple plays by many who fund research or hope to use it as a basis for policy making, it is unlikely that this proposition would have any currency at all. In anticipation of its demise, and foreseeing a time when teacher effectiveness research will serve as an aid to the formation of objectively reasonable beliefs, it would be wise to learn something of the subjectively reasonable beliefs of teachers. The next section of the argument lays the groundwork for doing so.

THE SUBJECTIVE REASONABLENESS OF TEACHERS' BELIEFS

What are the subjectively reasonable beliefs held by teachers? Is the character and quality of the evidence from teacher effectiveness research of the kind that serves the transformation from subjectively to objectively reasonable belief? That there is a connection between what it is subjectively reasonable to believe and the nature of the evidence presented to effect a transformation to objectively reasonable belief seems an obvious enough point—if the interaction between research and practice is understood as I have described it here. But since the interaction has not been generally conceived in this way, the point deserves a bit of emphasis. Some examples will illustrate the connection.

Suppose you believe that neither the United States nor the Soviet Union has ever put anyone on the moon. In your view, stories of manned moon landings are pure fabrication, hoaxes perpetrated by two governments trying to distract their citizens from crises of leadership. Suppose also that you suffer from a rare kidney disease. Your physician phones you, saying, ''Good news. I just returned from a medical conference, where I attended a seminar on space medicine. It seems that while one of the astronauts was on the moon, he experienced a rare kidney problem. The drug he took would normally not be effective, but apparently this drug produces an unusual body chemistry under very low gravity conditions. Anyway, he experienced relief within hours. I spoke with the NASA physicians at the conference, and they think they can help you. Any objections to my making an appointment for you at the space medicine facility in Houston?'' How credible is the evidence for a cure, *to you*, given your beliefs about men on the moon?

Consider another, more pertinent example. You are a teacher who believes that students can learn just about anything they want to, if they are given encouragement and the necessary resources. You are convinced that students should choose their own tasks, while you facilitate their attainment. Your principal, who has spent the summer taking courses toward the doctorate, calls a staff development meeting and says, ''There are things we can do to arrest the declining achievement scores at this school. It turns out that achievement in basic skills is very much a matter of how much time students spend actively engaged in academically appropriate tasks. Fortunately there are some very specific actions we can take to increase engaged time.'' Given your beliefs about teaching, what is the effect of this new evidence? Suppose you are not what Broudy (1972) calls ''existential humanist'' but see yourself as a classical humanist. You see education as the purpose of schooling and perceive your tasks to be

. . . the formation of habits of judgment and the development of character, the elevation of standards, the facilitation of understanding, the development of taste and discrimination, the stimulation of curiosity and wonder, the fostering of style and a sense of beauty, the growth of a thirst for new ideas and visions of the yet unknown. (Scheffler, 1976, p. 206)

How will you greet the principal's announcement that he has evidence for how the declining achievement scores may be arrested at your school?

These examples are illustrative of the connection between the kinds of evidence presented to teachers and the subjectively reasonable beliefs held by teachers. They indicate that if evidence is to have a transforming effect on a teacher, it must in some way be related to, or bear upon, the subjectively reasonable beliefs of the teachers to whom it is presented. In the absence of a relationship between the evidence and teachers' beliefs, we are forced to resort to the conversion schema to induce change; the transformation schema will not work under these conditions. Walter Dearborn, Bronfenbrenner's (1976) first mentor for his graduate studies, may have understood this when he said, ''Bronfenbrenner, if you want to understand something, try to change it'' (p. 164). The research team for Phase III of the BTES compiled with Dearborn's injunction when they set out to do an intervention study. In this study (Berliner et al., in press) the researchers shifted away from accounting for what makes teachers effective to trying to make teachers more effective than the data indicated they were.

The point of the intervention study was to take what had been learned about academic learning time (ALT) and use this knowledge to increase the effectiveness of a small sample of teachers. The study was not intended to be a tightly controlled experiment. To the contrary, teachers and researchers were to work cooperatively as colleagues, mutually committed to enhancing the cognitive achievement of the students. But as the study got underway, difficulties beyond the expectations of the researchers were encountered. They met with reluctance on the part of the teachers to try practices implied by the notion of ALT. On occasion, the reluctance became outright resistance. The diaries kept by the various members of the research team (that diaries were maintained is a marvelous stroke of forethought and of good fortune for those interested in the difference between studying teaching and changing teachers) provide ample indications of frustration, conflict, and misunderstanding—relieved now and again by feelings of goodwill and perceptions of progress being made. But what emerges very clearly is the ambiguity of role, uncertainty over whether the re-searchers were the bearers of rules or the presenters of evidence. There is an undercurrent of mixed metaphor: the researcher as therapist on the one hand (presumably concerned about the subjective beliefs of the teachers), and the researcher as management consultant on the other (presumably prepared to stip-ulate the rules for more efficient management of students' time).

Two groups of teachers were involved in the study. One was known as the weak intervention group; participating teachers were assembled in this group only for workshops on ALT, and there was no involvement of the researchers in the classrooms of these teachers. The other was the strong intervention group; here the researchers were actively involved in the classrooms of the participating teachers. In the weak intervention, the researchers simply met with the teachers to tell them of the results of the main study and to suggest some of the practical applications of these results. The very nature of the weak intervention ensured that the researchers would function as presenters of the evidence. The strong intervention, in contrast, invited mixed, ambiguous roles. Analysis of the data on student behavior indicates that both interventions did have an effect on the ALT–related practices of the teachers, but the weak intervention showed greater change in classroom processes productive of ALT than the strong intervention did.

Not evident in this study, or any other study based on a process-product design, is a concern for this question:

Q4   Why does the teacher engage in P_8 and P_9 (where P_8 and P_9 are performances not found to be effective for student success at K_1 and similar tasks)?

This question marks the beginning of an inquiry into the subjectively reason-able beliefs of teachers. It asks why teachers, given their experiences and the evidence available to them, consider P_8 and P_9 to be reasonable performances. Garden-variety common sense impels us to ask Q4–type questions under the most ordinary conditions, such as when a mother sets out to reprimand her son. The mother thinks the child's act ill-conceived but, before punishing him, asks why he did it. Upon hearing his answer, she reconsiders the punishment, as she now understands why such an action could appear to the child to be well conceived. Though Q4–type questions are often asked in everyday life, they are not prominent in many kinds of teacher effectiveness research (as will be noted later, there *are* categories of teacher effectiveness research in which Q4–type questions figure prominently). What accounts for the inattention to Q4–type questions in certain categories of teacher effectiveness research?

There are, I believe, two reasons why a consideration of subjectively reason-able belief has not been a primary concern of many teacher effectiveness researchers. Both reasons are part of the legacy of strong versions of be-haviorism; both are vestiges of an earlier era in educational research. The first is the subjectively reasonable belief of the educational researcher that what the teacher thinks is not the proper object of empirical inquiry. Rather, the proper object of study is what the teacher does. This thoroughgoing bifurcation of thought and action permits a researcher to concentrate exclusively on behavior, which is directly accessible by observation. Thought, in contrast, is accessible only by inference—a precarious and imprecise way to undertake controlled inquiry. The second reason is the view that the causative factors which account for a person's behavior are external to the person. This view of causation as outside the person, as exogenous, is prominent in process-product research, where explanations for student gains are sought by examining what teachers do. A researcher who supposes that exogenous causation is the scientifically proper way to account for an individual's behavior is not likely to entertain research designs or methodologies that deal with the subjectively reasonable beliefs of teachers.

Some care must be exercised in interpreting the idea of exogenous causation, else it will be misunderstood. There is a difference between intentionally setting out to determine whether school factors other than student background and aptitude determine student achievement, and presupposing that the only scientifically appropriate way to explain or predict a person's behavior is to look away from the person as an intentional agent. Process-product studies have been specifically addressed to determining whether school factors other than student characteristics account for the student's achievement. Given this concern, it is quite appropriate for this line of research to entertain only variables that impinge on the students while they are in school. Hence it is more or less in the nature of process-product studies to consider causative factors outside the student. Considerations of this kind are not what is meant here by exogenous causation. Rather, it is at the point of shifting from Q1 and Q2 to Q3 that exogenous causation becomes a critical consideration. The researcher who shifts from finding out what makes teachers effective to helping teachers be more effective, and does so merely by telling teachers that they should do P_1 and P_2 but not P_8 and P_9 in order to obtain student success at K_1 and similar tasks, is making the presupposition of exogenous causation. In the context of teacher effectiveness, this entails the view that what counts as effective is solely what has the effect of producing the outcomes considered desirable. The effect of presupposing exogenous causation is the idea that teachers become more effective by acting differently toward students (emitting different stimuli), as opposed to the idea that teachers become more effective by thinking and feeling differently about what makes the activity of teaching worthwhile.

Exogenous causation has a certain appeal in considering the apparently essential nature of basic skills. In the minds of many, basic skills are the primary task of schools. These skills are thought to be so essential that we may occasionally flirt with the idea that mastery of them justifies a degree of tyranny that would, under other circumstances, be unwise and inappropriate. We may even feel compelled to view the subjective beliefs of teachers as less worthy of consideration when the acquisition of basic skills is at stake. There is a temptation to justify the conversion schema on the grounds that mastery of some content is so important that it overrides attentiveness to the thoughts and feelings of those who teach this content. Those who think about the problems of effective teaching in this way often draw a distinction between teacher training and teacher education, contending that instruction at the primary school level is more a matter of training than of education. In training, the teacher is equipped with the skills deemed necessary (and hopefully effective) in aiding students to acquire mastery of the basic skills. In education, presumably, the teacher is prepared for sophisticated critical and reflective activities that elicit complex, high-order cognitive and affective responses from students. Such distinctions are seductive; they conjure up views of the world that rest comfortably within our preconceptions. But on scrutiny, they turn out to be neither profound nor useful.

Training is a word frequently chosen to describe the preparation of a person or animal for fairly routine, simple behavior, behavior that does not demand extensive logical or conceptual abilities. If we think of basic skills as simple routines, then we might naturally suppose that one who teaches basic skills need not be elaborately prepared for this work. That we may choose to think of basic skills and teacher training in this way does not entail that our conceptions are correct or that they might not be drastically upgraded. Scheffler (1976) has argued that the concept of basic skills is a bramble bush of confusion and that the way many persist in understanding this notion, at least as applied to mathematics, is misleading in the extreme. Though Scheffler does not specifically argue the point, a clear implication of his thesis is that the way we now handle basic skills in schools may *impair* the learner's ability to pursue advanced knowledge. Basic skills may be basic in the sense that they are needed to function at a most elementary level in a society, or they may be basic in the sense that these skills are needed to access more advanced knowledge. The two senses of the term do not amount to the same thing. If we understand basic skills in the latter, more clearly educative, sense, it should be obvious that teaching them is not a simple, routine, low-order task. However, even if basic skills were simple routines, the conclusion that teaching simple skills is a simple task is unsupported. An important part of the sophistication required for teaching resides in the ability to recognize the learner's source of error and confusion, not the source of success. Regardless of the simplicity or complexity of the objective, detecting and remediating error and confusion are skills of considerable magnitude.

The difficulties incurred by presupposing an exogenous concept of causation run even more deeply than is revealed in this discussion of basic skills and training versus education. Even if the conventional views of basic skills were correct, we would still not be justified in seeking teacher compliance to rules fabricated from theorems. If our purpose and intent are to change the practices of those who teach, it is necessary to come to grips with the subjectively reasonable beliefs of teachers. The conversion schema, the schema of preference for those adopting conventional views of basic skills and teacher training, merely ignores teacher beliefs or tramples upon them on its way to writing mandates and interdicts. The need to confront the subjectively reasonable beliefs of teachers is virtually unavoidable. This point could be argued for on empirical grounds, citing the recent literature on change (e.g., Berman & McLaughlin, 1977; Goodlad, 1975; Goodlad & Klein, 1970; Human Interaction Institute, 1976; Lieberman, 1977; McLaughlin, 1976a, 1976b; Sarason, 1971), which indicates that a necessary condition for the success of change and innovation in schools is an open and rational commitment from teachers. But in this case, the point is argued for on conceptual and normative grounds: to the extent that the preparation of teachers and the schooling of children is an educative activity, it requires, at a minimum, an accounting of the process of transforming belief. The subjective-objective transformation described here is a coherent, heuristically potent, and reasonably elegant manner of making this accounting.

If the argument to this point is sound, it should be evident that there is a critical difference between studying what makes teachers effective and teaching teachers to be effective. Though researchers may learn from their studies, the inquiry undertaken to account for teacher effectiveness is not an educational activity. But the act of teaching teachers is a potentially educative activity— potentially educative because there are ways of teaching teachers that are not educative. Adoption of the conversion schema destroys this potential. The conversion schema terminates in rulebound procedures, evocative of training programs of the most elementary nature. Not even the specter of basic skills justifies the program of training that follows from the conversion schema. The potential for education is realized when the results of the researcher's inquiry are used as evidence, as information, as sources of insight for teachers to consider along with their own experiences. If this much is clear and acceptable, then the stage is set for one more query and response before moving to the third and final section of this chapter.

The process-product research on teacher effectiveness lacks a normative theory of education; this research does not incorporate a conception or justification of what is ultimately worth knowing and doing, it includes no view or defense of right conduct or moral integrity, nor does it give consideration to or argument for the ethical obligations and reasonable expectations of persons who act in specific historical, social, political, and economic settings. The lack of such a theory is not necessarily a fault of this research, except when its results are converted from theorems to rules for teachers to follow. In the absence of a normative theory of education, there is no basis for determining whether the education of the students is advanced by the teachers who follow the rules. That the researcher has successfully linked the performance of some Ps with student success at some Ks, coupled with the statement that the public wants these Ks, is not an adequate justification for compelling teachers to obey rules of classroom performance. In our society, the findings of researchers and pollsters may have the effect of compelling teachers to obey rules (as exemplified by performance and competency-based teaching and teacher education), but these findings do not justify compulsion or obedience—especially given the problems of determining accurately what the public wants, of the validity of the research findings, and of establishing whether the Ks the pollsters say are the ones the public wants are indeed the Ks that produce what the public thinks it wants.

Suppose the conversion schema is dropped, and the transformation schema is used. Imagine that the full and complete results of the research summarized earlier are presented to teachers for their consideration. Under most circumstances, the maximum impact these results would have on the beliefs of teachers would be to alter some very specific ideas about how to deal with a restricted range of tasks. Success of this magnitude assumes that other, more fundamental beliefs held by teachers do not vitiate these results (recall the kidney patient who believed that no one landed on the moon). These results, as they stand, are unlikely to tap the most central and profound beliefs teachers have about their work. How much transformation can be accomplished under these circumstances? A researcher might answer, "Not much. But then Rome was not built in a day, and I'm not trying to change the world in a single stroke." But this researcher misses an intriguing possibility: Instead of waiting until the research is finished to bring the evidence to bear on the subjectively reasonable beliefs of teachers, these beliefs could be incorporated into the research itself.

AN INTENTIONALIST ACCOUNT OF RESEARCH ON TEACHER EFFECTIVENESS

This final section of the argument in this chapter marks off a conception of teacher effectiveness research that is designed to assist significantly in the transformation of teacher beliefs. I say *"mark off* a conception" because it would be overselling the argument to use words like *construct*, *define*, or *establish*. The territory to be marked off has been a difficult one for philosophers, social scientists, and scholars of the arts and letters. It has been so ravaged by great wars over the status of concepts like mentalism, purposiveness, determinism, reductionism, materialism, and teleology that the terrain looks different each time one visits it. Under these circumstances, only fools and geniuses would lay claim to elaborating a complete, formal system of inquiry based on work done and conclusions proved by those who regularly inhabit this territory. Believing myself to be neither idiot nor savant (a model case of subjectively reasonable belief), I shall only suggest what an alternative conception of educational research might look like. Systemization of the ideas will have to await the collaboration of colleagues in research methods, educational psychology, and sociology of education who become convinced that there may be something of worth here.

It is important to note that educational researchers have already staked out parts of the territory. But it is not always clear that they knew exactly where they were or how they got there. Medley (1977), on concluding his extensive collation of recent teacher effectiveness research, stated, "Somehow, . . . we must find and use a model in which the teacher's intent or purpose and the behavior of the individual pupil both play a part'' (p. 70). Frick and Semmel (1978), in their review of classroom observational measures, contended that "investigators often do not consider explicitly another important element—the observed subjects themselves. That is, human behavior is normally purposive or goal-oriented'' (p. 179). Magoon (1977) has reviewed, under the heading of "constructivist research,'' an extraordinary range of studies that purport to account for the intentional status of human behavior. Richer (1975), critical of conventional forms of sociological inquiry in education, argued that one can "discover the meaningful aspects of the school's operations by watching and listening to teachers and students alike, preferably with as few preconceptions as possible'' (p. 391). Toomey (1977) studied the curriculum planning of four grade 11 social studies teachers, trying to understand *their* grounds for the decisions they made. He found that "in the case of these four teachers, a decision about how one might conduct the lesson is preempted by some personal considerations about intention even if only at a relatively general level'' (p. 125).

Each of these writers is calling for or using a nascent form of the intentionalist thesis to study teaching. Each is contending, as possibility or as fact, that an intentionalist account offers a richer, more meaningful understanding of what is involved in the study of teaching. In his own way, each is directing our attention to a form of Q4, asking why teachers engage in the practices they do. What some of these writers realize, and others seem not to, is that they are calling for a lifting of the mantle of materialism and strong empiricism as the foundational metaphysics and epistemology for research on teaching. The metaphysics of materialism gives to matter, rather than mind or spirit, the position of primacy in consideration of the nature of reality (Campbell, 1967; Shaffer, 1971). The epistemology of strong empiricism (also called logical positivism) is that knowledge arises primarily out of experience (that which is outside of, and impinges upon us) rather than from the active reasoning of the mind (Ayer, 1947, 1959). Materialism and strong empiricism are the conceptual foundations for many of the explorations in the natural sciences. To the extent that the social sciences constructed their methods and logics isomorphically with those of the natural sciences, the social sciences assumed the same epistemological and metaphysical foundations. So long as all disputes over what counts as truth and validity are tried exclusively in the courts of matter and experience, an intentionalist thesis cannot gain standing in the research community. Whitehead (1925/1948) recognized the consequences of a strict adherence to materialism:

It is not wrong, if properly construed. If we confine ourselves to certain types of facts, abstracted from the complete circumstances in which they occur, the materialist assumption expresses these facts to perfection. But when we pass beyond the abstraction, either by more subtle employment of our senses, or by the request for meanings and for coherence of thoughts, the scheme breaks down at once. The narrow efficiency of the scheme was the very cause of its supreme methodological success. (p. 24)

Because many researchers no longer see the advantage in abstracting the facts from the complete circumstances in which they occur, and because these researchers seek more subtle employment of the senses and ask for meanings and coherence of thoughts, the intentionalist thesis shows signs of competing with the materialist thesis. If the intentionalist thesis is to become a foundational principle for the social sciences, a surgical excision of the materialist and strong empiricist theses will be required. That such surgery is feasible has been shown by Yankelovitch and Barrett (1971), who constructed a new metapsychology for psychoanalysis. Freud, in searching for a network of theory with which to explain what he had learned from clinical practice, adopted the materialist psychology of the Helmholtz school. Unfortunately, this supporting theory was inconsistent with the clinical results Freud had obtained. The clinical results implied an existential capability for human beings, while the Helmholtzian metapsychology locked persons into a strong determinism. Yankelovitch and Barrett stripped away the materialist metapsychology of Helmholtz, replacing it with a teleological account of human behavior and thereby restoring consistency between the clinical results and the theoretical underpinnings.

Preparation for a similar surgery begins when teacher effectiveness researchers initiate their inquiries with Q4–types instead of Q1–type questions (i.e., by questioning why teachers do what they do instead of asking whether what the teacher does produces certain predetermined effects). The researcher who asks Q4 and questions like it is seeking the teacher's subjectively reasonable belief for employing P_8 or P_9 (or *mutatis mutandis*, P_1 and P_2). The answer to Q4 is obtained by asking teachers why they perform in the manner they do. The answers will normally reveal the intent or purpose of the performances. The discovery of the intent clarifies, for the researcher, the teachers' conceptions of the relationship between their performances and their intentions. In other words, the teacher tells the researcher that he or she believes that doing P results in success at K, that the teacher intends that students succeed at K, and that therefore P is performed. Though the researcher may doubt that P results in success at K, or may even have evidence that P does not result in success at K, this skepticism or evidence is irrelevant for answering Q4. The point of asking Q4–type questions is to find out what connections the teacher believes obtain between Ps and Ks. Researchers who initiate their inquiries with Q4–type questions may find that the relationships posited by teachers, despite their subjectively reasonable character, are often as elegant and substantive as (or more than) any implied by the evidence or theories possessed by the researchers.

There are some relatively systematic attempts to study teaching that could be viewed as efforts to make use of an intentionalist thesis. One is the Corps Member Training Institute (CMTI) Impact Study, an evaluation and study of the 1975 Training Institute for tenth-cycle Teacher Corps interns. The purpose of the impact study was to examine the nature of the one-month training institute as a professional training activity and to assess its impact on the Teacher Corps interns. To do this, the research team used a wide range of investigatory devices, from time series surveys to photography and poetry. The data emerging from these multiple sources were to be synthesized and analyzed as a whole:

This meant that the relationship between quantitative and qualitative data was not considered to be one of simple effect and cause or of dependent and independent variables. Instead, observational descriptions, participant interview responses, survey results, and instructional intentions and instructor's underlying assumptions were to be considered together when interpreting the impact of CMTI. (Fox, 1976, p. vii)

A review of the impact study's technical reports indicates that it did not succeed in synthesizing quantitative and qualitative data too much differently from the way the rest of us do (with imagination and intuition, but not with rules that ensure intersubjectively verifiable conclusions). However, the research team did try to account for the transformation of the interns' aspirations, expectations, and goals as they moved through the training session and into the early period of the internship. This concern for the participants' intentions led to several insightful commentaries (e.g., Popkewitz, 1976; Popkewitz & Wehlage, 1977) on the interaction between intentions and social systems, about which more will be said shortly.

Another effort that might be thought relevant to an intentionalist account of ways to study teaching is the work of Shulman and Lanier (1977) at Michigan State University's Institute for Research on Teaching. The work of the institute is guided by Shulman's conception of teaching as clinical information processing (Shulman, 1974; Shulman & Elstein, 1975; Gage, 1975). This notion appears to be a blend of ideas from cognitive psychology, information processing theory, and the nature of clinical practice. Shulman contends that in order to grasp the practical implications of conceiving of teaching as clinical information processing, the researcher must be attentive to the mental life of the teacher: "How teachers behave and what they do is directed in no small way by what they think. It is the relationship between thought and action that becomes the critical issue in research on teaching" (Shulman & Lanier, 1977, p. 44). From Shulman's writing and from descriptions of research underway at the institute, it is evident that these researchers are not in sympathy with the conversion schema implicit in process-product designs for the study of teacher effectiveness. But though the institute's concern for the mental life of teachers may give the appearance of employing the intentionalist account, it is not at all clear that this is the case. (I have no reason to suspect that the institute has adopted or cares to adopt an intentionalist thesis, and hence the distinctions about to be drawn between the thesis and what the institute does are intended only to distinguish the thesis from points of view with which it may be confused.)

A concern for the mental life of teachers, for their thoughts and feelings, may or may not be consistent with an intentionalist account. If the concern for mental life is based on the assumption that cognitive psychology or information processing theory requires that the thoughts and feelings of teachers be considered, then this concern is unrelated to the intentionalist thesis. It may even be inconsistent with the thesis (Malcolm, 1977, identifies the grounds for the inconsistency, though he has not, in my view, proved the case). In cognitive psychology and in information processing theory, the thoughts and feelings of persons are used as *clues* to underlying developmental and information processing structures. In contrast, the intentionalist account uses the language of persons as *data* to explain why they do what they do. In their development of a nonmaterialist framework for the explanation of social behavior, Harré and Secord (1972) argue that "the things that people say about themselves and other people should be taken seriously as reports of data relevant to phenomena that *really exist* and which are *relevant* to the explanation of behavior" (p. 7). The intentionalist thesis argued for here is closely related to the position taken by Harré and Secord that "a person's use of ordinary language in describing his own and others' actions, in thinking about and preparing himself for action is vital to a proper behavioral science" (p. 299).

The primary interest of many cognitive psychologists has been to develop explanatory theories for the evolution of our capacity to acquire and use knowledge; to find, as Piaget (1971, p. 13) puts it, the "parallelism between the progress made in the logical and rational organization of knowledge and the corresponding formative psychological processes." The primary interest of the intentionalist researcher would be to develop explanations for psychosocial behavior. Information processing theorists, like cognitive psychologists, are disposed to develop structural accounts of epistemic operations. The intentionalist views any attempt to superimpose a structuralist theory on human action with the same suspicion as an attempt to superimpose some predetermined criterion of effectiveness on the performances of teachers. Either one would be an intrusion likely to defeat an inquiry aimed at identifying and accounting for the subjectively reasonable beliefs of persons.

At this point, consistency demands that the argument be cycled back to where it began, with the proposition that knowledge of what makes teachers effective constitutes knowledge of how to make teachers effective. The intentionalist thesis is a way to think about both, though the conclusion of the first section of the argument is not thereby breached. Generating knowledge, and getting people to use it appropriately and well, are two different activities. The former is an outcome of good research. The latter is an outcome of good education. A researcher may use an elaborated version of the intentionalist thesis to study teaching (in ways that are suggested by Harré and Secord, and Yankelovitch and Barrett), while the educator uses the same thesis as a source of foundational principles for guiding others in the formation of objectively reasonable beliefs. For both intentionalist researcher and intentionalist educator, the inquiries are initiated with Q4-type questions. The researcher's interest in Q4 is the study of the links teachers form between their intentions and their performances, determining the degree of evidence available for these links. The educator's interest in

Q4 is as the proper beginning of the process of belief transformation. Were it not for the fact that the teaching of concern to us here takes place in complex social settings called schools, one might conclude that the life of intentionalist researchers and educators is a relatively simple one.

But the educator engaged in the transformation learns quickly that holding objectively reasonable beliefs and being able to act on them are different phenomena. What seems objectively reasonable in the abstract can become debilitating and destructive in the concreteness of social systems like schools (Levy, 1970, provides a remarkably insightful account of just this kind of occurrence). The educator also faces another problem. Much of what is subjectively reasonable to teachers is subjectively reasonable because of their participation in schools; e.g., the belief that lots of practice is the surest road to mastery may be accounted for by the teacher's internalization of the school's insistence on order, routine, and relative quiet. If the school functions in ways that are alien to and unsupportive of beliefs shown to be objectively reasonable, and if the social system of the school is, in some sense, responsible for the formation of subjectively reasonable beliefs that are contrary to the evidence available, then how genuine and likely of success are the educator's efforts at the transformation of subjectively reasonable beliefs?

The researcher could assist the educator with these problems and by doing so add to our knowledge of teaching. The researcher could continue on from Q4–type questions and answers to find out whether the teacher's participation in the social system of the school does in fact account for the formation of certain subjectively reasonable beliefs. The researcher could study the question of whether particular characteristics of the social system are supportive of subjectively reasonable beliefs that have been determined to be objectively unreasonable. The researcher might then ask whether it is possible to modify the social system in order to diminish support for beliefs shown to be objectively unreasonable. If so, how might these changes be made? What features of the school social system are optimally supportive of teachers who hold objectively reasonable beliefs about the relationships between their performances and their intentions for students?

Educational researchers who received their disciplinary training in psychology may balk at these questions, contending that they are for sociologists and anthropologists. That's understandable, but not intentionalist. The intentionalist inquiry is guided by the concerns and interests of the subjects of the inquiry. If their problems fall into categories that transcend the disciplinary fences of academia, whose problem is that?

The territory is marked off as well as I am able to do it at this time. If the boundary lines are clearly perceived, then it is understood that, on an intentionalist account, the work of the researcher of teaching and the teacher of teachers is different, but complementary. The researcher is a generator of knowledge, a source of evidence for the teacher educator. The teacher educator is a transformer, and a source of problems for the investigatory talents of the researcher. These descriptions identify roles and do not necessarily demarcate the activities of two different persons. On the intentionalist thesis, the researcher of teaching cannot do research without in some ways participating in the education of teachers, nor can the teacher educator transform beliefs without participating in the study of teaching. The intentionalist thesis is a way of conceiving of the study of teaching so that the results of this study are more productive of knowledge that enhances education, in contrast to the simple acquisition of skills so characteristic of a training conception of teacher preparation and schooling. The researcher and teacher educator who view teaching through an intentionalist lens are not interested in peddling findings to high bidders for their talents, be these rule makers, policy makers, or policy administrators. On the contrary, their primary and mutually held concern is for the education of teachers that is expressive and evocative of the education they hope teachers will provide for their students.

REFERENCES

Arnstine, D. *Philosophy of education: Learning and schooling.* New York: Harper & Row, 1967.

Ayer, A. J. *Language, truth, and logic.* New York: Dover, 1947.

Ayer, A. J. (Ed.). *Logical positivism.* New York: Free Press, 1959.

Berliner, D. C., Filby, N. N., Marliave, R. S., & Weir, C. D. *Report of an intervention in classrooms following the Beginning Teacher Evaluation Study model of instruction* (Tech. Rep. VI-2). San Francisco: Far West Laboratory, in press.

Berliner, D. C., Filby, N. N., Marliave, R. S., Weir, C. D., & Fisher, C. W. *Description of classes and plan for an intervention study* (Tech. Note VI–1). San Francisco: Far West Laboratory, 1976.

Berliner, D. C., & Rosenshine, B. The acquisition of knowledge in the classroom. In R. C. Anderson, R. J. Spiro, & W. E. Montague (Eds.), *Schooling and the acquisition of knowledge.* Hillsdale, N.J.: Lawrence Erlbaum, 1978.

Berman, P., & McLaughlin, M. W. *Federal programs supporting educational change* (Vol. 7, *Factors affecting implementation and continuation*). Santa Monica, California: Rand, 1977.

Bronfenbrenner, U. The experimental ecology of education. *Teachers College Record,* 1976, *78*, 157-204.

Brophy, J., & Evertson, C. *Process-product correlations in the Texas Teacher Effectiveness Study: Final report* (Res. Rep. 74-4). Austin, Tex.: Research and Development Center for Teacher Education, 1974.

Brophy, J. E., & Evertson, C. M. Teacher behavior and student learning in second and third grades. In G. D. Borich (Ed.), *The appraisal of teaching: Concepts and process.* Reading, Mass.: Addison-Wesley, 1977.

Broudy, H. S. *The real world of the public schools.* New York: Harcourt Brace Jovanovich, 1972.

Calfee, R., & Calfee, K. H. Reading And Mathematics Observation System: Description and measurement of time usage in the classroom. *Journal of Teacher Education,* 1976, *27*, 323-325.

Campbell, K. Materialism. In P. Edwards (Ed.), *The encyclopedia of philosophy* (Vol. 5). New York: Macmillan, 1967.

Crawford, J., & Gage, N. L. Development of a research-based teacher training program. *California Journal of Teacher Education*, 1977, *4*, 105-123.

Cruickshank, D. R. Synthesis of selected research on teacher effects. *Journal of Teacher Education*, 1976, *27*, 57-60.

Dearden, R. F., Hirst, P. H., & Peters, R. S. (Eds.). *Education and the development of reason*. London: Routledge & Kegan Paul, 1972.

Dunkin, M. J., & Biddle, B. J. *The study of teaching*. New York: Holt, Rinehart, & Winston, 1974.

Elias, P., & Wheeler, P. Instructional activities as reported by teachers. *Journal of Teacher Education*, 1976, *27*, 326-328.

Ennis, R. H. *Logic in teaching*. Englewood Cliffs, N.J.: Prentice-Hall, 1969.

Far West Laboratory. *Proposal for Phase IIIB of the Beginning Teacher Evaluation Study*. San Francisco: Far West Laboratory, undated.

Filby, N. N., & Dishaw, M. *Construct validation of group-administered achievement tests through individual testing* (Tech. Note III-4). San Francisco: Far West Laboratory, 1977.

Fodor, J. A. Explanations in psychology. In M. Black (Ed.), *Philosophy in America*. Ithaca, N.Y.: Cornell University Press, 1965.

Fox, T. G. *Methodology* (1975 CMTI Impact Study). Madison, Wis.: 1976.

Frick, T., & Semmel, M. I. Observer agreement and reliabilities of classroom observational measures. *Review of Educational Research*, 1978, *48*, 157-184.

Gage, N. L. *Teacher effectiveness and teacher education: The search for a scientific basis*. Palo Alto, Calif.: Pacific Books, 1972.

Gage, N. L. (Ed.). *NIE conference on studies in teaching: Panel 2. Teaching as human interaction*. Washington, D.C.: National Institute of Education, 1974.

Gage, N. L. (Ed.). *NIE conference on studies in teaching: Panel 6. Teaching as clinical information processing*. Washington, D.C.: National Institute of Education, 1975.

Goodlad, J. I. *The dynamics of educational change: Toward responsive schools*. New York: McGraw-Hill, 1975.

Goodlad, J. I., & Klein, M. F. *Behind the classroom door*. Worthington: Ohio: Charles A. Jones, 1970.

Green, T. F. *The activities of teaching*. New York: McGraw-Hill, 1971.

Greene, M. *Teacher as stranger*. Belmont, Calif.: Wadsworth, 1973.

Harnischfeger, A., & Wiley, D. E. *Notes for a field study of instructional time* (Tech. Rep. 75-10-11). San Francisco: Far West Laboratory, 1975.

Harnischfeger, A., & Wiley, D. E. The teaching-learning processes in elementary school: A synoptic view. *Curriculum Inquiry*, 1976, *6*, 5-43.

Harré, R., & Secord, P. F. *The explanation of social behavior*. Oxford, England: Basil Blackwell, 1972.

Human Interaction Institute. *Putting knowledge to use: A distillation of the literature regarding knowledge transfer and change*. Los Angeles: Author, 1976.

Joyce, B. *Variables, designs, and instruments in the search for teacher effectiveness* (Tech. Rep. 75-10-4). San Francisco: Far West Laboratory, 1975.

Lambert, N. M., & Hartsough, C. S. APPLE observation variables and measures of teacher performance. *Journal of Teacher Education*, 1976, *27*, 320-323.

Lazersfeld, P. F. Philosophy of science and empirical social science research. In E. Nagel, P. Suppes, & A. Tarski (Eds.), *Logic, methodology, and philosophy of science*. Stanford, Calif.: Stanford University Press, 1962.

Levy, G. *Ghetto school*. New York: Pegasus, 1970.

Lieberman, A. Political and economic stress and the social reality of schools. *Teachers College Record*, 1977, *79*, 259-266.

Louch, A. R. *Explanation and human action*. Berkeley: University of California Press, 1966.

Magoon, J. Constructivist approaches in educational research. *Review of Educational Research*, 1977, *47*, 651-693.

Malcolm, N. The myth of cognitive processes and structures. *Thought and knowledge: Essays by Norman Malcolm*. Ithaca, N.Y.: Cornell University Press, 1977.

Marliave, R. *Observable classroom variables* (Tech. Rep. 1-2). San Francisco: Far West Laboratory, 1976.

Marliave, R., Cahen, L., & Berliner, D. C. *Prolegomenon to the concept of appropriateness of instruction* (Tech. Rep. IV-1). San Francisco: Far West Laboratory, 1977.

Marliave, R., Fisher, C., Filby, N. N., & Dishaw, M. *The development of instrumentation for a field study of teaching* (Tech. Rep. 1-5). San Francisco: Far West Laboratory, 1977.

McClellan, J. *Philosophy of education*. Englewood Cliffs, N.J.: Prentice-Hall, 1976.

McDonald, F. J., & Elias, P. J. *The effects of teaching performances on pupil learning* (Beginning Teacher Evaluation Study, Phase II, Final Rep.; 5 vols.). Princeton, N.J.: Educational Testing Service, 1975-1976.

McDonald, F. J., & Elias, P. *Executive summary report: Beginning Teacher Evaluation Study, Phase II, 1973-74*. Princeton, N.J.: Educational Testing Service, 1976.

McLaughlin, M. W. Implementation as mutual adaptation: Change in classroom organization. *Teachers College Record*, 1976, *77*, 339-351. (a)

McLaughlin, M. W. Implementation of ESEA Title I: A problem of compliance. *Teachers College Record*, 1976, *77*, 397-415. (b)

Medley, D. M. *Teacher competence and teacher effectiveness: A review of the process-product research*. Washington, D. C.: American Association of Colleges for Teacher Education, 1977.

Mill, J. S. *A system of logic: Ratiocinative and inductive* (8th ed.). New York: Harper & Bros., 1874.

Peters, R. S. *Ethics and education*. London: Allen & Unwin, 1966.

Peters, R. S. Chairman's remarks. In S. C. Brown (Ed.), *Philosophy of psychology*. London: Macmillan, 1974.

Piaget, J. *Genetic epistemology*. New York: Norton, 1971.

Popkewitz, T. *Teacher education as a process of socialization* (Tech. Rep. 18; 1975 CMTI Impact Study). Madison, Wis.: 1976.

Popkewitz, T., & Wehlage, G. Schooling as work: An approach to research and evaluation. *Teachers College Record*, 1977, *79*, 55-67.

Richer, S. School effects: The case for grounded theory. *Sociology of Education*, 1975, *48*, 383-399.

Rosenshine, B. Evaluation of classroom instruction. *Review of Educational Research*, 1970, *40*, 279-300. (a)

Rosenshine, B. The stability of teacher effects upon achievement. *Review of Educational Research*, 1970, *40*, 647-662. (b)

Rosenshine, B. Teaching behaviors related to pupil achievement: A review of research. In I. Westbury & A. A. Bellack (Eds.), *Research into classroom practice*. New York: Teachers College Press, Columbia University, 1971.

Rosenshine, B. Classroom instruction. In N. L. Gage (Ed.), *The psychology of teaching methods* (75th Yearbook of the National Society for the Study of Education; Part I). Chicago: National Society for the Study of Education, 1976. (a)

Rosenshine, B. Recent research on teaching behaviors and student achievement. *Journal of Teacher Education*, 1976, *27*, 61-64. (b)

Rosenshine, B. Review of teaching variables and student achievement. In G. D. Borich (Ed.), *The appraisal of teaching: Concepts and process*. Reading, Mass.: Addison-Wesley, 1977.

Rosenshine, B., & Berliner, D. C. Academic engaged time. *British Journal of Teacher Education*, 1978, *4*, 3-16.

Rosenshine, B., & Furst, N. Research on teacher performance criteria. In B. O. Smith (Ed.), *Research in teacher education: A symposium.* Englewood Cliffs, N.J.: Prentice-Hall, 1971.

Rosenshine, B., & Furst, N. The use of direct observation to study teaching. In R. M. W. Travers (Ed.), *Second handbook of research on teaching.* Chicago: Rand McNally, 1973.

Ryan, A. *The philosophy of the social sciences.* London: Macmillan, 1970.

Sarason, S. B. *The culture of the school and the problem of change.* Boston: Allyn & Bacon, 1971.

Scheffler, I. *The language of education.* Springfield, Ill.: Charles C Thomas, 1960.

Scheffler, I. *Conditions of knowledge.* Chicago: Scott-Foresman, 1965.

Scheffler, I. *Reason and teaching.* London: Routledge & Kegan Paul, 1973.

Scheffler, I. Basic mathematical skills: Some philosophical and practical remarks. *Teachers College Record,* 1976, *78,* 205-212.

Shaffer, J. A. *Reality, knowledge, and value.* New York: Random House, 1971.

Shulman, L. S. The psychology of school subjects: A premature obituary? *Journal of Research in Science Teaching,* 1974, *11,* 319-339.

Shulman, L. S., & Elstein, A. S. Studies of problem solving, judgment, and decision making: Implications for educational research. In F. N. Kerlinger (Ed.), *Review of Research in Education 3, 1975.* Itasca, Ill.: F. E. Peacock Publishers, Inc., 1975.

Shulman, L. S., & Lanier, J. E. The Institute for Research on Teaching: An overview. *Journal of Teacher Education,* 1977, *28,* 44-49.

Soar, R. S. An integration of findings from four studies of teacher effectiveness. In G. D. Borich (Ed.), *The appraisal of teaching: Concepts and process.* Reading, Mass.: Addison-Wesley, 1977.

Soar, R. S., & Soar, R. M. An attempt to identify measures of teacher effectiveness from four studies. *Journal of Teacher Education,* 1976, *27,* 261-267.

Soltis, J. F. *An introduction to the analysis of educational concepts* (2nd ed.). Reading, Mass.: Addison-Wesley, 1978.

Stallings, J. A. *Relationships between classroom instructional practices and child development.* Paper presented at the meeting of the American Educational Research Association, Washington, D.C.: March-April, 1975.

Stallings, J. A. How instructional processes relate to child outcomes in a national study of Follow Through. *Journal of Teacher Education,* 1976, *27,* 43-47.

Stallings, J. A. How instructional processes relate to child outcomes. In G. D. Borich (Ed.), *The appraisal of teaching: Concepts and process.* Reading, Mass., Addison-Wesley, 1977.

Toomey, R. Teachers' approaches to curriculum planning: An exploratory study. *Curriculum Inquiry,* 1977, *7,* 121-129.

Whitehead, A. N. *Science and the modern world.* New York: Mentor Books, 1948 (Originally published, 1925.)

Wiley, D. E., & Harnischfeger, A. Explosion of a myth: Quantity of schooling and exposure to instruction, major educational vehicles. *Educational Researcher,* 1974, *3,* 7-12.

Wilson, J. *Philosophy and educational research.* Bucks, England: National Foundation for Educational Research in England and Wales, 1972.

Wolman, B. B. Does psychology need its own philosophy of science? *American Psychologist,* 1971, *26,* 877-886.

Yankelovitch, D., & Barrett, W. *Ego and instinct.* New York: Vintage Books, 1971.

5

Bilingual/Bicultural Education

CHRISTINA BRATT PAULSTON
University of Pittsburgh

INTRODUCTION

Bilingual Education: A Controversial Field

This chapter (in line with the policy guidelines for the *Review of Research in Education* volumes) will survey the state of disciplined inquiry in the field of bilingual education (BE). This topic presents an unusually difficult task for a review chapter because the inquiry is frequently characterized by lack of discipline and rampant bias for or against issues, which range from bilingual education itself, its goals and objectives, to classroom techniques. Frequently this debate is carried out at a level of methodological development, when political ideology is actually the basic issue. To illustrate, the innocuous-sounding title of this chapter, assigned by the *Review* editor (no doubt in all innocence), has become a slogan which serves as the rallying cry of a particular interest group. At the federal level, only HEW agencies which work with civil rights legislation and Title VI funding ever use the term *bicultural education*. Title VII–funded programs officially eschew the use of the term *bilingual/bicultural education*; the statement by John Molina, former director of the Office of Bilingual Education of the Department of Health, Education, and Welfare, at a recent conference at the National Institute of Education is illustrative: "The United States government is in the business to teach language, not to teach culture." Needless to say, a great deal of caution is needed with research which grows out of such a controversial situation.

MERRILL SWAIN, Ontario Institute for Studies in Education, BERNARD SPOLSKY, University of New Mexico, and ROGER SHUY, Georgetown University, were editorial consultants for this chapter.

Note: Thanks to Karen Billingsley whose editing and intelligent typing again have been of great help to me. I gratefully acknowledge the influence and stimulation I have found in many discussions with Rolland G. Paulston on the topic of this paper and in his *Conflicting Theories of Social and Educational Change*.

At the world level, the field of research on bilingual education is characterized by disparate findings and inconclusive results. Typically this research uses psychometric data to establish intrinsic causation for certain language factors. Reduced to basic issues, the argument concerns (1) choice of medium of instruction, whether in L_1 (first language, mother tongue) or L_2 (second language; in the context of BE, usually an official or national language), and the consequent achievement of language skills, especially in initial reading; (2) achievement of subject matter knowledge in fields like mathematics and science in L_1 compared to L_2; and (3) concern about possible deleterious cognitive effects of following a curriculum in a second language. Engle (1975), after reviewing 25 studies, could only report that none had conclusively answered the questions posed in the first of these issues.

It makes little sense to review inconclusive findings again, and I will mention only a few. Among the more well-known and most often cited studies is Modiano's (1966) Chiapas, Mexico, study, which found that Indian children who had received initial reading in the vernacular and then in Spanish scored higher on tests of reading comprehension in Spanish after three years than those who had only been taught in Spanish. The Macnamara (1966) and Osterberg (1961) studies are often cited in support of Modiano's findings. The St. Lambert study (Lambert & Tucker, 1972) is frequently said to contradict Modiano's findings. This project is the prototype of the Canadian immersion programs wherein Anglophone children enter classes in which they are initially taught only in French. By the end of the second grade the students in the St. Lambert study were reading English as well as the English controls and were also able to read in French, and they maintained this achievement through the later grades. Studies cited in support of the St. Lambert findings, besides the other Canadian immersion studies (for a thorough account, see Swain, 1976a), which are remarkably in agreement with the St. Lambert data, are the Culver City studies (see Cohen, Fathman, & Merino, 1976, for the latest reference), Malherbe (1946), and Prator (1967).

Ramos, Aquilar, and Sibayan's (1967) Rizal experiment is occasionally cited to support instruction and initial literacy directly in L_2, as indeed the findings may be read to indicate. It was, by all indications, an excellent program, with the assistance of U.S. expertise. There were also some other interesting findings which are cited much less frequently. The socioeconomic indexes taken in grade 1 predicted achievement in English at the end of grade 4, as did the aptitude tests also taken in grade 1 (there is no mention of any correlation between these two variables). At the end of grade 6, "the covariate that has the highest correlation with the language tests is the socio-economic index" (Ramos et al., 1967, p. 94). It is interesting to look at the Philippine children who were not in the experimental program. A Literacy Survey conducted in Rizal Province among fourth-graders in 1964 found that "The percentage of pupils judged literate in English in the experimental classes was 79.42; in the non-experimental classes in the same schools it was 39.26. The percentage of pupils in the experimental classes judged literate in Filipino was 93.76; in the non-experimental classes, it was 69.04[*] (Ramos et al., 1967, p. 88). These figures illustrate two points which no data have been found to contradict. One is the importance of good programs (which often is a function of social class), and the other makes clear that in nonexperimental, mediocre programs it is easier to learn to read in the mother tongue. The Rizal experiment is a good example of a study whose findings can be taken for intrinsic support of either L_1 or L_2 medium of instruction, depending on the reader's bias.

And so it goes. A study can be found to support virtually every possible opinion, a not uncommon practice in review-of-the-literature endeavors. In this regard, a recent survey (Belkin, Graham, Paulston, & Williams, 1977) turned up considerable agreement of results in U.S. dissertations on BE programs. The U.S. BE programs without exception were found to increase achievement in Spanish reading when compared with control groups of Spanish-speaking children in monolingual English programs. In seven studies, the BE children did better in English reading or subject matter achievement than the controls did, and two studies found no difference. One study on Indian children favored the traditional English program. The programs increase the self-concept scores of the Latino children, as well as of the Anglo and Black children in the BE programs. The one program for Indian children failed to raise their self-concept scores. The findings on achievement in mathematics are contradictory; these studies show that skills in mathematics, especially computation, do not transfer across languages as do literacy skills in reading.

Recently the questions concerning bilingual education have begun to shift, and more attention is being paid to factors extrinsic to the programs as causal variables. It is generally recognized that the research findings are quite clear on one point. Upper- and middle-class children do perfectly well, whether they are schooled in the mother tongue or in the second language, although we don't really know why (C. B. Paulston, 1975a, p. 370). In this context, most scholars observe B. Gaarder's distinction between elitist bilingualism and folk bilingualism. Elitist bilingualism, he points out in an unpublished paper entitled "Political Perspective on Bilingual Education," is the hallmark of intellectuals and the learned in most societies, and, one might add, of upper-class membership in many societies, such as Western Europe. It is a matter of choice. This is not so for folk bilingualism, which is the result of ethnic groups in contact and competition within a single state where "one of the peoples become bilingual involuntarily in order to survive." Elitist bilingual education has never been an educational problem; consequently, North American BE research primarily deals with it as a result of folk bilingualism.[1]

Descriptive Definitions of Bilingual Education

The descriptive definitions of BE programs vary enormously, and care must be taken to avoid inadvertently comparing programs which differ in fundamental aspects, even though both are labeled as BE programs. There are three basic types of BE programs:

1. Programs where all classroom instruction is in the L_2, with the exception of a component on mother tongue skills. The Canadian early immersion programs are of this type.
2. Programs taught in L_1 with a second-language component; i.e., the target language is taught as a subject. There is a legitimate question whether these programs merit the name of bilingual education, but they do occur carrying that label.
3. Programs in which two languages are used as the medium of instruction. The standard U.S. Office of Education definition of bilingual education falls within the third type:

Bilingual education is the use of two languages, one of which is English, as mediums of instruction for the same pupil population in a well-organized program which encompasses part or all of the curriculum and includes the study of the history and culture associated with the mother tongue. A complete program develops and maintains the children's self-esteem and a legitimate pride in both cultures.

With only three basic types, and with the primary difference being in the medium of instruction, the variations among programs are primarily found in the arrangement and combination of components rather than in different components. The more obvious variables which can be used to distinguish among various models are:

1. The sequencing of languages: Is initial literacy taught in L_1 or L_2 or simultaneously? The U.S. Title VII programs teach initial reading simultaneously in the two languages or in L_1 first; the Canadian early immersion programs typically reverse the process and teach initial reading in L_2.

2. Time allotted, both in sequencing and within the curriculum. The U.S. programs typically do not delay more than one year in introducing reading in L_2 (if not taught simultaneously); the Canadian programs do not introduce reading in the mother tongue until 2nd grade, after two years of schooling (K, 1).

The definitions of bilingual education in Canada and Sweden are almost identical. In Canada: "Bilingual education can be defined as schooling provided fully or partly in the second language with the object in view of making students proficient in the second language while, at the same time, maintaining and developing their proficiency in the first language and fully guaranteeing their education development" (Stern, 1972, p. 1). In Sweden: "The goal of bilingual teaching in comprehensive school should be for the pupils to gain a parallel command of both languages'' (National Swedish Board of Education, 1973, p. 97). They both stress parallel proficiency in two languages, and only the time allocation in the curriculum of L1 and L2 makes the difference clear. A Canadian immersion fifth-grader experiences about 50% of classroom instruction in either L1 or L2, while an immigrant fifth-grader in Sweden usually spends about two hours a week in mother tongue instruction, which makes it very unlikely that the Swedish educational goals can be achieved.

Other variables concern the relative emphasis on the mother tongue culture of the children (the Canadian and Swedish definitions omit any reference to home culture, while the U.S. definition stresses it), and the medium of instruction of specific subjects, especially reading and mathematics. Reading seems to show transfer across languages using the same alphabet, but the findings on transfer between languages of mathematical skills are especially confusing (C. B. Paulston, 1977). Teacher ethnicity and competencies are still other variables which include such questions as whether: (1) the teacher is a member of the same ethnic group as the children, (2) the same teacher teaches in both languages, and (3) each language is taught by a native speaker, or the two languages are represented by a certified teacher on one hand and by a teacher's aide on the other. This variable is closely connected with another, that of good compared to bad programs. The issues involved concern such obvious matters as whether the teacher is fluent in the language being taught or whether the children have textbooks or just ''endless charts prepared by aides or teachers who guess at the orthography or rather at times invent it'' (Pascual, 1976, p. 6; my translation). ''Good'' vs. ''bad'' programs are difficult to operationalize in educational research, but at this simple level component teachers and adequate curricula and textbooks are important to keep in mind in attempts to interpret the research findings; often abysmal programs are compared with excellent programs. It should be reassuring to educators that children do better in good programs (Prator, 1967; Ramos, Aquilar, & Sibayan, 1967). Another variable, which is poorly understood and inadequately dealt with, concerns the language of the surrounding school and community. The immersion programs differ in this aspect from the U.S. ''submersion'' programs (Cohen & Swain, 1976), where non–English-speaking children find themselves in sink-or-swim types of programs.

Many more variables can be found to distinguish different types or models of BE programs, but I believe these are the more important ones. I advisedly say *believe* because these variables are rarely operationalized and observed within a coherent framework. The reader of the BE research simply has to keep these factors at the back of his mind, as it were, in interpreting the findings, and allow for failing to recognize them. My inclusion of these variables is just as informal; my experience with the BE literature indicates repeatedly that these factors tend to influence BE program output. Clearly what is needed is an empirically based feature analysis of models of BE programs (but see Fishman & Lovas, 1970; Fishman, 1977b; Mackey, 1970; Spolsky, 1978).

The Scope of the Chapter

I have restricted discussion in this chapter to sociolinguistic research on bilingual education, that is, research which draws heavily on the behavioral and social sciences, and have so excluded the literature relevant to bilingual education which falls within the discipline of straight linguistics on topics like semilingualism, language dominance, language proficiency and proficiency testing, bilingual language acquisition, error analysis, and interlanguage. Especially in implementing BE programs—in materials preparation, curriculum development, and teacher preparation—linguistics has important contributions to make, but those issues lie outside the topic of this chapter (see Ferguson, 1977; Center for Applied Linguistics, 1977, Vol. 2, Linguistics).

The reason I prefer a framework of sociolinguistic theory in formulating questions and finding answers about bilingual education is simple; in part it forms one of the two basic assumptions of this chapter. We can begin to understand these problems and questions only when we see bilingual education as the *result* of certain societal factors, rather than the *cause* of certain behaviors in children. Unless we attempt in some way to account for the sociohistorical, cultural, economic, and political factors which lead to certain forms of bilingual education, we will not be able to understand or to assess the consequences of that education. Swain rightly points out, however, that:

The reason bilingual education has been the independent variable is because educators, parents, etc., were worried about the possible harmful effects of bilingual education on their kids. The *evaluations* of the programs were undertaken to show that bilingual education was not harmful. In other words, research for immediate educational purposes necessarily has used bilingual education as the independent variable. Now if you want to develop a theory of bilingual education . . . then you have to take one step backwards (no negative connotation meant) and view bilingual education as the/a dependent variable. (Cited in C. B. Paulston, 1976, 239)

Parents, educators, and legislators want to know how children in BE programs are performing in school, and their first question concerns linguistic skills. We need a great number of case studies in order to develop a theory of bilingual education which will allow us to generalize the evidence from the individual studies and to account for the contradictory findings.

The other major assumption of this chapter is that the identification of the independent variables and the interpretation of outcomes depend on the world view of the researcher and on the particular theory employed to explain and predict phenomena. This chapter does not attempt an exhaustive review of the literature (for this see Engle, 1975; Fishman, 1977; C. B. Paulston, 1975a). Rather, after a brief historical introduction, it explores the theoretical perspectives on bilingual education so that the reader can recognize the implicit assumptions characteristic of specific theoretical orientations in his or her own further reading in the field. The chapter is partially a survey of research in the field, but it is primarily intended to aid the educator in making order of the disparate and contradictory findings which exist in this research.

It is obvious that I am including the Canadian research studies in this survey; the reasons·for this merit a brief mention. The studies are of excellent technical quality, and so are the programs they seek to evaluate, embarrassingly so at times in comparison with the U.S. work. They also contain systematic longitudinal data on the BE programs (one U.S. dissertation evaluates the effect of bilingual education after *eight* hours of "treatment"). Since the Canadian children are initially schooled in the L₂, and successfully so, these studies are frequently cited as evidence *against* bilingual education in the United States, and educators need to be familiar with the difference between the research and between the programs. It is my contention that a comparative approach allows us to test generalizations within a larger universe, to examine similar programs within different settings and different programs within similar settings, and so by systematic comparison to arrive at higher level generalizations in our attempts to account for the contradictory data on bilingual education.

THE LEGAL-HISTORICAL DEVELOPMENT OF BILINGUAL EDUCATION IN THE UNITED STATES

Bilingual education is a long-standing phenomenon in the world, and it is (as is not always recognized) also old in the United States. Bilingual education (elitist education excluded) tends to deal with two major concerns: on the one hand, the concern about mother tongue maintenance and a too-rapid shift to the other language; on the other hand, the concern that the children are not properly learning the official language of the nation. Early U.S. BE programs were of the former kind, and various forms of private bilingual schools were employed by different European groups for purposes of mother tongue retention, very often in connection with a local parish (Fishman, 1966). On the whole, these attempts at mother tongue maintenance among the European immigrant groups were not successful, and the bilingualism of these groups became the mechanism for massive and very rapid language shift (Lieberson, Dalto, & Johnston, 1975).

The experience of the Europeans was in sharp contrast to that of the Chicanos, the Puerto Ricans, the American Indians, and other ethnic groups whose lack of English has led to recent federal legislation which is frequently interpreted to mean bilingual education. As Heath (1976) discusses in her provocative paper, England never provided her American colonies with any comprehensive language policies vis-à-vis the Indians, and this English lack of evangelism and cultural emission, in sharp contrast to the Castile policy in Latin America, continued to characterize the independent United States in her contact with other ethnic groups. U.S. federal legislation concerning educational language policy is very late in the making, and it was only massive school failures of children which finally forced the authorities to acknowledge the existence of bilingualism or multilingualism and eventually to legislate into effect BE programs.

The actual state of BE legislation at the federal level seems somewhat confusing or ambiguous. The first piece of important legislation was the passage of Title VI of the Civil Rights Act of 1964, and as Teitelbaum and Hiller (1977) point out, not even the most prescient could have foreseen that this legislation was to "become a principal weapon of linguistic minorities in their battle to establish bilingual education and gain equal schooling" p. 140). It was followed by the so-called Bilingual Education Act in 1968, the Title VII amendment to the 1965 Elementary and Secondary Education Act, which provided the first federal funds for BE programs, and the Bilingual Education Act of 1974, in which Congress described these programs as those in which:

. . . there is instruction given in, and study of, English and to the extent necessary to allow a child to progress effectively through the educational system, the native language of the children of limited English-speaking ability, and such instruction is given with respect to elementary school instruction, such instruction shall, to the extent necessary, be in all courses or subjects of study which allow a child to progress effectively through the educational system. (Teitelbaum & Hiller, 1977, p. 139)

A report of the National Institute of Education points out that the Bilingual Education Act of 1968, intended for children of low-income families, actually is a misnomer, "since the long-range goal is not bilingualism but proficiency in English" (National Institute of Education, 1975, p. 6). From the legislators' viewpoint the programs are compensatory in nature and all U.S. Courts tend to view bilingual education this way. The objective for such programs is a more rapid and efficient acquisition of English, such programs have become known as the *transition model*. However, the programs may legally be transitional in nature, but the major proponents for them, especially those members of the ethnic groups involved in implementing the new directives, invariably refer to them as bilingual/bicultural and see the objectives as stable bilingualism with maintenance of the home culture as well as the home language. So far, as the NIE report points out, "the Guidelines for the Title VII programs have been interpreted loosely enough" to allow for *maintenance programs*, as they are known, as well as for transitional programs.

The landmark case in bilingual education was *Lau* vs. *Nichols*, in which a Chinese parent took the school board of San Francisco to court. As Teitelbaum and Hiller (1977) note, "It squarely presented to the courts the issue of whether non–English-speaking children who constitute national-origin minority groups receive an education free from unlawful discrimination when instructed in English, a language they do not understand" (p. 139). That is, are non–English-speaking children afforded an equal educational opportunity when instructed in a language they cannot understand? Teitelbaum and Hiller (1977) report that "The plaintiffs claimed that the absence of programs designed to meet the linguistic needs of such students violated both Title VII and the Equal Protection Clause of the Fourteenth Amendment to the Constitution" (p. 142). In 1974 the Supreme Court unanimously ruled in favor of Lau, avoiding the constitutional issue and relying solely on Title VI, "for students who do not understand English are effectively foreclosed from any meaningful education" (Geffert, Harper, Sarmiento, and Schember, 1975; p. 8). In other words, equal treatment does not constitute equal opportunity.

It is from this Supreme Court decision that some of the confusion about federal legislation on bilingual education is said to stem, because the Court never specifically required it as a remedy, instead stating: "Teaching English to the students of Chinese ancestry is one choice. Giving instruction to this group in Chinese is another. There may be others" (Geffert et al., 1975, p. 8). As Teitelbaum and Hiller (1977) point out, however, "It was wholly consistent with Supreme Court doctrine that no specific remedy was ordered in *Lau*. Remedies are almost always left to the trial court" (p. 144). Subsequently, the Office of Civil Rights of HEW appointed a task force which worked out a set of guidelines for implementing the *Lau* decision. These are the so-called *Lau* "remedies," which have caused considerable furor. At the elementary level the *Lau* "remedies" categorically reject English as a second language (ESL) techniques, stating again and again that an ESL program is not acceptable in a BE program. Some have mistakenly interpreted this to mean that the children are not to be taught English. The remedies conclude this section with a footnote which states that an ESL component is an integral part of a BE program. To this confusion is added the fact that the legal status of the *Lau* remedies is uncertain. The Office of Civil Rights has stated "that, although it does not look on the *Lau* remedies as a 'regulation with the force of law,' they are 'entitled to weight as an agency interpretation' . . . [however labeled], the *Lau* remedies clearly cannot be disregarded by school districts" (Teitelbaum & Hiller, 1977; p. 153).

The *Lau* remedies are implemented by the General Assistance Centers, Type B, the so-called Lau centers, which are under HEW. The federal government does have indirect control over the state's educational autonomy through the allocation of federal funding (total HEW expenditures on BE and/or ESL projects for fiscal year 1977 amounted to $118 million), and school districts which are judged out of compliance with the *Lau* decision stand the risk of losing all their federal funding, a most powerful argument for the implementation of BE programs.

So is continued litigation, which has served and is likely to continue to serve as a strategy for educational reform. Teitelbaum and Hiller, lawyers who represented Aspira in the New York City bilingual education case, *Aspira* vs. *New York*, point out that defending lawsuits costs money, and that school boards cannot ignore such costs. Bringing lawsuits, of course, also cost money, but they point out in a very interesting footnote that "Congress authorized as part of the Education Amendments of 1972 the award of attorneys' fees to prevailing parties in educational rights cases. In so doing, Congress intended to encourage private individuals to redress discrimination in schools through litigation" (Teitelbaum & Hiller, 1977; p. 155).

And so, slowly through *Lau* violation rulings, litigation, and also through voluntary action at the state level (Massachusetts was the first state legislature to pass statutes mandating BE programs, and the Massachusetts Transitional Bilingual Education Law of 1971 has served as a prototype for other states), BE programs are being implemented across the United States. In many cases, however, this is clearly a legal-political process rather than the pragmatic-educational policy that Congress presumably intended in its transitional Bilingual Education Act of 1968.

What is the future of bilingual education in the United States? Some see it as an economic boondoggle; when federal funding is reviewed in 1979 by Congress, it is certain that questions will be raised about the efficiency of BE programs in teaching children English. Others see bilingual education as disturbing to national unity; both the influential *New York Times*, in a series of hostile editorials (1975; November 1976; December 1976), and the equally influential *Washington Post* have questioned its worth. Asks the *Post's* Noel Epstein: "The question is whether the potential benefits outweigh the potential costs. Would the result be more harmony or more discord in American society?" (1977, p. 4). Others simply note the legal mandate and judge the BE programs

. . . by the standard of equal benefits, the touchstone of Title VI. Does bilingual education positively affect a student's self-concept? Does bilingual education hinder academic progress during the course of second-language acquisition? Does bilingual education improve achievement? The answers to these questions are significant in persuading a court to reject one remedy and adopt another. (Teitelbaum & Hiller, 1977, p. 169)

There are other questions one may ask as well. The balance of this chapter will examine the alternative questions asked about bilingual education in order to clarify the theoretical implications the selection of particular questions entails, as well as the theoretical perspectives which encompass particular questions. There is no single answer to questions in bilingual education. The very questions depend on the world view and bias—of whatever kind—of whoever poses them.

EQUILIBRIUM AND CONFLICT PERSPECTIVES ON BILINGUAL EDUCATION [2]

Most educators can probably agree on the basic phenomena which form the background to Title VII bilingual education programs in the United States and which gave rise to the original legislation of Title VII: there are a number of children from a low socioeconomic status (SES) background who speak no or poor English and who encounter massive school failure, with consequent early school dropout and low integration into the economic life of the nation. It is when we consider why this is so, what treatment these children should be accorded, and what outcomes should follow that considerable disagreement ensues. Such scholarly disagreement at times becomes public and divisive.

Although other fields of study have looked at scholarly strife within their disciplines from the notion of Kuhn's (1970) paradigm shift, I know of no attempt to understand the dimensions of bilingual education from a conceptual framework of paradigms. By paradigms, Kuhn means the way a scientific-professional community views a field of study, identifies appropriate problems for study, and specifies legitimate concepts and methods.

R. G. Paulston, drawing on the literature of social and educational change, posits two major paradigms: the functional or "equilibrium" paradigm, and the conflict paradigm. Theories (which admittedly cross and overlap) that fall within the equilibrium paradigm are evolutionary and neoevolutionary, structural-functionalist, and system analysis. Basically these theories are all concerned with maintaining society in an equilibrium through the harmonious relationship of the social components, and they emphasize smooth, cumulative change. Theoretical approaches which fall within the conflict paradigm are group conflict theory, cultural revitalization theory, and an anarchistic-utopian approach. According to R. G. Paulston (1976), these theories "emphasize the inherent instability of social systems and the conflicts over values, resources, and power that follow as a natural consequence" (p. 7). Major issues are economic conflict, conflicting value and cultural systems, and conflict arising from oppressive institutions and imperfect human nature.

Assuredly, all of these theoretical approaches are not equally represented in the attempts to delimit and comprehend the dimensions of bilingual education, and in this chapter I have limited the discussion to those theoretical orientations that occur most frequently in the literature (for a more inclusive discussion, see C. B. Paulston, 1977b). In examining studies for their underlying assumptions, basic questions, and putative solutions, it will be seen that each theoretical orientation identifies differently the key variables and their relationship, and consequently the answers they seek will differ. For the purpose of illustration, I have identified a number of studies which most clearly exemplify a particular approach. Granted, some studies incorporate aspects at random from more than one theoretical framework, and on the whole I have tended to avoid such studies. Furthermore, a very large number of studies on bilingual education are descriptive and atheoretical; such studies I have ignored.

The Equilibrium Paradigm

Structural-Functional Theory

Although the structural-functional, or S/F, framework is a discrete set of interrelated assumptions about values, norms, and appropriate questions and methods, it is to a considerable degree a twentieth-century version of evolutionary theory. But where the evolutionists placed primary emphasis on linked stages of socioeconomic and cultural development the S/F theorists focus on the homeostatic or balancing mechanisms by which societies maintain a "uniform state." Both theories view societies as essentially stable yet highly complex and differentiated. As the values embodied in institutions such as the educational sub-system are viewed as extremely durable, boundary exchanges between the sub-system and the environment will be equilibrating, i.e., they will tend toward balance. (R. G. Paulston, 1976, p. 13)

Structural-functional (S/F) theory, as exemplified by Merton (1957), Homans (1950), and Parsons (1951), cited in (Larkin, 1970), has been the dominant theory of social change in American social sciences and has had a strong influence on the interpretation of educational systems and valid educational reform.[3] I do not think it is an exaggeration to say that the majority of writings in the field fall under this category, as I shall attempt to illustrate. This approach tends to be the position (almost always tacitly assumed) of the ESL proponents in the ESL vs. BE controversy. And it is most certainly the position of the U.S. government.

In the Bilingual Education Act, Congress recognizes the problems of limited English-speaking children from low-income families and spells out the measures to be taken in order to cope with these problems:

. . . the Congress declares it to be the policy of the United States, in order to establish equal educational opportunity for all children (A) to encourage the establishment and operation, where appropriate, of educational programs using bilingual educational prac- tices, techniques, and methods, and (B) . . . to provide financial assistance to . . . educa- tional agencies . . . in order to . . . develop and carry out such programs, . . . which are designed to meet the educational needs of such children; and of demonstrating effective ways of providing, for children of limited English-speaking ability, instruction designed to enable them, while using their native language, to achieve competence in the English language (Geffert et al., 1975, p. 13).

The assumptions are clearly recognizable: (1) the lack of social and economic success on the part of these minority groups is due to "unequal opportunity," as manifest through different language, culture, and learning styles, and to a lack of scholastic success as a group because of poor English-speaking ability; (2) with the provision of English skills, merit and IQ will lead, through scholastic skills gained in a "meaningful education," to social and economic success.

The immediate objective of BE programs is then given: to equalize opportu- nity for children from limited English-speaking families by compensatory train- ing in English where such training can be theoretically interpreted as a balancing mechanism to maintain the equilibrium of society. In this approach "intra- system conflict is usually viewed as pathological, as an indicator of systemic breakdown" (R. G. Paulston, 1976, p. 13). Larkin (1970), writing from an S/F perspective, points out that in a technological society such as ours, "equilibrium is maintained by the educational institution" (p. 113), whose major function is seen as the socialization of youth. According to Larkin, the socialization process is two-dimensional. The instrumental aspect is the provision of technical compe- tence: Education is to provide the students with salable skills (for our purposes,

English language proficiency can be seen as the major skill). The expressive aspect is a "normative orientation in harmony with the values of society" (Larkin, 1970, p. 113), or in the terminology more frequently found in the literature on bilingual education, facilitating assimilation into the dominant, mainstream culture. But to the S/F theorists, the value transmission function of the schools serves a wider purpose than just assimilation, namely that of *pattern maintenance*, in Parson's terms.

According to Parsons, provision for pattern maintenance is a functional prerequisite of all societies: "the social system . . . depends on the requisite minimum of 'support' from each of the other systems. It must, that is, have a sufficient proportion of its component actors adequately motivated to act in accordance with the requirements of its rolesystem, positively in abstention from too much disruptive, i. e. deviant, behavior." (Parsons, 1959, p. 27). The expressive aspect of the socialization process is socialization of youth to a social order by instilling values necessary for the continuation of the social system. (Larkin, 1970, p. 113)

While this view of the function of schools is reminiscent of the legitimation process of Bowles and Gintis (1975), the two approaches differ profoundly in their attitude toward such a process. The S/F proponents see this process as highly functional in ensuring that the most qualified persons fill the most important positions, and they "contend that inequality is not only inevitable, but necessary and beneficial to all since individual survival is contingent on the survival and well-being of society" (R. G. Paulston, 1976, p. 13). Parsons no doubt would consider Bowles and Gintis's neo-Marxist viewpoint as "too much disruptive." The latter would be likely to agree with Hill-Burnett (1976) that:

The key to access to a position is not the competence of the performer but the answer to the question of who has authority to judge whether the performance meets the standards, and to the question of how the judge is linked to the other arrangements in the society for maintaining a given constellation of differentiated resources and power over resources. (p. 37)

One is reminded of the debate in bilingual education over teacher training and competencies. The major issues, on the surface, seem to be language proficiency in L_1 (here minority vernacular) and L_2 (here English) and professional educational training in order to meet state requirements for teacher certification. But the question of proficiency masks the real question which concerns ethnic group membership: Is the teacher an Anglo or a member of the L_1 ethnic group? Bilingual/bicultural education proponents typically claim that teachers should be members of the same cultural groups as the students and tend to ignore the teachers' proficiency in English as an important qualification. Their position, whether theoretical or not, tends to be one of conflict orientation, frequently tending toward utopian ideology. ESL proponents, on the other hand, typically insist on discussing issues at the level of method and technique, a characteristic of the S/F approach. They see fluency in English and a thorough training in the techniques of ESL as the major requirement among the competencies of the teacher of limited English-speaking children. They tend to exemplify Larkin's points that (1) innovation is threatening as it temporarily upsets the equilibrium and (2) any pressure for change will be met by resistance from those office holders who have vested interests.

Access to teaching jobs in BE programs becomes very much a question of "who has the authority to judge whether the performance meets the standard." The standards, of course, are determined by the perceived goals of bilingual education. The U.S. government and its legislators officially conceive of the goal to be assimilation of minority group members through transitional BE programs, where the emphasis can be interpreted from the viewpoint of S/F theory as maintaining vertical equilibrium "by translation of societal needs and goals into institutional goals. In turn, the institutions must be organized to efficiently and effectively implement these goals and satisfy societal needs" (Larkin, 1970, p. 113).

Efficiently and *effectively* are indeed the key terms for the major concerns of the research on bilingual education from an S/F perspective. As an ERIC search will quickly demonstrate, there is a pervasive technocratic concern with methods, techniques, curriculum, and teacher training, no doubt partially because these types of projects tend to get funded by the Office of Education. After a perusal of the literature as found in ERIC or in doctoral dissertations, one cannot avoid coming away with a vague feeling that the most important objectives of these programs are for the children to increase their standardized scores on tests in language arts, mathematics, and self-concept, in order to demonstrate that teaching in the mother tongue results in the more efficient learning of English.

While the research, whether of an equilibrium or a conflict theory orientation, which R. G. Paulston discusses is concerned primarily with social or educational change at the national level—Parsons's (1961) societal and institutional levels—the majority of research and writing on bilingual education, especially recent work in North America, tends to be at the programmatic-operational level. The research typical of the S/F approach usually treats the BE programs as the independent variable, as the causal factor which accounts for certain subsequent results, for certain behaviors in children. One problem with such research is that these studies carry in and of themselves virtually no generalizability to other programs, as Mackey (1972) and Macnamara (1974) are careful to point out. Nowhere is this problem seen more clearly than in a comparison of the S/F–oriented research on the Title VII bilingual education programs in the United States with the research on the immersion programs in Canada. Many descriptions and comparisons of these programs exist (Andersson & Boyer, 1970; Cohen & Swain, 1976; John & Horner, 1971; C. B. Paulston, 1975a, 1975b;

Swain, 1972; Swain & Bruck, 1976; U.S. Commission on Civil Rights, 1975) and need not be repeated here. Basically, the Title VII programs are for lower-class children from socially stigmatized ethnic minority groups; the immersion programs are for middle-class children from the Anglo majority, a group in social and economic power.

On the surface, both sets of studies show great similarity in research designs: both treat instruction as the independent variable; both tend to recognize IQ, age, and sex as intervening variables, and, when feasible, to match or control for these variables. Presumably the researchers also recognize the importance of merit (personality factors such as industry, perseverance, and motivation, but as a formal variable in research design, merit tends to be ignored, and indeed Swain (1976b) laments that the kind of psychometric data these studies collect masks individual achievement.[4] The major dependent variable or program outcome for both sets of studies is scholastic skills, primarily proficiency in the two languages (as measured by standardized tests in language arts) and in mathematics. Other additional dependent variables like cognitive development and self-concept can be found in many studies.

Because of their similarity of research design, of identically labeled variables in the same basic relationship, generalizations are frequently made from one set of studies to the other, or to be exact, from the Canadian studies to the U.S. children and to other minority group children as well. I consider the St. Lambert study (Lambert & Tucker, 1972) potentially dangerous, because its findings are often cited as a rationale against bilingual education for minority group members (see Spolsky, 1973). It is important therefore to examine how these studies differ, even though they share the same basic S/F perspective in their initial motivation, in the selection of relevant assumptions, and in long-range goals. The fact that these issues are rarely made explicit or discussed in these studies can be considered as an S/F characteristic to minimize, if not avoid, intrasystem conflict, as an attempt to seek a balancing mechanism to maintain a "uniform state" through adaptive change.

Although both the U.S. and the Canadian studies are concerned with language proficiency in L_1 and L_2, the interest in L_2 acquisition and proficiency stems from a widely disparate motivation. The U.S. studies (e.g., C. B. Paulston, 1977b, Appendix) attempt to demonstrate that children who are first taught to read in L_1 will eventually read better in L_2 than similar children in monolingual English programs. They also propose that these children will achieve a higher proficiency in L_2 through the medium of their mother tongue than children who go directly into an L_2 curriculum (submersion programs in Lambert's terms; for a discussion of the difference between immersion and submersion programs, see Cohen & Swain, 1976). The Canadian studies, on the other hand, undertake to demonstrate that initial reading in L_2 (i.e., initial literacy) will have no negative consequences on either later reading or language arts skills in L_1; they also seek to demonstrate that the L_2 proficiency of the children in immersion programs is superior to that found in traditional L_2 programs.

Not surprisingly, different assumptions motivate the undertaking of the two sets of research studies. These assumptions are rarely spelled out explicitly but rather are accepted axiomatically or tacitly taken for granted. We need therefore to examine these assumptions—and the long-range goals—of the two sets of studies in order to interpret the research findings better.

The major basic assumption which underlies the U.S. Title VII programs is that of "unequal opportunity," and the belief that bilingual education helps equalize such shortcomings. Anderson and Boyer (1970) outline some long-range implications for society of a national expansion of bilingual schooling:

A concern by all Americans for the elimination of poverty, based in the realization that the educational improvement of the poor (which include many speakers of other languages who are presently handicapped in English) helps to raise the socioeconomic level of the population. A higher income level can in turn benefit education, setting an upward spiral. (p. 144)

Anderson and Boyer also compare educational problems with the experience of foreign aid, citing Jacoby (1969), who defines *development* as "a complex socio-political-economic process whereby a people of a country progress from a static traditional mode of life toward a modern dynamic society" (p. 5).

Such statements are the hallmark of the liberal S/F position: Poor people from traditional ways of life will progress (the evolutionist position) to higher socioeconomic levels through educational improvement. These assumptions are echoed by the U.S. Commission on Civil Rights, which introduces a discussion of how bilingual bicultural education provides equal educational opportunity, by saying: "Emphasis is placed on the most important elements in any educational program: fostering self-concept and developing cognition, language expression, reading, and English skills" (1975, p. 30). We have a Supreme Court ruling that equal educational opportunity may imply partial education in the mother tongue, but I know of no research which investigates whether equal educational opportunity as manifest through BE programs really leads to raised socioeconomic status of the type Lopez (1976) has conducted on Spanish/English bilingualism. It is the major assumption of bilingual education, but in S/F research it remains not only untested but also unquestioned—it is a question outside the paradigm.

The second major assumption in Title VII figures is the importance of the culture contact situation in the schools. The very definition of bilingual education given above acknowledges the importance of the mother tongue culture. From this assumption follows the emphasis that the teacher should be from the same ethnic background as the children: "One way bilingual bicultural education further enhances self-concept is by utilizing language minority teachers to reinforce the child's background and culture" (U.S. Commission on Civil Rights, 1975, p. 39). Consequently, the ethnic identity of the teacher is occasionally a subvariable under the independent variable of instruction.

From this assumption also follows the interest in what is commonly called cross-cultural communication (although the focus often is on miscommunication). Other closely similar areas of interest and investigation include communicative competence (Hymes, 1972; C. B. Paulston, 1974), sociolinguistic competence (Ervin-Tripp, 1973, p. 293), interactional competence (Mehan, 1972), and social interaction (Grimshaw, 1973), all of which have in common the focus on the social meaning of language, on the social rules of language use, "the systemic sets of social interactional rules," in Grimshaw's terms (p. 109). Although most research on symbolic interaction in BE programs (Cicourel, 1970; Garfinkel, 1967; Goffman, 1959, 1961) is written from a conflict perspective, there is found in many S/F studies a concern, rarely studied systematically, that teachers may misinterpret their minority students' behavior because of contrasting interactional rules as in the use of space, eye contact, or voice level, and in permitted speech acts, like types of questions. The concern is also voiced that Anglo teachers may allow any kind of aberrant behavior from minority students out of misplaced cultural tolerance because they do not know what the acceptable norms are.

Future research is likely to give increased importance to the area of communicative competence because it not only is of interest to those whose primary concern lies in the interaction between members of different cultures but also holds significance for theoretical issues in language acquisition. A current assumption about L2 acquisition is that language must be used for purposes of communication if it is to be well learned, and a number of classroom techniques have been worked out which incorporate social interactional rules of the second language into classroom practices (Applegate, 1975; Holmes & Brown, 1976; Jacobson, 1976; C. B. Paulston & Bruder, 1976; White, 1974).

An elusive assumption of U.S. bilingual programs is that one method will eventually be found to be more effective than others, and studies occasionally incorporate method as well as medium under the independent variable, instruction. We know surprisingly little about methods of language teaching in elementary bilingual programs, compared with what we know about methods of teaching adults. Due to the S/F definition of the problem as one of limited English-speaking ability and of the perceived treatment as one of instruction, there is a pervasive tendency to look for solutions to problems *within* the programs. Future research is most likely to investigate methods of bilingual instruction more carefully than in the past, where medium of instruction has been the major variable of instruction.

Two less influential assumptions remain. S/F research tends to take for granted that ability and merit influence the attainment of scholastic skills and that once equal opportunity has been provided for through bilingual education, such ability will result in success in school. Research designs therefore tend to neutralize such causal influence on the findings by treating IQ, age, and sex (sex is subsumed under merit, as girls are perceived to be more strongly motivated, harder working, etc.) as intervening variables and, where possible, controlling for such influence by matching groups or by statistical techniques.

The other assumption holds that there is some relationship between language and cognition. Language is believed to be the "vehicle for complex thinking" (Finocchiaro & King, 1966), and the necessity to use the language the children know best then becomes axiomatic (U.S. Commission on Civil Rights, 1975, p. 44). But the section of the report of the U.S. Commission on Civil Rights on Cognitive and Language Development (pp. 41–47) is characteristic of other BE writings on this topic: It contains not one single reference to empirical work on cognitive development of children in bilingual programs. This topic remains poorly explored in these studies. The Scandinavian studies, the majority of which are in the S/F approach, are in sharp contrast with their exploration of the possible consequences of semilingualism on cognitive development (Loman, 1974; Skutnabb-Kangas & Toukomaa, 1976). It would appear that the question of language and cognition is perceived by many researchers as being outside the paradigm. The earlier studies (Darcy, 1953) on bilingualism and IQ still rankle, and the topic of language and cognition is frequently dismissed with vague comments on the invalidity of the instruments used in such research.

To sum up, the S/F research on bilingual education in the United States is characterized by two major assumptions: unequal opportunity and cultural diversity. I have attempted to show how these assumptions have structured the research studies. Two additional factors which have influenced the research are (1) that the majority of BE researchers are either educators or social scientists who, in contrast to the Canadians, draw primarily on linguistics, anthropology, and sociology, and (2) that the perceived long-range goals are those of harmonious integration—in Schermerhorn's (1970) terms, either economic incorporation or cultural assimilation—into the larger society by equalizing opportunity.

The Canadian immersion programs (see Swain, 1976c, for a bibliography) are very different from the Title VII programs. The long-range goal of the immersion programs, especially outside Quebec, is perceived by most parents to be maintenance of the family SES status quo; because of Canadian legislation regarding language, they see bilingualism in English/French as a necessary condition for their children to compete successfully in the job market. Others consider bilingualism a personal asset for cultural, intellectual, and social reasons (Melikoff, 1972, p. 221). The Canadian researchers, the majority of whom are psychologists, have tended to slight social factors in their research and to minimize the potential conflict situation between the English- and French-speaking groups, but they do acknowledge that there is "no doubt that the language policy at both the federal and provincial levels of Canadian government is helping to provide incentive for English-Canadian parents to enroll their children in French immersion programs" (Cohen & Swain, 1976, p. 49).

From the difference in long-range goals follows the difference in the underlying assumptions. Since the children in the immersion programs come from the socially and economically dominant Anglo group (Lieberson, 1970) and have managed perfectly well in the English-medium schools, all notions of unequal opportunity are irrelevant.

Similarly, the notion of cultural diversity is also irrelevant. No one is concerned that Anglo ideocultural behavior might become stigmatized and held against the children by their teachers. The Anglo parents, children, and researchers take their own culture for granted, and in the Canadian literature there is no counterpart to the writings on ethnic minority groups' culture and behavior in the schools which we find in the United States (Pialorsi, 1974; Turner, 1973). The programs are housed for the most part in Anglo schools. In fact, the children in class function in French with the communicative competence of English; that is, they are not expected to give up their social interactional ways of speaking, their cultural ways of being. As a trivial example, in a class I visited, in answer to a question from the teacher the children waved their hands and shouted *Je sais, Je sais* (in the sense of "Please call on me"). A French-Canadian child would have said *Moi, Moi*, as Guy Dumas pointed out to me later. The children were not corrected (C. B. Paulston, 1977a, p. 102).

Nor is there any emphasis on the target culture to compare with that found in the United States. The definition of bilingual education in *Bilingual Schooling* (Swain, 1972) contrasts clearly with the American in that there is no mention of culture. Nowhere is this perceived irrelevance of "cultural diversity" seen more clearly than in the teacher variable. As in the Title VII studies, the ethnic membership of the teacher is occasionally included as a variable under *instruction*; I do not know of a single Canadian study of the immersion programs that investigates teacher ethnicity as a variable. One reason is that there is no concern about the teacher's cultural background, as long as she or he is a natively fluent speaker of French. Many of the classrooms I have visited have had nonnative Canadians as teachers—Belgians, Moroccans, French, as well as French-Canadians. In fact, the speech of French-Canadians is occasionally criticized; to illustrate, after a classroom visit I recall my colleague disdaining the use of the calque *attaque de coeur* instead of the "proper" *crise cardiaque* and worse, the use of the masculine adjectival *-al* suffix in the plural. The program goal appears to be linguistic competence in standard French, not communicative competence in Canadian French. It hardly needs be added that none of these issues is tapped in the formal research designs.

The Anglophone Canadians do expect the children to show enhanced cultural tolerance and understanding for the Francophone-Canadians through the increasing knowledge of French. The St. Lambert children really do not demonstrate this; while views of French Canadians were generally more favorable among the experimental group than among English controls, this difference did not reach reliably significant proportions (Swain & Bruck, 1976, p. 491). After seven years, the researchers can only talk about trends in desired directions. Genesee (1974) found no difference between the immersion group and the control group. The only one to question the relationship between French proficiency and French culture tolerance is the usual *bête noire* Macnamara (whose work in general I make no attempt to type):

And the average English Canadian's understanding of French Canadians will have to become a lot deeper and less bigoted than it is at present. . . . It is unlikely that the mutual trust, sympathy, understanding, and friendship of the two linguistic groups will be achieved by schools alone. . . . This probably dooms the enterprise to failure. It may even be more sinister. It may tend to exploit the weakest sector of society, the sector least likely to resist. (1975, p. 8)

This quotation from Macnamara serves as a clear contrast; his assumptions are in profound opposition to those characteristic of the S/F approach.

The formal research primarily seeks to tap the implications which follow from the major assumption underlying the immersion programs: a second language can be learned fluently in the school only if it is used as a medium of instruction, as a means to an end, rather than studied as a subject, as an end in itself. Consequently, the children are taught from the beginning in L2 in language arts skills programs similar to those used for native-speaking children. The extensive testing, primarily by means of standardized tests, which is basically what the immersion research consists of, was undertaken to assure parents and administrators that the immersion programs work (the programs are voluntary). There is no question at all about the efficacy of the Canadian immersion programs, and, if anything, the amazing dexterity and charm of the children as they negotiate in French gets lost in the published data.

We see then that although the U.S. and Canadian research studies are similar in that they see instruction, especially medium of, as the independent variable and scholastic skills as the dependent variable, they vary in the order of introducing medium of instruction, so that the Canadian programs reverse the order of the American: $L_1 \rightarrow L_2$ to $L_2 \rightarrow L_1$. The Canadian programs eschew the ESL approach (here FSL, or French as a second language techniques), in favor of basic language arts training and consider cultural diversity as an irrelevant variable; consequently neither method nor teacher appears as a design variable in the Canadian studies.

It should be pointed out, however, that the perception of the ESL/language arts dichotomy (Greenfield, 1976; Tucker, 1977) is a considerable simplification of fact. It would be more correct to say that the immersion programs do not incorporate the ESL techniques that we associate with the audiolingual method, such as oral drills. But the early classes abound with ESL techniques from the direct method as well as from a cognitive code approach. To illustrate, in one third grade, a boy came up to me and said in perfect French: "Madame, could you tell me if this (pointing to a word) is a verb?" His task was a controlled composition in which he had to rewrite all the present-tense verbs in the imperfect. He had just gotten stung on *souvent* and wanted to make sure this time. The point is, of course, that controlled composition where the teaching point is a specific grammar pattern is an ESL technique par excellence.

It is misleading to imply that the immersion program students study language arts just as do native-speaking children; they do not in the early grades. The language teaching specialist in me cannot but wish for some systematic research on this aspect of the immersion programs. None exists, so these comments are based on class visits, discussions with teachers, administrators, and researchers, and a familiarity with the literature.

The topic is an urgent one in the United States, where I suspect many programs flounder between audiolingual techniques for adults used on children and the "concurrent translation" approach, which is likely to be directly detrimental to learning (Legarreta-Marcaida, 1975). It is my considered opinion that the American programs stand to benefit substantially from the Canadian experience, just at the level of ESL techniques. It would be a great pity if no one investigated the immersion programs from this angle because they are generally considered not to incorporate any ESL techniques. They certainly do, and we need to know a lot more about them.

We also find the familiar assumptions of a relationship between language and (1) cognition and (2) IQ, age, and sex. In my opinion, the Canadian studies are much more interesting than the American ones in their work on language and cognition; presumably, I should imagine, this is because the former researchers are not unduly worried about adverse results. Cummins's work is especially worth citing. He speculates, in "The Influence of Bilingualism on Cognitive Growth" (1976), that the lower level of verbal intelligence by the bilingual subjects in the earlier studies (Darcy, 1953) "may be a reflection of the fact that they are likely to have had less than native-like competence in both their languages" (Cummins, 1976, p. 36). Cummins hypothesizes that "the level of linguistic competence may mediate the effects of his bilingual learning experience on cognitive growth" (p. 37).

In other words, the bilingual's level of competence in L_1 and L_2 is posited by Cummins as:

. . . an intervening variable in the causal chain between cognitive development and more fundamental social, attitudinal, educational and cognitive factors. Specifically, there may be a threshold level of linguistic competence which a bilingual child must attain both in order to avoid cognitive deficits and allow the potentially beneficial aspects of becoming bilingual to affect his cognitive functioning. Bilingualism and unilingualism can both be thought of as instruments which individuals use to operate upon their environments. Because of its greater complexity, the bilingual instrument is more difficult to master, but once mastered has greater potential than the unilingual instrument for promoting cognitive growth. (Cummins, 1976, p. 37)

This direction of research looks exceedingly promising and may eventually account for a number of contradictory research findings. Barik and Swain's recent study (1976) supports Cummin's findings and points to a new course in research on bilingualism and cognition.

To sum up, although the U.S. and Canadian research studies frequently identify the same variables from the range of phenomena within bilingual education and see them in similar relationships, these studies illustrate the point that underlying assumptions so strongly influence the research design, the questions, and the interpretation of findings that one cannot, at this stage of the research, extrapolate from the results of one set of studies to the other.

My reservations as far as all those studies go are very simple and probably fairly characteristic of the conflict orientation: Unless we try in some way to account for the historical, cultural, economic, and political factors which lead to certain forms of bilingual education, we will never understand the consequences of that education. In other words, we need research which looks at bilingual education as the intervening [5] or dependent variable, along the lines suggested by Spolsky, Green, and Read (1976).

"The Distressed Liberal" Genre.   R. G. Paulston (1976) discusses what he terms "the largely atheoretical 'distressed liberal' genre which, while essentially S/F in world view, calls for basic educational reform as a strategy for meliorative social reform" (p. 24). This type of work avoids a discussion of the role of power and conflict and sees inequities and inefficiencies of the schools as the result of bureaucratic, teacher, or parent mindlessness or ignorance, but not as a consequence of social-class self-interest leading to structured inequality. "U. S. government agencies, foundations, and financial institutions, intervening both at home and abroad in the interests of poor people, continue to share the basic assumption of this genre, i.e., that educational reform will eventually lead in some enlightened, relatively conflict-free way to more equitable, democratic social relations and conditions" (R. G. Paulston, 1976, p. 24).

The writings on bilingual education are amply represented in this category; we have all probably at one time or another fallen into this camp. I have discussed, in "On the Moral Dilemma of the Sociolinguist" (C. B. Paulston, 1971), some of the concerns which can lead a linguist into this sort of a position. Because of the basically atheoretical nature of this genre of writing, I think we should recognize that it tends to weaken the research base and to trivialize scholarly support of bilingual education.

The Equilibrium Paradigm: Conclusion.   Bilingual education in the United States is necessarily closely tied to concerns of ethnic groups. We have lately experienced a resurgence of ethnic awareness which brings into question the goal of complete assimilation for these groups. Elazar and Friedman (1976) discuss this new development of ethnic affirmation in their perceptive book *Moving Up: Ethnic Succession in America*. They point out that ethnic identity has often been seen as a problem that must somehow be overcome. Social scientists have often considered religious and ethnic groups as "vestiges of a primitive past that are destined to disappear" (p. 4), but recent "writers on the 'new pluralism' have argued that racial, religious, and ethnic groups *are* a basic component of our social structure" (p. 5) who affect our institutions and are at times more powerful than economic forces in their influence.

What Elazar and Friedman are discussing in their study of ethnic groups is in fact a paradigm shift from equilibrium theory to a conflict perspective. Some recent BE work reflects that shift. As the S/F framework Larkin (1970) discusses would predict, there is considerable tension accompanying the implementation of bilingual education. However, equilibrium theory is not designed to deal well with such conflict. "With its limited ability to include, let alone explain, conflict in the calculus of change efforts, the equilibrium paradigm must now seriously compete with alternative views of social and educational reform that see change and instability as constant and unavoidable characteristics of all social organisms and relations" (R. G. Paulston, 1976, p. 24).

The Conflict Paradigm

Studies of socio-economic, cultural, and educational change using variants of conflict theory have increased significantly during the past decade or so (Coser, 1956; Dahrendorf, 1959; Zeitlin, 1968; Allardt, 1971; Collins, 1971; Boudon, 1974; Dreir, 1975). This work may be divided into three types of conflict "theory"—i.e., (1) Marxist and group conflict explanations of socio-economic conflict, (2) cultural revival or revitalization explanations of value conflict, and (3) the somewhat mixed bag of anarchist and anarchist-utopian explanations of institutional conflict and constraints on human development. (R. G. Paulston, 1976, p. 26)

Group Conflict Theory

. . . all variants of conflict theory reject the evolutionists' and functionists' image of society as a system of benign self-regulating mechanisms where maintenance of social equilibrium and harmony is "functional" and disruption of harmony is "dysfunctional". . . . Formal education is here viewed as a part of the ideological structure which a ruling class controls to maintain its dominance over the masses, and because formal education is dependent on the dominant economic and political institutions, it cannot be a primary agent of social transformation . . . it can only follow changes in the imperatives of the economic and political social order. (Gramsci, 1957; Zachariah, 1975) (R. G. Paulston, 1976, p. 26)

Studies of bilingual education using aspects or variants of conflict theory have increased during the past few years. The definition of the problem, from a conflict perspective, is no longer unequal opportunity per se but rather structured inequity, or "persistence of poverty, intractability of inequality of incomes and inequality of economic and social opportunity" (Bowles, Gintis, & Meyer, 1976, p. 263). Unequal opportunity, the existence of which is most certainly not denied, tends to be seen as a result of a condition of inequity rather than as a cause of school failure. Consequently, in conflict-oriented studies the solutions to the educational problems of bilingual programs are rarely sought in terms of technocratic efficiency; in fact, they are rarely sought within the programs themselves but rather are seen to lie *outside* the programs. Different language teaching methods are held to account for very little of achieved language proficiency.

It is in this context that we need to interpret the significance of Fishman's (1977b) discussion of the social dimensions of bilingual education, which found that "very few empirical studies have focused on particular social parameters and explored their relevance to bilingual education across schools or communities" (p. 17). One reason that this is so is that the majority of the BE research has followed the S/F approach, and if one assumes that improved efficiency of school programs will solve problems of scholastic achievement, then one looks to instruction rather than to social factors for elucidation. On the other hand, if one assumes that formal education cannot cope with the consequences of social injustice or social inequity (in this country, BE is one such consequence), then Fishman's (1977b) statement that "societal factors are not merely 'interesting' or 'enlightening' for an understanding of bilingual education but . . . they represent powerful forces governing the success and failure of such programs" (p. 19) points the major direction for BE research.

In this connection, a comment on Fishman's discussion of typologies of bilingual education is in order. Basically, the typologies fall into two categories: (1) those that are "school oriented" and classify by program and program outcomes (Fishman & Lovas, 1970; Fishman, 1977b; Spolsky, 1974); and (2) those that are "context oriented" and classify by the social factors which contribute to the establishment of bilingual programs (C. B. Paulston, 1975b; Schermerhorn, 1970; Spolsky, 1978). Mackey (1970) combines the two.

From a conflict perspective, it is the social factors which are seen to influence the success or failure of BE programs, and hence it is clearly the derivation of context-oriented typologies which holds the higher priority, since they are more likely to help facilitate the identification of salient social dimensions. When revised and improved, context oriented typologies can be seen to function at a higher level of theoretical abstraction (Pelto, 1970) than do school-oriented typologies, and this higher level accounts for the principal weakness of the former: the difficulty in operationalizing key concepts.

The long-range goals of the programs, seen from a conflict perspective, follow the definition of the problem; they are to maximize equity in the distribution of wealth, goods, and services. Hence the emphasis is no longer on *efficiency* but on *equity*. This necessarily leads to disagreement over the evaluation of BE programs. In the following discussion of such evaluations, adapted in part from an earlier paper (C. B. Paulston, 1977a),[6] I make no attempt at impartiality about the two paradigms. The discussion is clearly written from a conflict perspective (although I never thought of it in those terms at the time) and is illustrative of the concerns in this approach with equity rather than efficiency.

The National Institute of Education (1975) report stresses the need for aims and objectives to be "clarified and made explicit so that progress toward the goal can be evaluated" (p. 8). I don't share their concern. It is a functionalist technician's mistake to want consensual goals in order to assess the efficacy of bilingual education programs. The parents want access to goods and services for children, with the least degree of damage to their sense of self, and they will vary in their interpretation of the best means to achieve that goal.

Rather than using only standardized tests on school achievement to assess bilingual education programs in the United States, it makes a lot more sense to look at employment figures upon leaving school, figures on drug addiction and alcoholism, suicide rates and personality disorders—that is, indicators that measure the social pathology which accompanies social injustice. Many see BE programs as an attempt to cope with such social injustice rather than as an attempt at efficient language teaching—although the programs are that too. One of the best indicators with which to evaluate bilingual education programs is the student dropout rate. The dropout rate for American Indians in Chicago public schools is 95%; in the bilingual-bicultural Little Big Horn High School in Chicago the dropout rate in 1976 was 11% ("School in Chicago," 1976, p. 49), and I found that figure a much more meaningful indicator for evaluation of the bilingual program than any psychometric assessment of students' language skills.

The major assumption which underlies most work written within the conflict paradigm is that BE programs can only be understood in terms of the relationship between the various interest groups. That relationship is seen as basically one of power conflict: "The probability is overwhelming that when two groups with different cultural histories establish contacts that are regular rather than occasional or intermittent, one of the two groups will typically assume dominance over the other" (Schermerhorn, 1970, p. 68). Lenski's (1966) metaphor is suggestive of the difference in world view between the two paradigms: "where functionalists see human societies as social systems, conflict theorists see them as stages on which struggles for power and privilege take place" (p. 17). This viewpoint is most clearly seen in the militant/utopian writings on bilingualism and bilingual education, as in this 1976 editorial from *Defensa, Boletin de la Liga Defensora del Idioma Espanol:*

In other words, the *Québécois* have finally realized that if they don't say "That's enough" they will end up as third-class citizens in their own country. Put in another way, group bilingualism, imposed by the harsh necessity to eat, is like a wound which will not close and bleeds and will not stop bleeding. As we have said before: Money speaks louder than syntax. (My translation)

Clearly, the research designs from this perspective are not likely to consider instruction as the independent variable or to consider issues of language as the most salient aspects of bilingual education. There is as yet no generally accepted framework of BE research from a group conflict perspective, but Schermerhorn (1970) and my own paper drawing on Schermerhorn (C. B. Paulston, 1975a), are increasingly being cited in the literature on bilingualism and bilingual education (Churchill, 1976; Cummins, 1976; Greenfield, 1976; Skutnabb-Kangas, 1976; Skutnabb-Kangas & Toukomaa, 1976). Since Schermerhorn is the most carefully considered design for research on ethnic relations, I will review it briefly here, focusing on the designation of variables and their relationship.

To Schermerhorn, the central question in comparative research in ethnic relations is: What are the conditions that foster or prevent the integration of ethnic groups into their environing societies? By integration, he does not necessarily mean assimilation but rather an "active and coordinated compliance with the ongoing activities and objectives of the dominant group in that society" (1970, p. 14). Integration can include either assimilation/incorporation on the one hand or cultural pluralism on the other, as long as the dominant and subordinate groups agree on the collective goals for the latter.

Schermerhorn sees three major causal factors in determining the nature of the relationship between ethnic groups and the process of integration. He posits as independent variables (1) the origin of the contact situation between "the subordinate ethnics and dominant groups, such as annexation, migration, and colonization, (2) the degree of enclosure (institutional separation or segmentation) of the subordinate group or groups from the society wide network of institutions and associations," and (3) "the degree of control exercised by dominant groups over access to scarce resources by subordinate groups in a given society" (1970, p. 15).

Intervening or contextual variables which will modify the effects of the independent variables are: (1) whether the dominant and subordinate groups agree on the goals for the latter, (2) whether the groups share common cultural and structural features, and (3) forms of institutional dominance, i.e., polity dominating economy or vice versa. The dependent variables to be explained are the interweaving patterns of integration and conflict; the first two deal with the relationship between groups and are correlative, and the third operationalizes this relation. The first considers "differential participation rates of subordinates in institutional and associational life (including rates of vertical mobility) as compared with rates for the dominant groups." This is clearly the variable under which the institution of formal schooling and bilingual education programs are subsumed. The second dependent variable considers "the extent of satisfaction or dissatisfaction of both subordinate and dominant group members with the differential patterns of participation as they see them, together with accompanying ideologies and cultural values." This is the variable which subsumes the attitudes and reactions of all those involved in bilingual education: students, parents, community leaders, administrators, government officials, linguists and other researchers, and so on. The discussions and controversy about transitional or maintenance bilingual programs would fall under this variable where the type of program is seen as a *consequence* of the other factors just outlined, not as a factor *determining* program outcomes. The third considers "overt or covert behavior patterns of subordinates and dominants indicative of conflict and/or harmonious relations; assessments in terms of continued integration" (1970, pp. 15–16).

How these concepts are to be operationalized is far from clear. The major contribution of Schermerhorn's framework to BE research is to indicate its direction to make clear the futility of continued research which ignores the social and historical factors which lead to the establishment of bilingual education. At this time, the majority of work within the conflict paradigm considers BE programs as the dependent variable; presumably we need to work out a framework which will allow us to consider them as an intervening variable so the dependent variables to be explained can be both scholastic achievement and social integration. It remains to be demonstrated, as a neo-Marxist perspective would have it, that there is no relationship between the latter two variables; there well may be. Integration, that is, assimilation or cultural pluralism as a dependent variable, can be operationalized in terms of language maintenance and language shift. An early work on Title VII bilingual education programs, written from a group conflict perspective, was Kjolseth's (1972) seminal article, "Bilingual Education Programs in the United States: For Assimilation or Pluralism?" which considered "the *social* consequences of particular bilingual education strategies upon the changing patterns of community language use" (p. 116). Kjolseth echoes Gaarder's concern that the bilingual programs (because they are more efficient for a number of reasons in teaching the children English) may be a one-way bridge to English and complete language shift, although he looks favorably on bilingualism and cultural pluralism, in contrast to Gaarder. In Gaarder's view (1975, p. 7), it is best not to learn the dominant language, not to learn English. It is an extreme and utopian position, but nevertheless it is against this background of bilingual education and language shift that the controversy regarding transitional vs. maintenance programs is best interpreted.

The proponents of maintenance programs favor cultural pluralism and ethnic diversity and tend to see the world in terms of conflict and competition between interest groups. Recent development has seen mobilization along ethnic boundaries as one strategy in competition for rewards (Elazar & Friedman, 1976), and maintenance of the ethnic language is a very visible aspect of such mobilization. Language shift is a phenomenon which is poorly understood (Fishman, 1966; Lieberson et al., 1975), and the relationship between bilingual education and language maintenance and shift is no better understood today than when Kjolseth (1972) pointed out "that there is not a single study planned to determine program effects upon community diglossia" (p. 117). Fishman (1977, p. 16) is right in pointing out the seriousness of Gaarder's argument about the consequences of bilingual education for marked populations; we especially need to investigate the social factors which influence BE programs in contributing to language maintenance and shift. As a matter of fact, we do not even know whether they influence language maintenance or shift in any significant way.

An important question in studies written from a conflict perspective is *cui bono?*: "Who stands to gain?" (Gramsci, 1957), where "gain" can be operationalized as an indicator of which group in the power struggle benefits. The BE literature is noticeable for the almost complete absence of such questions. The pious assumption is, of course, that the children are the ones who stand to gain, with indicators like standardized tests scores on school achievement and self-concept. I have discussed other indicators like suicide rates and school attendance figures, and there are other obvious indicators such as budget allocations and salary schedules. The only studies I know which consider the issue of salaries in bilingual education are those of Spolsky, who says the economic impact on a local poor community "cannot be underestimated":

In the Navajo situation, the most important outcome of bilingual education is probably related to changes in the economic and political situation. At the moment, the 53,000 Navajo students in school, 90% of whom speak Navajo, are taught by 2,600 teachers, only 100 of whom speak Navajo. A decision to establish bilingual education, even a transitional variety for the first three grades, sets up a need for a thousand Navajo-speaking teachers. Whatever effects this may have on the educational or linguistic situation, it is clear that it immediately provides jobs within the community for a sizeable group of people. A thousand well-paying jobs on the reservation for Navajos would lead to a greater income not just for the teachers themselves but for the community as a whole and would immediately establish within the community a well-paid middle class whose potential influence on political development of the Navajo Nation is obvious. Whatever may then be the expressed goals of a bilingual education program, it is probable that its major effect will be in this area. (1978, pp. 23-24)

It is against this background that the controversy and discussions about ESL programs vs. BE programs are best understood. The attempt to carry out these discussions at a programmatic level of language teaching methodology (see the 1976 issues of *The TESOL Quarterly* and *The Linguistic Reporter*) only confuses the basic issue, which is one of competition for scarce jobs. Clearly it is possible to discuss ESL and BE programs in terms of language teaching methods and techniques. My point is that the source of the strife and acrimony which accompany these discussions has its origin, not in disagreement over methodology, but rather in the vested interests of the two groups, most clearly seen in the struggle for access to jobs and rewards. As an example, bilingual/bicultural program proponents typically hold it as axiomatic that the teachers should be bilingual teachers of the same ethnic group as the children, purportedly for methodological-pedagogical reasons. The result is drastically altered teacher qualification competency requirements and consequent institutionalized denial of access to jobs for Anglo teachers who no longer qualify to teach in the new programs (Campbell, Taylor, & Tucker, 1973; Spolsky, 1978).

My opinion is that this conflict is in part damaging to the development of bilingual education in the United States. I find the evidence that children under certain definable social situations should be instructed in the mother tongue as well as in the official language convincing, but I see no evidence which dictates fully bilingual teachers. I also see a great deal of harm done by such insistence. There are very few fully bilingual teachers, and the result is that the children again and again get saddled with teachers whose command of the children's mother tongue or of English is very poor. The children need and deserve native-speaking English teachers if they are to learn English well in the schools, and some of the opposition by Anglo school administrators to bilingual/bicultural programs stems from the poor English spoken by the teachers in the programs. The Canadian immersion programs are very careful to separate the two codes in the programs, not by topic but by individual teachers, who are always native speakers of the language in which they teach. We have a lot to learn from the Canadian programs at the methodological level, if the political pressures could be withstood.

Hill-Barnett's (1976) comment that the key to access to a position lies with "the answer to the question of who has the authority to judge whether the performance meets the standards" is of crucial interest, given that all groups are self-seeking and define "performance" in terms of furthering their own interests. The controversial *Lau* remedies are a case in point. There is no research on "who has the authority" in bilingual education, on the ideology and ethnic identification of administrators who control access to positions. It would seem that *who* holds control over such "authority" will have important implications in the definitions of goals, implementations of programs, and evaluation of outcomes, yet it is a question we have not asked. It is true that ethnic groups tend to see the necessity of community control over programs as axiomatic:

We call upon city, state, and Federal institutions . . . to insure that these programs are controlled by and responsive to the needs of Latino residents (Sevilla-Casas et al., 1973).

These [Cultural Education] Centres must be Indian controlled and operated, in view of the fact that they are established for Indian purposes and use (National Indian Brotherhood, 1972, p. 17).

Nevertheless, it is an issue which remains uninvestigated in formal research and one which is probably of importance in explaining and predicting BE phenomena.

Regardless of who gains from bilingual education, the children certainly do too, and the clearest evidence we have in the form of empirical research on language skills comes from the data on children from the Finnish working-class migrant population in Sweden. There is no research here which parallels these studies; to my mind, such research is urgent, as findings of this nature constitute compelling arguments for bilingual education, to S/F and conflict theorists alike. The Scandinavian data are particularly significant in that both Sweden and Finland are highly developed, industrialized, modern societies with school achievement norms for children in both countries. In addition, Sweden is a quasi-socialist society where problems of health care, diet, and unemployment are not intervening variables. Such conditions are often cited as contributary factors in the lack of school achievement by minority children.

In a report to UNESCO,[7] Skutnabb-Kangas and Toukomaa (1976) discuss a study in which 687 Finnish students in Swedish schools, divided among 171 classes, were tested:

The purpose of the study was to determine the linguistic level and development in both their mother tongue and Swedish of Finnish migrant children attending Swedish comprehensive school. Above all, attention was paid to the interdependence between skills in the mother tongue and Swedish, i.e., the hypothesis was tested that those who have best preserved their mother tongue are also best in Swedish. Partly related to this question, the significance of the age at which the child moved to Sweden was also determined. Do those who received a firm grounding in their mother tongue by attending school in Finland have a better chance of learning Swedish than those who moved to Sweden as pre-schoolers? A second important problem is the achievement of Finnish pupils in Swedish language schools. How do Finnish migrant pupils do in theoretical and what might be called practical subjects? Does one's skill in the mother tongue have any effect on the grade given in a Swedish-language school or on other school achievement? (p. 76)

On all nonverbal ability factors the migrant children tested out at normal or slightly above normal level; that is, they consistently test out at a normal level of intelligence. Between verbal and nonverbal factors, however, there is an "enormous gap." During the first four to five years of school the Finnish migrant pupils remained at a level "which in Finland had fewer than 10% of the poorest pupils judged in verbal tests." In other words, their Finnish is poor, and so is their Swedish; "the average level Finnish pupil had a test point score in Swedish on a level at which about 10% of the poorest Swedish pupils were placed" (p. 54).

The language development data are supported by findings from a study by Särkelä and Kuusinen (1975), who tested 182 subjects in Sweden with a rural control group in Finland. The migrant children were slightly more above average, as measured by the nonverbal Raven intelligence test.

On the other hand, the psycholinguistic ages determined by the ITPA (Illinois Test of Psycholinguistic Abilities) show that in their command of the Finnish language the pupils of Finnish-language classes in Sweden were on average 2.5–3 years behind the normal Finnish level and the Finnish pupils in Swedish-language classes were 3–4 years behind the normal Finnish level. (Skutnabb-Kangas & Toukomaa, 1976, p. 55)

In general, Skutnabb-Kangas and Toukomaa found that the children's rate of improvement in Swedish was not as fast as the regression in the mother tongue. Although ability factors influenced the learning of Swedish, it is very clear "that the better a pupil has preserved his mother tongue, the better are his prerequisites for learning the second language" (p. 78). Overwhelmingly, the better a student knew Finnish (as a function of having attended school for several years in Finland), the better he learned Swedish. An examination of language skills of siblings found that those who moved from Finland at an average age of 10 have preserved an almost normal Finnish language level, and they also approach the normal level in Swedish of Swedish pupils. Those who moved at the age of 12 also achieve language skills comparable to those of the Swedes, although learning the language takes place more slowly. Children who moved under the age of 6 or who were born in Sweden do not do as well. Their Swedish language development "often stops at the age of about 12, evidently because of their poor grounding in the mother tongue" (p. 75). Worst off are the pupils who were 7–8 when they moved to Sweden: "The verbal development of these children who moved just after school was beginning (children begin school at age 7 in Sweden) underwent serious disturbance after the move. This also has a detrimental effect on learning Swedish" (p. 75). The evidence is perfectly clear that mother tongue development facilitates the learning of the second language, and there are serious implications that without such development neither language may be learned well. The result is double semilingualism, the incomplete knowledge of either language.

In an examination of the school achievement of the Finnish students, it was found that they did relatively well in mathematics, in the upper level almost as well as their Swedish classmates. But more interestingly,

The Finnish-language skills shown by the test results are fairly closely connected with the grade in mathematics. In the upper level, Finnish seems to be even more important for achievement in mathematics than Swedish—in spite of the fact that mathematics, too, is taught in Swedish. This result supports the concept that the abstraction level of the mother tongue is important for mastering the conceptual operations connected with mathematics. . . . Subjects such as biology, chemistry and physics also require conceptual thinking, and in these subjects migrant children with a good mastery of their mother tongue succeeded significantly better than those who knew their mother tongue poorly. (Skutnabb-Kangas & Toukomaa, 1976, p. 69)

The Canadian data from Manitoba on French-speaking children also support the Finnish data. In a report entitled "Academic Achievement and Language of Instruction among Franco-Manitoban pupils," Hebert et al. (1976) also found that the pupils who did better in French, their mother tongue, also did better in English and in other academic courses. Intelligence, socioeconomic level, and motivation were controlled for in this study, so they could not be factors which influenced the findings. The evidence for the importance of mother tongue development seems clear, and one would wish for similar research in the United States. Basically structural/functionalist in research design, the Finnish studies nevertheless are motivated by the same concerns which are typical of a group conflict orientation. Skutnabb-Kangas's (1976) argument, based on her data, that it is highly functional within a capitalist system to withhold bilingual education from children who need it is clearly written from a conflict perspective:

In this way the educational system contributes to ensure the perpetuation of a class society. Educational systems in Western industrial countries function as factors which preserve the social structure of society. As the educational system functions in the interests of the majority, and as the majority even in the future will need workers at the assembly lines, the educational system reproduces the immigrants' work and social structure, even when the system's official objective is to give the migrant children the same possibilities which the children in the receiver (host) country have. From this point of view one can understand the function of the migrant children's semilingualism as a factor which transfers and increases social inequality. (p. 35; my translation)

The Finnish UNESCO report (Skutnabb-Kangas & Toukomaa, 1976) is interesting, then, in that its authors are able to combine the ideology and concerns of group conflict theorists with a research design typical of S/F research. It is in fact one of the few attempts at a dialectic orientation (Sherman, 1976) in BE research.

Cultural Revival and Social Movement Theory

The literature on culture change and culture conflict applied to educational change is exceedingly sparse. It may be recalled that functional theory assumes a high degree of normative consensus across social systems, while conflict theory posits normative consensus or an ethos shared across major social groups, i.e., the working class, the middle class, and conflict between classes. Cultural revitalization-theory, in contrast, focuses not on social classes but, according to Wallace (1956), on "deliberate organized conscious efforts by members of a society to construct a more satisfying culture." Such efforts are viewed as constantly recurring phenomena, a type of culture-creating activity in collective efforts of varying size which seeks social and cultural change that may take place at local or national levels. (R. G. Paulston, 1976, p. 30)

CULTURE CHANGE. The literature on culture change applied to bilingual education is even sparser, and we do not know what effect this education may have on the culture of ethnic groups. One obvious resource of ethnic groups which can be used in stressing ethnic awareness and identity of the members is the mother tongue. With the recent trend toward ethnic mobilization, we see both language maintenance programs and language revival programs in which the mother tongue serves to reinforce the ethnic boundaries of the group (Barth, 1969; Spolsky, 1978).

The function of bilingual education in ethnic revival movements is an important one, but one we know very little about. A group conflict perspective is not helpful in trying to account for culture change, as this theory focuses on conflict between the various groups. Wallace's (1956) framework allows us to focus on change within the group as it becomes "revitalized," but we need to explore the role of language within such revitalization movements, especially the function of language in the mechanism of ethnic boundary maintenance.

CULTURE CONFLICT. The literature on culture conflict applied to bilingual education at the national level is also exceedingly sparse, but a number of studies exist at the programmatic level. These studies of culture conflict differ from group conflict studies in that the latter tend to focus on conflict which is caused by structured inequality; that is, they focus on aspects of social structure, of major institutional activities of society, like economic and political life. The studies on culture conflict, on the other hand, tend to be ethnographic in nature and to focus on conflict which is caused by an incomplete knowledge and understanding of the other group's culture as its norms and values are expressed in overt behavior.

Hymes (1970) sketches a general theoretical framework for such research. Culture conflict in communication is interpreted as "interference not only between phonologies and grammars, but also between norms of interaction and interpretation of speech." Hymes notes that "The notion 'ways of speaking' calls particular attention to the fact that members of a speech community have a knowledge such that speech is interpretable as pertaining to one or another genre, and as instancing one or another speech act and event" (p. 74).

Philips (1970) used this framework in her work on the Warm Springs Indian Reservation to account for the children's failures in school. The children's native ways of speaking and strategies for learning are very different from those of the Anglo schools, and consequently, Philip found, "Indian children fail to participate verbally in the classroom interaction because the social conditions for participation to which they have become accustomed in the Indian community are lacking." Philips suggests:

Educators cannot assume that because Indian children (or children from other cultural backgrounds than that which is implicit in American classrooms) speak English, or are taught it in school, that they have also assimilated all of the sociolinguistic rules underlying interaction in classrooms and other non-Indian social situations where English is spoken. (Philips, 1970, p. 95)

Culture conflict or interference in the classroom is a topic of immense importance in teacher training, and much of this literature is directed at the teacher (Aarons et al., 1969; Abrahams & Troike, 1972; Burger, 1971; Cazden et al., 1972; C. B. Paulston, 1974; Spolsky, 1972; Turner, 1973). The assumption which underlies these studies is that once the teacher understands that the children function with other sociolinguistic rules, with other rules of communicative competence, he will adjust his ways, and culture interference in the classroom will be minimized. Philips is unusual in this regard:

The teachers who make these adjustments, and not all do, are sensitive to the inclinations of their students and want to teach them through means to which they most readily adapt. However, by doing so, they are avoiding teaching the Indian children how to communicate in precisely those contexts in which they are least able, and most need to learn how to communicate if they are to do well in school. (Philips, 1970, p. 88)

She ends her paper by saying that the children must be taught "the rules for appropriate speech usage," that is, they must be taught the ways of speaking that are acceptable to the dominant culture. This is a troublesome matter and an issue about which we know virtually nothing. In spite of all the rhetoric about bilingual/bicultural education, I do not know of any research on the Title VII programs which deals with the issue of bicultural teaching. To the degree that the bicultural component of Title VII programs is discussed, invariably aspects of the home culture of the children, the culture whose sociolinguistic rules the children already know, are dealt with. I know of no work on attempts to teach the children Anglo culture, yet Philips holds such teaching crucial for the scholastic success of the children, and she may be right.

Utopian Perspectives

Anarchistic and utopian theories of social change share the Marxian goal of radical social transformation, and the concern of cultural revival and revitalization movements for individual renewal. In marked contrast to all other previously noted theories seeking to explain and predict educational reform processes, they rarely bother to validate their call to reform with the findings and methods of social science, or to put their theory to practice (Idenberg, 1974). The utopians' often insightful critiques of existing inequalities and "evils" in education may serve to provoke impassioned discussion (Rusk; 1971, Graubard, 1972; Marin et al., 1975), but utopian analysis rarely takes into account how existing oppressive power relationships and lack of tolerance for "deviance" or change in any given social setting will influence reform efforts of whatever scope or magnitude (Freire, 1971). Typically the utopians begin with a critical analysis of socio-educational reality and rather quickly wind up in a dream world. (R. G. Paulston, 1976, pp. 33–34)

Because of the provocative nature of their work, names like Goodman (1960) and Illich (1971) are familiar, but none of these utopian theories has been used in any serious attempts to understand bilingual education. However, the literature on the topic abounds with its own utopian statements. These tend to fall into three categories; romantic/utopian, militant/utopian, and visionary/utopian.

A large share of the literature tends to romanticize what bilingual education is and can do:

A new humanism in education has very quickly brought revolutionary changes to the public school systems of the United States. . . . The remarkable dispatch with which bilingual educational projects have been implemented in this country during the past year bespeaks the altruism and idealism of teachers and administrators who have activated them. For in order to institute these programs, it has been necessary for the teachers themselves to write and develop their own teaching materials, translate textbooks, ... (Byrd, 1974:39)

"The truth is that the majority of the bilingual programs only limp along" (Pascual, 1976, p. 5). Pascual's comment is based on hundreds of classroom visits, and the discrepancy between the reality of the "salones de clase" where the children learn to read from experience charts—"endless charts prepared by aides or teachers who guess at the orthography or rather at times invent it" (p. 6; my translation)—and the view of altruistic teachers in pursuit of a new humanism is not very helpful. Bilingual education is not a search for the Holy Grail, and unrealistic expectations only harm its future development.

How helpful the militant/utopian statements are is a question which deserves to be studied in the context of ethnic mobilization. It may be simplistic to write off such statements as empty rhetoric, and we ought to know something of the process by which voters organize along ethnic boundaries and gain control of local schoolboards. The following citation directed to Mayor Daley and the Chicago City Council (Sevilla-Casas et al., 1973) is clearly a political document:

> Our conference brought together Latinos in Chicago who have fought to establish bilingual-bicultural human service programs that are responsive to and controlled by the Latino community.
>
> These programs were established both through battles with established institutions and by setting up alternative facilities which bypassed irrelevant institutional services. Each of these programs is staffed and controlled by Latino community residents.
>
> These bilingual-bicultural programs are desperately fighting to stem the tide of oppression by Anglo society and institutions as seen in an 80% dropout rate, poverty, and urban renewal.
>
> However, these programs are not enough. We call upon city, state, and federal institutions:
>
> 1. To allocate a fair share of its resources to bilingual-bicultural Latino programs.
> 2. To insure that these programs are controlled by and responsive to the needs of Latino residents.
> 3. To see to it that Anglo institutions stop pressuring Latinos to become "Americanized" but recognize that our country can be strengthened by many different languages and cultures.
> 4. To insure that institutions serving Latinos make significant changes in their programs, resources and staff so that they can more effectively serve our people.

We know nothing from any kind of organized research efforts about the effect of this and similar documents, nor do we know very much about mainstream tolerance for such cultural "deviance." But clearly the future of bilingual education in the United States is dependent upon such tolerance. An editorial in *The New York Times* (December 17, 1976) gave an indication of the extent to which we can expect such tolerance:

> In a recent editorial on bilingual education, we expressed concern over a growing tendency to misuse an essentially sound pedagogical tool toward the wrong educational and political ends. Specifically, we argued that the maintenance of non–English-speaking enclaves points the road to "cultural, economic, and political devisiveness." . . . There are clearly some who view non–English-speaking enclaves as attractive bases from which to enhance their own political power. Whatever short-term political pressures might be gained from such enclaves, those who in the process are denied speedy entry into the English-speaking mainstream are saddled with persistent economic and political disadvantages. . . . But none of these goals causes us to modify our position that the purpose of

bilingual education must be "to create English-speaking Americans with the least possible delay." (p. A26)

Finally, it should be noted that utopian writings on bilingual education usually are atheoretical in nature and so provide us with data on its course rather than with the means toward further understanding. The issues raised in the Chicago document and in the *Times* editorial lend themselves best to interpretation from a group conflict perspective. What utopian writings do best is to sketch a vision and to reaffirm the goodwill of decent men. An example is these words, written in 1912 by the president of the University of New Mexico:

I make no doubt that once the people of this State realize the importance of the [Spanish language] issue and the vast results which may accrue from it, both for State and Nation, a movement could be set on foot which, with representation properly made to the chief executive and the national legislature, would secure for New Mexico a federal appropriation sufficient to fund and endow for many years to come, a Spanish American College for the purpose of developing and utilizing to the utmost the inheritance of our fellow citizens in the Spanish language. While a proposal of this sort, considered as a mere act of tardy justice to a long neglected people, might fail of effect, yet the national advantage secured thereby would assuredly win sympathy and support for the plan. (Gray, 1912, p. 6)

CONCLUSION

I have attempted in this chapter to show that a discussion of the research on bilingual education must take into account a number of factors. First, and obviously, is a descriptive definition of the particular BE program under discussion as the programs vary along a wide range of factors and cannot just be compared one to the other. Second, in order to understand the climate of bilingual education in the United States today and the research which it fosters, one must have a notion of the legal mandate for this education and its historical development. Finally, and most important, one must take into account an analysis of the various theoretical frameworks which apply. Not only the formal research design but also the alternative assumptions, goals, and strategies follow from the theoretical perspective. An exploration of the range of various theoretical perspectives on bilingual education will allow:

1. An identification of the world view and ideological orientation which is inherent within each theoretical perspective. Science is not value free, and by being able to recognize the assumptions implicit in work characteristic of specific theoretical orientations, one can better deal with such values.
2. An examination of alternative questions and an understanding of the theoretical implications which the selection of particular questions entails.
3. Finally (which remains to be done), the development of a dialectical research perspective in bilingual education, which would help specify the

theoretical approach most likely to be fruitful in answering questions of a specified nature.

NOTES

1. Merrill Swain points out: "Generally speaking, Canadian programs have been for middle- to upper-middle-class kids, many of whom have not had contact with French Canadians. Many of the programs come much closer to *elitist* than *folk*, especially when not in Ottawa or Montreal regions" (personal communication). Although the Canadian programs are unusual in that they involve members of the upper rather than the lower social strata, they are nevertheless the consequence of folk bilingualism, as they result from ethnic groups in contact. The elitist characteristic of the immersion programs reflects the division between Anglophone socioeconomic power and Francophone political power in Quebec, where the immersion programs are the socioeconomically dominant middle-class response to legislated language policy.

2. The following discussion is an abbreviated version of "Theoretical Perspectives of Bilingual Education Programs," a paper I wrote for the National Institute of Education, Conference on the Dimensions of Bilingual Education, February 1977. It is appropriate to repeat here my acknowledgement in that paper to Rolland G. Paulston and the influence his *Conflicting Theories of Social and Educational Change: A Typological Review* (1976) has had on my thinking and interpretation of the research on bilingual education.

3. It should be pointed out that individual scholars cannot be typed according to specific theories; only individual works can be typed. So Larkin is careful to point out that Homans (1961) "has moved away from structural functionalism to a more social-psychological point of view as indicated by the content of his book, *Social Behavior: Its Elementary Forms* (Larkin, 1970, p. 112). Furthermore, some scholars write from a viewpoint which selectively incorporates elements from both equilibrium and conflict theories; this could certainly be an alternative interpretation of Fishman's paper (1977) which has been criticized by Nieves-Squires (1977) for its structural-functional orientation.

4. One conclusion reached at the Center for Applied Linguistics series of seminars on bilingual education was that classroom observation by informed participant-observers is a necessary counterpoint to psychometric data in research. See especially Hatch (1977) and Churchill (1976).

5. Wallace Lambert points out that I use the term *intervening variable* differently from how it is used by psychologists, and he is right. To psychologists, "Intervening variable is a term invented to account for internal and directly unobservable psychological processes that in turn account for behavior. . . an intervening variable is an 'in-the-head' variable. It cannot be seen, heard, or felt. It is inferred from behavior" (Kerlinger, 1973). Social scientists tend not to use the term (Pelto, 1970; Sjoberg and Nett, 1968), but Schermerhorn (1970) does so in the sense of contextual variables that modify the effects of independent variables and that help account for the conditions for and the modes of integration of ethnic groups. Intervening variables in this sense are perfectly observable variables, like cultural congruence. I use the term in this meaning.

6. "Viewpoints: Research," pp. 95-100 in *Bilingual Education: Current Perspectives*,

Vol. 2, *Linguistics,* pp. 95-100. (Arlington, Va.: Center for Applied Linguistics, 1977). Permission to use this material is gratefully acknowledged.
7. The discussion of this report is taken in part from C. B. Paulston, 1977, the reference cited in note 6. I am grateful to the Center for Applied Linguistics for permission to use this material.

REFERENCES

Aarons, A., Gordon, B., & Stewart, W. Linguistic-cultural differences and American education. *Florida FL Reporter*, 1969, *7*.

Abrahams, R. D., & Troike, R. C. *Language and culture diversity in American education.* Englewood Cliffs, N.J.: Prentice-Hall, 1972.

Allardt, E. Culture, structure, and revolutionary ideologies. *International Journal of Comparative Sociology*, 1971, *12*, 24-40.

American Institute for Research (AIR). *Evaluation of the impact of ESEA Title VII on Spanish/English bilingual education programs.* Palo Alto, Calif.: Author, 1977.

Andersson, T., & Boyer, M. *Bilingual schooling in the United States.* Austin, Tex.: Southwest Educational Development Laboratory, 1970.

Applegate, R. B. The language teacher and the rules of speaking. *TESOL Quarterly*, 1975, *9*, 271-281.

Barik, H. C., & Swain, M. A longitudinal study of bilingual and cognitive development. *International Journal of Psychology*, 1976, *11*, 251-263.

Barth, F. (Ed.). *Ethnic groups and boundaries.* Boston: Little, Brown, 1969.

Belkin, J., Graham, J., Paulston, C., and Williams, E. Appendix B: Excerpts from Abstracts of U.S. Dissertations on Bilingual Education. In C. B. Paulston, *"Research," Bilingual Education: Current Perspectives.* Arlington, Va.: Center for Applied Linguistics, 1977.

Boudon, R. *Education, opportunity, and social inequality: Changing prospects in Western society.* New York: Wiley-Interscience, 1974.

Bowles, S., & Gintis, H. *Schooling in capitalist America: Educational reform and the contradictions of economic life.* New York: Basic Books, 1975.

Bowles, S., Gintis, H., & Meyer, P. Education, I. Q., and the legitimation of the social division of labor. *Berkeley Journal of Sociology,* 1975–1976, *20*, 233-264.

Burger, H. G. *Ethno-pedagogy: Cross-cultural teaching techniques.* Albuquerque: N.M.: Southwestern Cooperative Educational Laboratory, 1971.

Byrd, S. Bilingual education: Report on the International Bilingual-Bicultural Conference, May 1974. *ADFL–Bulletin of the Association of Departments of Foreign Languages,* 1974, *6*.

Campbell, R. N., Taylor, D. M., & Tucker, G. R. Teachers' views of immersion type bilingual programs: A Quebec example. *Foreign Language Annals*, 1973, *7*, 106-110.

Cazden, C. B., John, V. P., & Hymes, D. *The function of language in the classroom.* New York: Teachers College Press, Columbia University, 1972.

Center for Applied Linguistics. *Bilingual education: Current perspectives* (5 vols.). Arlington, Va., 1977.

Churchill, S. Recherches recentes sur le bilinguisme et l'education des francophones minoritaires au Canada: L'example ontarien. In M. Swain (Ed.), *Bilingualism in Canadian Education* (Yearbook of the Canadian Society for the Study of Education), 1976.

Cicourel, A. The acquisition of social structure: Towards a developmental sociology of language and meaning. In J. Douglas (Ed.), *Existential Society*. New York: Appleton, 1970.

Cohen, A., Fathman, A., & Merino, B. The Redwood City Bilingual Education Project, 1971-1974: Spanish and English proficiency, mathematics, and language use over time. *Working Papers on Bilingualism*, 1976, *8*, 1-29.

Cohen, A., & Swain, M. Bilingual education: The 'immersion model' in the North American context. *TESOL Quarterly*, 1976, *10*, 45-53.

Collins, R. Functional and conflict theories of educational stratification. *American Sociological Review*, 1971, *36*, 1002-1008.

Coser, L. *The functions of social conflict*. New York: Free Press, 1956.

Cummins, J. The influence of bilingualism on cognitive growth: A synthesis of research findings and explanatory hypothesis. *Working Papers on Bilingualism*, 1976, *9*, 1-43.

Dahrendorf, R. *Class and class conflict in industrial society*. Stanford, Calif.: Stanford University Press, 1959.

Darcy, N. A review of the literature on the effects of bilingualism upon the measurement of intelligence. *Journal of Genetic Psychology*, 1953, *82*, 21-57.

Dreir, P. Power structures and power struggles. *The Insurgent Sociologist*, 1975, *5*, 233-237.

Elazar, D. J., & Friedman, M. *Moving up: Ethnic succession in America*. New York: Institute on Pluralism and Group Identity of the American Jewish Committee, 1976.

Engle, P. L. *The use of vernacular languages in education: Language medium in early school years for minority language groups*. Arlington, Va.: Center for Applied Linguistics, 1975.

Epstein, N. *Language, ethnicity, and the schools: Policy alternatives for bilingual bicultural education*. Washington, D.C.: Institute for Educational Leadership, George Washington University, 1977.

Erickson, D., et al. *Community school at Rough Rock: An evaluation for the* Office of Economic Opportunity. Springfield, Va.: U.S. Department of Commerce, Clearinghouse for Federal Scientific and Technical Information, 1969.

Ervin-Tripp, S. *Language acquisition and communicative choice*. Stanford, Calif.: Stanford University Press, 1973.

Ferguson, C. Linguistic theory. In *Bilingual education: Current perspectives* (Vol. 2, *Linguistics*). Arlington, Va.: Center for Applied Linguistics, 1977.

Finocchiaro, M., & King, P. *Bilingual readiness in earliest school years*. Washington, D.C.: U.S. Office of Education, 1966.

Fishman, J. A. *Language loyalty in the United States*. The Hague: Mouton, 1966.

Fishman, J. A. Bilingual education: The state of social science inquiry. Unpublished manuscript, Center for Applied Linguistics, Arlington, Va., 1977 (a).

Fishman, J. The social science perspective. In *Bilingual education: Current perspectives* (Vol. 1, *Social Science*). Arlington, Va.: Center for Applied Linguistics, 1977. (b)

Fishman, J. A., & Lovas, J. Bilingual education in sociolinguistic perspectives. *TESOL Quarterly*, 1970, *4*, 215-222.

Gaarder, B. Las Consecuencias del bilinguismo. Unpublished manuscript, 1975.

Gaarder, B. *Bilingual schooling and the survival of Spanish in the United States*. Rowley, Mass.: Newbury House, 1978.

Garfinkel, H. *Studies in ethnomethodology*. Englewood Cliffs, N.J.: Prentice-Hall, 1967.

Geffert, H. N., Harper II, R. J., Sarmiento, S., & Schember, D. M. *The current status of U.S. bilingual education legislation*. Arlington, Va.: Center for Applied Linguistics, 1975.

Genesee, F., et al. *Evaluation of the 1973–74 pilot grade XI French immersion class*. Montreal: Protestant School Board of Greater Montreal, 1974.

Goffman, E. *The presentation of self in everyday life.* New York: Doubleday, 1959.

Goffman, E. *Encounters: Two studies in the sociology of interaction.* Indianapolis: Bobbs-Merrill, 1961.

Goodman, P. *Growing up absurd.* New York: Alfred A. Knopf, 1960.

Gramsci, A. *The modern prince, and other writings.* London: Lawrence & Wishart, 1957.

Graubard, A. *Free the children: Radical reform and the free school movement.* New York: Pantheon Books, 1972.

Gray, E. D. McQ. *The Spanish language in Mexico: A national resource* (Bulletin, *1*, 2). Mexico City: University of Mexico, 1912.

Greenfield, T. B. Bilingualism, multiculturalism and the crises of purpose in Canada. In M. Swain (Ed.), *Bilingualism in Canadian Education* (Yearbook of the Canadian Society for the Study of Education), 1976.

Grimshaw, A. Rules, social interaction, and language behavior. *TESOL Quarterly*, 1973, 7, 99-115.

Hatch, E. Second language learning. In *Bilingual education: Current perspectives* (Vol. 2, *Linguistics*). Arlington, Va.: Center for Applied Linguistics, 1977.

Heath, S. B. Colonial language status achievement: Mexico, Peru, and the United States. In A. Verdoodt & R. Kjolseth (Eds.), *Language in sociology.* Louvain: Peeters, 1976.

Hebert, R., et al. *Summary: Academic achievement and language of instruction among Franco-Manitoban pupils.* Report to the Manitoba Department of Education, 1976.

Hill-Burnett, J. Commentary: Paradoxes and dilemmas. *Anthropology and Education Quarterly*, 1976, 7, 37-38.

Holmes, J., & Brown, D. Developing sociolinguistic competence in a second language. *TESOL Quarterly*, 1976, *10*, 423-431.

Homans, G. C. *The human group.* New York: Harcourt, Brace & World, 1950.

Homans, G. C. *Social behavior: Its elementary forms.* New York: Harcourt, Brace & World, 1961.

Hymes, D. Bilingual education: Linguistic vs. sociolinguistic basis. In J. Alatis (Ed.), *Bilingualism and language contact* (Report of the 21st Annual Roundtable). Washington, D.C.: Georgetown University, 1970.

Hymes, D. On communicative competence. In J. B. Pride & J. Holmes (Eds.), *Sociolinguistics.* Harmondsworth, England: Penguin Books, 1972.

Idenberg, P. J. Education and utopia. In R. Ryba & B. Holmes (Eds.), *Recurrent education: Concepts and policies for lifelong education.* London: Comparative Education Society of Europe, 1974.

Illich, I. *Deschooling society.* New York: Harper & Row, 1971.

Jacobson, R. Incorporating sociolinguistic norms into an EFL program. *TESOL Quarterly*, 1976, *10*, 411-422.

Jacoby, N. H. *The progress of peoples: Toward a theory and policy of development with external aid.* Santa Barbara, Calif.: Center for the Study of Democratic Institutions, 1969.

John, V. P., & Horner, V. M. *Early childhood bilingual education.* New York: Modern Language Association, 1971.

Kerlinger, F. M. *Foundations of behavioral research* (2nd ed.). New York: Holt, Rinehart, & Winston, 1973.

Kjolseth, R. Bilingual education programs in the United States: For assimilation or pluralism? In B. Spolsky (Ed.), *The language education of minority children.* Rowley, Mass.: Newbury House, 1972.

Kuhn, T. S. *The structure of scientific revolutions.* Chicago: University of Chicago Press, 1970.

Lambert, W. E., & Tucker, G. R. *Bilingual education of children: The St. Lambert experiment*. Rowley, Mass.: Newbury House, 1972.

Larkin, R. W. Pattern maintenance and change in education. *Teachers College Record*, 1970, *72*, 111-119.

Legarreta-Marcaida, D. *An investigation of the use or non-use of formal English-as-a-second language (ESL) training on the acquisition of English by Spanish speaking kindergarten children in traditional and bilingual classrooms*. Unpublished doctoral dissertation, University of California, Berkeley, 1975.

Lenski, G. E. *Power and privilege: A theory of social stratification*. New York: McGraw-Hill, 1966.

Lieberson, S. *Language and ethnic relations in Canada*. New York: John Wiley, 1970.

Lieberson, S., Dalto, G., and Johnston, M. E. The course of mother tongue diversity in nations. *American Journal of Sociology*, 1975, *81*, 34-61.

Loman, B. *Sprak och Samhälle*. Lund, Sweden: Gleerups Förlag, 1974.

Lopez, D. E. The social consequences of Chicano home/school bilingualism. *Social Problems*, 1976, *24*, 234-236.

Mackey, W. F. A typology of bilingual education. *Foreign Language Annals*, 1970, *3*, 596-608.

Mackey, W. F. *Bilingual education in a binational school: A study of equal language maintenance through free alteration*. Rowley, Mass.: Newbury House, 1972.

Macnamara, J. *Bilingualism and primary education*. Edinburgh: University Press, 1966.

Macnamara, J. The objectives of bilingual education in Canada from an English-speaking perspective. In M. Swain (Ed.), *Bilingual schooling: Some experiences in Canada and the United States*. Toronto: Ontario Institute for Studies in Education, 1972.

Macnamara, J. The generalizability of results of studies of bilingual education. In S. T. Carey (Ed.), *Bilingualism, biculturalism, and education*. Edmonton, Canada: University of Alberta, 1974.

Malherbe, E. G. *The bilingual school: A study of bilingualism in South Africa*. London: Longmans, Green and Co., 1946.

Marin, P., et al. *The limits of schooling*. Englewood Cliffs, N.J.: Prentice-Hall, 1975.

Mehan, H. Language using abilities. *Language Sciences*, 1972, *22*, 1-10.

Melikoff, O. Appendix A: Parents as change agents in education. In W. Lambert & R. Tucker, *Bilingual education of children*. Rowley, Mass.: Newbury House, 1972.

Merton, R. K. *Social theory and social structure*. New York: Free Press, 1957.

Modiano, N. *Reading comprehension in the national language: A comparative study of bilingual and all-Spanish approaches to reading instruction in selected Indian schools in the Highlands of Chiapas, Mexico*. Doctoral dissertation, New York University, 1966.

National Indian Brotherhood. *Indian control of Indian education*. Ottawa, Canada: 1972.

National Institute of Education. *Spanish-English bilingual education in the United States: Current issues, resources and recommended funding priorities for research*. Unpublished manuscript, 1975.

National Swedish Board of Education. The teaching of immigrant children and others. In *Curriculum for the comprehensive school* (Supplement). Stockholm: Author, 1973.

Natives in bilingual education: A disgrace. *Wassaja: A National Newspaper of Indian America*, January 1977.

Nieves-Squires, S. Viewpoints: Anthropology. In *Bilingual education: Current perspectives* (Vol. 1, *Social Science*). Arlington, Va.: Center for Applied Linguistics, 1977.

Osterberg, T. *Bilingualism and the first school language*. Umea: Vasterbottens Tryckeri, 1961.

Osterberg, T. *A review*. Washington, D.C.: Center for Applied Linguistics, 1976.

Parsons, T. *The social system*. New York: Free Press, 1951.

Parsons, T. The school class as a social system. *Harvard Educational Review*, 1959, *29*.

Parsons, T. An outline of the social system. In T. Parsons, E. Shils, K. D. Naegele, & J. R. Pitts (Eds.), *Theories of society: Foundations of modern sociological theory*. New York: Free Press, 1961.

Pascual, H. W. La educacion bilingue: Retorica y realidad. *Defensa*, 1976, *4, 5*, 4-7.

Paulston, C.B. On the moral dilemma of the sociolinguist. *Language Learning*, 1971, *21*, 175-181.

Paulston, C. B. Linguistic and communicative competence. *TESOL Quarterly*, 1974, *8*, 347-362.

Paulston, C. B. Ethnic relations and bilingual education: Accounting for contradictory data. In R. Troike & N. Modiono, *Proceedings of the first inter-American conference on bilingual education*. Arlington, Va.: Center for Applied Linguistics, 1975. (a)

Paulston, C. B. *Implications of language learning theory for language planning: Concerns in bilingual education*. Arlington, Va.: Center for Applied Linguistics, 1975. (b)

Paulston, C. B., with Bruder, M. N. *Teaching English as a second language: Techniques and procedures*. Cambridge, Mass.: Winthrop, 1976.

Paulston, C. B. Research. In *Bilingual education: Current perspectives* (Vol. 2, *Linguistics*). Arlington, Va.: Center for Applied Linguistics, 1977. (a)

Paulston, C. B. Theoretical perspectives on bilingual education programs. *Working papers in bilingualism*, 1977, *13*. (b)

Paulston, R. G. *Ethnic revival and educational change in Swedish Lapland*. Paper presented at the conference of the American Anthropological Association, Mexico City, 1972.

Paulston, R. G. *Conflicting theories of social and educational change: A typological review*. Pittsburgh, Pa.: University Center for International Studies, 1976.

Pelto, P. J. *Anthropological research: The structure of inquiry*. New York: Harper & Row, 1970.

Philips, S. Acquisition of rules for appropriate speech usage. In J. Alatis (Ed.), *Bilingualism and language contact* (Report of the 21st Annual Roundtable). Washington, D.C.: Georgetown University, 1970.

Pialorsi, F. (Ed.). *Teaching the bilingual: New methods and old traditions*. Tuscon, Ariz.: University of Arizona Press, 1974.

Prator, C. Language policy in the primary schools of Kenya. In B. W. Robinett (Ed.), *On teaching English to speakers of other languages*, Series III. Washington, D. C.: Teaching English to Speakers of Other Languages, 1967.

Prochnow, H. *Final evaluation accomplishment audit of the Harlandale Independent School District's bilingual education program* (Report No. ED. 081 1556). Harlandale Independent School District, San Antonio, Texas, 1973.

Ramos, M., Aquilar, J., & Sibayan, B. *The determination and implementation of language policy*. Dobbs Ferry, N.Y.: Oceana Publications, 1967.

Rusk, B. (Ed.). *Alternatives in education*. Toronto: General Publishing, 1971.

Särkelä, T., & Kuusinen, J. [The connection between the instruction given in one's mothertongue and the ability in languages.] Jyväskylä, 1975.

Schermerhorn, R. A. *Comparative ethnic relations: A framework for theory and research*. New York: Random House, 1970.

School in Chicago caters to Indians. *The New York Times*. June 16, 1976.

Sevilla-Casas, et al. Addenda of Chicanos and Boricuas to Declaration of Chicago, IX International Congress of Anthropological and Ethnological Sciences, September 7, 1973.

Sherman, H. Dialectics as a method. *The Insurgent Sociologist*, 1976, *6*, 57-64.

Sjoberb, G., & Nett, R. *A methodology for social research*. New York: Harper & Row, 1968.

Skutnabb-Kangas, T. Halvsprakighet: Ett medel att fa invandramas barn till lopande bandet? *Invandrare och Minoriteter*, 1976, *3-4*, 3136.

Skutnabb-Kangas, T., & Toukomaa, P. *Teaching migrant children's mothertongue and learning the language of the host country in the context of the sociocultural situation of the migrant family*. Helsinki: Finnish National Commission for UNESCO, 1976.

Spolsky, B. (Ed.). *The language education of minority children*. Rowley, Mass.: Newbury House, 1972.

Spolsky, B. Review of *Bilingual education of children: The St. Lambert experiment*, by W. E. Lambert & G. R. Tucker. *TESOL Quarterly*, 1973, *7*, 321-325.

Spolsky, B. American Indian bilingual education. In B. Spolsky & R. Cooper (Eds.), *Case studies in bilingual education*. Rowley, Mass.: Newbury House, 1978.

Spolsky, B., & Cooper, R. L. (Eds.). *Frontiers of bilingual education*. Rowley, Mass.: Newbury House, 1977.

Spolsky, B., & Cooper, R. L. (Eds.). *Case studies in bilingual education*. Rowley, Mass.: Newbury House, 1978.

Spolsky, B., Green, J., & Read, J. A model for the description, analysis, and perhaps evaluation of bilingual education. In A. Verdoodt & R. Kjolseth (Eds.), *Language in sociology*. Louvain: Edition Peeters, 1976.

Stern, H. H. Introduction. In M. Swain (Ed.), *Bilingual schooling: Some experiences in Canada and the United States*. Toronto: Ontario Institute for Studies in Education, 1972.

Swain, M. (Ed.). *Bilingual schooling: Some experience in Canada and the United States*. Toronto: Ontario Institute for Studies in Education, 1972.

Swain, M. Bibliography: Research on immersion education for the majority child. *The Canadian Modern Language Review*, 1976, *32*, 592-596. (a)

Swain, M. (Ed.). *Bilingualism in Canadian education: Issues and research* (Yearbook of the Canadian Society for the Study of Education), 1976. (b)

Swain, M. *Evaluation of bilingual education programs: Problems and some solutions*. Paper presented at the 20th Annual Convention of the Comparative and International Education Society, Toronto, 1976. (c)

Swain, M., & Bruck, M. (Eds.). Immersion education for the majority child. *The Canadian Modern Language Review*, 1976, *32*, 5.

Teitelbaum, H., & Hiller, R. J. Bilingual education: The legal mandate. *Harvard Educational Review*, 1977, *47*, 138-170.

Tucker, R. The linguistic perspective. In *Bilingual education: Current Perspectives* (Vol. 2, *Linguistics*). Arlington, Va.: Center for Applied Linguistics, 1977.

Turner, P. R. *Bilingualism in the Southwest*. Tucson, Ariz.: University of Arizona Press, 1973.

U.S. Commission on Civil Rights. *A better chance to learn: Bilingual bicultural education*. Washington, D.C.: U.S. Government Printing Office, 1975.

Wallace, A. Revitalization movements. *American Anthropologist*, 1956, *59*.

Zeitlin, I. M. *Ideology and the development of sociological theory*. Englewood Cliffs, N.J.: Prentice-Hall, 1968.

6

Language in Texts

MICHAEL MACDONALD-ROSS
The Open University

This review is the sequel to my review of graphics in text in Volume 5 of this series (Macdonald-Ross, 1978). Together the two chapters survey the field of research relevant to the design of printed curriculum materials. They also demark an area of applied research, namely, research which helps to develop the practical art of the communicator and hence may improve the quality of texts used for pedagogy.

Necessarily, this review has some limitations which ought to be kept in mind. Research into language is being published at an astonishing rate; no one could possibly be familiar with all of it, nor is there space to discuss each paper in detail. Therefore, this review is selective: I have chosen the research which seems to me important for its potential significance to the improvement of curricular texts. Wherever possible reviews and other key sources are quoted, and the reader can get access to the older literature by consulting these key works. The review is based on an extensive bibliography which lists all the sources in detail (Macdonald-Ross & Smith, 1978). Research workers will find this bibliography a source of further information.

The 20th century will doubtless be remembered in many ways—for its wars and its social changes, for atomic physics, for the start of genetic engineering, for the mass media, and for the first intelligent machines. Such great events do seize our imagination, but there are also quiet revolutions which are just as important in the long run. This century we have become conscious of *language*. In some sense we all know that the human race is the only form of life which uses

LAWRENCE FRASE, National Institute of Education, GEORGE KLARE, Ohio University, and JOHN RICKARDS, Purdue University, were editorial consultants for this chapter.

Note: My thanks to Professor George Klare, Dr. Lawrence Frase, and Dr. John Rickards, who acted as editorial consultants for this paper. My colleagues, Professor David Hawkridge, Neville Edwards, and Robert Waller also read the draft, and I am grateful for their comments and advice.

language (in the sense explained by Lennenberg, 1964, 1967, and Bronowski, 1977), but the full implications of this commonplace were not brought home to scholars until Frege, Peirce, and Wittgenstein showed how the great problems of philosophy were bound up with and perhaps caused by our habits of speech (see Dummett, 1973; Peirce, 1932/1960; Wittgenstein, 1922, 1953). After Wittgenstein's work no philosopher can treat language as a transparent problem-free medium of thought; when we have problems with our thought we now consider how these problems are connected to and partly caused by our habits of expression. This is a permanent change in outlook, an event in the history of man's culture. To find discoveries in language of comparable importance we must go back to Aristotle, who elucidated the basic parts of speech and hence laid the foundations of linguistics (see Aristotle, 1963).

The growth of linguistics as a real professional discipline is the second major influence on our understanding of language. After gradual progress in the preceding century (Johnson, 1836/1947; Muller, 1864–66; Pedersen, 1931/1962), the discipline of linguistics has been in full flood during the 20th century. So many great scholars have contributed to this work that one could hardly list them all; but by any score de Saussure (1915), Sapir (1921, 1949/1970), Jespersen (1922), Firth (1930, 1937), Bloomfield (1933), Vygotsky (1934/1962), and Chomsky (1957) are landmarks in the history of linguistic ideas.

Third, we have witnessed the growth of psychology as a discipline; from the start psychologists have identified language both as a tool of investigation and as a problem in its own right. This review will give some notion of the kind of contribution experimental psychology has made to the study of language (see also the outstanding review by Carroll, 1971). But while I have been formulating my own ideas on language research, a fourth set of ideas has invaded and reinvigorated the other three disciplines. This invasion by the conceptual framework of artificial intelligence is so striking that it cannot be ignored, yet so recent that its implications can hardly be assessed.

The reading situation entails a text, a reader, and some interaction between the two. In this review I start by considering ways and means of analyzing texts. The second part of the review is devoted to experimental studies with instructional texts.

THE ANALYSIS OF TEXTS

There is a widespread belief among instructional psychologists that the only way to get valid information about the quality of curricular materials is to try the materials out, in some more or less organized way, on the students they were meant for. This proposition has seemed so self-evident that it has almost never been questioned. The strongest form of this belief was stated by the Joint Committee on Programmed Instruction and Teaching Machines (Lumsdaine, 1966). Here quality was redefined as "effectiveness," and effectiveness was reduced to "achieving preset objectives." Thus, in this scheme the quality of learning material is decided entirely by whether or not the target population can achieve preset behavioral objectives.

Excerpts from the Joint Committee on Programmed Instruction and Teaching Machines (Lumsdaine, 1966):

Prospective users should evaluate each program on its own merits according to its demonstrated effectiveness in producing specified outcomes.

The publisher should state in detail the minimum objectives of his program, preferably in terms of specific behaviors or competences which its use is intended to achieve for specified kinds of learners.

The recommendations that follow are concerned primarily with the reporting of formal and rigorous assessment studies which are required for determining in some detail the performance characteristics of a program—that is, the specific outcomes which a program can be shown to be reliably capable of producing.

This simple, systematic approach to curriculum development still has many adherents; we see its influence in Scriven's formative vs. summative evaluation, a simple but memorable distinction which is a cornerstone of the curriculum movement (Scriven, 1966). Less directly we see the same influence in many studies by applied psychologists; for example, Rothkopf's research into questions in text (discussed later) started as a series of tests on the basic variables of programmed instruction.

Of course, it is necessary for curriculum developers to find out how their materials work in practice. Nothing I say here is meant to deny this truism. But when it is posed in its strong form—that is, student outcomes are *both necessary and sufficient* to show the merits and the defects of instructional materials—this proposition I believe to be completely false, seriously damaging to the production of good material and to the possibility of building sound practices of curriculum development.

The equation of quality with attainment of objectives is unsound in two ways: it is unsound conceptually, and it is unworkable in practice. Conceptually the equation fails because it is too grossly instrumental; the content of education is assumed to be nonproblematic and separable from the mechanics of teaching and learning. In fact the content of education is deeply problematic, and means and ends are almost inextricably intertwined. Furthermore, the equation rests absolutely on a strong version of the case for behavioral objectives, which has now been substantially demolished (Apple, 1972; Macdonald-Ross, 1973; Peters, 1973).

Also, there are practical difficulties which obstruct the simple empirical validation of quality. Developmental testing (formative evaluation) is expensive and time-consuming, and it rarely simulates realistic learning situations. For these reasons the notion of successive approximation is more honored by the breach than by the observance. Most textbooks, most national curriculum projects, and most distance-learning systems are not subjected to formative testing, or if the testing is done at all, it is perfunctory and in no way meets the strong procedures laid down in theory. When formative evaluation is done it rarely gives any insights that a skilled analyst could not have predicted; actually, most practical developers use the field data as a rhetorical device to gain acceptance for proposals they would have made in any case. The experimental approach of applied psychology also has its problems. To gain sufficient control over the experimental ·situation the text material of the learning situation is often simplified to the point of banality. Naturally, this makes the results difficult to interpret in practical situations. A more serious drawback is that after decades of detailed experimental work, we have obtained from this approach few deep or surprising insights.

One way to revitalize formative evaluation is to concentrate on recording the problem-solving protocols of individual students, as suggested by Newell and Simon (1972), or quite differently by Richards (1929, 1938). The use of individual records rather than summated pretest and posttest scores may seem at first sight just a nuance, but really it is an important shift of emphasis. From detailed records *diagnosis* can be achieved—and that is right at the heart of pedagogy.

Along with this more fruitful conception of formative evaluation there should be expert criticism of the text itself. The idea of using experts to analyze texts was severely criticized by the founding fathers of programmed learning, with the unfortunate consequence that this fruitful idea has been neglected until recently. The systematic and intelligent analysis of texts ought to be one of the central procedures of curriculum development: it is fast and relatively cheap, and if done by an expert analyst it has a creative potential that formative testing lacks. What techniques of analysis are available at present? In principle, there is no limit to the ways in which a text might be analyzed, but in practice the most important methods can be dealt with under these headings:

Readability Measures

Quantitative Content Analysis

Linguistic Analysis

Subject Matter Analysis

Readability Measures

The object of a readability measure is to predict the extent to which prose is likely to be read and understood. Such measures are of two kinds: readability formulae and direct measures. A *readability formula* uses one or more *indices* (such as word frequency or sentence length) which give a statistical prediction of reading difficulty. Since these formulae can be directly applied to the text and do not require the use of subjects, they are simple and cheap to use. They are also surprisingly reliable—for example, a formula is generally more reliable than the opinions of individual judges (Klare, 1976a). The second kind of readability measure, a direct measure, is obtained by testing prose on students; this is the cloze procedure, to be discussed later.

The importance of readable prose in practical learning situations can hardly be overestimated. If readers can freely choose whether or not to read on, or if they are relatively less skilled, or if they have limited time available for study, then the effect of readability can be quite crucial. For example, Murphy (1947a, 1947b) found readership of a farm newspaper increased from 45 to 66% with the more readable version of a split-run experiment. Swanson (1948) showed that in the more readable version of a newspaper nearly twice as many paragraphs were read. Sticht and his colleagues found that much military job-aid material was beyond the capacity of the intended users, and the actual use of printed sources was clearly related to the match between their readability and the reading ability of the users. As the gap between readability and reading ability increased, the men turned to each other for information instead of using the printed sources (Kern, Sticht, & Fox, 1970; Sticht, 1970, 1975; Sticht, Caylor, Kern & Fox, 1971; Vineberg, Sticht, Taylor, & Caylor, 1971.) Klare and his colleagues have also shown the clear relationship between readability and learner acceptability (Klare, Mabry, & Gustafson, 1955), and between readability and efficiency of reading (Klare, Shuford, & Nichols, 1957). Klare and Smart (1973) found a rank-order correlation of .87 between the readability level of correspondence material and the probability that students would send in all their lessons (with length held constant). Such decisively clear-cut field results are not to be put aside lightly.

From this evidence there is a strong argument for large-scale text producers to apply readability measures to their products. Centralized producers such as the armed forces, the larger textbook companies, and distance learning systems like The Open University have the resources and ought to protect their consumers by adequate monitoring. From the producer's point of view, monitoring by readability formulae is a filter or control device which predicts mismatches between the reader and the material being read.

The notion of "mismatch" or "literacy gap" should be considered warily. We do not always have good information about the reading ability of the target population, and if (as at The Open University) it is scattered across the whole country, giving reading tests to an adequate sample would be a most costly exercise. Reading tests for adults and older children are not adequate at present, so the choice of measuring rod is quite difficult and unsatisfactory. The degree of unreliability of readability formulae and reading tests can be sufficiently large for an apparent exact match between reading ability and readability to mask a real gap of two or three grades. The average classroom (or other target population) contains students with a wide range of reading ability, and individual textbooks are now known to contain extensive and erratic variations in readability level (Stokes, 1978). The professional research worker can cope with many of these difficulties, but the amateur is likely to fall into one or another pitfall. Thus there is a case for large-scale text producers to employ expert advisers who will tailor make a control system to the needs of a particular organization and its target audience. However, a readability "filter" (despite all these technical problems) is more reliable than the exercise of unaided human judgment. Since human judgment is costly and good editors are scarce, the alternative to a readability filter is usually no control system at all; that is, managers simply take it on trust that the texts their organization produces actually can be read and understood. The field evidence given above shows that this confidence is often not grounded in fact.

In general a readability formula is a tool of statistical prediction; its application to a particular reader or to a well-defined class of readers depends not only on their reading skill but also on their motivation, the time available for reading, and their prior knowledge of the subject matter. These factors obviously interact, as shown in the recent model of reading performance by Klare (1976b) illustrated in Figure 1.

One great merit of Klare's model is that it explains many of the no-difference results obtained in laboratory studies. As Klare says, researchers often take steps to raise readers' motivation, and if there is opportunity for this to take effect (for example, by providing generous reading time), then the experimental difference between texts of high and low readability may be washed out. By contrast, in the field motivation is much lower and the task may be abandoned—which obviously leads to a loss in comprehension. Klare's model also explains why Denbow (1973) found that improved readability caused relatively *less* information gain for the preferred content and for sessions conducted by regular instructors in their own classrooms. And it provides some guidelines for rewriting material; if there is a choice, the low-interest or least familiar material should be rewritten first. Klare's model pinpoints some of the key differences between laboratory experiments and field application, which is one of the perennial problems of applied psychology.

About the construction and choice of formulae, little needs to be said here. The standard reference works of Chall (1958) and Klare (1963) summarize the earlier work, and Klare's recent (1974–1975) review brings us up to date. Among expert readability researchers there is now an unusual consensus of opinion about the main issues. Computer text processing has already arrived, and we must assume that readability analysis will be a standard option in most software packages. In fact, most research laboratories have already automated their formulae (see Klare, 1974–1975). The choice of formula usually narrows down to Dale-Chall (1948) or Flesch (1948), both of which are available in updated and revalidated versions (Powers, Sumner, & Kearl, 1958), and the Dale/Chall formula is being revised by its authors. These are the best of the

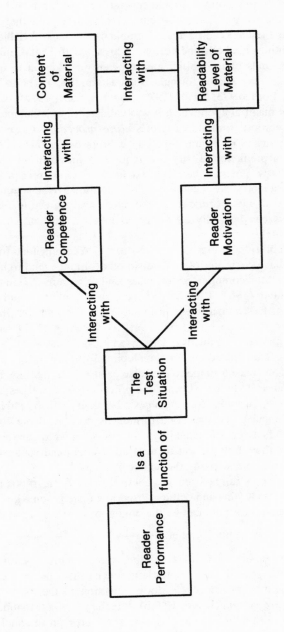

Figure 1. Some major factors interacting with readability measures in validity studies in Klare's model of reading performance. (From "A Second Look at the Validity of Readability Formulas," by G. R. Klare, *Journal of Reading Behavior,* 1976, *8,* 129-152.

two-variable formulae, that is, those that use a measure of work familiarity and also a measure of syntactic complexity (sentence length). The Dale-Chall formula is known to be the most reliable general-purpose formula, but because it is based on a word list it is somewhat cumbersome to apply either by hand or by machine. The Flesch Reading Ease formula is the most reliable of the faster (syllable-counting) methods and correlates highly with Dale-Chall.

Two other kinds of readability measures are in widespread use today. The special-purpose one-variable formula, such as HumRRO's FORCAST (Caylor, Sticht, Fox & Ford, 1973; Sticht, 1977, Sticht & Zapf, 1976), can be excellent for the kind of material upon which it was validated, but it cannot be used safely as a general-purpose formula. Taylor's *cloze procedure* is quite different in character (Taylor, 1953; Klare, Sinaiko, & Stolurow, 1972). Cloze is a direct measure, not a prediction. Every use requires a group of subjects; this is its strength and its weakness. The weakness is clear: Large text producers cannot and need not adopt such a cumbersome procedure when adequate predictive formulae are available. For the researcher cloze has interesting advantages. The filled-in blanks can be analyzed for error patterns, thus providing a tool for linguistic research.

Other readability measures cannot be strongly recommended for general use, though many have been proposed. The simpler formulae tend to be less reliable than Flesch, and the complicated formulae tend to require elaborate coding. For example, Bormuth (1967, 1969) developed some complex formulae using cloze as the criterion. He claimed these formulae have much greater predictive accuracy than even the Dale-Chall, but work by Coleman (1971) and especially Miller (1972) showed that this was largely an artifact caused by the use of cloze as a criterion. The procedure for developing formulae is quite standardized now—indeed, one reason so many formulae exist is because it fits nicely into the requirements for a Ph.D thesis! Since the procedure is so well established it can be used to develop formulae for languages other than English, and in many of the major world languages at least one formula is now available for use (Klare, 1974–1975). This aspect of readability research is bound to continue for the next decade or two, though at present there is no international center or agency for coordinating work and advising the smaller nations.

Readability scores can be used as a control device for textbook producers and to give feedback to writers and editors. Providing there is some knowledge of the target audience, the formula can be the engine of a writing-rewriting cycle:

Write ⟶ Apply formula ⟶ Revise ⟶ Apply formula

In this process the inexactness of the matching process must always be remembered; we should not aim for ultraprecise fits, but we should aim to eliminate gross misfits. The cycle draws attention to the distinction between *prediction* and *production* (Klare, 1976b). It is the job of a readability formula to predict reading difficulty; formulae do *not* show how prose should be written.

Writing is a complex art which cannot be reduced to a brief prescription. This confusion between an index (which predicts) and the art of writing prose has led many people to reject readability formulae altogether, and others to think that they should use only frequently used words and short sentences. Such a mechanical approach is definitely not advocated by readability research. Instead, readability research calls for linked but separate uses: the formula for prediction, and the human skills for production.

Quantitative Content Analysis

Quantitative procedures can be used to analyze the *content* of text discourse; this field of research is known in the United States simply as *content analysis*. The standard definition by Berelson (1952) is worth noting:

> Content analysis is a research technique for the objective, systematic and quantitative description of the manifest content of communication.

Most content analysis has been directed toward political ends—the tool has been the means of "objectifying" political analysis. During World War II Nazi propaganda in the United States was analyzed for legal and other reasons; after the war communist propaganda was analyzed during the Cold War period. More recently the content of political speeches and messages has been analyzed to reveal covert trends and other relevant content. These researches, techniques, and results are well described in the standard reference sources, such as Berelson (1952, 1954), Gerbner (1969), Holsti (1968, 1969), Lasswell & Leites (1949), Lasswell, Lerner, & Pool, (1952), North, Holsti, Zaninovich, & Zinnes (1963), Pool (1959), and Stone, Dunphy, Smith, and Ogilvie (1966, 1968).

So far the application of these methods to educational texts has been rather disappointing. It is rather easy to analyze textbooks for crude bias of race or sex, and a number of students have chosen this for their Ph.D. research (Kingston & Lovelace, 1977–1978). However, few senior researchers have done work on educational content analysis, and to my knowledge no major laboratory has a long-term research program to extend the techniques to the more subtle character of content that impedes or enhances learning. This neglect is bound to change as computer text handling comes of age. If all text is routinely processed by computer, then the major cost of computer text research (inputting the text) will be eliminated. Moreover, research in linguistics and artificial intelligence is already offering techniques far beyond those available a generation ago (Aiken, Bailey, & Hamilton-Smith, 1973; Hewitt, 1971; Mitchell, 1974; Wilks, 1972; Winograd, 1972; Winter, 1974). The stage is set for a fresh look at computer-based analysis of educational content.

Nevertheless, we must not get swept away by technologism. The heart of content analysis lies in the *choice of categories* and the *manner of coding*. These depend absolutely on the *questions* we pose rather than the technical state of the art. Therefore, content analysis will not be able to claim a central place in the tool kit of educational research until we learn what kinds of questions about educational texts are worth asking.

Linguistic analysis

Now I turn to *qualitative* methods, linguistic analysis being the first example. In general a qualitative method of analysis depends crucially upon the skill of the analyst, but to balance this apparent loss of objectivity there are certain vital gains. Analysts can use their experience and intuition (more formally, their tacit knowledge; see Polanyi, 1958) to highlight unexpected but important features of the text. This means that qualitative analysis can give deeper, more original, and more pertinent insights into the form and content of a text. In inexperienced hands the analysis can degenerate into clichés or political or methodological bias—but that is a problem long understood in disciplines in the humanities. The way to become a good text analyst is through a long, arduous apprenticeship to a master performer who will pass on the subtle discriminations (the ''connoisseurship,'' as Polanyi, 1958, calls it) necessary for the craft.

Until recently the trend of linguistic research was pointed so firmly away from the practical problems of communication that no results of any educational importance were obtained. Responsible for this sterility were the methodological rules which held sway over linguistics for more than 30 years, especially:

1. The Bloomfieldian restriction that the subject matter of linguistics is bounded by the sentence.
2. The primacy of syntax, or the belief that the interpretation of language is mainly driven by syntax-analyzing procedures.
3. The primacy of abstract general theories over detailed discriminations.
4. Avoidance of the study of language in use.

The social dominance of the two ''reductionist'' schools (first the behaviorist school of Bloomfield and then the transformational grammar school of Chomsky) was until recently so absolute that other approaches were scarcely tolerated, especially in the United States. Fortunately this situation has now changed, and as a result the field of linguistics is in a healthy turmoil.

The seed which sowed the destruction of the reductionist schools was the need to recognize linguistic *context*. It turns out that a proper treatment of context is absolutely necessary to explain the meaning of texts. This breaks Bloomfield's sentence restriction and thus ruins the possibility that linguistics will be reduced to an atomistic science. Furthermore, it turns out that the grammar of the sentence is needed, but in that grammar the idea of transformation plays a less significant role than was formerly proposed.

The sources of this renaissance of modern grammar and semantics include Fillmore's (1968, 1977) case grammar and the work of Halliday and his school (such as Halliday & Hasan, 1976). Other developments have been the advent of artificial intelligence machines that handle ordinary language (Hewitt, 1971;

Winograd, 1972), the publication of good modern texts on grammar (such as Quirk, Greenbaum, Leech, & Svartvik, 1972; Werlich, 1976), and the development of methods for analyzing between-sentence inferences (Crothers, 1975; Frederiksen, 1975). The sudden popularity of discourse analysis (Grimes, 1975), sociolinguistics (Shuy, 1977) and psycholinguistics (Anderson, Spiro, & Montague, 1977; Jenkins, 1974; Kintsch, 1974) has also contributed to the rebirth of interest.

For the purposes of educational research one of the most important recent developments is the publication of the work of Winter and his colleagues (Winter, 1971, 1974, 1977); other work is forthcoming. The key to Winter's ideas is his theory that human communication is possible because we share common presuppositions about the way information is structured, and these presuppositions are realized by the linguistics of clause structure. According to Winter, the meanings conveyed by individual sentences are semantically related to the meanings of the surrounding sentences which form the adjoining linguistic context. Part of the meaning of every sentence, therefore, must be located in the sentences which precede and follow it. The nature of this contextual relationship is realized in repeated clause structures between adjoining sentences. The systematic repetition of certain lexical items and structures between sentences in context is called *replacement*. Thus replacement entails studying the grammatical relations that obtain between adjoining sentences. A contextual relationship of this kind is realized within the *paragraph*, which consists of a sentence and its adjoining sentence or sentences (which may or may not coincide with the orthographic paragraph). In this strict, technical sense, the paragraph specifies the minimal meaningful context for the sentence.

Other constituents of text also have technical definitions. The *sentence*, for example, is defined as an orthographic unit which is comprised of one or more *clauses* between two full stops. *Sentence* and *clause* are therefore interchangeable. A *clause relation* refers to binary relation between *members*. Each member may comprise one or more sentences. Moreover, the presence of both members is necessary for an adequate understanding of a clause relation. The implication is that a sentence which is taken out of context has thereby lost its membership as a clause relation. Two important clause relations are *logical sequence* and *matching*. One example of logical sequence occurs when the first member precedes the second member in time. One of the meanings of matching is the comparing of lexical or grammatical items in adjoining clauses.

An important criterion by which to judge the nature of clause relations is the *question* (Winter, 1974). Questions, for example, form the items to which the second member of the clause relation is a reply. Thus the paragraph is contextually dependent on the adjoining paragraphs: It is a reply to the question(s) posed by the adjoining paragraphs.

The clause relations discussed so far are components of still larger clause relations. These are: *situation, problem, solution,* and *evaluation*. They organize the other clause relations so that they form the coherent "topic" of discourse. The two relations of matching and logical sequence, for example, are included within the larger semantic framework of situation and evaluation.

Clause relations are finite in number and are named by a special vocabulary. This vocabulary, which has been called Vocabulary 3 (Winter, 1977), has among its items the following: *achievement, affirm, cause, compare, deny, purpose, reason, similar, result, time,* and *true.* Vocabulary 3 is, technically speaking, on a continuum between open and closed system meaning. The theory of clause relations is concerned with describing the relations that are expressed by Vocabulary 3. The presence of one of its items in a sentence can *signpost* what kind of information is to be presented in the sentence or sentences which immediately follow it. This signposting function is called *anticipation,* and the information which is anticipated in this way is said to be *lexically realized* in the sentence or sentences that follow. A paraphrase relation exists between Vocabulary 3 and two-closed system vocabularies called Vocabularies 1 and 2, which are the *subordinators* and the sentence *connectors,* respectively. Among the items in Vocabulary 1 are the following: *after, as far as, at the same time as, because, before, given, that, which,* and *whereas.* Among those in Vocabulary 2 are: *accordingly, in addition to, also, however, indeed, similarly, yet, that is,* and *otherwise.* The paraphrase relation which obtains between Vocabularies 1 and 2 and Vocabulary 3 is the basis for the assertion that the corrective behavior of Vocabulary 3 must be of a closed-system kind.

According to the theory of clause relations, we, as encoders and decoders of text, share a finite set of structural meanings which are made explicit by these three vocabularies. The closed-system vocabularies of items which connect sentences in discourse inevitably place a limit on the number of ways in which we can interpret sentences in sequenced discourse so that we can communicate in a meaningful and *rule-governed* manner. This way of communicating is in fact proposed as a solution to the problem (identified by Chomsky) of the inherent uniqueness of sentences. We are constrained in our choices of what to say by the finite set of structural meanings represented by the three vocabularies (Winter, 1971, 1974, 1977).

In examining the effectiveness of texts we must be struck by the obvious fact that readers can "read" without understanding, or with confusion, or with positive misunderstanding. Some part of this, perhaps a large part, can be explained by supposing that some clause relations have been inadequately signaled or imperfectly realized. This would be the linguistic substance of the common intuition that in unsatisfactory prose individual sentences appear adequate when seen in isolation, yet the passage fails to fit together as a coherent whole.

Other Kinds of Qualitative Analysis

There are, in principle, an unlimited number of ways that texts can be analyzed. However, no one method of analysis is suitable for all purposes. Since any system of analysis must emphasize certain aspects of texts, it is automatically disqualified from universal application. This is an obvious point which is often forgotten.

Literary criticism is one important qualitative method. Here the crucial figure is Richards (1929, 1938), the father of modern literary criticism. Richards had a lifelong interest in education and came to believe that his methods were more likely to advance the cause of education than any amount of experimental psychology could:

What we want is the further development of what is already an advanced art, the art of intellectual discernment. For this reason . . . educational psychology is not what we want. (Richards, 1938, p. 9)

At first blush this might read to some as "antiempiricism," but it is not, for Richards gives many detailed protocols taken from teaching practice. Really the debate is about what *kind* of empiricism will help to improve pedagogy, the protocols collected by Richards giving vivid testimony to the state of discernment of which his students were capable. As Richards says:

"Every candid teacher knows . . . the majority of his pupils at the end of their schooling understand remarkably little of what they hear or read. But to reflect profitably on the modes and causes of these failures we need detailed examples rather than principles" (Richards, 1938, Preface).

Analysts of texts from the humanities and the social sciences will find Richards's work a storehouse of provocative and useful ideas. For a modern work by one of his disciples, see Empson (1951/1977), for an elementary introduction to the art of criticism some may find Williams (1950) a useful starting point.

Another tradition, more esoteric but also of great importance, is hermeneutics. *Hermeneutics* is the art or science of textual exegesis, born of the need for ways to adjudicate between alternative interpretations of the Bible. From the work of German biblical scholars nearly two centuries ago the hermeneutic movement has invaded history and the social sciences (Dilthey, 1913–1967; Hodges, 1944) and, more recently, literary criticism (Hirsch, 1967). Wach (1926–1933) is a history of early hermeneutics, and Palmer (1969) provides a good modern introduction in English. Most of the central issues of textual analysis (such as whether analysis can be systematized and whether it can be applied to all kinds of texts) are dealt with by hermeneutic thinkers better than those in any other tradition I know of.

Many researchers now realize the pressing need for ways to summarize the *conceptual structure* of texts. Usually this has been done indirectly by eliciting conceptual maps from human subjects. For example, Johnson and Shavelson have used nonmetric multidimensional scaling to show the pattern of relationships between stimulus words in physics (Johnson, 1964; 1971; Shavelson, 1972, 1974). Gagné and his co-workers use task analysis to derive their hierarchies (Gagné, 1965, Resnick, 1973), and Pask and his co-workers interrogate subject matter experts to externalize their conceptual structure as "entailment nets" (Pask, 1975a, 1975b, 1976). Of these methods, I believe Pask's has the soundest theoretical grounding. He has shown that knowledge has a netlike structure and that hierarchies are special cases of such nets. Furthermore, his distinction between knowledge and behavior is profound and (so it seems to me) fundamentally correct. Since all three methods use human subjects rather than texts as their source of information, they are not directly helpful as methods of text analysis, but they do show what a "summary conceptual structure" might look like.

I have made a series of attempts to analyze the conceptual structure of subject matter. The first idea (reported briefly in Macdonald-Ross, 1974) was to develop a notational system for deriving conceptual nets from text material; the basic formats were networks and matrices (which are, of course, interchangeable— actually isomorphic). The atoms of this analysis are technical terms, which are the most stable and least ambiguous parts of the public structure of any discipline. The basic network then consists of technical terms and their interrelations. This can be done objectively because there are certain formal occasions when the connection between terms is spelt out publicly, for example, in definitions and in certain key equations. Examples, counterexamples, and tasks can be attached to relevant parts of the network, and theories, laws, and problems are regarded as discourse over more or less well-defined parts of the network.

The results of this work were in general consistent with the results obtained by Johnson and Pask, thus showing that (as expected) the texts examined had an internal conceptual structure which reflects the conceptual structure of subject matter experts. Two useful insights were obtained. First, there are some obvious differences between texts and experts as sources of data. The text is available for detailed scrutiny and remains stable and public (so that others can check the validity of the analysis). On the other hand, the text is whatever it is—if certain questions are not dealt with, they remain unanswered. Here Pask's interrogation procedure has more creative scope.

Second, this work highlighted the differences between disciplines and within disciplines. Obviously, the most compelling differences exist between mathematics and the natural sciences on the one hand and the humanities and social sciences on the other. A discipline like chemistry has one world view, and consequently the definition of key terms like *valency* or *hydrocarbon* is fairly well settled. Contrast the situation of a discipline like sociology, where key terms like *class* are certain to be defined differently in each world view. This much ought to be expected without any detailed analysis, but some other results were perhaps not so obvious. Terms in the natural sciences are related to just a few other terms—there is a severe restriction on possible pathways in the net. On the other hand, terms in the social sciences may be related to dozens of other terms. Thus terms in the natural sciences can be clearly distinguished from one another, whereas terms in the social sciences overlap and may differ in nuance only.

The soundness of this finding can be demonstrated by a simple experiment. First choose any basic concept in the natural sciences and work out its relationships; for example:

$$\text{Force} = \text{Mass} \times \text{Acceleration.}$$

This can be graphed as:

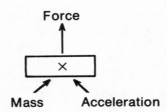

Note that to define force, only two other technical terms and one (fairly complex) relation are needed. Contrast this with any basic concept in the social sciences, for example the concepts of learning, or class, or attitude. Far more terms are needed to define any single term in the social sciences, so many that the whole idea of representing this kind of discipline by concept networks may be seriously inadequate because it fails to reduce the discourse to a manageable level of complexity. The utility (the parsimony) of a network goes down as the number of interconnections goes up, and much more depends then on the way in which the net is traversed.

This brings me to an interesting point. If texts in the humanities and social sciences are to be analyzed, and if this analysis is to do justice to the original, then more attention must be paid to the manner of argumentation in the text. This manner of argumentation corresponds to the way in which the author chooses to traverse an extremely complex net. In fact, we need a kind of rhetorical analysis. I have argued in some preliminary reports (Macdonald-Ross, 1975, 1977a, 1977c) that since reasoning in the social sciences is predominantly concerned with *persuasion*, analysis of the means of persuasion must be central to any judgment of educational quality. The term *educational rhetoric* is the way I have described this phenomenon. By this I mean the *dynamics of argument* used by the author to persuade the reader to the author's point of view. This analysis does depend upon the skill or experience of the analyst, but it is not arbitrary. For example, a checklist covering the main features of argument found in a survey of Open University social science texts provides an effective guide for the classification of new material and acts as a way to partly objectify the process of analysis.

This kind of work is directed not only toward the classic problem of comprehension but also toward the issue of *quality*, whether what is being learnt is worth learning. I argue that poor-quality curricular material can be understood only too well by students who unerringly assimilate its wicked (but covert) message: that shallow, slack explanations are the norm; that evidence should be handpicked to support predestined conclusions; that key terms should be covertly redefined wherever it suits the author; that the choice of problem should be governed mainly by the conclusions required; that counterarguments and counterevidence should be ignored or blocked. All this and more are learnt too well for comfort.

Evidence from student essays and from observation of tutorial groups shows that students start to mimic the language of their teacher within the first few weeks of a course (for instance, *place* is quickly ousted by *spatial location* in a geography course). By itself this might not be bad, except that acceptance of a system of terminology implies acceptance of the presuppositions and theories that were the original reason for the growth of the terminology. The only counter to this would be the students' awareness of the bias, especially their awareness of alternative schemes of explanation. Unfortunately, the evidence we have collected shows that most students are not aware of the bias in their social science courses, nor are they aware of the full range of alternative views which might be brought to bear on a particular subject. For example, the first unit of our Foundation Course in Social Science (D101) at The Open University is on unemployment. This unit treats this issue entirely from the point of view of Keynesian economics, without indicating anywhere that quite different kinds of analysis are possible and, indeed, are widely discussed today. When asked "Did you detect any bias in this unit? If so, of what kind?" only 1 out of 128 respondents managed to identify the Keynesian slant. This bias is, incidentally, not repaired later in the course.

I do not suggest that this difficult educational issue has any simple solution, but there are reasonable ways such a problem might be tackled. My contribution is simply to make the sinews of the argument more visible by offering the analyst ways to identify the argumentative maneuvers used in texts. Though bias of argument is just one block which prevents the attainment of quality in educational texts, it is crucial in the social sciences and in those institutions that (directly or indirectly) restrict the range of acceptable opinions which their students are effectively able to study. Naturally, the arguments I have presented here are suggestive rather than conclusive. They are meant to open out the range of debate to include issues which are certainly of educational significance, though they are not often tackled by research groups. Other relevant thoughts on quality can be found in the delightful Pirsig (1974).

It is also possible for the analyst to tackle the traditional problem of comprehension by asking, in an organized and professional manner, what *sources of confusion* are present in the text. This work can be divided into two parts, analysis of the general discourse (the actual teaching material), and analysis of the educational superstructure (the objectives, instructions, in-text questions, feedback). The educational apparatus (which Rothkopf [1970] calls *mathemagenic devices*) are the easiest to handle because fairly explicit rules exist in the literature for judging their quality. These rules are "minimal standard" rules which ensure that no serious source of confusion exists. For example, an instruction to do something must satisfy these requirements:

1. The instruction must be intelligible.
2. The task must be do-able.
3. The student must know when a satisfactory performance has been achieved.

If an instruction fails, it fails because one or more of these criteria are not met. Sometimes all these criteria can be met in one sentence: "Stop at the red light." Sometimes the instruction is virtually undoable; some putative science experiments cannot be done with the time, the equipment, or the mental resources of the student. Sometimes understanding the question may be the hardest part of the task. The analyst must learn to distinguish, identify, and separate these causes of confusion so that clear guidance can be given to authors on how to revise their manuscripts.

Some questions are bound to be asked: How are such procedures validated? How do we know that the supposed defects would indeed have caused misunderstanding? What proportion of defects is left undiscovered? Is analysis more or less effective than (for instance) formative evaluation? That these questions of empirical verification can be answered at all is partly due to the work of The Open University's Institute of Educational Technology. Staff members of this institute have analyzed hundreds of texts during the past decade and have been able, from time to time, to check their predictions with various kinds of field data. Much of this work is unfortunately not published or is available only as internal memoranda, but this may be the most extensive experience of qualitative analysis in the history of curriculum development. Therefore, some summary remarks are appropriate.

In the first place, there is a remarkable degree of consensus among text analysts. More experienced analysts will usually spot problems that are invisible to the less experienced, but there is usually no difference of opinion about the most serious defects in a text. This "interjudge reliabilty" is due to consensus about the criteria for judging adequacy of the various parts of a text, and also— an obvious point—because anything that is unclear to the analyst is almost certainly going to be unclear to the student.

Most of the text difficulties identified during formative evaluation can be identified beforehand by the analyst. Since analysis is usually quicker and cheaper than field trials, the curriculum developer must have good reasons before going in for empirical testing. I notice that many educational psychologists who practice formative evaluation do so in order to provide "objective" evidence of points they were going to make in any case. It is certainly not sensible for the parent organization to fund such exercises routinely; an occasional demonstration should suffice. There is something to be said for the writer himself testing out the material on small groups of students, however. He will not learn anything the analyst could not have told him, but the psychological force of recognizing the students' learning difficulties will be much greater.

One potential benefit of formative evaluation is the possibility of collecting, classifying, and analyzing student errors and misapprehensions. This information provides quite strong guidelines for the subsequent revision of the text. One potential benefit of skilled analysis is the uncovering of those deep issues of quality that by their very nature are almost invisible to the student. Thus good analysis has a creative potential which is extremely valuable. The general guideline is that formative evaluation makes the most of what there is, whereas the analyst is able to comment on what is not present but might be. My own conclusion based on this experience at The Open University is that the qualitative analysis of teaching material is one of the most valuable (and also one of the most underused) possibilities in curriculum development.

EXPERIMENTS WITH PEDAGOGIC MATERIAL

The psychology of learning from meaningful prose has blossomed in the past 20 years. Much of this work has been done on the instructional apparatus that surrounds the main discourse—the objectives, organizers, questions, and other pedagogic devices. We now have at least a dozen important recent reviews of this work, certain testimony to its practical importance and also (as we shall see) to the difficulty of interpreting the empirical studies. These reviews mainly summarize the empirical results, though some deal with the methodology of research design and interpretation; this is fortunate, for it enables me to center my remarks around the main issues of curriculum development. In a nutshell: How do good teaching texts get written, and of what use is the research to the process of their development?

This field of research contains several hundred publications, so it does represent an impressive body of empirical knowledge. There are, in my opinion, three important characteristics which occur often and limit the possible value of this research. These defects of methodology must be discussed before any analysis of the empirical details.

In the first place most studies have revealed (directly or by implication) an over-simple model of what ordinary language is and what it can do. No doubt this was partly caused by the methodological sterility of linguistics discussed above. However, the state of literary criticism and other disciplines in the humanities is extremely healthy—indeed, one is tempted to think that more open contact with good literature would surely have alerted the researchers to the way they were underestimating the flexibility and complexity of written discourse, and hence underestimating the potential contribution of the art of writing.

We are all used to the style of modern instructional material in which the devices that are supposed to help the learner—the objectives, instructions, questions, feedback, overviews, advance organizers—are *clearly marked* by typography, position, and style. This visual separation of the educational apparatus from the main subject matter discourse has become the norm: indeed, if ever this visual marking is not absolutely clear (as with advance organizers), researchers have been in great confusion as to whether or not the entity actually exists.

There are three possible explanations for this state of affairs which may be partly or wholly true:

1. Such devices may actually help learners to master the main features of the discourse.
2. Such devices may act as access structures (see discussion below).
3. Such devices may be cultural descendants of the structure of programmed learning material and may be perpetualized by tradition as well as (or even instead of) by proven function.

Is it conceivable that the instructional functions of these devices could be attained by continuous prose with no such typographic markers to set them off? Surely it is; any kind of good literature does all that is claimed for these instructional devices—and much more besides. It would be easy to assemble examples of the astonishing possibilities of prose; for example:

It is a truth universally acknowledged, that a single man in possession of a good fortune, must be in want of a wife (first sentence of Jane Austen's *Pride & Prejudice*).

No doubt this does achieve the function of an "advance organizer," but in just one sentence a great deal more is achieved. Most important, we feel encouraged to *read on*. I mention this because it is a consideration so singularly lacking in the design of many psychological experiments. That the drive to read on can be stimulated by sharply defined expression (and not just by the content) can be seen in brilliant accounts of extremely distressing content, such as the various pieces written by Oscar Wilde from Reading Gaol (for example, "The Case of Warder Martin: Some Cruelties of Prison Life," in which Wilde reveals the effect of prison on children and lunatics, and the dilemma of decent men administering a cruel system). This review is not the place to pursue this question in detail, though surely the broad outline of my thesis—that prose is a rich vehicle capable of all the essential functions necessary for human communication—must be granted. And if that is granted, then the skill of the writer is one of the prime variables in curriculum development.

The great range and variety of prose should suggest how subtle and complex problems can be clearly displayed without any external aids to learning. To many people this would seem quite uncontroversial—a truism, perhaps. Yet the fact remains that researchers have come to draw a clear distinction between what is said (the discourse) and aids to learning what is said (the various devices such as in-text questions). How has this come about? We can get some idea from the work of Rothkopf, who has had a great influence on the field of modern instructional psychology. In one of his earlier papers he draws the distinction in neutral terms:

The most interesting feature of the conceptual model is the notion of mathemagenic behavior. It divides the domain of written instruction into two related classes of problems. The first of these is how the instructive material must be arranged to produce efficient learning. The second problem concerns itself with . . . what must be done to assure that the content of an instructive document is effectively used. (Rothkopf, 1964, p. 216)

According to Rothkopf, it is the second problem which is more amenable to solution:

It is a commonplace observation that, given certain circumstances, humans will learn from instructive documents that are very badly prepared . . . discovering the conditions that will keep the student working and teaching the student how he should study are the most practical approaches toward making written documents useful instructive tools. (Rothkopf, 1965, p. 216)

In the management of [learning], instructional materials are accepted as *givens*. (Rothkopf, 1968, p. 129)

What is being claimed is that the analysis of the structure of the text is not the most important source of prediction about learning. The analysis of the subject's activities while he is exposed to the text is certainly at least as important. (Rothkopf, 1972, p. 323)

These remarks are important. Indeed, they are central to Rothkopf's work and to the wider audience of instructional psychologists who have generally accepted the second problem (the management of learning) as more important, or at any rate more amenable to change, than the first problem (the structure of the main discourse). But I think these remarks come close to error; if not read with skepticism they might be quite misleading. For instance, although it is true that in certain *rare* circumstances people *must* (and therefore do) read boring, illiterate, and maybe rather illegible prose, *in most cases they do not*. The evidence from field studies on readability (quoted above) is fairly conclusive on this point (see also Educational Testing Service, 1978; Murphy, 1973). Moreover, the difficulty people have with badly designed forms and poorly written documents is quite well known—indeed, it is an everyday experience (Lewis, Horabin, & Gane, 1967; Wright, 1977, 1978).

If it is impossible to influence the *construction* of learning materials, then, only the *use* of these materials can be influenced by psychologists. But in many situations the psychologist has an open choice as to how to deploy his or her effort; and it would be unwise to preempt this decision, which ought to be taken with all the available information pertaining to the particular circumstance. We can agree on the significance of the subject's activities while exposed to the text, though exactly what counts as an activity may be rather opaque. The question is what roles are played by the structure of the discourse and by the aids to learning in controlling and enhancing appropriate cognitive activities. Rothkopf's "strong" claim ("the analysis of the structure of the text is not the most important source of prediction about learning") may turn out to be empirically untrue in many cases. It is difficult to tell, because for so long the attention of researchers was directed away from the analysis of text structure. But now the situation is changing, and appropriate means of text analysis are beginning to be developed.

Some interesting comments were made by leading researchers after the presentation of Rothkopf's 1968 and 1972 papers:

DR. GAGNE: It is true, isn't it . . . that one thinks of textbooks as being written with a literary style criterion, as one writes a novel. Literary standards are not the same as pedagogical or instructional standards.

DR. ROTHKOPF: Yes, I agree. Take as an example the criteria of clarity . . . the relationship between how well a sentence reads and how effective it is in teaching has to my knowledge never been tested. Personally, I am very suspicious of very smooth, beautiful prose as a carrier of denotative meaning. (Rothkopf, 1968, p. 133)

This exchange calls to mind the situation discussed in my earlier review of graphic communication (Macdonald-Ross, 1978). There it was shown how researchers and designers are often at cross-purposes, and in particular how researchers tend to ignore the existence of tacit skills or to hold them in contempt. This does not mean that *any* designer has these skills; many do not. However, some designers can show (by being able to repeat effective performance at will) that their tacit skills are real and are backed up by substantial knowledge, albeit not always well articulated. It was suggested in this review that instead of denying or denigrating this skill researchers might usefully identify master performers and help to externalize the bases of their work so that the public processes of discussion, criticism, and testing could become more fruitful.

An exactly analogous situation holds with instructional psychologists on the one hand and skilled writers and editors on the other. It is true that much textual learning material is badly written; we know from many years of readability research that this does make a difference to the reader. We also know that readability formulae (though more reliable than most individual judgments of prose difficulty), do correlate highly with pooled judgments of professional editors (Klare, 1976a). Those of us who live close to the nuts and bolts of curriculum development must have, I think, more respect for the art of writing. For most authors the struggle to attain a deep grasp of their subjects and to get insights into the process of learning is intertwined with the struggle to achieve intelligible and pertinent expression. This complex triad cannot be reduced by ignoring either the deep issues residing in the subject matter or the art of explicating these issues in vivid prose. If this is so, then the comments by Gagné and Rothkopf are suspect and misleading. Some support to my point of view is given in these extracts from the discussion following Rothkopf's (1972) paper:

Carroll, Scriven and Crothers thought that Rothkopf may have been overstating his claim that *structural* features of text play almost no role in self-paced instructional settings. As examples, they suggest that sentences that have been thoroughly scrambled . . . will almost certainly be hard or impossible to comprehend. . . . Rothkopf suggested that in the extreme cases just mentioned it is probably true that ''structure'' can be shown to influence comprehension, but for the kinds of materials he has been dealing with he thought his claim was defensible. (Rothkopf, 1972, p. 333)

Winter's work, as discussed above, suggests strongly that the structure of text plays a primary role in the comprehension of all meaningful informative prose (Winter, 1971, 1974, 1977). If this is so, Rothkopf's suggestion is not correct. Of course, prose is not just one simple entity; that point was made earlier. Structure will play a less important role in material with high fact but low conceptual content, especially if the criterion tests concentrate mainly on more or less rote recall questions (Level 1 in Bloom, 1956). Material of this kind has often been used by instructional psychologists because it lends itself to manageable experiments; perhaps this helps to explain the difference of opinion as to the relative importance of the structure of the main discourse. Rothkopf's recent (1976) paper gives an account of his present position on the main themes discussed in this section. My own ideas are closer to those of Medawar: ''No one who has anything original or important to say will willingly run the risk of being misunderstood; people who write obscurely are either unskilled in writing or up to mischief'' (Medawar, 1974, p. 29).

Behavioral Objectives

The original purpose of behavioral objectives was to prescribe the construction of programmed instructional material and the associated achievement test items (Mager, 1962). Another function—to help students organize their learning activities—became necessary for learning materials when the student behavior was not so strongly constrained. Curriculum systems such as the Keller plan (Keller, 1974) concentrate effort on the objectives and test items and use existing texts as well as tailor-made materials. This extra degree of freedom for the student is perhaps rather minimal (the student is still strongly constrained), but still any degree of free choice by the student offers the scope for study guides of one sort or another. If indeed the achievement test is based on well-specified objectives, it makes sense to alert the student to this fact. Whether the achievement test *should* be so derived is another question, however. There are good reasons for thinking that the conceptual flaws in the behavioral-objective approach are so serious that they will never be repaired (Apple, 1972; Macdonald-Ross, 1973; Peters, 1973).

The empirical research into behavioral objectives has been reviewed by Ammerman and Melching (1966) and Duchastel and Merrill (1973). The last five years have not added much to the literature, and little is gained by resurrecting issues that for most curriculum experts are no longer live or interesting. However, a few summarizing remarks may be helpful. First, the *content* of the subject matter makes an essential difference in the validity of stating goals in behavioral terms. A course in economics cannot be adequately summarized as a list of behaviors, for example, but mending a car may be (even so, note that the tasks are interrelated and backed up by conceptual knowledge). Consequently, any attempt to generalize across the board is not justified (in saying this I am especially rejecting the idea that the concept of education can be reduced to training).

The typographic position of the objectives in the learning package is a practical but nevertheless important question. Since 1970 objectives have been placed at the front of The Open University Science Faculty courses, consistent with the systematic procedures of the objectives model (Kaye, 1973; Melton, 1977a, 1977b). In such a position the objectives are supposed to act as attention directors, in behaviorist language, or goal statements, in cognitive language. However, the evidence we have collected by questionnaire surveys suggests that objectives are not used in this way by students. This had led my colleague Robert Waller to suggest that lists of objectives should instead be seen as part of the *access structure* of texts (see below). In this case they should be placed at the end of the teaching material as a checklist (as done, for example, by Games & Klare, 1967), with page numbers for back reference.

Since most of the empirical research on objectives ignores or glosses over the main conceptual problems, no simple summary is sufficient to sort out the confusion. I am inclined to agree with Wittrock and Lumsdaine (1977) that "giving the learner behaviorally defined, specific or narrow objectives has not fulfilled its early promise" (p. 422).

Advance Organizers

Another field of research which has ground to a halt, at any rate for the present, is Ausubel's notion of "advance organizers" (Ausubel, 1960, 1963; Ausubel & Fitzgerald, 1961, 1962; Ausubel & Robinson, 1969; Ausubel, Schpoont, & Cukier, 1957). The review by Barnes and Clawson (1975) and the reply by Lawton and Wanska (1977) show all too clearly how empirical research gives conflicting results which cannot be interpreted because the conceptual foundations of the research are too loosely formulated. The central problem is that, to quote Hartley and Davies (1976), "There is currently no acceptable way of generating or recognizing advance organizers . . . further serious research must await this problem of operationalizing the concept." Quite right; but no concept in science can be made operational in a *satisfactory* way until and unless deep and appropriate conceptual analysis has been done. The sequence of events which occurs so often is:

> Good commonsense notion→Empirical testing→Conflicting results→Confusion→Realization of need for operational definition→Conflicting operational definitions→Realization of need for clearer thought

As a result, much painstaking work has gone to waste. Though no simple program guarantees good science (it is essential to recognize this proviso), experience suggests that a more cautious approach might lead to more substantial progress. In particular, *thinking* (conceptual analysis) should be given a higher priority, and no hypotheses should be tested unless and until the conceptual framework has been clarified. Much more needs to be said, of course. Other activities (such as careful observation of the problem domain, using master performers as a source of operational knowledge, and selecting critical issues based on a grounded taxonomy of the problem domain) should be welded into a coherent set of activities. Where almost all the nonexperimental activities are ignored (as in so many studies in educational psychology), there is almost no hope of laying a sound foundation. In fact, the more experiments are done the less the agreement, because in the absence of a strong conceptual framework experiments which at first sight seem to be aimed at the same problem turn out to be firing at all kinds of targets.

The research on advance organizers is no better and no worse in this respect than research in many other fields. It does, however, provide an excellent example of the tendency of weakly grounded empirical research to produce more confusion, the more experiments are conducted. Ausubel's early work seemed to show good evidence for "the facilitating influence of advance organizers on the incorporability and longevity of meaningful learning material" (Ausubel, 1960, p. 271). Now that more research has been done, however, the results conflict and are almost impossible to sort out (Barnes & Clawson, 1975; Lawton & Wanska, 1977; Novak, Ring, & Tamir, 1971; Ring & Novak, 1971; West & Fensham, 1974).

Ausubel's framework can be broken down into these interconnected components:

1. A hierarchical theory of cognitive structure: "Cognitive structure is hierarchically organized in terms of highly inclusive concepts under which are subsumed less inclusive subconcepts and informational data" (Ausubel, 1960, p. 267).
2. A hierarchical model of the subject matter in which higher level concepts and propositions subsume lower level concepts and data. Material which (it is hoped) will act as an organizer must be of "a much higher level of

abstraction, generality and inclusiveness than the latter passage itself"
(Ausubel, 1960, p. 268).

3. A cognitive theory as to the organizing process: "New [potentially] meaningful material becomes incorporated into the cognitive structure insofar as it is subsumable under relevant existing concepts" (Ausubel, 1960, p. 267).

4. An unstated assumption about the reading process; or at any rate an assumption about the way reading affects cognition. The criteria of *typographic* priority (that is, potential organizing material comes first) is not strictly entailed by Ausubel's cognitive theory; it assumes a once-read-through model, which is not consistent with what is now known about quasi-naturalistic reading (Augstein, 1971; Pugh, 1974; Thomas, Augstein, Deans & Moore, 1970; Waller, 1977a, 1977b).

All of these components seem to be either incorrect or vague or both vague and incorrect; this is the main reason for the apparently conflicting results of empirical studies. However, Ausubel deserves admiration for two correct and important decisions: His theory is a cognitive theory, albeit limited by the primitive state of cognitive psychology 20 years ago, and his experiments were conducted with realistic learning material. In both these respects Ausubel was ahead of his time.

For all that, his framework is seriously flawed. Most importantly, neither the structure of subject matter nor the process of cognition can be adequately modeled as a hierarchy. Modern theories of cognition vary in detail and in language, but they do agree that a *heterarchy* is the basic logical structure of cognition. The basic fact is that while on a certain occasion for a particular purpose one procedure may control another (here a concept is considered to be a procedure), on another occasion for another purpose the previously superordinate procedure may be called upon as a lower order subroutine. Thus an appearance of hierarchy results from confusing the set of behaviors appropriate to a particular situation with the structure which generated those behaviors. The same consideration applies to the structure of subject matter (which is, in a special sense, independent of particular cognitions—see Popper, 1972). For recent work on cognitive structure see Johnson-Laird and Wason (1977) and Pask (1975a, 1975b, 1976).

From the inadequate models of cognition and the subject matter in Ausubel follows a vague and shallow account of the act of mastering new but related information (i.e., subsumption). Again, the great stimulus given to cognitive theory by artificial intelligence (Boden, 1977) should enable us to reformulate this problem in a more fruitful and more correct manner. Another flaw in Ausubel's framework is that there is no particular cognitive reason for the typographic primacy of organizers, unless the structure and function of the potential organizers are so tightly defined (by semantic and linguistic methods) as to determine its priority. Otherwise the initial position of the organizer is conflated with an unjustified assumption that effective reading consists of starting at the top, reading everything once, and finishing at the end. Everything we know about effective readers suggests that their strategies are far more sophisticated than this. However, as my colleague Waller points out, it may make sense to put organizers in a consistent place so they can be accessed easily. This is a different reason from the one given by Ausubel and may be more convincing.

The accumulated effect of all these problems is devastating (but note Ausubel's recent defense, 1978). To do Ausubel justice, he does notice and acknowledge many of the consequent subproblems, for example:

The pedagogic value of advance organizers obviously depends in part upon how well organized the learning material itself is. If it contains built-in organizers . . . much of the potential benefit derivable from advance organizers will not be actualised (Ausubel, 1963, p. 82).

Thus if an organizer can first delineate clearly, precisely, and explicitly the principal similarities and differences between the ideas in a new learning passage, on the one hand, and existing related concepts in cognitive structure on the other, [there would be] fewer ambiguities . . . and fewer misconceptions suggested by the learner's prior knowledge of the related concepts (Ausubel, 1963, p. 83).

This is the problem in a nutshell. Although empirical research has done little to solve these problems, there have been great conceptual advances in cognitive psychology during this time. Surely an attempt should be made to reformulate Ausubel's notions in a modern conceptual framework. The rewards for even partial success would be considerable, for the problems Ausubel addresses are right at the heart of pedagogy.

Adjunct Questions and Mathemagenics

Work on questions in texts (usually called "adjunct" or "in-text" questions) has been steadily progressing for the past 15 years. This research was also started in the days of programmed learning, though gradually the behaviorist framework has been shed, and the problems now addressed by researchers have to do with the effects of questions on cognitive processing. There have been several excellent reviews of this work (the most recent being Rickards & Denner, 1978), so again I will discuss the research mainly from the viewpoint of curriculum development.

The notion of adjunct questions is difficult to separate from an important concept of Rothkopf's, namely, *mathemagenic behavior*. In his early papers Rothkopf conceived of this idea in extremely broad terms. Any activities of the subject in the learning situation are called mathemagenic *activities;* they might include both behaviors relevant to learning and nonrelevant behaviors:

Mathemagenic activities refer to the activities of the student in the instructional situation . . . such activities as reading, asking questions . . . and mentally reviewing a recently seen motion picture. Mathemagenic activities also include looking out of the classroom window, yawning, turning the pages of a textbook without reading . . . and sleeping, either in class or in a library carrel. (Rothkopf, 1968, p. 116)

Mathemagenic behaviors include gross postural adjustment of the head and body toward the printed page and the movement of the eyes over the page. It is assumed that there are other mathemagenic activities that cannot be observed directly and which must be inferred. These inferred activities are in many respects more interesting than the directly observable aspects of mathemagenic behavior. (Rothkopf, 1965, p. 199)

These are extremely broad definitions, but in practice the operational definition used by Rothkopf in his experiments was comparatively strict; it depended upon an important distinction between the direct effect of questions and their indirect effect upon unquestioned material:

Basically, the adjunct question experiments at the Bell Telephone Laboratories were incidental learning studies. At the simplest level they involved measurement of performance changes on reading material that was not directly related to the text components on which the experimental questions were based. Hence any measured behavioral changes could not be attributed to the direct-instructive-effects of questions' content. The changes were ascribed instead to changes in presumed mathemagenic activity during inspection of the text. (Rothkopf, 1970, p. 333)

Early results (summarized in Rothkopf, 1968) suggested a small but definite mathemagenic effect for questions placed after relevant text segments. This effect was much smaller than the direct instructive effect, and a difference of opinion arose as to whether these results were sufficient to permit the conclusions Rothkopf drew from them (Carver, 1972; Ladas, 1973; Rothkopf, 1974). As guides to curriculum development, these experiments have some weaknesses. The size of the mathemagenic effect was of marginal statistical significance, whereas the curriculum developer looks for large effects which are robust enough to withstand the extraordinary variety of field learning situations. Certainly these results do not lend weight to Rothkopf's opinion that mathemagenic variables were more significant than structural variables, for, as discussed above, we know that structural variables can produce quite striking effects. A second, and perhaps more decisive, query concerns the nature of the text material and the nature of the adjunct questions. The material had a "relatively high factual content" (Rothkopf, 1968, p. 120). As Frase (1969) remarks: "Many of the studies . . . employed only factual questions, which is unfortunate if the researcher's interest is in a variety of behaviors that can produce learning." Finally, the experimental method constrains the subjects not to look back at the material after seeing the adjunct questions. This is "ecologically suspect;" in other words, it does not correspond to the normal reading process.

Later research has to some extent tackled these problems and has produced results which are more applicable to real curricular texts. In particular, researchers have made determined efforts to use adjunct questions which elicit higher order cognitive strategies. Frase (1969, 1970, 1971) found that readers given inferential prequestions retained more passage material than those given verbatim prequestions. Watts and Anderson (1971) found that "application of principle" postquestions induced a more thorough processing of the material than did other kinds of questions. Similar results were obtained by Rickards and DiVesta (1974) and Mayer (1975); Rickards and Denner (1978) conclude on this evidence:

It has been repeatedly demonstrated that high level questions provide more and better organized recall of passage information [but] a consistent position effect for the conceptual questions has not been found.

Some effort has been made to separate out different kinds of process effects. Here the work of McGaw and Grotelueschen (1972), Rothkopf and Billington (1974), and Rickards and DiVesta (1974) led Rickards and Denner (1978) to distinguish these basic processes:

1. A specific review process: mental review of questioned material.
2. A general review process of nonquestioned material close to or related to the questioned material.
3. A learning set process focusing attention on the kind of information being questioned in paragraphs following the postquestions.
4. A general stimulating process, resulting in increased attention to subsequent paragraphs.

Some interesting work by Shavelson, Berliner, Loeding, Portens, and Stanton (1974) and Shavelson, Berliner, Ravitch, & Loeding (1974), and also by Rickards and Hatcher (in press), has shown an interesting trait-treatment interaction. Good readers can effect higher order processing without the stimulus of adjunct questions; the greatest effect of higher level questions is seen with the less competent readers.

The field of adjunct questions has been reviewed by several leading instructional psychologists (especially Anderson & Biddle, 1975; Faw & Waller, 1976; Rickards & Denner, 1978). So far no recent research has used text material and questions as complex as those in The Open University correspondence texts, and most experimental designs have not allowed subjects to reread material after receiving the adjunct questions (but see Hiller, 1974; Gustafson & Toole, 1970; and Washburne, 1929, for exceptions). Moreover, though it is encouraging to see the general adoption of cognitive theory, the particular cognitive models adopted in this research have so far been rather primitive.

On balance, this research supports the practice of inserting into texts higher level (not rote recall) questions after the relevant teaching material. This practice was adopted at The Open University in 1969 on grounds of common sense, teaching experience, and the distilled experience of practical work on programmed instruction. This convergence of experiment and praxis is occurring in language research, just as it has in graphic communication (see remarks in Macdonald-Ross 1977b, 1978). In the long run a science that could not improve on common sense might be considered a waste of time; but instructional psychology is not an advanced science, and the progress made is perhaps acceptable. Further progress on adjunct questions depends upon *conceptual advances*, especially to meet these needs:

1. We need better ways to analyze the semantic (conceptual) structure of texts and the questions derived from texts. Without well-founded classification we cannot know we are conducting experiments.

2. We need to apply the latest ideas in artificial intelligence and cognitive psychology to experimental design. In particular, experimental designs which use rote recall postquestions are both ecologically invalid and cognitively uninteresting. As one suggestion, problem-solving tasks should be set and records of process (protocols) analyzed as in de Groot (1965) and Newell and Simon (1972).

3. We need more information about the effect of questions upon the process of reading. This undoubtedly means more emphasis on ways and means of recording the natural reading processes and ways of interpreting these records in the light of modern cognitive theories.

Feedback

Closely connected with in-text questions is *feedback*, a term which includes both the behaviorist concept of *reinforcement* and the cognitive concept of *knowledge of results*. It now seems clear that there is a real distinction between reinforcement and knowledge of results (KR); this difference is seen most clearly in studies of temporal contiguity, that is, the time which elapses between the performance and the feedback. Reinforcement studies of animal learning showed the overriding importance of giving feedback immediately after the distinctive response (see Grice, 1948, for example, and Renner, 1964, for a general review). On the other hand, feedback to human subjects about cognitively meaningful responses is dependent mainly on the informational appropriateness of the feedback. Annett (1964) concluded:

It is suggested that 'reinforcement' be restricted to those usages outlined by English and English (1958) and should not be used arbitrarily as a substitute for other related terms such as knowledge of results.

The whole field of research into feedback is the subject of a booklength review by Annett (1969); Kulhavy (1977) is also a valuable source. The great weakness of our knowledge about KR is exactly the same as that found so often in applied psychology. There is a lack of *how-to* and *when-to/when-not-to* information. Unless authors can be given fairly explicit procedures for identifying the best places to use KR and then shown how to construct the feedback, we are left with little more than individual intuition, which varies more than somewhat. Questions like this need detailed study along these lines:

1. Analysis of the structure of communications.
2. Collection and analysis of the confusions and mistakes exhibited by learners.
3. Identification of master performers (in this case), people who showed repeated capacity to design effective KR elicitation; and discussion, criticism, and testing of this skill.

Such a research program has hardly been started.

Research on the Substantive Discourse

Research on the structure of the main discourse has been rare, except for the readability studies mentioned earlier. There are some good reasons for this, as Frase (1973, 1975) has pointed out. The complexity of prose and the lack of good analytic procedures for decomposing its structure is one agenda of problems. Another set of unanswered questions surrounds the natural history of the reading process. Given these difficulties, it is perhaps not surprising that large-scale studies on meaningful learning material have been few and far between. I have chosen one of the largest such studies for close scrutiny, partly because its problems are typical and interesting, and partly because it seems this study has not been closely examined in any other review paper.

The study of popular science writing by Funkhouser and Maccoby (1970, 1971a, 1971b) was conducted in two phases, the first being a *correlational* study and the second being an *experimental* study. For the first phase ten short articles on enzymology were commissioned, nine from professional science writers and the tenth from a subject matter expert. The authors were allowed to treat the subject in their own way, within certain limits; they were told which facts to cover and how long the article was to be (eight typewritten pages). The aim was to get ten articles with the same basic content but with variations of style, though in fact there were some disparities of content as well as style. The articles were read by undergraduates in the liberal arts or social studies (a total of 773 subjects), and the effectiveness of each article was measured in terms of:

Information gain (multiple-choice questions)

Reader enjoyment (simple scales)

Attitude change (semantic differential format)

Information seeking (opinions and behavior associated with a desire for further information)

The experimental design was "after only" in style, the authors judging that prior knowledge would be negligible and that pretesting would be a significant learning experience in its own right. Subjects were assigned to article groups and test materials by quasi-random procedure (for details see the original report, Funkhouser & Maccoby, 1970).

The ten articles were analyzed quantitatively in these categories:

1. Vocabulary analysis
   1.1. Function words (50 most common words in English; Francis, 1964)
   1.2. Science words (technical terms)
   1.3. Activity words (verbs, etc., denoting action)
   1.4. Concrete words (nouns describing objects)
2. Readability analysis
   2.1. Dale-Chall
   2.2. Flesch
   2.3. Farr, Jenkins, and Paterson's (1951) "short form" of Flesch
   2.4. Cloze
3. Subject matter analysis
   3.1. Percentage of space given to specified topic
   3.2. Test items which could be answered from the article
4. Style analysis
   4.1. Examples
   4.2. Analogy
   4.3. Definition
   4.4. Conclusion
   4.5. Introduction
   4.6. Elaboration
5. Text organization
   5.1. Length in words
   5.2. Length in lines
   5.3. Words per sentence
   5.4. Words per paragraph
   5.5. Source citation frequency
   5.6. Division into sections
   5.7. Percent of multicontent lines

Some of this content analysis is open to criticism as being rather unsubtle (for example, the equation of "function words" with the 50 most common words). Some categories overlap, while others could be analyzed more deeply (for example, more could be done with "subject matter analysis"). These conceptual difficulties do not necessarily vitiate the investigation; provided the investigators concentrated on large-scale effects (which by and large they did), the design is fairly robust.

The main results of Phase I were:

1. The four factors of effective communication (information gain, enjoyment, attitude change, and information seeking) were positively correlated.

2. These audience effects were highly correlated with manipulable text variables. Therefore, in principle, it should be possible to tailor science articles to specifications.

3. There were substantial differences in the effectiveness of the ten different articles.

Analysis of the text variables brought these further conclusions:

4. Readability (and in particular the Dale-Chall method) was related in the same direction to all four response (effectiveness) variables. This shows again the common finding that readability scores are good predictive indices of both reader enjoyment and information gain.

5. Percentage of activity words was strongly related to all the effects measures.

6. Percentage of science words was negatively related to all four response variables.

7. Percentage of lines of examples was the highest correlate of information gain.

8. Percentage of lines of nonscience topics was highly related to information seeking and reader enjoyment (but for a contrary view, see Klare et al., 1955). It was not correlated with information gain. (Flesch's Human Interest Score measures this text variable; see Flesch, 1948)

9. Percentage of lines of analogy was negatively correlated with information gain. The authors wisely conclude that "the evidence recommends not a complete abhorrence of analogy, but only that the writers be judicious in its use."

10. Percentage of lines of definition had a positive correlation with reader enjoyment.

11. Percentage of lines of conclusion was negatively correlated with all the response measures, but none of these correlations was statistically significant.

12. Percentage of concrete words had positive correlation with reader enjoyment, favorable attitude, and information seeking.

13. Division of articles into sections with section headings had negative correlations with all four response variables, though these correlations were not statistically significant. However, this is not especially surprising: the key function of a section heading is to enable the reader to identify particular topics, that is, the *access function* (see below). The value of an access device is not fully realized unless the subjects read selectively under conditions of restricted time allowance.

Phase II of the investigation took the form of a "true" experimental design (Funkhouser & Maccoby, 1971b). This design manipulated two kinds of variables: *gross variables*, involving the whole article, and *information-gain variables*, which contrasted two different ways of presenting individual pieces of information. The test materials were similar to those used in Phase I; multiple-choice questions for information gain, a general questionnaire eliciting demographic information and prior interest in science, and an attitude survey.

Some crucial facts are worth noting about the way the test materials were written. The procedure started with the construction of the test items, that is, the items were in hand before the alternative versions were written. (The authors explicitly say they used the tests as the basis for writing the materials.) The articles on a topic contained exactly the same information, and the alternate version was constructed by the investigators and not, for example, by the best professional writers as identified in Phase I. These three facts have a crucial bearing on the results obtained and on the way we should interpret these results. For example, the plasma physics article contains this example vs. analogy alternate, embedded, of course, in the whole article (p. 43):

Example Version:

Besides positive and negative particles, plasmas may contain neutral atoms or molecules, and also electromagnetic radiation. For example, hydrogen is the simplest atom known. It can be ionized to a single positive particle and a single negative particle. We can make a plasma of hydrogen gas by ionizing it, but in addition to the ionized particles there would be neutral hydrogen atoms and hydrogen (H_2) molecules present.

Analogy version:

Besides positive and negative particles, plasmas may contain neutral atoms or molecules, and also electromagnetic radiation. In a way, a plasma is like a herd of cattle in a field. A lot of "neutral" elements like grass, sagebush, cowboys and prairie-dogs are intermixed with them. Although these may have some effects on our "bovine particles" their presence is irrelevant to the fact that it is a "herd of cattle."

It seems obvious that a plasma is in no real way "like a herd of cattle in a field," and I doubt whether any competent science writer would have drawn such a comparison. The test item corresponding to this manipulation (p. 62) is:

In addition to positive and negative ions, a plasma may consist of

A. neutral atoms and molecules
B. neutral ions
C. electrons
D. nothing: positive and negative ions are the only possible constituents

---

This item can be answered by rote recall of the first sentence of the paragraph, that is, without reference to the structure or content of either the example or the analogy. Rather surprisingly, there was a significant advantage for the analogy variable with one student group (but only at the $p < .5$ level); but it seems that nothing can be inferred from this result. No doubt analogy is a powerful explanatory device when used appropriately, and no doubt the use of examples is also an important device; however, nothing was learned from this experiment that could be sensibly used by the practicing communicator.

Another interesting comparison was "starting with question vs. not starting with question." There was a slight advantage for the second (no-question) version, but once again it would be unwise to draw any conclusions before looking closely at the actual experimental material:

Starting with Question:	*Starting without Question*
Where do these miraculous molecules originate? Simply enough . . .	These miraculous molecules of course have an origin. Simply enough . . .

If we regard questions as problem statements or as requisites for explanations, then both versions are semantically almost identical. Small wonder, then, that no advantage was found for the "starting with question" version; indeed one of the two student groups showed a marginal advantage for the "without question" version (but $p < .05$ only). It seems that these comparisons are almost worthless unless preceded by a careful semantic and linguistic analysis to dissect out exactly what questions (or examples or analogies) are, what kinds exist, and where their use seems most appropriate.

It seems that no practical conclusions can be drawn from the manipulation of information-gain variables. Above all, the "no significant difference" results do not refute the hypotheses under test and in at least some cases were definitely to be expected. However, one further comparison made by Funkhouser and Maccoby did turn out to be rather illuminating. The Phase II materials were tried out on 272 professional scientists. These tests showed clearly that the more knowledgeable readers learned most from the articles (Table 1), and also (Table 28 in Funkhouser & Maccoby, 1971b) that the manipulated variables had no significant effect on the measures. The authors conclude (p. 126) that "Evidently, scientists do not need the advantage of good exposition nearly as much as students do for adequate comprehension." This fits quite well with Klare's readability model, which states that if subjects have increased motivation and/or increased reading skills, the effect of readability differences will be reduced.

TABLE 1
Rounded Gain Scores Derived from Funkhouser and Maccoby (1971b).

Populations	Crude Gain	Adjusted Gain	p
Scientific ($n = 179$)	30%	60%	.001
Stanford students (262)	25	40	.001
de Anza students (279)	20	30	.001

The chief lessons to be learned from this analysis are methodological. Readability formulae once again turn out to be reliable predictors of comprehension difficulty, and once again the absence of good text analysis procedures is exposed. Experimental alternatives must be of the highest possible quality; the second part of this investigation was almost completely vitiated by the poor quality of the materials. The essential questions to pose are when to/when not to and how to/how not to questions. It is not sensible to test, for instance, "examples" versus "analogies" across the board, since no answer to such a test is meaningful. What we need is clarification of the conditions and rules for appropriate use—and that, unfortunately, is the kind of applied research which is conspicuous by its rarity.

Although studies which deal with the main structure of the discourse are rather scarce, there are some others that are worth attention, especially the work of Hiller (1968; Hiller, Marcotte, & Martin, 1969) and Meyer (1975). Hiller showed that vagueness was negatively correlated to writing and lecturing effectiveness, a finding of considerable ecological validity and interest. Meyer showed that the memorability of concepts was connected to their position in the conceptual framework of the whole passage; if the embedded paragraph was conceptually central, it was remembered more easily. Both these experiments show a good "feel" for the main issues of real-life instruction, though admittedly both designs could be improved with recent knowledge in linguistics and cognitive psychology (for a discussion of Meyer's work, see Carter, 1977).

Access Structure

My colleague Waller (1977b) has been developing the notion of *access structure*. He criticizes the model of reading as a once-through, top-left to bottom-right process. This model is implicit or explicit in almost all studies of reading; for example, most experimental designs prevent readers from going back and reviewing the text they have read before answering the text questions (Frase, 1973). Observation of macro strategies in reading shows them to be quite complex (Hatt, 1976; Pugh, 1974; Thomas, 1976; Whalley, 1977; Whalley & Fleming, 1975). Second, models of reading must take notice of research on learning styles (Cronbach & Snow, 1976; Mager, 1961). Third, in most real-world situations students are overloaded with work and therefore *must* adopt selective reading strategies (for example, Blacklock, 1976).

These considerations have led Waller to see the reader as active, not only because he is struggling to understand what he reads but also because he is *selective* in what he reads. This leads to a radically different view of the devices which surround the prose discourse (listed in Figure 3). They are not there to assist comprehension (at any rate not directly); they are there to *help the reader find his way about*. Hence the term *access structure*.

According to Waller, access devices fall into two broad classes, according to their function in the reading process. There are those devices that help the reader *plan* his reading strategy, for example contents, objectives, study guides. Then there are the devices that help the reader *execute* his strategy (Waller calls these "orienting" devices). Examples of the latter are headings, page and section numbers, indexes, and any typographic device which signals the status of the communication to the reader.

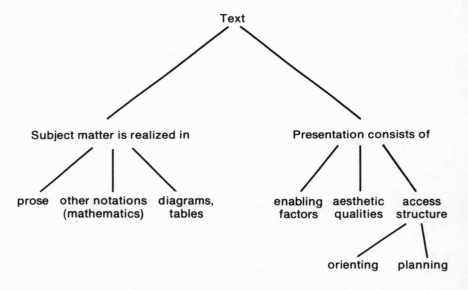

Figure 2. Text structure. (From *Three Functions of Text Presentation* [Notes on Transforming, 2], by R. Waller. Milton Keynes, U.K.: Institute of Educational Technology, The Open University, 1977.)

Some categories serve more than one function; for example, binding has both an ergonomic and a stylistic function; contents lists can also be used for orienting purposes; illustrations can be both decorative and informative.

At present, Waller's classification is a contribution to the content analysis of educational texts, but like all taxonomies it does direct attention to certain theoretical issues and away from other issues. In particular, his taxonomy emphasizes questions of how the reader selects and uses information. We can see this scheme as a kind of *macrotypography* of the book as a whole, in contrast to

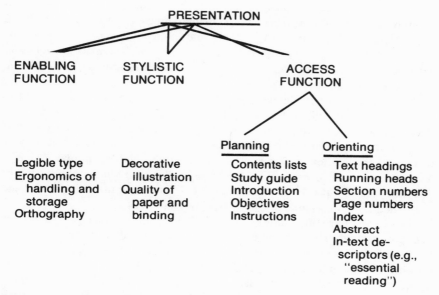

Figure 3. Text presentation functions. (From *Three Functions of Text Presentation* [Notes on Transforming, 2], by R. Waller. Milton Keynes, U.K.: Institute of Educational Technology, The Open University, 1977.)

the more traditional *microtypography*, which concentrates on the details of prose setting.

CONCLUSION

Since Carroll's (1971) review of verbal discourse, research has increased in quantity, but certain difficulties continue to obstruct progress. There is a general consensus that the causes which make for difficulty in experiments on the study of language in texts include:

1. Ungrounded or weakly grounded empiricism.
2. Impoverished prose as experimental material.
3. Excessive and unjustified reliance on rote-memory tasks.
4. Failure to control for ecologically important variables, such as study time and motivation.
5. Failure to distinguish between statistical significance and ecological significance.

Though easy to identify, such flaws are difficult to correct. For example, if low-level rote-recall passages are rejected, the experimenter must face the full complexity of prose (which is, of course, what the educator deals with all the time). To characterize complex prose, better linguistic techniques are needed; this is one of the present-day limitations to valid research. Again, the simple rote-recall multiple-choice test is not appropriate for asking many kinds of cognitive questions; some record of the reading process is needed, as well as a measure of terminal competence. Much more attention must be paid to the "ecological validity" of the proposed design. Many of the remarks of Johnson-Laird and Wason (1977), Neisser (1976), and Newell and Simon (1972) should be carefully digested.

In general, text research during the past ten years has reinforced the standard procedures of curriculum design but has not transformed it. This is maybe a tribute to the intuition and skill of curriculum practitioners, but it suggests that many of the research questions have not been fruitful, and that new directions should be tried. There is a notable lack of how-to and when-to/when-not-to information; on the other hand, too much research is done without the support of adequate theory. Thus all too often research has failed to be useful in practice and also failed to be interesting as theory (see Wright, 1978).

Researchers have often shown a lack of discrimination in their handling of the stimulus material. This has had a seriously debilitating effect on the validity of much empirical work as this review has shown. Clearly if researchers choose to do work on natural texts they must develop a suitable sense for the subtlety and complexity of natural language. Backed up by appropriate procedures of content analysis, this grounded understanding would help the researcher steer through the hidden reefs of language structure.

One area of practical research has come through this review with a surprisingly good record: readability research. One central theoretical issue which is starting to bear fruit is the representation of cognitive strategies. And the healthy turmoil in linguistics is bound to give us insights and practical tools of analysis. At present these exciting prospects are not always connected to the immediate concerns of the practitioner. Nevertheless, our ideas do condition the way we think and work. In the next ten years, the flowering of cognitive theory is bound to affect us all.

REFERENCES

Aiken, A. J., Bailey, R. W., & Hamilton-Smith, N. *The computer and literary studies.* Edinburgh: Edinburgh University Press, 1973.

Ammerman, H. L., & Melching, W. H. *The derivation, analysis and classification of instructional objectives* (HumRRO Tech. Rep. 66–4, Task INGO). Washington, D.C.: George Washington University, 1966.

Anderson, R. C., & Biddle, W. B. On asking people questions about what they are reading. In G. Bower (Ed.), *Psychology of learning and motivation* (Vol. 9). New York: Academic Press, 1975.

Anderson, R. C., Spiro, R. J., & Montague, W. E. *Schooling and the acquisition of knowledge.* Hillsdale, N.J.: Lawrence Erlbaum, 1977.

Annett, J. The role of knowledge of results in learning: A survey. In J. P. DeCecco (Ed.), *Educational technology.* New York: Holt, Rinehart & Winston, 1964.

Annett, J. *Feedback and human behaviour: The effect of knowledge results, incentives and reinforcement on learning and performance.* London: Penguin Books, 1969.

Apple, M. W. The adequacy of systems management procedures in education. *Journal of Educational Research*, 1972, *66*, 10-18.

Aristotle. *Categories* (Categoriae) & *De interpretatione*. (J. L. Ackrill, trans.). London: Oxford University Press, 1963.

Augstein, S. *Reading strategies and learning outcomes*. Unpublished doctoral dissertation, Brunel University, Uxbridge, Middlesex, U.K., 1971.

Ausubel, D. P. The use of advance organisers in the learning and retention of meaningful verbal material. *Journal of Educational Psychology*, 1960, *51*, 267-272.

Ausubel, D. P. *The psychology of meaningful verbal learning*. New York: Grune & Stratton, 1963.

Ausubel, D. P. In defense of advance organizers: A reply to the critics. *Review of Educational Research*, 1978, *48*, 251-257.

Ausubel, D. P., & Fitzgerald, D. The role of discriminability in meaningful verbal learning and retention. *Journal of Educational Psychology*, 1961, *52*, 266-274.

Ausubel, D. P., & Fitzgerald, D. Organizer general background and antecedent learning variables in sequential verbal learning. *Journal of Educational Psychology*, 1962, *53*, 243-249.

Ausubel, D. P., & Robinson, F. G. *School learning: An introduction to educational psychology*. New York: Holt, Rinehart & Winston, 1969.

Ausubel, D. P., Schpoont, S. H., & Cukier, L. The influence of intention on the retention of school materials. *Journal of Educational Psychology*, 1957, *48*, 87-92.

Barnes, B. R., & Clawson, E. U. Do advance organizers facilitate learning? Recommendations for further research based on an analysis of 32 studies. *Review of Educational Research*, 1975, *45*, 637-659.

Berelson, B. R. *Content analysis in communication research*. Glencoe, Ill.: Free Press, 1952.

Berelson, B. R. Content analysis. In G. Lindzey and E. Aronson (Eds.), *Handbook of social psychology*. Reading, Mass.: Addison-Wesley, 1954.

Blacklock, S. *Workload: A summary of student workload on courses for which feedback was collected by the Survey Research Department 1971–1975*. Internal paper, Institute of Educational Technology, The Open University, U.K., 1976.

Bloom, B. S. (Ed.). *Taxonomy of educational objectives*. New York: David McKay, 1956.

Bloomfield, L. *Language*. New York: Holt, 1933.

Boden, M. A. *Artificial intelligence and natural man*. Hassocks, Sussex: Harvester Press, 1977.

Bormuth, J. R. New developments in readability research. *Elementary English*, 1967, *44*, 840-845. (Reprinted in J. R. Bormuth [Ed.], *Readability in 1968*. Champaign, Ill.: National Council of Teachers of English, 1968.)

Bormuth, J. R. *Development of readability analyses* (Final Rep. Project No. 7-0052, Contract No. OEC 3-7-070052-0326). Washington, D.C.: Office of Education, U.S. Department of Health, Education, and Welfare, 1969.

Bronowski, J. *A sense of the future*. Cambridge, Mass.: MIT Press, 1977.

Carroll, J. B. *Learning from verbal discourse in educational media: A review of the literature* (ETS Research Bulletin 71-61). Princeton, N.J.: Educational Testing Service, 1971.

Carroll, J. B., & Freedle, R. C. (Eds.). *Language comprehension and the acquisition of knowledge*. Washington, D.C.: V. H. Winston, 1972.

Carter, J. F. Comments on Chapter 6: The structure of prose, by B. J. F. Meyer. In R. C. Anderson, R. J. Spiro, and W. E. Montague (Eds.), *Schooling and the acquisition of knowledge*. Hillsdale, N.J.: Lawrence Erlbaum, 1977.

Carver, R. P. A critical review of mathemagenic behaviors and the effect of questions upon the retention of prose materials. *Journal of Reading Behavior*, 1972, *4*, 93-119.

Caylor, J. S., Sticht, T. G., Fox, L. C., & Ford, J. P. *Methodologies for determining reading requirements of military occupational specialties* (HumRRO Tech. Rep. 73-5). Alexandria, Va.: Human Resources Research Organization, 1973.

Chall, J. S. *Readability, an appraisal of research and application.* Columbus: Ohio State University Press, 1958.

Chomsky, N. *Syntactic structures.* The Hague: Mouton, 1957.

Coleman, E. B. Developing a technology of written instruction: Some determiners of the complexity of prose. In E. Z. Rothkopf and P. E. Johnson (Eds.), *Verbal learning research and the technology of written instruction.* New York: Teachers College Press, Columbia University, 1971.

Cronbach, L. J., & Snow, R. *Aptitudes and instructional methods.* New York: Irvington, 1977.

Crothers, E. J. *Paragraph structures description.* Boulder: Institute for the Study of Intellectual Behavior, University of Colorado, 1975.

Dale, E., and Chall, J. S. A formula for predicting readability. *Educational Research Bulletin,* 1948, *27,* 11-20, 28.

De Groot, A. D. *Thought and choice in chess.* The Hague: Mouton, 1965.

Denbow, C. J. *An experimental study of the effect of a repetition factor on the relationship between readability and listenability.* (Doctoral dissertation, Ohio University, 1973). (University Microfilms No. 74-13, 128)

De Saussure, F. *Cours de linguistique générale.* Lausanne: Payot, 1915.

Dilthey, W. *Gesammelte Schriften* (14 vols.). Gottingen: Vandenhoeck & Ruprecht, 1913-1967. (Reissued, Stuttgart: B. G. Teubner, 1958.)

Duchastel, P., & Merrill, P. The effects of behavioral objectives on learning: A review of empirical studies. *Review of Educational Research,* 1973, *43,* 53-69.

Dummett, M. *Frege: Philosophy of language.* London: Duckworth, 1973.

Educational Testing Service. *Focus 4: Learning to read.* Princeton, N.J.: Author, 1978.

Empson, W. *The structure of complex words* (3rd ed.). London: Chatto & Windus, 1977. (Originally published, 1951.)

English, H. B., & English, A. C. *A comprehensive dictionary of psychological and psychoanalytical terms: A guide to usage.* London: Longmans, Green, 1958.

Farr, J. N., Jenkins, J. J., & Paterson, D. G. Simplification of the Flesch Reading Ease formula. *Journal of Applied Psychology,* 1951, *35,* 333-337.

Faw, H. W., & Waller, T. G. Mathemagenic behaviors and efficiency in learning from prose materials: Review, critique and recommendations. *Review of Educational Research,* 1976, *46,* 691-720.

Fillmore, C. The case for case. In E. Bach and R. T. Harms (Eds.), *Universals in linguistic theory.* New York: Holt, Rinehart & Winston, 1968.

Fillmore, C. The case for case reopened. *Syntax and Semantics,* 1977, *8,* 59-82.

Firth, J. R. *Speech.* London: Benn, 1930.

Firth, J. R. *The tongues of men.* London: Watts, 1937.

Flesch, R. F. A new readability yardstick. *Journal of Applied Psychology,* 1948, *32,* 221-233.

Francis, W. N. A standard sample of present-day edited American English, for use with digital computers. Providence, R.I.: Brown University, Department of Linguistics, 1964.

Frase, L. T. Structural analysis of the knowledge that results from thinking about text. *Journal of Educational Psychology,* 1969, *6,* part 2. (Monograph 60)

Frase, L. T. Boundary conditions for mathemagenic behavior. *Review of Educational Research,* 1970, *46,* 337-348.

Frase, L. T. Effect of incentive variables and type of adjunct questions upon text learning. *Journal of Educational Psychology,* 1971, *62,* 371-375.

Frase, L. T. On learning from prose. *Educational Psychologist,* 1973, *10,* 15-23.

Frase, L. T. Prose processing. In G. H. Bower (Ed.), *The psychology of learning and motivation* (Vol. 9). New York: Academic Press, 1975.

Fredericksen, C. H. Representing logical and semantic structure of knowledge acquired from discourse. *Cognitive Psychology*, 1975, *7*, 371-458.

Funkhouser, G. R., & Maccoby, N. *Communicating science to nonscientists: Phase I. A correlational study of textural variables and audience effects.* Stanford, Calif.: Institute for Communication Research, Stanford University, 1970.

Funkhouser, G. R., and Maccoby, N. Communicating specialized science to a lay audience. *Journal of Communication*, 1971, *21*, 58-71. (a)

Funkhouser, G. R., & Maccoby, N. *Study on communicating science information to a lay audience: Phase II.* Stanford, Calif.: Institute for Communication Research, Stanford University, 1971. (b)

Gagné, R. M. *The conditions of learning.* New York: Holt, Rinehart & Winston, 1965.

Games, P. A., & Klare, G. R. *Elementary statistics: Data analysis for the behavioral sciences.* New York: McGraw-Hill, 1967.

Gerbner, G. (Ed.). *The analysis of communications content.* New York: John Wiley, 1969.

Grice, G. R. The relation of secondary reinforcement to delayed reward in visual discrimination learning. *Journal of Experimental Psychology*, 1948, *38*, 1-16.

Grimes, J. E. *The thread of discourse.* The Hague: Mouton, 1975.

Gustafson, H. W., & Toole, D. L. Effects of adjunct questions, pretesting, degree of student supervision on learning from an instructional test. *Journal of Experimental Education*, 1970, *39*, 53-58.

Halliday, M. A. K., & Hasan, R. *Cohesion in English.* London: Longmans, 1976.

Hartley, J., & Davies, I. K. Preinstructional strategies: The role of pretests, behavioral objectives, overviews and advance organizers. *Review of Educational Research*, 1976, *46*, 239-265.

Hatt, F. *The reading process: A framework for analysis and description.* London: Bingley, 1976.

Hewitt, C. *Description and theoretical analysis (using schemas) of PLANNER: A language for proving theorems and manipulating models in a robot.* Unpublished doctoral dissertation, Massachusetts Institute of Technology, 1971.

Hiller, J. H. *An experimental investigation of the effects of conceptual vagueness on speaking behavior* (Doctoral dissertation, University of Connecticut, 1968). (University Microfilms No. 69-2144)

Hiller, J. H. Learning from prose text: Effects of readability level, inserted question difficulty and individual differences. *Journal of Educational Psychology*, 1974, *66*, 202-211.

Hiller, J. H., Marcotte, D. R., & Martin, T. Opinionation, vagueness, and specificity-distinctions: Essay traits measured by computer. *American Educational Research Journal*, 1969, *6*, 271-286.

Hirsch, E. D. *Validity in interpretation.* New Haven, Conn.: Yale University Press, 1967.

Hodges, H. A. *Wilhelm Dilthey: An introduction.* London: Routledge & Kegan Paul, 1944.

Holsti, O. R. Content analysis. In G. Lindzey and E. Aronson (Eds.), *Handbook of social psychology.* Reading, Mass.: Addison-Wesley, 1968.

Holsti, O. R. *Content analysis for the social sciences and humanities.* Reading, Mass.: Addison-Wesley, 1969.

Jenkins, J. J. Remember that old theory of memory? Well, forget it. *American Psychologist*, 1974, *29*, 785-795.

Jespersen, O. *Language: Its nature, development and origin.* London: Allen & Unwin, 1922.

Johnson, A. B. *A treatise on language.* (D. Rynin, Ed.) Berkeley: University of California Press, 1947. (Originally published, 1836.)

Johnson, P. E. Associative meaning of concepts in physics. *Journal of Educational Psychology,* 1964, *55,* 84-88.

Johnson, P. E. Experimental analysis of written instruction. In E. Z. Rothkopf and P. E. Johnson (Eds.), *Verbal learning research and the technology of written instruction.* New York: Teachers College Press, Columbia University, 1971.

Johnson-Laird, P. N., & Wason, P. C. *Thinking: Readings in cognitive science.* London: Cambridge University Press, 1977.

Kaye, A. R. The design and evaluation of science courses at The Open University. *Instructional Science,* 1973, *2,* 119-191.

Keller, F. S. *PSI, The Keller Plan handbook: Essays on a personalized system of instruction.* Menlo Park, Ca.: W. A. Benjamin, 1974.

Kern, R. P., Sticht, T. G., & Fox, L. C. *Readability, reading ability and readership* (HumRRO Professional Papers 17-70). Alexandria, Va.: Human Resources Research Organization, 1970.

Kingston, A. J., & Lovelace, T. Sexism and reading: A critical review of the literature. *Reading Research Quarterly,* 1977-1978, *13,* 133-161.

Kintsch, W. *The representation of meaning in memory.* New York: John Wiley, 1974.

Klare, G. R. *The measurement of readability.* Ames: Iowa State University Press, 1963.

Klare, G. R. Assessing readability. *Reading Research Quarterly,* 1974-1975, *10,* 62-102.

Klare, G. R. Judging readability. *Instructional Science,* 1976, *5,* 55-61. (a)

Klare, G. R. A second look at the validity of readability formulas. *Journal of Reading Behavior,* 1976, *8,* 129-152. (b)

Klare, G. R., Mabry, J. E., & Gustafson, L. M. The relationship of human interest to immediate retention and to acceptability of technical material. *Journal of Applied Psychology,* 1955, *39,* 92-95.

Klare, G. R., Sinaiko, H. W., & Stolurow, L. M. The Cloze procedure, a convenient readability test for training materials and translation. *International Review of Applied Psychology,* 1972, *21,* 77-105.

Klare, G. R., Shuford, E. H., and Nichols, W. H. The relationship of style difficulty, practice and ability to efficiency of reading to retention. *Journal of Applied Psychology,* 1957, *41,* 222-226.

Klare, G. R., Sinaiko, H. W., & Stolurow, L. M. The Cloze procedure, a convenient tional materials. *Journal of Educational Research,* 1973, *67,* 176.

Kulhavy, R. W. Feedback in written instruction. *Review of Educational Research,* 1977, *47,* 211-232.

Ladas, H. The mathemagenic effects of factual review questions on the learning of incidental information. *Review of Educational Research,* 1973, *43,* 71-82.

Lasswell, H. D., & Leites, N. (Eds.). *Language of politics: Studies in quantitative semantics.* New York: Stewart, 1949.

Lasswell, H. D., Lerner, D., & Pool I. de S. *The comparative study of symbols.* Stanford, Calif.: Stanford University Press, 1952.

Lawton, J. T., & Wanska, S. K. Advance organisers as a teaching strategy: A reply to Barnes and Clawson. *Review of Educational Research,* 1977, *47,* 233-244.

Lenneberg, E. H. *New directions in the study of language.* Cambridge, Mass.: MIT Press, 1964.

Lenneberg, E. H. *Biological foundations of language.* New York: John Wiley, 1967.

Lewis, B. N., Horabin, I. S., and Gane, C. P. *Flow charts, logical trees, and algorithms for rules and regulations.* (H.M. Treasury: Centre for Administrative Studies, Occasional Papers No. 2.) London: Her Majesty's Stationery Office, 1967.

Lumsdaine, A. A. (Ed.). *Recommendations for reporting the effectiveness of programmed instruction materials*. Washington, D.C.: Division of Audiovisual Instruction Service, National Education Association, 1966.

Macdonald-Ross, M. Behavioural objectives: A critical review. *Instructional Science*, 1973, *2*, 1-52.

Macdonald-Ross, M. *Glass beads and geometric monsters: The problem of representing knowledge*. Paper presented at the meeting of the Association for Educational Communications and Technology, Atlantic City, N.J., 1974.

Macdonald-Ross, M. The quality of course materials. In *Evaluating teaching in higher education*. London: Institute of Education, University Teaching Methods Unit, University of London, 1975.

Macdonald-Ross, M. Content analysis. In *Course evaluation* (Conference Papers No. 7, Manchester Polytechnic Staff Development and Educational Methods Unit). Proceedings of a conference held at Manchester Polytechnic, Great Britain, May 26, 1977. (a)

Macdonald-Ross, M. How numbers are shown: A review of research on the presentation of quantitative data in texts. *Audio-Visual Communication Review*, 1977, *25*, 359-409. (b)

Macdonald-Ross, M. *The quality of course materials*. Contribution to a conference on curriculum development sponsored by the Ford Foundation, 1977. (Available from the author.) (c)

Macdonald-Ross, M. Graphics in text. In L. S. Shulman (Ed.), *Review of research in education 5*. Itasca, Ill.: F. E. Peacock Publishers, Inc., 1978.

Macdonald-Ross, M., & Smith, E. *Graphics in text: A bibliography*. Milton Keynes, U.K.: Institute of Educational Technology, The Open University, 1977.

Macdonald-Ross, M., & Smith, E. *Language in text: A bibliography*. Milton Keynes, U.K.: Institute of Educational Technology, The Open University, 1978.

McGaw, B., and Grotelueschen, A. Direction of the effect of questions on prose material. *Journal of Educational Psychology*, 1972, *63*, 586-588.

Mager, R. F. On the sequencing of instructional content. *Psychological Reports*, 1961, *9*, 405-413. (Reprinted in I. K. Davies and J. Hartley (Eds.), *Contributions to an educational technology*. London: Butterworth, 1972.)

Mager, R. F. *Preparing instructional objectives*. Palo Alto, Calif.: Fearon, 1962.

Mayer, R. E. Toward transfer of different reading strategies evoked by test-like events in mathematics text. *Journal of Educational Psychology*, 1975, *67*, 165-169.

Medawar, P. B. *The hope of progress*. London: Methuen, 1972.

Melton, R. F. Course evaluation at The Open University: A case study. *British Journal of Educational Technology*, 1977, *8*, 97-102. (a)

Melton, R. F. *Resolution of conflicting claims concerning the effect of behavioural objectives on student learning*. Paper presented to the annual meeting of the American Educational Research Association, New York City, April 1977. (b)

Meyer, B. J. F. *The organization of prose and its effects on memory* Amsterdam: North-Holland, 1975.

Miller, L. R. *A comparative analysis of the predictive validities of four readability formulas*. Unpublished doctoral dissertation, Ohio University, 1972. (University Microfilms No. 73-04240)

Mitchell, J. L. *Computers in the humanities*. Edinburgh: Edinburgh University Press, 1974.

Müller, F. M. *The science of language* (based on lectures delivered at the Royal Institute in 1861 and 1863). London: Longmans, Green, 1864-66.

Murphy, D. R. How plain talk increases readership 45 per cent to 66 per cent. *Printer's Ink*, 1947, *220*, 35-37. (a)

Murphy, D. R. Tests prove short words and sentences get best readership. *Printer's Ink*, 1947, *218*, 61-64. (b)

Murphy, R. T. *Adult functional reading study* (Final Rep., Project No. 0-9004, Grant No. OEC 0-70-4791 [508] PR73-48). Princeton, N.J.: Educational Testing Service, 1973.

Neisser, U. *Cognition and reality: Principles and implications of cognitive psychology.* San Francisco: W. H. Freeman, 1976.

Newell, A., & Simon, H. A. *Human problem solving.* Englewood Cliffs, N.J.: Prentice-Hall, 1972.

North, R. C., Holsti, O. R., Zaninovich, M. G., & Zinnes, D. A. *Content analysis: A handbook with applications for the study of international crisis.* Evanston, Ill.: Northwestern University Press, 1963.

Novak, J. D., Ring, D. G., & Tamir, P. Interpretation of research findings in terms of Ausubel's theory and implications for science education. *Science Education*, 1971, *54*, 483-526.

Palmer, R. E. *Hermeneutics: Interpretation theory in Schleiermacher, Dilthey, Heidegger and Gadamer.* Evanston, Ill.: Northwestern University Press, 1969.

Pask, G. *Conversation, cognition and learning: A cybernetic theory and methodology.* Amsterdam: Elsevier, 1975. (a)

Pask, G. *The cybernetics of human learning and performance.* London: Hutchinson, 1975. (b)

Pask, G. Styles and strategies of learning. *British Journal of Educational Technology*, 1976, *46*, 128-148.

Pedersen, H. *The discovery of language: Linguistic science in the nineteenth century.* Bloomington: Indiana University Press, 1962. (Originally published, 1931.)

Peters, R. S. (Ed.). Aims of education: An interdisciplinary inquiry. *London Educational Review*, 1973, *2*, 1-80.

Peirce, C. S. *Collected papers.* Cambridge, Mass.: Harvard University Press, 1960. (Originally published, 1932.)

Pirsig, R. M. *Zen and the art of motorcycle maintenance.* New York: William Morrow, 1974.

Polanyi, M. *Personal knowledge.* London: Routledge & Kegan Paul, 1958.

Pool, I. de S. (Ed.). *Trends in content analysis: Papers.* Urbana: University of Illinois Press, 1959.

Popper, K. R. Epistemology without a knowing subject. In K. R. Popper (Ed.), *Objective knowledge: An evolutionary approach.* Oxford: Clarendon Press, 1972.

Powers, R. D., Summer, W. A., and Kearl, B. E. A recalculation of four adult readability formulas. *Journal of Educational Psychology*, 1958, *49*, 99-105.

Pugh, A. K. *The design and evaluation of reading efficiency courses.* Unpublished doctoral dissertation, University of Leeds, Great Britain, 1974.

Quirk, R., Greenbaum, S., Leech, G. N., & Svartvik, J. A. *A grammar of contemporary English.* London: Longman, 1972.

Ravetz, J. R. *Scientific knowledge and its social problems.* London: Oxford University Press, 1971.

Renner, K. E. Delay of reinforcement: A historical review. *Psychological Bulletin*, 1964, *61*, 341-361.

Resnick, L. Hierarchies in children's learning: A symposium. *Instructional Science*, 1973, *2*, 311-362.

Richards, I. A. *Practical criticism.* London: Routledge & Kegan Paul, 1929.

Richards, I. A. *Interpretation in teaching.* London: Routledge & Kegan Paul, 1938.

Rickards, J. P., & Denner, P. R. Inserted questions as aids to reading text. *Instructional Science*, 1978, *1*, 313-346.

Rickards, J. P., & DiVesta, F. J. Type and frequency of questions in processing textual materials. *Journal of Educational Psychology*, 1974, *66*, 354-362.

Rickards, J. P., & Hatcher, C. W. Meaningful learning post-questions as semantic cues for poor readers. *Reading Research Quarterly*, in press.

Ring, D. G., & Novak, J. D. The effects of cognitive structure variables on achievement in college chemistry. *Journal of Research in Science Teaching*, 1971, *8*, 325-333.

Rothkopf, E. Z. Some theoretical and experimental approaches to problems in written instruction. In J. D. Krumboltz (Ed.), *Learning and the educational process.* Chicago: Rand McNally, 1965.

Rothkopf, E. Z. Two scientific approaches to the management of instruction. In R. M. Gagné and W. J. Gephart (Eds.), *Learning research and school subjects.* Itasca, Ill.: F. E. Peacock Publishers, Inc., 1968.

Rothkopf, E. Z. The concept of mathemagenic activities. *Review of Educational Research,* 1970, *40*, 325-326.

Rothkopf, E. Z. Structural text features and the control of processes in learning from written text. In J. B. Carroll and R. O. Freedle (Eds.), *Language comprehension and the acquisition of knowledge.* Washington, D.C.: V. H. Winston, 1972.

Rothkopf, E. Z. Barbarism and mathemagenic activities: Comments on criticism by Carver. *Journal of Reading Behavior*, 1974, *6*, 3-8.

Rothkopf, E. Z. Writing to teach and reading to learn: A perspective on the psychology of written instruction. In N. L. Gage (Ed.), *The Psychology of Teaching Methods* (75th Yearbook of the National Society for the Study of Education; Part I). Chicago: University of Chicago Press, 1976.

Rothkopf, E. Z., & Billington, M. J. Indirect review and priming through questions. *Journal of Educational Psychology*, 1974, *66*, 669-679.

Rothkopf, E. Z., & Johnson, P. E. *Verbal learning research and the technology of written instruction.* New York: Teachers College Press, Columbia University, 1971.

Sapir, E. *Language: An introduction to the study of speech.* New York: Harcourt, Brace & World, 1921.

Sapir, E. *Culture, language and personality, selected essays* (D. G. Mandelbaum, Ed.). Berkeley: University of California Press, 1970. (Originally published, 1949).

Scriven, M. *Primary philosophy.* New York: McGraw-Hill, 1966.

Shavelson, R. J. Some aspects of the correspondence between content structure and cognitive structure in physics instruction. *Journal of Educational Psychology*, 1972, *63*, 225-234.

Shavelson, R. J. Methods for examining representations of a subject matter structure in a student's memory. *Journal of Research in Science Teaching*, 1974, *11*, 231-249.

Shavelson, R. J., Berliner, D. C., Loeding, D., Portens, A. W., & Stanton, G. C. *Adjunct questions, mathemagenics and mathematics.* Paper presented at the American Psychological Association annual convention, New Orleans, 1974.

Shavelson, R. J., Berliner, D. C., Ravitch, M., & Loeding, D. Effects of position and type of questions on learning from prose material: Interaction of treatments with individual differences. *Journal of Educational Psychology*, 1974, *66*, 40-48.

Shuy, R. W. Sociolinguistics. In R. W. Shuy (Ed.), *Linguistic theory: What can it say about reading?* Newark, Dela.: International Reading Association, 1977.

Sticht, T. G. *Literacy demands of publications in selected military occupational specialties* (HumRRO Professional Paper 25-70). Alexandria, Va.: Human Resources Research Organization, 1970.

Sticht, T. G. *Reading for working: A functional literacy anthology, a compilation of research on job-related literacy.* Alexandria, Va.: Human Resources Research Organization, 1975.

Sticht, T. G. Comprehending reading at work. In M. Just and P. Carpenter (Eds.), *Cognitive processes in comprehension.* Hillsdale, N.J.: Lawrence Erlbaum, 1977.

Sticht, T. G., Caylor, J. S., Kern, R. P. and Fox, L. C. *Determination of literacy skill requirements in four military occupational specialties* (HumRRO Tech. Rep. 71-23). Alexandria, Va.: Human Resources Research Organization, 1971.

Sticht, T. G., & Zapf, D. W. *Reading and readability research in the armed services* (HumRRO FR-WD-CA-76–4). Alexandria, Va.: Human Resources Research Organization, 1976.

Stokes, A. The reliability of readability formulae. *Journal of Research in Reading*, 1978, *1*, 21-34.

Stone, P. J., Dunphy, D. C., Smith, M. S., & Ogilvie, D. M. *User's manual for the computer approach to content analysis.* Cambridge, Mass.: MIT Press, 1966.

Stone, P. J., Dunphy, D. C., Smith, M. S., & Ogilvie, D. N. *User's manual for the General Inquirer.* Cambridge, Mass.: MIT Press, 1968.

Swanson, C. E. Readability and readership: A controlled experiment. *Journalism Quarterly*, 1948, *25*, 339-343.

Taylor, W. L. Cloze procedure: A new tool for measuring readability. *Journalism Quarterly*, 1953, *30*, 415-433.

Thomas, L. F. *The self-organised learner and the printed word.* Centre for the Study of Human Learning, Brunel University, Uxbridge, Middlesex, U.K., 1976.

Thomas, L. F., Augstein, S., Deans, T., & Moore, H. *An experimental approach to learning from written material.* Centre for the Study of Human Learning, Brunel University, Uxbridge, Middlesex, U.K., 1970.

Vineberg, R., Sticht, T. G., Taylor, E. N., & Caylor, J. S. *Effects of aptitude (AFQT) job experience and literacy on job performance: Summary of HumRRO work units UTILITY and REALISTIC.* Alexandria, Va.: Human Resources Research Organization, 1971. (ERIC Document Reproduction Service No. ED 050 311)

Vygotsky, L. S. *Thought and language* E. Hanfmann and G. Vakar (Eds. and trans.). Cambridge, Mass.: MIT Press, 1962. (Originally published, 1934.)

Wach, J. *Das Verstehen: Grundzuge einer Geschichte der hermeneutischen Theorie im 19 Jahrhundert.* Tubingen: Mohr, 1926-1933.

Waller, R. *Three functions of text presentation* (Notes on transforming, 2). Milton Keynes, U.K.: Institute of Educational Technology, The Open University, 1977. (a)

Waller, R. *Typographic access structures for educational texts.* Institute of Educational Technology, The Open University, 1977. (b)

Washburne, J. N. The use of questions in social science material. *Journal of Educational Psychology*, 1929, *20*, 321-359.

Watts, G. H., & Anderson, R. C. Effects of three types of inserted questions on learning from prose. *Journal of Educational Psychology*, 1971, *62*, 387-394.

Werlich, E. *A text grammar of English.* Heidelberg: Quelle & Meyer, 1976.

West, L. H. T., and Fensham, P. J. Prior knowledge and the learning of science: A review of Ausubel's theory of this process. *Studies in Science Education*, 1974, *1*, 61-81.

Whalley, P. C. *Aspects of purposive reading: The analysis of reading records.* Milton Keynes, U.K.: Institute of Educational Technology, The Open University, 1977.

Whalley, P. C., and Fleming, R. W. An experiment with a simple recorder of reading behaviour. *Programmed Learning and Educational Technology*, 1975, *12*, 120-124.

Wilde, O. *Collected works.* London: Methuen, 1909.

Wilks, Y. A. *Grammar, meaning and the machine analysis of language.* London: Routledge & Kegan Paul, 1972.

Williams, R. *Reading and criticism* (Man and Society Series). London: Muller, 1950.

Winograd, T. *Understanding natural language.* Edinburgh: Edinburgh University Press, 1972.

Winter, E. *Connection in science material: A proposal about the semantics of clause relations* (CILT Papers and Reports, No. 7). London: Centre of Information, Language and Teaching, 1971.

Winter, E. *Replacement as a function of repetition: A study of some of its principal features in the clause relations of contemporary English.* Unpublished doctoral dissertation, University of London, London, Senate House, 1974.

Winter, E. Clause-relational approach to English texts: A study of some predictive lexical items in written discourse. *Instructional Science*, 1977, *6*, 1-92.

Wittgenstein, L. J. J. *Tractatus logico-philosophicus.* London: Routledge & Kegan Paul, 1922.

Wittgenstein, L. J. J. *Philosophical investigations.* Oxford: Blackwell, 1953.

Wittrock, M. C., and Lumsdaine, A. A. Instructional psychology. *Annual Review of Psychology*, 1977, *28*, 417-459.

Wright, P. Presenting technical information: A survey of research findings. *Instructional Science*, 1977, *6*, 93-134.

Wright, P. Feeding the information eaters: Suggestions for integrating pure and applied research on language comprehension. *Instructional Science*, 1978, *7*, 249-312.

III

POLICY

7

About Educational Indicators: Statistics on the Conditions and Trends in Education

RICHARD M. JAEGER
University of North Carolina—Greensboro

In the early 1960s the National Aeronautics and Space Administration granted funds to the American Academy of Arts and Sciences to study the societal impact of the space program. A major product of that grant was a book entitled *Social Indicators* (Bauer, 1966), now acknowledged to be the cornerstone of the *social indicators movement* (Sheldon, 1975).

In the decade since Bauer's work appeared, hundreds of published and presented papers and dozens of books have been produced on social indicators (Frisbie, 1975; Magura & Ball-Rokeach, 1975; Meile & Haese, 1969; Myers & Guttman, 1974), indicators of life quality (Holz & Glitter, 1975; Skogan, 1974; Stetson & Wright, 1975), health indicators (Derogatis, Yevzeroff, & Wittelsberger, 1975; Siegler, 1974; Taylor, Aday & Anderson, 1975; Tissue, 1972), environmental indicators (Dye, 1975), indicators of social mobility (Duncan, 1968), employment indicators (Berkowitz, 1973; Dillman & Christenson, 1974), religious indicators (Finner, 1970), welfare indicators (Angrist, 1974; Flax, 1971; Merriam, 1968), leisure indicators (Ennis, 1968; Noe, 1972; Room, 1972), and, yes, educational indicators (Beyer & Snipper, 1974; Duncan, 1968; Glitter & Peterson, 1970; Irvine, 1968; Swift, 1967).

Despite the voluminous literature on indicators, or perhaps because of it, indicators are not clearly distinguished from statistics. They hold no exalted place. Further, the literature contains much discussion of their potential application but little evidence of their utility. Finally, although the label may be newly rediscovered, the existence of educational indicators can be traced throughout history (Goody, 1968; Impara, 1977; Lockridge, 1974; MacManus, 1944).

JAMES IMPARA, Virginia Polytechnic Institute and State University, and KENNETH LAND, University of Illinois, were editorial consultants for this chapter.

Having set the record straight at the outset—educational indicators are neither unique nor novel, and they may not be useful in practice—is it pointless to go on? I think not. The recent history of American education suggests that information on its aggregate condition is sorely needed and will become even more important in the future. Despite the traditional (if not legal) precept of local control, schooling in America has been the target of a barrage of state and federal legislation in recent years. In California, evaluation of teachers was mandated through the Stull bill in 1972; and in North Carolina, preparation of individualized educational plans for "gifted and talented" students was required under the Creech bill in 1976. In 1976–77, 31 of the 50 states had legislatively-mandated statewide assessment programs in operation. In 1977, Representative Harrington of Massachusetts introduced H.R. 6776, a bill intended "to promote the rights of individuals who take standardized educational tests," and Representative Mottl of Ohio introduced H.R. 6088 and H.R. 7116, bills that would "amend the Elementary and Secondary Education Act of 1965 to require state educational agencies to establish basic standards of educational proficiency applicable to secondary school students." The Senate Education Subcommittee on the Quality of Education has considered development of a standardized minimum competency test by the federal government. These are but a few examples of such legislation; the list could go on for many pages. Some of these legislative "remedies" are attempted responses to perceptions of the changing condition of education, such as recent statistics on the ten-year decline of Scholastic Aptitude Test score averages. Most others were formulated in the absence of adequate data. As long as decisions that affect the schooling of millions are to be made by state governments and federal lawmakers, the case for sound, trustworthy, and extensive data on the aggregate condition of education in the various and collective United States is clear. Whether such statistics, when refined, distilled, and otherwise massaged, should be termed educational indicators is unimportant.

This chapter is composed of three sections. In the first, various definitions of social and educational indicators included in the literature are described and examined. A summary will show them to be eclectic, and often contradictory. The second section is devoted to a variety of technical considerations in the definition and use of indicators. These considerations include: (1) the aggregative nature of indicators, together with problems that follow from attributing summary information on the collective characteristics of observed units to a larger population; (2) construct validity problems that arise when indicators are interpreted as measures of broad, unobservable attributes of populations (constructs); (3) systematic (bias) and unsystematic (random) errors that accompany generalizations of findings on aggregations of units to populations of interest; and (4) methodological problems that are unique to statistical time series—the interpretation of sequences of supposedly identical measurements, taken on a common aggregate of units. The third section is devoted to the brief literature on the application of indicators and some comments on avenues of research that may prove fruitful in the future.

A review of specific educational statistics and indicators has been omitted intentionally, since several recent sources consider that topic. Jaeger and Jaeger (1978) discuss readily available data, missing information, and proposed schema for comprehensive systems of indicators. A collection of time series on education is provided by Ferriss (1969), and the series of reports entitled *The Condition of Education* published annually by the National Center for Education Statistics (U.S. Department of Health, Education, and Welfare, 1976a, 1977) since March 1975 contains an impressive collection of statistics, time series, and facts on formal schooling in the United States and elsewhere. These reports are organized by level of education (elementary, secondary, and postsecondary) and incorporate data collected by a number of government agencies and federally funded projects such as the National Assessment of Educational Progress, the National Institute of Education, the Bureau of the Census, the National Center for Education Statistics, the Department of Labor, and the U.S. Office of Education. Available statistics and indicators can be compared with one conception of needed information by reviewing a proposal for a comprehensive system of indicators prepared by Richard Stone (United Nations, 1975).

WHAT IS AN INDICATOR?

Alternative definitions of an indicator

Most social scientists would regard our formal education system as one sector of a larger social system. As Gooler (1975, p. 11) has suggested, educational indicators can be regarded as social indicators applied to the education sector. Keeping this suggestion in mind, we will consider the relatively abundant literature on social indicators as we seek a definition of educational indicators.

The term *social indicator* has been used, off and on, since the 1920s. Since their rediscovery by Raymond Bauer and his colleagues in 1966, social indicators have been the subject of thousands of published papers and dozens of books. Most authors of these publications assume that the meaning of the term is known. Those who have attempted to define it have stopped short of operational clarity. The giants in the field do not agree on what is essential. One person's indicator is another person's statistic, and a third person's variable. Indicators have no special place beside ordinary statistics, except in the conceptual schema of their proposers.

Following are some definitions that have appeared in the literature and some comments on them. From Clemmer, Fairbanks, Hall, Impara, & Nelson (1973, p. 2):

> [an indicator is] a descriptor, in quantifiable terms, of the status at a specified point in time of a significant condition or variable which provides evidence useful for an analysis of progress towards a goal or objective.

The Clemmer et al. report suggests that an indicator is not inherently evaluative, must have constant meaning over time, and need not be validated through a specific causal model. However, an indicator must be quantitatively measurable, must be related to some goal or objective that is of interest to educators in the state (presumably, consensus judgment would be used to determine whether a statistic meets this requirement), and must be measurable at various time points.

So numbers are within the domain of definition, verbal impressions and nonnumerical qualitative descriptions are not, utility is essential, and relationship to time is a key factor. These characteristics appear in the definitions offered by several contributors to the field but are noticeably absent, or contradicted, in other definitions.

Otis Dudley Duncan, in a memorandum entitled "Developing Social Indicators" (no date) defines social indicators as

> . . . quantitative descriptions and analyses of social conditions and trends, designed both to inform public decision-making and to advance our knowledge and understanding of society.

The social indicator definition suggested by Duncan has a lot in common with the one proposed by Clemmer et al. Both demand numbers. Usefulness is a key element in both definitions, but the contexts in which the definitions appear lead to different criteria for utility. Clemmer demands that an indicator be useful in judging progress toward some educational goal or objective, and Duncan demands that it be designed, more generally, to inform decision makers or to aid in an understanding of society. Duncan omits any reference to time, except in his suggestion that we consider social trends.

Land and Spilerman (1975, p. 1) state:

> The label "social indicators" has been with us for nearly a decade. It is now generally applied to indices of various social conditions within particular communities or societies; that is, to measurements of the contexts of the social life of members of a society.

This definition is so general as to exclude almost nothing. It surely encompasses economic statistics, as well as verbal impressions of the quality of the environment in which individuals conduct their affairs—to the degree that these impressions can be measured. The general objects of measurement are specified, but no proscriptions on type of measurement, utility, or relationship to time are imposed. Perhaps the key to the definition is the word *indices*, but lacking definition of this term, we are at a loss to set consistent boundaries on social indicators.

In a report issued by the United Nations (1975), Stone provides a definition for social indicators that delimits only through perceived utility and a focus on some aspect of social interaction:

> . . . social indicators are constructs, based on observations and usually quantitative, which tell us something about an aspect of social life in which we are interested or about changes taking place in it. Such information may be objective in the sense that it purports to show what the position is or how it is changing; or it may be subjective in the sense that it purports to show how the objective position, or changes in it, are regarded by the community in general or by different constituent groups.

Many of the delimiting criteria that have been encountered in previous definitions are contradicted or omitted in Stone's definition. According to Stone, a social indicator is usually quantitative but need not be so; indeed, subjective impressions, provided they are collective, are admissible. Also, social indicators are not necessarily related to time. They may illustrate change or trends but may also show position or status.

Purpose of a different sort enters the definition suggested by Bauer (1966, p. 1):

> This volume is devoted to the topic of social indicators—statistics, statistical series, and all other forms of evidence—that enable us to assess where we stand and where we are going with respect to our values and goals, and to evaluate specific programs and determine their impact.

It is clear that, according to Bauer, an indicator is different from a statistic or a variable only to the degree that it provides information on status or progress in relation to goals, values, or programs. An indicator need not be quantitative (since forms of evidence other than statistics generally are not) and need not be related to time.

In an address before the 1968 annual meeting of the American Statistical Association, Wilbur J. Cohen, then Secretary of Health, Education, and Welfare, called for

> . . . statistics which indicate clearly and present precisely conditions in our society, including, for example, the magnitude of existing social problems and their rate of change. . . .

He termed these statistics *social indicators*.

From Cohen's definition of social indicators several requisite characteristics can be identified. If social indicators are to reflect rates of change in existing social problems, they must be related to time. Since they are statistics, they must obviously be quantitative. To represent the magnitude of a social problem, one must have a value structure that permits placement of normative interpretations on data. This latter characteristic has not been found in previous definitions of social indicators. It is, perhaps, the most restrictive component of Cohen's definition. The notion of inherent evaluative capacity was emphasized even more strongly in a definition of social indicators that appeared in a later Department of Health, Education, and Welfare publication.

In 1969, the Department of Health, Education, and Welfare was so deeply committed to the concept of social indicators that a position with the title Deputy Assistant Secretary for Social Indicators existed in the department hierarchy. A task force in the department, operating under the direction of Secretary Cohen, produced a publication entitled *Toward A Social Report*. On page 97 the following elaborate definition of a social indicator can be found:

> A social indicator, as the term is used here, may be defined to be a statistic of direct normative interest which facilitates concise, comprehensive and balanced judgments about the condition of major aspects of a society. It is in all cases a direct measure of welfare and is subject to the interpretation that, if it changes in the "right" direction, while other things remain equal, things have gotten better or people are "better off." Thus statistics on the number of doctors or policemen could not be social indicators, whereas figures on health or crime rates could be.

As Land (1975a, p. 15) points out, this definition of a social indicator has received considerable criticism from prominent social science researchers. Sheldon and Freeman (1970, p. 98) suggest that a variable that is of normative interest now may be of little concern in the future because societies and their perceived problems change. Their second criticism concerns the restriction of social indicators to "direct measures of welfare," since this precludes labeling as indicators variables that are exogenous in complex causal models. Duncan (1969, pp. 3–4) suggests that the HEW definition of a social indicator restricts consideration to highly aggregated quantities, and some disaggregation might be useful and necessary at this stage of social indicators development.

Beyond these well-founded criticisms, the HEW definition shares several elements in common with other definitions cited above. It delimits indicators to quantitative variables. It states that variables must be of major importance to the user to be labeled as indicators.

Amenability to normative interpretation, despite the criticism advanced by Sheldon and Freeman, also appears in the definition of social indicators offered by Hauser (1975):

> . . . social indicators involve not only quantitative measurement of an aspect of the social but also its interpretation in relation to some norms against which the statistic represents advance or retrogression.

This definition is clearly less restrictive than that proposed by HEW, but many common elements can be identified: restriction to quantitative variables, focus on social conditions, and the requirement of normative bases for interpretation.

Campbell and Converse (1972, pp. 2–3) propose as defining characteristics of social indicators:

> (1) the capacity to assess the "evolving quality of American social life" and (2) amenability to "manipulation through policy change."

Like the criteria in other definitions cited above, these are both restrictive and vague. An indicator must be inherently normative and evaluative if it is to have the capacity to assess the quality of American social life. If a simple input-output model of social reality is considered, Campbell and Converse would allow some output variables to be labeled social indicators, but all input variables would be excluded. Although many variables are potentially manipulable through policy change, a vast array of important, explanatory context variables are not. Many demographic variables, for example, are necessary to an understanding of trends in manipulable output variables. To exclude such variables from the social indicators domain seems both unwise and unnecessarily restrictive.

In summarizing a review of various definitions of social indicators, Sheldon and Freeman (1970, p. 97) state:

> . . .there is little agreement on the defining characteristics of social indicators beyond the following: (1) social indicators are time-series that allow comparison over an extended period; (2) social indicators are statistics that can be disaggregated (or cross-classified) by other relevant characteristics.

Unfortunately, much of the more recent literature on social indicators cited above contradicts both of these conclusions. Many definitions admit variables that are current status indices, with no requirement for earlier or later data. Other definitions admit highly aggregated summary statistics that could not be cross-classified with other variables. For example, under the Clemmer et al. definition, such summary statistics as the proportion of the population aged 18–21 that voted in the most recent general election might be used as an indicator of the success of a citizenship education program. Such a statistic, in its summary form, could not be cross-classified with other variables.

Land (1971) attempted to formulate a definition of social indicators that would strike a balance between those he regarded as overly restrictive and those that were so general they admitted essentially all variables. The essence of his criteria is captured in the following citation (p. 323):

> I propose that the term *social indicators* refer to social statistics that (1) are components in a social system model (including sociopsychological, economic, demographic and ecological) or of some particular segment or process thereof, (2) can be collected and analyzed at various times and accumulated into time-series, and (3) can be aggregated and disaggregated to levels appropriate to the specifications of the model. Social system model means conceptions of social processes, whether formulated verbally, logically, mathematically, or in computer simulation form. The important point is that the criterion for classifying a social statistic as a social indicator is its informative value which derives from its empirically verified nexus in a conceptualization of a social process.

This definition contains many of the criteria that have appeared in other definitions, plus a new ingredient that is deemed essential by Land. Introduction of the concept of social system models is, on the one hand, restrictive, and on the other, liberating. It specifies the kinds of variables that will be considered social indicators in a given application—only those variables that are integral to some conceptual model of a particular social process—but allows specific variables to be admitted for some applications and excluded for others. Thus a variable can be termed a social indicator for some applications, even though it would not be so defined for others.

Land (1975a) expanded on his earlier definition of social indicators and attempted further to "solve this problem of definition" (p. 18). He proposed a classification system for social indicators that would, presumably, ease the problem of identification, and suggested the uses to which social indicators could be put. He first proposed three types of indicators, as follows:

(1a) *Output descriptive indicators:* These are measures of the end products of social processes and are most directly related to the appraisal of social problems and social policy.

(1b) *Other descriptive indicators:* These are more general measures of the social conditions of human existence and the changes taking place therein.

(2) *Analytic indicators:* These are components of explicit conceptual models of the social processes which result in the values of the output indicators.

Land then went on to describe a generic social system model that incorporates each type of indicator and to identify subcategories of his three indicator types. Two types of other descriptive indicators were called *policy instrument descriptive indicators* and *nonmanipulative descriptive indicators*. Land's output descriptive indicators were subdivided into what he called *output or end-product descriptive indicators* and *side-effect descriptive indicators*.

From Land's perspective, the purpose of social indicators research is to explore and heighten understanding of the status and dynamics of social processes. His generic model is reminiscent of many nonrecursive causal path models (Kerlinger & Pedhazur, 1973) used to estimate relationships among variables and their mutual influences. In causal path models, and in Land's generic model, a set of exogenous variables—those that are outside the influence of other variables in the model—are causally related to ultimate endogenous variables (typically termed output variables) through one or more sets of mediating variables. Land identifies two classes of exogenous variables: those that can be manipulated as a result of policy action (such as increasing the per-pupil expenditure in a school system), and those that cannot be manipulated through policy but are nonetheless influential. An example of the latter type is the proportion of males and females who seek educational services in a particular school system.

Land also divides endogenous variables into two categories. His output or end-product descriptive indicators identify the social condition that is of central concern to the researcher, or, equivalently, the output of the social process that is of primary interest to the researcher. Side-effect descriptive indicators describe results of social interventions that are either unplanned or are not of principal interest to the researcher. Nonetheless, they constitute ultimate endogenous variables. Suppose, for example, a school system increases its expenditures for basic skills education (a policy instrument descriptive indicator), and uses these funds to purchase curriculum materials that emphasize drill and practice in fundamental arithmetic operations and English grammar. Suppose, then, that reading and arithmetic achievement scores subsequently increase (these would be output or end-product descriptive indicators), but that attitudes of students toward school and toward arithmetic and English become extremely negative (these would be side-effect descriptive indicators).

Land's generic social system model incorporates two classes of analytic indicators. The major class consists of variables that mediate the relationships between the exogenous descriptive indicators and what are here termed ultimate endogenous variables (the output and side-effect descriptive indicators). In the brief example cited above, these indicators would characterize the curriculum and the instructional process and context. They would thus relate per-pupil expenditure for education, and a set of context-descriptive and demographic variables (the nonmanipulable descriptive indicators), with the achievement and attitude variables (the output and side-effect indicators). Land's smaller class of analytic indicators relates his end-product descriptive indicators and his side-effect descriptive indicators. These Land terms *second-order impact analytic indicators*. His model shows a two-headed arrow connecting the end-product descriptive indicators and the side-effect descriptive indicators. This suggests the absence of a directional causal relationship between these two classes of indicators.

Land's descriptions of various types of indicators, and his requirement that indicators be identifiable as components of a social system model, serve to reduce the ambiguity that remains when other social indicators definitions are used. However, Land's definition may well be overly restrictive. When the purpose of social indicators research is analysis of the impact of social policy, or when causal analysis of changes in social conditions is the objective, Land's schema would appear to be quite useful. When social reporting is the research objective, however, development or identification of a social system model would seem to be beyond the purpose of the research. For example, the National Assessment of Educational Progress (NAEP) can be justified purely as a response to the need to determine what American children and adults know. It is an educational report, nothing more or less. For some research purposes, it will be necessary to relate scores on NAEP test instruments to changes in policy variables (such as educational funding information), to curriculum information, and to demographic data. Indeed, it is not difficult to conceive of an educational system model that incorporates all of these variables. By Land's definition, such a model would justify labeling each of these variables an indicator, whereas the

NAEP results would not qualify for such recognition were they to be presented as an independent report on the status of societal knowledge.

Land (1975a) also retains his earlier (1971) requirements that social indicators data be collected and analyzed at various times and accumulated into time series, and that they be amenable to aggregation and disaggregation to levels consistent with the purposes of the research. The latter requirement does not appear to be unreasonably restrictive, but the former would eliminate some otherwise useful reports of societal status.

SUMMARY AND CONCLUSIONS

Offerings of the literature in response to the question of what an indicator is are anything but clear and consistent. Review of a dozen definitions has produced much that is contradictory and little that is concise and illuminating. By way of summary, Table 1 arrays characteristics proposed for social indicators against the entire set of definitions discussed above. A check mark in the table indicates that a given characteristic is a component of a referenced definition. In all, 12 sources suggest nine different criteria in their definitions of social indicators. Only two of these criteria—that social indicators must be quantitative, and that social indicators must be measures of social conditions—are common to a majority of the definitions. The other criteria appear to stem from the authors' answers to the question of why social indicators research ought to be pursued. Those who propose that social indicators can be used to evaluate federal programs or to judge the impact of large-scale social policies typically suggest that indicators must be inherently normative. Those who propose to use social indicators in exploring the causes of or interrelationships among social phenomena typically suggest that social indicators must be components of social system models. For this class of users, it is essential that indicators can be aggregated and disaggregated, since cross-tabulation of indicators and calculation of indices of relationship among indicators is not possible unless statistics can be disaggregated to some degree. Among the authors cited above, there is a near-even split on the requirement that social indicators be related to time or be expressible as time series. Certainly, repeated measures on a variable permit many kinds of analyses that would otherwise be impossible, but it is also quite likely that the title *social indicator* can properly be applied to a single measurement on a variable that was central to a social phenomenon under investigation.

At this point, the reader may be thinking "So what?" and that is my conclusion as well. Perhaps some variables should be termed indicators, while others should not—for if all variables were called indicators, there would be no need for an additional term. I would suggest that a given variable deserves the label *indicator* in some situations and does not deserve it in others. I propose that all variables that (1) represent the aggregate status or change in status of any group of persons, objects, institutions, or elements under study, and that (2) are essential to a report of status or change of status of the entities under study or to

TABLE 1
Defining Criteria for Social Indicators Proposed by a Variety of Authors

Source of Definition	Quantitative	Time Related or Time Series	Utility	Measure of Social Condition	Value or Goal Related	Inherently Normative	Manipulable through Policy	Amenable to Disaggregation or Aggregation	Components of a Social System Model
Bauer (1966)	Typically		✓		✓				
Campbell & Converse (1972)				✓		✓	✓		
Cohen (1968)	✓	✓	✓	✓		✓			
U.S. Dept. HEW (1969)	✓		✓	✓		✓			
Hauser (1975)	✓			✓		✓			
Land (1971)	✓	✓						✓	✓
Land (1975a)	✓	✓						✓	✓
Land & Spilerman (1975)				✓					
O. D. Duncan (undated)	✓	Maybe		✓					
Clemmer et al. (1973)	✓	✓	✓						
Sheldon & Freeman (1970)	✓	✓						✓	
U.N. (1975)	Typically		✓	✓	✓				

an understanding of the condition of the entities under study, should be termed indicators. I would not require that reports of status or change in status be in quantitative form, for narrative is often a better aid to comprehension and understanding of phenomena than is a numeric report.

To impose additional restrictions on indicators does not appear to be helpful or useful. The additional criteria suggested by the sources cited above tend to restrict the use of indicators to particular kinds of investigations. At this point in the development of the indicators movement, there is little evidence that indicators are uniquely suited to the pursuit of some types of research, to the exclusion of others. In fact, there is scant evidence on their utility for any purpose.

TECHNICAL CONSIDERATIONS IN THE USE OF EDUCATIONAL INDICATORS

Interpretive Generalizations

Interpretation of educational indicators is an act of generalization from measurements taken on some aggregate of units to status of or trends in some characteristics of a population. Such generalizations are complex and involve several dimensions. When the generalization is to population status, two dimensions are involved. These could be termed *statistical generalization* and *substantive generalization*. When the generalization is to trends in characteristics of populations, a third dimension—*temporal generalization*—must be considered as well.

Statistical generalization occurs in the interpretation of all sample survey results. It involves considerations of sample representativeness (freedom from bias errors) and sampling adequacy (control of random errors).

Substantive generalization and statistical generalization are qualitatively different. If measurements of a particular variable were available for every element of a population of interest, no statistical generalization would be required. However, interpretation of indicators typically goes beyond a simple report on the value of a population parameter. When statistical results are interpreted as indicators of complex variables and phenomena, questions of validity arise. Do the measurements of observable attributes and characteristics truly represent the phenomena described in their interpretation? Can resulting inferences be supported? Such construct validity questions routinely arise in psychometric research and must be considered in indicators research as well. For example, if per-pupil educational expenditures were measured for every school system in the nation, no statistical generalization would be involved in computing the mean per-pupil expenditure over the entire population of districts. However, substantive generalization issues would arise if the resulting mean were to be interpreted as an indicator of the average district's *level of effort* in supporting education.

The third dimension of generalization suggested above, temporal generalization, arises when sequences of measurements are interpreted as trends in a characteristic of a population. Threats to valid temporal generalization include random measurement errors over time, changes in contexts of measurement as a function of time, and temporal changes in the definitions of variables. Assumptions on the stability of contexts and definitions are essential to valid temporal generalization.

No educational indicators are inherently better than others. Some educational indicators will support some generalizations better than would other indicators, and some will do a less adequate job of supporting other generalizations. Questions on quality must be faced anew with every application and desired interpretation. The dimensions of evaluation will be common to most interpretations, but the results of indicator evaluation will typically be unique.

Dimensions of generalization involved in the interpretation of educational indicators are illustrated in Figure 1. The balance of this section is a discussion of threats to valid interpretation and techniques useful in reducing those threats.

Statistical Generalization

Sample Representativeness. A great deal of indicators research seeks information on the status of, or trends in, some characteristics of a population. The work often involves reanalysis of data in existing files. Even in situations affording the opportunity to collect new data, the match between populations of interest and available sampling frames (Cochran, 1963; Jaeger, 1973; Moser & Kalton, 1972) may not be exact. One of two situations may occur: Either the population of interest will be a subset of the population for which data are obtainable, a situation that sampling researchers would term *overregistration*, or the population of interest will subsume the population for which data are obtainable, a situation that would be termed *underregistration*. Moreover, overregistration and underregistration can occur simultaneously. In any of these cases, inference to the population of interest on the basis of obtainable data will result in some degree of bias.

As an example of underregistration and the resulting inferential dilemma, suppose we are interested in plotting the trend in constant-dollar expenditures for the education of children aged 5 to 17 during the decade 1965–1975. Conceptually, organization of such data is simple. We would list the types of education made available to all children in the age range of interest and the cost of each type, and then we would aggregate expenditures for each year. But the simplicity is deceptive, since education extends well beyond the boundaries of formal schooling. As Stone (United Nations, 1975, p. 93) suggests, private instruction by qualified teachers complements the formal schooling system by providing remedial education and education in subjects not offered in the formal schools. In addition, parental instruction in the home supplements the in-school learning of many children aged 5 to 17. Surely, these educational processes cost money and should be counted in a listing of expenses for education of the age cohort. But no listing of educational units such as these exists, much less data on their costs. So

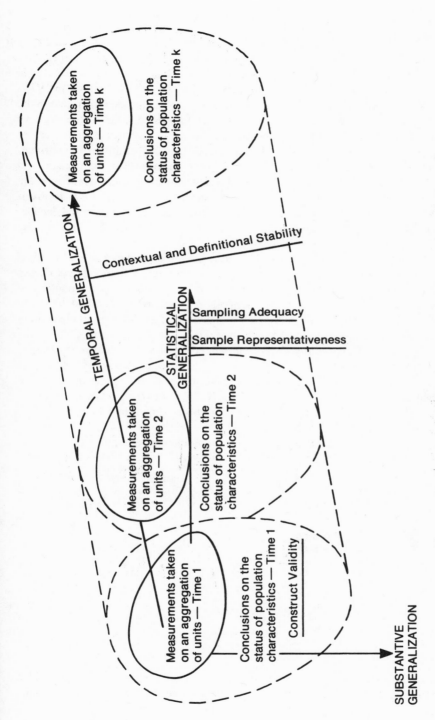

Figure 1. Dimensions of generalization in the interpretation of educational indicators.

we would have to make do with statistics for public and nonpublic elementary and secondary schools such as those provided by the U.S. Department of Health, Education, and Welfare (1977, pp. 171-172), which show total expenditures in 1975–76 dollars rising from $49.3 billion in 1964–65 to $73.5 billion in 1974–75. If interest lies in the pattern of expenditure over the decade rather than in the absolute expense figures, the available data might suffice. That is, the negative bias might be proportional over the entire time span. But current social history suggests otherwise. White flight from the public schools resulting from enforcement of the Civil Rights Act of 1964 was not uniform over the decade, and statistics on educational expenditures through so-called white academies are likely to be incomplete. Also, there is no reason to believe that other forms of private, nonschool instruction existed in proportional amounts over the decade. Thus the pattern of the trend, as well as the trend level, may be differentially biased over the time span of interest.

Overregistration, the converse of underregistration, also carries the potential of substantial bias in interpretation of results. Fortunately, the National Center for Education Statistics (NCES) reports trends in expenditures for public and nonpublic schools separately. But suppose that we were interested solely in public school expenditures, and the only obtainable data were for all elementary and secondary schools in the United States, regardless of control. Clearly, the absolute level of expenditures would be biased upward. But would the bias be proportional over the years 1964–65 to 1974–75? If so, expenditures for nonpublic schools, in constant dollars, would have to be in strict proportion to total expenditures over the time period. Using NCES data (U.S. DHEW 1977, pp. 171–172), the proportions were computed to be as shown in Table 2.

TABLE 2
Nonpublic School Expenditures as a Proportion of Total Elementary and Secondary School Expenditures, 1964-65 to 1974-75

Academic Year	Non–Public School Expenditures as a Proportion of Total Expenditures
1964–65	.12
1965–66	.11
1966–67	.11
1967–68	.11
1968–69	.10
1969–70	.10
1970–71	.10
1971–72	.10
1972–73	.11
1973–74	.11
1974–75	.11

In this example, use of expenditure data for all elementary and secondary schools, rather than data for public elementary and secondary schools, would seem to inflate estimates by a slightly fluctuating amount over the time period of interest. If knowledge of the shape of the expenditure curve over time were desired rather than knowledge of its absolute level, bias due to overregistration might well be tolerable. However, this example is atypical, and problems resulting from overregistration will often be more severe. As with underregistration, no general solutions can be suggested. Use of auxiliary time series to adjust results will often be the only recourse. In the present case, if data for public and nonpublic school expenditures had not been available separately, enrollment time series for public and nonpublic schools might have been used, together with the assumption that per-pupil expenditures were independent of type of school control, to adjust the total expenditure figures.

Even when the population we wish to describe with an indicator matches the labeled aggregation of elements for which data are available, bias errors can confound resulting analysis. Whether we work with existing data files or collect new data, it is unlikely that reports for every element in the population of interest, or for a representative sample of that population, will be found. Nonresponse is a part of every data collection procedure, and the usual remedy is to aggregate reports from the units for which data were obtained. Among others, Cochran (1963, p. 355 ff.) describes the serious effects of nonresponse on the precision and accuracy of aggregate estimates. After presenting results on a variety of combinations of response rates, sample proportions, and tolerable error limits, Cochran concludes that a response rate as low as 90% can be tolerated, provided one is willing to double the sample size that would be required with 100% response and would be satisfied with estimates that are in error by as much as 20%. If precision requirements are more stringent, no amount of increase in sample size will compensate for the substantial bias attributable to nonresponse. If data are newly collected through a survey procedure, techniques for reduction of nonresponse can be found in numerous books on survey research and sampling theory (Cochran, 1963; Hansen, Hurwitz, & Madow, 1953; Moser & Kalton, 1972; Murthy, 1967; Raj, 1968; Sukhatme & Sukhatme, 1970). Rogers, Folsom, Kalsbeek, and Clemmer (1977) provide a detailed illustration of methods of assessing bias due to nonresponse in surveys. Since their investigation makes use of data from the National Assessment of Educational Progress, it is particularly relevant to the study of educational indicators. If data from existing files are used to form indicators, we can only hope for sufficient information to determine the potential magnitude of sampling bias. Little can be done to compensate for its effects.

Sampling Adequacy. Unless the indicators under study apply to very small populations of units—such as all states and territories of the United States—data probably will be collected from only a sample of units. Summary statistics on the aggregate of sampled units will then be used as estimates of population parameters of interest. For example, the National Assessment report on the proportion of 9-year-old children who can successfully answer a science test item on how liquids expand when heated is based on a supposedly representative sample of that age group, not on administration of the item to all 9-year-olds in the nation.

Except in rare and atypical cases, sample statistics differ from the population parameters they estimate. Even when samples are truly representative of populations of interest and the statistics computed are not systematically biased, unsystematic (random) errors will generally be found. When new data for the development of indicators are to be collected, random error can be estimated and controlled, on the average, through the judicious selection of sampling plans and estimation procedures. Excellent guides to efficient practice can be found in the sampling theory literature (Cochran, 1963; Hansen et al., 1953; Jaeger, 1973; Kish, 1965; Murthy, 1967; Raj, 1968; Sukhatme & Sukhatme, 1970). When indicators are based on data in existing files, and data on individual units are obtainable, the magnitude of random error may be estimable even if the sampling plan used for collection of data is unknown. A variety of direct assessment procedures, such as the jackknife procedure (Mosteller & Tukey, 1968) or balanced half-sample replications, can be applied to assess the variability of estimates across samples of a given size.

In some circumstances, published summary statistics may be used to form indicators or may be directly interpreted as indicators. In these cases, the size of random error components cannot be judged unless such information is provided, along with the statistic of primary interest. Reputable statistical agencies routinely provide information on the reliability of their statistics as a part of their reports. For example, in a report on the condition of education compiled by the National Center for Education Statistics (U.S. DHEW, 1976a, p. 277) we find the information on data collected through a survey termed the Consolidated Program Information Report (CPIR) which is shown in Table 3. The entire NCES table has not been reproduced here. Instead, a full range of entries has been selected to illustrate the type of random error data given and to provide a basis for further discussion. Suppose that educational expenditures for American Indian children in reservation schools were tabulated in a time series, based on CPIR data, to form an indicator of investment in Indian education. If the annual current-dollar figure were around $100,000,000, the sampling error data in Table 3 indicate that a relative error of 6% could be expected. Or, in other terms, one would be approximately 95% confident that the estimated annual expenditure figure would be within $12 million of the true figure in any given year. If the trend in funding of reservation schooling for American Indians showed small variation across years, CPIR estimates might miss the trend entirely, since the magnitude of random error is so large. In all fairness it should be noted that this example is fictitious, since the CPIR was not developed for the purpose described. The point to be made is that excessive random error may prevent detection of minor trends in time series indicators. Therefore, estimates of the magnitude of random error are needed before it is possible to draw valid conclusions on the absence of change.

TABLE 3
Approximate Relative Sampling Errors versus the Size of an Estimate
for Participants or Staff and for Expenditures, 1973 CPIR

Estimated No. of Participants or Staff	Relative Sampling Error (Percent)	Estimated Expenditures	Relative Sampling Error (Percent)
1,000	25%	$1,000,000	23%
5,000	16	$5,000,000	14
20,000	12	$20,000,000	9
100,000	8	$100,000,000	6
1,000,000	4	$1,000,000,000	2
10,000,000	1	$10,000,000,000	1

Unit of Analysis.   If data from existing files are used to form indicators, lack of correspondence between the desired unit of analysis and the available sampling unit looms as a potential problem. If the level of aggregation available in the file is too high (e.g., data on individual students are desired but classroom averages are available), there is no general solution. Some types of analyses, such as cross-tabulations of achievement by student background characteristics, will have to be foregone. If the level of aggregation in the file is lower than that desired (e.g., data on school systems are desired but data on schools are available), it may be possible to estimate observations for the units of interest. If data are available for all subunits of interest, the solution is obvious, provided the subunits can be identified by unit. For example, if data on all schools identified by district are contained in a file, simple addition will yield data for school districts. Since census reports for large populations are rare, aggregation to higher level units through simple addition often will not be possible. But other procedures, such as weighting of totals across observed subunits to yield estimates for units, can be employed.

For many types of indicators research, different units of analysis may well lead to different conclusions. For example, the American Telegraph and Telephone Company published, in *Business Conditions*, June 1977, a record of the unemployment rate in the United States from 1971 through 1977. Two time series were shown: unemployment as a percentage of the total civilian labor force, and unemployment as a percentage of the total number of heads of households. Not unexpectedly, the two time series suggest problems of markedly different severity. The peak unemployment rate in the first case occurred in 1975, with a maximum level of about 9%. For the second time series, the peak occurred slightly later and reached only 6%. Clearly, one way a U.S. president could suggest an improvement in the unemployment situation would be to change the reporting unit.

As another example, consider statistics on current expenditures for elementary and secondary education by school district and by state (U.S. DHEW, 1976a). The average expenditure per pupil for the United States was reported as $1,281 in the 1973–74 school year (p. 154), while the median of per-pupil expenditures by school district was reported as $1,008 in the same school year (p. 157), suggesting a positively skewed distribution for school systems. Direct comparison of expenditures by states and by districts within states might also lead to different conclusions. For example, in 1973–74, the median of school district expenditures per pupil was $1,236 in Colorado and $1,143 in Connecticut. But 15.6% of Colorado districts spent less than $900 per pupil in that year, while only 6.3% of Connecticut districts had expenditures that low. If numbers or percentages of students receiving low levels of educational expenditure were the statistics of real interest, statewide data and district-level data would present very different pictures.

Substantive Generalization

As suggested above, indicators research extends statistical reporting by attempting to infer conceptual meaning and form phenomenological generalizations from data summaries. A statistical report may contain data on higher education enrollment, by school year, in the United States; the indicators researcher uses these data to speak of *educational demand*. Like many other concepts arising in indicators research, educational demand is an unobservable variable that exists in the mind of the researcher. Psychometric researchers would label it a *construct*—a constructed variable that serves as a label for many highly related observables in a particular model of reality.

As Sheldon and Moore (1968, p. 9) suggest, the attribution of meaning to numbers is fraught with problems:

The measurement of social change shares with other targets for measurement a congeries of statistical hazards. The first of these rests in the relation between numbers and meaning. Statistical analysis deals with numbers produced by certain operations and conclusions, based on numbers relating to both the processes producing them and to the explanatory context from which they derive and to which they refer. No item of information, no measure or series of measures, is self-explanatory.

Thus when meaning is attributed to data we must understand the context in which the data were produced and the phenomena to which the data refer. De Neufville (1975, pp. 57–68) suggests that we must have models or theories upon which to base interpretations of data. She warns that observations of reality are mediated by a host of implicit assumptions. When we use data collected by others we must be assured that their perceptions of reality are similar, that their labels for categories have the same meaning, and that their definitions of universes are the same.

When we speak of educational demand on the basis of enrollment data, we make the assumption that the measured variable encompasses the whole of the unobservable phenomenon, and thus the observable variable can be substituted for the unobservable one. In short, we are asserting that enrollment ''acts like'' educational demand in all of the latter variable's relationships with other phenomena. Like de Neufville, Boulding (1966) warns against blindly substituting the observable for the conceptual without examining underlying assumptions and the theoretical underpinnings of generalization.

We might be tempted to suppose that problems of conceptual representation are endemic to the so-called "soft" sciences, and that social and educational indicators are exclusively vulnerable to interpretive problems. Some illustrations of similar problems with well-known economic indicators should dispel that view. In a discussion of the inadequacy of the gross national product as an indicator of economic expansion, Sametz (1968) has argued the case for a new set of economic measures that would allow adjustments based on the quality of products, reflect the "purchase" of leisure time through the use of new work-saving products, and take into account the increased costs of product development due to growth of bureaucracy in government and the stress of urbanization. Solow (1975) suggests that the wholesale price index should be revised to reflect prices of services as well as goods and to eliminate double counting of some products.

Apart from extensive theoretical underpinnings in the philosophy of science (Frank, 1956; Kaplan, 1964), much of the practical work on validation of measures exists in the psychometric literature (Bechtoldt, 1959; Campbell, 1960; Campbell & Fiske, 1959; Cronbach, 1971; Cronbach & Meehl, 1955; Cureton, 1951; Ebel, 1961; Lennon, 1956; Messick, 1975; Shavelson & Stanton, 1975). Cronbach (1971, p. 443) suggests that validity considerations apply equally well to interpretations of test scores, observations, questionnaires, protocols, summaries of qualitative observations, and ratings of artistic products. I contend that they apply especially well to interpretations of social and educational indicators.

We could readily adapt Cronbach's summary description of construct validity (1971, p. 446):

> Does the test measure the attribute it is said to measure? More specifically: the description of the person in terms of the construct, together with other information about him and in various situations; are these implications true?

to the context of social and educational indicators. A revised description might read as follows:

> Does the social or educational indicator measure the phenomenon it is claimed to measure? More specifically: the description of the population in terms of the indicator, together with other kinds of information on the population; are these implications true?

When speaking of tests, Cronbach notes that it is not the test itself that is validated, but the interpretation of data arising from use of the test in the context of a specific measurement procedure that must be validated. A parallel distinction exists when we speak of validating a social or educational indicator. It would be folly to attempt to "validate" a procedure for collecting, reducing, editing, analyzing, and presenting data. Some interpretations of the results of such a process could be supported and justified (hence validated), while others would be highly suspect, and still others would have to be rejected. So in the realm of social and educational indicators, we cannot validate an indicator, or a process for generating an indicator, but must attempt to validate the interpretation attached to an indicator.

Construct Validation Procedures.   Among the references on validation of measures cited above, Cronbach and Meehl (1955) and Cronbach (1971) provide the most detailed reviews of construct validity theory and procedures. Shavelson and Stanton (1975) illustrate the application of a particular validation criterion to a unique educational measurement problem, in addition to providing a well-documented review of modern procedural literature.

Construct validation resolves to a set of procedures for investigation of the question: Do measures behave in accordance with theoretical predictions for the phenomena supposedly represented? Although this question is very general, accumulation of evidence in support of an answer can be approached systematically by considering a set of common rules:

1. Supposedly interchangeable measures of the same phenomenon should be highly related across units of analysis.
2. Measures of theoretically related phenomena should show a substantial degree of association across units of analysis. Also, the direction of association—direct or inverse—should be consistent with theoretical expectations.
3. Measures of theoretically unrelated phenomena should show a limited degree of association across units of analysis.
4. Measures of theoretical phenomena should respond to historical interventions in theoretically expected ways.

These rules will be discussed individually, together with some examples of their application.

Since most constructs represent a complex of observable variables, it is likely that alternative measures can often be developed. If we have access to two or more measures of the same phenomenon, it is reasonable, and consistent with theory, to expect them to be highly associated across units of analysis. For example, if mother's educational level was considered to be one component of an index of the socioeconomic status of students' families, and number of educational possessions in the home (newspaper, dictionary, encyclopedia, etc.) was considered to be another, we would expect these variables to be positively and highly correlated across students. If, for a representative sample drawn from the student population for which the index was to be interpreted as an indicator of socioeconomic status, the variables show negligible or negative correlation, we would question the construct validity of one or both measures. A substantial positive correlation between the variables, however, would not constitute sufficient evidence to conclude that either was a measure of socioeconomic status in the population of interest. Construct validity is established through a series of investigations, and a "proof" is never complete. The results of a single investigation can provide sufficient basis for reexamining a construct validity claim but cannot provide a sufficient basis for the acceptance of such a claim.

If accepted theory suggests that two constructs are related in a specified way, we would expect measures of these constructs to be similarly related. For example, theory suggests that average verbal aptitude levels and average reading comprehension levels should show a substantial positive correlation across a random sample of elementary schools. Were we to find that examinations that were claimed to be measures of these constructs had mean scores which were not highly correlated across elementary schools, four avenues of investigation would be in order:

1. We could examine the claim that one examination measures verbal aptitude.
2. We could examine the claim that the other examination measures reading comprehension (for example, assessment of correlations of individual scores or mean scores for schools with those on other, known measures of these constructs would be appropriate).
3. We could examine the claim that the correlation was computed across a representative sample of U.S. elementary schools. Aberrations in sampling design and procedure might lead to a nonrepresentative sample of schools for which the relationship between the measures and the constructs was anomalous.
4. We could reconsider the theory that suggests a substantial and positive relationship between the constructs, verbal aptitude and reading comprehension. This course is unlikely to be fruitful, since relationships between these constructs are well documented for students in U.S. elementary schools.

Since social and educational indicators are often represented by time series (in contrast to educational and psychological measures on individuals, which are often made only once), they offer unique opportunities for investigating theoretically expected relationships. Theories involving relationships among variables often involve causal hypotheses, and causal relationships suggest temporal orderings among constructs. For example, if teachers' expectations contribute to modification of students' achievement levels, one would expect to see changes in achievement *after* teachers' expectation levels are changed. If we had a series of measurements on a teacher's expectation of a student's achievement level, together with a series of measurements on that student's achievement, the construct validity of the measures could be explored by computing correlations between the teacher's expectation level measure in one time period and the student's achievement measure one or more time periods later. Correlations close to zero, or negative correlations, would be inconsistent with theoretical expectations, whereas positive correlations would support the construct validity of the measures. These types of cross-lagged correlations between series of measurement are common in time series analysis work (Glass, Wilson, & Gottman, 1972; Hannan, 1960) but are not found in the psychometrically based literature on construct validation.

When we search for positive correlations among supposed measures of the same construct or among measures that should be directly related according to theory, we are applying what is often termed a *convergence criterion* (Campbell & Fiske, 1959; Cronbach, 1971; Loevinger, 1957). But some theoretical relationships are not convergent. Measures of some constructs should, according to theory, show negligible relationships in some populations. Measures of other constructs should show strong or moderate relationships in some populations, but negligible relationships in others. As Cronbach (1971, p. 467) suggests, evidence of convergence is generally insufficient to demonstrate construct validity; discriminant validation is also necessary. Discrimination is evidenced by the presence of low correlations when absence of relationship is theoretically expected. For example, theory would predict a substantial relationship between measures of capacity to support education (fiscal capacity) and measures of educational expenditure per student, for school districts in states where local revenues are the principal source of educational support. However, in states with substantial state foundation programs, measures of local fiscal capacity and per-student educational expenditure should show much smaller relationships (Johns, Alexander, & Jordan, 1971). Failure to conform to these expectations would be cause to reexamine the claimed construct validity of the measures used, or the theoretical operation of state foundation programs.

When exploring the construct validity of indicators, it is usually impossible to create experimental interventions. However, it often is possible to capitalize on historical events in analogous investigations. Consider, for example, the claim that the proportion of 18- and 19-year-olds enrolled in higher education in a given year is an indicator of educational demand. We would expect demand for education to vary, depending on alternative opportunities for and demands on members of the 18- and 19-year-old age cohort. Demand for education should rise if the availability of low-skill jobs decreases, or if the marriage rate among teenagers decreases. As a historical event, elimination of military service exemptions for 18- and 19-year-old male college students should have reduced demand .for higher education among men in that age cohort. That is, removing an opportunity to avoid compulsory military service should have dissuaded many male students from attending colleges and universities simply to avoid the draft, thereby lowering demand for higher education among the age cohort. If it had been found that proportionate higher education enrollments were unaffected by elimination of the exemption, we would be forced to question the use of enrollment as an indicator of educational demand. (One could posit a more complex explanation: asserting an increase in educational opportunity for females as a result of decreased male enrollment, thus stabilizing total enrollment and eliminating the effect of termination of compulsory military service.) The use of historical events in the interpretation of indicators, and relationships among higher education enrollments and other time series are discussed in Ferriss (1974).

In summary, substantive generalization from measures to indicators cannot be accepted without challenge. Evidence in support of such claims must be carefully assembled, in accordance with a network of theoretical propositions. The task is never complete. Theories and validity claims are always subject to discovery of new evidence.

Temporal Generalization

Advantages of Time Series. Many indicators are interpretable only because they have a known performance history; the Dow Jones Industrial Average is a case in point. Computation of the index is lost on the public, yet even novice investors and would-be investors respond to its level because it is prominently reported in most nightly news broadcasts and daily newspapers. Other indicators have arbitrarily chosen scales that preclude interpretation of their status. Only change in the indicator over a period of time allows formation of value judgments. For indicators such as these, repeated collection and reporting of data in the form of a series of measurements taken at fixed time points is essential.

The National Assessment of Educational Progress provides concise examples of statistics that gain meaning only as they change over time. Consider writing performance data for examinees at ages 9, 13, and 17. In the U.S. DHEW (1976a) report of these statistics, reported scores are based on holistic appraisals of the quality of essays, rated on a scale with values ranging from 1 to 9 (p. 202). For 9-year-old examinees, the mean writing score was 3.8 in 1970 and 4.1 in 1974, a gain of .3 points, or an improvement of 8%. The 13-year-olds had a mean writing score of 5.0 in 1969 and a mean of 4.7 in 1973, a drop of .3 points, or 6%. For 17-year-olds, the 1969 mean score was 5.1 and the 1974 mean score was 4.9, a loss of .2 points, or 4%. Since the scale points are undefined, the status data are not directly interpretable. Nor can the performances of 9-, 13-, and 17-year-olds be compared in any given year. There is no assurance that any scale point has the same meaning for essays produced by examinees of two different ages. However, assuming the judgment criteria and scales applied in 1969–70 and in 1974 were comparable within age groups, it could be said that 9-year-olds showed better writing performance in 1974 than in 1970, but representatives of the older age groups showed better performance in 1969.

National Assessment mathematics performance data are equally perplexing when viewed as a status report. For example, the 1976a U.S. DHEW report showed that 9-year-olds answered 36.7% of mathematics items correctly, 13-year-olds answered 51.3% correctly, 17-year-olds answered 57.1% correctly, and adults answered 59.3% correctly (p. 203). Unfortunately, it cannot be concluded that mathematics performance improves monotonically with age, since somewhat different mathematics items were used with the various age groups. Further, there is no a priori basis for defining "acceptable" or "good" mathematics performance for any age group. If the mathematics items given 9-year-olds were typified by $2 + 2 = ?$, we would be horrified by their performance. Conversely, if the items were well represented by $(364)^{1/2} = ?$, we might be delighted. In fairness, it should be stated that National Assessment reports (e.g., 1975) do provide sample test items; these interpretative aids were not reproduced in the U.S. DHEW document cited above. However, assuming the NAEP mathematics items are generally appropriate for the various examinee age groups, changes in the statistics reported above will be interpretable even in the absence of sample items, once test results for a second time point are compared with the original results. Here again, time series reporting permits interpretation that would otherwise be difficult or impossible.

Some indicators are weighted composites of quantities that are not directly comparable. Time series analysis permits interpretation and comparison of the change patterns of such indices, provided they are expressed in the form of indices that are standardized in the same base year. Sheldon and Moore (1968, p. 10) suggest that longitudinal studies are needed in almost all societal sectors and that the use of index numbers is a promising method of comparing changes in phenomena that would otherwise defy comparison.

Pitfalls in Time Series Interpretation.   Although time series analyses permit investigations that would otherwise be impossible, they impose a unique set of methodological and interpretive problems. Unfortunately, ready solutions are not available for many of these problems, and this discussion must resolve into a set of warnings.

When scales of measurement are arbitrary or are constructed in the form of index numbers, interpretations are often based on relative changes. An example is the oft-cited inflation rate. Comparison of relative changes across indicators can often be misleading, since so-called floor and ceiling effects can limit advancement or decline. More generally, the significance of a change in an indicator depends on the value of the starting point (Harris, 1963). Growth in the mean Law School Admissions Test scores of successful applicants to Stanford Law School, from 1976 to 1977, cannot be substantial, since the 1976 mean probably exceeded 775 on a test with a scale range of 200 to 800. Conversely, the 9-year-old writing scores reported above for the 1970 NAEP testing had more room to advance than to decline; they averaged 2.8 scale points above the lower scale limit and 5.2 scale points below the upper limit.

When external characteristics of society change, the definitions of variables that compose indicators must be changed accordingly. Otherwise, we cannot attribute the same meaning to indicators at different time points. We must also guard against, and compensate for, changes in the definition of populations and units over a period of time. For example, Kaestle (1977) describes the difference between ''private'' and ''public'' schools in the early 1800s and the 1970s. The earlier public school is today's private school.

Finally, use of time series indicators presents a set of operational problems. De Neufville (1975) suggests that indicators are typically defined in terms of preconceived solutions of social and educational problems (e.g., reports of participation in higher education by socioeconomic status group). But judgments of problems change with time. An important indicator today may well be passé in 10 years, and it is likely that one will have failed to collect time series data today that will be useful then. How to foresee needs a decade or so ahead?

Even if the ''right'' data were to be collected to form the ''right'' time series, the problem of how often to collect such data must be faced. Sheldon and Moore (1968, p. 11) suggest that data should be collected as often as the budget allows, and then less frequently if the time series shows little fluctuation: ''There is simply no a priori basis for determining the frequency of observation of any aspect of social behavior or function. Such a premise would require precisely what we lack—rates of change and their shape over various periods of time.''

USES OF INDICATORS AND NEEDED DEVELOPMENTS

Proposed Applications of Indicators

Unfortunately, the literature does not abound with examples of the successful application of social or educational indicators. It cannot be denied that social and educational statistics have influenced the formation of government policy and the allocation of public sector resources. Conversely, it cannot be proven that any given policy was formulated in direct response to any given indicator or set of indicators. As suggested by Parke and Sheldon (1973), Sheldon and Parke (1975), and Miller (1977), among others, formulation of public policy is a political process that is selectively served by objective data. The theoretical models of operations research and systems theory, with clearly defined objective functions and multiequation constraint sets, contribute little to practical decision making in the public sector. Yet the feeling remains that most lawmakers desire to do ''good'' in some public-spirited sense of that term. Surely informed decisions are better than those made in the absence of information. Even without demonstrations of effect, it would be illogical to deny the potential value of social and educational indicators.

The indicators literature is rich with commentary on the potential value of the movement and its products. The list of uses suggested for indicators is very long, but three broad categories appear repeatedly: (1) program evaluation (Bauer, 1966; U.S. DHEW, 1969); (2) policy analysis (Biderman, 1966; Parke & Sheldon, 1973; Land, 1975a); and (3) social system monitoring (Miller, 1977; Sheldon & Freeman, 1970). These categories will be described in some detail, and the use of educational indicators for each purpose will be considered individually.

Program Evaluation

The use of social indicators in evaluating the consequences of government programs was strongly suggested by Bauer (1966) and his colleagues at the inception of the social indicators movement. In fact, evaluation of the second-order effects of the space program was the genesis of NASA funding of Bauer's research. Federal government interest in using social indicators for program evaluation was reaffirmed in *Toward a Social Report*, a 1969 publication of the Department of Health, Education, and Welfare.

In a series of papers that reflect the consistent position of the Russell Sage Foundation and the Social Science Research Council, Eleanor Sheldon and her colleagues have repeatedly emphasized the futility of using social and educational indicators for program evaluation (Sheldon & Freeman, 1970; Sheldon & Parke, 1975; Miller, 1977). They suggest that program evaluation requires collection of data under experimental conditions that allow control of extraneous variables and influences. They equate program evaluation with impact analysis (Rivlin, 1971), and claim that problems of multicollinearity, undetected exogenous variables, and confounding of input and context variables preclude the attribution of changes in output variables to programmatic inputs.

Although the assertions of Sheldon and associates are well taken, their conclusions stem from an overly narrow conception of the goals of program evaluation and a consequent oversimplification of evaluation procedures and purposes. In this discussion, a program will be defined as a government funding mechanism, based on specific legislative authorization, that supports a coherent set of service-delivery activities. An excellent example in the area of education is provided by Title I of the Elementary and Secondary Education Act of 1965, a program intended to provide compensatory education to "educationally deprived" children in the age range 5 to 17. Evaluation of a program will be defined as the systematic collection, analysis, and interpretation of data that bear on the effectiveness, sufficiency, and efficiency of the program in meeting its goals or otherwise providing a public good in the absence of public harm.

Sheldon and associates are correct in asserting that some evaluative questions cannot be answered unequivocally on the basis of social and educational indicators research. For example, were educational indicators to show a substantial decline in the differential educational performance of children from low-income families and children from high-income families over the years 1966–1976, no manipulation of the data would support the unequivocal conclusion that Title I, ESEA, was responsible for the improvement. The targeting of educational services to children from low-income families under Title I, ESEA, would support the suggestion that the program *might have contributed* to the reported improvement, but it would not rule out a variety of plausible alternative explanations.

Conversely, consider the equally important question of whether the Title I, ESEA program, in conjunction with any other intervention programs operating during the decade 1966–76, was sufficient to overcome the educational performance deficit of children from "educationally deprived" families. That is, has the association between educational background of parents and the educational performance of children been broken by the Title I program, as it operates in the context of a variety of regular and targeted education programs throughout the United States? Educational indicators surely bear on this important evaluative question. Several indicators provided by the National Assessment of Educational Progress (1975) suggest that the relationship between parental background and student performance continues to be quite strong. Those 17-year-olds whose parents had not graduated from high school performed from 6 to 11% below the national average on National Assessment exercises in the seven subject areas tested in the first five years of the program: science, writing, citizenship, reading, literature, music, and social studies. In contrast, 17-year-olds whose parents have some post–high school education performed from 4 to 8% above the national average on National Assessment exercises in these subject areas. In science, scores of students aged 9, 13, and 17 whose parents had some post–high school education averaged 6% above the national percent correct. Scores of students at these ages whose parents had no high school education averaged 8 to 12% below the national percent correct. On reading exercises, the corresponding advantages for students whose parents had some post–high school education were 6 to 7%; deficiencies for students whose parents had no high school education were 9 to 12%. Results in other National Assessment subject areas were similar.

From these indicators the conclusion might be drawn that Title I, ESEA, has not provided sufficient remedy for all students in the United States, ages 5 to 17, who come from "educationally deprived" families. Counterarguments are obvious: Title I services have been concentrated, by regulation and guidelines, in the lower elementary grades. Older children did not have the opportunity to benefit from the program when they were in these grades. A large percentage of the children represented by the National Assessment sample received no services under Title I. Basic skills education—reading and arithmetic—has been emphasized under Title I, and science, music, literature, and citizenship results are irrelevant to judgments of programmatic success.

I agree that educational indicators cannot be used to draw the conclusion that Title I, ESEA, or any other targeted education program, was ineffective. But they can support judgments on sufficiency of effect and thereby support decisions on residual need. To this degree, at least, educational and social indicators can be useful in program evaluation.

Policy Analysis

Policy analysis is a popular term that encompasses a multitude of activities, including study of the effects of previous government policies, studies focused on the detection of social problems, research on alternative solutions to social problems, and analysis of the anticipated consequences of policy decisions

(President's Commission on Federal Statistics, 1971). Researchers have long anticipated the usefulness of indicators in such studies. Bauer (1966, p. 19) stated:

. . .we see that the purpose of social indicators is not primarily to record historical events but to provide the basis of planning for future policies. Such planning should not be based on the assumption of the single most probable outcome, nor should it confuse the probability with the seriousness of the outcome. Rather it should take into account the range of important consequences that can be anticipated, and both their probability and their importance should also be considered. Data series then become the basis for reassessment of these anticipations.

Biderman (1966) defined three distinct uses of data: *information*, intended for use at the operational level; *intelligence*, intended for use by management or administrators for tactical planning and monitoring; and *enlightenment*, intended for informing public understanding and to support the formulation of general policies. He suggested that the third level of data constitutes social indicators. Land's (1971; 1975a; 1975b) conception of indicators as components of social system models suggests their use in explaining and exploring a variety of social phenomena, including the consequences of policy actions. His definition (1975a, p. 18) of one class of indicators as "policy instrument descriptive indicators" (exogenous variables that are manipulable by social policy) reinforces the conclusion that he had one type of policy analysis in mind as a principal application of social indicators.

The line between policy analysis and program evaluation is fuzzy and broad, since many government programs are direct manifestations of identifiable public policies. However, I conceive of policies as general positions that may or may not have the benefit of resource investments. Policies can emerge in the form of sanctions, laws, rhetoric, or investments, whereas programs are, by definition, investments for a specific purpose.

As an example of the use of educational indicators in analyzing the consequences of a major educational policy, consider assessment of the degree to which equality of educational opportunity has been realized in the United States. This policy emerged from a variety of sources, including *Brown* vs. *Board of Education* (1954) and the Civil Rights Act of 1964. It is a broad policy, with implications at all levels of education, from infant education programs to postgraduate programs. Its realization cannot be assessed through any single educational indicator, since the construct is complex and inclusive, whereas indicators are unitary and narrow.

Equality of educational opportunity can be considered variously as (1) equality of access to education, by geographic region, degree of urbanism of residence, race, sex, socioeconomic class, or state of residence; (2) equality of public investment in education; (3) provision of education of comparable quality; or (4) equality of the results of education. This last suggestion is undoubtedly the most controversial. One could argue that inequality of outcomes (level of educational attainment or level of educational achievement) is prima facie evidence of inequality of investment. The argument rests on assertions analogous to a "cycle of poverty" theory, and it acknowledges the need for added investment in the education of certain minorities to overcome the residual effects of earlier inequitable investments. The counterargument is that educational investment and provision of educational services should be comparable for all, regardless of race, sex, urbanism of residence, and so on, and that such comparability is sufficient.

Clearly, no single indicator will allow adequate monitoring of progress toward equality of educational opportunity. But many series of educational data, some new and others routinely collected for years, can aid in analysis of this policy issue. For example, data on trends in participation in college, by race and region of residence of student, are provided in the 1977 *Condition of Education* report (U.S. DHEW, 1977, p. 203). In 1970, the percentage of the population aged 18 to 34 enrolled in college was substantially different for blacks than for whites in every region of the United States. The largest difference in percentage was 16.5% for whites and 8.8% for blacks in the Northeast; the smallest was 12.9% for whites and 9.1% for blacks in the Southeast. By 1975 the differences in college participation rates for these groups had all but disappeared. The largest remaining difference was in the Southeast, with participation of 13.5% for whites and 11.6% for blacks. In the central states, 16.2% of blacks in the 18–34 age group were enrolled in college, and the corresponding figure for whites was 16.0%. These figures are highly aggregated, and they may well mask inequities based on type and quality of college attended, full-time and part-time enrollment, and remaining differences in smaller demographic regions. Nonetheless, they suggest progress toward achievement of one aspect of equality of educational opportunity for one age group.

Another time series that provides information on equality of educational opportunity was prepared by the Bureau of the Census (Series P–20, *School Enrollment: Social and Economic Characteristics of Students*). This series reports, among other facts, the percentage of the population in various age ranges that is composed of those who are not high school graduates and are not enrolled in school. The series allows comparison of high school dropout rates by race and sex. Here too, some progress toward equality between the races is evident. But in contrast to college enrollment data, the rate of progress is small. Between 1967 and 1975, the proportion of white high school dropouts aged 14–24 remained relatively stable; for white males in 1967 it was 11.6% and in 1975, 9.9% for white females, in 1967 it was 13.1% and in 1975, 11.0%. Intermediate years show some fluctuation in these percentages, and the 1975 data do not represent minima. For blacks, the series also show some year-to-year fluctuation, but a negatively sloped trend is more clearly evident. For black males aged 14–24, there were 23.9% dropouts in 1967 and 18.1% dropouts in 1975; for black females, the corresponding figures were 21.9 and 18.9%.

Denial of equality of educational opportunity through unequal allocation of public school funds was the subject of a series of state and federal Supreme Court cases in the early 1970s. The *Serrano* vs. *Priest* case in California (1971) resulted in a decision by that state's supreme court in favor of the plaintiff's claim that children residing in school districts with low capacity to support education were denied equal protection of the law through the state's failure to equalize educational expenditures among school districts. In the same year, the Minnesota school finance plan was held to be unconstitutional on similar grounds in *Van Duzartz* vs. *Hatfield*. In *Rodriguez* vs. *San Antonio*, a federal court ruled the Texas school finance system unconstitutionally discriminatory, but the U.S. Supreme Court refused to uphold the decision in 1973. Data reported in the *Education Directory* compiled in 1976 by the National Center for Education Statistics (U.S. DHEW, 1976) confirm the continued disparity in expenditures for public education within most states, despite the revision of many state foundation support plans following the litigation mentioned above. In all but the most impoverished states, variation in per-pupil expenditures across school systems was prevalent during the 1974–75 school year. In New York, for example, almost 20% of the school systems spent between $1,100 and $1,500 per pupil, while nearly 25% of the systems spent more than $2,000 per pupil. In Illinois, about 20% of the school systems spent less than $900 per pupil, while over 20% spent more than $1,300 per pupil. In Wyoming, nearly 30% of the systems spent less than $1,100 per pupil, and nearly 12% spent more than $2,000 per pupil.

Between-state disparities in per-pupil expenditures are also substantial, and time series reported in the (U.S. DHEW, 1976a) *Condition of Education* report suggest ever-widening gaps among states (p. 154). During the 1969–70 school year, the minimum average expenditure per pupil was $503 in Alabama and the maximum was $1,420 in New York. Corresponding figures for the 1974–75 school year were $921 for Mississippi and $2,241 for New York. Thus the range increased from $917 to $1,320 over the five years. (Note that these figures are not in constant 1969–70 dollars, and inflation would contribute to the growth of the expenditure range.)

From these few time series alone, it is obvious that the picture of progress toward equality of educational opportunity is clouded. It appears that progress is being made on some important variables, while ground is being lost on others.

Not open to question is the value of educational indicators in exploring important aspects of policy attainment. Although Land's (1975a, 1975b) desire for exploration of relationships among inputs, mediating indicators, and outputs may not be feasible here, analysis of status and trends in complementary indicators is clearly informative.

Social System Monitoring

A group of social indicators researchers working under the auspices of the Russell Sage Foundation or the Social Science Research Council has long claimed that indicators are most useful for what they term *social system monitoring* (Sheldon & Freeman, 1970; Sheldon & Parke, 1975; Miller, 1977). The meaning of the term varies somewhat among authors, but it generally includes such activities as informing the public of the status of various social conditions, descriptive reporting on trends in social phenomena, analytic studies of social change, and informal predictions of future trends and conditions. The distinction between social system monitoring and some forms of policy analysis is unclear. Perhaps the difference lies in the extensiveness and rigor of the relational models required. Descriptive reporting could rely on interpretation of a single time series or a small set of series, with little attempt to impute cause. Prediction of the future might rely on such methods as autoregression and cross-lagged correlation, with little attempt to explain why certain relationships obtained. In short, such studies serve to show what exists and how the present compares with the past, rather than seeking explanations of how or why society came to be as it is or was. Description is sufficient, and causal analysis is secondary.

Collection and dissemination of educational statistics for purposes of describing the condition of education in the United States was the original raison d'etre of the U.S. Office of Education. Bureaus with similar missions exist in almost all developed nations and in several international bodies, such as UNESCO and OECD, and have existed for decades. If the indicators movement has had any influence on the collection and dissemination of statistics for monitoring the condition of education, it may be through such ideas as the need to build extensive and consistent time series; the need to unify definitions of populations, levels of aggregation, and units of analysis; and the need to begin collection of large categories of educational data that were previously ignored. Such influences are impossible to document, and they probably have resulted in quantitative rather than qualitative changes in existing data collection systems. In short, educational statistics have been used for the purposes espoused by Sheldon and associates for many decades, and it is difficult to find new ideas in the writings of those who advocate the use of indicators for social system monitoring.

Needed Developments

Despite my skepticism, the social and educational indicators movement appears to be in no danger of an early death. The Social Science Research Council maintains a Center for the Coordination of Research on Social Indicators. Its monthly *Social Indicators Newsletter* suggests the continued growth of the movement and, if some news items are carried to their logical extreme, perhaps the birth of a discipline. The December 1977 issue of the *Newsletter* contained an announcement of a master's degree program in social indicators research at the University of Guelph in Canada. It also contained reports on a dozen new social indicators reports produced by the U.S. government, university-based researchers in the United States, and several foreign governments. It lent further support to the assertion made earlier in this chapter that social statistics are indistinguishable from social indicators.

In considering needed developments in the educational indicators movement, work from which we should be spared can be as clearly identified as work that might contribute to progress. We need no more papers exhorting individuals or agencies to develop social and educational indicators. Nor are future debates on the definition of social or educational indicators likely to prove fruitful. It is likely that generic social and educational system models have seen their day. Such models typically have been unsupported by theories and often have not been prescriptive of variables, data, and relationships among them. These assertions would seem to reflect negatively on a large portion of the social indicators movement, but such is not my intent. As Land (1978) suggests, the extensive rhetoric of the early social indicators movement was probably necessary to the growth of data on social conditions and trends that occurred over the past 15 years. We have many more social (noneconomic) time series now than were available in 1962, when the Bauer (1966) project began. It seems likely that the federal agencies primarily responsible for the collection of social data would not have expanded their programs in the absence of political pressure that grew out of the social indicators movement.

It must also be noted that generic indicator models that portray relationships among classes of social indicators are useful definitional tools. But the state of development of the indicators movement would seem now to call for models that specify theoretically based variables and the relationships among them.

Compelling needs, as I see them, fall into two categories: demonstrations and data. It is time to provide clear demonstrations of the utility of educational indicators in support of persistent claims of their advocates. In the areas of program evaluation and policy analysis, convincing evidence might be found in retrospective legislative reviews. At the federal level, in particular, most of the public debate that precedes legislative enactment is well documented in the form of transcripts of committee hearings, transcripts of speeches before the Congress, administrative reports to the Congress, and documents inserted into the *Congressional Record*. Such materials could be reviewed systematically to determine which social statistics and what types of analytic treatments, if any, influenced the formation of policy and ultimately formed the basis for public law.

Demonstrations of another sort would build on the recent work of Land and his colleagues at the University of Illinois (Felson & Land, 1977; Land & Felson, 1976, 1977; Pampel, Land, & Felson, 1977). The first paper contains a definition of "dynamic macro social indicator models" and an illustration of one such model in the area of public safety. Such models posit formal relationships among aggregated time series and make use of statistical procedures (such as least squares regression analysis) to estimate the strength and direction of relationships. Land and Felson (1976) suggest the use of parsimonious stochastic difference equations representing functional relationships among logically or theoretically connected indicators of major social conditions or processes. In their example, they predict the reported property crime rate in a given year, on the basis of the reported property crime rate in the preceding year, the proportion of the total population composed of males between the ages of 15 and 24, the consumer price index, the dollar value of the gross national product per 100,000 persons in the U.S. population, and the total of federal, state, and local expenditures for police services per 100,000 in the U.S. population. They justify their choice of variables through an extensive logical argument and appeal to sound sociological theory. Through ordinary least squares regression analysis, they estimate the coefficients of a linear model and achieve an extraordinarily high coefficient of multiple determination (explained in large part by the use of autoregression and the existence of a strong linear trend in the dependent variable). Land and associates apply these logical and statistical procedures to the prediction of changes in the United States in educational enrollments, educational attainments, and the number of educational institutions; in occupational structure; and in marriage, family, and population conditions. In each application, a system of regression equations is used to define relationships among endogenous variables in the domain of central interest and indicators of more general social and economic conditions and trends.

Although this recent work provides an impressive demonstration of the ability of one team of social scientists to develop parsimonious functional equations involving important social indicators, the results are subject to all of the criticisms generally aimed at regression models. These models typically provide excellent predictions of the values of their dependent variables one or two time increments beyond the period of their data bases. But long-term predictions are generally lacking, and accuracy probably cannot be expected, given the likelihood that many coefficients are subject to temporal variation. As explanatory models, these results must be critically scrutinized in the light of such problems as specification bias, multicollinearity, and the use of surrogates for more basic or fundamental causes. Land and Felson (1976, pp. 594–595) are certainly mindful of these problems, and they suggest they are breaking ground in a field that requires considerably more attention.

Data available on education in the United States are overwhelmingly represented in cross-sectional studies of public schools, colleges, and universities. Apart from Project Talent and the current longitudinal study of the high school class of 1972 being conducted by the Department of Health, Education, and Welfare, there are no nationally based longitudinal studies of school-age youth. Such studies are essential to an understanding of the consequences of schooling and the relationships among school experiences and the activities of later life. No collection of cross-sectional studies can provide an adequate substitute for the more expensive and complex longitudinal study, since important relational analyses are precluded. In fact, the types of data required by adequate models of educational processes will probably necessitate longitudinal studies.

Large classes of data are either missing from currently available collections of educational statistics or are seriously underrepresented. Remediation of these deficiencies should be considered a high priority. Data on education outside the formal system of schooling are virtually nonexistent, despite suspicions that such education is increasing. With a shift in the age composition of the population in the United States will come greater demands for education beyond the traditional school years. Coupled with a movement to a technically based service economy and the concomitant acceleration in technological change, these demands will create a serious need for lifelong instruction. Considerable education now takes place in private industry, specialized proprietary schools, and on-the-job training. In view of population trends and technological development, these forms of instruction can be expected to grow.

Although the National Assessment of Educational Progress provides some interesting and important statistics on the results of education, its data are limited in subject matter and amenability to disaggregation. It is not possible to relate National Assessment results to the school experiences of students of any age, so any inferences to the effects of schooling are seriously weakened. Further, as Stake (1970) suggests, the subjects encompassed by National Assessment and the exercises used to measure knowledge of those subjects are limited by the consensual agreements of many special-interest groups and, as a result, are often sterile or intentionally noncontroversial. Additional measurements of the results of education are clearly needed. It is to be hoped they will be collected in the context of longitudinal studies that permit analyses of relationships between in-school and out-of-school experiences, educational programs and investments, and short- and long-term educational effects. Presently available data are particularly deficient in measures of noncognitive effects of education, such as values, interests, motivation, and attitudes.

Finally, presently available data include very little information on what takes place in education in and out of schools. We have many measures of educational expenditures, facilities, and personnel, but few descriptors of instructional processes and curricula. Thus measures of Land's (1975a) analytic indicators are hardly present in current data banks. Without such measures, it is unlikely that educational system models can be evaluated.

CODA

This chapter began with the assertion that educational indicators are not new and are virtually indistinguishable from the kinds of educational statistics that have been assembled in government offices for decades. Various definitions of social indicators were reviewed and contrasted, to the conclusion that indicators are aggregated measures of social or educational variables of interest. Since indicators are interpreted as characteristics of populations, a variety of technical, methodological issues accompany their use. Statistical and substantive generalization from data collected on a sample of units to the characteristics of a population of interest imposes statistical and psychometric hazards such as intolerably large bias and random errors and lack of construct validity. Although many claims for the utility of social and educational indicators can be found in the voluminous literature of the movement, clear demonstrations are lacking. Some important evaluative questions are amenable to attack through indicators research, but others are not. Indicators might prove useful in investigating the realization of social policy goals but probably will contribute little to causal policy analyses. They are likely to be most useful in describing the status of social and educational conditions and illustrating trends in such conditions but are less likely to be useful in illuminating the reasons for the existence of various conditions. As to the future of the indicators movement, the advocates appear to be gaining strength. Their cause would be substantially aided by clear demonstrations of the usefulness of indicators in affecting the formation of educational policies or in modeling significant educational processes. Barring such demonstrations, it is unlikely that the centuries-old tradition of collecting educational statistics will soon be abandoned. Whether such statistics are termed educational indicators is probably of little consequence.

REFERENCES

Angrist, S. S. Dimensions of well-being in public housing families. *Environment and Behavior*, 1974, *16*, 495-516.

Bauer, R. (Ed.). *Social indicators*. Cambridge, Mass.: Massachusetts Institute of Technology Press, 1966.

Bechtoldt, H. P. Construct validity: A critique. *American Psychologist*, 1959, *14*, 619-629.

Berkowitz, W. R. The impact of anti-Vietnam demonstrations on national public opinion and military indicators. *Social Science Research*, 1973, *2*, 1-14.

Beyer, J. M., & Snipper, R. Objective versus subjective indicators of quality in graduate education. *Sociology of Education*, 1974, *47*, 541-557.

Biderman, A. D. Social indicators and goals. In Raymond A. Bauer (Ed.), *Social indicators*. Cambridge, Mass.: MIT Press, 1966.

Biderman, A. D., & Drury, T. F. *Measuring work quality for social reporting*. Washington, D.C.: Bureau of Social Science Research, 1976.

Boulding, K. E. The ethics of rational decision. *Management Science*, 1966, *12*, 161-169.

Campbell, A., & Converse, P. E. (Eds.). *The human meaning of social change*. New York: Russell Sage, 1972.

Campbell, D. T. Recommendations for APA test standards regarding construct, trait, or discriminant validity. *American Psychologist*, 1960, *15*, 546-553.

Campbell, D. T., & Fiske, D. W. Convergent and discriminant validation by the multitrait-multimethod matrix. *Psychological Bulletin*, 1959, *56*, 81-105.

Clemmer, R., Fairbanks, R., Hall, D., Impara, J., & Nelson, C. *Indicators and statewide assessment*. Salem, Ore.: State Department of Education, 1973.

Cochran, W. G. *Sampling techniques* (2nd ed.). New York: John Wiley, 1963.

Cohen, W. J. Social indicators: Statistics for public policy. *The American Statistician*, 1968, *22*, 14.

Cronbach, L. J. Test validation. In R. L. Thorndike (Ed.), *Educational measurement* (2nd ed.), pp. 443-500. Washington, D.C.: American Council on Education, 1971.

Cronbach, L. J., & Meehl, P. E. Construct validity in psychological tests. *Psychological Bulletin*, 1955, *52*, 281-302.

Cureton, E. E. Validity. In E. F. Lindquist (Ed.), *Educational Measurement* (1st ed.), pp. 621-694. Washington, D.C.: American Council on Education, 1951.

De Neufville, J. I. *Social indicators and public policy: Interactive processes of design and application*. Amsterdam: Elsevier Scientific Publishing Company, 1975.

Derogatis, L. R., Yevzeroff, H., & Wittelsberger, B. Social class, psychological disorder, and the nature of the psychopathologic indicator. *Journal of Consulting and Clinical Psychology*, 1975, *43*, 183-191.

Dillman, D. A., & Christenson, J. A. Toward the assessment of public values. *Public Opinion Quarterly*, 1974, *38*, 206-221.

Duncan, O. D. Social stratification and mobility: Problems in the measurement of trend. In E. B. Sheldon & W. E. Moore, *Indicators of social change: Concepts and measurements*, pp. 675-719. New York: Russell Sage, 1968.

Duncan, O. D. Toward social reporting: Next steps. *Social Science Frontiers*, 1969, *2*, 2-8.

Duncan, O. D. Developing social indicators. Department of Sociology, University of Arizona, Tucson (undated).

Dye, T. R. Population density and social pathology. *Urban Affairs Quarterly*, 1975, *11*, 265-275.

Ebel, R. L. Must all tests be valid? *American Psychologist*, 1961, *16*, 640-647.

Ennis, P. H. The definition and measurement of leisure. In E. B. Sheldon & W. E. Moore, *Indicators of social change: Concepts and measurements*, pp. 525-572. New York: Russell Sage, 1968.

Felson, M., & Land, K. C. *Social, demographic and economic interrelationships with educational trends in the United States: 1947–74*. Paper presented at the Annual Meeting of the American Sociological Association, Chicago, August 1977.

Ferriss, A. L. *Indicators of trends in American education*. New York: Russell Sage, 1969.

Ferriss, A. L. Monitoring and interpreting turning points in educational indicators. *Social Indicators Research*, 1974, *1*, 73-84.

Finner, S. L. Religious membership and religious preference: Equal indicators of religiosity? *Journal for the Scientific Study of Religion*, 1970, *9*, 273-279.

Flax, M. J. *Blacks and whites: An experiment in social indicators*. Washington, D.C.: Urban Institute, 1971.

Frank, P. (Ed.). *The validation of scientific theories*. Boston: Beacon, 1956.

Frisbie, P. Measuring the degree of bureacratization of the societal level. *Social Forces*, 1975, *53*, 563-573.

Glass, G. V., Wilson, V. W., & Gottman, J. M. *Design and analysis of time-series experiments*. Boulder: University of Colorado, 1972.

Glitter, A. C., & Peterson, R. R. *Toward a social indicator of education: A pilot study* (CRC Report No. 44). Boston: Boston University, 1970.

Goody, J. (Ed.). *Literacy in traditional societies*. Cambridge, Mass.: Cambridge University Press, 1968.

Gooler, D. The development and use of educational indicators. In *Educational indicators: Monitoring the state of education* (Proceedings of the 1975 Educational Testing Service Invitational Conference), pp. 11-27. Princeton, N.J.: Educational Testing Service, 1975.

Hannan, E. J. *Time series analysis*. London: Methuen, 1960.

Hansen, M. H., Hurwitz, W. N., & Madow, W. G. *Sample survey methods and theory* (2 vols.). New York: John Wiley, 1953.

Harris, C. W. *Problems in measuring change*. Madison: University of Wisconsin Press, 1963.

Hauser, P. M. *Social statistics in use*. New York: Russell Sage, 1975.

Holz, R. F., & Glitter, G. A. Assessing the quality of life in the U.S. Army. *Catalog of selected documents in psychology*, 1975, *5*, 207.

Impaia, J. C. *Are indicators the yellow brick road?* Paper presented at the annual Meeting of the American Educational Research Association, New York; April 1977.

Irvine, D. J. *Performance indicators in education*. Albany: New York State Education Department, 1968.

Jaeger, R. M. *A primer on sampling for statewide assessment*. Princeton, N.J.: Educational Testing Service, 1973.

Jaeger, R. M., & Jaeger, J. *Indicator, statistic, datum and fact: A journey through the house of mirrors*. Princeton, N.J.: ERIC Clearinghouse on Tests, Measurement, and Evaluation, 1978.

Johns, R. L., Alexander, K., & Jordan, K. F. (Eds.). *Planning to finance education*. Gainesville, Fla.: National Educational Finance Project, 1971.

Kaestle, C. F. *Recent methodological developments in the history of American education*. Unpublished manuscript, Department of History, University of Wisconsin, Madison, Wisconsin, 1977.

Kaplan, A. *The conduct of inquiry*. San Francisco: Chandler, 1964.

Kerlinger, F. N., & Pedhazur, E. *Multiple regression in behavioral research*. New York: Holt, Rinehart, & Winston, 1973.

Kish, L. *Survey sampling*. New York: John Wiley, 1965.

Land, K. C. On the definition of social indicators. *American Sociologist*, 1971, *6*, 322-325.

Land, K. C. Social indicator models: An overview. In K. C. Land & S. Spilerman, (Eds.), *Social indicator models*. New York: Russell Sage, 1975. (a)

Land, K. C. Theories, models and indicators of social change. *International Social Science Journal*, 1975, *27*, 7-37. (b)

Land, K. C. Personal communication. March 18, 1978.

Land, K. C., & Felson, M. A general framework for building dynamic macro social indicator models: Including an analysis of changes in crime rates and police expenditures. *American Journal of Sociology*, 1976, *82*, 565-604.

Land, K. C., & Felson, M. A dynamic macro social indicator model of changes in marriage, family, and population in the United States: 1947–74. *Social Science Research*, 1977, *6*, 328-362.

Land, K. C., & Spilerman, S. (Eds.). *Social indicator models*. New York: Russell Sage, 1975.

Lennon, R. T. Assumptions underlying the use of content validity. *Educational and Psychological Measurement*, 1956, *16*, 294-304.

Lockridge, K. A. *Literacy in colonial New England: An enquiry into the social context of literacy in the early modern west*. New York: W. W. Norton, 1974.

Loevinger, J. Objective tests as instruments of psychological theory. *Psychological Reports*, 1957, *3*, 635-694.

MacManus, S. *The story of the Irish race*. New York: Devin-Adair, 1944.

Magura, S., & Ball-Rokeach, S. J. Is there a subculture of violence? *American Sociological Review*, 1975, *40*, 831-836.

Meile, R. L., & Haese, P. N. Social status, status incongruence and symptoms of stress. *Journal of Health and Social Behavior*, 1969, *10*, 273-274.

Merriam, I. C. Welfare and its measurement. In E. B. Sheldon & W. E. Moore, *Indicators of social change: Concepts and measurements*, pp. 721-784. New York: Russell Sage, 1968.

Messick, S. The standard problem: Meaning and values in measurement and evaluation. *American Psychologist*, 1975, *30*, 955-966.

Miller, R. B. Tools for evaluation or for the study of social change? Paper presented at the Annual meeting of the American Educational Research Association, New York, April 1977.

Moser, C. A., & Kalton, G. *Survey methods in social investigation* (2nd ed.). New York: Basic Books, 1972.

Mosteller, F., & Tukey, J. Data analysis, including statistics. In G. Lindzey & E. Aronson (Eds.), *Handbook of social psychology* (Vol. 2, *Research Methods*; 2nd ed.). Reading, Mass.: Addison-Wesley, 1968.

Murthy, M. N. *Sampling theory and methods.* Calcutta: Statistical Publishing Society, 1967.

Myers, J. H., & Guttman, J. Life style: The essence of social class. In W. D. Wells (Ed.), *Life style and psychographics.* Chicago: American Marketing Association, 1974.

National Assessment of Educational Progress. *Update on education.* Denver: Education Commission of the States, 1975.

Noe, F. P. *Leisure life styles: Indicators of social class.* Unpublished doctoral dissertation, State University of New York at Buffalo, 1972.

Pampel, F. C., Land, K. C., & Felson, M. A social indicator model of changes in the occupational structure of the United States: 1947–74. *American Sociological Review*, 1977, *42*, 951-964.

Parke, R., & Sheldon, E. B. Social statistics for public policy. *Proceedings of the American Statistical Association*, Washington, D.C., 1973.

President's Commission on Federal Statistics. *Federal statistics* (Vol. 1), chap. 3. Washington, D.C.: U.S. Government Printing Office, 1971.

Raj, D. *Sampling theory.* New York: McGraw-Hill, 1968.

Rivlin, A. M. *Systematic thinking for social action.* Washington, D.C.: Brookings Institution, 1971.

Rogers, W. T., Folsom, R. E., Jr., Kalsbeek, W. D., & Clemmer, A. F. Assessment of nonresponse bias in sample surveys: An example from national assessment. *Journal of Educational Measurement*, 1977, *14*, 297-311.

Room, R. Drinking patterns in large U.S. cities: A comparison of San Francisco and national samples. *Quarterly Journal of Studies on Alcohol*, 1972, *6*, 28-57.

Sametz, A. W. In N. Baster (Ed.), *Measuring development: The role and adequacy of development indicators.* London: F. Cass, 1968.

Shavelson, R. J., & Stanton, G. C. Construct validation: Methodology and application to three measures of cognitive structure. *Journal of Educational Measurement*, 1975, *12*, 67-85.

Sheldon, E. B. The social indicators movement. In *Educational indicators: Monitoring the state of education* (Proceedings of the 1975 Educational Testing Service Invitational Conference), pp. 3-10. Princeton, N.J.: Educational Testing Service, 1975.

Sheldon, E. B., & Freeman, H. E. Notes on social indicators: Promises and potential. *Policy Sciences*, 1970, *1*, 16-19.

Sheldon, E. B., & Moore, W. E. (Eds.). *Indicators of social change: Concepts and measurements.* New York: Russell Sage, 1968.

Sheldon, E. B., & Parke, R. Social indicators. *Science*, 1975, *188*, 693-699.

Siegler, I. C. *Threats to external validity in survey research with the elderly: The effects of selective dropout on health, morale, social relations and environmental circumstances.* Unpublished doctoral dissertation, Syracuse University, 1974.

Skogan, W. G. The validity of official crime statistics: An empirical investigation. *Social Science Quarterly*, 1974, *55*, 25-38.

Solow, R. M. The intelligent citizen's guide to inflation. *Public Interest*, 1975, *38*, 30-66.

Stake, R. E. *National assessment* (Proceedings of the 1970 Invitational Conference on Testing Problems), Princeton, N.J.: Educational Testing Service, 1970.

Stetson, D. M., & Wright, G. C. The effects of laws on divorce in American states. *Journal of Marriage and the Family*, 1975, *37*, 537-547.

Sukhatme, P. V., & Sukhatme, B. V. *Sampling theory of surveys with applications* (2nd ed.). London: Asia Publishing House, 1970.

Swift, D. F. Family environment and 11 + success: Some basic predictors. *British Journal of Educational Psychology*, 1967, *37*, 10-21.

Taylor, D. G., Aday, L. A., & Anderson, R. A social indicator of access to medical care. *Journal of Health and Social Behavior*, 1975, *16*, 39-49.

Tissue, T. Another look at self-rated health among the elderly. *Journal of Gerontology*, 1972, *27*, 91-94.

United Nations. *Towards a system of social and demographic statistics* (Studies in methods, Series F, No. 18). New York: United Nations, 1975.

U.S. Department of Health, Education, and Welfare. *Toward a social report*. Washington, D.C.: U.S. Government Printing Office, 1969.

U.S. Department of Health, Education, and Welfare. *The condition of education, 1975*. Washington, D.C.: U.S. Government Printing Office, 1975.

U.S. Department of Health, Education, and Welfare. *The condition of education, 1976*. Washington, D.C.: U.S. Government Printing Office, 1976. (a)

U.S. Department of Health, Education, and Welfare. *The condition of education, 1977*. Washington, D.C.: U.S. Government Printing Office, 1977.

U.S. Department of Health, Education, and Welfare. *Education Directory*. Washington, D.C.: U.S. Government Printing Office, 1976. (b)

U.S. Department of Labor. *New perspectives on manpower problems and measures*. Washington, D.C.: U.S. Government Printing Office, 1968.

IV

METHODOLOGY

8

An Evolving Logic of Participant Observation, Educational Ethnography, and Other Case Studies

LOUIS M. SMITH
Washington University

INTRODUCTION

The aspiration of the author in this chapter is straightforward but wide ranging: to provide a context and logic for the discussion of the genre of research that is coming to be known by such varied labels as educational ethnography, participant observation, qualitative observation, case study, or field study. For the most part, I will use these terms as synonyms.

Such an aspiration is warranted for several reasons. First, the method seems very simple, and some methodologists perceive it this way. Biddle (1967) called it "the broadest and simplest methodology used in classroom studies." The researcher goes into an educational setting with a pencil and pad, makes a few observations, takes some notes, and writes a report, a dissertation, or a book. For some it seems almost this easy; others stumble about and have incredible difficulty. Second, a growing group of researchers, evaluators, and policymakers (e.g., NIE's Experimental Schools, NIE's School Capacity for Problem Solving, Nuffield Humanities Evaluation, OECD's Center for Educational Research and Innovation, and NSF's Case Studies in Science Education) have been urging inquiry and evaluation using these techniques. Third, several major methodologists have disparaged the use of such procedures: the two most significant statements are Scriven's (1967) classic paper on evaluation and Campbell and Stanley's (1963) classic chapter on experimental research in education. The former attacked "process studies" and "noncomparative evalua-

FREDERICK ERICKSON, Harvard University, and PAUL DIESING, State University of New York— Buffalo, were editorial consultants for this chapter, and special thanks are due to Paul Pohland and Lee Shulman.

tion.'' The latter took a moral stand on the design these authors call X–O, or the ''one-shot case study.''

The Campbell and Stanley (1963) position on the one-shot study is:

Much research in education today conforms to a design in which a single group is studied only once, subsequent to some agent or treatment presumed to cause change. Such studies might be diagrammed as follows:

XO

As has been pointed out (e.g., Boring, 1954; Stouffer, 1949) such studies have such a total absence of control as to be of almost no scientific value. The design is introduced here as a minimum reference point. Yet because of the continued investment in such studies and the drawing of causal inferences from them, some comment is required. . . .

In the case studies of Design 1, a carefully studied single instance is implicitly compared with other events casually observed and remembered. The inferences are based upon general expectations of what the data would have been had the ''X'' not occurred, etc. Such studies often involve tedious collection of specific detail, careful observation, testing, and the like, and in such instances involve the error of *misplaced precision*. How much more valuable the study would be if the one set of observations were reduced by half and the saved effort directed to the study in equal detail of an appropriate comparison instance. *It seems well-nigh unethical at the present to allow, as theses or dissertations in education, case studies of this nature* (i.e., involving a single group observed at one time only). (pp. 176–177; italics added)

Being faced with such an edict, and with accumulating contradictory personal research experience, posed an interesting dilemma to which we responded in various ways. In part we quoted other authorities. George Homans (1962) for example, introduced his discussion of the strategy of industrial sociological research with the epigrammatic comment: ''People who write about methodology often forget that it is a matter of strategy, not of morals. There are neither good nor bad methods, but only methods that are more or less effective under particular circumstances in reaching objectives on the way to a distant goal'' (p. 257). And we referred to the more devastating style and argument of Howard Becker (1970) that methodology is ''too important to be left to the methodologists,'' and to his data, a presentation of the minimal overlapping of the research methods of the chairmen of the American Sociological Association's section on methodology and the methods used by the winners of the most prestigious sociological research awards (pp. 3–7).

In addition, we have tried to confront the issue directly with students and colleagues at Washington University in St. Louis. At one point some years ago, the following question was part of a set of Ph.D. examinations there:

Gouldner's books, *Patterns of Industrial Bureaucracy* and *Wildcat Strike*, are classics in the eyes of some social scientists. The methodology seems to be what Campbell and Stanley have called the ''X–O'' or ''one-shot case study'' (attached is a quote from their discussion). They state explicitly, "It seems well nigh unethical" to permit such research. Take a position on the apparent dilemma and indicate how you would reason through toward a solution. Illustrate with reference to the substance of Gouldner's monographs.

In an important sense, this chapter attempts to develop a broader position within education, social science, and philosophy and to join the debate in the educational research community. The goal is to isolate significant methodological issues which can be examined in some detail, both theoretically and empirically.

In a recent unpublished version of his Kurt Lewin Award address, Campbell (1974) backed off from his earlier position. In a brief paragraph he makes the following points regarding qualitative case studies: (1) "such studies regularly contradict the prior expectations of the authors" (p. 24), (2) [such studies] "are convincing and informative to skeptics like me to a degree which my simpleminded rejection doesn't allow for" (p. 24), (3) "such a study [is given] a probing and testing power which I had not allowed for" (p. 25). In a concern for the division of labor in most large-scale projects, with the resulting partial knowledge of the several specialists, he also comments: "A project anthropologist, sociologist, or historian, assigned the task of common sense acquaintance with the overall context, including the social interactions producing the measures, could often fill this gap" (p. 25). While at heart Campbell remains a quantitative experimentalist and quasi experimentalist, his more general points are "Social knowing . . . is a precarious and presumptuous process" (p. 29), and "If we are to be truly scientific, we must reestablish this qualitative grounding of the quantitative in action research" (p. 30).

My point in raising the Campbell and Stanley position and the reactions to it has to do with the difficulties in any prescription of research methods and procedures. The implications are several. First, such prescriptions are changing and evolving standards, group norms, if you like, of research communities and subcommunities within education and social science which are also evolving and changing. As such they may have a kinship with moral prescriptions. There are now a number of commentaries on the sociology of knowledge and scientific communities (Crane, 1972; Hagstrom, 1965; Kuhn, 1970; Lakatos & Musgrove, 1970; Ziman, 1968). These changing communities are one meaning of the "evolving logic" stipulated in the title to this chapter.

A second implication of the illustration, and of the title of the essay, is pedagogical. I will draw heavily on my own and my colleagues' research and methodological reflections to illustrate many of the general issues and problems. In a sense this is a reflexive mode of presentation, an attempt to try out Becker's suggestion for a "natural history." In this way a concrete, integrated, and contextual statement explicating the general arguments will be provided. Thus I believe I am stating, in a particular setting, Toulmin's (1972) more general point:

This thesis can be summed up in a single, deeply held conviction: that in science and philosophy alike, an exclusive preoccupation with logical systematicity has been destructive of both historical understanding and rational criticism. Men demonstrate their rationality, not by ordering their concepts and beliefs in tidy formal structures, but by their preparedness to respond to novel situations with open minds—acknowledging the shortcomings of their former procedures and moving beyond them. . . . The philosophical agenda proposed here sets aside all such assumptions in favor of patterns of analysis which are at once more historical, more empirical and more pragmatic. (pp. vii–viii)

The theory under consideration in this essay is a theory of methodology within education and social science. It is a theory constructed to help solve methodological problems in studying teachers, curricula, classrooms, and schools.

Such a methodological description and analysis should culminate in a provisional codification of criteria and procedures which indicates a little about ''how to do an educational ethnography or a participant observer case study,'' and it should present to a judge of ethnographic research proposals, or a reader of participant observer project reports, an image of a provisional set of criteria for a ''good observational case study'' or a ''good educational ethnography.''

DOMAINS OF KNOWLEDGE

General Overview

The general educational research community has only recently discovered participant observational research. A corollary to this discovery is the lack of knowledge of the substantial body of research that has been carried out with this genre of methods. In some quarters the belief seems to be that there is little precedent for such work and that there have been minimal attempts to speak to the methodological issues underlying the inquiry. To rectify this impression, four tables of references are presented here. While they are not exhaustive, they should destroy the belief regarding little precedent, and the citations are numerous enough to enable the reader to begin his own program of criticism or self-training. In rough fashion they have been grouped into four clusters. Table 1 includes general references: studies of non-Western culture, modern communities, formal organizations, and informal small groups. Mostly they have been carried out by anthropologists, sociologists, and political scientists. Table 2 presents studies of educational settings: school and community, school systems, elementary and secondary schools, classrooms, and curricula and special programs. Table 3 lists major, seminal, methodological statements from fields other than education, and Table 4 lists those from education, many of which would be described as educational evaluation.

The most obvious limitation of these tables occurs in the slighting of the traditional anthropological research. In addition, the huge case study literature in clinical and individual psychology has been omitted (e.g., Freud, Erickson, and Piaget). Finally, the related large body of literature on comparative psychology and animal ethology has not been included. For an early statement see Scott

TABLE 1

Domains of Observational Case Studies: General

Non-Western Cultures	Modern Communities	Formal Organizations	Informal Groups
Firth (1957, 1959)	Arensberg and Kimball (1940)	Arensberg & MacGregor (1942)	Becker (1970)
Malinowski (1922, 1935)	Barker & Wright (1954)	Blau (1955)	Festinger, Riecken, & Schachter (1956/1964)
Mead (1930)	Bruyn (1963)	Goffman (1959, 1961)	Gump, Schoggen, & Redl (1957)
Radcliffe-Brown (1922/1948)	Kimball and Pearsall (1954)	Gouldner (1954a, 1954b)	Homans (1950)
	Warner & Lunt (1941)	Lipset (1950); Lipset, Trow, & Coleman (1962)	Humphreys (1975)
		Polsky (1962)	Liebow (1967)
		Redl & Wineman (1957)	Whyte (1955)
		Selznick (1949, 1952)	Whyte (1953)
		Yunker (1977)	

TABLE 2
Observational Studies of Educational Systems

School and Community	School Systems and Interorganizational Educational Systems	Schools	Classrooms	Curricula and Program Evaluation	Teaching Careers and Student Teaching
Henry (1963, 1966)	CERI (1973)	Atwood (1960)	Cazden, John, & Hymes (1972)	Applegate (1971)	Becker (1951)
Singleton (1967)	Lutz (1962)	Barker & Gump (1964)	Cicourel (1974)	Beittel (1972, 1973)	Eddy (1969)
Spindler (1963)	Pohland (1970)	Becker, Geer, Hughes, & Strauss (1961)	Delamont (1976)	Berlak, A., et al (1975)	Finch (1978)
Warren (1967)	Schumacher (1975)	Charters, Everhart, Jones, Packard, Pellegrin & Wacaster (1973)	Elliott & Adelman (1977)	Eisner (1975)	Iannaccone (1963)
Wax, Wax & Du Mont (1964)	Smith (1977b)	Cusick (1973)	Gump (1967)	Easley (1974)	Sarason, Davidson, & Blatt (1962)
Wolcott (1967)		Iannaccone (1958)	Henry (1957, 1966)	Hall & Thurnau (1975)	
		Jackson (1968)	Leacock (1969)	Hamilton (1977)	
		McPherson (1972)	Lipnick (1976)	Munro (1977)	
		Mercurio (1972)	Rice (1964)	Reid & Walker (1975)	
		Reynolds (1973)	Smith & Geoffrey (1968)	Russell (1969)	
		Rist (1973)	Tikunoff, Berliner, & Rist (1975)	Seif (1971)	
		Sarason (1971, 1972)		Smith & Carpenter (1972)	
		Smith & Keith (1971)		Smith & Pohland (1974)	

TABLE 2

Observational Studies of Educational Systems—Continued

School and Community	School Systems and Interorganizational Educational Systems	Schools	Classrooms	Curricula and Program Evaluation	Teaching Careers and Student Teaching
		Walker (1932)		Smith & Schumacher (1972)	
		Wolcott (1977)		Soloman (1971)	
				Stake and Easley (1978)	
				Walker (1971)	
				Wolfson (1974)	
				Wolcott (1977)	

TABLE 3

Methodological Statements on Participant Observation Field Studies: General

Papers and Chapters	Monograph and Books	Collections
Becker (1958)	Becker (1970)	Adams & Preiss (1960)
Becker & Geer (1957)	Bruyn (1966)	Casagrande (1960)
Denzin (1971)	Denzin (1970)	Epstein (1967)
Glaser & Strauss (1965)	Glaser & Strauss (1967)	Garfinkel (1967)
Gump & Kounin (1959–1960)	Junker (1960)	Habenstein (1970)
Kimball (1955)	Pelto (1970)	Hammond (1964)
Kluckhohn (1940)	Powdermaker (1966)	Jacobs (1970)
Malinowski (1922)	Walker & Adelman (1975)	McCall & Simmons (1969)
Meehl (1971)	Wax (1971)	Naroll & Cohen (1970)
Merton (1947, 1957)		Vidich, Bensman, & Stein (1964)
Scott (1965)		
Van Velsen (1967)		
Vidick & Shapiro (1955)		
Whyte (1971)		

TABLE 4

Methodological Statements on Participant Observation: Education

Papers and Chapters	Monographs and Books	Collections
Adelman (1976)	Beittel (1973)	Adelman (n.d.)
Atkin (1973)	Lutz & Iannaccone (1969)	Hamilton, Jenkins, King, MacDonald, & Parlett (1977)
Burnett-Hill (1973)	Parlett & Hamilton (1972)	Pohland (1972)
Easley (1974)		Roberts & Akinsanya (1976)
Erickson (1973)		Tikunoff & Ward (1977)
Hamilton (1976)		
Lutz & Ramsey (1974)		
Magoon (1977)		
Sindell (1969)		
Smith (1967)		
Smith & Pohland (1976)		
Wilson (1977)		

(1950), and for a recent review see Miller (1977). In fact, these tables have a personal quality, representing the gradually accumulating collection of materials I have read and found stimulating. Nonetheless, inherent in them, and well beyond, are important empirical problems in the sociology and psychology of knowledge. Genealogies, communities, and individual perspectives of these research workers and their interrelationships deserve empirical attention, much as Crane (1972) has done for mathematicians and rural sociologists.

A Personal Story

Every research worker has an interesting story to tell on the evolution of his or her own work. I believe that more of these stories need to be told if we are to have a useful and potent theory of methodology. The accounts of recommended training programs, not to mention the uncollated statements in graduate school catalogs, often have ironical contrasts with personal histories as they are recounted in various forms (Becker, 1970; Homans, 1962; Homans & Bailey, 1959; Murchison, 1961; Skinner, 1956).

My own experience in participant observation of natural settings began in discussions with Laurance Iannaccone and W. W. Charters, Jr. From them I came to know Homans' book *The Human Group* (1950), and soon I was into the literature of the overlapping groups of social scientists in the Society of Fellows at Harvard and Warner's Yankee City group. From Iannaccone and Charters also I learned of Robert Merton's *Social Theory and Social Structure* (1957) and the case study work of a cluster of his students, Blau, Gouldner, Selznick, and Lipset. A major center of activity existed in Chicago: Blumer, Hughes, Becker, Bruyn, Geer, Goffman, Lortie, Strauss, and the Waxes. Harvard, Chicago, and Columbia traded some people back and forth over the years. Some of these individuals began studying educational settings and problems. Most notable were Kimball and his students, Iannaccone and Hill-Burnett and their students. At Stanford, Spindler was training such people as Wolcott, Singleton, and Warren and developing his highly regarded series of monographs on education and culture. Recently several of these strands have become institutionalized in the Council on Anthropology and Education of the American Anthropological Association and in Division G, Social Context of Education of the American Educational Research Association, as earlier some had flowed together in the founding of the Society of Applied Anthropology.

My own background—a mixture of Minnesota dustbowl empiricism in the Psychology Department and a kind of clinical educational psychology in the College of Education's Psycho-educational Clinic—had acquainted me with *none* of the anthropological and sociological investigators but with a variety of researchers doing case studies of individuals. That line of case study work has intersected very little with the more sociological and anthropological case studies. At one point (Smith, 1972) I informally tried to check the references to Piaget's clinical method in the various methodological statements by participant observers. There were none. More recently, people like Gardner (1972, 1973) have been bridging those domains. Finally, and again personally, an interest in the arts and aesthetic education raised the possibility of some additional kinds of case studies. Once again the ubiquitous Becker was already there empirically ("The Dance Musician," 1966) and theoretically ("Art as Collective Action," 1974). Beittel's seminal case studies (1972, 1973) on producing art seem unknown to most educationists. Hamilton and his colleagues (Hamilton, Jenkins, King, MacDonald, & Parlett, 1977) have produced a reader in educational evaluation, *Beyond the Numbers Game,* whose saucy and irreverent continuity tells a part of the "illuminative evaluation" story—complete with a manifesto and a prediction of a paradigm shift in educational evaluation.

These personal socialization sequences and casual observations of evolving networks, invisible colleges, and gradual institutionalizations deserve more formal attention than the informal curiosity which can be satisfied by reading prefaces, footnotes, and references and engaging in casual conversations concerning struggles for an intellectual perspective, for a peer reference group, and for legitimacy.

In summary, these comments are small but important examples of the evolving nature of scientific ideology and practice. They make the points that moral principles ("It seems well-nigh unethical") in research are norms of communities and subgroups of scholars in the social sciences and education, and that deviancy from community standards has some parallels to deviancy in other groups (Becker, 1966; Festinger, Schachter, & Back, 1950; Schachter, 1953). They also suggest that methodological pluralism has some benefits as well as hazards. For this chapter they indicate the labyrinthian and somewhat tortuous route one investigator took in searching for a theoretical-methodological rationale to solve the problems he was confronting. Traveling that path has helped to focus many of the more general perspectives of this essay.

Reference to a half dozen of our observational studies will occur throughout this essay, and a brief introduction to these should facilitate the analysis. They can be grouped into three periods: initial forays, a CEMREL period, and a recent period. Substantively they reflect a research serial which might be called an evolving ethnography of schooling. Theoretically they represent a cluster of middle-range theories which might one day cumulate in a general theory of education.

Early on, the Office of Education, in its small contract program, supported three of our studies: *The Complexities of an Urban Classroom* (Smith & Geoffrey, 1968), *Anatomy of Educational Innovation* (Smith & Keith, 1971), and *Patterns of Student Teaching* (Connor & Smith, 1967b). *Complexities* was an attempt to look at how a middle-class teacher coped with a group of lower-class children in a sixth-and-seventh-grade classroom of an urban elementary school. Procedurally it was our first attempt to implement a qualitative participant observer methodology. Through a series of commonsense decisions and lucky accidents we hit on the "inside/outside stance" of William Geoffrey, the teacher, insider, and true participant, and Smith, the outsider, nonparticipant, and observer. We developed a device which we called "interpretive asides," which called for the inclusion of insights in the observational record. We split our records into in situ "field notes" and out-of-setting "summary observations and interpretations." The latter we dictated into a portable stenorette while driving to and from the school, which involved a half hour of critical time each way. Leaving the site, the percepts and ideas would be popping in a thousand directions. Capturing these before they were lost seemed essential. Early the next morning, on the way in, the residue that remained could be commented on when one felt fresh and relaxed. Some of the results of the study which still seem important were concerns about the way the school year began; the teacher's role in that beginning; the development of the social structure of the classroom, especially the roles played by individual children; the conceptualization of teacher as decision maker and actor; and the characteristics of children from an inner-city neighborhood as these presented themselves to a teacher whose responsibility was to help the children learn.

From this class of Geoffrey's we moved to Kensington and the study of the first year in the life of an innovative suburban elementary school. *Anatomy* became a study of issues in innovation and organizational structure and process, a story of a group of educators attempting to build and implement the new elementary education. The significant results were descriptions and analyses of organizational development, of formal doctrine, and of the alternative of grandeur as a strategy of innovation. Considerations included the key themes of open-space building design, democratic administration, team teaching, and individualized curriculum and instruction, major elements in the new elementary education.

William Connor and I, intrigued with the unusual pattern of student teaching at City Teacher's College, spent a semester following a dozen apprentices around. Their "two by two" apprenticeship program included two weeks in a kindergarten, two weeks in a first grade, two weeks in a second grade, and so on through the eighth grade. Methodologically we became more serious about interviewing and began to think about triangulation and what we later came to see as an elaboration of the Campbell and Fiske (1959) multitrait, multimethod approach to valid data. Substantively, a variety of issues arose—"the nine trials phenomenon," aspects of anxiety, an analogy to psychomotor skills, and a model of socialization into the teaching profession.

The CEMREL period reflected an early commitment by Wade Robinson, the president of the Regional Laboratory, to the possibilities of alternative modes of educational inquiry and their relationship to educational practice. I spent a decade there, mostly with half-time appointments and released time from Washington University. One study continued directly the earlier line of work. Pat Brock and I began and still have several unfinished drafts of *Teacher Plans and*

Classroom Interaction. We wanted to attack issues in the intellectual life of classrooms, we wanted to continue and extend the micro analysis of classroom discourse, we wanted to critique the stance of various in-vogue systems of classroom observation—Flanders, B. O. Smith, Taba, Medley and Mitzel, and Bellack, we wanted to move toward quantification, and we wanted to remain with a processual rather than a structural analysis. Consequently we tape-recorded a full semester of her first-hour Science I class, we took field notes along the way, and we have her daily pre- and poststatements about plans and results. CEMREL published our major methodological statement *"Go Bug Go": Methodological Issues in Classroom Observation* (Smith & Brock, 1970).

However, most of the CEMREL work was a series of forays into formative and summative evaluation using qualitative observational procedures, sometimes independently and sometimes triangulated with experimental and survey procedures in a three-legged evaluation model. The initial example (and perhaps most important) of these was "Education, Technology, and the Rural Highlands" (Smith & Pohland, 1974), a study of a computer-assisted instruction program. A series of papers (Smith & Pohland, 1974, 1976) grew out of that work. Substantively we were into community analysis, interorganizational theory, and the wonders of technology—both its doctrine and its realities. Methodologically we came to terms with "standard" participant observation technique, a phenomenon which does not exist, in our view. We elaborated the multimethod, multitrait position. And we tried to reanalyze and synthesize the Glaser and Strauss (1967) grounded theory position with our own.

Pat Carpenter and I spent a year in the formative evaluation of a social exchange token economy program in an urban school. In *General Reinforcement Project: Qualitative Observation and Interpretation* (1972), we raised critical issues in the implicit value stand of a behavior modification position, the simplistic doctrine of token economies and the complex behavior of the teachers, and some similarities and differences with Kounin's (1970) classroom management position.

Finally we were involved in several studies related to the Aesthetic Education Program. Sally Schumacher and I spent a year on *Extended Pilot Trials: A Description, Analysis, and Evaluation of the Aesthetic Education Program* (Smith & Schumacher, 1972). Later I observed a weeklong workshop for administrators (Smith, 1974), began toying with a variation of Piagetian clinical method (Smith, 1975b) as an evaluation technique, and took the observational role of learner in *Mrs. Kaye's Drawing Class: Some Theoretical Thoughts on Curriculum, Teaching, and Learning* (1975a). The perspective of the pupil seems an unexploited stance.

Our major recent activity has been an involvement in Robert Stake and Jack Easley's *Case Studies in Science Education* (1978), supported by the National Science Foundation (NSF). We studied the Alte School District (Smith, 1977b) an older suburban, upper-middle-class school district with the reputation of having a good science program. Key issues arose in district history, in the politics of curriculum change, in the nature of the strong teacher (as well as the prima donna syndrome), and in the conceptualization of curriculum at the district level. Currently we have two studies planned and underway: "Improving Urban Education: Federal Policy in Action" and "Kensington Revisited: A 15-Year Follow-Up of an Innovative School and Its Faculty." The former is an attempt to describe and understand a major effort in knowledge development and utilization in urban education. The latter is a simple "What's happened?" inquiry at the innovative Kensington School, including an attempt to find the original faculty, who are now scattered about the country, and to inquire into their current views of educational innovation and change. Both of these investigations are being supported by the National Institute of Education.

In summary, outside the dominant educational psychological paradigm in educational research, a large body of research exists within the qualitative, ethnographic, participant observational genre. Its roots lie especially in anthropology and in several traditions within sociology. A brief overview of one educational research practitioner's use of these methods suggests its applicability to a broad array of problems within education—schools, classrooms, curriculum development, and evaluation.

COGNITIVE PROCESSES IN EDUCATIONAL ETHNOGRAPHY

A number of stories can be told regarding the intellectual processes in doing educational ethnography, participant observation, and other case studies. On several occasions symposia at APA, AERA, and AAA, and in appendices to books and technical reports, we have tried to speak to issues in the cognitive processes involved in qualitative observational research. These attempts have usually been reflexive, that is, they have grown out of our musings and reflections as we have tried to use the methods in particular projects. In an important sense they have been attempts to indicate the dynamics of ethnography by attending to the creative processes in learning from a field work project. In this section I will summarize these thoughts. Once again this is a personal statement; it should be read as a semiintegrated collection of hunches and hypotheses open to more careful tests by empirically oriented students of social science methodology. How one does that testing is an interesting commentary on one's assumptions, practices, and theory of methodology.

Preliminary Phases

Origins of Problems.   The vagaries in the origins of our research problems are captured best in the title of a recent short paper, "Accidents, Serendipity, and Making the Commonplace Dramatic" (Smith, 1978). The general point is that the problems are all around; they pass by the investigator in varying guises and for the most part need only to be recognized for their possibilities. A brief example or two must suffice. William Geoffrey was an MA student in a summer school course entitled "The Classroom as a Social System." As one of the activities each student took the Minnesota Teacher Attitude Inventory (MTAI) as part of a discussion of teacher variables in the classroom system. As Geoffrey turned his paper in he commented that this was how he felt but it had little to do with the way he taught. Such needling provoked a conversation, led to an invitation to see what it's like in an urban classrom, and eventually developed into *Complexities*. While observing Geoffrey's class I met an apprentice who was in this "funny two by two" student teaching program which was so different from the "regular" program at Washington University. Two programs which had common goals but such different structures just had to be interesting, so Connor and I set out on *Patterns*. When Cohen and Shelby approached me to get involved studying the Kensington School, it looked like a beautiful opportunity to see the origins of an elementary school faculty peer group, a phenomenon that was a very important part of Geoffrey's life at the Washington School. *Anatomy* grew out of that.

It might be argued that the three illustrations suggest an absurd model for the origins of research studies. Be that as it may, that's the way it seems to happen. It might be argued also that this is an applied extension of Underwood's (1949) old notion of "I wonder what would happen type" origin of research problems.

The Intuitive Feel of the Problem. When funding agencies, colleagues at other universities, practicing professionals (superintendents, principals, teachers), or graduate students considering dissertations raise with me the possibility of "the study of *X, Y* or *Z*," there occurs an almost immediate perceptual reaction-evaluation that it is or is not a good problem. Strangely perhaps, almost as an animal sniffing the air in an unusual setting, it comes out silently to myself as "It smells like a good problem." I have the impression that I could, at a minimum, defend it, or at a maximum get truly excited by it and be willing to commit one or more years to working on it. Usually the perceptual reaction is accompanied by a feeling of "Why didn't I see that or think about it before?" I don't understand the dynamics of the reaction, but it happens. It seems functional.

Guiding Models and Images of an End in View. Usually very quickly also there comes to mind a particular piece of research which captures the essence of what seems implicit in the problem and which serves as a kind of guide for what might be done. *Guide* is perhaps too limited an image, for not only does it give direction to the intellectual work but it brings a kind of confidence to the task; it legitimates the activity: "If we can do it as well as Jones did, it will be a worthwhile contribution." Several brief illustrations come to mind. In *Complexities,* a "simple" image dominated our orientation: Do an educational case study that would fit the half dozen presented and analyzed in Homans's *Human Group*. The logic was simple—a teacher and a classroom are just another group, as was the Irish farm family, the street corner society, or the bank wiring group.

Further, Homans provided methodological and procedural guidelines, a conception of social science theory, a view of explanation, and a set of concepts and hypotheses appropriate to a middle-range theory of groups (and possibly a basis for a more general and abstract theory of sociology). In *Alte* the model was McKinney and Westbury's (1975) attempt to consider a school district and its curriculum from a historical perspective. We were on the hunt for a way of looking at science education in the Alte schools. Currently we have begun a new study entitled "Improving Urban Education: Federal Policy in Action." As soon as the label was generated it immediately raised an association with a study I'd casually known from years ago, "Project Camelot." A search in the library found it unavailable, but its author, I. L. Horowitz, had co-authored another book with J. E. Katz, *Social Science and Public Policy in the United States* (1975). A quick skimming (one section dealt with "Project Camelot") provided an initial guiding model.

Foreshadowed Problems.   One of Malinowski's major contributions to the logic of ethnography was his distinction between "foreshadowed problems" and "preconceived solutions." As he put it a half century ago:

Good training in theory, and acquaintance with its latest results, is not identical with being burdened with "preconceived ideas." If a man sets out on an expedition, determined to prove certain hypotheses, if he is incapable of changing his views constantly and casting them off ungrudgingly under the pressure of evidence, needless to say his work will be worthless. But the more problems he brings with him into the field, the more he is in the habit of molding his theories according to facts, and of seeing facts in their bearing upon theory, the better he is equipped for the work. Preconceived ideas are pernicious in any scientific work, but foreshadowed problems are the main endowment of a scientific thinker, and these problems are first revealed to the observer by his theoretical studies. (Malinowski, 1922, pp. 8–9)

In a sense, Malinowski's statement calls the investigator to an awareness of the key problems, issues, and debates in that corner of the intellectual world in which the setting and the problem lie. The foreshadowed problems represent initial and partial analyses of the problem, the tenor of thinking of people who are working in related and relevant areas, and provisional modes of thinking. By way of illustration, at one time we joked about what one needed to know before starting a theory-generating observational study. Since we had just finished an educational psychology text (Smith & Hudgins, 1964) this seemed an appropriate spot to begin. The advice became, "Go write an ed psych text, then you are ready for a classroom observational study!" In retrospect, the truth in that advice seems to be in the residual questions after one has tried to read and synthesize several hundred research references (not to mention those that didn't make the bibliography). In the best sense these were Malinowski's foreshadowed problems.

Equally important for me has been the experience of teaching in an education department. My students have been undergraduates just moving into the teacher education program and experienced teachers in the M.A. and Ph.D. program in elementary and secondary education, administration, psychology, and guidance. As they raise their most perplexing questions, I store them away to ask the data from Geoffrey's class, from the Kensington School, from the Alte District, or wherever else we have been or are contemplating entering. In working with students as they try to learn the methodology of educational ethnography, a major problem arises if they do not have a wide background of problems generated by attempts to puzzle through large amounts of related but difficult-to-integrate literature, by an array of personal experiences or by difficult questions posed by colleagues. Dealing with that is one of the more intractable problems in teaching and learning participant observation.

Competing Theories.   Many students and critics have found the conception of foreshadowed problems not adequate to their concerns for selectivity of data, seeing what one wants to see, and implicit theoretical biases. One of our further procedures has been to describe the tenor of the theoretical concerns that we have "gone in with." The best illustration of this comes from *Complexities*. In our educational psychology text we drew heavily on such theorists as McClelland, Homans, and Skinner. A more precise conceptualization of that position can be seen in the table of contents of that book, and contrasts and similarities can be seen in the table of contents of *Complexities* and, perhaps even more significantly, *Anatomy*. While elements of continuity exist, the real world of the classroom and school pulled us some distance from our initial stance. This acquaintance with prior theory reflects not only the early position of Malinowski but a similar more recent statement by Diesing: "The prospective field worker will acquaint himself with a variety of theories (the more the better) that may be applicable to his case" (1971, p. 142). Now, in long retrospect, the point of emphasis is slightly different. I believe we were implicitly running several alternative general theories against each other, that is, putting them in competition. In a sense we were unwittingly initiating an ethnographic paradigm for falsification. In addition, we were not only selecting from the several stances but also moving toward the beginnings of our own position.

Discussions with colleagues (Nolan, 1975) suggest a further illustration. In a project involving the genesis of a community college, one alternative would be to enter this deliberately from the point of view of a sociologist such as Parsons and to look to the resolution of the functional problems and pattern variables and further clarification and development of that point of view. In keeping with the principle of competing theories, one might become as well versed in Homans's brand of interaction theory, Merton's functionalism, and March and Simon's organizational theory. As the events play themselves out in the natural setting, particular hypotheses within one position or another will be found to be less tenable than others. These beginnings of falsification, in the context of competing theories, seem to be the latent logical thrust of the Malinowski, Diesing, and Becker rules of thumb. Stated alternatively, approaching a setting with several competing theories, to each of which one is only partially committed, allows one to explore more fully the conceptual realities of the events in the setting. As events occur which the several theories omit, neglect, or speak to only minimally, the generation of one's own position comes to the forefront.

Thinking during Data Collection

While we are in the field observing directly, informally talking with and listening to participants, collecting and reading documents, a variety of discriminable intellectual operations seems to be occurring.

Immersion in Concrete Perceptual Images. One of the exciting and often unexpected events for a novice field worker comes from his/her immersion in concrete perceptual images. The day-in, day-out involvement in the setting produces an ocean of images of the phenomenon, a wealth of particulars—people, situations, events, occasions, and so on. The human condition, in all of its varied, idiosyncratic, unusual, mundane, exotic aspects, plays itself out before one's eyes. The potency of this overwhelming flood of unorganized data to disturb one's cognitive map of structures, hypotheses, and point of view cannot be overestimated. One sits in wide-eyed and "innocent" wonder and tries to capture, as much as possible, in the field notes and the summary observations and interpretations the drama going on.

The Interpretive Aside. Along the way, a variety of ideas, insights, and interesting associations of ideas, events, and people arise. We tend to jot these down into the notes as "(Obs- ...)". They seem to "pop out" in the normal give-and-take of observing and talking with people in the setting. Often they have a free-associational quality ("reminds me of...") and sometimes they are simple perceptual comparisons or contrasts. This technique or procedure we sort of "fell into" while beginning *Complexities*. It seemed sensible to make at least a quick note of the "insights" or "bright ideas" that seemed to be arising effortlessly along the way. My hunch is that many get lost if not jotted down at the time. Later we found these to be very useful in that part of the analysis process we have called "generating concepts and hypotheses." Students whose notebooks are full of these seem to move the analysis along much easier than those whose notes are more limited.

Conscious Searching. Concomitantly with the almost unconsciously determined items of the interpretive asides there is the omnipresent question, "What does it all mean?" This is a search for overall patterns, for broad themes which seem to break the phenomenon into large chunks or domains. This is an active searching for order. Sometimes, as with the historical emphasis in the case study of science education in the Alte District, it came early, from reading Toulmin in general and Westbury in particular. It seemed to "keep working for me" in the sense of methodologically guiding me toward interesting data and, substantively, in turning up interesting problems and perspectives. It became a major theme of the final report. Further, it left me with a bit of unresolved tension: ''Next time, or soon at least, I want to do a *for real* historical study.'' That brings us back full circle to a foreshadowed problem (in this instance, a mix of problem and procedure) and means that the next study is already cracked open enough to have a beginning point of attack. Such events remind me of Henry Murray's concept of serial, a longer-term unit in a theory of personality. He illustrates with friendships, marriages, and careers. More recently Beittel (1973) has adapted the concept for studying creativity in drawing. His argument is that understanding the production of any one piece of art requires knowledge of prior work and intended future work, an artistic serial. The parallels to cumulative research seem obvious. The conscious searching for patterns, in effect, is not only within the single project but also throughout the series of projects over time.

The conscious search for analytical or interpretive meaning moves concurrently with data collection. Glaser and Strauss (1967) have called the process ''theoretical sampling'': ''data collection for the purpose of generating theory whereby the analyst jointly collects, codes, and analyzes his data and decides what data to collect next and where to find them, in order to develop his theory as it emerges'' (p. 45). A number of concepts are subsumed under the generic concept of theoretical sampling. Among these are saturation, slices of data, and depth. By saturation, Glaser and Strauss mean that no additional data are found which contribute to the properties of the categories under consideration. This is a useful but tricky concept. It assumes that one knows in advance or along the way what the key categories are and where the locus of information is. We have not found it quite that easy. As we work in a particular context or setting we try to exploit that setting for all of the information and all of the ideas we can find. In a sense, we keep looking until we can generate no more ''insights'' and ''interpretive asides.'' It is at that point that we tend to quit. In this situation our experience has been that beyond the initial focus, the narrative or story line soon carries us into a whole variety of other problems and issues that we had not anticipated in our preliminary entrance to the problem. This is moving from the foreshadowed problems into the theoretical issues. The ''Rural Highland'' project was a beautiful example of this. Initially we had conceived the project in terms of the psychology of mathematics teaching. As we began carrying out our observation, however, the exigencies of the situation shifted the focus of investigation to the politics of education, interorganizational issues, the problems of introducing sophisticated 20th-century technology into an underdeveloped region, and the like. In a very real sense, the twin concepts of saturation and flexibility run parallel courses in the field work.

As is becoming explicit in the several items in this discussion of cognitive processes, data analysis occurs throughout the project, and also the social context of the project impinges on the intellectual aspects of the work. In our reflections on the *Alte* case study (Smith, 1977b), we raised the idea of ''project press'':

"the short time line on CSSE produced enormous pressure to move quickly, to begin intensive attempts at conceptualizing early, to seek workable outlines. This produced a series of stresses, some of which were toward conceptualization and interpretation" (p. 128). We were on a one-semester, portal-to-portal time line: enter in January, final report due the first of June. We were finished (in several senses) on the first of July. Some of our colleagues in the other case studies were on shorter time lines—a month's observation and interviewing, with varying deadline dates. In every project we have been on, deadlines were posed by aspects of the projects themselves, by contracts for final reports, by AERA presentations, by new activities, by recurring responsibilities at the Graduate Institute of Education. These have exerted a press to finish particular pieces of work, and variations on the form of the intellectual processes of data collection, analysis, and write-up have developed. These were felt most intensely while still in the setting.

In one form or another these cognitive activities, along the way, appear in accounts of most field workers. They are vivid and potent experiences which contrast dramatically with images created by Campbell and Stanley's brief account of the one-shot case study. They seem more akin to an extended and sometimes multiple time series quasi experiment.

Final Analysis and Writing

The overall image I'm trying to arouse in this section on cognitive processes is intended to be one of creative thinking, the generation and construction of concepts, perspectives, and theories from an initial set of problems, through a long period of sought and unsought percepts and experiences in the field setting, to some final kind of order which appears as a written report. Its open-ended quality frightens some novices and critics and exhilarates others.

The Case as an Instance of a Class of Events. Eventually, if not early on, comes one of the most difficult and elusive problems, locating the case as an instance of a more general class of events. I think this gives researchers from other traditions great difficulty with the early stages of participant observer research, particularly as done by neophytes (e.g., doctoral students), because they cannot specify their problems clearly enough. The outsider seldom is content with "a description and analysis of X," for X is usually a particular concrete setting (e.g., Geoffrey's class, the first year of the Kensington School, science education in the ALTE School District). In a hypothesis-testing sense, there is no problem. The difficulty that neither the student nor the critic perceives is the theoretical complexity in coming to grips with what is the substantive problem in the investigation.

We tried to address the issue in the project entitled "Mrs. Kaye's Drawing Class" (Smith, 1975a). In coping with the "problem" under investigation, I constructed an abstraction ladder of one element, the kind of learning under consideration. At the most concrete level, I, as student-participant-observer, was learning to sketch wine bottles with charcoal. Sketching wine bottles is one instance of charcoal drawing, which is an instance of one kind of representational drawing. Learning representational drawing is an instance of a broader class of learning artistic skills, which in turn is an instance of an even broader class, productive learning, wherein one produces something. In that study, I eventually decided that I wanted to work at the level of a theory of productive learning, interrelated with conceptions of curriculum and teaching. Alternatively, that research might have been conceptualized as a study in representational drawing or a study in artistic skills.

I believe this kind of process occurs throughout social science but that it is neither well recognized nor dealt with effectively in most observational research, or for that matter in other genres of educational research. Paul Meehl speaks to a similar problem in *Clinical vs. Statistical Prediction* (1954). Prediction, for Meehl, requires that an individual event be put into a class of events for which probabilities exist. Predictions of whether Jane Doe will go to a movie on Friday night will vary, depending on whether you know frequencies of Friday night movie attendance, of women attending Friday night movies, of women having dates, or of women with a recently broken leg attending Friday night movies. Jane Doe could be classified correctly into any one of those cells, but each would give a different probability. Other instances come to mind. Some years ago, in reading Skinner's *The Behavior of Organisms* (1938), one of the most brilliant and stunning, and, in hindsight, possibly misguided illustrations of this occurs in the first 60 pages, Chapters 1 and 2. For those interested in a model of theory building, his discussion of the experimental box as "environment," of white rat as "organism," of bar press as "operant," and of operant as "spontaneous behavior" is breathtaking.

For our purposes, Diesing (1971) captures best the importance of the issue under examination:

If I had to generalize at this premature stage, I would be inclined to point to the problem of the One and the Many as the essential problem of scientific method. Any scientific account of human society must somehow deal not only with the uniqueness of which human history and individual life histories consist, but also with the regularities of various sorts that appear in history. If I were to work out this problem in detail to determine how adequately various methods deal with it, case study methods would come out on top. They include both the particular and the universal within science instead of consigning the particular to intuition, practical application, or history; they exhibit the universal within the particular instead of segregating the two in one way or another; and they move from particular to universal and back by gradual steps rather than in one grand jump. (p. 296)

As we have indicated throughout this essay, such thoughts are continually salient. In the final analysis, if not before, the researcher must stake out the domain in what often seems like the shifting sands of multiple levels of abstraction across domains of theory.

Skimming the Cream: An Initial Overview. In the appendix to our study of the extended pilot trials of an aesthetic education program (Smith & Schumacher, 1972) we used a metaphor we called "skimming the cream." In a sense this is another perspective on what kind of a case one has. Here the procedure is more inductive and more "quick and dirty." In my view, metaphors from other occupations, life-styles, and eras probably do not carry the full meaning one intends, but they help. One of the consequences of research in a bureaucratic organization is being faced with deadlines. A second is limited time to do a task. The situation was this. During our last week of data collection we had to make a brief presentation of results to the several parties of the larger project we were investigating; these individuals were making decisions regarding the form the project would take in the succeeding years. The tactic we adopted was a simple one. In a local coffee shop, for a period of a couple of hours, we asked ourselves: "What are the major things we have learned from our year in the field?" As we brainstormed these ideas, with no reference to our file drawer of notes, interpretive asides, or summary interpretations (some of which were still untyped on tapes because of organization resource problems), we gradually accumulated a list of ideas, findings. We pushed and pulled on these until they gradually fell into reasonable broader topics and differentiated outlines. Points of debate were joined and countered with images recalled from classroom observations and informal conversations (interviews) with children, teachers, and supervisors. The most intriguing methodological question this raises is suggested by the "skimming the cream" metaphor. In this simple procedure, can the really significant rich items be obtained? Do the labored procedures suggested by Becker et al. (1961) in the *Boys in White* analysis and by Glaser and Strauss (1967) in their constant-comparative method yield more creative, more comprehensive, or more reliable theory and interpretations? Our guess is that the differences in creative propositions are probably minimal. Some comprehensiveness is probably lost by cream skimming. The reliability of interpretation, or perhaps better, the confidence in the interpretation, probably drops off more sharply. For students of methodology this is obviously a testable empirical problem.

Another, related aspect of cream skimming involves the preparation of initial statements of parts of the report. Here we have been caught with limited time to do the report—two months instead of a year. Essentially we have picked up on the brainstormed issues, returned to the notes to check them, elaborate them, and refine them. This is in marked contrast to alternative procedures of quick total review of all notes and careful page-by-page reading with cumulating analysis, or careful reading, categorizing, and tabulating as done in the constant-comparative approach. The empirical question remains. Does the quick and dirty cream skimming yield 20, 50, 70, or 90% of the total from the more systematic analysis?

Developing Individual Sections. From one perspective, the methods of data analysis I use seem terribly inefficient and unsystematic. After such processes of skimming our recollections for key items, and after the files have been organized into a chronology with separate sections for my field notes, my summary observation notes, the notes of colleagues and assistants, and the various kinds of documents, and after I have done some reviewing of the specific contents of the overall project, I usually start back at the beginning of the notes. I read along and seem to engage in two kinds of processes—comparing and contrasting, and looking for antecedents and consequences.

The essence of concept formation is—and somehow I'd never quite seen it back in the days when I was administering the Wechsler and WISC—"How are they alike, and how are they different?" As items appear in the perceptual images, as verbal comments are recorded, as situations appear, as events come and go, one asks a simple two-sided question: How are they alike, and how are they different? The similar things are grouped and given a label that highlights their similarity. The different things are grouped, insofar as possible, and given labels. There always is a large "miscellaneous" category of items which seem important but which do not fit anywhere. The *seem* is critical. There is always a hunch lurking behind the *seem* and, given more data, more time, and more thought, the pieces find a place in relation to one another. Earlier we called this the "jigsaw puzzle analogy" (Smith, 1967). This metaphor reflected not only the multiple pieces of a jigsaw one was trying to put together, but the very important aspect of actually shaping the individual pieces themselves. In time, these similarities and differences come to represent clusters of concepts, which then organize themselves into more abstract categories and eventually into hierarchical taxonomies.

Concurrently, a related but different process is occurring. Some time ago, I was impressed by Robert Merton's insight into social theory and social structure. The item that came to represent the totality was the beautiful label "latent and unanticipated dysfunctional consequences." My psychological background had urged a search for causes, for reasons, for determinants of a child's reading problem, for disaffection in school, for family difficulties. The conscious search for the consequences of social items, in all their combinations—latent and manifest, anticipated and unanticipated, functional and dysfunctional—seemed to flesh out a complex systemic view and a concern for process, the flow of events over time. In addition it seemed to argue for a more holistic, systemic, interdependent network of events at the concrete level and concepts and propositions at an abstract level. Zetterberg's argument for multiple ways of ordering propositions—inventories of determinants, inventories of consequences, chain patterns, and finally axiomatic formats—blended the theoretical with the concrete flow. At a practical level, while in the field, the thinking, searching, and note recording reflected not only a consciousness of similarities and differences but also an attempt to look for unexpected relationships, antecedents, and consequences within the flow of items.

These twin processes seem to capture the best of concept formation, in contrast to concept attainment, and of hypothesis development, in contrast to hypothesis testing. For us, they specify, almost operationally, the meaning of Glaser and Strauss's beautiful idea and label, "the discovery of grounded theory" and Diesing's equally apt term, "patterns of discovery."

There is a social dimension to these. No project occurs in isolation, at least when one studies social phenomena in one's own society. The importance of this for the gradually developing analysis and the progressive refocusing of data collection seems obvious to most field workers, and it is underestimated by most investigators using more set designs, whether experimental, quasi experimental, or survey. One illustration conveys the general point. As we were observing events at the Kensington School and talking casually with Professor Edwin Bridges, he took items about the fervor of the participants, the total time commitments, and the enthusiasm, and suggested that they sounded like Hoffer's (1951) true believers. Immediately the relevance of the more general conception was obvious. Later, Pat Keith found extensions to Klapp's (1969) crusades. Every project we have undertaken has always rippled in and out of other events in our professional lives. Such experience makes the "one-shot case study" label a serious misnomer. Everyday in the field is a new quasi experiment, guided and enriched by an intellectually stimulating environment of persons, supportive and critical; of ideas, mundane and all encompassing; of chores and opportunities. These events play in and through the field experience.

Collapsing Outlines. In every participant observer study we have undertaken we have experienced a further phenomenon, one we have called "collapsing outlines." As we have begun analyzing the data, usually in terms of the foreshadowed problems which initially guided our entry and data collection, we have come upon interpretative asides and latent theoretical issues which seem a vital part of the setting and our understanding of it. As pieces are developed, we keep making tentative outlines that put some larger meaningful and logical order into the interpretation. Invariably the tentative outlines collapse in the face of more complex data and ideas. This seems another, later stage item in the definition and redefinition of the problems as a theoretical issue. Empirically, the dated sequences of outlines as we grappled with the meaning of our problem would be a helpful addition to this discussion.

Collapsing outlines seems very similar to a number of accounts of creativity in various artistic disciplines (Beittel, 1972; Gribble, 1970; Housman, 1933). While most artists begin a work with an initial idea, the gradually developing picture, poem or novel seems to develop something of a life of its own. Resolutions to particular problems create structures which not only constrain future decisions but also often suggest options which the individual creator had not perceived earlier. So it seems with problems, data, and analysis in participant observation. The initial problems are jarred by the interpretative asides. Recalcitrant pieces of data and negative instances are there and demand to be integrated. Finally, and most devastatingly, large, reasonably intact outlines tend to collapse because the weight of the data and the developing ideas in the analysis are too much for the earlier formulated conceptual structure. Eventually we have an outline which holds. It has a structure reflecting three major dimensions: integrity, complexity, and creativity. By integrity I mean it has a theme, a thesis, a point of view. The pieces fit together as an interrelated part-whole relationship. By complexity, I mean the outline has enough discriminable pieces to cover the major themes and the minor nuances, the large elements, and the nooks and crannies necessary to do justice to the system under study. Finally, by creativity, I mean the outline conveys some novel and important ideas to some relevant audience—the people in the system, the educational research community, and/or some practitioner who is teaching, administering, or working in the educational community.

Summary

As should be obvious by now, we have wrestled with and been guided by a number of field workers: Homans, Malinowski, Becker, Bruyn, Glaser and Strauss, Denzin, McCall and Simmons, Whyte, Iannaccone, Van Velsen, and others. All of them kept speaking to and answering questions we kept running into. Perhaps the most amazing experience has been rereading some of the early favorites (e.g., Homans and Whyte) and finding how much Homans and Whyte had learned and had to teach the second and third time through, several years later.

CLUSTERS OF MULTIPLE DIMENSIONS OF PARTICIPANT OBSERVATION

To this point I have argued that the educational research community exemplified by Campbell and Stanley has focused on the experiment and the quasi experiment as the dominant mode of knowing. I have suggested that such a view may represent the norms of the major community in education and psychology but that other social science communities—in anthropology and parts of sociology, especially—have developed their own traditions. Within education, a smaller subcommunity has evolved which has attracted a number of practitioners, researchers, and theorists and has begun to institutionalize itself more formally. More particularly I have described in some detail one researcher's attempt to implement, through a series of studies, this strand of participant observer research. Now, I intend to distance myself from those particular experiences and formulate a more abstract structure for analyzing and evaluating research work within this genre. This task seems both difficult and necessary. Regarding the difficulties, early on we thought that there might be a unitary phenomenon called "standard participant observation procedures" which could be used as a paradigm for analyzing and eventually judging any particular piece of educational ethographic research. Paul Pohland and I (Smith & Pohland 1974, 1976) disabused ourselves of that hope. We argued then that on such dimensions as emphasis on the descriptive narrative, generation of theory, verification of theory, and quantification, important participant observer studies varied quite markedly. As a consequence, I am more inclined to ask for a clear statement of actual procedures and an intellectual cost/benefit analysis of those procedures for the problems at hand and the purposes in mind. In this section, four related clusters of concerns will be used to chart the multiple dimensions of participant observation.

While these clusters of concern pattern themselves like a piece of woven cloth, for analytical purposes they can be broken into warp, weft, colors, and textures. In order of increasing abstraction they include these levels: (1) data, (2) descriptive narrative, (3) analytical-theoretical-interpretive, and (4) metatheoretical. The necessity of such efforts arises in the needs of various individuals and groups who must make decisions in training students, in reviewing project proposals, and in judging research reports for publication.

The Data Level

In analyzing and judging a piece of observational research, a series of questions can be raised concerning the data and how they were collected. The resulting cluster of dimensions—direct on-site observation, freedom of access, intensity of observation, triangulation and multimethods, sampling, and attention to muted cues and unobtrusive signs—seems to comprise the major conditions assuring valid data.

Direct On-site Observation. At the simplest and most basic level, participant observation, in the sense of "being in" or "living in" the setting, involves the researcher directly in the social behavior under study. Being on site is the sine qua non of ethnographic research. It distinguishes the research from surveys, from interview studies, from laboratory studies, from testing studies. Such direct on-site observation assumes several conditions in social life. For instance, individuals in institutions, organizations, and groups often mask what is happening in the setting, for a number of reasons. That is, they create formal doctrines, develop facades, or perhaps "wallpaper over" significant issues and events. On such occasions any researcher faces major problems at the data level in regard to what is "really" going on. This masking cannot be done so easily when one is observing directly at meetings, talking informally to participants at coffee klatsches, and taking part as people relate to one another in situ. While useful for many purposes, questionnaires, tests, and formal reports of events, insofar as they attest to social behavior and events, are indirect observations of those events and are susceptible to all kinds of distortions, both conscious and unconscious. The makers of K, L and F scales on the MMPI and other tests are wont to indicate this possibility when individuals fake good or fake bad, both consciously and unconsciously. In other settings and on other occasions individuals have been known to "stonewall," to lie, and to develop fictional reports to hide organizational realities.

The magnitude of importance of these points is so fundamental yet so "obvious" that it seems unnecessary to elaborate further. It emphasizes and reemphasizes our continual preoccupation with valid data of social events. In part our later discussion amounts to means to control or lessen possible difficulties in learning from such simple direct observation.

Freedom of Access.   Conversations with observers—particularly short-term evaluators of educational programs— indicate a concern that they are being steered toward particular teachers, or classes, or schools or that they do not have access to other particular settings, people, or events. Usually these issues are settled at the time of entry; usually they are an interrelated function of the initial foreshadowed problems, the boundaries of the system under study, the more general purposes undergirding the research, and the evolving social relationships of the researcher in the setting. For instance, in *Complexities* the formal agreements that I had with the superintendent and the principal of the Washington School were that I would be in Geoffrey's class and go with him wherever his duties took him—lunch duty, yard duty, and so on. I was not to go into any other classroom unless invited. Our basic interest was his classroom, and that's where I spent most of my days. However, the clique of teachers with whom he associated included the eighth-grade "teacher in charge" and the clerk in the main office. Geoffrey set up a coffee bar where a number of teachers congregated and gossiped before school and at recess. We lunched usually with a group of the men teachers. I became good friends with several teachers and we chatted on several occasions through lunch and through their free period when the children were with the physical education teachers. While the focus was on Geoffrey's class, I was socialized more generally into the faculty of the Washington School. At Kensington, our agreements were such that all meetings—general, faculty, teams, PTA, and so on—were open to us, as well as all classes, curricular areas, and lessons. We were free to talk with anyone who was willing to talk to us. More recently in the Alte School District, in our study of science curriculum (Smith, 1977b), some of the staff had been in class with me at the university. We had discussed participant observer research in detail. When the project began they opened conversation with comments such as "You'll probably be interested in some of this..." and brought out stacks of curriculum guides, reports, newsletters, and so on. Once again, as part of the informed-consent procedures, teachers willing to participate, after a discussion of the project, signed consent forms describing the kind of access we hoped for.

The main point: In studying schooling most field workers negotiate broad access relevant to the questions under study. Insofar as the relations among problem, purpose, settings, and events have been perceived initially, they are able to gather relevant data. A subcondition we try to emphasize is the freedom to come to classes, meetings, and other events unannounced or without prior arrangements. Partly this represents convenience in maximizing use of time. Partly it broadens the basis of seeing normal or usual events and increases the validity of the data we are obtaining. When access is limited, for whatever reasons, questions arise regarding the adequacy of the data.

Intensity of Observation. Invariably one of the first and most critical questions regarding the validity of the data concerns the intensity of observation of the system under study. In general, field work is a labor-intensive research mode. In our own work on *The Complexities of an Urban Classroom*, I was there, "almost all day, every day for a semester," sitting in the back of the classroom, taking notes. Geoffrey, as teacher-researcher, was there all day everyday. In *Anatomy*, the intensity of involvement was recorded in a footnote to the study:

During the study, school was in session 177 days from September to June. The workshop had involved four weeks in August. The observers have field notes from 153 *different* days at the school or in the district and 247 total entries. The latter indicates the overlap when both of us were in the field. Although it is possible to speak of 247 man-days of observation, this is faulty in the sense that some of the entries reflect part days and some reflect early morning to mid-night days. One of our colleagues phrased it colloquially but cogently when he commented, "You were all over that school." The intensity of involvement is a key issue in the validity of the data. (Smith & Keith, 1971, p. 10)

Several implications follow upon the issue of intensity of observation. First, the possibility of individuals "faking" their behavior, intentionally or unintentionally, seems less probable. The multiple actors are caught in a thick web of historical and contemporaneous interconnections. As observer, I kept listening and looking for offhand comments, raised eyebrows, hints that any one was behaving uncharacteristically. Reactions from pupils who had been in class the prior year, from teachers a grade below or a grade above, and from staff friends were constantly being scanned at the odd moment and setting of lunch or recess. Becker (1970) makes similar points in contrasting field work with the laboratory experiment. In the latter setting, the "subject" is totally removed from the social constraints of real life and is susceptible to experimenter intentions and nuances of experimenter behavior, as Orne (1962) and other have argued. In such a context the "pristine" qualities of laboratory data and results take on other shades of meaning.

The intensity of observation, in the sense of length of time in the field, interacts with the conceptual, theoretical stance one takes. In most of our work we have had a concern for processes over time, a theory of action. Early on, it was more implicit; more recently we have been trying to make it explicit. In regard to our data collection, we have tried to be around for a period of time that reflects commonsense boundaries—a semester, a year, the life of a project, and so forth. I suppose such units are comparable to the annual cycle in the life of a primitive group. Schools, in part, have an annual or semiannual opening or beginning; an establishment of order, structure, and routines; a long steady state period; and a closing or termination of the year. By observing throughout such a cycle one is privy to the special problems of phases in the social activities of the system, and one sees particular actors—administrators, teachers, pupils—coping with each other at critical, different points in time. Early on we had an intuitive feel that these data were more critical for teachers and administrators in our classes, in the sense of giving them help in thinking about their problems. Now we see this as a part of a larger theory of action conception.

The main point is that there is a need for a statement of the intensity of observation so that readers can assess the credibility of the results. A secondary point is a caution in moving toward a simple checklist-type judgment. The amount of time interacts with the scope and focus of the problem. A tertiary point is a common concern for adequacy of data across modalities of social science.

Qualitative and Quantitative Data.   Traditionally, participant observers and educational ethnographers have shied away from quantitative data—from tests, questionnaires, or structured interviews. In my own case, early on I deliberately did so because I did not want to defend what we were doing in terms of the canons of the quantitative test literature. I had spent a year attending to the validity of children's personality and adjustment tests (Smith, 1958). I thought I was on to a very different kind of problem; I wanted it judged on another set of criteria. Now I think many of the arguments about qualitative and quantitative data are pseudo issues. Some field workers, such as Blau (1955), count kinds of interaction to make specific points. Others, such as Becker et al. (1961), quantify field note records regarding particular issues; on occasion we have taken issue with such procedures (e.g., Smith & Geoffrey, 1968, pp. 255–256, the two realities problem).

Some educational anthropologists (Cazden, John, & Hymes, 1972; Cicourel, Jennings, Jennings, Leiter, Mackay, Mehan, & Roth, 1974; Erickson, 1975), pursuing more specific substantive problems in the "new ethnography" rather than the broader, more holistic study of a group or a community, have moved to audio and video tapes of classroom events and the beginnings of quantitative analyses of these. From these records, they reconstruct the implicit meanings in speech and nonverbal behavior. My guess is that this tradition will gradually merge with the time-sampling tradition of study begun in child development by Goodenough (1928), Olson (1930), and others. In addition it will probably merge with the large literature on quantitative observation of teaching and classroom events, work well summarized in Dunkin and Biddle (1974) and Simon and Boyer (1967). A quick, nonquantitative survey of Dunkin and Biddle's book on teaching and Cicourel et al.'s (1974) book on language and school performance suggests a minimal overlap in reference citations. The work of Barker and his colleagues (1954, 1964) stresses direct observation of social settings and quantified records, but it too has remained as a nearly independent tradition. I find these to be puzzlements in the social science of knowledge.

Triangulation and Multimethods.   Even though one tries to stay at the data level, the phenomena keep dragging one back to one's purposes and one's more general conceptions. Briefly I have indicated some of the dimensions of participant observation at the data level which enable one to analyze any piece of work and to begin to see the methodological structure of any project. A further argument needs to be entertained—that is, the nature of combining and synthesizing the multiple kinds of data implicitly and explicitly raised in the discussion.

Our attempts to deal with the issue have been mainly an outgrowth of Campbell and Fiske's (1959) multimethod, multitrait approach to construct validity in psychological measurement and Denzin's (1970) concept of triangulation. By triangulation, Denzin means the use of multiple kinds of data brought to bear on a single problem or issue. At an initial level, all of our studies combine direct observation interviews and conservations and document analysis, all of which we bring to bear on the issues at hand. A similar but more sophisticated analysis is made by Campbell and Fiske (1959). Their argument is simple and powerful. In checking the validity of psychological tests to give a picture of an individual, one needs multiple instruments dealing with multiple traits. The pattern of intercorrelations allows one to detect reliability coefficients and two kinds of validity coefficients: convergent coefficients, where the several instruments measuring the same trait should be high, and divergent coefficients, where the test formats are similar but the traits are different and the coefficients should be low. At the time of their writing, and probably now as well, the psychometric data available on most instruments was severely limited.

In our work we think we are pursuing a similar paradigm, even though our data are qualitative and even though they are more a patchwork of partially filled cells and inferences. Figure 1 presents our elements of a multimethod, multiper-

1. Methods
   1.1 Observation
   1.2 Informal interviews
   1.3 Documents: lesson materials, computer printouts, et cetera
2. Persons
   2.1 Pupils
   2.2 Cooperating teachers
   2.3 Principals
   2.4 Other teachers
   2.5 Multiple incumbents of multiple positions in multiple organizations
3. Situations
   3.1 Pupils at terminals
   3.2 Classroom teaching: announced and unannounced visits
   3.3 Multiple parts of the curriculum, in addition to arithmetic
   3.4 Multiple schools
   3.5 Multiple organizations
   3.6 Multiple parts of the country
4. Variables
   4.1 Individual: schemas, traits, motives
   4.2 Group: classroom interaction, activity, sentiments
   4.3 Organizational: schools, universities, R & D, Title III

Figure 1. Elements of a multimethod, multiperson, multisituation, and multivariable matrix. (Smith & Pohland, 1974).

son, multisituation, and multivariable matrix. The picture of the phenomenon—for instance, Geoffrey's classroom, the innovative Kensington School, the computer-assisted instruction in the rural highlands, or science education in Alte—involves the interrelation of data from different sources (observation, interviews, documents), different people (teachers, administrators, school board members), different situations (classrooms, schools, board meetings), and different variables and concepts—systems, norms, interactions, individual schemas.

When the items fit, agree, or are congruent, the picture evolves confidently. In the Alte High School, as I was trying to come to grips with the nature of social science, it was revealing that most of the faculty had degrees in history, that the psychology courses (and instructor) were not listed as part of the social science department, and that the social science department office sign said "History Department." Such items led to several interpretations about a dimension, degree of breadth, in social science at Alte High School. The central thrust of the multimethod approach seems to be an argument for internal consistency; the data hang together, the correlations would be high if data were scaled and quantified.

When the data do not hang together, one cannot throw out the tests or items and go back to the drawing boards. The problem is more difficult. Usually it sends one back for more data. Is an individual lying, seeing only part of the system, or ignorant of a whole set of events? Is the principal conveying his own wishful thinking of what science education is in his building? Is the faculty sketching out "what they are reaching for," "trying to do," rather than the day-to-day realities? Or is it, as the test makers might see it, that there is another trait or variable involved? In an important sense, one begins to reconstrue one's conception of the phenomenon. In a brief but powerful statement, Charters and Jones (1973) caution about the risk of appraising nonevents in program evaluation. Specifically, they ask: "When has an innovation been adopted?" Their analysis produces a conceptualization of four levels of organizational activity: institutional commitment, structural context, role performance, and learning context. Such a conception puts order into the discrepant data one finds in formal documents and institutional plans, in discussion of administrative strategy and tactics, in teachers' day-to-day activities, and in pupil activities. The new conception sends one back for more data to check its adequacy. If the distinctions are sound, the data should diverge, just as correlations should be low on tests measuring traits which are independent (e.g., intelligence and weight).

Attempts to triangulate or to build multimethod matrices with qualitative data often result in congruencies which strengthen the validity of the picture one is drawing. When the data do not converge then one checks the points with more data, reconstrues the phenomenon, that is, makes more subtle distinctions than one began with, and then one goes for more data to recheck the new descriptive model, conceptual system, or interpretation. Van Velsen (1967), in discussing the final report and its credibility, argues for inclusion of lengthy excerpts from field notes. These notes, which include some context beyond the central point entered by the author, permit the reader to regroup and reorder them for her or his own analytical and verificational purposes. Van Velsen's label for this is "situational analysis."

In short, these investigators are arguing for a common criterion—data from multiple methods brought together on common issues and presented in a way that the reader can perceive each source clearly and can begin to weigh the overall credibility and significance of the analytic interpretation.

The Sampling Problem at the Data Level. Whenever one cannot be everywhere in the system all of the time, one is faced with the sampling problem just as other social scientists doing more quantitative survey or experimental research are faced with the problem of sampling. Our comments here intertwine with earlier remarks (e.g., intensity of observation) and with later remarks on the descriptive and theoretical purposes of the particular projects. In the case study of science education in the Alte School District we were trying for a descriptive, analytic account of the nature of science education (math, natural science, and social science) in kindergarten through grade 12. Even for a small district, a hopelessly large task. With the problem stated—"What is the nature of science education in the district?"—a tentative sampling plan, Figure 2, was conceived.

SAMPLING DOMAINS

1. Principals

2. Schools and teachers

3. Classes and teachers by weeks:

	Cycle 1	Cycle 2 Social	Cycle 3	Cycle 4 Alternative
High School	Science	Science	Math	high school
Junior High	Team 1, 7th	Team 2, 8th	Team 2, 7th	Team 1, 8th
Elementary	School A	School B	School C	School D

4. Elementary Curriculum Committee: Science, Math, Social Studies

5. High School committees preparing for North Central Evaluation: Policy, Math, Science, Social Studies

6. Special circumstances:
   a. Citizens, school board members
   b. Knowledgeable professionals who have contacts in the district
   c. Faculty meetings, PTA meetings, etc.
   d. Special events, programs, activities

Figure 2. An early sampling plan for the Alte study (Adapted from *Science Education in the Alte Schools,* by L. M. Smith (NSF Case Studies in Science Education), 1977).

The logic of the plan was quite simple and was built on conventional wisdom about schools in general and Alte in particular. I talked with each of the principals. Typically, this was in the form of an open-ended oral history interview: What's science education like in your building? This usually had several components: an hour of taped comments; a walk through the building with running comments on facilities, materials, and staff; an armful of documents; and initial meetings with particular teachers by chance and design. In effect they conveyed, at least initially, their perspective of science education—curricularly and organizationally, hopes and realities, problems and successes. It seemed that I needed to see teaching and learning in process; consequently I devised a possible way of cycling through schools, levels, and domains of science during the semester of field work. Early on I found there were curriculum committees and, even more importantly, by chance, that Alte High was in its self-study year, getting ready for a North Central Evaluation. I was permitted to and did join some of those 7:15 a.m. discussions. A number of special circumstances also arose. I interviewed people with special perspectives on the district—long-term residents, parents, school board members, professionals who enter the schools for various reasons (psychologists, university professors, etc.), and districtwide central office personnel. Some of these were early "Tell me about science education in Alte," and some were more exit interviews. The latter started with "Tell me" and soon evolved into a series of "How about . . .?" wherein I raised interpretive hypotheses. The major point here, however, is that we had a rough initial image of the territory. We tried, through interviews, observation, and document analysis, to cover that territory.

Time restrictions in Alte caused us to modify in several ways the more formal plan outlined in Figure 2. For instance, the classroom observations shifted to an initial concentration on the junior high school—every science, math, and social studies teacher was observed at least once, and a number were observed several times. Usually these were intertwined with brief to several-hour interviews. Most of the elementary school observations were concentrated in two schools. At the high school I observed several teachers in each department—usually a mix of those I had known and not known. Typically these were of the unannounced "May I sit with you this morning?" type. No request was refused; often there were comments such as "Today's a lab . . . a review . . . a film" and so forth. I said "Fine" and went in to see what was happening. Usually I was given a copy of the text or lab materials, and a brief comment or two locating the lesson in the broader perspective of the course, department offerings, or grade-level sequences. Similarly, I hunted documents—high school yearbooks, curriculum guides, reports of curriculum committees, and, significantly, the *Alte School News*, a newsletter to the citizens of the community. Some of these I scanned, some I read intensely with particular questions in mind. Again they presented a sampling problem.

Most participant observers don't speak to the issues of sampling. In our view it lurks behind every decision the investigator makes when he elects to be here or there, to spend more time here rather than there, and decides what array of documents to read, of people to interview, of settings to hang around. At the data level, the question is always, "Have I seen the nooks and crannies of the system as well as the main arenas, to give a valid picture of the system?" The main criterion we strive to meet is to know the total system better than any participant, who is often restricted to a particular niche or position in the system. As we learn more about the system at its concrete level, we find areas we hadn't anticipated, and we find we have to shift plans. This shift in plans has been called "progressive refocusing" by Parlett and Hamilton (1972) and speaks to the flexibility of the methodology. Similarly, Glaser and Strauss (1967) have spoken of "theoretical sampling." In their discussion, they are attending to the problems of the kinds of ideas and theory being generated and the shift in activities at the data level as the more abstract problems under investigation are clarified. My central point is that the participant observer, in a procedures chapter or a methodological appendix, needs to convey to the reader his initial plans and intentions, the changes along the way, and the final resolutions and accompanying reasons. In this manner, the reader, or the skeptic who wants to replicate, can see clearly how and why he did what he did.

Muted Cues and Unobtrusive Signs. Close observation in a setting produces what Andrew Halpin (1966) has called "muted cues" and what Webb, Campbell, Schwartz, and Sechrest (1966) have called "unobtrusive measures." When the clerk in the Washington School sat silently "working" within earshot while I had my entry conversation with the principal, and two weeks later she thought it would be a good joke on the principal to make out a central office timecard for me to sign first and then for him to sign, I began to form an image that she had more to do with the social structure of the school than the formal organization chart indicated. In spite of my initial anxiety, it turned out to be a good joke, she thought, and thereafter she cheerfully volunteered neighborhood and school stories and items "for your book": items from the mailman who walked through the community daily, from local shopkeepers, and from parents, not to mention items from downtown office personnel that came by her desk. In effect, the muted language, the unobtrusive traces of social life, suggest a host of important, often unverbalized issues that enhances the quality of data available to the directly observing inquirer, in contrast to the inquirer not in the setting. In project proposals, which are based on some pilot observations, I look for data reflecting muted cues and unobtrusive measures. Final reports which don't contain such data seem less significant than those that do.

Summary. In the analysis of the structure of participant observation at the data level, my contextualist bias has encroached to demand that other elements and the multiple interrelations among the elements be stressed. Careful analysis of the project's data does begin to locate it in a position from which judgments of quality can be initiated.

The Descriptive Narrative: A First-Level Interpretation

In considering the multiple dimensions of participant observation, we have been inquiring first into the adequacy of the data generated by the researcher, in the course of which we have commented necessarily but fragmentarily on the uses to which the data are put. Since first reading Homans's *The Human Group*

(1950), I have been struck with the impact of his descriptive accounts, in everyday language, of a group, organization, or society under consideration, and with his attempts to conceptualize these events in more abstract concepts and propositions. Most of the groups we have studied have evolved over time, and we have usually wanted to grapple with the change processes in the group during these periods. The latent agenda seemed to be a belief that the process issues (in contrast to the structural) are more critical for teachers, school administrators, and curriculum developers, our usual audiences. This has led us to argue for "telling the story" of the characters, settings, incidents, and on occasion the drama of conflict, crisis, and denouement. More recently we have been persuaded by White's (1963) analysis of the logic of historical narrative that there is not "a" narrative or "the" narrative; rather, multiple narratives might be written.

White's Analysis.   In his "The Logic of Historical Narration" (1963), White makes a half dozen points which clarify the nature and assumptions of the descriptive narrative in participant observation. He sets the stage with a definition of history:

> . . . every history is a history of some entity which existed for a reasonable period of time, . . . the historian wishes to state what is literally true of it in a sense which distinguishes the historian from a teller of fiction or mendacious stories, and the task of the narrator is to give a connected account of the entities' development in time. (p. 4)

Participant observers, particularly those of us interested in processes of education, should have little difficulty with this initial statement.

Next White distinguishes "a chronicle" from "a history." The former is "a conjunction of non-explanatory empirical statements which expressly mention that subject and which report things that have been true of it at different times" (p. 5). A history is distinguished from the chronicle in that a history employs the notion of explanation. At this level the chronicle is close to our data level. His comments regarding facts in the narrow sense, statements about conditions and statements about events, follow upon this. For White a chronicle is true insofar as its component statements are true. Even as chronicles move toward historical narrative, he expressly indicates that this requires no necessary commitment to a covering law or regularity model of explanation. Nor, in his judgment, is it a commitment to explanation by causes.

Third, he embarks on a major discussion of the meaning of one history being better than another, when both are "true" in the sense of the truth of the items in the chronicle. He comments that historians have developed reasonably clear statements of alternative positions regarding this level of their histories. The list of labels includes subjectivism, essentialism, big battalion history, encyclopedianism, and scientism. Again they seem congruent with various stances on ethnography and participant observation.

Fourth, he argues that calling one history a superior or better history than another piece of work involves more than judgments of truth of facts and truth of causal statements. Finally, regarding historical memorability, he leaves the analyst with a relativistic and contextualist problem: "I know no rock or historical practice or usage upon which to rest some definition of historical memorability" (p. 26). In my judgment, that takes the participant observer, insofar as his descriptive narrative is like an historical narrative, back to a broader contextualist stance of his purposes, his priorities, his problems, and his situation, and the purposes, priorities, problems and situations of his multiple audiences. In a sense this is every researcher's concern. In another sense, I am arguing that the participant observer has a special and potentially very powerful stance toward these issues.

Beittel's Analysis: Presentational Modes. Explicating Kenneth Beittel's approach to participant observation constitutes an exercise in the totality of the methodology. However, his point of view regarding the several narratives which might be written is central to his analysis and provides a complement as well as supplement to White's historical analysis of narrative. In contrast to most participant observers, Beittel focuses on the individual rather than the group. The individual in this case is in an interesting setting, a basement laboratory in the art education building at Pennsylvania State University, and he is involved in "the making of art," a series of drawings using pencil, charcoal, and ink. The laboratory permits time-lapse photographs, notes on the process, and interviews stimulated by the photos. The two-hour weekly sessions continue for ten weeks. Some individuals return for several semesters. Beittel's major assumptions are twofold: ". . . to study the making of art one must move as closely as possible . . . to the creating stream of consciousness, and [secondly] . . . a special participant observer role is essential to this closeness" (1973, p. 8). At the data level, Beittel has (1) mute evidence, that is, the pictures themselves; (2) iconic representations, videotapes and motion pictures of the artist in action; (3) process representations of the evolving art work; that is, the time-lapse still photographs of the developing picture; and (4) the notes kept by the observing researcher and recordings of the interviews between the observer and the artist.

From these data, Beittel argues that several kinds of narratives can be developed. Several of these remain very close to the data. The "first-person singular narrative" is an attempt to "reunite the available information on a drawing's evolution as though the artist were thinking to himself as he works" (1973, p. 34). His examples, such as this one of Larry's, graphically convey the portrayal: "Let's see . . . I'd like to try to get that bad downtown Baltimore feeling. I can see it. How to begin? Like I'm right in the middle, everything stronger than me. But how to get it on the page? What line to hang it on? They need to fan out like. Guess I'll just jump in. Stronger, bolder strokes. There . . . better watch how I mix black and white paints. I'll lose that grunginess of outdoors against that black, black inside feeling—the bar, the strip show. The black's gotta count . . ." (1973, pp. 36–37). But as gripping as the narrative is, it loses for Beittel some of the broader context, both in the long-term serial perspective and in the host of additional elements of meaning and feeling about "downtown Baltimore."

Beittel tries next for what he calls a "multiple consciousness narrative." The artist, Beittel, an assistant, and a visiting psychologist all have taken part in the participant observation of the drawing process. The descriptive narrative produced by these multiple consciousnesses stays at the educated layman's level as the several individuals come to grips with the events and conditions of "a unique time-space artistic process."

Beittel labels a third kind of narrative "literary psychology." It represents an observer with a particular theory in mind which guides his perceiving and reporting but which still remains couched in the language of the general culture. Frequently used theories are those of Freud, Jung, Langer, and so forth. This mode of narration gives Beittel great difficulty. His problem, so it seems to me, is his own creativity. Consider, for example, the following comment:

My procedure, in actual practice, has been that of coining new terms and labels to aid my perception and description of the individual case, arriving at these neologisms as inductively as possible. Since, however, I use the new terms for more than one case, they function somewhat like principles from psychological theory. In truth, they function more usefully when I discuss the problem of representing individual cases in the abstract, or in the general. When I actually speak of a given individual, the terms do not occur as readily. In this book, for example, I have spoken of "artistic causality," "idiosyncratic meaning," and "intentional symbolization." (1973, p. 44–45).

If I read him correctly, Beittel has the beginnings of major sensitizing concepts which reflect both inner and outer perspectives and which have considerable power in thinking about artistic creativity. Informally we have tried to test this potency hypothesis by equating artistic creativity, teacher creativity, and researcher creativity and looking for analogues to Beittel's concepts in these other domains. But my major point is that the generation of these concepts plays back into his observing and narrating. As a consequence, the literary psychology narrative begins to take on a considerably more theoretical appearance.

In what he calls "historical and interpretive modes twice removed from the artist's stream of consciousness," Beittel distances himself in time and specific occasion to develop narratives which I am more inclined to call analytical or theoretical accounts. They continue to have a curious blend of the artist and the observer. In essence he tries to draw out the "artist's conceptualization about making art" as the artist reflects on what he's done. The analogue seems to be similar to our several attempts to capture a teacher's theory of teaching or a principal's theory of administration, that is, to determine what are the working concepts and propositions. Finally, in some if not most or all artists, Beittel pushes toward what the depth psychologists are prone to call more basic or fundamental levels of functioning, and what he calls "the artist's superordinate concepts on the making of art or idiosyncratic artistic myths." These are the more all-inclusive accounts of the meshing of an individual's life and his art. His major examples are autobiographical, "the Bach-music landscape theme" and "the river theme." In time they stretched over decades; in space they ranged from the Susquehanna River to the battlefields of France; and in meaning they captured the full reaches of an evolving life perspective.

Finally, he takes a major position on the observer's relation to the individual(s) he studies. This he labels the "formative hermeneutic mode," a stance which seems close to a Rogerian counseling relationship. Understanding and helping intertwine. The narrative takes on an action perspective.

This commitment to a narrative as one of the outcomes of participant observer research has further major implications on the kind of sociological and psychological theory that one generates and uses. I'm reminded of Becker's arguments in the preface to *Sociological Work* (1970), wherein he sees society as collective action, people doing things together, and sociology as a study of the forms of collective action. Any talk of structures and functions must come back eventually to individuals doing something together. Similarly, Homans's (1950) early admonitions about the "big" words of sociology—status, role, culture, authority—must eventually lead back to human beings doing things in particular times and places. In psychology, Henry Murray's (1938) concerns for persons, situations, actions, proceedings, and serials, not to mention needs and presses, reflect a point of view, a theory, which is compatible with results presented in narrative form. More recently, Sarbin (1977), in the *Nebraska Symposium on Motivation*, has argued that psychological theory needs to be reconstructed around a root metaphor or world view of contextualism which implies, for him, a dramaturgical perspective, units built on historical events and interacting individuals, and concepts such as scenes, plots, roles, and actors if one is to deal with creativity, novelty, and change in the human condition. By implication he is arguing that other theories are less amenable to these issues.

Summary. This discussion of the descriptive narrative has shown how complex and problematic is what we once thought was a necessary but simple task—telling the story of the case under investigation. By appealing to White's analysis of the historical narrative and Beittel's imaginative set of alternatives, we now see a fuller set of distinctions about the narrative. The implications for the kind of psychological and sociological theory are also apparent. The data problems, the metatheoretical dilemmas, and the theoretical stance all contribute a context to the narrative. The individual ethnographer in doing his work is faced with a series of contingent decisions. He who would judge a particular piece of ethnography faces a task no less complex. To think otherwise is to make a serious mistake.

The Theoretical-Analytical-Interpretive Level

In the discussion of clusters of dimensions which can be used for analyzing and evaluating participant observer research, the argument has proceeded from the concrete to the abstract. A number of concerns were raised regarding the quality of the data. At the next level of abstraction, it was argued, most participant observers want to "tell the story" of a group, an organization, a community. To some, such as Erickson (1975), Lévi-Strauss (1963), and Wolcott (1975a), this is the core definition of ethnography. Most researchers, however, want to move more abstractly into what is typically called theory, analysis, or interpretation. At this point, the field splits apart and almost all commonality is lost. For purposes of clarity I propose to describe briefly the evolving position we have taken in much of our work, and then to indicate alternative positions. The arguments for the pros and cons of those positions involve a series of metatheoretical dilemmas, controversies which have plagued social science and philosophy for a long time and which seem to have no clear solutions.

In recent years we have been urging our students to make explicit the theory that is implicit in their studies; that is, we have asked a student, Jones: "What is Jones' theory of . . .?" Over the past few years this has yielded Wood's (1977) theory of localist educational task groups, Yunker's (1977) theory of professional socialization of police officers, Finch's (1978) theory of the teacher and the change process in schools, and Wolfson's (1974) and Lipnick's (1976) theory of post–Bar Mitzvah religious education, to list just a few.

Asking the question, What is your theory of . . .? forces the inquirer to attend to issues such as: What is meant by theory? What are the differences between generating and verifying (proving, falsifying) theory? What stance—inner or outer—do you take? What is meant by explanation? What are the boundaries of your case? Of what is your case an instance?

I do not believe that these questions are inapplicable to other research modes, but educational ethnography or participant observation research is an innovative and evolutionary development in most schools of education. The questions take on different meanings in this new context. Trying to justify a different set of activities demands a consciousness of issues that most others can handle by assumption or by appeal to the status quo. Further, in making a judgment of the adequacy of a piece of qualitative research, one important criterion is theoretical coherence of one's point of view. Such internal consistency runs through these metatheoretical issues.

In our first attempts at participant observation (Smith & Geoffrey, 1968; Smith & Keith, 1971), we were confident that what we sought was the beginnings of a theory of classroom teaching in the one instance and a theory of educational organizational innovation in the other. We were operating well within the logical positivist's conception of theory. Some of this had roots in Feigl (1945) and the early debate regarding operational psychology, Bridgeman (1927), and Boring (1945). Zetterberg's *On Theory and Verification in Sociology* (1965) is a simple, coherent account of this position: Concepts are abstractions of reality; some are categorical or class labels, and others are dimensions or variates. Propositions are relations between two or more concepts. Those propositions that are tentative are hypotheses, and those that are more strongly corroborated are laws. When two or more propositions are joined together, one has a theory. Zetterberg described several variations—inventory of antecedents, inventory of determinants, chain structures, and axiomatic formats. We have developed this position in considerable detail in Chapter 1, "The Nature of Classroom Microethnography," in *Complexities*.

Such a conception led us in several directions. We developed glossaries of concepts with theoretical and operational definitions and pictorial models of miniature and middle-range theories. It led us to a conception of explanation, which later we found formalized in Hempel's (1965) covering law model, both deductive nomological (DN) and inductive statistical (IS). The conception legitimated our emphasis on theory generation in the case study, with later verification/falsification in more classical experimental and quasi-experimental designs. Figure 3 depicts this sequence.

Our conception of theory also led us to see educational principles as one piece of social science and social science as part of the larger general fabric of natural laws produced by science. In turn, this was part of a lawful determined universe. This point of view was influenced, illustrated, and legitimated by several books of George Homans: *English Villagers of the 13th Century* (1941), *The Human Group* (1950), *Sentiments and Activities* (1962), *The Nature of Social Science* (1967), and *Social Behavior: Its Elementary Forms* (1961). All in all, this conception provided a very powerful, integrated stance.

In recent years, this intellectual structure has begun to unravel. The unraveling has not been the simple pulling of a single thread; the fabric was snagged in multiple places and in multiple ways. Early on, it was a major puzzlement in *Complexities*.

A serious discontinuity exists within educational psychology. The language of learning theory—Hull, Mowrer, Skinner, or other behaviorists—used to analyze the behavior of children cannot easily be used by the teacher to analyze and alter his own behavior. As we see it, the problem focuses on the pupil as an object, a complex of operant and respondent behavior controlled by the environment, a part of which is the teacher. The child's "rationality" and autonomy are minimized as the program and the reinforcing contingencies are accented. The teacher, however, usually is implored to be rational, to plan carefully, to meet the child's needs, and so forth, as though the locus of control lay within himself. The teacher who thinks about his own behavior as a series of operants has difficulty in synthesizing these positions. We believe the issue lies fundamentally in the heart of contemporary social science theory, and we do not propose anything like a basic solution. Rather, we are going to present a way of talking about teaching that has seemed "comfortable" to us at this fundamental level. It has provided a congruence between the experience of observing and participating in teaching and the language available for describing teaching. As we meet the traditional problem areas of educational psychology we will try to rephrase them from this point of view. (Smith & Geoffrey, 1968, pp. 87–88)

This puzzlement is in part the genesis of this chapter and the innumerable activities between then and now.

Snags occurred in reading Bruyn's *Human Perspective* (1963); he makes a case for participant observation as *the* method of sociology, based on the central criterion that it respects the nature of the subject matter, the human condition. He contrasts it with the "traditional empiricist" position. I found myself doing what I thought was participant observation, yet doing it from a rationale which he saw as a polar opposite. Table 5 is from his account.

TABLE 5
The Human Perspective: Methodological Dimensions

	Inner Perspective (*Participant Observer*)	Outer Perspective (*Traditional Empiricist*)
Philosophical background	Idealism	Naturalism
Mode of: Interpretation	Concrete procedures	Operational proced- ures
Conceptualization	Sensitizing concepts	Formal concepts
Description	Synthesis	Analysis
Explanation Principles	Telic	Causal
Models	Voluntarism	Determinism
Aims	Sensitively accurate interpretation and *explanation* of man's social and cultural life	Accurate measurement and *prediction* of man's behavior

Source: *The Human Perspective in Sociology: The Methodology of Participant Observation*, by S. T. Bruyn (Englewood Cliffs, N.J.: Prentice-Hall, 1966, p. 49).

The Homanian rationale is heavily on the side of traditional empiricism. In addition, Bruyn argued from a broader position in the humanities. The Aesthetic Education Program (Smith & Schumacher, 1972) literature became increasingly salient. The central point, however, remained—Homans and Bruyn, the major exponents of case studies, qualitative observation, and generation of grounded theory, were operating from highly divergent metatheoretical positions.

Quandaries occurred in trying to formalize a concept of explanation. As I read Hempel (1965) and saw the linkages to earlier reading of Feigl (1945), I cheered at the more philosophical underpinnings of Homans and Zetterberg. The major villains that Hempel was flogging were Scriven and Dray, so I went back to their original papers (Scriven, 1959; Dray, 1957). In his characteristic style, a style not known for understatement, Scriven (1959) blithely stated his thesis:

Such, in brief, is the argument that ties together the certainty of explanations with the possession of laws and the possibility of predictions. In its most convincing form, it is due to Professor C. G. Hempel. I refer to it as the deductive model of explanation because it proposes as a criterion for good explanations the deducibility of a statement of the facts to be explained from statements of the antecedent condition and relevant laws. *I have the greatest respect for its powers, its interest, and its adherents, but I shall argue that it is wrong, not only in detail but in conception.* (pp. 444–445; italics added)

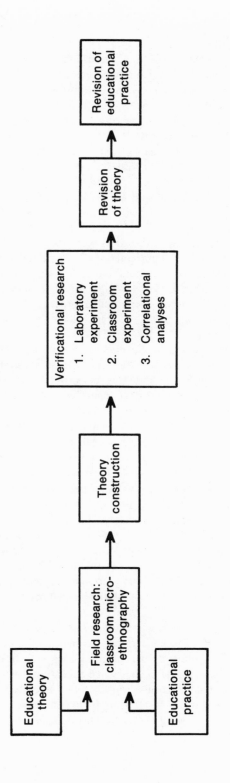

Figure 3. A process model integrating educational research styles, educational practice, and educational theory. (From *The Complexities of an Urban Classroom*, by L. M. Smith and W. Geoffrey. New York: Holt, Rinehart & Winston, 1968, p. 246.)

On the one hand it is reassuring to find philosophy of science, like other intellectual domains, riven with conflicting positions among major theorists. On the other hand, this is troublesome when one is trying to put one's intellectual house in order. And particularly it is troublesome when one is trying to justify a departure from the norms of inquiry in the educational research community.

In part, too, the unraveling occurred as I read more intensively in the philosophy and social science of science—particularly the splendid series by Toulmin and Goodfield (1961, 1963, 1965). The diversity of what was and is scientific method and theory is startling to behold. Stories that I knew before as isolated fragments from high school and college science were elaborated and arranged into a complex design. Variations in inquiry across subject matter areas and across centuries were pieced together. The incredible celestial forecasting of the Babylonians was dust bowl empiricism at its best. The invention of theory by the Greeks spanned a multitude of "interpretations" of celestial affairs before the current synthesis, or present-day common sense. The discovery of time, the Darwinian revolution, the implication for "the present state of nature and humanity as temporary products of a continuing process developing through time" (Toulmin and Goodfield, 1965, p. 246) challenged the fixity of the 17th-century religious-scientific world view. This broader history intermingled with Snow's *The Two Cultures and the Scientific Revolution* (1959), Kuhn's *The Structure of Scientific Revolutions* (1970), and Ziman's *Public Knowledge* (1968), all accounts of scientific communities and how they function.

At a personal level, I found myself challenged by Professor Beittel, both in conversation and in coming to terms with his provocative work on the production of art. He was doing his own variant of participant observer research; he had read our work as carefully as anyone, and he was chastising us for not seeing the full implications of what we were doing. Our lack of vision concerned the incompatibility of our stance at the root metaphor level of contextualism, and the very important problem of individual creativity. In an important way he provided an artistic educational instance of Bruyn's more general sociological perspective. This he did while we were doing an evaluation of an aesthetic education program and more generally starting a series of inquiries into psychological aspects of aesthetic education (Smith & Schumacher, 1972; Smith, 1975a & b, 1977a). It was timely, troublesome, and stimulating to be told that the world view, the root metaphor, the major polar principle, was incompatible with the logic of the methodology we were using and with the central procedural activities in which we were engaged.

Then there came an internal tearing apart of the fabric by the dominant group of educational researchers. As an educational psychologist, I have been taken aback with a number of my most respected colleagues who have expressed a malaise with the theoretical outcome of traditional educational and psychological research, even when done at a highly sophisticated level (Cronbach, 1975; Jackson; Jenkins, 1974; Sarbin, 1976.) The major statement, however, is Cronbach's (1975) address on receiving the APA Distinguished Scientific Award.

He makes several points skeptical of scientific theory in education.

First, Cronbach observes that the aptitude treatment interaction problem seems unsolvable as regards more complex and higher order interactions: "Once we attend to interactions, we enter a hall of mirrors that extends to infinity" (p. 119). Second, he suggests the time element—which decade the data were gathered—as a source of interaction of great importance to educational affairs. Many empirical propositions, especially those involving open systems, have a short half-life. Once again he develops a powerful metaphor to make his point: "It is as if we needed a gross of dry cells to power an engine and could only make one a month. The energy would leak out of the first cells before we had half the battery completed. So it is with the potency of our generalizations" (p. 122). Third, this view has major consequences for his early work on construct validity, in which he and Meehl imported an epistemological rationale from a logical positivist view of social science as a part of natural science (Cronbach & Meehl, 1956). Fourth, as he shies away from "enduring theoretical structures" and "theoretical palaces," he moves toward "interpretations in context." These are more heavily descriptive and more sharply tied to local situations. He, too, accents the analogy to historical inquiry and to the generation of a perspective or point of view. Finally, as he argues that broad and enduring theories about man in society are unlikely on the horizon, he sets forward two goals for the educational inquirer: "One reasonable aspiration is to assess local events accurately, to improve short-run control. . . .The other . . . is to develop explanatory concepts, that will help people use their heads" (p. 126). More and more Cronbach seems to be moving toward what Bruyn (1966) calls "concrete universals," meanings in the local culture, and "sensitizing concepts," which link the scientist's world to the conventional world.

In an interesting sense these more recent educational psychology points of view seem to come full circle, back to Scriven's early confrontation with Hempel. In his conclusion, as he argues for truisms as grounds for historical explanation, Scriven quoted, then rejected, Boswell: "Great abilities are not requisite for an Historian. . . ." Rather, Scriven (1959) felt: "To get the facts ready to one's hand, to avoid invention in reporting them, to penetrate their meaning and illuminate their presentation it might well be said that these *are* tasks to tax the greatest powers of the human mind"(p. 471). Cronbach, referring to Scriven, made his final point:

The special task of the social scientist in each generation is to pin down the contemporary facts. Beyond that, he shares with the humanistic scholar and the artist in the effort to gain insight into contemporary relationships, and to realign the culture's view of man with present realities. To know man as he is is no mean aspiration.

To someone who has been arguing for "theory generation" as the goal of qualitative field research, this is not a happy state to be in.

Finally, I have been strongly influenced by what I've come to call the Hirst

(1966), O'Connor (1973), and Struthers (1971) debate, the degree to which educational theory is mostly scientific, mostly ethical, or some combination of the two. The position one takes on this metatheoretical issue determines quite strongly the logic of the argument one derives from one's data and analysis. If the key terms of the theory—for example, education, curriculum, and teaching—contain value statements in their very structure (as Peters, 1965; Scheffler, 1971; Green, 1971; and Gowin, 1976, among others, argue) then an "objective," "scientific" theory of education is impossible. An educational theory which has ethical components in its core concepts is a very different theory from one which is "scientific." Such a view ripples through such practical items as making recommendations from research studies, dealing with multiple and sometimes conflicting values in evaluation, analyzing divergent interests in the politics of education, and making discriminations among such activities as teaching, instructing, and indoctrinating.

In conclusion, the more involved I became in observational studies, in reading methodological rationales of other observational inquirers, in keeping up with the activities of educational and social science colleagues, and in trying to ground the theoretical rationale in more philosophical conceptions, the more difficulties and irresolvable dilemmas arose. Nonetheless, as I read observational reports, the criteria I tend to focus on at the theoretical level are these: First, insightful distinctions, that is, novel concepts, propositions, and perspectives that tell me something about the phenomenon that I did not know before. Second, clear definitions of new concepts, at the semantic or theoretical level and at the operational, index, or concrete example level. Third, a cumulating glossary of these ideas within a specific project and across projects, that is within the investigator's research serial. Fourth, the interrelations of ideas into patterns or concatenations, as Kaplan (1964) calls them, or more abstract formal deductive systems, as Hempel (1965) calls them. Fifth, I want the findings to be useful, that is, helpful in solving problems when I'm working in the same broad domain, either as a researcher or a practitioner. All this seems to be a way of saying that the theory should be novel, comprehensive, internally consistent, and functional, a reasonably conservative view of theory.

Metatheoretical Issues: Assumptions in the Phrasing of Results

To ask what has been learned from an observational project is to pose the theoretical-analytical-interpretive issue in a slightly different form. To have a rationale for the manner in which one phrases those results moves one into a series of metatheoretical dilemmas. To be called on to judge observational research proposals, as one might do on an NIE panel, or to judge reports of observational projects, as one might do as a book or journal editor, demands a stand on these issues.

Root Metaphors. Implicit in the structuring of one's results are more general assumptions, stances, and perspectives, analogies and metaphors from which individuals operate and which guide thinking over troublesome spots and implicitly make some events but not others problematic. Stephen Pepper (1942), the philosopher-aesthetician, speaks of these as root metaphors. He argues that four or five of these have currency in contemporary thought: mechanism, organicism, formism, and contextualism. To conceive of human events in terms of clocks and pendula or billiard tables, balls, and cues, is to adopt a mechanistic root metaphor. Behaviorism, in his view, is a psychological theory grounded in a metaphor which solves many problems but has more trouble coping with problems of creativity, of opinion, of choice, of tragedy. Organicism or growth metaphors undergird many counseling and personality theories (e.g., self actualization). Formism or structural metaphors give legitimacy to trait theories and classical individual-difference psychology. Contextualism raises images of historical happenings, events, contexts, and syntheses. Goffman's (1959) brand of symbolic interactionism and Burke's (1945) grammar of motives would be others. In brief, the hypothesis I'm proposing is that a critic, judge, or evaluator brings one or another of these root metaphors to his task, just as the inquirer brings one or another to his task. Most participant observers are probably contextualists. When mismatches occur, the critic or judge defines almost unconsciously the inquiry out of the domain of legitimacy.

Inner vs. Outer: Observer Stance and Theoretical Perspectives. When Geoffrey and I first began thinking about what we were doing methodologically, we began to talk about our "inside-outside" stances. This seemed to make uncommonly good sense in understanding what was going on in the classroom. I was the objective outsider; he was the insider, privy to the entire system. Later we were to find that Gold (1958) and Junker (1960) had a taxonomy of such roles, that Bruyn (1967) spoke of involvement and detachment, and that Powdermaker had a book entitled *Stranger and Friend* (1966). She stated the task for the outsider in lucid prose in the preface:

To understand a strange society, the anthropologist has traditionally immersed himself in it, learning, as far as possible, to think, see, feel, and sometimes act as a member of its culture and at the same time as a trained anthropologist from another culture. This is the heart of participant observation method—involvement and detachment. Its practice is both an art and a science. Involvement is necessary to understand the psychological realities of a culture, that is its meanings for the indigenous members. Detachment is necessary to construct the abstract reality: a network of social relations including the rules and how they function—not necessarily real to the people studied. (p. 9)

Once again, we find that the kind of "learnings" one desires from one's inquiry keep tugging at the kind of data. For Powdermaker, "meanings for indigenous members" and "construct the abstract reality" constitute the twin goals. Others (Bruyn, for instance) stay more with the meanings for the participants, while some (Homans, for instance) are more behavioristic natural scientists looking for general truths and hypotheses. I have never lived comfortably with the dichotomy between the inner perspective—the world as viewed from the point of the agent—and the outer perspective—the agent viewed as one part of the natural world.

A resolution or synthesis, if it be that, seems awkwardly simple, perhaps overly simple. It lies in the continual transformation of the internal perspective through knowledge from the external perspective. For instance, in our early study of an urban classroom we approached the setting, in part, as descriptive behaviorists. The analogue between the Skinner box and the classroom box was very real. Equally, Geoffrey's point of view, especially his decision making, seemed very critical. Our hope was, and is, that insofar as we could say some important things about the regularities of his classroom, regularities that were generalizable to other classrooms, other teachers could be taught to think and act in terms of these regularities. Their internal perspectives would be enhanced by such knowledge.

This same position is reflected in a point of view about consulting which derives in part from Gouldner's (1961) comments on the theoretical requirements of applied social science. First, one needs to carefully understand the client's purposes, internal perspective, and statement of the problem. Second, these ideas must be translated into one's own theoretical point of view and solved in one's own terms. Third, the "results" must be translated back into a framework useful to the clients. Usually a fourth step occurs, one of mutual adaptation. The experience teaches both parties things they hadn't known before—enlarges and differentiates their repertory of ideas.

If I read the Toulmin and Goodfield (1961) point of view correctly, they are arguing that the conventional wisdom, the common sense of an era, has evolved over the recorded history of man. As they say in regard to the fabric of the heavens, "Common sense is a powerful mould. . . . One century's common sense is an earlier century's revolutionary discovery which has since been absorbed into the natural habits of thought" (1961, pp. 15–17). People with commonsense ideas that heavenly bodies are of different orders, such as stars, planets, and meteors; that atoms are not the ultimate particles sought by the Greeks; and that human history antedates Adam and Eve are in some important respects different from people of earlier generations. The most important aspect of this difference is that outer perspectives developed by cumulating applications of intelligence and rationality to problems have created social structures which in turn create individuals with different internal perspectives. Scriven (1972) takes an even stronger position and argues for sidestepping the entire debate: "I want to suggest that once again we should be willing to forget the dichotomy of external/internal, subjective/intersubjective, and think of these as claims that *both* require and refer to internal states *and* external ones" (p. 114). All of these arguments seem to concur with, but go a step further than, Campbell's discussion of qualitative knowing, which we cited earlier.

Miniature Theories vs. General Theories. Because case studies of classes or schools often have a holistic or systemic quality, they tend to get caught in dilemmas regarding the scope of the theory. Various labels have been coined, such as miniature theories, middle-range theories, and substantive theories, to contrast with abstract theory, formal theory, or general theory (Glaser & Strauss, 1967; Merton, 1957; Zetterberg, 1965). In our work we have tended to solve the problem in several ways. First, we accent the building of pictorial models of smaller pieces of the educational world under study. These might be described as miniature theories of pupil roles, such as court jester, or pupils on contract (Smith & Geoffrey, 1968), or miniature theories of facade and individualized curriculum and instruction (Smith & Keith, 1971). The major concepts within these miniature theories become parts of larger and more abstract clusters within the same research study. Increasingly, and with some difficulty, we are attempting to link them across studies. For instance, in the *Alte* investigation in 1977 I picked up the concept "idiosyncratic styles of teaching," which had come up almost tangentially a decade before in our apprenticeship study (Connor & Smith, 1967; Smith, 1972). The hope is that these larger integrations will culminate in a more general theory of education.

Pattern Explanation vs. Deductive Explanation. If one can believe the philosophers of science (Hempel, 1965; Kaplan, 1964; Scriven, 1958, 1959), a large controversy exists in the phrasing of abstract social science results. We got mixed up in it in several ways. First, the Homanian approach, which is essentially grounded in a deductive nomological rationale, was one of our guides. Second, Becker's (1958) early paper on problems of inference and proof in participant observation suggested a four-step procedure: (1) selection and definition of problems, concepts, and indices, (2) checking the frequency and distribution of phenomena, (3) construction of social system models, and (4) presentation of results. It, too, was influential and pushed us toward patterns, configurations, and concatenations. Early on, Geoffrey, Keith, and I struggled with the various diagrams, models, and miniature theories in *Complexities* and *Anatomy*. We tried, unwittingly at times, for more abstract, deductive, covering law statements and at other times for more concrete, systemic, configurations or patterns. The dilemma has remained. We have found each mode to be informative at different points as we reached for understanding.

Educational Rather than Social Science Theory. Traditionally, and particularly in its research efforts, education has borrowed from the social sciences. The methods, measures, apparatus, and ideas of anthropology, sociology, and particularly psychology have been brought to bear on the teacher, the classroom, the school, and the curriculum. At this time it seems appropriate to ask whether education has profited substantially from the stepsister relationship, and whether it may now be time to take seriously such terms as teaching, curriculum, steering group, lesson, and recitation and to build a genuinely educational theory with core primitive terms, derived terms, and sensitizing concepts of its own. Participant observer research seems uniquely suited to this task because of its efforts to understand events in a culture and system from the point of view of the practitioners in the system. Ferreting these out, codifying the shades of meaning, building them into configurations and propositions, using them to solve significant problems seems a worthy objective. A vigorous application of such a criterion by journal editors or funding committees would change the nature of educational jargon and maybe eventually the phenomena themselves.

Social and Educational Theory: Natural or Artifactual.   Basic to the formulation of one's results is a belief concerning the formulation of social science generalizations as natural science laws or as more artificial or artifactual principles dependent on human institutions which are constructed for individual and collective purposes. In a sense this seems a form of emergence, that is, living organisms and events are different in some important ways from inorganic events, and human beings are different in some important ways from other animals. As one moves into social events of human beings, the openness and indeterminancy loom larger and larger. Natural law seems less and less applicable, so the argument goes. Within educational theory Cronbach (1975) and Gowin (1976) have voiced a variant of this more explicitly than most of their fellows.

The is/ought problem is solved classically by splitting science and ethics, with science trying to describe the world as it "really is" and with ethics trying to clarify the good or the ideal, the world as it "should be." As social theory is conceived more toward the artificial or artifactual, it often takes on aspects of practical theory or a theory of action (Schwab, 1969, 1971, 1973). This raises old arguments that are sometimes posed as historical explanation vs. scientific explanation. Dray (1957) and Scriven (1958, 1959, 1972) have had a running argument with Hempel (1965) for several decades over these issues. In a recent paper, within a long series of essays attacking the more formalist position of the logical positivists, Scriven (1972) argues again the nature of historical knowledge as the prototype for education in particular and social science in general. He is referring to "weak knowledge claims . . . a knowledge claim of a rather different kind from the usual ones." He argues:

One would thus expect it to be the norm in history and, if this approach is logically sound, it does something to rescue history from the choice between (usual conceptions of) the Scylla of science and the Charybdis of literature. We can, for instance, answer the question, what do we learn from history, without having to produce absurd or trivial laws, or bare particulars about the past, or murmur mysteriously about deepening our understanding of man. What we most importantly learn from history is a range of possibilities—not of probabilities, not of certainties. And of course these are not mere possibilities, of the kind that one has in mind when one says, Oh, anything is possible! They are significant possibilities, ones that have shaken empires or cabinets before and may do so again for all that we know to the contrary. They are thus most deserving of our respect, and with our knowledge of them we can plan more rationally for the future. If we wish to make a certain outcome more likely, then we can try to bring about those conditions which on previous occasions, not demonstrably irrelevant to the present case, did bring about that outcome. If we wish to prevent an outcome, what we can do is to make it less likely; we try to eliminate those circumstances which have in the relevant past brought about this result or repeat those circumstances that have previously frustrated it. We rarely have much idea about how much effect such actions will have, speaking precisely, but we sometimes know that they have a ''good chance,'' or are a ''desperate hope,'' and to suppose that we shall ever be much better off than that in human engineering a history-conscious world is pipe dreaming. The sad thing is that we could have done so much and done it so much better if we had been willing to learn the lessons from history that are there to be learned, instead of going in search of some Holy Grail whose contents would give us the same kind of predictive reliability in history that we have in astronomy. (p. 115)

If I understand him correctly he is arguing the more general epistemological case of knowledge in a theory of action.

In summary, educational research workers differ on a number of often implicit dimensions and configurations, which might be called metatheoretical issues. A half dozen of these seem particularly important:

1. The root metaphor within which one works—mechanical, organic, formal, or contextual.
2. The inner or outer perspective one chooses, that is, a stance from the subject's point of view or the outside observer's point of view.
3. A theory which is more limited in scope and time to a local context versus one that is more general.
4. A level of abstraction that is more descriptive and concrete or more abstract and interpretive.
5. A model of explanation that is more covering law versus one that is configurational or contextual.
6. A theory that is more action oriented and more ethical versus one that is more descriptive and analytical.

It is my contention that a reader of participant observer reports, as he positions himself at one or another of the poles in these metatheoretical dilemmas and as he treats these positions as value laden—good, appropriate, desirable—will make varying judgments on the quality of any particular piece of research. It is my contention also that while these issues separate various ethnographic researchers from each other, they also represent major differences between the ethnographer and the larger community of educational researchers. As such they are problems needing more general attention in the educational research community.

CONCLUSIONS

This essay has been directed largely to the educational research community, perhaps most thoroughly represented by AERA. Most basically, the hope has been to widen and deepen the discussion of a broad methodological stream of inquiry—educational ethnography, participant observation, and other case studies. More by implication than direct analysis, the assumption is that the dominant paradigm—experimental, quantitative, positivistic, and behavioral—has been too restrictive to cope with the ideas, the problems, and the interests of what is called education and of people who call themselves educators.

More positively, the analysis and its several lines of argument have tried to make several major points. A large, interesting, and provocative literature, both substantively and methodologically (Tables 1–4 and the reference list) exists within this field study tradition. As the activities reflected in those tables engendered conversations and communications, individuals began to coalesce in conferences, groups, communities, and invisible colleges. Witness, for example, the Cambridge Evaluation Conferences of 1972 and 1975 and the recent publication of *Beyond the Numbers Game* (Hamilton et al., 1977), a reader in alternative methods of educational evaluation. The elements in a theory of research methodology, as items or patterns, can be viewed as group norms or mores of those evolving communities. Over time, the larger research communities and subcommunities evolve and change, as in the development of Division G, Social Context, in AERA and the Council on Anthropology and Education in AAA. In time, the theory of research methodology, as with any theory, evolves and changes, perhaps on occasion dramatically enough to be labeled a revolution, as Kuhn calls the paradigm shifts.

Second, a reflexive overview of the cognitive processes in field work suggests a perspective on the methodology. It is one person's idiosyncratic ''how to do it.'' It, like the methodology, builds on one participant's actions and observation of the process, reading about other persons' observations, and then describing, analyzing, and interpreting that experience. It is its own kind of grounded theory of methodology. Experientally, the phases and the discriminable items within the phases are very real. They have a public quality in being sharable, communicable, and meaningful to other field workers. They seem to help our students in learning to do similar work. They seem to lead to knowledges and understandings that are useful to a variety of persons engaged in educational activities.

Third, and more specifically within the educational ethnographic, participant observation tradition, the essay presents a patterned analysis of the genre of research. The major domains considered were at four levels of abstraction, data, descriptive narrative, theoretical, and metatheoretical. The framework presents a way of talking about any piece of research in the tradition. Such a perspective is one step toward a guide to evaluation. Audiences can discern relative kinds and amounts of attention to data, to narrative, to theory in a piece of work. If they value portrayals more than conceptual models, for instance, then one piece will be judged better than another; conversely, if they value model development and they find only a portrayal, the evaluation will be different. Each of the levels of analysis contains several discriminable subissues. All of these are linked in multiple and sometimes contradictory ways to other research traditions in education, social science, and philosophy. Overall the framework suggests the kinds of things the practicing inquirer might consider as he is developing his own line of research. Particular positions of the author were presented in considerable detail as one configuration of possibilities. For now that seems enough.

REFERENCES

Adams, R. N., & Preiss, J. J. (Eds.) *Human organization research: Field relations and techniques.* Homewood, Ill.: Dorsey Press, 1960.

Adelman, C. (Ed.) *Uttering, muttering: Collecting, using and reporting talk for social and educational research.* Reading, England: Bulmershe College of Education, n.d.

Adelman, C., Kemmis, J., and Jenkins, D. *Rethinking case study: Notes from the Second Cambridge Conference.* Unpublished manuscript, Center for Applied Research in Education, Norwich, England, 1976.

Allport, G. W. *The use of personal documents in psychological science.* New York: Social Science Research Council, 1942.

Applegate, J. *A description and anlysis of role playing as a student activity in an elementary classroom.* Unpublished Ph. D. dissertation, Washington University, 1971.

Arensberg, C. M., & Kimball, S. T. *Family and community in Ireland.* Cambridge, Mass.: Harvard University Press, 1940.

Arensberg, C. M., & MacGregor, D. Determination of morale in an industrial company. *Applied Anthropologist,* 1942, *1,* 12-34.

Atkin, J. M. Practice-oriented inquiry: A third approach to research in education. *Educational Researcher,* 1973, *2,* 3-4.

Atwood, M. S. *An anthropological approach to administrative change.* Unpublished doctoral dissertation, Columbia University, 1960.

Barker, R. G., & Gump, P. V. *Big school, small school: High school size and student behavior.* Stanford, Calif: Stanford University Press, 1964.

Barker, R., & Wright, H. F. *Midwest and its children. The psychological ecology of an American town.* Evanston, Ill.: Row, Peterson, 1954.

Becker, H. S. *Role and career problems of the Chicago public school teacher.* Unpublished doctoral dissertation, University of Chicago, 1951.

Becker, H. S. Problems of inference and proof in participant observation. *American Sociological Review,* 1958, *28,* 652-660.

Becker, H. S. *Outsiders: Studies in the sociology of deviance.* New York: Free Press, 1966.

Becker, H. S. *Sociological work: Method and substance.* Chicago: Aldine, 1970.

Becker, H. S. Art as collective action. *American Sociological Review,* 1974, *39,* 767-776.

Becker, H. S., & Geer, B. Participant observation and interviewing: A comparison. *Human Organization,* 1957, *16,* 28-32.

Becker, H. S., Geer, B., Hughes, E., & Strauss, A. *Boys in white: Student culture in medical school.* Chicago: University of Chicago Press, 1961.

Beittel, K. R. *Alternatives for art education research: Inquiry into the making of art.* Dubuque, Iowa: William C. Brown, 1973.

Beittel, K. R. *Mind and context in the art of drawing.* New York: Holt, Rinehart & Winston, 1972.

Berlak, A., Berlak, H., Bagenstos, N. T., & Mikel, E. K. Teaching and learning in English primary schools. *School Review,* 1975, *83,* 215-243.

Biddle, B. J. Methods and concepts in classroom research. *Review of Educational Research,* 1967, *37,* 337-357.

Blau, P. M. *The dynamics of bureaucracy: A study of interpersonal relations in two government agencies.* Chicago: University of Chicago Press, 1955.

Blumer, H. *Symbolic interactionism: Perspective and method.* Englewood Cliffs, N.J.: Prentice-Hall, 1969.

Boring, E. G. The nature and the history of experimental control. *American Journal of Psychology,* 1954, *67,* 573-589.

Boring, E. G. The use of operational definitions in science. *Psychological Review,* 1945, *52,* 243-245, 278-281.

Bridgeman, P. *The logic of modern physics.* New York: Macmillan, 1927.

Bruyn, S. T. *Communities in action: Pattern and process.* New Haven: College and University Press, 1963.

Bruyn, S. T. *The human perspective in sociology: The methodology of participant observation.* Englewood Cliffs, N.J.: Prentice-Hall, 1966.

Burke, K. *A grammar of motives.* Berkeley: University of California Press, 1969. (Originally published, 1945.)

Burnett-Hill, J. Event description and analysis in the microethnography of the classroom. In F. Ianni and E. Storey (Eds.), *Cultural relevance and educational issues.* Boston: Little, Brown, 1973.

Campbell, D. T. *Qualitative knowing in action research.* Kurt Lewin. Award address presented at the Society for the Psychological Study of Social Issues, 1974.

Campbell, D. T., & Fiske, D. W. Convergent and discriminant validation by the multitrait-multimethod matrix. *Psychological Bulletin,* 1959, *56,* 81-105.

Campbell, D. T., & Stanley, J. C. Experimental and quasi-experimental designs for research in teaching. In N. L. Gage (Ed.), *Handbook of research in teaching.* Chicago: Rand McNally, 1963.

Casagrande, J. B. *In the company of man: Twenty portraits by anthropologists.* New York: Harper & Bros., 1960.

Cazden, C., John, V. P., and Hymes, D. (Eds). *Functions of language in the classroom.* New York: Teachers College Press, Columbia University, 1972.

Center for Educational Research and Innovation. *Case studies of educational innovation* (4 vols.). Paris: Organization for Economic and Cooperative Development, 1973.

Charters, W. W., Jr., Everhart, R., Jones, J., Packard, J., Pellegrin, R., and Wacaster, C. *The process of planned change in the school's instructional organization.* Eugene, Ore.: CASEA, 1973.

Charters, W. W., and Jones, J. On the risk of appraising nonevents in program evaluation. *Educational Researcher,* 1973, *2,* 5-7.

Cicourel, A. V., Jennings, K., Jennings, S., Leiter, K., MacKay, R., Mehan, H., & Roth, D. *Language use and school performance.* New York: Academic Press, 1974.

Connor, W. H., & Smith, L. M. *Analysis of patterns of student teaching* (Final Rep. No. 5-8204). Washington, D.C.: U.S. Office of Education, 1967.

Crane, D. *Invisible colleges: Diffusion of knowledge in scientific communities.* Chicago: University of Chicago Press, 1972.

Cronbach, L. J. The two disciplines of scientific psychology. *American Psychologist,* 1957, *12,* 671-684.

Cronbach, L. J. Beyond the two disciplines of scientific psychology. *American Psychologist,* 1975, *30,* 116-127.

Cronbach, L. J., & Meehl, P. E. Construct validity in psychological tests. In H. Feigl and M. Scriven (Eds.), *The foundations of science and the concepts of psychology and psychoanalysis.* Minneapolis: University of Minneapolis Press, 1956.

Cusick, P. A. *Inside high school: The student's world.* New York: Holt, Rinehart & Winston, 1973.

Delamont, S. *Interaction in the classroom.* London: Methuen, 1976.

Denzin, N. K. *The research act: A theoretical introduction to sociological methods.* Chicago: Aldine, 1970.

Denzin, N. K. The logic of naturalistic inquiry. *Social Forces,* 1971, 50, 166-182.

Diesing, P. *Patterns of discovery in the social sciences.* Chicago: Aldine-Atherton, 1971.

Dray, W. *Laws and explanation in history.* London: Oxford University Press, 1957.

Dunkin, M. J., & Biddle, B. J. *The study of teaching.* New York: Holt, Rinehart & Winston, 1974.

Easley, J. A. The structural paradigm in protocol analysis. *Journal of Research in Science Teaching,* 1974, *11,* 281-290.

Eddy, E. M. *Becoming a teacher: The passage to professional status.* New York: Teachers College Press, Columbia University, 1969.

Eisner, E. Curriculum development in Stanford's Kettering Project: Recollections and ruminations. In J. Schaffarzick & D. H. Hampson (Eds.), *Strategies for curriculum development.* Berkeley, Calif.: McCutchan, 1975.

Elliot, J., & Adelman, C. *Classroom action research* (Ford Teaching Project). East Anglia, England: Center for Applied Research in Education, 1977.

Epstein, T. E. (Ed.). *The craft of social anthropology.* New York: Barnes & Noble Books, 1967.

Erickson, F. What makes school ethnography "ethnographic?" *Council on Anthropology and Education Newsletter,* 1973, *4,* 10-19.

Erickson, F. Gatekeeping and the melting pot: Interaction in counseling encounters. *Harvard Educational Review,* 1975, *45,* 44-70.

Erickson, F. Personal communication, 1978.

Feigl, H. Operationism and scientific method. *Psychological Review,* 1945, *52,* 250-259, 284-288.

Festinger, L., Riecken, H. W., & Schachter, S. *When prophecy fails.* New York: Harper Torchbook, 1964. (Originally published, 1956.)

Festinger, L., Schachter, S., and Back, K. *Social pressures in informal groups: A study of human factors in housing.* New York: Harpers, 1950.

Finch, M. E. *Behind the teacher's desk: A study of the teacher and the change process.* Unpublished doctoral dissertation, Washington University, 1978.

Firth, R. W. *Social change in Tikopia: Re-study of a Polynesian community after a generation.* New York: Macmillan, 1959.

Firth, R. W. *We, the Tikopia: A sociological study of kinship in primitive Polynesia.* Boston: Beacon Press, 1957.

Gardner, H. *The quest for mind; Piaget, Lévi-Strauss, and the structuralist movement.* New York: Alfred A. Knopf, 1972.

Gardner, H. *The arts and human development: A psychological study of the artistic process.* New York: John Wiley, 1973.

Garfinkel, H. *Studies in ethnomethodology.* Englewood Cliffs, N.J.: Prentice-Hall, 1967.

Glaser, B. & Strauss, A. L. Discovery of substantive theory: A basic strategy underlying qualitative research. *American Behavioral Scientist,* 1965, *8,* 6, 5-12.

Glaser, B. G., & Strauss, A. L. *The discovery of grounded theory: Strategies for qualitative research.* Chicago: Aldine, 1967.

Goffman, E. *The presentation of self in everyday life.* New York: Anchor Books, 1959.

Goffman, E. *Asylums: Essays on the social situations of mental patients and other inmates.* New York: Anchor Books, 1961.

Gold, F. L. Roles in sociological field observations. *Social Forces,* 1958, 36, 217-223.

Goodenough, F. Measuring behavior traits by means of repeated short samples. *Journal of Juvenile Research,* 1928, *12,* 230-35.

Gouldner, A. W. *Patterns of industrial bureaucracy.* Glencoe, Ill.: Free Press, 1954(a).

Gouldner, A. W. *Wildcat strike.* New York: Harper & Row, 1954. (b)

Gouldner, A. W. Theoretical requirements of the applied social sciences. In W. Bennis, K. D. Benne, and R. Chin (Eds.), *The planning of change.* New York, Holt, Rinehart, & Winston, 1961.

Gowin, D. B. Is educational research distinctive? In L. G. Thomas (Ed.), *Philosophical redirection of educational research.* Chicago: National Society for the Study of Education (NSSE), 1972.

Gowin, D. B. On the relation of theory to practice in educational research in IDM. In *relating theory to practice in educational research.* Bielefeld, Germany: Inst. für Didaktile der Mathematik der Universitat Bielefeld, 1976.

Green, T. A typology of the teaching concept. In Hyman, R. T. (Ed.), *Contemporary thought on teaching.* Englewood Cliffs, New Jersey: Prentice Hall, 1971.

Gribble, J. Logical and psychological considerations in the criticism of F. R. Lewis. *British Journal of Aesthetics,* 1970, *10,* 1, 39-57.

Gump, P. V. *The classroom behavior setting: Its nature and relation to student behavior* (Project No. 2453). Washington, D.C.: U.S. Office of Education, 1967.

Gump, P. V., & Kounin, J. S. Issues raised by ecological and "classical" research efforts. *Merrill-Palmer Quarterly,* 1960, *6,* 145-153.

Gump, P. V., Schoggen, P., & Redl, F. The camp milieu and its immediate effects. *Journal of Social Issues,* 1957, *13*(1), 40-46. (Issues not continuously numbered)

Habenstein, R. W. (Ed.). *Pathways to data: Field methods for studying ongoing social organizations.* Chicago: Aldine, 1970.

Hagstrom, W. *The scientific community.* New York: Basic Books, 1965.

Hall, B., & Thuernau, P. Formative evaluation in the aesthetic education program. *Council for Research in Music Education,* 1975, No. 43, 50-64.

Halpin, A. W. *Theory and research in administration.* New York: Macmillan, 1966.

Hamilton, D. *In search of structure: Essays from an open plan school.* Edinburgh: Scottish Council for Research in Education, 1977.

Hamilton, D. *A science of the singular?* Unpublished mimeo, 1976.

Hamilton D., & Delamont, S. Classroom research: A cautionary tale. *Research in Education,* 1974, *11,* 1-16.

Hamilton, D., Jenkins, D., King, C., MacDonald, B. and Parlett, M. (Eds.). *Beyond the numbers game.* London: MacMillan Education Ltd., 1977.

Hammond, P. E. (Ed.). *Sociologists at work: Essays on the craft of social research.* New York: Basic Books, 1964.

Hempel, C. G. *Aspects of scientific explanation and other essays in the philosophy of science.* New York: Free Press, 1965.

Henry, J. Attitude organization in elementary school classrooms. *American Journal of Orthopsychiatry,* 1957, *27,* 117-133.

Henry, J. *Culture against man.* New York: Random House, 1963.

Henry, J. *Jules Henry on education.* New York: Vintage Books, 1966.

Hirst, P. H. Educational theory. In J. W. Tibble (Ed.), *The study of education.* London: Routledge & Kegan Paul, 1966.

Hirst, P. H. The nature and scope of educational theory: (2). Reply to D. J. O'Connor. In G. Langfeld and D. J. O'Connor (Eds.), *New essays in the philosophy of education.* London: Routledge & Kegan Paul, 1973.

Hoffer, E. *The true believer: Thoughts on the nature of mass movements.* New York: Harper & Bros.,1951.

Homans, G. C. *English villagers of the thirteenth century.* Cambridge, Mass.: Harvard University Press, 1941.

Homans, G. C. The strategy of industrial sociology. *American Journal of Sociology,* 1949, *54,* 330-337.

Homans, G. C. *The human group.* New York: Harcourt, Brace, 1950.

Homans, G. C. *Social behavior: Its elementary forms.* New York: Harcourt, Brace & World, 1961.

Homans, G. C. *Sentiments and activities: Essays in social science.* New York: Free Press of Glencoe, 1962.

Homans, G. C. *The nature of social science.* New York: Harcourt, Brace & World, 1967.

Homans, G. C., & Bailey, O. T. The Society of Fellows, Harvard University 1933-1947. In C. Brinton (Ed.), *The society of fellows.* Cambridge, Mass: Harvard University Press, 1959.

Horowitz, I. L., & Katz, J. E. *Social science and public policy in the United States.* New York: Frederick A. Praeger, 1975.

Housman, A. E. *The name and nature of poetry.* New York: Macmillan, 1933.

Hsu, F. L. K. (Ed.). *Psychological anthropology: Approaches to culture and personality.* Homewood, Ill.: Dorsey Press, 1961.

Hull, C. L. *Principles of behavior.* New York: Appleton-Century, 1943.

Humphreys, L. *Tearoom trade: Impersonal sex in public places.* Chicago: Aldine, 1970.

Iannaccone, L. *The social system of an elementary school staff.* Unpublished doctoral dissertation, Teachers College, Columbia University, 1958.

Innaccone, L. Student teaching: A transitional stage in the making of a teacher. *Theory into Practice,* 1963, *2,* 73-80.

Jackson, J. M. Structural characteristics of norms. In N. B. Henry (Ed.), *The dynamics of instructional groups* (59th Yearbook of the National Society for the Study of Education. Chicago: University of Chicago Press, 1960.

Jackson, P. *Life in classrooms.* New York: Holt, Rinehart & Winston, 1968.

Jackson, P. *The promise of educational psychology.* Chicago, n.d.

Jacobs, G. (Ed.). *The participant observer.* New York: George Braziller, 1970.

Jenkins, J. J. Remember that old theory of memory? Well, forget it! *American Psychologist,* 1974, *29,* 785-795.

Junker, B. H. *Field work: An introduction to the social sciences.* Chicago: University of Chicago Press, 1960.

Kaplan, A. *The conduct of inquiry: Methodology for behavioral science.* San Francisco: Chandler, 1964.

Kimball, S. The method of natural history and educational research. In G. D. Spindler (Ed.), *Education and anthropology.* Stanford, Calif.: Stanford University Press, 1955.

Kimball, S. T., & Pearsall, M. *The Talladega story: A study in community process.* University: University of Alabama Press, 1954.

Klapp, O. E. *Collective search for identity.* New York: Holt, Rinehart & Winston, 1969.

Kluckhohn, F. The participant observer technique in small communities. *American Journal of Sociology,* 1940, *46,* 331-343.

Kounin, J. S. *Discipline and group management in classrooms.* New York: Holt, Rinehart & Winston, 1970.

Kuhn, T. S. *The structure of scientific revolutions* (2nd ed.). Chicago: University of Chicago Press, 1970.

Lakatos, I., & Musgrove, A. (Eds.). *Criticism and the growth of knowledge.* Cambridge: Cambridge University Press, 1970.

Leacock, E. B. *Teaching and learning in city schools: A comparative study.* New York: Basic Books, 1969.

Lévi-Strauss, C. *Structural anthropology.* New York: Basic Books, 1963.

Liebow, E. *Tally's corner: A study of Negro streetcorner men.* Boston: Little Brown, 1967.

Lipnick, B. *An experiment that works in teenage religious education.* New York: Bloch, 1976.

Lipset, S. M. *Agrarian socialism; The Cooperative Commonwealth Federation in Saskatchewan: A study in political sociology.* Berkeley: University of California Press, 1950.

Lipset, S. M., Trow, M., and Coleman, J. *Union democracy: The internal politics of the International Typographical Union.* New York: Anchor Books, 1956.

Lutz, F. W. *Social systems and school districts.* Unpublished doctoral dissertation, Washington University, 1962.

Lutz, F. W., & Iannaccone, L. *Understanding educational organizations: A field study approach.* Columbus, Ohio: Charles E. Merrill, 1969.

Lutz, F., & Ramsey, M. The use of anthropological field methods in education. *Educational Researcher,* 1974, *3,* 5-9.

MacDonald, B., and Walker, R. *Changing the curriculum.* London: Open Books Ltd., 1976.

MacDonald, B., and Walker R. (Ed.). *SAFARI: Some interim papers.* Norwich, England: Center for Applied Research in Education, 1974.

MacDonald, B., & Parlett, M. *Rethinking evaluation: Notes from the Cambridge conference.* Norwich, England: Center for Applied Research in Education, 1973.

Magoon, A. J. Constructivist approaches in educational research. *Review of Educational Research,* 1977, *47,* 651-693.

Malinowksi, B. *Argonauts of the western Pacific.* London: Routledge, 1922.

Malinowski, B. *Coral gardens and their magic: A study of the methods of tilling the soil and of agricultural rites in the Trobriand Islands.* Bloomington, Ind.: Indiana University Press, 1965. (Originally published, 1935.)

Malinowski, B. *Coral gardens and their magic (Vol. 11, The language of magic and gardening).* Bloomington, Ind.: Indiana University Press, 1955. (Originally published, 1935.)

Maslow, A. H. Observing and reporting education experiments. *Humanist,* 1965, *25,* 13.

Maslow, A. H. *The psychology of science: A reconnaissance.* New York: Harper & Row, 1966.

McCall, G. J., & Simmons, J. L. (Eds.) *Issues in participant observation.* Reading, Mass.: Addison-Wesley, 1969.

Mckinney, W. L., & Westbury, I. Stability and change: The public schools of Gary, Indiana, 1940-1970. In W. A. Reid and D. F. Walker (Eds.), *Case studies in curriculum change: Great Britain and the United States.* London: Routledge & Kegan Paul, 1975.

McPherson, G. H. *Small town teacher.* Cambridge, Mass.: Harvard University Press, 1972.

Mead, M. *Growing up in New Guinea.* New York: William Morrow, 1930.

Meehan, E. J. *Explanation in social science: A system paradigm.* Homewood, Ill.: Dorsey Press, 1968.

Meehl, P. E. *Clinical versus statistical prediction: A theoretical analysis and a review of the evidence.* Minneapolis: University of Minnesota Press, 1954.

Meehl, P. E. Law and the fireside inductions: Some reflections of a clinical psychologist. *Journal of Social Issues,* 1971, *27* (4), 65-100.

Meehl, P. E. Second-order relevance. *American Psychologist,* 1972, *27,* 932-940.

Meehl, P. E. *Psychodiagnosis: Selected papers.* Minneapolis: University of Minnesota Press, 1973.

Mercurio, J. A. *Caning: Educational rite and tradition.* Syracuse, New York: Syracuse University Press, 1972.

Merton, R. K. Selected problems of field work in the planned community. *American Sociological Review,* 1947, *12,* 304-312.

Merton, R. K. *Social theory and social structure* (Rev. ed.). Glencoe, Ill.: Free Press, 1957.

Miller, D. B. Roles of naturalistic observation in comparative psychology. *American Psychologist, 1977, 32,* 211-219.

Mischel, T. (Ed.). *Human action: Conceptual and empirical issues.* New York: Academic Press, 1969.

Munro, R. *Innovation: Success or failure?* London: Hodder & Stoughton, 1977.

Murchison, C. A. *A history of psychology in autobiography.* New York: Russell & Russell, 1961.

Murray, H. A. *Explorations in personality.* New York: Oxford University Press, 1938.

Murray, H. A., & Kluckhohn, C. Outline of a conception of personality. In C. Kluckhohn et al., *Personality in nature, society and culture.* New York: Alfred A. Knopf, 1954.

Naroll, R., & Cohen, R. (Eds.). *A handbook of method in cultural anthropology.* Garden City, New York: Natural History Press, 1970.

Nolan, P. Personal communication, 1975.

O'Connor, D. J. *An introduction to the philosophy of education.* London: Routledge & Kegan Paul, 1957.

O'Connor, D. J. The nature and scope of educational theory. In G. Langfeld & D. J. O'Connor (Eds.), *New essays in the philosophy of education.* London: Routledge & Kegan Paul, 1973.

Olson, W. C. *Problem tendencies in children: A method for their measurement and description.* Minneapolis: University of Minnesota Press, 1930.

Orne, M. T. On the social psychology of the psychological experiment: With particular reference to demand characteristics and their implications. *American Psychologist, 1962, 17,* 776-784.

Parlett, M., & Hamilton, D. *Evaluation as illumination: New approaches to the study of innovative problems* (Occasional Paper No. 9). Edinburgh: Center for Research in the Educational Sciences, University of Edinburgh, 1972.

Pelto, P. *Anthropological research: The structure of inquiry.* New York: Harper & Row, 1970.

Pepper, S. C. *World hypotheses: A study in evidence.* Berkeley: University of California Press, 1942.

Peters, R. S. Education as initiation. In R. D. Archambault (Ed.), *Philosophical analysis and education.* London: Routledge & Kegan Paul, 1965.

Piaget, J. *The child's conception of the world.* Paterson, N.J.: Littlefield Adams & Co., 1960. (Originally published, 1929.)

Piaget, J. *Genetic epistemology.* New York: W. W. Norton, 1971.

Pohland, P. A. *An interorganizational analysis of an innovative education program.* Unpublished doctoral dissertation, Washington University, 1970.

Pohland, P. A. Participant observation as a research methodology. *Studies in art education, 1972, 13,* 4-15.

Polsky, Howard W. *Cottage six: The social system of delinquent boys in residential treatment.* New York: Russell Sage, 1962.

Powdermaker, H. *Stranger and friend: The way of an anthropologist.* New York: W. W. Norton, 1966.

Radcliffe-Brown, A. R. *The Andaman Islanders.* Glencoe, Ill.: Free Press, 1948. (Originally published, 1922.)

Redl, F., & Wineman, D. *The aggressive child.* Glencoe, Ill.: Free Press, 1957.

Reid, W. A., & Walker, D. F. (Eds.). *Case studies in curriculum change.* London: Routledge & Kegan Paul, 1975.

Reynolds, L. J. *Problems of implementing organizational change in the elementary school: A case study.* Unpublished doctoral dissertation, University of Oregon, 1973.

Rice, R. *Toward a general conceptualization of interest grouping and its impact on the social system of the classroom.* Unpublished doctoral dissertation, Washington University, 1964.

Riegel, K. F. The dialectics of human development. *American Psychologist,* 1976, *31,* 689-700.

Rist, R. C. *The urban school: A factory for failure; A study of education in American society.* Cambridge, Mass.: MIT Press, 1973.

Roberts, J., and Akinsanya, S. A. *Educational patterns and cultural configurations.* New York: David McKay, 1976.

Roebuck, M., Bloomer, J., and Hamilton, D. *Project PHI: Independent learning materials and science teaching in small schools in the highlands and islands of Scotland.* Glasgow: University of Glasgow, 1974.

Russell, H. (Ed.). *Evaluation of computer assisted instruction program.* St. Ann, Mo.: CEMREL, Inc., 1969.

Sarason, S. B. *The culture of the school and the problem of change.* Boston: Allyn & Bacon, 1971.

Sarason, S. B. *The creation of settings and the future societies.* San Francisco: Jossey-Bass, 1972.

Sarason, S. B., Davidson, K. S., and Blatt, B. *The preparation of teachers: An unstudied problem in education.* New York: John Wiley, 1962

Sarbin, T. Contextualism: A world view for modern psychology. In Cole, J. (Ed.). *Nebraska Symposium on Motivation,* Vol. 24, 1976. Lincoln, University of Nebraska Press, 1977.

Schachter, S. Deviation, rejection and communication. In D. Cartwright & A. Zander, *Group dynamics.* Evanston, Ill.: Row Peterson, 1953.

Scheffler, I. Philosophical models of teaching. In R. T. Hyman (Ed.), *Contemporary thought on teaching.* Englewood Cliffs, N. J.: Prentice-Hall, 1971.

Schumacher, S. *Political processes in education: A case study of an interagency curriculum evaluation and diffusion project.* Unpublished doctoral dissertation, Washington University, 1975.

Schwab, J. J. The practical: A language for curriculum. *School Review,* 1969, *78,* 1-23.

Schwab, J. J. The practical: Arts of eclectic. *School Review,* 1971, *79,* 493-542.

Schwab, J. J. The practical: Translation into curriculum. *School Review,* 1973, *81,* 501-22.

Scott, J. P. (Ed.). Methodology and techniques for the study of animal societies. *Annals of the New York Academy of Science,* 1950, *51,* 1001-1122.

Scott, W. R. Field methods in the study of organizations. In J. March (Ed.), *Handbook of organizations.* Chicago: Rand McNally, 1965.

Scriven, M. A possible distinction between traditional scientific disciplines and the study of human behavior. In H. Feigl & M. Scriven (Eds.), *Minnesota studies in the philosophy of science, Vol. 1.* Minneapolis: University of Minnesota Press, 1956.

Scriven, M. Definitions, explanations and theories. In H. Feigl et al., *Concepts, theories, and the mind-body problem* (Minnesota Studies in the Philosophy of Science, Vol. 2). Minneapolis: University of Minnesota Press, 1958.

Scriven, M. Truisms as the grounds for historical explanations. In P. Gardiner (Ed.), *Theories of history.* New York, Free Press, 1959.

Scriven, M. *Primary philosophy.* New York: McGraw-Hill, 1966.

Scriven, M. The methodology of evaluation. In R. W. Tyler, R. M. Gagné, and M. Scriven (Eds.), *Perspective of curriculum evaluation.* Chicago: Rand McNally, 1967.

Scriven, M. Objectivity and subjectivity in educational research. In L. G. Thomas (Ed.), *Philosophical redirection of educational research.* Chicago, National Society for the Study of Education, 1972.

Seif, E. *A conceptual analysis of thought processes and instructional strategies based on field observations of elementary school classrooms.* Unpublished doctoral dissertation, Washington University, 1971,

Selznick, P. *TVA and the grass roots: A study in the sociology of formal organization.* Berkeley, Calif.: University of California Press, 1949.

Selznick, P. *The organizational weapon: A study of Bolshevik strategy and tactics.* New York: McGraw-Hill, 1952.

Shulman, L. The psychology of school subjects: A premature obituary. *Journal of Research in Science Teaching,* 1974, *11,* 319-339.

Simon, A., & Boyer, E. G. (Eds.). *Mirrors for behavior.* Philadelphia: Research for Better Schools, 1967.

Sindell, P. S. Anthropological approaches to the study of education. *Review of Educational Research,* 1969, *39,* 593-605.

Singleton, J. C. *Nichū: A Japanese school.* New York: Holt, Rinehart & Winston, 1967.

Skinner, B. F. *The behavior of organisms.* New York: Appleton Century, 1938.

Skinner, B. F. *Walden two.* New York: Macmillan, 1948.

Skinner, B. F. *Science and human behavior.* New York: Macmillan, 1953.

Skinner, B. F. A case history in scientific method. *American Psychologist,* 1956, *11,* 221-233.

Smith, L. M. The concurrent validity of six personality and adjustment tests for children. *Psychological Monographs,* 1958, *72* (No. 457).

Smith, L. M. The micro-ethnography of the classrooom. *Psychology in the Schools,* 1967, *4,* 216-221.

Smith, L. M. *Dilemmas in educational innovation: A problem for anthropology as clinical method.* New York: American Educational Research Association, 1971.

Smith, L. M. Classroom social systems in teacher education. In B. Joyce and Marcia Weil (Eds.), *Perspectives for reform in teacher education.* Englewood Cliffs, N.J.: Prentice-Hall, 1972.

Smith, L. M. *An aesthetic education workshop for administrators: Some implications for a theory of case studies.* Paper presented at the annual meeting of the American Educational Research Association, Chicago, 1974. (a).

Smith, L. M. Images and reactions: A personal report on "An 8 Day Week." In S. Madeja et al., *Working papers: Final report on the institute in aesthetic education for administrators.* St. Louis, CEMREL, Inc., 1974. (b).

Smith, L. M. Reflections on trying to theorize from ethnographic data. *CAE Quarterly,* 1974, *5,* 18-24. (c)

Smith, L. M. *Mrs. Kaye's drawing class: Some theoretical thoughts on curriculum, teaching and learning.* St. Louis, Mo.: CEMREL, Inc., 1975.(a)

Smith, L. M. Psychological aspects of aesthetic education: Some initial observations. *Bulletin of the Council for Research in Music Education,* 1975, *43,* 92-115. (b)

Smith, L. M. Relating theory to practice in educational research: Some personal notes. In IDM, *Relating theory to practice in educational research.* Bielefeld, Germany: Institut für Didadtik der Mathematik, 1976.

Smith, L. M. Effective teaching: A qualitative inquiry in aesthetic education. *Anthropology and Education Quarterly,* 1977, *8,* 127-129. (a)

Smith, L. M. *Science education in the Alte schools: A kind of case study* (NSF Case Studies in Science Education). 1977. (b)

Smith, L. M. *Accidents, serendipity, and making the commonplace dramatic.* Unpublished manuscript. Washington University, 1978.

Smith, L. M., & Brock, J. A. M. *"Go, Bug, Go": Methodological issues in classroom observational research* (Occasional Paper Series No. 5). St. Ann, Mo.: CEMREL, Inc., 1970.

Smith, L. M., & Carpenter, P. *General reinforcement project: Qualitative observation and interpretation.* St. Ann, Mo.: CEMREL, Inc., 1972.

Smith, L. M., & Geoffrey, W. *The complexities of an urban classroom.* New York: Holt, Rinehart & Winston, 1968.

Smith, L. M., & Hudgins, B. B. *Educational psychology*. New York: Alfred A. Knopf, 1964.

Smith, L. M., & Keith, P. *Anatomy of educational innovation*. New York: John Wiley, 1971.

Smith, L. M., & Pohland, P. A. Education, technology, and the rural highlands. In D. Sjogren (Ed.), *Four evaluation examples: Anthropological, economic, narrative and portrayal*. Chicago: Rand McNally, 1974.

Smith, L. M., & Pohland, P. Grounded theory and educational ethnography: A methodological analysis and critique. In J. Roberts and S. K. Akinsanya (Eds.), *Educational patterns and cultural configurations*. New York: David McKay, 1976.

Smith, L. M., & Schumacher, S. *Extended pilot trials of the aesthetic education program: A qualitative description, analysis and evaluation*. St. Louis, Mo.: CEMREL, Inc., 1972.

Snow, C. P. *The two cultures and the scientific revolution*. Cambridge, England: University Press, 1959.

Soloman, W. *Toward the development of a theory of teaching: A participant observer's study of the experimental trial of lessons from a social studies curriculum project*. Unpublished doctoral dissertation, Washington University, 1971.

Spindler, G. Personality, sociocultural system, and education among the Menomini. In G. D. Spindler (Ed.), *Education and culture: Anthropological approaches*. New York: Holt, Rinehart & Winston, 1963.

Stake, R., and Easley, J. *Case studies in science education* (Final Rep.). Urbana, Ill.: University of Illinois, 1978.

Stouffer, S. A. (Ed.). *The American soldier* (2 vols.). Princeton, N.J.: Princeton University Press, 1949.

Stouffer, S. A. Some observations on study design. *American Journal of Sociology*, 1950, *55*, 355-361.

Struthers, M. Educational theory: A critical discussion of the O'Connor-Hirst debate. *Scottish Educational Review*, 1971, *4*, 71-78.

Tikunoff, W., Berliner, D., & Rist, R. *An ethnographic study of the forty classrooms of BTES known sample*. San Francisco: Far West Laboratory, 1975.

Tikunoff, W., and Ward, B. (Eds.) Exploring qualitative/quantitative research methodologies in education. *Anthropology and Education Quarterly*, 1977, *8*, 37-163.

Toulmin, S. *Human understanding* (Vol. 1). Princeton, N.J.: Princeton University Press, 1972.

Toulmin, S., & Goodfield, J. *The fabric of the heavens*. London: Hutchinson, 1961.

Toulmin, S., & Goodfield, J. *The architecture of matter*. London: Hutchinson, 1963.

Toulmin, S., & Goodfield, J. *The discovery of time*. London: Hutchinson, 1965.

Underwood, B. J. *Experimental psychology*. New York: Appleton-Century-Crofts, 1949.

Van Velsen, J. The extended-case method and situational analysis. In A. L. Epstein, (Ed.), *The craft of social anthropology*. London: Tavistock Publications, 1967.

Vidich, A. J., & Shapiro, G. A comparison of participant observation and survey data. *American Sociological Review*, 1955, *20*, 28-33.

Vidich, A. J., Bensman, J., and Stein, M. R. (Eds.). *Reflections on community studies*. New York: John Wiley, 1964.

Walker, D. F. A naturalistic model for curriculum development. *School Review*, 1971, *81*, 51-65.

Walker, R., and Adelman, C. *A guide to classroom observation*. London: Metheun, 1975.

Walker, W. *The sociology of teaching*. New York: John Wiley, 1932.

Warner, W. L., & Lunt, P. S. *The social life of a modern community*. New Haven, Conn.: Yale University Press, 1941.

Warren, R. *Education in Rebhausen: A German village*. New York: Holt, Rinehart & Winston, 1967.

Wax, M., Wax, R., & DuMont, Jr., R. V. Formal education in an American Indian community. Supplement to *Social Problems*, 1964, *11* (4), 1-115.

Wax, R. H. *Doing fieldwork: Warnings and advice*. Chicago: University of Chicago Press, 1971.

Webb, E., Campbell, D., Schwartz, R., and Sechrest, L. *Unobstrusive measures: Nonreactive research in the social sciences*. Chicago: Rand McNally, 1966.

White, M. The logic of historical narration. In S. Hook (Ed.), *Philosophy and history: A symposium*. New York: New York University Press, 1963.

Whyte, W. F. *Street corner society: The social structure of an Italian slum* (2nd Ed.). Chicago: University of Chicago Press, 1955.

Whyte, W. F. *Leadership and group participation: An analysis of the discussion group*. Ithaca, N.Y.: Cornell University Press, 1953.

Wilson, S. The use of ethnographic techniques in educational research. *Review of Educational Research*. 1977, *47*, 245-265.

Wolcott, H. F. *A Kwakiutl village and school*. New York: Holt, Rinehart & Winston, 1967.

Wolcott, H. F. *The man in the principal's office: An ethnography*. New York: Holt, Rinehart & Winston, 1973.

Wolcott, H. F. Criteria for an ethnographic approach to research in schools. *Human Organization*, 1975, *34*, 111-128. (a)

Wolcott, H. F. (Ed.). Ethnography of schooling. *Human Organization*, 1975, *34*, 109-215. (b)

Wolcott, H. F. *Teachers vs. technocrats: An educational innovation in anthropological perspective*. Eugene, Ore.: Center for Educational Policy and Management, University of Oregon, 1977.

Wolfson, R. *A description and analysis of an innovative living experience in Israel: The dream and the reality*. Unpublished doctoral dissertation, Washington University, 1974.

Wood, C. J. *The attempted use of participatory strategies in a localist educational task group: A description and analysis*. Unpublished doctoral dissertation, Washington University, 1977.

Yunker, R. *Police field training: The analysis of a socialization process*. Unpublished doctoral dissertation, Washington University, 1977.

Zetterberg, H. On theory and verification in sociology (3rd ed.). Totowa, N.J.: Bedminster Press, 1965.

Ziman, J. M. *Public knowledge: An essay concerning the social dimensions of science*. London: Cambridge University Press, 1968.

Name Index

Aarons, A., 218, 223
Aaronson, M., 79, 85, 90, 91, 115
Abrahams, R. D., 223
Adams, R. N., 323, 367
Aday, L. A., 276, 315
Adcock, D., 79, 90, 112
Adelman, C., 321, 323, 324, 367, 369, 376
Adkins, D. C., 87, 88, 98
Advisory Panel on Scholastic Aptitude Test Score Decline, 37, 40
Ahammer, I. H., 132, 150
Aiken, A. J., 237, 266
Ainsworth, M. D. S., 52, 54, 56, 62, 63, 64, 93, 98, 99, 100
Akinsanya, S. A., 324, 374
Akiyama, M., 74, 107
Alcalde, E., 19, 40
Aldous, J., 65, 73, 99
Alexander, K., 298, 313
Alford, R. W., 88, 99
Allardt, E., 208, 223
Allport, G. W., 367
American Academy of Arts and Sciences, 276
American Anthropological Association, 325, 366
American Educational Research Association, 325, 366
American Institute for Research, 223
American Sociological Association, 317
American Statistical Association, 280
Ammerman, H. L., 251, 266
Anderson, R., 276, 315
Anderson, R. B., 14, 45

Anderson, R. C., 239, 256, 266, 274
Andersson, T., 199, 201, 223
Andrews, S. R., 80, 81, 82, 85, 88, 89, 91, 99
Angrist, S. S., 276, 311
Annett, J., 257, 266
Apfel, N., 47-98
Appelbaum, M. I., 63, 64, 65, 70, 71, 74, 111
Apple, M. W., 231, 251, 266
Applegate, J., 321, 367
Applegate, R. B., 202, 223
Appleton, T., 63, 99
Aquilar, J., 187, 188, 190, 227
Arango, M., 79, 90, 112
Arenberg, D., 138, 139, 150
Arensberg, C. M., 320, 367
Aristotle, 230, 267
Arkin, A. M., 62, 63, 104
Arnstine, D., 168, 182
Aronfreed, J., 63, 65, 76, 99
Astin, A. W., 13, 40
Atkin, J. M., 324, 367
Atkinson, J. W., 132, 150
Atwood, M. S., 321, 367
Augstein, S., 253, 267, 274
Austen, J., 247
Ausubel, D. P., 251, 252-4, 267
Averch, H. A., 13, 40
Ayer, A. J. 177, 182

Bache, W. L., 80, 81, 82, 85, 88, 89, 91, 99
Back, K., 326, 369
Backman, M. E., 26, 40
Badger, E., 86, 89, 90, 98, 99

Badger, E. D., 81, 88, 108
Baer, D. M., 75, 77, 106, 114
Bagenstos, N. T., 321, 367
Bailey, O. T., 325, 371
Bailey, R. W., 237, 266
Bajema, C. J., 39, 40
Bakeman, R., 66, 69, 99, 102
Bakwin, H., 52, 74, 99
Bakwin, R. M., 74, 99
Baldwin, A. L., 61, 99
Ball-Rokeach, S. J., 276, 313
Baltes, P. B., 120, 124, 125, 129, 130, 132, 137, 142, 147, 150, 152, 154, 155
Ban, P., 56, 110
Bandura, A., 76, 77, 97, 99
Banfield, E. C., 57, 99
Barash, D. P., 30, 40
Barbrack, C. R., 86, 100
Barik, H. C., 206, 223
Barker, R. G., 320, 321, 344, 367
Barker, W. B., 23, 45
Barnes, B. R., 251, 252, 267
Barnett, J. T., 69, 106
Barrett, W., 178, 180, 185
Barth, F., 217, 223
Bauer, R., 276, 278, 280, 286, 301, 302, 304, 308, 311
Baumrind, D., 58, 61, 62, 65, 67, 72, 73, 97, 100
Bayley, N., 10, 40, 58, 63, 65, 72, 74, 100, 114, 115
Beason-Williams, L., 75, 117
Bechtoldt, H. P., 295, 311
Becker, H. S., 317, 320, 321, 323, 325, 326, 333, 337, 340, 343, 353, 363, 367
Becker, W. C., 61, 62, 65, 67, 68, 100
Beckwith, L., 58, 61, 63, 64, 65, 70, 100
Bee, H. L. 58, 100
Beittel, K. R., 321, 324, 326, 334, 339, 351-3, 367
Belkin, J., 188, 223
Bell, B., 136, 152
Bell, R. Q., 66, 92, 93, 100
Bell, R. W., 50, 100
Bell, S. M., 62, 63, 64, 93, 99, 100
Bell, T. H., 48, 100
Beller, E. K., 68, 85, 87, 88, 100, 116
Belmont, L., 18, 40

Belsky, J., 68, 101
Bengtson, J., 133, 150
Bennett, O., 55, 113
Bensen, J. F., 98, 101
Bensman, J., 323, 376
Benson, L., 85, 100
Bereiter, C., 17, 34, 37, 40
Berelson, B. R., 237, 267
Berg, A., 19, 40
Berger, M., 85, 101
Berkowitz, B., 81, 101
Berkowitz, W. R., 276, 311
Berlak, A., 321, 367
Berlak, H., 321, 367
Berliner, D., 149, 150, 157, 321, 376
Berliner, D. C., 160, 162, 163, 164, 171, 182, 184, 256, 273
Berman, P., 175, 182
Bernal, J., 62, 101
Bettelheim, B., 17, 40
Beyer, J. M., 276, 311
Biddle, B. J., 157, 160, 183, 316, 344, 367, 369
Biddle, W. B., 256, 266
Biderman, A. D., 301, 304, 311
Biller, H. B., 59, 101
Billingsley, K., 186
Billington, M. J., 256, 273
Bing, E., 72, 101
Birch, H. G., 19, 40, 66, 117
Birkhill, W. R., 130, 145, 150
Birns, B., 57, 105
Birren, J. E., 120, 121, 125, 137, 150
Bishop, D. W., 67, 101
Bissell, J. S., 14, 45
Blacher-Dixon, J., 82, 106
Black, A. E., 62, 65, 100
Blacklock, S., 263, 267
Blatt, B., 321, 374
Blau, P. M., 320, 325, 368
Bloch, M., 48, 107
Block, J. H., 25, 40
Block, N. J., 4, 26, 40
Bloom, B. S., 11, 37, 40, 70, 101, 131, 148, 151, 250, 267
Bloom, K., 75, 97, 101
Bloomer, J., 374
Bloomfield, L., 230, 267
Blumenthal, J. B., 80, 81, 82, 85, 88, 89, 91, 99
Blumer, H., 325, 368

Bobbitt, R. A., 51, 118
Boden, M. A., 253, 267
Boger, R. P., 85, 86, 89, 101
Boismier, N. O., 91, 105
Bond, J. T., 81, 82, 85, 88, 89, 91, 98, 109
Boring, E. G., 317, 354, 368
Bormuth, J. R., 236, 267
Bossio, V., 52, 53, 113
Boswell, 359
Botwinick, J., 126, 138, 143, 151
Boudon, R., 208, 223
Boulding, K. E., 295, 311
Bowlby, J., 49, 52, 53, 54, 101
Bowles, S., 198, 208, 223
Boyd, E. F., 78, 93, 105
Boyer E. G., 344, 375
Boyer, M., 199, 201, 223
Brackbill, Y., 75, 101
Bradford, C., 15, 41
Bradley, R., 64, 72, 73, 104
Bradley, R. H., 58, 63, 72, 73, 101
Brazelton, T. B., 55, 66, 101
Breese, F. H., 61, 99
Breland, H. M., 18, 40
Bridgeman, P., 354, 368
Bridges, E., 339
Brim, O. G., 48, 60, 71, 87, 89, 101, 102
Brock, J. A. M., 328, 375
Brock, P., 327
Brodbeck, A., 53, 102
Brodway, K. P., 10, 40
Brody, G. F., 61, 102
Broman, S. H., 74, 118
Bronfenbrenner, U., 48, 49, 60, 61, 71, 72, 78, 81, 83, 88, 102, 171, 182
Bronowski, J., 230, 267
Bronson, W. C., 68, 102
Brophy, J., 161, 182
Brophy, J. E., 162, 182
Brossard, M., 74, 102
Broudy, H. S., 171, 182
Brown, D., 202, 225
Brown, J. V., 66, 69, 99, 102
Brown, M. A., 122, 151
Brozek, J., 19, 40
Bruck, M., 200, 204, 228
Bruder, M. N., 202, 227
Bruner, J. S., 140, 151

Bruyn, S. T., 320, 323, 325, 340, 356, 358, 359, 361, 368
Bryan, J. H., 64, 75, 76, 102
Buech, B. U., 128, 155
Buium, N., 75, 117
Burger, H. G., 218, 223
Burke, K., 361, 368
Burnett-Hill, J., 324, 368
Burns, D., 90, 98, 99
Burns, R. W., 151
Burstein, L., 157
Burt, Cyril, 7, 28
Byrd, S., 219, 223

Cahen, L., 149, 150, 163, 184
Cairns, R. B., 50, 51, 102
Caldwell, B. M., 57, 58, 61, 62, 63, 64, 72, 73, 101, 102, 104, 117
Calearo, C., 137, 151
Calfee, K. H., 162, 182
Calfee, R., 162, 182
California Commission, 160, 162
Campbell, A., 282, 286, 311
Campbell, D., 349, 377
Campbell, D. T., 69, 81, 102, 114, 295, 298, 311, 316-18, 327, 335, 340, 345, 362, 368
Campbell, E. Q., 13, 22, 23, 24, 26, 34-5, 41, 103
Campbell, K., 177, 182
Campbell, R. N., 213, 223
Carew, J. V., 21, 41, 63, 65, 102
Carew Watts, J., 20, 46
Carnegie Commission on Higher Education, 121, 134, 151
Carnegie Council on Children, 48, 108
Carpenter, P., 321, 328, 375
Carroll, J. B., 230, 250, 265, 267
Carroll, S. J., 13, 40
Carter, J. F., 263, 267
Carver, R. P., 255, 267
Casagrande, J. B., 268, 323
Casler, L., 74, 102
Castell, R., 68, 103
Cattell, R. B., 127, 151
Cavanaugh, P. J., 97, 115
Caylor, J. S., 233, 236, 267, 273
Cazden, C., 58, 64, 103, 321, 344, 368
Cazden, C. B., 218, 223
Center for Applied Linguistics, 191, 222, 223

Center for Educational Research and Innovation, 321, 368,
Cerra, T. R., 14, 45
Chace, C. A., 67, 101
Chall, J. S., 234, 236, 268
Chamberlin, R. W., 61, 103
Chan, I., 63, 65, 102
Chandler, M. J., 74, 115
Charters, W. W., Jr., 321, 325, 346, 368
Chesler, D., 66, 108
Chess, S., 66, 117
Chicago City Council, 220
Chilman, C. S., 87, 88, 89, 90, 97, 103
Chiriboga, D., 145-6, 153
Chomsky, N., 230, 240, 268
Christenson, J. A., 276, 312
Churchill, S., 210, 222, 223
Cicirelli, V. G., 14, 41
Cicourel, A., 202, 223, 344
Cicourel, A. V., 321, 344, 368
Cisin, I. H., 88, 107
Clark, D. H., 23, 43
Clarke, A. D. B., 17, 41, 49, 53, 54, 55, 74, 103
Clarke, A. M., 17, 41, 49, 53, 54, 55, 74, 103
Clarke-Stewart, A., 80, 86, 87, 88, 89, 90, 91, 98, 108
Clarke-Stewart, K. A., 47-98, 103
Clausen, J. A., 68, 109
Clawson, E. U., 251, 252, 267
Cleary, T. A., 26, 41
Clemmer, A. F., 291
Clemmer, R., 278-9, 282, 286, 311
Clifton, R., 63, 99
Cochran, W. G., 288, 291, 292, 311
Coelen, C. G., 81, 86, 87, 88, 89, 110
Cohen, A., 187, 190, 199, 200, 203, 224
Cohen, R., 323, 330, 373
Cohen, S. E., 63, 64, 65, 100
Cohen, W. J., 280, 286, 311
Cohler, B. J., 61, 73, 117
Coleman, E. B., 236, 268
Coleman, J., 320, 372
Coleman, J. S., 13, 22, 23, 24, 26, 34-5, 41, 48, 103, 133-4, 151
Collins, R., 208, 224
Connolly, K. J., 140, 151

Connor, W. H., 326, 327, 330, 363, 368
Converse, P. E., 282, 286, 311
Cooper, R. L., 228
Corps Member Training Institute, 178
Corso, J. F., 136, 137, 151
Coser, L., 208, 224
Costello, J., 48, 107
Coulson, J. E., 15, 41
Craik, F. I. M., 138, 139, 148, 151
Crandall, V. C., 60, 103
Crandall, V. J., 63, 64, 103
Crane, D., 318, 325, 368
Crane, W. D., 69, 103
Cravioto, J., 19, 40
Crawford, J., 165, 183
Cronbach, L. J., 149, 151, 263, 268, 295, 296, 298, 311, 312, 358-9, 364, 368
Cropley, A. J., 121, 132, 133, 151
Cross, A. D., 67, 111
Crothers, E. J., 239, 250, 268
Crowell, D. C., 87, 98
Cruickshank, D. R., 160, 183
Cukier, L., 251, 267
Cummins, J., 206, 210, 224
Cureton, E. E., 295, 312
Curtiss, S., 17-8, 41, 54, 103
Cusick, P. A., 321, 368

Dahrendorf, R., 208, 224
Dale, E., 234, 236, 268
Dalto, G., 192, 212, 226
Daley, Mayor, 220
Danish, S. J., 120, 147, 150
Darcy, N., 203, 206, 224
Darwin, 30
Datan, N., 135, 154
Dave, R., 151
Dave, R. H., 58, 103, 121, 151
Davenport, R. K., 49, 50, 104, 114
David, J., 14, 44
Davids, A., 61, 104
Davidson, K. S., 321, 374
Davies, I. K., 251, 269
Davis, K., 17, 41, 53, 104
Day, M. C., 81, 85, 88, 89, 118
Deans, T., 253, 274
Dearborn W., 171
Dearden, R. F., 168, 183
Décarie, T. G., 74, 102

DeFries, J. C., 8, 9, 10, 30, 41
DeGroot, A. D., 12, 41, 257, 268
Delamont, J., 370
Delamont, S., 321, 368
DeLeeuw, L., 59, 119
Denbow, C. J., 234, 268
Denenberg, V. H., 50, 100
DeNeufville, J. I., 294, 295, 301, 312
Denner, P. R., 254, 256, 272
Dennis, W., 52, 53, 54, 74, 104
Denzin, N. K., 323, 340, 345, 369
Derogatis, L. R., 276, 312
DeSaussure, F., 230, 268
Deutsch, C. P., 57, 104
Dewey, R., 63, 103
Diesing, P., 316, 332, 333, 336, 339, 369
Dillman, D. A., 276, 312
Dilthey, W., 241, 268
Dishaw, M., 163, 183, 184
DiVesta, F., 149, 151
DiVesta, F. J., 145, 154, 256, 272
Dodd, B. J., 75, 104
Doherty, W. J., 15, 41
Donaldson, G., 142, 143, 152
Donaldson, T. S., 13, 40
Downey, J., 87, 88, 104
Dray, W., 356, 264, 369
Dreir, P., 208, 224
Drurry, T. F., 311
Dubin, S., 122, 123, 148, 152
Dubin, S. S., 152
Duchastel, P., 251, 268
Duck, G. A., 15, 41
Dumaret, A., 9, 45
Dummett, M., 230, 268
DuMont, R. V., Jr., 321, 377
Duncan, O. D., 32, 41, 276, 279, 286, 312
Dunkin, M. J., 160, 183, 344, 369
Dunn, J. F., 64, 104
Dunphy, D. C., 237, 274
DuPan, R. M., 53, 104
Duyme, M., 9, 45
Dworkin, G., 4, 26, 40
Dye, H. B., 16, 45, 53, 116
Dye, T. R., 276, 312
Dyer, J. L., 82, 88, 111

Easley, J., 322, 328, 376
Easley, J. A., 321, 324, 369

Eaves, L. J., 11, 41, 43
Ebel, R. L., 295, 312
Eckland, B. K., 24, 41
Eddy, E. M., 321, 369
Educational Testing Service, 248, 268
Edwards, N., 229
Eisner, E., 321, 369
Elardo, R., 58, 63, 64, 72, 73, 101, 104
Elazar, D. J., 207-8, 212, 224
Elderton E. M., 8, 41
Elias, P., 162, 164, 183, 184
Elias, P. J., 162, 184
Ellett, F., 157
Elliot, J., 321, 369
Elliot, O., 50, 104
Elstein, A. S., 179, 185
Emerson, P. E., 62, 63, 64, 67, 115
Empson, W., 241, 268
Endsley, R. C., 64, 104
Engel, M., 62, 63, 104
Engle, P. L., 187, 191, 224
English, A. C., 268
English, H. B., 268
Ennis, P. H., 276, 312
Ennis, R. H., 168, 183
Epstein, A. S., 67, 86, 91, 104
Epstein, N., 195, 224
Epstein, T. E., 323, 369
Erickson, D., 224
Erickson, F., 316, 319, 324, 344, 354, 369
Erickson, M. T., 75, 101
Ericson, D., 157
Erlanger, H. S., 57, 58, 59, 60, 104
Erlenmeyer-Kimling, L., 11, 41
Ervin-Tripp, S., 202, 224
Escalona, S., 61, 104
Esposito, A., 97, 101
Etaugh, C., 59, 105
Etzel, B. C., 75, 93, 105
Evans, E., 132, 152
Evans, J. L., 86, 91, 104
Evans, J. W., 14, 41
Everhart, R., 321, 368
Evertson, C., 161, 182
Evertson, C. M., 162, 182
Eysenck, 4

Fairbanks, R., 278-9, 282, 286, 311
Falconer, D. S., 6, 41

Falender, C. A., 91, 105
Far West Laboratory, 162, 163, 183
Farr, J. N., 259, 268
Fathman, A., 187, 224
Faw, H. W., 256, 268
Feigl, H., 354, 356, 369
Fein, G., 69, 80, 83, 86, 87, 88, 89, 90, 91, 98, 108
Feingold, J., 9, 45
Fels, 10
Felson, M., 308, 309, 312, 313, 314
Fensham, P. J., 252, 274
Fenstermacher, G. D., 157-82
Ferguson, C., 80, 85, 86, 90, 191, 224
Ferguson, T., 52, 105
Ferriss, A. L., 278, 299, 312
Feshbach, N., 76, 105
Feshbach, S., 76, 105
Festinger, L., 320, 326, 369
Fifer, G., 23, 43
Figueroa, R. A., 24, 43
Filby, N. N., 157, 163, 171, 182, 183, 184
Fillmore, C., 238, 268
Finch, M. E., 321, 354, 369
Finkelstein, N. W., 75, 105
Finner, S. L., 276, 312
Finocchiaro, M., 203, 224
Firkowska, A., 25, 41
Firth, J. R., 230, 268
Firth, R. W., 320, 369
Fisher, C., 162, 163, 182, 184
Fishman, B., 209, 212, 222, 224
Fishman, J. A., 190, 191, 192, 209, 212, 222, 224
Fiske, D. W., 295, 298, 311, 327, 345, 368
Fitzgerald, D., 251, 267
Flavell, J. H., 125, 132, 147, 152
Flax, M. J., 276, 312
Fleming, R. W., 263, 274
Flesch, R. F., 234, 236, 260, 268
Fodor, J. A., 158, 183
Folsom, R. E., Jr., 291, 314
Ford, J. P., 236, 267
Forehand, R., 58, 97, 119
Forest, I., 105
Forgays, D. G., 49, 105
Forgays, J. W., 49, 105
Forrester, B. J., 91, 105
Fox, L. C., 233, 236, 267, 270, 273

Fox, T. G., 179, 183
Fozard, J. L., 136, 152
Francis, W. N., 268
Frank, P., 295, 312
Frase, L. T., 229, 255-6, 258, 263, 268, 269
Fredericksen, C. H., 239, 269
Fredrickson, W. T., 66, 102
Freeberg, N. E., 64, 105
Freedle, R., 57, 110
Freedle, R. C., 267
Freeman, H. E., 282, 286, 301, 302, 307, 314
Freeman, P. K., 81, 85, 88, 89, 118
Frege, 230
Freire, 219
Freud, 178, 319
Frick, T., 177, 183
Friedman, M., 207-8, 212, 224
Friedrich, D. K., 126, 152
Frisbie, P., 276, 312
Fulker, D. W., 7, 28, 41, 43
Fuller, J. L., 50, 115
Funkhouser, G. R., 258-9, 260-3, 269
Furfey, P. H., 79, 115
Furst, N., 160, 185

Gaarder, B., 188, 212, 224
Gage, N. L., 33, 41, 160, 165, 179, 183
Gagné, R. M., 242, 249-50, 269
Galper, A., 132, 156
Galton, F., 36, 39, 41
Games, P. A., 251, 269
Gane, C. P., 248, 270
Garber, H., 16, 41, 55, 106
Gardner, H., 326, 369
Garfinkel, H., 202, 224, 323, 369
Garland, J. A., 55, 113
Garner, A. P., 64, 104
Gaulin-Kremer, E., 66, 105
Geer, B., 321, 323, 325, 337, 367
Geffert, H. N., 194, 197, 224
Genesee, F., 204, 224
Genie, 17-8
Geoffrey, W., 321, 326-7, 330, 332, 335, 342-3, 344, 346, 354, 355, 357, 361, 362, 363, 375
George, J. S., 123, 152
Gerbner, G., 237, 269
Gesell, A., 17, 42

Gewirtz, J. L., 75, 76, 78, 93, 105, 114
Ghodssi, M., 74, 107
Gilmer, B., 88, 89, 92, 98, 105
Gintis, H., 198, 208, 223
Glaser, B., 334, 369
Glaser, B. G., 323, 328, 337, 339, 340, 349, 363, 369
Glass, G. V., 15, 42, 298, 312
Glick, J., 80, 82, 85, 88, 112
Glitter, A. C., 276, 312
Glitter, G. A., 276, 313
Goffman, E., 202, 225, 320, 325, 361, 369
Gold, F. L., 361, 369
Goldberg, S., 56, 63, 64, 65, 99, 105, 110
Goldberger, A. S., 7, 13, 42
Golden, M., 57, 105
Goldfarb, W., 52, 105
Gomber, J. M., 50, 105
Gomez, H., 16, 44
Gonda, J. N., 130, 140, 153
Goodenough, F., 344, 369
Goodfield, J., 358, 362, 376
Goodlad, J. I., 175, 183
Goodman, P., 219, 225
Goodson, D. B., 48, 83, 85, 86, 87, 88, 89, 106
Goody, J., 276, 312
Gooler, D., 278, 312
Gordon, B., 223
Gordon, B. N., 80, 81, 91, 109
Gordon, C., 129, 152
Gordon, E., 35, 42
Gordon, I. J., 79, 80, 82, 85, 86, 88, 89, 91, 106
Gottman, J. M., 69, 106, 298, 312
Gouldner, A. W., 320, 325, 362, 369, 370
Goulet, L. R., 126, 152
Gowin, D. B., 360, 364, 370
Graham, J., 188, 223
Gramsci, A., 208, 212, 225
Grandon, G., 18, 46
Granick, S., 137, 152
Graubard A. 219, 225
Gray, E. D. McQ., 221, 225
Gray, S. W., 16, 42, 81, 82, 85, 88, 89, 91, 92, 98, 105, 106, 109
Graziano, A., 81, 101

Green, J., 207, 228
Green, R. F., 142, 152
Green, T. A., 360, 370
Green, T. F., 167-8, 183
Greenbaum, C. W., 93, 106
Greenbaum, S., 239, 272
Greenberg, M., 67, 106, 168
Greene, D., 97, 110
Greene, M., 183
Greenfield, T. B., 205, 210, 225
Gribbin, K., 126, 130, 141, 155
Gribble, J., 339, 370
Grice, G. R., 257, 269
Griffin, G., 49, 106
Grimes, J. E., 239, 269
Grimshaw, A., 202, 225
Grotelueschen, A., 256, 271
Grotevant, H. D., 30, 42
Grusec, J., 49, 117
Grusec, J. E., 76, 99
Guinagh, B., 79, 85, 88, 89, 91, 106
Gump, P. V., 320, 321, 323, 344, 367, 370
Gustafson H. W., 256, 269
Gustafson, L. M., 233, 260, 270
Gutelius, M. F., 85, 86, 106
Guttman, J., 276, 314

Habenstein, R. W., 323, 370
Haese, P. N., 276, 313
Hagen, E., 4, 46
Hagstrom, W., 318, 370
Halcomb, R. A., 10, 41
Halfar, C., 63, 65, 102
Hall, B., 321, 370
Hall, D., 278-9, 282, 286, 311
Halliday, M. A. K., 238, 269
Halpin, A. W., 349, 370
Hamenway, J. A., 15, 41
Hamilton, D., 321, 324, 326, 349, 366, 370, 373, 374
Hamilton-Smith, N., 237, 266
Hamm, P. M., Jr., 92, 106
Hammond, P. E., 323, 370
Hanes, S. D., 15, 41
Hanks, C., 67, 113
Hannan, E. J., 298, 312
Hansen, M. H., 291, 292, 312
Hanson, R. A., 63, 64, 65, 70, 71, 106
Hantman, S. A., 81, 85, 88, 89, 118
Harlow, H. F., 49, 50, 51, 106, 112

Harnischfeger, A., 162, 183, 185
Härnqvist, K., 12, 42
Harper, L. V., 51, 106
Harper II, R. J., 194, 197, 224
Harré, R., 180, 183
Harrell, J. E., 59, 106
Harrington, Rep., 277
Harris, C. W., 300, 312
Harris, F. R., 75, 106
Harrison, A. N., 78, 115
Harte, T. J., 79, 115
Hartley, J., 251, 269
Hartsough, C. S., 162, 183
Hasan, R., 238, 269
Haskins, R., 82, 106
Hatch, E., 222, 225
Hatcher, C. W., 256, 273
Hatt, F., 263, 269
Hauser, P. M., 286, 313
Havighurst, R. J., 125, 146, 152
Hawkridge, D., 229
Heath, S. B., 192, 225
Hebb, D. O., 49, 106
Heber, F. R., 16, 41
Heber, R., 55, 91, 105, 106
Hebert, R., 216, 225
Hegmann, J. P., 10, 41
Hein, A., 49, 107
Heinicke, C. M., 87, 107
Heinig, C., 59, 119
Heinstein, M. I., 61, 62, 107
Held, R., 49, 107
Hellmer, L. A., 67, 68, 100
Hempel, C. G., 355, 356, 359, 360, 363, 364, 370
Henry, J., 321, 370
Hepler, R., 66, 102
Hernstein, R. J., 4, 24-5, 42
Heron, W., 49, 117
Herscher, L., 61, 117
Hertz, T. W., 92, 93, 100, 107
Hertzig, M. E., 66, 117
Herzog, E., 59, 88, 107
Hess, R. D., 48, 83, 85, 86, 87, 88, 89, 106, 107
Hewett K., 81, 86, 87, 88, 89, 110
Hewitt, C., 237, 238, 269
Hickey, L., 132, 152
Hickey, T., 132, 152
Hiemstra, R., 121, 152
Hildreth, G. H., 8, 42

Hill-Burnett, J., 198, 214, 225, 325
Hiller, J. H., 256, 263, 269
Hiller, R. J., 193, 194, 195, 228
Hinde, R. A., 49, 50, 51, 107
Hindley, C., 57, 58, 107
Hines, B., 88, 99
Hines, R. P., 80, 85, 86, 91, 110
Hirsch, E. D., 241, 269
Hirst, P. H., 168, 183, 359, 370
Hobson, C. J., 13, 22, 23, 24, 26, 34-5, 41, 103
Hodges H. A., 241, 269
Hodgins, A., 90, 98, 99
Hodgins, A. S., 81, 88, 108
Hoffer, E., 339, 370
Hoffman, L. W., 59, 96, 107, 112
Hoffman, M. L., 61, 107
Hogarty, P. S., 11, 44, 63, 64, 65, 70, 71, 74, 111
Holland, J. L., 134, 152
Holmes, J., 202, 225
Holsti, O. R., 237, 269, 272
Holz, R. F., 276, 313
Homans, G. C., 197, 222, 225, 317, 320, 325, 331, 332, 340, 349-50, 355, 356, 361, 370, 371
Honig, A. S., 85, 86, 88, 89, 91, 109
Honzik, M. P., 58, 67, 68, 69, 71, 72, 107
Horabin, I. S., 248, 270
Horn, J. L., 142, 143, 152
Hornblum, J. N., 133, 152
Horner, V. M., 199, 225
Horowitz, F. D., 85, 107
Horowitz, I. L., 331, 371
Houle, C. O., 121, 132, 134, 149, 152
House, E. R., 15, 42, 148
Housman, A. E., 339, 371
Hoyer, W. J., 138, 152
Hsu, F. L. K., 371
Hubbell, R., 82, 83, 85, 86, 88, 89, 110
Hubel, D. H., 50, 118
Huberman, M., 135, 149, 152
Hudgins, B. B., 331, 376
Hughes, E., 321, 325, 337, 367
Hulicka, I. M., 139, 153
Hull, C. L., 355, 371
Hultsch, D. F., 138, 140, 153
Human Interaction Institute, 175, 183
Humphreys, L., 320, 371

Humphreys, L. G., 26, 41
Hunt, J. McV., 11, 37, 42, 49, 57, 60, 74, 107, 117
Hurlburt, N., 11, 44
Hurley, J. R., 62, 108
Hurwitz, W. N., 291, 292, 312
Hymel, S., 78, 113
Hymes, D., 202, 218, 223, 225, 321, 344, 368
Hymovitch, B., 49, 108

Iannaccone, L., 321, 324, 325, 340, 371, 372
Idenberg, P. J., 219, 225
Illich, I., 219, 225
Impara, J., 276, 278, 282, 286, 311
Impara, J. C., 276, 313
Institute of Educational Technology, 245, 265
Interagency Panel on Early Childhood Research and Development, 79
Irvine, D. J., 276, 313
Irwin, O. C., 53, 102

Jacklin, C. N., 25, 44, 51, 111
Jackson, 358
Jackson, J. M., 371
Jackson, P., 321
Jacob, T., 96, 108
Jacobs, G., 323, 371
Jacobson, R., 202, 225
Jacoby, N. H., 201, 225
Jaeger, J., 278, 313
Jaeger, R. M., 276-311, 313
Jaffe, J., 66, 108
Jantz, R., 132, 156
Jarvella, R., 66, 114
Jarvik, L. F., 11, 41
Jencks, C., 10, 11, 13, 24, 27, 42, 48, 108
Jenkins, D., 324, 326, 366, 367, 370
Jenkins, J. J., 239, 259, 268, 269, 358, 371
Jennings, K., 344, 368
Jennings, S., 344, 368
Jensen, A. R., 3, 4, 6, 7, 14, 17, 22-4, 26, 27, 28, 31, 34, 35, 36-7, 39, 42, 43, 70, 108
Jensen, G. D., 51, 118
Jerauld, R., 66, 108
Jespersen, O., 230, 269

Jester, R. E., 79, 85, 89, 106
Jinks, J. L., 7, 11, 12, 43
John, V. P., 199, 218, 223, 225, 321, 344, 368
Johns, R. L., 298, 313
Johnson, A. B., 230, 270
Johnson, D. L., 80, 85, 86, 91, 110
Johnson, P. E., 241-2, 270, 273
Johnson-Laird, P. N., 253, 266, 270
Johnston, M. E., 192, 212, 226
Johnstone, J., 122, 153
Joint Committee on Programmed Instruction and Teaching Machines, 230-1
Jones, J., 321, 346, 354, 368
Jones, S. J., 57, 64, 72, 73, 108, 112
Jordan, K. F., 298, 313
Joyce, B., 160, 183
Junker, B. H., 323, 361, 371

Kadushin, A., 55, 108
Kaestle, C. F., 300, 313
Kagen, J., 10, 43, 56, 57, 58, 72, 74, 108, 111, 112, 117, 132, 153
Kahan, A. J., 80, 85, 86, 91, 110
Kalhorn, J., 61, 99
Kalish, R., 132, 152
Kalsbeek, W. D., 291, 314
Kalton, G., 288, 291, 314
Kamin, L. J., 4, 7, 8, 12, 27, 28, 32, 43, 140, 153
Kaplan, A., 295, 313, 360, 363, 371
Karnes, M. B., 81, 88, 108
Katkovsky, W., 63, 103
Katz, J. E., 331, 371
Katz, S. H., 23, 45
Kaufman, I. C., 51, 108
Kausler, D. H., 68, 117
Kaye, A. R., 251, 270
Kaye, K., 69, 108
Kaye, Mrs., 335
Kearl, B. E., 234, 272
Keele, T., 74, 111
Keith, P., 321, 326, 339, 343, 354, 363, 376
Kelleher, C., 123, 153
Keller, F. S., 250, 270
Kemmis, J., 367
Kendrick, S. A., 26, 41
Keniston, K., 48, 108
Kennedy, M. M., 14, 43

Kennedy, W. A., 22, 43
Kennell, J. H., 66, 108, 109, 114
Kerlinger, F. M., 222, 225, 313
Kerlinger, F. N., 283
Kern, R. P., 233, 270, 273
Kessen, W., 69, 80, 83, 86, 87, 88, 89, 90, 91, 98, 108
Keynes, M., 264, 265
Kiesling, H. J., 13, 40
Kifer, E., 56, 58, 64, 109
Killian, G. A., 61, 62, 63, 64, 65, 71, 72, 103
Kimball S., 323, 325, 371
Kimball, S. T., 320, 367, 371
King, C., 324, 326, 366, 370
King, F. J., 149, 153
King, P., 203, 224
Kingston, A. J., 237, 270
Kinsbourne, M., 138, 153
Kintsch, W., 239, 270
Kirchner, E. P., 132, 153
Kirk, S. A., 74, 109
Kish, L., 292, 313
Kjolseth, R., 212, 225
Klapp, O. E., 339, 371
Klare, G. R., 229, 233, 234, 235, 236, 249, 251, 260, 269, 270
Klaus, M. H., 66, 108, 109, 114
Klaus, R. A., 16, 42, 81, 82, 85, 88, 89, 92, 106, 109
Kleban, M. H., 137, 152
Klein, M. F., 175, 183
Klein, R. E., 56, 108
Klein, R. L., 146, 153
Klinghammer, E., 50, 109
Kluckhohn, C., 373
Kluckhohn, F., 323, 371
Knowles, R. T., 48, 107
Knox, A. B., 121, 122, 134, 153
Kogan, K. L., 80, 81, 82, 91, 109
Kogan, N., 143, 156
Kohlberg L., 63, 76, 77, 109, 120, 125, 146, 153
Kohn, M., 58, 109
Kohn, M. L., 68, 109
Kolb, S., 75, 119
Koluchová, J., 17, 43, 54, 109
Konig, E., 137, 153
Konner, M., 56, 109
Kopp, C. B., 63, 64, 65, 100
Korn, S., 66, 117

Korner, A. F., 75, 117
Koslowski, B., 66, 101
Kotelchuck, M., 67, 109
Kounin, J. S., 323, 328, 370, 371
Krauss, I. K., 142, 153
Kreger, N. C., 66, 108
Kreling, B., 78, 115
Kropp, R. P., 149
Kuhn, T. S., 109, 196, 225, 318, 358, 371
Kulhavy, R. W., 257, 270
Kuusinen, J., 215, 227

Labouvie, G. V., 128, 130, 152, 155
Labouvie-Vief, G., 127, 129, 130, 140, 153, 155
Ladas, H., 255, 270
Lakatos, I., 318, 371
Lakin, M., 61, 109
Lally, J. R., 85, 86, 88, 89, 91, 109
Lamb, M. E., 67, 109
Lambert, N. M., 162, 183
Lambert W. E., 187, 200, 222, 226
Lambie, D. Z., 81, 82, 85, 86, 88, 89, 91, 98, 109
Land, K. C., 276, 279, 282-5, 286, 301, 304, 306, 308, 309, 310, 312, 313, 314
Laudau, R., 93, 106
Lanier, J. E., 179, 185
Largay, D., 48, 107
Larkin, R. W., 197-8, 199, 208, 222, 226
Lasater, T. M., 80, 85, 90, 109
Lasswell, H. D., 237, 270
Lau, 193-5, 214
Lawton, J. T., 251, 252, 270
Lay, M., 132, 153
Lazar, I., 82, 83, 85, 86, 88, 89, 110
Lazersfeld, P. F., 157, 183
Lazzaroni, A., 137, 151
Leacock, E. B., 321, 371
Lebo, C. P., 136-7, 153
Leckie, M.S., 58, 100
Leech, G. N., 239, 272
Legarreta-Marcaida, D., 206, 226
Leiderman, P. H., 55, 110
Leiter, K., 344, 368
Leites, N., 237, 270
Leler, H., 80, 85, 86, 91, 110
Lengrand, P., 121, 151

Lenneberg, E. H., 230, 270
Lennon, R. T., 295, 313
Lenski, G. E., 210, 226
Lepper, M. R., 97, 110
Lerner, D., 237, 270
Lesser, G., 23, 46
Lesser, G. S., 23, 43
Levenstein, P., 79, 80, 81, 82, 85, 86, 88, 89, 91, 92, 110, 111
Levenstein, S., 79, 81, 111
Lévi-Strauss, C., 354, 371
Levin, H., 61, 115
Levine, J. A., 58, 111
Levy, D. M., 61, 66, 110
Levy, G., 181, 183
Lewis, B. N., 248, 270
Lewis, H. N., 55, 61, 110
Lewis, M., 56, 57, 64, 65, 67, 110
Lewontin, R. C., 4, 27, 31, 32, 43
Lieberman, A., 175, 183
Lieberson, S., 192, 203, 212, 226
Liebow, E., 320, 371
Lindzey, G., 10, 11, 19, 23, 27, 38, 43
Lipnick, B., 321, 354, 371
Lipset, S. M., 320, 325, 372
Lipton, E. L., 61, 117
Lipton, R. C., 52, 53, 113
Lloreda, P., 16, 44
Lockridge, K. A., 276, 313
Loeding, D., 256, 273
Loehlin, J. C., 7, 9, 10, 11, 19, 23, 27, 30, 38, 43
Loevinger, J., 298, 313
Lohnes, P. R., 26, 43
Loman, B., 203, 226
Lonbard, A. D., 87, 89, 110
London, R., 80, 82, 85, 88, 112
Long, H., 121, 122, 134, 153
Lopez, D. E., 201, 226
Lorenz, K. Z., 50, 110
Lortie, 325
Louch, A. R., 158, 183
Lovas, J., 190, 209, 224
Love., J. M., 81, 86, 87, 88, 89, 110
Lovelace, T., 237, 270
Lowe, J. C., 146, 154
Lowenthal, M. F., 145-6, 153
Lumsdaine, A. A., 230-1, 251, 270, 275
Lunt, P. S., 320, 377

Luria, Z., 67, 68, 100
Luscher, K., 48, 60, 111
Lutz, F. W., 321, 324, 372
Lyle, J. G., 74, 111
Lyman, D. A., 92, 106
Lynn, D. B., 59, 67, 111
Lytton, H., 64, 68, 111

Mabry, J. E., 233, 260, 270
MacArthur, R. S., 26, 44
Maccoby, E. E., 25, 44, 51, 61, 111, 115
Maccoby, N., 258-9, 260-3, 269
MacDonald, B., 324, 326, 366, 370, 372
Macdonald-Ross, M., 229-66, 271
MacGregor, D., 320, 367
MacKay, R., 344, 368
Mackey, W. F., 190, 199, 209, 226
MacManus, S., 276, 313
Macnamara, J., 187, 199, 204-5, 226
Madden, J., 79, 81, 111
Madow, W. G., 291, 292, 312
Mager, R. F., 250, 263, 271
Magoon, A. J., 31, 44, 324, 372
Magoon, J., 177, 184
Magura, S., 276, 313
Main, M., 66, 101
Malcolm, N., 180, 184
Malherbe, E. G., 187, 226
Malinowski, B., 320, 323, 331, 332, 333, 340, 372
Malone, P., 80, 85, 86, 90, 109
Mangus, S., 92, 93, 107
Mann, A. J., 92, 93, 107
March, 332
Marciano, R., 14, 44
Marcotte, D. R., 263, 269
Marcy, T. G., 63, 64, 65, 100
Marin, P., 219, 226
Marjoribanks, K., 20, 44, 69, 72, 118
Marliave, R., 160, 163, 184
Marliave, R. S., 171, 182
Marolla, F., 19, 46
Marolla, F. A., 18, 40
Marquette, B. W., 125, 145, 155
Martin, B., 81, 90, 97, 111
Martin, M. J., 64, 104
Martin, T., 263, 269
Martin, W., 247
Maslow, A. H., 372

Mason, M. K., 17, 44
Matarazzo, J. D., 142, 153
Mathey, F. J., 141, 153
Mautz, R. K., 136, 154
Mayer, R., 120, 153
Mayer, R. E., 256, 271
McAlpine, W., 66, 108
McAskie, M., 7, 28, 44
McCall, G. J., 323, 340, 372
McCall, R. B., 11, 44, 63, 64, 65, 69, 70, 71, 74, 111
McCarthy, J. L. G., 87, 89, 111
McClellan, J., 168, 184, 332
McDonald, F. J., 162, 164, 184
McFall, R. M., 69, 106
McGaw, B., 256, 271
McGee, R. K., 49, 111
McGurk, F. C. J., 22, 44
McKay, A., 16, 44
McKay, H., 16, 44
McKinney, J. P., 74, 111
McKinney, W. L., 331, 372
McLaughlin, H., 55, 113
McLaughlin, M. W., 175, 182, 184
McLean, L. D., 15, 42
McNemar, Q., 21, 44
McPartland, J., 13, 22, 23, 24, 26, 34-5, 41, 103
McPherson, G. H., 321, 372
Mead, M., 320, 372
Mease, W., 86, 101
Medawar, P. B., 250, 271
Medley, D. M., 160, 175, 184
Meehan, E. J., 372
Meehl, P. E., 295, 296, 312, 323, 336, 359, 368, 372
Mehan, H., 202, 226, 344, 368
Meier, G. W., 49, 111
Meile, R. L., 276, 313
Melching, W. H., 251, 266
Melikoff, O., 203, 226
Melton, R. F., 251, 271
Menlove, F. L., 76, 99
Menzel, E. W., 50, 104
Mercer, J., 26, 44
Mercurio, J. A., 321, 372
Merino, B., 187, 224
Merriam, I. C., 276, 313
Merrill, J., 136, 154
Merrill, P., 251, 268

Merton, R. K., 197, 226, 323, 325, 332, 338, 363, 372
Messenger, K. P., 81, 85, 88, 89, 118
Messick, S., 295, 313
Meyer, B. J. F., 263, 271
Meyer, P., 208, 223
Michigan State University Institute for Research on Teaching, 179
Mikel, E. K., 321, 367
Mill, J. S., 165-6, 168, 184
Miller, D. B., 325, 373
Miller, J. O., 88, 89, 92, 98, 105, 111
Miller, L. B., 82, 88, 111
Miller, L. R., 236, 271
Miller, R. B., 301, 302, 307, 314
Miller, S. J., 92, 111
Miller, S. M., 35, 44
Milner, E., 61, 111
Minton, C., 58, 111
Mischel, T., 373
Mitchell, J. L., 237, 271
Modiano, N., 187, 226
Mohandessi, K., 74, 107
Molina, J., 186
Monge, R., 120
Montague, W. E., 239, 266
Mood, A. M., 13, 22, 23, 24, 26, 34-5, 41, 103
Moore, H., 253, 274
Moore, J. W., 146, 154
Moore, W. E., 294, 300, 301, 314
Moray, N., 139, 153
Morgan, S. T., 66, 102
Morris, A. G., 80, 82, 85, 88, 112
Morris, N., 67, 106
Morton, N. E., 11, 44, 45
Moser, C. A., 288, 291, 314
Moses, S., 122, 154
Moss, H. A., 10, 43, 57, 58, 61, 64, 66, 72, 73, 77, 108, 112, 114, 132, 153
Mosteller, F., 13, 44, 314
Mottl, Rep., 277
Mowrer, 355
Moynihan, D. P., 13, 44
Müller, F. M., 230, 271
Muller, H. J., 39, 44
Munroe, R., 321, 373
Munsinger, H., 8, 28, 44, 45
Murchison, C. A., 325, 373
Murphy, D. R., 233, 271

Murphy, R. T., 248, 272
Murray, E. J., 68, 112
Murray, H., 82, 83, 85, 86, 89, 110, 334, 353
Murray, H. A., 373
Murthy, M. N., 291, 292, 314
Musgrove, A., 318, 371
Mussen, P. H., 76, 112
Myers, J. H., 276, 314

Nardi, A. H., 146, 154
Naroll, R., 323, 373
National Academy of Sciences, 48, 59, 112
NASA, 170, 302
National Assessment of Educational Progress, 284-5, 291-2, 299, 300, 303, 310, 314
National Center for Education Statistics, 278, 290, 292
National Indian Brotherhood, 214, 226
National Institute of Education, 160, 186, 193, 209, 222, 226, 316, 329
National Science Foundation, 316, 328
National Society for the Study of Education, 48, 112
National Swedish Board of Education, 190, 226
Natives in bilingual education, 226
Nauta, M. J., 81, 86, 87, 88, 89, 110
Novojsky, B. J., 66, 114
Nechlin, H., 62, 63, 104
Neisser, U., 266, 272
Nelson, C., 278, 282, 286, 311
Nelson K., 58, 64, 65, 112
Nelson, K. E., 75, 112
Nelson W. H., 149, 153
Nesselroade, J. R., 125, 150
Nett, R., 222, 228
Neugarten, B. L., 134, 135, 146, 154
Newcomb, C. H., 88, 107
Newell, A., 232, 257, 266, 272
Nichols, R. C., 3-40, 43, 44, 62, 112
Nichols, W. H., 233, 270
Nieves-Squires, S., 222, 226
Nimnickt, G., 79, 90, 112
Noe, F. P., 276, 314
Nolan, P., 332, 373
North, R. C., 237, 272

Novak, J. D., 50, 252, 272, 273
Novak, M. A., 112
Nowlis, V., 72, 116
Nye, F. I., 59, 112
Nyman, A. J., 49, 112
Nyman, B. A., 58, 100

O'Connor, D. J., 360, 373
Odom, A. H., 64, 104
OECD, 307, 316
Office of Bilingual Education, 186
Ogilvie, D. M., 237, 274
Okun, M. A., 145, 154
O'Leary, S., 67, 113
Olim, E. G., 58, 112
Olson, W. C., 344, 373
O'Malley, J., 87, 88, 98
Orne, M. T., 343, 373
Osofsky, J. D., 66, 112
Osterberg, T., 187, 226
Ostrowska, A., 25, 41
Overton, W. F., 133, 152
Ozenne, D. G., 15, 41

Packard, J., 321, 368
Paden, L. Y., 85, 107
Page, E. B., 18, 19, 44, 46
Pakstis, A. J., 23, 45
Palmer, 89
Palmer, F. H., 49, 112
Palmer, R. E., 241, 272
Pampel, F. C., 308, 314
Parelius, A., 154
Parham, I. A., 127, 128, 129, 130, 143, 154, 155
Parke, R., 301, 302, 307, 314
Parke, R. D., 60, 67, 68, 69, 76, 78, 112, 113, 115
Parker, A. L., 76, 112
Parkman-Ray, M., 82, 113
Parlett, M., 324, 326, 349, 366, 370, 372, 373
Parmelee, A. H., 63, 64, 65, 100
Parsons, T., 197, 198, 199, 227
Pascual, H. W., 190, 219, 227
Pask, G., 242, 253, 272
Pastalan, L. A., 136, 154
Paterson, D. G., 259, 268
Paulston, C., 188, 223
Paulston, C. B., 186-223, 227

Paulston, R. G., 186, 196-7, 198, 199, 207, 208, 217, 219, 222, 227
Payne, 64, 105
Payne, S., 145, 154
Pearlstone, A., 138, 156
Pearsall, M., 320, 371
Pedersen, F., 57, 58, 112
Pedersen, F. A., 63, 64, 67, 68, 72, 113, 119
Pedersen, H., 230, 272
Pedhazur, E., 283, 313
Peery, J. C., 66, 108
Peirce, C. S., 230, 272
Pellegrin, R., 321, 368
Pelto, P., 323, 373
Pelto, P. J., 209, 222, 227
Peng, S. S., 36, 45
Penney, C. G., 139, 154
Pepper, S. C., 361, 373
Peters, R. S., 158, 168, 183, 184, 231, 251, 272, 360, 373
Peterson, D., 121, 154
Peterson, D. R., 67, 68, 100
Peterson, R. R., 276, 312
Philips, S., 218, 227
Phillips, D. C., 157
Phillips, J. R., 64, 113
Piaget, J., 124, 132-3, 140, 154, 180, 184, 319, 325, 373
Pialorsi, F., 204, 227
Pierce, J. E., 82, 106
Pincus, J., 13, 40
Pineiro, C., 19, 40
Pirsig, R. M., 244, 272
Plemons, J. K., 130, 154
Plomin, R., 8, 9, 30, 41
Podolsky, S., 136, 152
Pohland, P., 316
Pohland, P. A., 321, 324, 328, 340, 345, 373, 376
Polanyi, M., 238, 272
Polivanov, S., 10, 45
Polsky, Howard W., 320, 373
Pool I. deS., 237, 270, 272
Popkewitz, T., 179, 184
Popper, K. R., 253, 272
Portens, A. W., 273
Powdermaker, H., 323, 361, 373
Powell, L. F., 75, 113
Powell, M., 157
Power, T., 78, 113

Powers, R. D., 234, 272
Prator, C., 187, 190, 227
Preiss, J. J., 367
President's Commission on Federal Statistics, 304, 314
Preston, A., 63, 64, 103
Price, G. M., 78, 113
Pringle, M. L. K., 52, 53, 113
Prochnow, H., 227
Proper, E. C., 14, 45
Provence, S., 52, 53, 113
Pugh, A. K., 253, 263, 272

Quayhagen, N., 135, 155
Quirk, R., 239, 272

Rabbitt, P., 138, 154
Rabson, A., 63, 64, 103
Radcliffe-Brown, A. R., 320, 373
Radin, N., 63, 67, 69, 72, 87, 88, 89, 104, 113, 114
Radke-Yarrow, M., 77, 118
Raj, D., 291, 292, 314
Ramey, C. T., 75, 82, 105, 106, 118
Ramos, M., 187, 188, 190, 227
Ramsey, M., 372
Rao, D. C., 11, 45
Rathburn, C., 55, 113
Ravetz, J. R., 272
Ravitch, M., 256
Read, J., 207, 228
Rebelsky, F., 67, 113
Reddell, R. C., 136-7, 153
Redican, W. K., 52, 114
Redl, F., 320, 370, 373
Rees, J., 53, 54, 55, 117
Reese, H. W., 125, 150
Reid, W. A., 321, 373
Reinert, G., 124, 154
Renner, K. E., 257, 272
Renner, V. J., 125, 150
Resnick, L., 242, 272
Reynolds, L. J., 321, 373
Rheingold, H. L., 53, 74, 75, 114
Rice, R., 321, 373
Richards, I. A., 232, 241, 272
Richards, M. P. M., 62, 101
Richer, S., 177, 184
Richmond, J. B., 61, 117
Rickards, J. P., 229, 254, 256, 272, 273

Ridley, C. A., 59, 106
Riecken, H. W., 320, 369
Riegel, K. F., 131, 154, 374
Riessen, A., 49, 114
Rimland, B., 28, 45
Ring, D. G., 252, 272, 273
Ringler, N. M., 66, 114
Risley, T. R., 75, 77, 114
Rist, R., 321, 376
Rist, R. C., 321, 374
Rivera, R., 122, 153
Rivlin, A. M., 302, 314
Roberts, J., 324, 374
Robertson, E. A., 138, 150
Robinson, F. G., 251, 267
Robinson, M., 60, 114
Robinson, W., 327
Robson, K. S., 57, 58, 61, 66, 67, 112, 113, 114
Roebuck, M., 374
Rogers, C. M., 49, 50, 104, 114
Rogers, W. T., 291, 314
Rogosa, D., 120
Rogosa, D. R., 69, 114
Romberg, T., 157
Room, R., 276, 314
Rosche, M., 82, 83, 85, 86, 88, 89, 110
Rosenberg, M., 73, 114
Rosenblatt, J. S., 51, 114
Rosenblum, L. A., 51, 108, 114
Rosenfeld, A., 55, 110
Rosenow, E. C., 123, 154
Rosenshine, B., 157, 160, 164, 182, 184, 185
Ross, H. W., 75, 114
Roth, D., 344, 368
Roth, S., 53, 104
Rothkopf, E. Z., 231, 245, 248-50, 254-5, 256, 273
Royce, J., 82, 83, 85, 86, 88, 89, 97, 110, 117
Rozelle, R. M., 69, 114
Rubenstein, J., 63, 114
Rubenstein, J. L., 63, 64, 72, 119
Rudinger, G., 141, 154
Ruopp, R. R., 81, 86, 87, 88, 89, 110
Rusk, B., 219, 227
Russell, H., 321, 374
Russell Sage Foundation, 302, 306

Rutter, M., 49, 50, 52, 54, 55, 62, 63, 68, 114
Ryan, A., 166-7, 185

Sackett, G. P., 69, 115
Saenger, G., 19, 46
St. Pierre, R. G., 14, 45
Saltz, R., 74, 115
Sameroff, A. J., 74, 97, 115
Sametz, A. W., 295, 314
Sanders, N., 149, 151
Santilli, M., 97, 115
Sapir, E., 230, 273
Sarason, S. B., 175, 185, 321, 374
Sarbin, T., 353, 358, 378
Särkelä, T., 215, 227
Sarmiento, S., 194, 197, 224
Sattler, J. M., 68, 115
Sawin, D. B., 78, 115
Saxe, R. M., 63, 115
Sayegh, Y., 74, 104
Scarr, S., 3, 7, 8, 9, 10, 21, 23, 45
Scarr-Salapatek, S., 8, 28, 30, 42, 45, 71, 115
Schachter, S., 320, 326, 369, 374
Schaefer, E. S., 58, 62, 63, 65, 72, 79, 85, 90, 91, 100, 115
Schaffer, H. R., 62, 63, 64, 67, 115
Schaie, J. P., 128, 141, 155
Schaie, K. W., 120-50, 154, 155
Scheffler, I., 168, 171, 174, 185, 360, 374
Scheidt, R. J., 142, 155
Schember, D. M., 194, 197, 224
Schermerhorn, R. A., 203, 209, 210-12, 222, 227
Schiff, M., 9, 45
Schiller, J. S., 14, 41
Schlieper, A., 58, 115
Schlossman, S. L., 48, 90, 98, 115
Schoggen, P., 320, 370
Schpoont, S. H., 251, 267
Schultz, C., 149, 151
Schumacher, S., 321, 322, 328, 337, 356, 358, 374, 376
Schwab, J. J., 364, 374
Schwartz, R., 349, 377
Scott, J. P., 50, 104, 115, 319, 323, 374
Scott, P., 59, 119
Scott, P. M., 76, 119

Scott, W. R., 374
Scriven, M., 231, 250, 273, 316, 356, 359, 362, 363, 364, 374
Seagoe, M. V., 36, 45
Seagull, A., 68, 112
Sears, P. S., 72, 116
Sears, R. R., 61, 72, 115, 116
Sechrest, L., 349, 377
Secord, P. F., 180, 183
Seefeldt, C., 132, 156
Seif, E., 321, 374
Seltzer, R. J., 57, 116
Selznick, P., 320, 325, 375
Semmel, M. I., 177, 183
Serock, K., 132, 156
Sevilla-Cases, 214, 220, 227
Shaffer, J., 134, 156
Shaffer, J. A., 177, 185
Shapiro, G., 323, 376
Shavelson, R. J., 157, 241-2, 256, 273, 295, 296, 314
Shaw, J. L., 66, 105
Shearer, M. S., 80, 92, 116
Shelby, 330
Sheldon, E. B., 276, 282, 286, 294, 300, 301, 302, 307, 314
Sheppard, H. L., 123, 156
Sherman, H., 217, 227
Shipman, V. C., 70, 72, 73, 116
Shockley, W., 39, 45
Shoemaker, D. J., 67, 68, 100
Shuford, E. H., 233, 270
Shulman, L., 316, 375
Shulman, L. S., 179, 185
Shumener, B., 157
Shuy, R., 186
Shuy, R. W., 239, 273
Sibayan, B., 187, 188, 190, 227
Siegel, 89
Siegler, I. C., 129, 156, 276, 314
Siemen, J. R., 148, 156
Simmons, J. L., 323, 340, 372
Simon, A., 332, 344, 375
Simon, H. A., 232, 257, 266, 272
Sinaiko, H. W., 236, 270
Sindell, P. S., 324, 375
Singleton, J. C., 321, 325, 375
Sinisterra, L., 16, 44
Sjoberg, G., 222, 228
Skeels, H. M., 16, 45, 53, 54, 69, 74, 116

Skelly, 48, 96
Skinner, B. F., 325, 332, 336, 355, 375
Skodak, M., 54, 69, 116, 119
Skogan, W. G., 276, 314
Skutnabb-Kangas, T., 203, 210, 214, 215-7, 228
Slaughter, D. T., 81, 82, 83, 86, 89, 116
Sloane, H. N., 92, 111
Smart, K., 233
Smith, E., 229, 271
Smith, L. M., 316-67, 368, 375, 376
Smith, M. S., 14, 45, 237, 274
Smith, R. T., 7, 45
Smolak, L. M., 68, 116
Snipper, R., 276, 311
Snow, C. E., 64, 116
Snow, C. P., 358, 376
Snow, R., 263, 268
Snow, R. E., 149, 151
Snyder, P. A., 66, 102
Soar, R. M., 161, 185
Soar, R. S., 161-2, 185
Social Science Research Council, 302, 306, 307
Society of Applied Anthropology, 325
Society of Fellows, 325
Sociobiology Study Group of Science for the People, 30, 45
Sokolowska, M., 25, 41
Soloman, W., 322, 376
Solow, R. M., 295, 314
Soltis, J. F., 168, 185
Sonquist, H., 80, 86, 90, 91, 116
Spencer-Booth, Y., 50, 107
Spilerman, S., 279, 286, 313
Spindler, G., 321, 325, 376
Sprio, R. J., 239, 266
Spitz, R. A., 52, 61, 116
Spock, B., 60, 116
Spolsky, B., 186, 190, 200, 207, 209, 213, 217, 218, 228
Sprott, R. L., 10, 45
Spuhler, J. N. 10, 11, 19, 23, 27, 38, 43
Sroufe, L. A., 58, 116
Staats, J., 10, 45
Stake, R., 322, 328, 376
Stake, R. E., 310, 314
Stallings, J. A., 161, 162, 185

Stanford Research Institute, 161
Stanley, J. C., 69, 81, 102, 316-7, 318, 335, 340, 368
Stanton, G. C., 273, 295, 296, 314
Starr, S., 69, 80, 84, 86, 87, 88, 89, 90, 91, 98, 108
Stayton, D. J., 63, 99
Stebbins, L. B., 14, 45
Stedman, D. J., 82, 87, 106, 116
Steffa, M., 66, 108
Stein, M. R., 323, 376
Stein, Z., 19, 25, 41, 46
Stern, C., 86, 87, 116
Stern, D., 60, 66, 117
Stern, D. N., 66, 108
Stern, G. G., 61, 117
Stern, H. H., 189, 228
Stetson, D. M., 276, 315
Stevenson, H. W., 75, 117
Stewart, J., 9, 45
Stewart, N., 24, 46
Stewart, T. R., 145, 154
Stewart, W., 223
Sticht, T. G., 233, 236, 267, 270, 273, 274
Stodolsky, S., 120
Stodolsky, S. S., 23, 46
Stokes, A., 234, 274
Stollak, G. E., 63, 115
Stolurow, L. M., 236, 270
Stolz, L. M., 59, 117
Stone, P. J., 237, 274
Stone, R., 278, 280, 288
Stormsdorfer, E. W., 36, 46
Stouffer, S. A., 317, 376
Strain, B. A., 67, 113
Strauss, A., 321, 337, 367
Strauss, A. L., 323, 325, 328, 334, 337, 339, 340, 349, 363, 369
Streissguth, A. P., 58, 100
Strike, K., 157
Strother, C. R., 130, 137, 155
Struthers, M., 360, 376
Studley, W. M., 88, 108
Sudia, C. E., 59, 107
Sukhatme, B. V., 291, 292, 315
Sukhatme, P. V., 291, 292, 315
Summer, W. A., 234, 272
Summers, D. A., 145, 154
Suomi, S. J., 49, 117
Super, C. M., 56, 117

Susser, M., 19, 25, 41, 46
Svartvik, J. A., 239, 272
Swain, M., 186, 187, 190, 199, 200, 203, 204, 206, 222, 223, 224, 228
Swanson C. E., 233, 274
Swift, D. F., 276, 315

Talland, G. A., 138, 156
Tamir, P., 252, 272
Taylor, D. G., 276, 315
Taylor, D. M., 213, 223
Taylor, E. N., 233
Taylor, W. L., 236, 274
Teitelbaum, H., 193, 194, 195, 228
Terman, L. M., 3, 36, 37, 46
Teska, J., 108
Teska, J. A., 81, 88, 108
Thomae, H., 141, 156
Thoman, E. B., 51, 66, 75, 105, 117
Thomas, A., 66, 117
Thomas, L. F., 253, 263, 274
Thompson, C. W., 10, 40
Thompson, W. R., 49, 117
Thorndike, E. L., 3, 29, 46
Thorndike, R. L., 4, 46
Thuernau, P., 321, 370
Thurlow, M., 75
Thurnher, M., 145-6, 153
Tikunoff, W., 321, 324, 376
Till, R. E., 137, 156
Tinsley, B., 78, 113
Tissue, T., 276, 315
Tizard, B., 53, 54, 55, 117
Tizard, J., 53, 117
Toca, T., 19, 40
Toffler, A., 122, 156
Tomkiewicz, S., 9, 45
Tomlinson-Keasey, C., 133, 156
Toole, D. L., 256, 269
Toomey, R., 177, 185
Torres, M., 80, 85, 86, 91, 110
Torshen, K. P., 148, 156
Toukomaa, P., 203, 210, 214, 215-7, 228
Toulmin, S., 318, 333, 358, 362, 376
Trapp, E. P., 68, 117
Troike, R. C., 218, 223
Troll, L. E., 123, 134, 135, 156
Trotter, R., 16, 46
Trow, M., 320, 372
Tryon, R. C., 10, 46

Tucker, G. R., 187, 200, 213, 223, 226
Tucker, R., 205, 228
Tuddenham, R. D., 37, 46
Tukey, J., 314
Tulkin, S. R., 55, 58, 59, 61, 73, 110, 117
Tulving, E., 138, 156
Turner, P. R., 204, 218, 228
Turnure, J. E., 75, 117
Turvey, M. T., 137, 156
Tyler, L. E., 24, 46

Underwood, B. J., 330, 376
United Nations, 278, 279, 286, 288, 315
UNESCO, 214, 307
U.S. Bureau of the Census, 305
U.S. Commission on Civil Rights, 13-14, 46, 200, 201, 203, 228
U.S. Dept. of Health, Education & Welfare, 186, 194, 278, 280, 286, 290, 293, 299, 300, 301, 302, 305, 306, 309, 315
U.S. Dept. of Labor, 315
U.S. Office of Child Development, 48
U.S. Office of Education, 48, 189, 199, 278, 307
Updegraff, B., 74, 116
Urbach, P., 5, 46
Uzgiris, I. C., 57, 117

Van De Riet, V., 22, 43
Van Egeren, L. F., 58, 100
Van Horne, K. R., 126, 152
Van Velsen, J., 323, 340, 346-7
Vance, S., 68, 116
Vandenberg, S. G., 29, 46
VenderStoep, L., 61, 62, 63, 64, 65, 71, 72, 103
Velandia, W., 18, 46
Vidich, A. J., 323
Vineberg, R., 233, 274
Vopova, J., 86, 88, 89, 97, 117
Vygotsky, L. S., 230, 274

Wacaster, C., 321, 368
Wach, J., 241, 274
Wachs, T. D., 57, 117
Wade, N., 7, 28, 30, 46
Wagner, C. S., 92, 93, 107

Wahler, R. G., 75, 118
Walberg, H. J., 69, 72, 118
Wald, I., 25, 41
Walker, D. F., 15, 42, 321, 322, 373, 376
Walker, K. E., 67, 118
Walker, R., 323, 372, 376
Walker, W., 322, 376
Wallace, A., 217, 228
Wallach, M. A., 143, 156
Waller, J. H., 25, 46
Waller, R., 229, 251, 253, 263, 264, 265, 274
Waller, T. G., 256, 268
Wallston, B., 59, 118
Walsh, D. A., 137, 148, 156
Wandersman, A., 86, 118
Wandersman, L. P., 86, 118
Wanska, S. K., 251, 252, 270
Ward, B., 324, 376
Warner, W. L., 320, 377
Warren, R., 321, 325, 377
Washburn, S. L., 31, 46
Washburne, J. N., 256, 274
Wason, P. C., 253, 266, 270
Watson, J. S., 75, 118
Watts, G. H., 256, 274
Watts, J. C., 65, 118
Wax, M., 321, 325, 377
Wax, R., 321, 325, 377
Wax, R. H., 323, 325, 377
Waxler, C. Z., 76, 77, 118, 119
Weale, R. A., 136, 156
Webb, E., 349, 377
Webb, N., 69, 114
Weener, P., 149, 151
Wehlage, G., 179, 184
Weikart, D. P., 81, 82, 85, 88, 89, 91, 98, 109
Weinberg, R. A., 8, 9, 10, 21, 30, 42, 45
Weinfeld, F. D., 13, 22, 23, 24, 26, 34-5, 41, 103
Weinraub, M., 67, 110
Weir, C. D., 163, 171, 182
Weisberg, P., 75, 80, 85, 86, 90, 93, 109, 118
Weiss, A. D., 137, 152
Wellman, B., 74, 116
Wenar, C., 63, 118
Werboff, J., 50, 102

Werlich, E., 239, 274
Werner, H., 124, 156
Wesman, A., 26, 41
West, L. H. T., 252, 274
Westbury, I., 331, 372
Westinghouse Learning Corp., 14, 46
Whalley, P. C., 263, 274
Wheeler, P., 162, 183
White, 48, 96, 119, 202
White, B. L., 20, 46, 48, 65, 70, 74, 118
White, J. C., Jr., 22, 43
White, M., 350-1, 353, 377
White, S. H., 81, 85, 88, 89, 118
Whitehead, A. N., 177, 185
Whiting, J. W. M., 72, 116
Whyte, W. F., 320, 323, 340, 377
Wiener, G., 80, 81, 82, 85, 88, 89, 91, 99
Wiesel, T. N., 50, 118
Wilde, O., 247, 274
Wiley, D. E., 183, 185
Wilks, Y. A., 237, 274
Willerman, L., 9, 74, 118
Williams, E., 188, 223
Williams, H. M., 74, 116
Williams, M. V., 137, 156
Williams, R., 241, 274
Williams, T. McB., 92, 118
Willis, S. L., 120-50, 154
Wilson, C. D., 57, 110
Wilson, E. O., 30, 46
Wilson, J., 158, 185
Wilson, S., 324, 377
Wilson, V. W., 298, 312
Wineman, D., 320, 373
Winograd, T., 237, 239, 274
Winter, E., 237, 239, 240, 250, 274, 275
Wittelsberger, B., 276, 312
Wittgenstein, L. L. J., 230, 275
Wittrock, M. C., 251, 275
Wohlwill, J., 147, 152
Wohlwill, J. F., 126, 156
Wolcott, H. F., 321, 322, 325, 354, 377
Wolf, E., 136, 152

Wolf, M. M., 75, 106
Wolfe, H., 66, 108
Wolfheim, J. H., 51, 118
Wolfson, R., 322, 354, 377
Wolins, M., 53, 118
Wolkind, S., 53, 118
Wolman, B. B., 157, 185
Wood, C. J., 354, 377
Woodruff, D., 120, 121, 148, 150, 156
Woods, M. E., 67, 118
Wright, G. C., 276, 315
Wright, H. F., 320, 344, 367
Wright, P., 248, 266, 275
Wright, W. R., 88, 108
Wroczynski, R., 122, 133, 156
Wyer, R. S., 68, 118

Yankee City Group, 325
Yankelovitch, D., 96, 178, 180, 185
Yankelovich, Skelly and White, Inc., 48, 96, 119
Yarrow, L., 47
Yarrow, L. J., 52, 63, 64, 67, 72, 113, 119
Yarrow, M. R., 59, 60, 76, 93, 119
Yee, S., 11, 45
Yevzeroff, H., 276, 312
Yogman, M., 67, 119
York, R. L. 13, 22, 23, 24, 26, 34-5, 41, 103
Yunker, R., 320, 354, 377

Zachariah, 208
Zajonc, R. B., 18-9, 46
Zaninovich, M. G., 237, 272
Zapf, D. W., 236, 274
Zegiob, L. E., 58, 97, 119
Zehrbach, R. R., 108
Zeitlin, I. M., 208, 228
Zelazo, N. A., 75, 119
Zelazo, P. R., 75, 97, 119
Zetterberg, H., 338, 354-5, 356, 363, 377
Ziman, J. M., 318, 358, 377
Zimmermann, R. R., 51, 106
Zinnes, D. A., 237, 272

Subject Index

Academic achievement: definition of, 162-3

Academic aptitude: and age, 144; and intelligence, 3, 140-3; and IQ scores, 4, 26

Academic Learning Time hypothesis, 163, 171-2

Academic performance: and age, 144; and attitude, 132; and bilingual education, 195, 199-201, 209, 212, 216; and birth-order, 18-19; and discipline, 161-2; and feedback, 257-8; and heredity, 30; and IQ, 4, 34, 36; and language, 344; and motivation, 143-6; and parental behavior, 56, 60, 63-4, 94-5; and parental education, 47-9, 59, 296, 303; and quality of schools, 13; and race, 33-4, 36, 94; and socioeconomic status, 58, 94, 161, 302-3, 327; and teacher effectiveness, 162-82; and time, 161, 162-3, 171-2, 299-300; improvement of, 37-8; see also Academic aptitude, Compensatory education, Education, IQ, Learning ability

Access structure, 263-4

Achievement test, 250

Achieving preset objectives, 230-1

Achieving stage, 145

Acquisition, 138,

Acquisitive stage, 145

Adjunct questions, 254-7

Adoptions: and heritability, 8-10, 30; and IQ, 8-10, 20-1, 28, 54-5, 69-70; and social adjustment, 55; transracial, 9-10

Adult education, 121, 134-5; and age, 124-5, 130-42; and cognitive development, 145-6; and development, 124-5; level attained, 121-2, 128; motivation for, 143-6, 148-9; relevance of, 142; statistics on, 121-2, 134-5; teaching, 149; see also Education, Lifelong learning

Adult stability model, 127

Advance organizers, 251-4; components of 252-3

Age: and academic aptitude, 140, 144, 147-9; and academic performance, 143-6; and attitude, 132; and bilingual education, 215-16; and cognitive development, 145-6; and development models, 127-9, 130-1; and education, 120-1, 124-7, 130-42; and educational goals, 147; and IQ, 10-11, 16, 18-19, 23, 128-30, 142-3; and learning ability, 127-9, 135-46; and learning motivation, 143-6, 148-9, and memory, 138-40, 148; and occupation, 122-3; and perceptual function, 135-8; and perceptual masking, 137-8; and risk taking, 143-5; and sensory function, 135-41; and social conformity, 146; and teaching techniques, 149; vs development, 124-5, 130-1, 132

Alte School, 331, 332, 334, 335, 342, 345, 347, 348, 363

Anecdotal Process for Promoting Learning Experience, 162

Animal research: birds, 50; dogs, 50; mammals, 50; monkeys, 49-50, 52

Animals: environment and, 49-50; heritability and, 10; parental behavior and, 51-2; reinforcement and, 257; social development of, 51; sociobiology and, 30-1

Anthropology, 181, 319, 320, 340, 344, 361, 363

Applied psychology, 230, 232, 234, 257

Art, 166, 168, 334, 335, 336, 339, 351, 352, 358, 361

Attitude: and aging, 132; and learning, 132; and occupation, 132

Auditory acuity, 136-7, 139

Basic skills, 165, 171, 173-4, 175, 303

Beginning Teacher Evaluation Study, 160, 162, 171

Behavior: and heredity, 30-1

Behavioral objectives, 250-1; purpose of, 250

Bicultural education: see Bilingual education

Bilingual education: and academic performance, 195, 199-201, 209-10, 212, 216; and age, 215-16; and conflict paradigm, 199, 208-21; and cross-cultural communication, 201-2, 204; and culture conflict, 217-21; and employment, 210; and English proficiency, 193-5, 197, 198-9, 200, 201, 210, 213; and equilibrium paradigm, 196-208; and immersion programs, 187, 189, 190, 199-200, 204, 205; and integration, 211-12; and IQ, 203, 215; and language sequence, 189; and medium of instruction, 187; and motivation, 200; and political power, 220; and self-concept, 188, 195, 201, 212; and self-esteem, 189; and siblings, 215-16; and social adjustment,197-8, 209-210, 212; and socioeconomic status, 187-8, 195-6, 197, 199-200, 201, 203, 209, 210, 213, 216-17, 222; and student dropout, 210; and submersion programs, 190, 199-200; and teacher ethnicity, 190, 198-9, 201, 204, 213; and teacher training, 198, 217; and time, 189; and Utopian perspectives, 219-21

definition of, 188-90, 204; goals of, 209; history of, 192-5; kinds of: Elitist, 188, 222; Folk, 188; objective of, 197-8, 200; typologies of, 209; variables of, 189-90, 191, 200

Canada, 187, 189-90, 192, 199, 200, 203, 204-5, 206, 214, 216; Finland, 216; Mexico, 187, 199; Philippines, 187-8; Sweden, 189-90, 203, 214-15; U.S., 188, 189-90, 192-3, 195-7, 199, 200, 203, 204, 206, 212, 218-21; see also Compensatory education

Bilingual Education Act, 193, 197

Biometrical genetic analysis, 11-12

Birth order, 18-19

Black box, 60

Blacks: see Race

California Achievement Test, 162

Career education, 121

Case studies, 318-40

Child behavior: and parental attitude, 61-2

Child development: and environment, 47-96; and parental behavior, see Parental behavior, problems of; observation of, 68-74

Child-focused programs, 87

Child-rearing: and working mother, 48, 57-60, 96-7; discipline and, 61-2, 65, 72-3, 76; education for, see Parental education; African, 56; Guatemalan, 56; Mayan, 55; see also Child development, Parental behavior

Chronicle: definition of, 350

Citizenship, 303

Civil Rights Act, 193, 290, 304

Classroom Observation Instrument, 161

Clause relation, 239-40; definition of, 239

Climbing control group, 81-2

Cloze procedure, 233, 240, 259; definition of, 236

Cognitive Abilities Test, 4

Cognitive ability, 14, 91, 125, 132, 140, 141, 143, 147-8, 161-2, 171, 200, 201, 203, 206, 253

Cognitive and Language Development, 203

Cognitive development: stages of, 145-6

Cognitive process, 329-40

Cognitive psychology, 253-4, 256, 257, 263

Cognitive structure, 252, 253

Cognitive theory, 253-4, 256-7, 266

Cohort-sequential, 126, 128

Coleman Report, 22-4

Collapsing outlines, 339-40; dimensions of, 340

College Admissions Test, 26

Communication: effective factors of, 259

Compensatory education: and race, 13-17, 25, 33-6, 79; and socioeconomic status, 25, 57, 79, 201; effects of, 13-17, 25, 33-6, 79, 80-4, 132; *see also* Bilingual education

Competence: definition of, 140

Concept formation, 338

Concept of serial, 334

Conceptual advances, 257

Concurrent translation, 206

Conflict paradigm, 196-221

Confluence theory, 18-19

Consolidated Program Information Report, 292

Constant-comparative method, 337

Construct validity, 294-9, 359; rules of, 296; theory of, 296

Content analysis: of textbooks, 237-8, 259-63; definition of, 237

Contextualism, 361

Continuity of developmental function, 69-70

Convergence criterion, 298

Conversion schema, 168-9, 174-5, 176, 179

Corps Member Training Institute Impact Study, 178-9

Covering law model, 355

Creativity, 62, 339, 340, 352, 358

Creech bill, 277

Cross-cultural communication, 201-2, 204

Cross-sectional method, 125-6, 127, 142, 309

Cross-sequential, 126, 127-8, 142-3

Cultural bias, 26-7

Culture conflict, 217-21

Curriculum development, 231; and texts, 232; variables in, 247

Dale-Chall formula, 234, 236, 259, 260

Data level, 341-9, 351

Decrement with compensation, 128-9, 131

Descriptive narrative level, 349-53

Development, 124-5; definition of, 201; models of, 130-1

Differentiated U, 161

Direct instruction, 164

Direct measure, 233

Discipline, 61-2, 65, 72-3, 76, 161, 172

Discovery of grounded theory, 339

Distressed Liberal Genre, 207

Dropouts, 210, 305

ECNI, 9

Education: and age, 120-1, 124-7, 130-46; and aging, 131-43, 148-9; and attitude, 132; and IQ, 12-17, 31, 140-3, 148-9; and life-competency, 133-4; and motivation, 143-6, 148-9; and occupation, 25; and population, 121-2; and race, 13, 23-4, 305; and real-life problems, 133, 141; and scientific theory, 358, 359; and sex, 141; and social change, 131, 147; and social transformation, 208; and sociobiology, 31-9, 133; and socioeconomic status, 201, 216-17, 296; and teacher effectiveness, 157-82; and teacher variables, 330; and texts, 229-66; of adults, 121-3, 133-5; of children, 131-2; of parents, 47-9, 59, 296, 303; of women, 135.

aim of, 120, 130; case studies of, 318, 320-40; content of, 231; definition of, 159; effects of, 12-17; equality in, 35; evaluation of, 323, 326; financing of, 288-94, 306; goals of, 147; kinds of: individualized, 277; lifelong, 120-50, 310; vocational, 133-4; life-span models of, 124-31; philosophy of, 167-8; setting of, 321; theory of, 159; *see also* Adult education, Academic performance, Bilingual education, Com-

pensatory education, Vocational education
Education for Parenthood, 98
Educational Aptitude, 143
Educational ethnography: cognitive processes in, 329-40; goals of, 359; logic of, 331
Educational indicators, 276-311; and population characteristics, 287, 299-301; and population status, 287, 288-99; and time, 297-301, 305-6 application of, 301, 304-5; interpretive generalizations of, 287-8; statistical generalizations of, 288-94, 307; substantive generalizations of, 294-9; temporal generalizations of, 299-301; use of, 287-310; variables in, 294-6; *see also* Indicators
Educational rhetoric: definition of, 243
Elementary and Secondary Education Act, 277, 302
Elitist, 188, 222
Emergency School Aid Act, 15
Employment: *see* Occupation
ESL, 194, 197, 198-9, 205, 213
English proficiency, 193-5, 198-9, 200, 201, 210, 213
Environment: and adult development, 128-9; and child development, 51-96; and heritability, 6-7, 16; and IQ, 4, 9-10, 11, 12-21, 23, 27, 34, 36, 37-8, 69-70, 78, 128-9; and retardation, 16-18
Environmentalist, 4-5, 36-8
Equality of Educational Opportunity, 13, 23, 34, 193-4, 208, 304-6
Equilibrium paradigm, 196-208
Ethnicity: and integration, 211; of bilingual education, 192-5, 207; of bilingual teachers, 190, 198-9, 201, 204
Ethnography: definition of, 354
Evaluation: definition of, 302
Exogenous causation, 173, 174
Family: and child IQ, 19-21; *see also* Heritability, Parental behavior, Siblings
Feedback, 257-8
Feral children: and IQ, 17-18
First-person singular narrative, 351

Flanders Interaction Analysis, 161
Flesch Reading Ease Formula, 236, 259
Flexibility, 334
Florida Parent Education Infant and Toddler Program, 79
Folk, 188
FORCAST, 236
Force, 243
Foreshadowed problems, 331, 334, 342
Formative evaluation, 231-2, 245-6
Formative hermeneutic mode, 353
Formative vs summative, 231-2
Formism, 361

Genetics: and behavior patterns, 30-1; and heritability, 6-7; and IQ, 4-12, 22-3, 38-9
Geography, 244
Government: *see* Politics
Graduate Record Examination, 13
Group conflict theory, 208-17
Group differences: equalizing of, 35; IQ, 21-7, 33

Head Start, 14
Hereditarian, 4-5, 36
Heredity: and behavior patterns, 30-1; and IQ, 4-12, 18, 27, 33, 36, 37-9; *see also* Heritability
Heritability: and adoptions, 8-10; and animals, 10, 30-1; and siblings, 7-8; and twins, 6-7; and race, 24-5 of intelligence, 5-12, 24-5, 27-33; of interest, 29-30; of personality, 10, 29-31; definition of, 5-6, 29; measurement of, 6, 17; *see also* Heredity
Hermeneutics, 241
History, 364; definition of, 350
Human being: definition of, 3
Humanities, 242, 243, 246, 356
Hypothesis development, 338

Idiosyncratic styles of teaching, 363
Immersion programs, 187, 189, 190, 199-200, 204, 205, 214, 222; goal of, 203
Inclusive fitness, 30
Indicators: and construct validity, 294-9; and politics, 301; and pro-

gram evaluation, 302-3; application of, 301; definition of, 278-9, 301; uses for, 301-7; variables of, 300, 308; *see also* Educational indicators, Social indicators

Individual differences: in intelligence, 3-28, 31-9, 148-9; *see also* IQ

Infant Education Research Project, 79

Inside-outside, 327, 361

Insights, 334

Institutionalization: effects of, 52-3, 74

Instructional psychology, 248, 249, 250

Integration: and ethnic groups, 211-12; definition of, 211

Intellectual Responsibility Scale, 161

Intelligence: and academic aptitude, 140-3; and environment, 12-21; and heredity, 4-12; heritability of, 5-12, 24-5, 27-9; measurement of, 3-4; definition of, 3, 140; *see also* Academic performance, IQ

IQ: and academic aptitude, 140-3; and academic performance, 4, 34, 36; and adoptions, 8-10, 20-1, 28, 54-5, 69-70; and age, 10-11, 16, 23, 127-30, 142-3; and bilingual education, 203, 215; and birth order, 18-19; and compensatory education, 13-17, 25, 33-6, 79; and discipline, 61-2, 65; and education, 12-17, 31, 148-9; and environment, 4, 9-10, 11, 12-21, 23, 27, 34, 37-8, 51-2, 70, 78, 94, 129; and family characteristics, 20-1; and family size, 19; and feral children, 17; and genetics, 4, 22-3; and heredity, 4-12, 18, 27, 33, 37-9; and infant care, 55-6; and institutionalization, 52-3; and maternal behavior, 63-5, 70, 87-8, 90-2; and nutrition, 19-20; and old age, 128-130; and parental behavior, 73-4, 82, 94; and parental education, 25, 78, 80, 83, 85-6, 87-8; and parental occupation, 25, 58; and paternal behavior, 63-5, 67, 70-1; and politics, 3-39; and race, 16, 19, 22-5, 26-7, 31, 33; and retardation, 16-18, 70-1; and sex, 25-6; and siblings, 7-8, 9, 20, 23, 71; and socioeconomic status, 20-1, 22, 24-5, 38,

58, 78; and twins, 6-7, 28; changes in, 16-18, 94; culture bias of, 26-7; group differences in, 21-7; kinds of: animal, 10; parental, 9, 20-1; 25; racial, 22, 24; religious, 22, 24; raising of, 37-8; stability of, 10-1; variance in, 17, 27; tests of, 3-4, 9, 11, 13, 14, 16, 19, 20, 25, 26-7, 128, 141, 143, 161, 187, *see also* Academic performance, Intelligence

Intentionalist thesis, 170-82

Interagency Panel, 81

Interests: and heredity, 29-31

Interjudge reliability, 245

Interpretive asides, 327, 333, 334

Intervening variable: definition of, 222

Inverted U, 161

Iowa Test of Basic Skills, 161

Irreversible decrement, 128, 131

Isolation: effects of, 49-51, 53-4

Jigsaw puzzle analogy, 338

Kensington School, 329, 330, 332, 335, 339, 342, 346

Klare's model, 234-5, 262

Knowledge of results, 257

Language: and academic performance, 344; and sequencing of, 189; and teacher, 244; and teaching, 186-7, 193-5, 198-9, 200, 201; and texts, 229-66; mother tongue, 187-8, 189, 192, 198-9, 200, 201, 216, 217; second language, 187-8, 189, 192, 194, 198-9, 200, 201, 205; *see also* Linguistics

Language Curriculum, 84, 86-7

Lau remedies, 194, 214

Lau vs Nicholas, 193-4

Law School Admissions Test, 300

Lazar Consortium on Developmental Continuity, 83

Learning ability: and age, 135-49; *see also* Academic aptitude, Academic performance, IQ

Life-competency roles, 134

Lifelong learning, 121-50, 310

Life-span models: cross-sectional, 125-6, 127, 142; longitudinal, 125-6, 127, 142-3; sequential, 125-7, 142-3

Linguistis analysis: of textbooks, 238-40; rules of, 238

Linquistic performance, 18, 26, 53, 63-4, 75, 79, 84, 85, 86-7, 125, 133, 138, 147, 180, 187-9, 191, 200, 201-2, 203, 205, 206, 215-16

Linguistics: and applied psychology, 230, 263; and art of writing, 246-7; development of, 229-30

Literacy gap, 233

Literacy Survey, 187

Literary criticism, 241, 246, 249

Literary psychology narrative, 352

Literature, 303

Longitudinal method, 125-6, 127, 142-3, 192, 309, 310

Maintenance programs, 193, 198, 212

Mathemagenic activities, 254-5

Mathemagenic behavior, 254-7

Mathemagenic devices, 245, 248

Mathematical comprehension, 18, 24, 25, 26, 125, 161, 163-4, 187-8, 190, 199, 200, 216

Mathematics, 242, 245, 284, 300, 303, 334, 347, 348

Meaningfulness of content, 138-9

Mechanism, 361

Memory: and age, 138-40, 148

Metatheoretical level 360-65; issues of, 365

Metropolitan Achievement Test, 14, 161

Minnesota Teacher Attitude Inventory, 300

Minorities: *see* Race

Mismatch, 233

Misplaced precision, 317

Modeling, 76-8

Mother Child Home Program, 79

Mother-focused programs, 87

Mother-infant interaction, 62-6

Motivation: and learning, 143-6, 148; and readability formula, 234

Multiple consciousness narrative, 352

Music, 303

Muted cues, 349

National Assessment of Educational Progress, 291, 299-300, 303, 310

National Longitudinal Study, 36

Nature-nurture, 32

Nine trials phenomenon, 327

Nonverbal tests, 22, 148

Number ability: *see* Mathematical comprehension

Nutrition: and IQ, 19-20

Occupation: and age, 122-3; and attitude, 132; and IQ, 25, 58; and women, 123, 135

One and the Many, 336

One-shot case study, 317-19, 335, 339

Open University, 233, 243, 244, 245, 246, 251, 256

Organicism, 361

Overregistration, 288, 290-1

Paced tasks, 138

Paradigms, 196

Paragraph: definition of, 239

Parent Child Development Centers, 80

Parent-child interaction, 66, 71-4, 77, 84, 90-2, 94; and race, 73; and socioeconomic status, 73-4

Parent Child Toy Library Program, 79

Parental behavior: and attitude, 61-2, 85-6, 95; and child academic performance, 94-5; and child behavior, 75-8, 82, 93; and child development, 54-74, 94-5; and child IQ, 63-5, 70-1, 82, 91-2, 94; and child sex, 72-3; and discipline, 61-2, 65, 72-3, 76; and infant, 64, 66-7, 75, 77, 93, 97; and mother-focused programs, 87-8; and parental education, 80-4, 85; and race, 73; and socioeconomic status, 57-60, 73-4; kinds of: maternal, 61, 62-6 72, 76-7, 83, 84, 85-6, 97; paternal, 66-8, 78; modeling of, 76-8; modification of, 77-8; problems of observation of, 68-74

Parental education: and child IQ, 25, 47, 78, 80, 83, 85-6 87-8, 91-2; and siblings 98; assumptions of, 89-92; effects of, 80-4, 85-92, 95-6; kinds of: child-focused, 87; mother-focused, 87, 90-2; programs of, 78-92

Parental IQ: and child IQ, 9, 20-1, 38-9, 70-1

Parental occupation: and child development, 58; and child IQ, 25
Participant observation, 319-65; levels of, 340-65; methodology of, 325-9; studies of, 320-40, 349-53
Pattern maintenance, 198
Patterns of discovery, 339
Peabody Picture Vocabulary Test, 27
Perceptual function: and age, 135-8
Perceptual masking, 137-8
Personality: and cognitive tasks, 141; and heredity, 29-31
Philosophy, 318, 319, 354
Philosophy of mind, 159, 177
Piagetian Theory, 79, 125, 132, 133, 140-1, 328
Play Curriculum, 84, 86-7
Policy analysis, 303-6; uses of data of, 304, 308
Politics: and bilingual education, 200; and indicators, 301; and IQ, 3-39; and social indicators, 302; and textbooks, 237
Population characteristics: and educational indicators, 299-301
Population status: and educational indicators, 288-99
Preconceived ideas, 331-332
Preconceived solutions, 331
Prediction, 336
Primary Mental Abilities, 20, 128, 143
Prior knowledge: and reading formula, 234
Problem solving, 125
Process-product research, 160, 165, 167, 168, 173, 175, 179
Program: definition of, 302; evaluation by indicators, 302-3, 304, 308
Programmed instructional material, 231, 250
Programmed learning, 231, 232, 254
Progressive Matrices, 19
Progressive refocusing, 349
Project Camelot, 331
Project Follow Through, 14-16, 161
Project Press, 334
Project Talent, 24, 26, 36, 309
Psychology, 230, 248, 338, 340, 353, 363

Quantitative content analysis, 237-8,

259-63; computer-based, 237; *see also* Content analysis

Race: and academic aptitude, 26; and academic performance, 33-4, 36, 94-5; and adoption, 9-10; and compensatory education, 13-17, 22-4, 25, 79; and cultural bias, 26-7; and dropouts, 305; and education, 13, 305; and IQ, 16, 19, 22-5, 26-7, 31, 33; and parent-child interaction, 73, 97
Raven Progressive Matrics, 18, 25, 27, 161
Reading and Mathematics Observation System, 162
Readability analysis, 259-60
Readability formula, 232-7; and comprehension, 263; and motivation, 234; and prior knowledge, 234; and time, 234; and unreliability of, 233-4; kinds of: one-variable, 236; two-variable, 234, 236
Readability measures, 232-7; and reading ability, 233; kinds of, 232-3, 234, 236; objects of, 232
Reading ability, 233; and adjunct questions, 256-7
Reading performance, 18, 161, 187-8, 190, 200, 201, 233, 254-5, 263, 284, 303; Klares model, 234-5
Real-life situations: and education, 133, 141, 263
Reasoning ability, 12, 24, 133, 167, 177
Reductionist schools, 238
Reinforcement, 257
Reintegrative stage, 145-6
Replacement, 239
Representative equality, 35
Responsible stage, 145
Retardation: changes in, 16, 17-18, 54-5; effect on offspring, 70-1; *see also* IQ
Rizal experiment, 187-8
Root metaphors, 360-1

St. Lambert study, 200, 204
Saturation, 334
Scholastic Aptitude Test, 277
School: *see* Education

Science, 166, 168, 187, 242, 303, 329, 331, 334, 335, 336, 342, 346, 347, 348, 355, 361, 364; philosophy of, 157, 158, 159, 295, 318, 358, 363
Scientific theory, 358, 359
Self-care, 26, 125
Self-concept, 188, 195, 199, 200, 201, 212
Self-esteem, 189
Sensitive periods, 50
Sensory function: and age, 135-40, 141, 148
Sentence: definition of, 239
Sequential method, 125-7, 142-3, 189
Sex: and dropouts, 305; and IQ, 25-6; and learning ability, 141; of child and parent behavior, 72-3
Siblings: and academic performance, 18-19; and bilingual education, 215-16; and heritability, 8, 29-30; and IQ, 7-8, 9, 18-19, 20, 23, 71; and parental education, 98; see also Twins
Single celled, 92
Skimming the cream, 337-8
Sniper approach, 59
Social adjustment, 55, 85, 94, 97, 125, 133, 197-8, 209
Social change: and education, 131, 147, 208-9, 212, 276-87, 294
Social competence, 62
Social conformity: and age, 146; definition of, 146
Social Curriculum, 84, 86-7
Social indicators, 276-87; and policy analysis, 304; and politics, 302; and time, 297, 308; classification of, 283; criteria for, 286; definition of, 279-86; models of, 308-9; purpose of, 304; types of, 283; variables of, 283-5; see also Indicators
Social philosophy, 159
Social privation, 49-51
Social science, 166-7, 177, 178, 242-3, 244, 303, 318, 325, 331, 336, 340, 344, 346, 347, 348, 354, 355, 358, 359, 362, 363, 364
Social Science Theory, 363-4
Social system monitoring, 306-7
Social theory, 364-5

Sociobiology: and education, 31-9; definition of, 30-1
Socioeconomic status: and ability to learn English, 187, and ability to learn second language, 188; and academic achievement, 58, 94-5, 161, 296, 302-3, 327; and bilingual education, 195-6, 197, 199-200, 203, 209, 213, 216-17, 222; and child-rearing, 48, 57-60; and compensatory education, 25, 57, 79, 133; and IQ, 20-1, 22, 24-5, 38, 58, 78; and parent-child interaction, 73-4; and teaching, 326
Sociolinguistic theory, 191
Sociology, 181, 242, 318, 329, 331, 340, 363
South Carolina Observation Record, 161
Spatial ability, 24, 25, 26
Stability model, 125-7, 131
Stability of individual differences, 69-70
Stanford-Binet, 3, 16, 20
Sterilization, 39
Structural-functional theory, 196-207; definition of, 196-7
Student teaching, 327
Stull Bill, 277
Style analysis, 259
Subject matter analysis, 259-63
Submersion program, 190, 199-200

Teacher: and learner's age, 149; and socioeconomic status, 326; and student mimic, 244; behavior of, 328, 329, 355, 362; creativity of, 352; effectiveness of, 157-82; evaluation of, 277; mental life of, 179-80; subjective reasonable beliefs of, 170-6, 181; transformation of beliefs of, 176-82; training of, 160-70, 174-6, 181-2; see also Bilingual education
Teacher education: definition of, 174
Teacher Practices Observation Record, 161
Teacher training: definition of, 174-6
Teaching: bilingual, 189-222; purpose of, 167; see also Teacher Team teaching, 327
Tests: construct validity of, 295-9; in

textbooks, 231-2, 250; of intelligence, *see* IQ Texts

Texts: and advance organizers, 251-4; and content analysis, 237-8, 259-63; and experimental psychology, 230, 232; and instructional psychology, 248-9, 250; and linguistic analysis, 238-40; and qualitative analysis, 238-46; and subject matter analysis, 259-63; access structure of, 251, 263-4; analysis of, 230-66; bias of, 244-5; conceptual structure of, 241-2; confusion in, 244-5; effectiveness of, 258-63; formative evaluation of, 232; language in, 229-66; organization of, 259; programmed, 231; questions in, 231, 254-7; readability of, 232-7, 248-9; structure of, 248-50; tests in, 231-2, 250; variables of, 260-1

Theorem of the combination of circumstances, 166

Theoretical-Analytical-Interpretive level, 353-60

Theoretical sampling, 334, 349

Theory generation, 359-60

Time: and academic performance, 161, 162-3, 171-2, 299-300; and bilingual education, 189-90; and educational indicators, 297-301, 305-6; and educational research, 337; and feedback, 257; and readability formula, 234; and social indicators, 297

Time series analysis, 299-301, 305-6

Time-sequential, 126, 129

Transformation schema, 169, 176

Transition model, 193, 212

Triangulation, 344-5, 346

Triple play, 165, 168

Twins: and heritability, 6-7, 29; and IQ, 6-7, 28

Two by two, 327, 330

Underregistration, 288, 290-1

Unobtrusive measures, 349

Verbal comprehension, 12, 18, 22, 24, 25, 206

Visual acuity, 135-6, 139

Vocabulary analysis, 259

Vocabulary, 1, 2, and 3, 240

Vocational education, 133-4

Wait-controls, 81

War on Poverty, 13, 78

Wechsler, 3

White flight, 290

Winter's theory, 239

WISC, 9

Women: employment of, 123-4, 135; *see also* Sex

Work Diaries, 162, 171

Writing, 246-7, 299, 300, 303

X-O, 317-19

THE BOOK MANUFACTURE

Computer-assisted composition (RCA VideoComp 800), offset printing, and binding of *Review of Research in Education, 6, 1978* were by Kingsport Press. The paper is Glatfelter B32 Litho. Internal and cover design were by John Goetz. The type is Times Roman with Helvetica display.